FIRE DEPARTMENT
DEPLOYMENT ANALYSIS

PUBLICATIONS IN OPERATIONS RESEARCH SERIES
Saul I. Gass, *Editor*

Volume 1
MANPOWER PLANNING MODELS
  Richard C. Grinold and **Kneale T. Marshall**

Volume 2
FIRE DEPARTMENT DEPLOYMENT ANALYSIS
  The Rand Fire Project

FIRE DEPARTMENT DEPLOYMENT ANALYSIS
A Public Policy Analysis Case Study

The Rand Fire Project

Editors

Warren E. Walker
Jan M. Chaiken
Edward J. Ignall

Contributing Authors

Rae W. Archibald   **Peter J. Kolesar**
Edward H. Blum   **Kenneth L. Rider**
Grace M. Carter   **John E. Rolph**
Jan M. Chaiken   **Arthur J. Swersey**
Edward J. Ignall   **Warren E. Walker**

Editorial Consultant
Barry Richman

NORTH HOLLAND
New York • Oxford

The manuscript for this book was prepared under contract H-2351 from the Office of Policy Development and Research, Department of Housing and Urban Development (HUD). The statements and conclusions contained herein are those of the authors and do not necessarily reflect the views of the sponsor. Neither the United States nor HUD makes any warranty, expressed or implied, or assumes responsibility for the accuracy or completeness of the information herein, or assumes liability with respect to the use of any method herein.

Elsevier North Holland, Inc.
52 Vanderbilt Avenue, New York, New York 10017

Distributors outside the United States and Canada:

Thomond Books
(A Division of Elsevier/North-Holland Scientific Publishers, Ltd.)
P.O. 85
Limerick, Ireland

© 1979 by The Rand Corporation

Library of Congress Cataloging in Publication Data

Rand Fire Project.
    Fire department deployment analysis: a public policy analysis case study
    (Publications in operations research series; 2)
    ([A Rand Corporation research study])

    Bibliography: p.
    Includes index.
    1. Fire-departments—Management. 2. System analysis. I. Walker, Warren E. II. Chaiken, Jan M. III. Ignall, Edward J. IV. Archibald, Rae W. V. Title. VI. Series: Operations Research Society of America. Publications in operations research; 2. VII. Series: Rand Corporation. Research study.
TH9145.R36   363.3'7   79-19522
ISBN 0-444-00335-5

Printed in the United States of America

Contents

Foreword
Preface
Acknowledgments

**PART I INTRODUCTION TO FIRE DEPARTMENT
DEPLOYMENT ANALYSIS**   1

Chapter 1   Public Fire Protection   3
Edward H. Blum

1.1 Introduction   3
1.2 Increasing Demands for Fire Protection   7
1.3 Money, Management, and Manpower   12
1.4 Fire   20
1.5 Improving Fire Protection   27
1.6 Measuring Fire Protection   39

**Chapter 2   Fire Department Organization and Firefighting
Operations**   47
Arthur J. Swersey

2.1 Firefighting Resources   48
2.2 From Alarm Receipt Until Dispatch   52
2.3 Fighting the Fire: From Dispatch Until Overhaul   60
2.4 After the Fire: Fire Reporting Systems and Statistics   62
2.5 Fire Department Field Organization and Manpower
     Scheduling   63
2.6 Fire Prevention and Other Fire Department Activities   64

Chapter 3   An Introduction to Deployment Analysis   68
Warren E. Walker

SYNOPSIS   68
3.1 What is Deployment Analysis?   69
3.2 Step 1: Identifying the Problem   72

3.3	Step 2: Specifying the Objectives	77
3.4	Step 3: Choosing the Criteria	79
3.5	Step 4: Selection of Alternatives	87
3.6	Step 5: Analysis of Alternatives	88
3.7	Step 6: Comparison of Alternatives	96
3.8	Step 7: Implementation of Results	97
3.9	Step 8: Monitoring and Evaluating the Results	98

Chapter 4 Organizing for Deployment Analysis   100
Rae W. Archibald

SYNOPSIS		100
4.1	Introduction	101
4.2	Establishing an Analytical Team	102
4.3	Problem Assessment	114
4.4	Taking Stock of the Department	119
4.5	Summary	123

Chapter 5 Managing Change in the Fire Department   125
Rae W. Archibald

SYNOPSIS		125
5.1	Introduction	126
5.2	The Challenge of Change in the Fire Department	127
5.3	Organizations	130
5.4	Strategies for Change	137
5.5	Change in Organizations	143

PART II BASIC TOOLS AND TECHNIQUES   155

Chapter 6 Travel Time and Travel Distance Models   157
Peter J. Kolesar

SYNOPSIS		157
6.1	Introduction	160
6.2	Estimating Point-to-Point Travel Distances	161
6.3	Estimating Point-to-Point Travel Times	164
6.4	The Square-Root Law for Estimating Average Regional Travel Distances	177
6.5	Estimating Average Travel Times in a Region	199

Chapter 7 Probabilistic Models of Fire Company Availability and Dispatching   202
Jan M. Chaiken

SYNOPSIS		202
7.1	Basic Elements of Queuing Theory	204
7.2	Number of Companies Busy in a Region	218
7.3	Deciding Which Companies to Dispatch	234
7.4	Deciding How Many Companies to Dispatch	243
Appendices		246

Contents

Chapter 8	**Analyzing the Demand for Fire Department Services**	255
	Grace M. Carter and John E. Rolph	
SYNOPSIS		255
8.1	Introduction	257
8.2	Data Collection	261
8.3	Displays of Fire Data	265
8.4	Statistical Inference	280
8.5	A Model for Predicting Alarm Rates	291
8.6	Predicting the Probability that an Alarm Signals a Serious Fire	308
Appendix		318

PART III   APPLICATIONS TO FIRE DEPARTMENT PROBLEMS   321

Chapter 9	**Allocating Fire Companies**	323
	Kenneth L. Rider	
SYNOPSIS		323
9.1	Introduction	325
9.2	Approaches to Determining the Number and Location of Fire Companies	326
9.3	The Parametric Allocation Model	330
9.4	Formal Description of the Parametric Allocation Model	340
9.5	Using the Allocation Model to Reallocate Fire Companies in Jersey City, New Jersey	349
Appendix		366
Glossary of Symbols		371

Chapter 10	**Locating Firehouses**	372
	Warren E. Walker	
SYNOPSIS		372
10.1	Introduction	373
10.2	Two Descriptive Models	374
10.3	A Prescriptive Model	401
10.4	Using the Siting Model in Trenton, New Jersey	403

Chapter 11	**Initial Dispatch**	416
	Edward J. Ignall and Kenneth L. Rider	
SYNOPSIS		416
11.1	Introduction	417
11.2	The Evaluation of Initial Dispatch Policies	420
11.3	Traditional Approaches and Their Implications	430
11.4	A Simple Adaptive Approach	436
11.5	An Algorithm for Initial Dispatch	444
Glossary of Symbols		457

Chapter 12	**Relocation**	459
	Peter J. Kolesar	
SYNOPSIS		459
12.1	Introduction	460
12.2	Mathematical Formulation of the Problem	464

12.3	Solving the Problem: A Heuristic Algorithm	480
12.4	An Example	483
12.5	Testing the Algorithm	486
12.6	On-line Implementation of the Algorithm in New York City	492
12.7	Using the Algorithm to Generate Preplanned Relocations	494

Chapter 13 The Fire Operations Simulation Model   495
Edward J. Ignall

SYNOPSIS		495
13.1	Overview	496
13.2	Program Design	499
13.3	Input Needs	506
13.4	Output Information	511
13.5	Experimental Design	532
13.6	Statistical Analysis	537
13.7	The Use of Simulation to Validate an Analytic Model	545

Chapter 14 Deployment Case Studies   549
Arthur J. Swersey

SYNOPSIS		549
14.1	The Deployment of Firefighting Resources in Yonkers, New York	550
14.2	Locating Firehouses in Denver, Colorado	568
14.3	Using the Parametric Allocation Model in Tacoma, Washington	581
14.4	Workload Problems in the New York City Fire Department	588
14.5	Reducing Dispatching Delays in a New York City Communications Office	607

Research History of The Rand Fire Project	629
Glossary	641
Bibliography	653
Index	663
Selected Rand Books	669
Biographies	671

Foreword

In the face of rising costs, more calls for help, and population and business shifts, local executives and fire chiefs are increasingly turning to systems analysis to find economical ways to provide high-quality fire service.

Based on ten years of research and testing in local governments, this book describes an important advance in the field of systems analysis to help fire departments solve their deployment problems. There is sufficient detail for readers to understand the basic formulation of the analytical techniques and to learn when and how to use them effectively. Going beyond the technical aspects, the book treats organizational and political issues and provides guidance on how to turn the results of analysis into action.

In 1969, the Office of Policy Development and Research (PD&R) of the U.S. Department of Housing and Urban Development first began testing ways to help local officials and practitioners improve services and make more effective decisions. The initial questions were: Can systems analysis, previously applied successfully to defense and industrial operations, be adapted to urban problem-solving and services? Are there rational methods to evaluate alternative policies and choose an appropriate course of action?

The Office of Policy Development and Research first looked at the work being done by Rand in cooperation with the Fire Department of New York City where new methods were being developed and used to examine station siting and dispatch policy options. The next question was: Can other local governments use these deployment analysis methods?

Years of HUD-funded research allow PD&R and others to answer these questions with a yes, in every case.

This book documents the answers, consolidates into a single volume already published technical guides, case studies, and training manuals, and adds previously unpublished accounts along with recent experiences of a variety of communities in deployment analysis and planning.

About one hundred communities have now used some form of the analytical techniques and reported significant benefits in fire service operations. The Office of Policy Development and Research is confident that this book will become a regularly consulted desk-top reference for those who wish to effect change and improvement in the delivery of public services. The authors and all those who participated in these efforts are to be thanked for their very significant contribution to HUD's ongoing efforts to stimulate innovation in decisionmaking on the local level.

Hartley Campbell Fitts
Chief, Community Management and
  Productivity Improvement Research
  Program
Office of Policy Development and
  Research
U.S. Department of Housing and
  Urban Development

Alan R. Siegel
Director, Division of Government
  Capacity Building
Office of Policy Development and
  Research
U.S. Department of Housing and
  Urban Development

Preface

This book is about fire department deployment—deciding how many firehouses and fire companies a department should have, where they should be located, which companies should be dispatched as incidents occur, and how and when to relocate them. We hope that the book will be equally useful to readers whose work is directly related to fire department operations and readers who are more broadly interested in applications of systems analysis to public policy problems.

The book is unique in the scope and depth of its contents. Some topics discussed here have national, and even international, implications. Others concentrate on administrative and operational concerns in local government, with particular reference to fire departments. At the finest level of detail, the book describes practical procedures for data collection, the mathematical formulation of deployment models, and related aspects of analysis.

Readers belonging to any of the following groups should find material directly related to their interests:

Analysts (uniformed or civilian) who work for municipal or county fire departments or budget offices;

Fire department managers and operating personnel;

City managers, mayors, councilmen, directors of public safety bureaus, state fire marshals, and others who deal with or exercise authority over fire departments;

Students, teachers, and researchers in policy analysis, operations research, public administration, urban technology, fire science, and fire protection engineering;

Employees of engineering and systems analysis firms who work on fire protection problems.

Others involved in municipal fire protection should find parts of the book valuable as a source of background or reference information—researchers who study the physics and chemistry of fire, manufacturers of communication and information systems, and members of the fire insurance industry or regulatory agencies. This information should also prove useful to officials in national agencies or practitioner organizations who establish standards or priorities for fire service equipment, codes and formats for collecting data, or research.

ABOUT THE "AUTHOR": THE RAND FIRE PROJECT

This book is an outgrowth of a large body of research conducted by the Rand Fire Project. The project began in 1968, when The Rand Corporation entered into its first contract with the City of New York to undertake studies for the Fire Department.[1] From 1969 through 1975, this work continued at The New York City-Rand Institute, a nonprofit corporation established jointly by Rand and the City.

The research for the New York City Fire Department served as a nucleus for other fire-related studies at the Institute. These smaller research efforts—not specifically focused on New York City problems—were funded by the U.S. Department of Housing and Urban Development, the National Science Foundation, and the cities of Trenton, New Jersey and Yonkers, New York. The applicability of the material in this book to small as well as large fire departments is largely due to the work sponsored by these agencies, although the central concepts and methods were nearly all developed under New York City funding.

All the people who made major substantive contributions to fire deployment studies as employees or consultants of The New York City-Rand Institute are collectively the "author" of this book, the Rand Fire Project. Their names are in Table P.1.[2] All of them, whether or not they have written one of the chapters of the book, share in the authorship: their ideas are represented on these pages and the book often freely draws on their writings.

HOW THE BOOK WAS WRITTEN

When The New York City-Rand Institute closed in late 1975, there were no longer any major fire studies at Rand. The members of the Fire Project moved on to other kinds of research; many of them were no longer employed by Rand. But much of the product of the project remained unpublished or was accessible only in scattered papers that would be

---

[1] A research history of the Rand Fire Project is given at the end of the book.

[2] A few Institute staff members who worked on fire-related studies are not listed in the table. They worked in fields other than deployment analysis, such as research on fire insurance, program budgeting, and fire prevention activities.

TABLE P.1. Members of the Rand Fire Project who worked on deployment analysis.

Member	Fields of Expertise
Rae Archibald[a]	Planning, administration, implementation
Edward Blum[a]	Engineering, management, operations research
Grace Carter[b]	Operations research, simulation
Jan Chaiken[b]	Mathematics, operations research
Hope Corman	Economics
Colleen Dodd	Computer programming
Peter Dormont	Computer programming
Edward Ignall[b]	Operations research
Jack Hausner	Operations research
Joan Held	Computing and information systems
Thomas Hendrick[c]	Management, operations research
Ralph Keeney[c]	Utility theory
Peter Kolesar[b]	Operations research
Donald Plane[c]	Management, operations research
Kenneth Rider[a]	Operations research
John Rolph[b]	Statistics
Carol Shanesy	Computing and information systems
Anne (Sandy) Stevenson	Data analysis
Arthur Swersey[a]	Operations research
Richard Urbach	Operations research
Warren Walker[a]	Operations research
Robert Yin	Neighborhood studies

[a] Contributing authors who directed Fire Project at some time.
[b] Other contributing authors.
[c] Consultants to The Rand Corporation.

difficult to assemble and read. Recognizing the importance of rewriting, updating, and publishing this material in a single volume, Warren Walker, acting on behalf of ten previous members of the Fire Project, who became the contributing authors, obtained a contract to write this book from the Office of Policy Development and Research, U.S. Department of Housing and Urban Development (HUD).

The book was prepared under the general supervision of the three editors, HUD's contract monitors, and the members of our advisory board; the last, named in the acknowledgments, represent fire service practitioners, researchers, and municipal officials. Authors for the chapters were selected on the basis of their availability as well as their past work and writings in the fields covered here. Their task was not to write about their own work, but rather to summarize the most important information about the assigned topic. Consequently, the methods presented in a chapter were not necessarily developed by the chapter's author, but rather were the work of the people cited in the references. To emphasize the distinction between chapter authorship and "intellectual title" to the material, we have adopted the term "contributing authors" to refer to those who wrote chapters.

The book's editors attempted to achieve consistency and completeness in the final manuscript by establishing format and content requirements and by resolving overlaps and omissions in the drafts submitted by the contributing authors. Moreover, each member of the advisory board was assigned overall responsibility for a specific group of chapters.

For the most part, the recommendations of the editors and the advisory board were simply conveyed to the authors, who incorporated them as they saw fit. In some instances the editors moved material from one chapter to another or wrote additional sections where they were needed. Maintaining stylistic consistency, common use of terminology, and readable prose was the thankless task of Barry Richman, also a colleague of the authors at the Institute. Thus, the text as you see it here is the result of a collaborative integrative effort and is not simply a collection of individual papers.

GUIDE TO THE BOOK

There are many ways to read this book. Everyone should read Chapter 1 —quickly or carefully as their interests dictate—for an overall picture of the problems of the fire service and the context within which deployment analysis is performed. Chapter 2 is intended primarily for readers who are unfamiliar with the operations of a fire department, although even fire professionals may find it a convenient reference for terminology used in the rest of the book[3] or for descriptions of operations they have never personally observed, such as those in a dispatching office.

Beginning with Chapter 3, the easiest way to find material of interest is to read the synopses of the chapters. These are nontechnical overviews of the contents that will give the reader a broad introduction to fire deployment analysis. Then the chapters can be read in nearly any order, using the internal cross references to identify related or prerequisite material to pursue.

The book is organized to be most convenient for readers who are fire service practitioners responsible for undertaking deployment analyses in their own departments. They can read the material from the beginning to find out what tasks must be performed during the analysis, the types of technical skills needed on the project team, techniques for organizing and managing a project, basic principles of modeling, and data requirements. Case histories showing how models and computer programs can and have been used are presented in the final chaiter.

In general, the material within each chapter is presented in order of increasing technical complexity. Each chapter starts with the important points that can be presented without recourse to mathematical formulations. Readers without advanced mathematical skills should have little

---

[3] The Glossary also serves this purpose.

trouble with the few tables, graphs, and equations presented in the early, basically nontechnical, chapters. In later chapters they will reach a point where the mathematical details become too burdensome and should skip to the beginning of the next chapter.

The technically trained reader may find the early chapters somewhat frustrating because they lack mathematically precise formulations of models, and they review, in tutorial fashion, already familiar information—such as descriptions of systems analysis, use of road networks to estimate travel times, and elementary principles of queuing theory. Such readers will find the last few sections of chapters after Chapter 5 most pertinent to their interests. They should skip lightly over the beginnings of these chapters until they reach the desired technical level.

For students and others who want to learn the techniques of systems analysis, this book is a complete, nearly self-contained lesson in how systems analysis can be applied to public policy issues. All the steps are included here, from identification of objectives and appropriate measures of effectiveness, through mathematical tools and models, to implementation of the findings in the political arena. A full-year course for upper-class undergraduates or beginning graduate students can be designed using the book as a text. (It has already been used in operations research applications courses at Columbia University and U.C.L.A.) Such a course will provide a firm foundation for later work in other areas.

Figure P.1 illustrates the relationships among the chapters and their technical content. A line connecting a section in one chapter with a section in another indicates that the material at the start of the line is a prerequisite for understanding the material at the end of it. Generally, technical content labeled "moderate" requires the reader to be familiar with algebra and basic concepts of probability and statistics. Technical content labeled "substantial" requires familiarity with calculus, queuing theory, linear programming, or similar techniques.

Part I of the book, consisting of Chapters 1 to 5, contains general background material related to all the later chapters. Part II, consisting of Chapters 6 to 8, contains basic concepts and models that can be used by themselves in deployment analysis and that also serve as components of models presented in Part III. The last part contains details of a number of fire deployment models and their applications.

The sections indicated by cross hatching as having substantial technical content are never prerequisites for later material. They can always be skipped without loss of continuity. Some of the sections labeled as having moderate technical content, namely Sections 6.3–6.5 and 7.1, should be read—or at least skimmed—for a full understanding of the material in Part III. However, the remaining sections with moderate technical content can be skipped by a reader who is not interested in the details of models.

For the convenience of the reader who wants to find material related to special topics in deployment analysis, there is an Index in Table P.2.

FIGURE P. 1. RELATIONSHIPS AMONG CHAPTERS

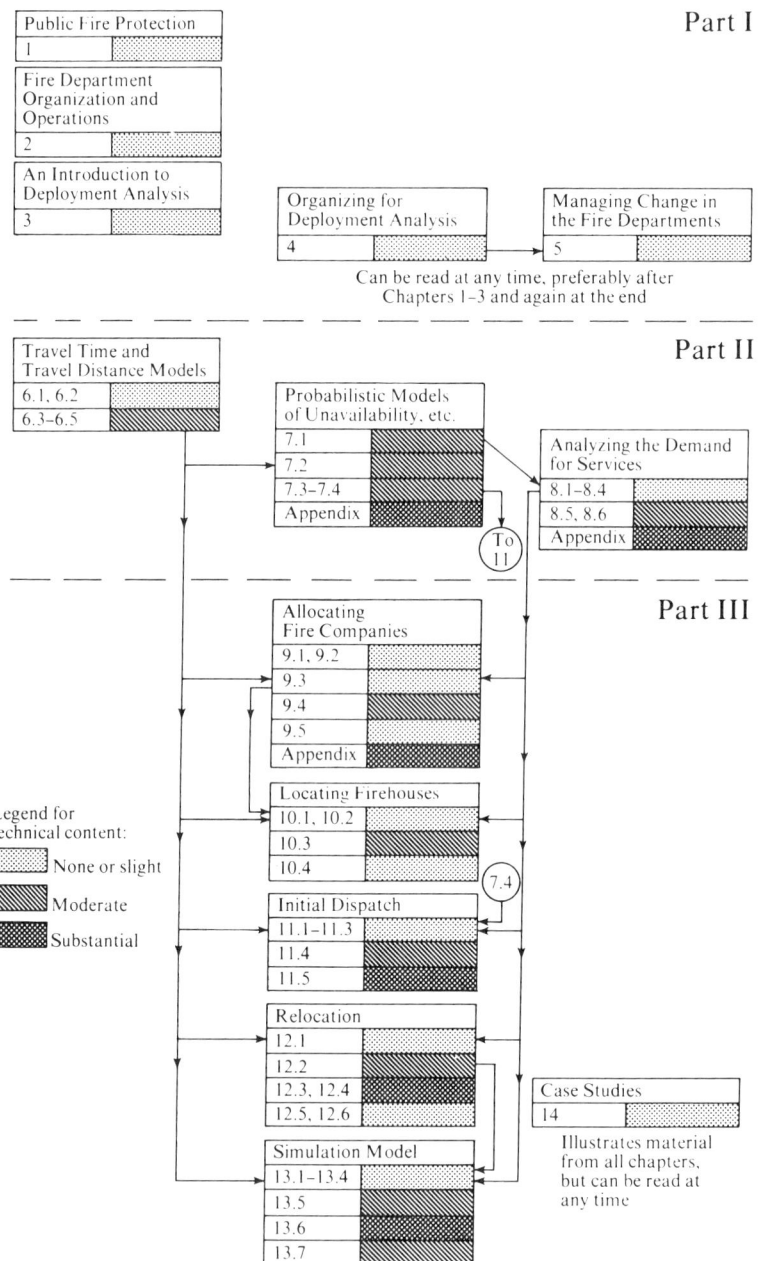

TABLE P.2. Index of selected topics.

Topic	Sections and Chapters
Administration of fire departments and analytical teams	1.3, 4, 5, 14
Data	1.2, 1.5, 2.1, 2.2, 2.4, 3.2, 6.3, 6.4, 8.2, 8.3, 8.5, 8.6, 13.3, 13.4, 14
Data analysis	6.3, 8.1–8.6, 9 Appendix, 13.3, 14
Fire department operations	1.5, 2, 11.2
Implementation of models	1.5, 4, 5, 14
Measures of cost and effectiveness	1.4, 1.6, 3.2, 11.2, 13.4
Models	
Basic models and rules of thumb	6, 7.2–7.4
Computer programs	7.2, 7 Appendix, 9.3–9 Appendices, 10.2, 10.4, 11.4, 11.5, 12, 13
Principles of deployment analysis and modeling	3, 7.1–7.3, 8.1, 8.4, 9.2, 9.3, 11.2, 11.3, 12.1, 12.2, 13.1, 13.2, 13.5
Validation of models	6.3–6.5, 8.5, 11.4, 12.5, 13.7, 14

Fire Department Deployment Analysis presents the current state of the art in applying systems analysis to fire department deployment problems. While we have worked hard to achieve simplicity and clarity, we have resisted glossing over the harder parts. The book alone will not make anyone an accomplished deployment analyst. But we hope that the reader will obtain an understanding of the capabilities and limitations of the field.

Warren E. Walker
Jan M. Chaiken
Edward J. Ignall

Acknowledgments

Preparation of this book was sponsored by the Office of Policy Development and Research, U.S. Department of Housing and Urban Development (HUD). We are grateful to Alan Siegel and Hartley Fitts of HUD's Community Development and Management Research Division, who supported not only our work on this book but also many of our earlier studies that are described here. Robert Baumgardner worked closely with them in recent years and provided valuable guidance. Their sustained interest in our fire deployment research made this book possible.

They wisely recommended that we appoint an advisory panel to review our outlines and draft manuscripts, and to meet with the editors for discussions of the order in which topics would be presented, the technical level of the material, and the content of the book. Fortunately, five highly qualified people agreed to serve on the panel, and we wish to thank them for their conscientious assistance:

Murray Geisler, Operations Researcher, Logistics Management Institute

Anthony Granito, Technical Marketing Director, National Fire Protection Association

Marc Leopold, Manager of Operations Research, Division of Planning and Operations Research, Fire Department of the City of New York

Francis Ronan, Assistant Professor of Fire Protection Technology, Monroe Community College and Assistant Chief (retired), Fire Department of the City of New York

Jack Watts, Assistant Professor, Department of Fire Protection Engineering, University of Maryland.

They made substantial contributions by pointing out topics we had inadvertently omitted in early drafts, suggesting major reordering and condensation in some chapters, and helping us adopt currently accepted fire service terminology.

Other reviewers of partial or complete draft manuscripts included William Donaldson, City Manager of Cincinnati, Ohio; David Jaquette, The Rand Corporation; James Reiser, Chief (retired), Tacoma Fire Department; Peter Rydell, The Rand Corporation; Philip Schaenman, United States Fire Administration; and Robert Burns, Chief, Mountain View Fire Department. Our thanks to all of them for their interest and help.

Particular thanks must go to the New York City Fire Department for providing us with detailed information, letting us observe its operations freely, and giving our analyses and proposed deployment methods critical but constructive attention. We are especially grateful to Commissioner John T. O'Hagan, for providing continuous and unswerving support to the Rand Fire Project over its eight-year life. The Department assigned high-ranking chiefs as liaison officers, who worked closely with the project staff, and we owe much of our practical knowledge to them: Francis Ronan,[4] Lester Snyder, Robert Brown, Joseph Hess, Homer Bishop, and Elmer Chapman. Other members of the Department who had a strong influence on our work were Commissioner Robert Lowery, Assistant Commissioner Paul Canick, Director of Training Lewis Harris, Fire Communications Director Nicholas Reinhardt, Chief Dispatchers Frederick Grant and Russell Ramsey, and Manager of Operations Research Marc Leopold.[4]

When Rand opened its New York office in 1968, two of our strongest supporters in city government were Mayor John Lindsay and Budget Director Frederick O'R. Hayes. Without their assistance, and that of their staffs, the Fire Project would never have begun. The first president of The New York City-Rand Institute, Peter Szanton, provided warm guidance and encouragement to many of us, and he should share in our accomplishments. His successors, Gustave Shubert, Bernard Gifford, and Robert Levine, led us ably through the development and application of our work. The last president of The New York City-Rand Institute, Marshall Davie, helped us complete our work, providing support and a professional environment even though the Institute was closing its doors.

Two cities other than New York funded parts of our fire deployment research: Trenton, New Jersey and Yonkers, New York. In addition, we received close cooperation from officials in four other cities where we conducted HUD-funded testing and development of our models: Denver, Colorado; Jersey City, New Jersey; Tacoma, Washington; and Wilmington, Delaware. All of this work was performed in 1974 and 1975. In Trenton, we wish to thank Mayor Arthur Holland, Business Administrator Brian Baxter, Chief Daniel George, and management analyst Jim Allison; in Yonkers, Chiefs Wallace Brown and James Ryan, and Budget

---

[4] Previously mentioned as a member of the advisory panel.

Acknowledgments xxi

Director James Carney. In Denver, the principal researchers were Thomas Hendrick and Donald Plane, who later were consultants to Rand; they have been listed in the Preface as members of the Rand Fire Project because their report is excerpted in this book. The Denver project team was headed by Chris Tomasides, Denver's Deputy Finance Director, and F. William Heiss, Director of the Denver Urban Observatory, and it included David Monarchi and Chief Myrle Wise. In Jersey City, our thanks go to the Director of Public Safety, Nicholas Fargo. In addition, close cooperation, including coauthorship of the final report, was provided by Captain Robert Shortell, Battalion Chief John Bligh, and Captain Thomas Candiloro. In Wilmington, two members of the project team were also coauthors of the final report: David Singleton, Director of Program Analysis in the Department of Planning and Development, and Bruce Smith, a fiscal consultant in the Office of the Mayor; other supporters and participants included Mayor Thomas Maloney, Fire Chief James Blackburn, and Captains Donald Donovan and Joseph Green.

Some of the work of the Rand Fire Project was funded by the National Science Foundation, whose support we gratefully acknowledge.

Administration of the business and secretarial aspects of producing this book was ably handled by Rachel Hockett and Diane Moore of Urbatronics, Inc. They successfully kept track of the numerous revisions of the manuscript, and of the authors who were spread throughout the world. At the Rand Corporation, which provided facilities and resources for converting the final manuscript into a published book, John Hogan was especially helpful with his guidance and efforts on our behalf.

Two classes of graduate students, one at Columbia University and the other at the University of California, Los Angeles, used the typed manuscript as a textbook and made many helpful suggestions for clarifications.

A special note of gratitude goes to our spouses, children, parents, and roommates, who cheerfully tolerated smoky clothes, computer terminals that tied up the telephones, large maps spread over the living room floors, late night forays to dispatching centers, and our absence when we were writing our reports and book chapters.

Affiliations mentioned in this section were current at the time of interaction with the Fire Project.

FIRE DEPARTMENT
DEPLOYMENT ANALYSIS

PART I
INTRODUCTION TO FIRE DEPARTMENT DEPLOYMENT ANALYSIS

Chapter 1
Public Fire Protection

1.1 INTRODUCTION

Despite occasional nostalgia for the good old days, public fire protection has improved substantially in the last 100 years. Conflagrations such as those that swept Chicago, San Francisco, and Baltimore have become rare. Mass tragedies such as the Triangle Shirtwaist Company fire[1] and the Coconut Grove fire[2] have motivated fire safety codes designed to prevent similar disasters. As gas lighting and kerosene heaters have disappeared from homes, so have the hundreds of serious fires and deaths they have caused each year. Fire-resistant construction, fire doors, and automatic sprinklers now help confine and limit fire damage. When fires do occur, firefighters can usually rely on municipal water supplies, powerful motor-driven vehicles, high-volume pumps, hydraulically operated ladders, aerial elevating platforms, self-contained breathing equipment, and radio communications.

There is little solid information, however, to show what effects these improvements have had in this country.[3] Data for France (Chesnais, 1974 and *Fire Journal*, November 1974) indicate a decrease of more than 70

---

[1] The Triangle Shirtwaist Company fire occurred in New York City, March 25, 1911. It killed 145 people, predominantly women employees, and led to major changes in building and fire-safety codes.

[2] The Coconut Grove nightclub in Boston burned on November 28, 1942, killing 491 people. Many of those who died were crushed in the panic to escape.

[3] Even current U.S. fire loss and fire death figures suffer from incomplete and inconsistent reporting—a problem the National Fire Data Center of the United States Fire Administration (USFA) is working to overcome (see *Fire in the United States*, 1978). The sources of reports, the reliability and accuracy of reports, the definitions of "fire-related" loss and death, and past adjustments for incomplete reporting have varied greatly, making long-term comparisons especially difficult.

percent in the fire death rate over the past 107 years—from 2.5 fire-related deaths per 100,000 people in 1866 to 0.7 in 1973. This progress has come largely from advances in technology and in the legal, economic, and administrative means of putting it into practice.

Some of the advances, both in the United States and overseas, have been initiated by local officials and fire protection specialists who want to provide the best fire protection possible. Others have been forced into practice by political and economic pressure, often during periods of high public awareness of fire. The identification of new hazards and the perception of new risks have also played important roles. But getting significant advances has usually been difficult. Some have required major changes in policy, operating procedures, and skills. Some, especially those directly involving the public, have met resistance and have required years to take root.

Significant problems still exist. The United States Fire Administration (USFA) has estimated that about 7500 Americans still die annually in fires, and roughly 300,000 are scarred or injured (*Fires in the United States*, 1978).[4] The American rate of about 3.5 fire-related deaths per year per 100,000 people is more than twice the recent British rate and about five times the current Italian rate (Figure 1.1). Indeed, the current American fire death rate is greater than the French rate of a century ago.

Fire is the leading cause of catastrophic accidents (those in which five or more people die) in the United States (*Fire in the United States*, 1978), and the third most frequent cause of all fatal accidents. Fire annually destroys approximately $4 billion in property and costs the total economy an estimated $13.6 billion (*Fire In the United States*, 1978). These losses occur in spite of approximately $5 billion spent annually on public fire departments and still another several billion dollars invested each year in equipment, material, and structural design to meet increasingly stringent regulations and codes.

Moreover, some of the underlying problems are becoming more severe. Technological change has created new fire risks, some of unprecedented size and complexity. Serious deterioration in many cities has spawned rising numbers of fires in buildings where traditional fire prevention approaches no longer work. Simultaneously, in most cities, money is

---

[4] The National Fire Protection Association (NFPA) has recently estimated that approximately 8800 fire fatalities occurred in the United States in 1976 (Derry, 1977). Both the USFA and NFPA estimates are considerably lower than the previously accepted estimate of 12,000 fire deaths per year (see, for example, *America Burning*, 1973). Much of the difference is attributable to errors in previous methods for estimating the number of motor vehicle fire deaths.

1.1 Introduction

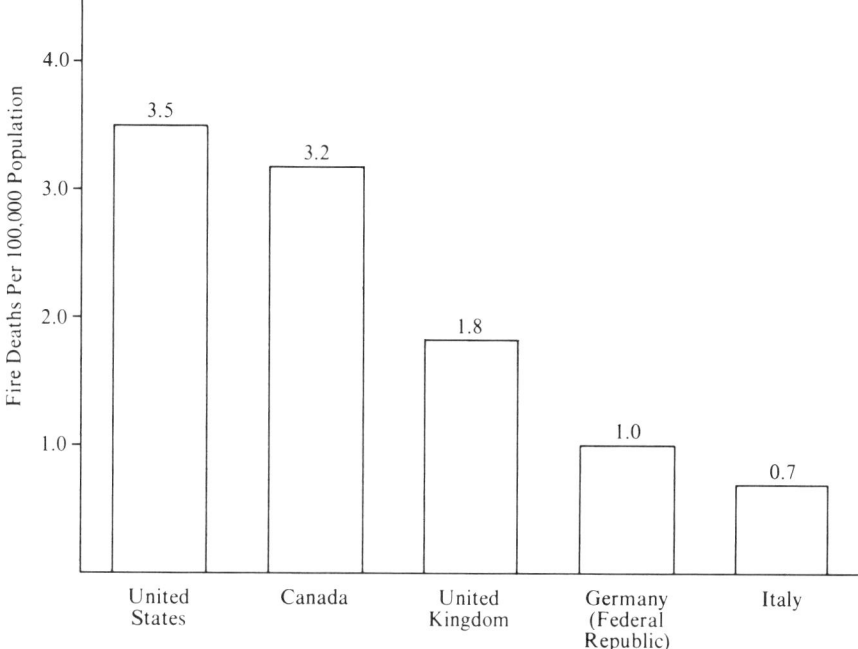

FIGURE 1.1 International fire death rates per 100,000 population. The United States estimate is for 1975 and is from *Fire In the United States* (1978). Other estimates are 1972–1974 averages based on World Health Organization data, and are reported in Rardin and Mitzner (1977).

becoming scarcer, fire personnel are rejecting traditional motivations, and management is becoming more complex and difficult.

The fire protection system in a community is quite broad, encompassing among other things the fire prevention and suppression activities of the fire department, the community's building codes and its water supply system, the private investment of building owners, and the activities of the occupants of the buildings. This book concentrates on the role of the municipal fire department in suppressing fires. It presents a new approach to the problems of deploying firefighting resources (i.e., deciding how many firehouses and fire companies a fire department should have, where they should be located, which companies should be dispatched as incidents occur, and how and when to reposition them). The approach, called "systems analysis," applies scientific techniques and modern computer methods to the problems of operating systems.

The use of systems analysis need not be confined to deployment problems. In fact, fire protection master planning, which is being promoted by the United States Fire Administration,[5] applies systems analysis to the evaluation and improvement of a community's entire fire protection system. The basic elements of system analysis are described in Chapter 3.

Systems analysis closely links policy aims and plans with results. It attempts to show how to shape policies to achieve particular goals, how to test potential policies and programs inexpensively and at low risk, how to strengthen them to maximize the desired effects (or to minimize undesirable effects), and how to tailor them to suit local circumstances or meet changing conditions. Overall, it increases the likelihood that changes will be improvements.

Looking toward the future, systems analysis can help identify targets for improvement. This is done by pinpointing areas in which given levels of investment can achieve the largest gains in public fire protection. It thus expands the capacity to explore and innovate, while controlling the cost and risks of innovation.

Applications of systems analysis to the fire service are relatively recent. They have been made chiefly in intensive work conducted since 1968 by fire departments and fire protection agencies working with public sector research organizations. By 1976, however, systems analysis was in use in several dozen cities, ranging in population from 20,000 to over 7,000,000. These cities have helped refine the key methods and have developed the ability to use them on important problems without outside assistance. The result has been new policies and procedures, many of which have already been implemented. Some have been operational long enough to be carefully evaluated, and they have been found to work well. Several important examples of this experience are described in detail in subsequent chapters, especially Chapter 14.

Like other innovations that preceded it, systems analysis will be brought into use both as an internal initiative and as a response to external pressures. Some public administrators and fire professionals will recognize its advantages for their jurisdictions. They themselves will take the necessary steps to apply analysis to their fire protection problems. Others will be pushed to consider putting it into practice. Some will be compelled by political pressures from constituent communities, citizens' groups, and firefighters' unions. Some will be pressed economically by the tightening squeeze between scarce municipal funds and rising service costs. And some will be induced to respond to the external pressures imposed by rising alarm rates, increased hazards, and other problems.

This book has two major objectives: (1) to present the elements of

---

[5] See, for example, *A Basic Guide For Fire Prevention and Control Master Planning* (1978).

systems analysis in the context of the deployment of firefighting resources; and (2) to provide a practical detailed guide to its effective application. The focus on deployment is sensible because:

- The fire service controls its deployment policies (and the operating decisions that make them effective) more completely than it controls other key aspects of fire protection.
- Of the key aspects of fire protection, fire service deployment has attracted the greatest analytic attention (and proved especially amenable to analysis).

With this focus, therefore, the book can present not only techniques but also completed analyses and operating experience showing how well the analytical results work in practice.

However, before narrowing the focus to deployment analysis, we devote the remainder of this chapter to an overview of a community's entire fire protection system, with particular emphasis on urban fire protection.

1.2 INCREASING DEMANDS FOR FIRE PROTECTION

The demand for fire protection is increasing, and the nature of the demand is intimately related to the kind of service needed. Unlike education and recreation, which create social "goods," fire protection is inherently a preventive and remedial service, designed to combat social ills and physical failures. The nature and dimensions of these factors determine the nature and dimensions of the service. For example, where there is little chance that a fire could endanger life or destroy property, little fire protection is needed. Conversely, where the potential losses are great, much fire protection is needed.

The demand for fire protection takes two forms. First, the potential for loss creates a *latent demand* (often called *potential demand*) for fire protection. Fire companies must be available to respond in case a fire occurs. Second, when fires actually occur, latent demand is converted into *realized demand*—events that (in principle) require the fire department to respond and put the fires out.

The physical objects giving rise to latent demand are called *hazards*. Every hazard has the following attributes:

1. A probability that a fire will actually occur during a specified time interval (i.e., the *risk* of a fire).
2. The magnitude of the possible loss.
3. The consequences of the loss.

These attributes shape the entire fire protection process. Each is the target of specialized activities. *Fire prevention* aims to reduce the likelihood that fires will occur. Particular buildings or classes of buildings are selected for inspection, and an attempt is made to separate things that could start fires from things that could burn. A component of what is usually called fire prevention is actually *preresponse damage limitation*, steps taken before a fire occurs to try to reduce the magnitude of the possible loss. Fire detectors, fire doors, and sprinklers fall into this category, as do exit requirements and fire drills. Once a fire occurs, and is detected and reported, the fire department responds by rescuing people and putting the fire out. The department's *response and firefighting* is a critical emergency activity whose objective is to reduce the magnitude of the actual loss. Sometimes, even while the ashes are still warm, the fire department, insurance companies, physicians, and groups such as the Red Cross begin *treatment of the consequences*, to minimize net losses.

The net loss at a fire depends on the original value of the hazard, as modified successively by the four stages of fire protection activity shown in Figure 1.2. A city's hazards thus determine the fire protection it needs to provide. All fire protection is driven by demand—mostly by latent demand, though fire departments and other organizations that intervene after a fire has occurred are also affected by realized demands. The nature of a city's demands and the ways they shape fire protection needs are major management and planning considerations. Chapter 8 describes these demands in detail.

1.2.1 Latent Demands

All across the United States (and in many other industrially advanced countries), new technology is creating large, complex fire hazards. These hazards, in turn, are creating needs for new fire protection strategies. Major fires are relatively rare events, but they can inflict large, even crushing losses when they occur.

The new hazards causing the largest increase in latent demands for fire protection arise largely from three technological advances. First, construction techniques enable large numbers of people to be present in the same enclosed space. These include sealed high-rise buildings, large apartment houses, enclosed shopping centers, enclosed stadiums, airport terminals, jumbo aircraft, subway systems, large exhibition centers, large warehouses, semipartitioned manufacturing buildings, and large hospitals. These enclosures confine enormous collective potentials for losses in relatively small spaces. Such enclosures have relatively short times for serious fire growth and spread, and their environmental control systems contain and circulate both heat and life-threatening combustion products.

Second, technologies have created very valuable properties that are difficult to protect by conventional means. These include computer sys-

1.2 Increasing Demands for Fire Protection

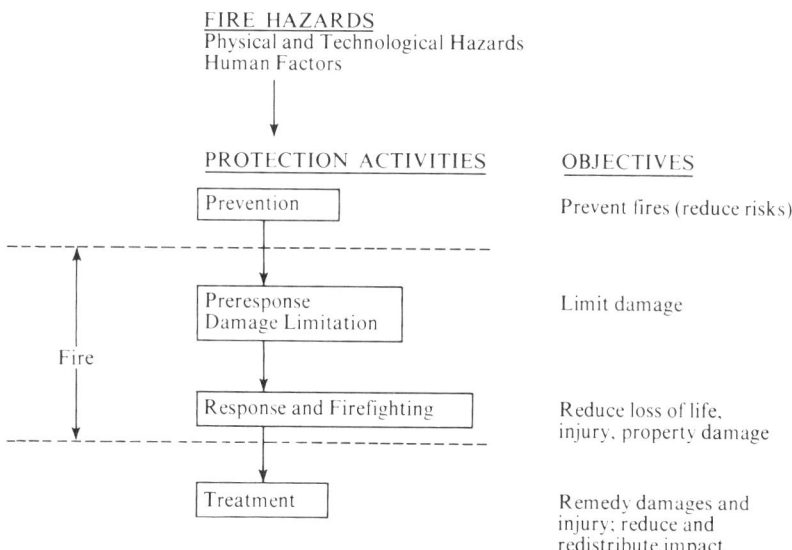

FIGURE 1.2. Stages of fire-service activity, related to risks, objectives, and consequences.

tems (the computers themselves and their libraries of flammable magnetic tape, which now form the indispensable core of many businesses), automated warehouses without windows or space for firefighting, port facilities, giant fuel storage tanks (not only oil and gasoline but also liquefied petroleum and natural gases, which require unusual protective techniques), and nuclear reactors. For these hazards, the property value at stake may be tens or even hundreds of times the value at risk in most fires. Seemingly minor damage may cause much or all of the value to be lost, and the risks of damage from firefighting may be as great as those from the fire itself.

Third, new materials increase the potential release of heat, toxic gases, and corrosive gases. The use of plastics for furniture, finishings, and insulation is growing rapidly. This greatly increases the potential "fuel loading," that is, the potential heat a fire would release per cubic foot. Greater heat increases the chance that a seemingly small fire will spread and that a moderate fire will become an inferno. When burned, these plastics often generate much larger and more toxic and corrosive volumes of gases than the materials they have replaced. Even very small fires in such materials—smoldering seat cushions, for example—have generated enough poisonous gases to kill sleeping families.

The safety technology required to cope with the fire problems created by these technological advances has not kept pace with their development, thereby contributing to their potential for catastrophic loss.

1.2.2 Realized Demands

The volume of calls for fire service—fires, emergencies, and false alarms—and their geographic and temporal variation, have changed dramatically since 1960. In many American cities, the total number of calls has increased much faster than the population or the number of buildings. Indeed, the number of incidents per thousand people more than doubled between 1960 and 1970 in nearly all the largest cities. In some cities, the trend has leveled off in the 1970's; in others, it has kept going.

Increases in the number of urban fires, especially those deliberately set, appear to stem largely from housing decay and social tensions. In many cities, false alarms, rubbish fires, nonfire emergencies, fires set in vacant or abandoned buildings, and arson or "protest" fires now outnumber the accidental fires in relatively well-maintained buildings, which used to be the principal justification for the fire service and which used to generate its principal realized demands. Most of these problems are concentrated in slum areas, where they seem closely tied to inadequately maintained housing and facilities, overcrowding, and other accumulating social ills.

So, the demands on the fire service in urban areas are reflections of more basic social and economic problems, such as sagging urban economic conditions, long-term unemployment among certain groups, inadequate national housing and welfare policies, declining pride in neighborhoods, and disregard for property. These problems are not likely to yield soon to anything that might be done by individual fire departments or even by the fire profession as a whole.

A major frustration for the fire service is that it lacks control over many of the realized demands for its services. Generally, less than one-third of all fires, or even of fatal fires, can be traced to technical origins. Smoking, children playing with matches, cooking, and careless handling of flames have headed national lists of causes for years. Mounting educational and awareness programs to counter these causes has proved difficult, and clearly identifiable, sustained successes are rare.

The recent changes in the incidence of fire alarms have caused serious deployment problems for many fire departments. Calls for service have more than doubled average workloads in the larger cities since 1960. The number of alarms received during peak periods (summer evenings, for example) in some cities has grown to the point where dispatching and response capabilities are sometimes strained. The increasing concentration of calls in high-demand areas, as well as rapid changes in the incidence of alarms, has forced city and fire department management to reconsider station sizes and locations.

The standard policy of routinely dispatching large numbers of firefighters and equipment to answer an alarm is also being questioned. A prime motivation for the questioning is the skyrocketing false-alarm rate that so plagues firefighters. Many cities have tried to minimize their response to high false-alarm boxes.[6] However, where high false-alarm activity and serious fires occur in the same vicinity, as they often do, such a policy can be extremely risky. More flexible response policies are clearly necessary, but they are not simple to devise. Chapter 11 discusses flexible response policies and suggests when they might be appropriate.

1.2.3 The Relationship Between Demand and Fire Department Resources

The increase in latent and realized demands described above has important implications for the firefighting resources that fire departments must deploy to respond to the demands. Three considerations primarily determine the level of resources needed by a fire department. First, the *types of hazards involved* (for example, lumberyards, apartment houses, nursing homes, row houses, and single-family homes on large lots). These determine the kind of firefighting equipment needed and the desired proximity of firefighting units. They also influence the number of personnel that should be assigned to engines, ladders, and special units. What attributes of the hazards matter? Generally, the potential for loss of life, the potential for crippling economic loss, the likelihood of rapid fire spread, the difficulty of evacuation or rescue, the number of firefighters likely to be needed, the difficulty of extinguishment, and the potential for conflagration are the most important, though any chief could add a dozen more.

Second, the *geography of the area protected*, especially as it affects the time vehicles require to reach the site of a fire once they are notified to respond. Ease of access is also important. Extra protection may be needed for isolated locations (peninsulas, ridges) or points where access may become difficult or restricted (single access roads, narrow streets, heavy traffic, critical bridges, tunnels, or mountain roads).

Third, *peak-period alarm rates*, especially when a sizeable part of the firefighting force may be out at the same time. Very heavy peak-loads may require extra personnel and equipment to handle the simultaneous demands for service, or to relieve the heavy workload.

The methods presented in this book show how fire departments can plan for these factors. Initially, that may be all one can do. These methods also show, however, the gains that would result from changing these factors or altering their implications for service.

---

[6] The term "box" here refers to street alarm boxes, which transmit mainly or exclusively telegraphic signals identifying the particular box that has been activated. Newer boxes that permit voice communication with the dispatcher perform like telephones.

1.3 MONEY, MANAGEMENT, AND MANPOWER

1.3.1 Fiscal Pressures

The recent changes in latent and realized demand have imposed new burdens on fire departments. They include evaluating the new dangers and hazards; reconsidering equipment, manning needs, and locations; adding new training programs; upgrading technical abilities; reassessing standards of service; and absorbing increased activity and workloads. To the extent that all this implies a need for more resources, the issue is money—and the money may not be available. If it is not available, top management may be squeezed hard, especially if the jurisdiction is seeking budget cuts. One of the few graceful short-run solutions is to *do as well as possible in meeting demands for fire protection with the resources that are or will be available.* In general, this means that the jurisdiction must do one or more of the following:

Maintain current levels of service with lower budgets.

Keep costs from rising as fast as before.

Improve levels of service at lower cost than would be possible using traditional means.

Reduce service, if necessary, while keeping the increase in fire losses to a minimum and gaining maximum financial benefits.

Shift more of the costs of providing fire protection to the private sector.

The methods presented in Chapters 3 through 14 can help in any of these approaches. They can also ease planning and management headaches within fire departments. The specific areas they address include how to handle shifting alarm patterns, heavy peak-loads of alarms concentrated in a few hours, and false alarms; the best response to serious fires; and how to make move-ups (relocations) to balance coverage during busy periods. In addition, they address important problems in planning and implementing plans, choosing or evaluating firehouse sites, analyzing and interpreting call and alarm records, and using real-time command and control systems for dispatching and relocating firefighting resources. In collective bargaining, the methods can help provide a common basis of information for use in negotiation, which can improve the quality of the agreement reached, if not necessarily the ease of obtaining it.

1.3.2 Personal Services

Fiscal pressures and the accompanying management problems can be particularly severe for fire departments because of the nature of the services they provide. Despite the familiar hardware—engines, hoses,

1.3 Money, Management, and Manpower

tools, and ladders—the fire service is still basically a personal service provided at widely distributed local sites by groups of firefighters having specialized interests, skills, and physical capabilities. They lay hoses and advance them. They open up buildings, to expose flames to hose streams and to ventilate heat and smoke. They brave heat, flames, toxic gases, and collapsed structures to perform rescues. And they command these operations at the scene. Facilities and equipment are neither insignificant nor inexpensive, but the primary strength of a fire department is in its manpower, and the preponderant annual expenditure is still on personnel.

Indeed, in most paid fire departments, manpower costs amount to more than 90 percent of the total budget. Increases in costs have often followed increased demands for protection. Combined with the growing strength of municipal labor unions, these have sometimes led to larger forces and more often to higher salaries, pensions, and fringe benefits. As a result, to supply, staff, and operate one fire company—keeping the unit ready and running 24 hours a day, seven days a week—now costs from $250,000 to $750,000 per year, depending on manning levels and salaries.

Consider, for example, a firefighting unit staffed by four firefighters and an officer. In a more-or-less typical city, this unit might have a 52-hour work week (some cities work more hours per week, some fewer), 20 days paid vacation per year (some cities have more, some less), and 9 annual paid holidays or equivalent time off. In addition, they might use an average per individual of 15 days per year for total sick leave, military leave, training duty, and other approved time out of the firehouse.

If, for accounting purposes, the days off are considered to have 10 hours (regardless of the actual shifts followed), then the firefighters are not available for 44 days—440 hours—per year. This time is 16.3 percent of 2704 hours per year for which they are nominally on duty. Averaged over the full year, then, the effective time per week on duty is $52 \times (1 - 0.163) = 43.5$ hours. To fill a single position full-time (168 hours per week) requires $168/43.5 = 3.9$ firefighters actually on the payroll. Two units each with five firefighters on the apparatus thus require a total of 39 firefighters on the payroll.

In many jurisdictions, the average total cost of a firefighter (including officers and allocated support and administrative personnel) is roughly $20,000 per year. This includes salary, pension contributions, and fringe benefits such as insurance, but excludes the time off already accounted for. In these jurisdictions, the personnel cost of the five-firefighter unit staffed full-time would be $390,000 per year. If the average total cost were $30,000 per individual, the unit's personnel cost would be $585,000 per year.

In contrast, a fire station housing one unit might cost $400,000, but might last 40 years. Amortized at 7 percent interest, with normal maintenance, such a station might cost roughly $45,000 per year. The fire apparatus and associated equipment might cost about $70,000 and have a 15-year life. Amortized, with maintenance, they would cost roughly $10,000 per year. Together, the firehouse, apparatus, and equipment, with maintenance, would cost about $55,000 per year. This figure is 12.4 percent of the total cost of the unit if personnel costs $20,000 per individual per year, and 8.6 percent if it runs $30,000 per individual per year.

Costs for manpower, facilities, and equipment have all risen rapidly in the past decade, pushed in part by general inflation. Many departments have met the rising capital costs by continuing to use aging firehouses and apparatus past the point of normal replacement. But no such simple devices exist to reduce the effective cost of personnel.

As the calculation above shows, personnel costs are directly determined by:

(a) Average work week (for example, 52 hours per week).
(b) Average time off from firefighting duty (for example, 44 ten-hour days per year, or an average of 8.5 hours per week).
(c) Average time during the week that firefighters must be available on duty (for example, 168 hours per week).
(d) Average staffing of units on duty (for example, 4 firemen and 1 officer = 5 firefighters).
(e) Total manpower cost per firefighter (for example, $20,000 per year).
(f) The number of firefighting units.

Indeed, the calculation above can be written as

$$\text{cost per unit} = \frac{(c)}{(a) - (b)} \times (d) \times (e).$$

The total personnel cost for the firefighting units in a jurisdiction is:

$$\text{total cost} = \text{cost per unit} \times (f).$$

These quantities are not all equally amenable to change. The average work week may be set by custom or negotiation. There have been nationwide pressures for shorter work weeks, especially in the private sector. Municipal work weeks have tended to shrink notably over recent decades, though this trend may have been halted or reversed by severe fiscal pressures in some cities.

Time off is usually determined as a component of fringe benefit policy, which is negotiated in some jurisdictions. Sick leave and other absences may vary greatly over time, depending in part on job safety practices, management policies and practices, and firefighter morale.

In virtually all cities, firefighting units must be staffed seven days a week, 24 hours a day. In a few cities, however, there may be some flexibility as major hazards periodically change (e.g., in office buildings at night and on weekends), permitting modification of coverage at those times. Also, alarm rates may be high enough to warrant additional units on duty at peak times, but not at others.

Manning levels vary considerably from locality to locality, even on similar units handling similar hazards. Moreover, manning needs clearly depend on local firefighting tactics, the kinds of fire problems faced, the firefighting technology available, the skills and experience of the firefighters, and the organizational and response strategies followed. Major opportunities for flexibility clearly exist, but they need to be considered in the context of the overall deployment of a fire department's resources.

Manpower costs depend largely on salaries and pension contributions, which are usually set either by policy or by negotiations. To the extent that overhead or administrative costs are significant, reducing them can reduce the average cost per active firefighter. Otherwise, these costs tend mainly to increase in the long run and to be relatively inflexible in the short run.

The number of firefighting units (engines, ladders, squads, and special units) in a jurisdiction can usually be changed somewhat at any given time and can be changed substantially over longer periods of time. Decisions about the number of units are intimately tied to manning. With 20 men available on a given shift, for example, one can organize four 5-man units or five 4-man units. Or one might try four 4-man units and two 2-man minipumpers (as some cities have done), stationing the latter in areas where large volumes of water or large numbers of men are not likely to be immediately needed.

New units are readily created, though finding suitable firehouse space may create initial difficulties. Existing units are not easily consolidated or eliminated. Conflicts may arise if firefighters feel their jobs are being threatened or if people in the community feel they are being deprived of adequate protection.

1.3.3 Possible Productivity Improvements

Fire protection costs can be reduced by improving the productivity of the firefighting resources. Some productivity improvements that relate to improving a fire department's response and firefighting are described in Section 1.5.3. In this section we discuss approaches that reduce the amount of idle or "insurance" time charged to the fire department's budget.

In most localities, fire companies spend less than 5 percent of their time actually responding to or working at alarms. The rest of the time they provide insurance against major catastrophe and loss of life by being available and close-by when a fire occurs.[7] One way to capitalize on this "insurance time" is to use the same corps of men to serve multiple functions. Examples are:

On-duty inspections by firemen. Many American fire departments use "insurance time" to perform fire prevention duties, inspect hydrants, and check alarm boxes. This work not only helps prevent or limit fires, it also familiarizes the men with potential problem situations and buildings, and helps build closer ties with the community.[8]

Joint fire-ambulance work with crews trained thoroughly in both services and assigned flexibly to respond with whichever unit most needs men at the time. This practice is followed by most fire departments in northern Germany.

Joint fire-ambulance-rescue-towing work, as provided by Falck-Zonen throughout much of Denmark.

Joint fire-police service, as now practiced in some small-to-medium American cities. This is a controversial and often hotly debated approach.

Another method of improving productivity is through "consolidation." In regional consolidation, localities merge their fire departments. The idea is to improve the use of available firefighters, coordinate or centralize dispatch, provide a wider range of equipment, and create a more professional command. It is also possible to consolidate only selected functions. County fire inspection services can be instituted, for example, while individual communities continue to do the firefighting. Consolidated inspection teams, including fire, building, health, and environmental inspectors, can make a unified "pass" through a building. The virtue of this approach is its ability to take care of problems that otherwise might fall between jurisdictions. For firefighters, this is much like on-duty inspections, except that the joint teams alter the nature of the firefighters' work, and presumably increase the overall service provided.

Fire protection may also be combined with profitable functions, such as light manufacturing or craft industry. In Scottsdale, Arizona, the private fire department makes the special plastic garbage cans that the city provides for households. This saves the city what it would otherwise

---

[7] All emergency services spend large parts of their time being ready to respond to serious calls for assistance whenever they may occur. Police and ambulance services typically receive more calls per unit than fire services, and thus have less apparent "idle" time.

[8] Though the services performed are quite different, on-duty fire inspections can be considered analogous to the "preventive" or "deterrent" patrols that police often conduct between calls.

have to pay for labor. Work is easy to interrupt when the fire bell rings, as it must be to avoid conflict with the firefighters' primary function.

Still another approach is to use part-time personnel who can be mobilized quickly when problems are anticipated or begin to develop. For example, public employees on flexible jobs (such as public works) may agree to serve as reserve firefighters, to be put on standby when needed, or to respond to special fires when called via radio or paging device. Some men may regard this as a form of job enrichment; others receive extra pay for the time spent in training and service. Volunteer firefighters may be on call. This is done in much of Great Britain and parts of Germany and France. These groups may have professional officers or they may elect one of their own members to serve as commanding officer, as is done in many small American towns. Auxiliary firefighters and firefighter reserves can also help. This category includes civil defense personnel, armed forces personnel, college students (in college towns), and National Guard reservists. Full-time firefighters on another town's payroll can help if they can be called upon in emergencies to help neighboring towns. Two ways by which this is accomplished are "mutual aid" (in which neighboring fire companies are special-called to an alarm) and "automatic aid" (in which the neighboring companies automatically respond to alarms originating in certain locations).

Complementary personnel in the private sector, paid for by private funds, can also help shift some of the financial burden from the fire department. For example, industrial fire brigades are required in most European countries, and are relatively common in some parts of the United States. They are often trained and equipped to work with public firefighters. Fire liaison officers on payrolls of office buildings and universities can be trained according to public fire protection standards. Modest beginnings in this direction have been made in New York City. Insurance associations have for many years provided special salvage units to protect the property of their clients, although most of these units are now apparently being phased out.

1.3.4 Fire Service Personnel

Perhaps more than any other municipal service, the fire service is linked together by a sense of fraternity and tradition, the keystones of which are reliability, dedication, *esprit de corps*, heroism, and self-sacrifice. This tradition underlies much of the fire service's effectiveness, particularly in the grueling and dangerous operations required to save lives and limit damage in serious fires. So much indeed does the spirit of altruism and selfless dedication still survive that in thousands of communities where other services are paid, the fire service is still largely or entirely volunteer.

But many American volunteer fire departments have been eroding under the influence of suburban mobility and decreasing community ties, leaving a potentially serious fire protection gap in the nation's fastest-growing regions. In the cities, fire service traditions are beginning to seem antiquated. Public adulation, even support or sympathy for the firefighter, has been waning. And in the larger cities, demands on the fire service have increasingly become conspicuous symptoms of deeper social ills.

Firefighters have become increasingly disturbed because their traditions and the values they represent appear to be disintegrating. Changing public attitudes, fragile relations with minority communities, and increasing bureaucratization, even in smaller departments, have dimmed the luster of the job and have shaken the firefighters' self-image. Feeling that they are denied respect and prestige, many have channeled their resentment into demands for more tangible rewards—more money, shorter hours, easier work, more pleasant working conditions. These feelings have helped to increase militancy and to foster a previously unthinkable willingness to strike.

The same underlying conditions have also affected fire service management. Recruiting the most highly qualified men and women has become difficult. Labor-management and community relations have become increasingly important concerns. Costs have risen while voter resistance to increased budgets and taxes has stiffened. And management itself has become more difficult and more complex now that tradition alone no longer suffices to motivate and guide personnel.

Yet nearly everywhere certain traditions still dominate: for example, the only route to the top of the larger fire departments is from within, and few training programs are available to teach management and organizational skills. Moreover, even among officers, the orientation toward putting out fires is so decided that many of the best men prefer field command to top administrative or staff jobs.

1.3.5 The Fire Service, Local Government, and the Public

The fire service, the local government, and the public are all critical participants in creating fire protection services. Each has distinct perspectives, interests, and roles. Each influences the services provided and the results achieved in distinctive ways.

One way of looking at these mutual influences is to consider what each group gives in exchange for what it gets. If each group feels it is receiving more in value than it is giving, the exchange, and hence the entire fire protection system, will be stable. If one or more of the groups feel they

1.3 Money, Management, and Manpower

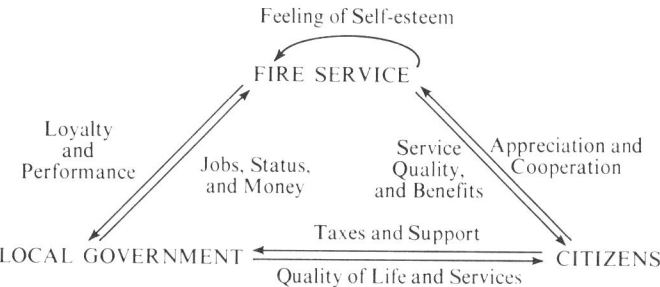

FIGURE 1.3. Exchange relationships among the fire service, local government, and the public.

are being short-changed, then instabilities can develop that must be remedied by revising or rebalancing the exchanges.[9]

In simplified form, the relations between the fire service, local government, and the public are represented as sides of a triangle in Figure 1.3. It is important to note that the relations treated in greatest detail in the chapters that follow—fire service performance for local government, and service quality and benefits for citizens—constitute parts of two sides of the triangle. Though the book concentrates on these two parts, it should not be forgotten that all the other parts must also be effective if the system as a whole is to work well.

The increasing role (and strength) of local community interests in the fire protection system now commands more consideration than in the past. This raises serious questions of equity, and even discrimination, in planning and providing services, and forces reexamination of local needs. Planners find themselves rethinking the balance of protection for business and residential areas, deteriorating and solid neighborhoods, center-city and outlying areas. Traditional formulations of need for protection may no longer be acceptable.

Moreover, community interests, especially in cities with well-educated, well-informed citizens who seek initiative and an active role in their government, increasingly create pressures for community participation in what formerly were unilateral decisions. Perhaps no American cities have progressed as far as Japan, where citizen consensus in public policy matters pervades public management. But local policy formulation has clearly been affected.

Sometimes, of course, there are conflicts, even within the community,

---

[9] More details about exchange relationships and their relevance to devising and "marketing" public service programs are given in Kotler (1975); Chapter 2, pp. 27–29, deals with fire departments.

that may test the diplomatic skills of fire service management. A neighborhood may want a new firehouse to improve its protection, but the people who live around the best or most feasible site may just as vocally oppose having it *there*. Any change, whether increasing or decreasing protection, or simply realigning locations to meet changing needs, may stimulate public meetings and partisan rallies. Such interest is surely preferable to apathy. But fire service management accustomed to unilateral modes of action may come to feel that rational decisionmaking has ceased to exist.

1.4 FIRE

1.4.1 The Nature of Fire[10]

To plan fire protection, it is important to consider the nature of fire and the protective tasks it imposes. To begin, a fire needs primarily two things: a "fuel," technically a substance that will give off heat when it reacts chemically, and some energy, usually in the form of heat. This initial extra energy serves two purposes: (a) to get the material hot enough locally so that it will be able to react, and (b) to keep the material hot enough to continue reacting even while the first reaction (for paper, wood, or fossil fuels, breaking down big molecules into smaller ones) soaks up the heat. If things get past this stage, there must still be enough energy left for the partially reacted material to react further, this time with oxygen from the air. These three prerequisites—fuel, heat, and oxygen[11]—are known popularly as the three sides of the "fire triangle."

If the fuel-oxygen compatibility is right, things begin to happen quickly at this stage. The heated materials react with the oxygen, giving off more heat. This heats them even more, causing them to react faster, giving off heat faster. If the heat cannot get away, the sequence becomes a spiral: give off heat, get hotter, react faster, etc. The point at which the reaction takes off on this spiral and at which the temperature and heat release-rate jump, is called "ignition."

If conditions are right for ignition, a new-born fire, sometimes called an "incipient" fire, has started. Now it needs more fuel and oxygen to grow. If both are within its reach, it begins to consume them, absorbing

---

[10] This brief section is intended for those unfamiliar with fire, to introduce concepts and terms used later on. Readers familiar with fire and firefighting may want to skip to Section 1.4.3. For a more complete, but still nontechnical, description of the nature of fire, see Lerup, Cronrath, and Liu (1977).

[11] Some fuels can be burned by chemical oxidizers other than oxygen, and others by "electron deficient" substances such as fluorine. We confine attention here, however, to the most common situation—fuels burning in air.

1.4 Fire

them to feed the growing spiral. Soon, if conditions remain favorable, the fire attains adolescence. The air around it gets hot, and, should the fire be in a building, begins rising to the ceiling, across the ceiling, down the walls, out the door to the next room. As the air moves, it carries along heat and reaction products (some of which may be solid particles, which if numerous enough become visible as smoke). This is often called the "smoldering" stage.

As the fire grows and gets hotter, it gets hot enough to glow and produce a flame.[12] It is not yet hot enough to warm surfaces near it by the energy radiating from its glow. Now it can spread many ways—by consuming more fuel nearby, by sending out warm tendrils of air containing burnable toxic gases (and perhaps smoke), and by radiant heating.

If conditions remain right, it does spread. New surfaces not next to the flame get hot enough to begin burning themselves, and shortly the room as a whole becomes ripe for ignition. Its temperature leaps upward and a sheet of flame seems to erupt and sweep across everything. This is "flashover." The odds are that anything once living in the room is now

---

[12] Some fires heat up so rapidly that flames may become visible almost immediately, even before the surrounding air has had time to warm and begin rising. Others smolder for hours before flame appears.

dead. The fire is now mature, and a raging menace to life and property, growing and consuming fuel exponentially with time.

How long the fire takes to grow to and through these stages depends on an enormous number of factors, most of them not yet well understood. How much a fire burns, what kind of damage it causes, how many people it injures or kills, and how fast it can spread if not contained thus depend greatly on circumstances. The aim of prevention and planned damage-limitation programs is to make circumstances unfavorable for ignition, growth, and spread.

1.4.2 Fighting a Fire

Any of a fire's characteristics can give it away: the early reaction products, the particles of smoke in the air, the toxic gases, the visible flame, or the rise in temperature. These can be detected by properly located, well-designed devices (detectors or sensors), or by animals or people. When the fire is detected, an alarm is sent to the fire department—electronically, mechanically, on foot; by pull-box, call-box, or telephone.

When the alarm is received, the most conspicious part of the fire service springs into action: fire vehicles with lights, bells, and sirens, carrying pumps, hoses, axes, hooks, ladders, and often much other equipment, speed to the scene of the fire. At a structural fire, firefighters rescue and evacuate people who are or may be endangered, and put out the fire—most often with water, but occasionally with special chemicals if the fire is unusual or small.[13] In many departments, once the fire seems to be out the tedious work of "overhauling" begins—finding and quenching embers and hot spots from which the fire could reignite, and putting the property in order. The fire department has the prime responsibility for all these activities, from the time the alarm is first received until the embers are cool.

1.4.3 The Cost of Fire

By the time a fire department learns about a fire, much of the damage may already have been done. Recent studies[14] have confirmed the widely held belief that roughly 90 percent of all people who die in fires in the

---

[13] Putting out (or extinguishing) a fire entails breaking the chain of events described above, which permit a fire to start and grow. Heat can be removed by cooling the fuel (e.g., by the heat water absorbs in vaporizing to steam); oxygen can be shut off (e.g., by smothering the fire in foam); the nature of the heat-liberating chemical reactions can be altered (e.g., by special chemicals); fuel can be removed (e.g., by closing a natural gas valve; by cutting a fire break in a forest fire).

[14] See, for example, Berl, Fristrom, and Halpin (1975).

United States die not from burns but from the toxic gases, mostly carbon monoxide, and are already dead or beyond recovery by the time the fire department receives the alarm. Unlike most other accidents, fires kill disproportionately the very young and very old—those who do not know they must escape, or how to escape; those who may be infirm; and those most susceptible to smoke, heat, and carbon monoxide.

Another cost of fire is property damage,[15] the extent of which often depends on how long it takes for the fire to be detected and reported after ignition. A fire that could have been put out with a glass of water or a fire extinguisher when it was small may become a raging inferno. It may destroy a building or an entire shopping center if no one notices it before the windows break and smoke or flames are widely visible. As long as the fire department depends primarily on people to detect and report fires, losses will depend at least partly on luck, as well as on fire department performance.

Property damage involves immediate economic losses, the destruction of assets, which must be repaired or replaced if possible. But there may also be other, less tangible losses. For example, when a home burns, the psychological damage to its owners may be as important as the physical damage. A business that depends on critical physical assets—special machinery, tools, or even files—may be closed for months, or even permanently, if money cannot replace them. The same may be true of a business that depends on its location to distinguish it from otherwise very similar competition. These indirect losses, which may far exceed the direct losses, are sometimes estimated, but more often are not.[16] The figures reported officially for fire losses tend, therefore, to understate the true impact of fire.

When a neighborhood is already marginal, or when a fire sweeps a substantial portion of a block, there may be secondary effects. Unless the damaged buildings are repaired properly (or are promptly demolished), they may begin to blight their surroundings, not only to disfigure them with blackened ruins but also to attract debris, vandals, and other undesirables. This acceleration of decay is a cost of fire.

Costs associated with fire insurance are also important. If, because of inflation or other factors, losses increase to the point where total insurance company costs exceed premium revenues, rates are increased, usually via a regulatory process that varies from state to state. Payments for fire losses thus always come from someone's premiums—this year's

---

[15] Direct property damage in the United States is estimated to be $4.2 billion per year (*Fire In the United States*, 1978).

[16] Munson and Ohls (1978) have estimated the indirect monetary losses from residential fires, including medical costs, temporary shelter costs, and costs due to missed work, are approximately $300 million per year.

or past years' if they fall within normal experience, next year's if losses overall are increasing.

The total costs of fire to society thus include:

Deaths and personal injuries.

Property damage, much of which is included in the premiums of fire insurance.

Uncompensated, secondary, and intangible losses.

The cost of administering and operating the fire insurance system. (Usually about 60 to 70 percent of the premiums for fire insurance are paid out to compensate for losses. The remainder covers brokers' commissions, inspections, loss adjustments and overall administration, contingency reserves, and profits.)

The cost of providing public fire protection, through the fire department and associated services (such as water supply). Some of these are capital investments paid for by bonds. Most are annual operating costs paid for by annual tax revenues.

The costs of private activities to prevent fires and limit damage, including those for materials, building design, protective devices, private fire protection, and fire safety training.

To some extent, these costs can be substituted for one another. Increasing private activities, for example, can ultimately reduce the number and severity of fires. Such a reduction immediately reduces uncompensated losses, and over time reduces insurance costs, since these are related to compensated losses. Moreover, if the general risk level in the city declines, so may the level of public fire protection provided. Over time, therefore, these costs too could decrease; the increase in private costs may, therefore, reduce the total costs to society.

Economic theory tells us that private activities should be increased until we reach the point at which total costs (public and private) cease decreasing and begin to rise. That is, we should keep spending until a dollar for private protection buys exactly a dollar decrease in the total of other fire costs. In practice, of course, only public and insurance costs are known with any accuracy, so that such a prescription is useful mainly in principle.

However, even though this cost/benefit approach cannot prescribe the best solution in detail, it can serve as a useful guide. First, it suggests that since American levels of private activity are well below those in much of Europe and Japan, increases in private fire protection investments are likely to prove highly beneficial.

Second, this approach emphasizes that the net social gains will not be realized immediately, but rather over an extended period of time. In an era of high interest rates, this extended pay-back period must be taken seriously and ways must be found to offset its effects on investment decisions. The society, after all, goes on for generation after generation, and if each generation sees benefits accruing mainly to the next, highly beneficial decisions may never be made.

Third, it raises a serious policy question. If increasing private fire protection leads to a decrease in the public costs, what happens the other way around? Over the long run, perhaps an increase in public fire protection would lead people to relax their private efforts, since the consequences of a fire would presumably be less severe than at the previous, lower levels of fire protection. Conversely, if public fire protection is perceptibly decreased, perhaps there would be a compensating increase in private activity. In the short run, this latter relationship seems to be valid. When fire protection has been conspicuously and drastically curtailed, during firefighter strikes and severe snowstorms for example, news accounts suggest that the public becomes more careful. But thus far there is no evidence, one way or the other, about what the long-term effects would be, since the curtailments have all lasted for only a short time.

Within this framework, it is also easy to see the trade-off between increased fire department expenditures and reduced insurance costs. In the short run, fire insurance costs may decrease if a city buys what it needs to change its category on the *Grading Schedule for Municipal Fire Protection* (1974).[17] Over the long run, the question is more like, what expenditures will best improve real fire protection and reduce losses, thereby improving conditions and ultimately building a case for lower rates? Of course, for obvious reasons, most political decisions are made for the near future. The methods presented in this book will be helpful in taking the broader perspective accurately into account.

1.4.4 Fire Insurance

A large loss matters much more to most people than the equivalent loss spread out in small amounts. The small amounts are often barely noticed and are almost always easily absorbed, while a large loss all at once may be ruinous. So people join groups or "pools" to share their risks. Each contributes a small amount regularly to reduce the net loss to any member of the group unlucky enough to be struck by a catastrophe. This is the principle underlying fire insurance; the contributions are the "premiums," which are pooled (after expenses and profits) to reimburse contributors financially for the losses they suffer when a fire occurs.

---

[17] Fire insurance and the role of the Grading Schedule in determining fire insurance rates are discussed in Section 1.4.4.

This is also the principle underlying public fire protection. Here, the "contributions" or "premiums" are the fire service's share of tax revenues. These are pooled to provide *physical insurance*—specialized equipment and people that reduce the likelihood of fires occurring and limit the size of losses when they do. The greater the risks, the greater the physical insurance required, and the greater the premiums that must be paid.

Fire insurance is essentially a means of redistributing losses, with the fortunate subsidizing the unfortunate. Fire protection also is redistributive. But it is primarily directed toward reducing realized losses, per se, and thus generating net economic benefits. Both fire insurance and fire protection also substitute a degree of certainty (e.g., regular, relatively small payments, and limited loss potential) for the uncertainty of rare—but possibly large—losses.

In the United States, the fire insurance industry consists of regulated profit-making firms. The decisions made by these firms affect the delivery of both public and private fire protection services. In the public sector, insurance industry decisions affect fire departments, water supply departments, building departments, and housing and development agencies. In the private sector, the availability and adequacy of fire casualty coverage can be critical to investment in housing and commercial development. Although the fire insurance industry strongly influences the level of fire protection that exists, the manner in which these influences arise is not well understood. Nor is the extent to which insurance industry practices support (or defeat) good fire protection known.

The insurance rate for an individual building in a particular city is determined by its characteristics (construction, use, etc.) and by the grade assigned by the Insurance Services Office (ISO)[18] to the city in which the building is located. The factors that determine a city's grade are described in ISO's *Grading Schedule for Municipal Fire Protection* (1974). They include: the number, location, and manning of the city's fire companies; the fire department's equipment and communications facilities; and the city's water supply, building codes, and fire prevention activities. The rationale behind the grading system and the resulting fire insurance premiums is simple. For two identical buildings in two different cities, other things being equal, one would expect the loss in a city with

---

[18] The Insurance Services Office (ISO) is a national organization established in 1971 by the property and liability insurance industry to provide a range of advisory, acturial, rating, statistical, research, and other support services to insurers, state fire organizations, and others. It is licensed as a fire rating organization in most states, and operates as an advisor to state fire organizations in all others. It grades the fire protection levels of most major cities in the Unites States, and all smaller municipalities and fire districts in the states in which it is licensed as a fire rating organization. Additional information about ISO is contained in *ISO Today* (1972).

an inadequate water supply and a fire department with low manning, poor equipment, and high response times, to be greater than the loss in a city with an excellent water supply and a fire department with high manning, good equipment, and low response times. So, in principle, the rate should be lower in the city with the better grade. The extent to which actual loss statistics bear this out is not known, so it is not clear that insurance rates determined in this manner are reasonable reflections of the hazards and risks of individual properties.

What is clear is that the insurance industry's evaluation of a community's fire protection system is exclusively related to protecting the insurance industry's interests. Although this is as it should be, the fire protection needs of a community will usually be different from those of the insurance industry. For example, life safety is not the primary concern of the fire insurance industry, while it is the primary concern of the community. Thus, the insurance industry may recommend different fire suppression levels or different fire prevention activities than those that the community decides are in its best interests.

In recent years, ISO's grading schedule has come under fire from a number of sources (see, for example, Homer et al., 1977). ISO is responding to this criticism by modifying its rate-making practices to shift the basis for setting insurance premiums away from arbitrary input requirements to actual fire losses. Some cities are also considering alternatives to the private provision of fire insurance because of the nonresponsiveness of the fire insurance industry to their needs in fire prevention and control. The Institute for Local Self-Government has recently examined the political, legal, and economic feasibility of municipal fire insurance (*Municipal Fire Insurance,* 1977).

1.5 IMPROVING FIRE PROTECTION

As noted earlier, fire protection has four major components: prevention, preresponse damage limitation, response and firefighting, and treatment. Of these, the first two offer the greatest potential for improving protection. Obviously, fires that do not occur cannot kill or cause damage. And, other things being equal, the sooner remedial action begins, the less chance there is that a fire will cause death, serious injury, or property damage. The problem is making prevention and preresponse damage limitation effective.

Both are now limited by a technological base that is universally inadequate. Much work remains to be done to understand the physics, chemistry, and engineering of fire initiation, spread, and extinguishment, and the chemical, medical, and human factors (psychology and man-technology relations) that influence injury and death. In the United States, both prevention and preresponse damage limitation are also hindered by economic, political, legal, and institutional obstacles that keep much of what is already known from being used.

1.5.1 Fire Prevention

In general, a firm commitment to fire prevention has not been made in the United States, whereas European countries stress preventive policies (see Section 1.5.5 for some examples). Preventing fires means preventing their ignition. Since, as described earlier, ignition can occur only when a suitable source of energy comes close enough to a potential fuel, there are basically four types of preventive actions:

1. *Change the potential source of energy,* so that it will not be hot enough or intense enough to ignite the fuels with which it is likely to come in contact.
2. *Change the potential fuel,* so that it will be less likely to ignite, or to sustain a flame if ignition does occur.
3. *Separate potential sources of energy from potential fuels.*
4. Institute more general measures to *prevent ignition and propagation* (for example, measures to accelerate heat removal, thereby raising the threshhold of additional energy needed to attain ignition).

Once the preventive technique (for example, impregnating fabrics to make them resist ignition) has been identified, the really difficult questions arise. What means exist to get it into use? At whom are these means directed, or at whom should they be directed to be most effective? In short, how can the technological possibility be brought into practice and made effective?

As a first step, one might categorize the principal means and targets. In the American system, the principal means of effecting change in prevention are:

A. *Legal,* by legislative, executive, or judicial actions (such as codes and regulations).
B. *Economic,* through financial incentives such as subsidies, taxes, tax credits, and fines.
C. *Social, political, and psychological,* through social pressures, political pressures, and appeals to responsibility or self-interest.
D. *Technological,* by changing the nature of the technical environment.

Each of these means can be directed at some or all of the principal targets:

i. *Individuals,* in their roles as owners, operators, and users of fire hazards, as potential accessories to ignition, and as potential victims of fire.

1.5 Improving Fire Protection

ii. *Items* (and their producers), representing the potential sources of energy (matches, electrical cable, etc.) and the potential fuels (fabrics, finishes, etc.).
iii. *Systems of hazards,* such as buildings, building subsystems (electrical, heating, etc.), and neighborhoods.

Thus, there are potentially 48 classes of prevention policies, one for each combination of action, means, and targets (Figure 1.4). For example, no-smoking regulations would fit in class 3-A-i; campaigns to observe them would fit into 3-C-i. Flammable fabrics regulations fit into 2-A-ii. Building codes fit into several classes, since their components include actions 1, 2, and 3, means A and B (and perhaps traces of D) and targets ii and iii.

From the standpoint of a municipality, which classes of fire prevention policy are most important to pursue? First, it should be pointed out that only certain classes can be pursued by municipalities; many require the legal, economic, or persuasive powers of higher levels of government. Second, not all classes are directed at fires that affect the overall service that the municipality and its fire department must provide. Of the remaining classes, those having the greatest potential for reducing fire losses at the smallest cost should be emphasized. It may be possible to obtain a great reduction in the likelihood of large fire losses by reducing

FIGURE 1.4. Alternative prevention policies.

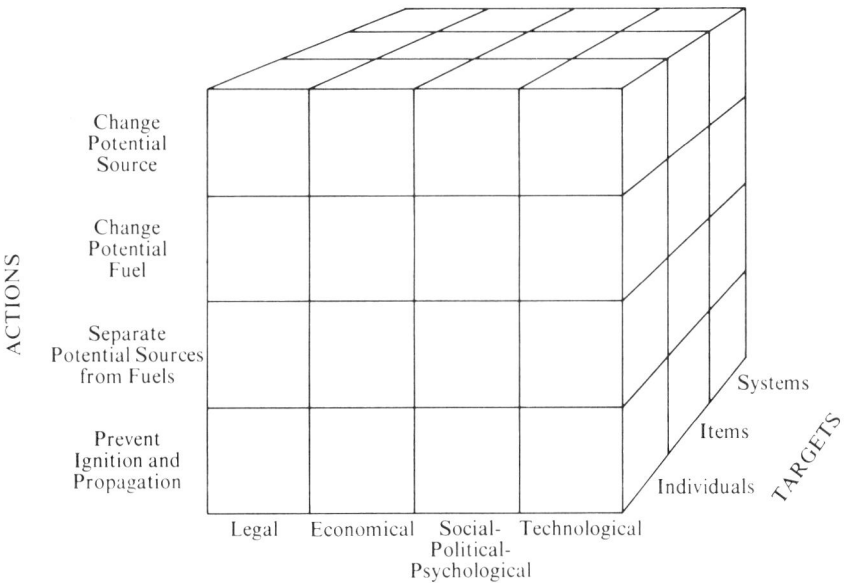

the risk associated with only a small number of buildings or industrial locations. If this is true, then these sites should be the first targets for any fire prevention efforts.

1.5.2 Preresponse Damage Limitation

If a fire cannot be prevented, it should be extinguished before it can cause much damage. In general, fires are extinguished by firefighters and special equipment sent to the site to extinguish them. But before response occurs, many things can be done to limit the damage a fire can cause.

Preresponse damage limitation can be examined and categorized systematically following the procedure used for prevention; that is, classifying alternatives in terms of *actions, means,* and *targets*. Following this procedure, possible damage-limiting actions are:

1. *Speeding human response,* typically by detecting a fire early and warning potential victims. Some devices also call the fire department directly. If warned early enough, potential victims can escape and perhaps begin fighting the fire themselves if it is still small enough.[19]
2. *Containing the fire,* typically by interposing physical barriers (such as fire walls, fire doors, and intumescent paints) or by attempting to extinguish it (sprinklers, halogenated gas discharge, and dry chemical agents).
3. *Limiting the exposure or reducing the maximum possible loss,* typically by helping victims escape or restricting hazards by building and zoning regulations.

The means of achieving preresponse damage-limiting actions, and the targets for these means, are the same as those depicted in Figure 1.4. There are thus 36 possible categories of preresponse damage-limiting policies that can be constructed simply by changing the labels along the vertical axis in Figure 1.4 and identifying the boxes as above.

1.5.3 Response and Firefighting

Improving response and firefighting implies improving the ways fire companies are dispatched and how they work at fires. This includes changing dispatching procedures in the communications office (see Chapter 14),

---

[19] Many American fire officials are reluctant to advocate citizen firefighting efforts for fear that people who try to put out their own fires will delay notifying the fire department and unnecessarily jeopardize their safety. Many European officials, on the other hand, stress the importance of prompt local firefighting activity and encourage it wherever possible. Some feel that on-the-scene efforts before the fire service arrives are critical in keeping losses relatively low.

1.5 Improving Fire Protection

changing the response policy (see Chapter 11), revising fireground procedures, and improving the ability of firefighters to perform by providing better tools and training.

The interaction between technology and manning is particularly important. One ladder truck carrying six men equipped with hand-held radios and power tools may be able to do many jobs that normally require two ladder trucks each with four or five men less well equipped. A four-man engine company with automatic pumper control may be able to perform the work that ordinarily requires five men. These improvements would not merely save time and effort at fires; they would enable men to be used far more effectively, and thus to provide better overall protection. For example, if four 5-man pumpers without automatic control can be turned into five 4-man pumpers with automatic control, one additional unit is "created" without decreasing the firefighting ability of the initial four units.

Another approach to improving the response to fires is in some ways the easiest: Improve the allocation of resources to match supply and demand. In many cases, measures based on this approach can be developed and implemented in weeks, whereas the other approaches mentioned usually require months to years. This approach is based on the principle that supply and demand should be in balance. One way to achieve the balance is to match the number of men on duty to the demands anticipated in the forthcoming time period. For example, manpower scheduling can be designed with overlapping or split shifts. Also, sophisticated on-duty and off-duty patterns can be used to ensure that more men are on duty when peak loads are expected, without having extra men on duty when they are not needed. Such tailored scheduling is relatively common in police departments and is also used, for example, by the Metropolitan Toronto Ambulance Service and the Washington D.C. Emergency Ambulance Service. It has also been used by the New York City Fire Department and the Rural Fire Protection Company in Scottsdale, Arizona.

It is also possible to use multilocation units, which move from areas where they may be needed during the day but not at night (a central business district having few residences, for example), to areas where they are needed more at night (high-risk residential neighborhoods and sports arenas, for example).

Supply and demand may also be balanced by matching the number and type of units dispatched to the best estimate of the need at the site. Adaptive response policies, such as those described in Chapter 11, are designed to do exactly that—to ensure that serious incidents receive more immediate coverage than they might otherwise get, while less serious incidents receive less.

Another way of balancing supply and demand is to dynamically match the coverage in a region to the current status of its fire companies and the demands expected in the next hour or so. Such dynamic balancing of coverage to demand is achieved by the relocation policies described in Chapter 12.

1.5.4 Treatment

Once a fire has been extinguished, the job of treatment begins. Generally, treatment attempts to achieve three broad goals:

1. *Limit the lasting consequences,* typically by the immediate provision of medical services, counseling and psychological assistance, the relocation of occupants, immediate efforts to shore up (or demolish) weakened buildings, employment assistance, and salvaging property.
2. *Repair the damage,* typically by medical treatment, property repairs and debris removal.
3. *Redistribute the economic and social burdens,* typically through insurance payments, unemployment insurance, business assistance, and area rehabilitation (where damages are widespread).

1.5.5 International Perspective

Though cultures, economies, and governmental structures differ among countries, fire protection is a universal need that in many respects must be satisfied the same way everywhere. International differences occur principally over (a) which fire protection components are emphasized, (b) how they are emphasized, (c) what compromises are made when fire protection conflicts with other societal goals (such as economic development), and (d) what institutional forms permit policies to be developed and put into practice.

Do these differences matter in determining the ultimate quality of fire protection? The record is clouded somewhat by the differences in definitions of fire losses and fire-related deaths (even within the United States the definitions vary greatly from state to state and city to city), and by statistics of widely varying quality. But the overall comparison is clear: *the United States experiences more serious fires and more fire-related deaths per capita than any other comparably advanced nation* (see Table 1.1).[20]

Nationally, the rate of American fire-related deaths is more than twice those in Great Britain and France. The same relations hold when cities are compared. The fire death rate in New York City, which is quite

---

[20] Additional international comparisons are described in Rardin and Mitzner (1977).

1.5 Improving Fire Protection

compatible with the rate for the entire U.S., is more than twice the rate in Vienna, more than three times the rate in West Berlin, more than four times the rate in Amsterdam, and more than six times the rate in Hamburg and Munich.[21]

Part of the reason must lie in the greater number of fires, and serious fires, that Americans suffer. New York City, for example, experiences roughly 600 structural fires per 100,000 population per year. In contrast, Munich and West Berlin have fewer than 200 structural fires per 100,000 people per year, and Hamburg, Vienna, and Amsterdam all have fewer than 260. These figures match well the data for all of Great Britain and France, which experience less than 280 structural fires annually per 100,000 people. As a result, European cities typically operate with many fewer firefighters per capita than American cities do, and incur much smaller expenditures per capita for public fire protection.

Serious fires are more difficult to define consistently, but the contrasts here are similar: American cities experience far more serious fires per capita than any of their European counterparts.

The much smaller number of European fires appears largely attributable to very strong emphasis on prevention and preresponse damage limitation.[22] Virtually all of the advanced European countries and Japan stress preventive policies and programs, which are firmly integrated into their cultural patterns and their economic, administrative, and legal systems. These countries have been willing to grant to national and local authorities powers over new construction, existing buildings, and potentially hazardous operations that Americans thus far have been unwilling to cede.

Some regulations not typically found in the United States include:

Virtual prohibition of wooden structural frames or external surfaces in buildings or homes in urban areas.

Occupancy certification laws that require all buildings to meet current

---

[21] Though all cities differ, especially those in different cultures, these European cities are comparable in many ways to their United States counterparts of similar size. Most have sizeable minority populations, which are often transient (and composed at least partly of aliens) and are usually housed in run-down areas. Most are experiencing population declines and financial strains, plus terrorism and other modern social ills. The differences in fire experience are so large, however, that even very rough comparability makes the basic point clear.

[22] Some of the emphasis on prevention may be implicit, almost a subliminal part of the culture. Perhaps because of the long history of disastrous conflagrations, fire is treated as a disgrace—nearly a crime—in some countries, whereas in the United States fire-related negligence is often dismissed or even condoned by permissive insurance laws and community sympathy. These differences should not obscure the factors that may be transferable, however, or encourage despair about improving American fire protection.

TABLE 1.1. Comparison of international fire experience.

Place	Population[a]	Annual Structural Fires[b]		Annual Serious Fires[c]		Annual Fire-Related Deaths[d]	
		No.	No. Per 1000 Persons	No.	No. Per 10,000 Persons	No.	No. Per 100,000 Persons
		COUNTRIES					
USA[e]	210,000,000	1,200,000	5.7	N.A.	N.A.	7,500	3.5
England and Wales[f]	49,000,000	128,209	2.6	N.A.	N.A.	775	1.6
France[g]	50,000,000	138,705	2.8	16,500	3.3	310	0.6
		U.S. CITIES					
New York City[h]	7,600,000	49,533	6.5	4,523	6.0	295	3.9
Tacoma, Washington[i]	155,000	740	4.8	64	4.1	6	3.9
Trenton, New Jersey[j]	101,000	947	9.4	N.A.	N.A.	5	5.0
Wilmington, Delaware[k]	80,000	846	10.6	208	26.0	3	3.8
		EUROPEAN CITIES					
Amsterdam[l]	770,000	1,957	2.5	115	1.5	8	1.0
Hamburg[m]	1,800,000	4,429	2.5	664	3.7	11	0.6
Munich[n]	1,300,000	1,913	1.4	241	1.8	2	0.2
Vienna[o]	1,600,000	3,547	2.2	685	4.3	27	1.7
West Berlin[p]	2,100,000	4,034	1.9	251	1.2	26	1.2

[a] Most recent estimate or census report of full-time resident population, rounded to two or three significant figures. For all cities (except West Berlin), workday population can be as much as one-third higher because of commuting workers, shoppers, and visitors.

[b] Generally defined to be fires occurring in buildings. Figures from England and Wales include fires involving other kinds of enclosed property, such as automobiles, ships, and airplanes. Figures for France include all fires requiring firefighting or response by firefighters.

[c] Generally, fires where more than one hose line was used in extinguishment. For Vienna, fires involving some danger or rescue. For France, fires with "serious consequences."

[d] Total civilian deaths attributed to fire. Typically, 80–90 percent occur in buildings.

[e] *Fire In the United States*. U.S. Fire Administration, Washington, D.C., 1978.

[f] *Home Office Report of Her Majesty's Chief Inspector of Fire Service for the Year 1973*. London: Her Majesty's Stationery Office, Cmnd. 5674, October 1974.

[g] Chesnais, J. C. "La Mortalité Par Accidents en France Depuis 1826." *Population*, Vol. 29, No. 6, 1097–1135, 1974. Also, *La Protection Civile*. Paris: Ministère de L'Intérieur, Service Nationale de la Protection Civile, 1975, pp. 10–22.

[h] *Fire Department of New York Annual Statistics, 1973*. New York: New York City Fire Department, 1974.

[i] *1974 Annual Report, Tacoma Fire Department*. Tacoma, Washington: Tacoma Fire Department, 1975.

[j] *1974 Annual Report of the Trenton Fire Division*. Trenton, New Jersey: Trenton Fire Division, 1975.

[k] *Wilmington Fire Department, Annual Report, 1972–1973*. Wilmington, Delaware: Wilmington Fire Department, 1973.

[l] *Verslagen der Bedrijven Diensten en Commissies van Amsterdam, Jaarverslagen 1970, 1971, 1972, 1973*. Amsterdam Brandweer, 1971, 1972, 1973, 1974. Fire statistics are for 1973. Death figures are the average for 1970–1973; the annual death figures were 15, 9, 4, 6, respectively.

[m] *Notruf 112: Erfahrungen der Feuerwehr Hamburg 1968–1971*. Hamburg, 1972 and "Taetigkeit der feuerwehr Hamburg im Kalenderjahr 1974," in *Feuerwehr Hamburg*, Hamburg, 1975. Death figures given are the average for 1968–1971; fire statistics are for 1974, but do not differ greatly from the average for 1968–1971.

[n] *Feuerwehr der Landeshauptstadt Muenchen im Jahresbericht 1973*. Munich, 1974.

[o] *Feuerwehr der Stadt Wien im Jahresbericht 1973*. Vienna, 1974 and *Statistischer Jahrbuch der Stadt Wien*. Vienna: Magistrat der Stadt Wien, 1974.

[p] *Berliner Feuerwehr im Jahresbericht 1974*. West Berlin, 1975.

fire codes, regardless of when they were built, and that can shut down buildings of all sizes and occupancies if they do not comply.

Criminal and civil negligence laws aimed at those whose actions (or inaction) contribute(s) to serious fires.

Strong fire codes backed by substantial engineering expertise in local building and fire departments, and special administrative judges to speed adjudication of disagreements.

Requirements for local fire prevention officers and firefighters, backed by professional inspection, at all major industrial installations.

These requirements (and rigorous code enforcement) are believed to raise building and operating costs moderately, though it is difficult to estimate the effect quantitatively. And, as all laws do, they restrict individual freedom, though not to an extent that has generated strong protests, or even noticeable feelings of limited freedom. In return, they have evidently induced the design and construction of buildings less likely to burn, and have stimulated citizens, owners, and managers to be more careful and more concerned about fire.

Fire service institutional arrangements vary greatly. Most countries have local fire service, as the United States does. But Great Britain has consolidated its forces to cover relatively large regional areas providing considerable national coordination through the Home Office in London. Recent West German laws have shifted legal authority and codes to the state level, though the fire service itself is still local. The civil service structure of the professional fire service in Germany has long been uniform within states, however, and has permitted movement of personnel between states as well. Most mobility appears to be at the highest ranks. The French fire service is strongly centralized, as is much of the French government. Indeed, the Paris fire brigade is supplied by the Army, and that in Marseille, by the Navy. In Denmark, on the other hand, most of the fire service outside Copenhagen is provided by a nationally regulated private corporation, Falck-Zonen, which also provides ambulance, rescue, and automotive towing services to localities, all on a contract basis.

On the European continent, fire departments have two-tier personnel systems. Rank and file firemen, without college degrees but with some technical skills, occupy one ladder, while officers, who must have college degrees (usually in engineering or architecture), occupy another. Officers enter laterally at their higher ranks, depending on their education, training, and experience, though they must be apprenticed for several years before they can assume command at fires. The officers' advanced technical backgrounds lead to a strong technological emphasis in all aspects of their work, and to the use of some more sophisticated equipment (for example, automatically controlled pumpers) than is readily available in the United States.

Another notable feature is the extensive use of volunteer firefighters as an adjunct to professionals, even in the major cities. In West Germany, volunteers man all the stations in the relatively less dense (usually outlying) sections of major cities. They use the same or slightly less complex equipment, and are supported by the professional force, which provides training, supervision, and help at any incidents that threaten to get out of hand. German fire chiefs say this practice greatly enhances the fire protection they can supply, and also helps build and maintain close ties between the professional fire service and the community it serves.[23]

1.5.6 Obstacles to Innovation in the Fire Service

Although fire protection has advanced significantly over the past century, innovation in fire protection often comes slowly, especially within the fire service itself. Even with the advent of motorized equipment and mobile radio communications, for example, basic fire department practices inherited from the past continue widely in traditional forms, and most use manpower generously.

Fire departments are essentially line-operating agencies. Such agencies are often ill-equipped in outlook, skills, and organization to undertake novel or significant change.[24] Though their members willingly accept major personal risks in firefighting, organizationally they are often unwilling to undertake efforts that involve more than minimal uncertainty and bureaucratic risk. The rewards for success within the organization and its political setting are usually small, and the price of failure disproportionately high.[25]

External obstacles raise the barriers to innovation even higher. To be effective, the fire service depends heavily upon others, for whom fire protection is typically a secondary objective: those who formulate and administer the building codes; architects and building contractors; fire insurance companies; telephone companies; alarm services; and equipment manufacturers and suppliers. Within local government, the fire service depends upon other agencies' programs that deal with: housing, particularly those policies aimed at preventing deterioration and aban-

---

[23] A more extensive international comparison of fire protection systems and fire losses is contained in Rardin and Mitzner (1977).

[24] This is clearly not always so, as the significant changes introduced by many departments demonstrate. The other side of the coin is that fire departments also can be tightly organized, relatively monolithic organizations that may respond quickly to leadership in situations having commonly perceived goals and outcomes.

[25] See Chapter 5.

donment; trash collection, especially in yards, halls, and vacant lots; water supply; land-use and zoning; and social policies at all levels of government.

As noted above, technological change could contribute significantly to some aspects of fire protection, either by changing the basic nature of the service the fire department must provide (for example, by creating less flammable bedding and furnishings, or comprehensive early fire detection and warning systems) or by increasing the service capability of each firefighter. But such technological changes in fire protection have occurred slowly, even where suitable technology already exists, principally because normal market forces work against them. The changes add to costs, and there have been neither financial incentives nor strong regulations to stimulate adoption.[26]

Given the magnitude and seriousness of fire-related problems that ultimately affect nearly everyone in our society, it might be imagined that the fire profession is united in a common struggle. This is not the case. Despite their common interests, the fire protection industry, fire insurance companies, fire departments (further divided by size and by whether they are predominantly paid or volunteer), and firefighting unions have tended to view themselves as rivals as much as partners. Leading interest groups (such as the NFPA) and universities have tried to bring order to the field, but have had limited resources. The establishment in 1974 of the National Fire Prevention and Control Administration in the Department of Commerce was an important positive step. Despite its promising beginning, however, the leverage it and its successor, the United States Fire Administration (established in 1978), can exercise over the most significant problems remains to be seen.

American public management has entered a period of serious public skepticism, which further complicates the already complex processes of innovation. After several decades of urgent calls to action, bold ventures, and reform, many Americans have become unusually disenchanted with the disparity between political promise and performance. Real incomes, educational levels, life expectancy, and opportunities for self-expression have increased notably for many citizens. Yet serious problems that were to be eliminated have persisted and even grown worse. Programs begun with great fanfare and expenditures are now branded failures; still others are simply marking time. Money and good intentions have often been applied lavishly, but seem not to have sufficed.

---

[26] The major leverage over such technological changes exists at national rather than local levels, because most of the relevant markets that must be influenced are national in scale. Federal activity thus appears to be essential if the basic nature of urban fire protection is to change.

In this climate of public skepticism, it is increasingly necessary to be sure that proposed policies and programs will actually work. Once essentially taken for granted, this ancient and honorable criterion is experiencing renewed emphasis. Proponents more and more will be pressed to convince skeptics and nonbelievers that what they suggest: (a) will accomplish what it is supposed to accomplish; (b) will minimize unwanted side effects—or clearly yield social benefits much greater than costs; (c) can be administered efficiently and fairly; and (d) once implemented, can be kept running correctly as long as desired with only routine maintenance. Satisfying these criteria is not simple, as experienced managers know.

The principal means of developing such ideas or establishing such evidence are likely to be analysis and analogy. Analysis can provide the means to develop rational solutions to problems. Analogy can help to transfer principles and ideas from one context to another. When the differences are sufficiently small or well understood, experience in one context can be used to estimate what it could be in others.

The analytical and analogical methods presented in this book thus represent more than an advance in the ability to provide fire protection. They also help management to develop and *pretest* new ideas safely and inexpensively before proposing them to the public.

1.6 MEASURING FIRE PROTECTION

Clearly, to improve fire service or even to determine objectively whether it needs improving, measures of service performance are needed. Since fire protection has many intangible attributes, measuring is something of an art, as well as a science. A detailed discussion of many measurement issues and problems is contained in a recent NFPA publication by Schaenman and Swartz (1974).

1.6.1 Quality and Quantity

In a critical service such as fire protection, the quality of the service matters as much as the quantity. Each of two fire departments may be able to field a hundred men, but one group may do a much better job of firefighting than the other. The reason may be basic ability, training, command, tools, *esprit de corps*, or all of these. But what matters is that the firefighting is better, the service is better, the quality is higher.

Of course, a word like "quality," which is subject to various interpretations, must be tied down by specific measures. What are they? Some quality measures may be quantitative, such as the time taken to control and extinguish a "standard" kind of fire. Of course, such measures are not completely quantitative since, although two fires may be similar they are almost never identical. Some quality measures may be qualitative, even subjective. An example is the poise of the lead ladder man as he climbs onto a burning roof laden with tools, or the calmness with which he descends with an unconscious person over his shoulder.

Quantitative measures are usually preferred to qualitative measures. They are (or are at least capable of being) more objective and uniform, and have generally agreed meanings, which value-laden words do not. Moreover, there are accepted methods for working with numbers and transforming them to yield information, whereas the methods for transforming words into other words are usually concealed within people's heads or are difficult to explain. Still, one should always ask of any number: How is it defined? How was it measured? Can you really measure what the number purports to represent (e.g., gallons of water used at a fire, percentage of structure saved)? What assumptions are included? Were the rules of statistics followed in testing and interpreting it, and if not, why?

The purpose of a measure is to represent compactly information that otherwise would be difficult to depict (i.e., a list of response times replaces videotapes of the actual responses.) Such information can be qualitative or quantitative, as can the measure. The central question is: how faithful is the representation to what really matters about what it portrays?

1.6.2 Basic Criteria

Any public service must be measured by three criteria that reflect the essential social values underlying the service. They are:

Effectiveness—how well the service achieves its stated goals.

Efficiency—how well key resources are used in providing the service.

Equity—how fairly costs and benefits are distributed.

The first two, effectiveness and efficiency, are often assumed to mean much the same thing. But there is a significant difference between them: effectiveness is concerned with the basic reason for providing the service (protection from fires), while efficiency is concerned with the resources that are being consumed (the use of skilled man-hours, for example). A fire department may be effective (that is, provide excellent fire protection) without being efficient; another department may be efficient (i.e., economical) but not highly effective.

The third criterion, equity, is often called the "political" criterion, though it reflects interests more basic than that implies. It concerns the relationship between those who pay and those who benefit. The equity

1.6 Measuring Fire Protection

question may also be put in the form: Is the distribution of payments and benefits one that society considers fair?

How are these basic criteria translated into measures, and how does one use them? Let us consider some simple examples, beginning with the simplest criterion—efficiency. *Efficiency* is an economic criterion that identifies how well scarce resources are used in performing particular services. It is most often applied to small parts of service operations that are critically limited by one or more scarce items, although it can be applied to the entire service as well. Generally, money is the scarcest item in the fire service, so that one operation is said to be more efficient than another if, for comparable levels of "output," it is less expensive (or for the same expense yields more). In special situations, such as a disaster, special skills and equipment may be more scarce than money; then the most efficient operation is not necessarily the least expensive, but the one that makes the best use of the scarce equipment, doctors, and rescue crews.

Measures of *equity*, on the other hand, look at variations or differences in service among groups. Which groups matter depends, of course, on local concerns. Typically, fire service equity concerns city neighborhoods or geographic subdivisions; it could also concern economic levels, racial or ethnic groups, or other identifiable subsections of society. For example, if one wished to allocate fire stations to minimize the response time to the actual fires that occur, one would tend to group the stations in the high alarm rate areas. This allocation would lessen coverage in the areas that call for service less often (because they are more careful, better constructed, or whatever). Such a distribution might be considered inequitable or unfair to the people who have fewer fires, since response times to the few alarms that do occur in the low-alarm neighborhoods could be undesirably long, while response times in high-alarm areas might be shorter than they need be. Consideration of equity shows that an otherwise reasonable criterion (based on effectiveness) should not be used alone.[27]

Effectiveness is the measure of how well a service does what it is supposed to do. To the extent that the fire service is intended to meet diverse objectives, any effectiveness measure will have a number of components. For example, a straightforward list of the purposes of a fire department includes:

Public Orientation

Minimize damage, injury, and loss of life from fire.

Provide physical security and enhance citizens' sense of security.

---

[27] Chapter 9 deals with this issue in some detail.

Monitor the building stock and potentially dangerous activities for fire hazards.

Provide assistance in nonfire emergency situations.

Internal Orientation

Maintain men and equipment in the best appropriate condition.

Maintain *esprit*, commitment, and managerial direction.

To the extent that all these purposes matter, components of the effectiveness measure should be developed for them. For example, consider inspections. One simple measure is a count of the number of inspections made. But this would not reflect the quality of the inspections (superficial vs. thorough, whether the property owner or manager was involved, etc.) or the relation of the numbers to potential dangers to be discovered and corrected. Inspections relative to past history of fires, or inspections relative to perceived fire risk would seem more informative and better related to the information desired.

If one is really interested in effectiveness, however, it is necessary to look beyond the immediate event to its consequences. What happens after the inspection? What is the distribution of time from inspection to next fire? What evidence is there that the inspections made a difference? The measures need not be complicated or require massive data collection. But they must be sharply focused on the basic question that underlies the activity: Does the service really accomplish what it set out to accomplish?

1.6.3 Measurement Levels

It is often tempting to define the broadest possible goal for the service at the highest level, and define effectiveness as the extent to which that goal is met. Such a broad definition is rarely operationally useful. For one thing, some key services, such as prevention, are intended to be cumulative, to reap their benefits over an extended period of time. Today's fires reflect the cumulated deficiencies of months and years of prevention activity, in some cases dating back to the time the offending buildings were constructed. The true success of the service at the broadest level can be determined only many years after it is provided. Such a formulation may well be of long-term interest, but can hardly provide the information needed to improve service on a time scale that is operationally and politically meaningful.

Moreover, since the kinds of decisions that are made vary from level to level within the city and the fire department, both "global" and "local" measures are needed to reflect these differences. Most operating decisions about deploying service are not made, after all, at the level of the mayor or city manager, or even at the level of commissioner of chief, nor should they be. When the administrative system works properly, major policy guidelines are established at the top levels, but basic decisions about where to put resources are not. They are usually made at working levels a step or two down in the hierarchy. Whereas relatively broad objectives and measures of effectiveness are needed to form good high-level policies, they may be confusing or useless at lower levels.

Take, for example, the objective of minimizing total social costs. This is an appropriate objective for the head of the United States Fire Administration, or even for a mayor or city manager. For the fire chief, however, it is merely frustrating: he does not control enough of the key factors that affect the objective, and hence measures of its attainment. His subobjective relates to what he can control: the "avoidable damage" and "avoidable loss of life" from fires, taking into account the unknown and currently uncontrollable time before detection and alarm. His subordinates, however, do not have even this scope. The dispatchers, together with the area commanders, make the decisions that affect the number of men on duty in particular locations at particular times, and the number dispatched to particular alarms. The local commander arriving at the fire to find an inadequate response can only demand more help. He is responsible for what he does with the units he gets; if they are understaffed or late, that responsibility lies elsewhere. "Local" measures thus are needed to reflect true accountability.

1.6.4 The Service Process and Measures

The service process consists of the stages by which basic resources (men, materials, money, and information) are converted into the desired effects. In aggregate, there are five stages:

1. *Inputs*—budget allocations.
2. *Intermediate inputs*—the things money immediately buys: manpower, equipment, firehouses. They are the labels that appear on budget lines. These intermediate inputs are also the items counted in the ISO grading schedule.
3. *Outputs*—what the fire department produces with the intermediate inputs. For example, coverage, company availability, response times, numbers of men on the scene, and hose lines active.
4. *Effects or Impacts*—what the fire department's activities produce, together with the inputs from other city services, private investments, and private activities. These include reductions in deaths, property damage, total loss to the community, and lasting injuries.
5. *Perceptions*—people's views of these effects, which influence how often the service is requested and its level of public support. Public

perception of how well a fire department is doing may count as much as the facts about output or effects.

Each stage generates its own measures: dollars, men and equipment, response times, damage, degree of satisfaction. Which ones should be used, and how? Ultimately, of course, the "measure" of interest is the total social cost. At the fire department level, the key part of total social cost is the effect of fire protection, usually measured, unfortunately, by the results of lack of protection. This is expressed in the following simple equation:

Damage Prevented by the Fire Department

= Damage Without Fire Protection − Actual Damage That Occurs.

We can measure observed damage, but we want to know the damage prevented or saved by the fire department (if the fire department and not all of society is our immediate concern). Unfortunately, we do not know the second factor in the equation, the damage that would have occurred without "protection." The question is, without how much protection? With no fire department at all, and no consequent adjustments in private investment? Or with a minimal fire department; enough, say, to prevent a conflagration?

The choice of "savings" due to fire protection is akin to that made by the man who came puffing into city hall, late for a meeting. As he plopped into his chair he gasped, "Sorry I'm late. I forgot my wallet and had to run all the way. But I ran next to a bus, and saved forty cents." "Well," said the chairman, "If you had run next to a taxi all the way, you could have saved five dollars!" Anytime the standard for comparison is arbitrary, "savings" estimates are also arbitrary and may obscure more than they reveal.

A number of attempts have been made to establish more precisely the relationship between fire department output and ultimate effects or impacts. One can distinguish three general approaches: (1) engineering models of fire growth and spread for particular buildings, with factors representing fire department activities; (2) "quantified intuition" models, which represent systematically the intuitive experience and feelings of senior fire chiefs; and (3) statistical models, which retrospectively analyze losses from and response times to past fires, and try to fit the data statistically to "reasonable" representations of the major effects involved.

Of these, the engineering models are extremely complex and as yet still in their infancy so far as fire department applications are concerned. The "quantified intuition" models yield interesting relationships, but

1.6 Measuring Fire Protection

cannot tie the inputed "value of response time" to dollars, lives, or more general measures people understand.[28] The last approach is best exemplified by the work of the Scientific Advisory Branch of the British Home Office, which has derived and published a number of curves for loss versus response-time using aggregate data from Great Britain.[29] For a fuller description and review of these approaches see Swersey et al. (1975).

This last set of results has been applied by the Home Office group to compute fire service allocations to minimize the sum of losses and fire brigade expenditures, assuming private investment to be constant in the short run. The resulting curves of total costs versus numbers of units are surprisingly flat—that is, remarkably insensitive to the number of units and stations—over rather a wide range. Whether this result is realistic is, of course, open to question. It does seem to show, however, that the best allocations of men and equipment are not extremely sensitive to the exact numbers used in the response time versus loss relations, or to their exact forms (as one can readily check), as long as the curves remain generally of the form the British group has used.

If that is so for the best relations yet derived, one is tempted to ask, why become ensnared in the details of losses versus response time? This is especially so in view of the preceding discussion: the base for loss versus response-time calculations is essentially arbitrary at present; the variation in time before detection and reporting is likely to mask the effects of the much smaller variations in response times; and the loss figures will in any case have to be adjusted for specific buildings (skyscrapers versus shacks) to reflect relative valuations. If not dollars and lives, what then?

Let us take the viewpoint of the fire chief. When the call comes into the fire department, the best he can do is to affect the margin with which he can work: other things being equal, the faster the needed men and equipment respond to a serious fire, the lower the losses and deaths. Minimizing response times, therefore, is minimizing losses and deaths—at the controllable margin.

In much of this book we work with output measures, recognizing their limitations, but integrating them into a logical framework that minimizes these limits while exploiting their advantages. In subsequent chapters, we make extensive use of measures such as response time, coverage, availability, initial response adequacy, and fire company workloads. We

---

[28] Interested readers with mathematical training can pursue this work in Keeney (1973).
[29] Recent reports presenting the data and analyses include Hogg (1973) and Hogg (1975). These require some mathematical background in order to be read easily.

do so because, as noted earlier, (a) the book concentrates on the deployment of firefighting resources, for which such output measures are most appropriate, and (b) experience has shown that output performance measures, properly interpreted, capture the essence of what one needs to know for management policy and programs.

Chapter 2
Fire Department Organization and Firefighting Operations

In this chapter we describe how a typical fully paid fire department is organized and how it operates. This sets the stage for what follows by defining the operating environment and many of the terms that are used throughout the book.

We devote most of the chapter to the fire suppression aspects of a fire department's operations since deployment questions revolve around these activities. But municipalities are becoming increasingly concerned with other aspects of a fire department's activities. They are beginning to realize that there may be more cost effective ways of reducing loss of life and property from fire than by spending ever-increasing amounts of money on their fire suppression systems. For example, increasing attention is being paid to public education, building inspections, developing and enforcing fire protection codes and standards, and encouraging the use of sprinklers and automatic detection devices. These important fire department functions will also be discussed briefly in this chapter.

In order to provide a framework for describing a fire department's suppression activities, we consider the events that occur from the start of a fire until it is extinguished. The sequence of events, which is shown in Figure 2.1, begins with ignition. After some time the fire is detected (by a person or an automatic device) and is reported to the department. The alarm is processed by one or more dispatchers who notify fire companies to respond. Men and equipment speed to the scene, where they operate to extinguish the fire. The effectiveness of the fire department in minimizing loss of life and property depends in part on the elapsed time between ignition and extinguishment. There are a range of alternative ways of reducing this time. Among them are:

1. faster detection
2. the use of sprinklers
3. better dispatching procedures

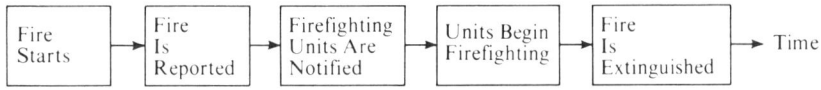

FIGURE 2.1. A typical sequence of events in a fire, from ignition to extinguishment.

4. improved deployment of fire companies
5. more effective firefighting tactics.

This book concentrates on alternatives 3 and 4.

2.1 FIREFIGHTING RESOURCES

2.1.1 Fire Companies

For rescue and extinguishment, firefighters and equipment are organized into companies that are deployed throughout a jurisdiction and are dispatched from firehouses to fires and other incidents as needed. A company usually consists of a vehicle that carries equipment and a complement of firefighters led by a company officer. The two basic types of fire companies are the engine (or pumper) company and the ladder (or truck) company. To accomplish their primary function of extinguishment, engine company personnel deliver water onto the fire using a variety of nozzles, connections, and different diameter hoses. Water is drawn from a hydrant (or sometimes from a natural body of water, if there are no hydrants around) and pumped under pressure through hose lines. The main pump on an engine generally can deliver between 500 and 2000 gallons of water per minute. Most engines also have a small booster

pump connected to a tank containing about 300 to 500 gallons of water. This supply of water is normally sufficient to extinguish a small fire, and it can be applied extremely quickly.

The firefighters in a ladder company ride a vehicle that is usually equipped with a hydraulically operated aerial ladder, between 65 and 100 feet in height. Their primary mission is to rescue trapped or unconscious victims, and to remove heat, smoke, and gases from a burning building. Ladder companies carry portable ladders of various sizes, axes, forced entry devices, and other special tools and equipment.

In addition to engine and ladder companies, many departments have a number of special-purpose units. The most common of these are "rescue" companies and "squad" companies. Both perform special functions and are assigned to cover a wide area. The rescue company carries large jacks, generators, mechanical winches, and other tools that are useful in unusual circumstances, such as when a building collapses. Squad companies are usually used to provide additional manpower at fires, and may ride a conventional pumper or a vehicle that carries only the men and their protective equipment. Other special-purpose units maintained in some jurisdictions are searchlight companies and marine companies.

Although the above descriptions of fire companies apply to most departments, the details differ from department to department. For example, in some cases an engine company consists of two vehicles (a pumper and a hose wagon). In many departments conventional aerial ladders are augmented by vehicles equipped with an elevating platform, which has a bucket attached at the end of a boom. One type of elevating platform

has an articulating boom and is called a "snorkel"; another has a telescoping boom, and is called an "aerialscope" or "tower ladder." In either case, the platforms usually reach to between 75 and 85 feet (although some in excess of 100 feet are in service) and have built-in piping so that they can deliver a stream of water directly onto the fire.

2.1.2 Chief Officers

At the scene of an incident, firefighters are under the command of their company officer. If several companies are working together at an incident the company officer will be commanded by a higher ranking officer from another company or by a chief officer who ranks higher than any company officer. The rank above a company officer is often call a battalion chief (or district chief). The battalion chief responds to sufficiently serious incidents in his assigned area and directs the operations of perhaps four to six companies.[1] At incidents requiring more companies there may be several battalion chiefs, who are in turn commanded by higher ranking officers called division chiefs, deputy chiefs, or assistant chiefs. At the largest fires the chain of command extends to the chief of the entire department.

---

[1] The battalion chief also has certain administrative responsibilities. These are described in Section 2.5.1.

2.1.3 The Geographic Distribution and Manning of Fire Companies

The number of firefighters assigned to engine and ladder companies varies from locality to locality. Table 2.1 illustrates the extent of this variation by showing the number who were normally on duty (including the officer) in fifteen American cities in 1972. The number varied from a high of eight men in some ladder companies and seven in some engine companies in New York[2] to a low of three men in some ladder companies in Phoenix and four men in engine companies in a number of cities.

The number and distribution of companies also varies from locality to locality, and companies are generally not distributed uniformly within a locality. Figure 2.2 shows the distribution of firefighting resources in Washington, D.C. in 1974, when there were 32 engine companies, 17 ladder companies, three rescue squads, and eight battalions.

2.1.4 Response Areas

Most fire departments in large cities at one time operated a network of telegraph-type alarm boxes located on street corners, and many still do. Typically, in such systems there would be an alarm box on every other

---

[2] As a result of New York's recent fiscal crisis, its ladder companies now have six men assigned, and its engine companies have either five or six. The numbers may also have changed in some of the other cities, but significant variations in manning levels still exist among cities.

TABLE 2.1. Number of men normally assigned to engine and ladder companies in major American cities. The data are from an unpublished survey by the Citizens Budget Commission (New York City, 1972).

		Number of Men Assigned	
City	Population (millions)	Engine Companies	Ladder Companies
New York	7.90	5–7	7–8
Los Angeles	2.82	5–6	5–6
Philadelphia	1.95	5	6
Detroit	1.51	4	5
Houston	1.23	5	5
Dallas	.84	5	5
Washington, D.C.	.76	5	6
Milwaukee	.72	5	5
San Francisco	.72	5	6
San Diego	.70	4	6
San Antonio	.65	4	5
St. Louis	.62	5	5
Phoenix	.58	4–5	3–4
Columbus	.54	5	5
Buffalo	.46	5	6

corner. In Washington, D. C., there are 1600 such boxes. In addition, alarm boxes may be located in hospitals, schools, and other public buildings.

For each alarm box there is an "alarm assignment card" or "running card" that lists the units that are assigned to respond to alarms at that box. (In Section 2.2 we describe this card and show how it is used for dispatching purposes.) In areas where there are no alarm boxes or the distribution of street boxes is sparse, certain locations can be designated as "phantom" or "dummy" boxes, and an alarm assignment card would list the companies assigned to that location even though there is no box there. In these cases we use the term "alarm box" to refer to a street intersection or a range of street addresses, rather than a physical box.

Each fire company's primary or "first-due" response area is the set of boxes (locations) to which it is the closest company of its type (in time, if not in distance). Similarly, each company has regions where it is second-due, third-due, etc.

2.2 FROM ALARM RECEIPT UNTIL DISPATCH

In this section we describe the events that typically occur between receipt of an alarm and the dispatch of fire companies. Although the details will differ from locality to locality, the general procedure is the same.

2.2 From Alarm Receipt Until Dispatch

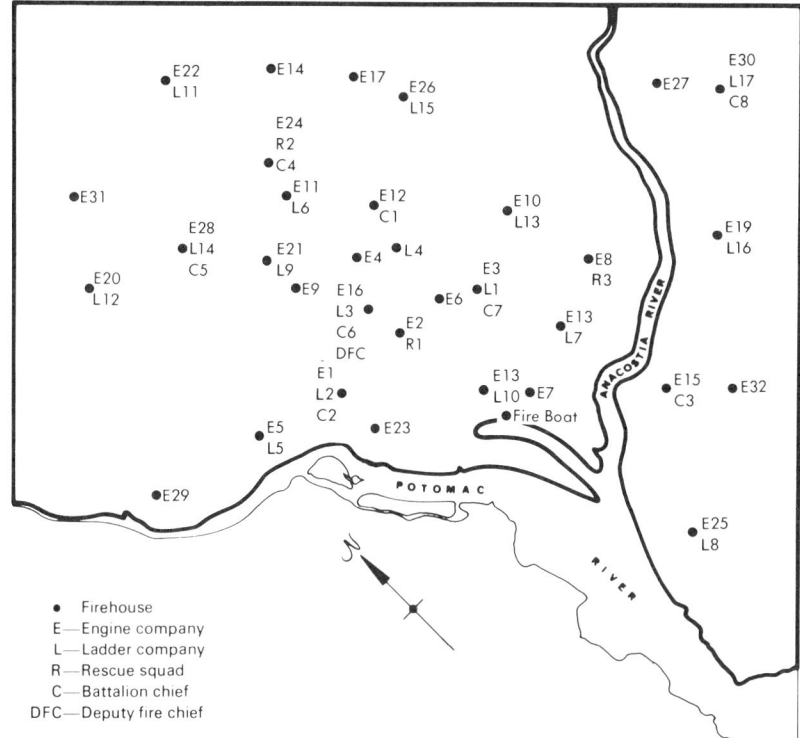

FIGURE 2.2. Fire company locations in Washington, D.C., 1972.

2.2.1 Receiving Alarms

Most fire alarms are reported by telegraph-type street boxes or by telephone.[3] The signal or call is received at a central facility, which is usually called a communications office or dispatching office. Most cities have one communications office that processes all of its alarms, but large cities may have several. New York City, for example, has five, one for each borough; Los Angeles had three until recently; Chicago has two. Most cities have one dispatcher on duty; the busiest offices in New York City have as many as ten.

Pulling the handle of a street box produces a signal in the communications office—a series of rings that identify the number of the box. As the alarm is being received the dispatcher counts the number of rings. At

---

[3] Some cities use telephone-type call boxes while others use radio systems. In addition, some alarm boxes are located off the street in premises such as hospitals and schools, and some are connected directly to detectors and sprinklers.

144	15th and H Streets, N. W.			
ENGINE COMPANIES	TRUCK COMPANIES	CHIEFS	R.S.	AMB.
16, 2, 23, 1	3, 2	6	1	
4, 6, 9, 3	4, 1	2		
13, 12, 21, 7	10, 9	1		
11, 5, 18, 8	- -	-		
10, 24, 28, 26	- -	-		

FIGURE 2.3. A Washington, D.C. alarm assignment card.

the same time, the number is usually recorded on a paper tape or similar device. At that point, the alarm assignment card corresponding to that alarm box is retrieved. If someone calls by telephone to report a fire, the dispatcher asks what is on fire and at what address. Then he (or another dispatcher) looks up the address in a street address file to determine the corresponding alarm assignment card. Figure 2.3 is an example of a card used in Washington, D.C. On the left side it lists the engine companies and ladder companies in order of their distance from the location (in this case, Alarm Box 144, located at 15th and H Streets, in the northwest part of the city). In other departments, information equivalent to that shown in Figure 2.3 will be available to the dispatchers, but it may not appear on a card. For example, the information could be on microfiche or in a computer file.

2.2.2 Deciding on the Initial Response

The dispatcher determines if the alarm represents a new incident. If so, he uses the alarm assignment card to determine which units to send. The first line of the card shown in Figure 2.3 lists the first-alarm assignment, in this case the four closest engine companies, the two closest ladder companies, and the closest battalion chief. Generally the first-alarm assignment consists of the number of units judged to be needed initially if an alarm at the given location is a serious fire. Table 2.2 shows the first-alarm assignments of a number of major American cities in 1972. For example, in Philadephia and Washington the assignment was four engine companies and two ladder companies, while in Detroit the assignment was two engine companies and one ladder company. Often the first-alarm assignment depends on whether the alarm box is in a high risk area (e.g., the business district). For example, in San Diego, four engine companies

2.2 From Alarm Receipt Until Dispatch

TABLE 2.2. First-alarm assignment of engine and ladder companies in major American cities. The data are from an unpublished survey by the Citizens Budget Commission (New York, 1972).

City	Populations (millions)	High Risk Area		Other Areas	
		Engines	Ladders	Engines	Ladders
New York	7.90	3	2	3	2
Philadelphia	1.95	4	2	4	2
Detroit	1.51	2	1	2	1
Houston	1.23	4	2	3	1
Baltimore	.91	4	2	3	1
Dallas	.84	3	2	2	1
Washington, D.C.	.76	4	2	4	2
Cleveland	.75	3	2	2	1
Milwaukee	.72	3	2	3	1
San Francisco	.72	3	2	3	1
San Diego	.70	4	2	3	1
San Antonio	.65	3	1	3	1
Boston	.65	3	2	3	2
Memphis	.62	4	2	2	1
St. Louis	.62	3	1	3	1
Phoenix	.58	3 or 4	1 or 2	2	1
Columbus	.54	3	2	2	1
Buffalo	.46	3	2	3	2

and two ladder companies are dispatched to high-risk areas, while other areas receive an initial dispatch of three and one.

A telephone report of a structural fire would receive the complete first-alarm assignment. If one or more of the assigned units were not available, the dispatcher would usually substitute the closest available units. Telephone alarms for incidents other than structural fires would receive the response that appears to be required. In some cases (an auto fire or rubbish fire, for example) the decision is easy; in others (a report of someone smelling smoke, for example) the judgment of the dispatcher is required.

For alarms received from street boxes (without a confirming telephone call), the initial response is generally less than the full first-alarm assignment. The response policy to box alarms varies from city to city, and within cities it may vary by time of day and geographical area. Fewer units are sometimes dispatched in areas in which false alarms are a problem during times when these unnecessary calls are most likely to occur. Alarms from telephone or radio call boxes are treated like telephone alarms; that is, they receive what appears to be required, except when someone activates the box but does not speak. In cases of no voice contact some cities do not respond at all; others send only the closest engine company.

In Chapter 11 we discuss methods for determining the initial response to alarms, showing that it is possible to improve upon the strategies commonly used. In particular, we discuss the importance of predicting whether an alarm signals a structural fire. In Chapter 8 we develop methods for making these predictions.

2.2.3 Notifying the Units to Respond

If the dispatcher decides that an alarm represents a new incident and units should be sent to it, he first determines the status of the assigned companies. The method of recording status varies from city to city. For example, in Washington, D.C. until recently, status information was displayed on two wall panels—one listing units available in quarters; the other listing units available "on the air" (i.e., units that can be contacted by radio).[4] There also was a large wall map showing the locations of all engine and ladder companies, with colored lights indicating their current status. The map was used primarily to determine when one or more companies needed to be temporarily moved to fill gaps in coverage.

Once the status of the assigned companies has been determined, those that are available in quarters are notified to respond by telegraph signal (i.e., ringing bells), voice communication, or both. In some departments the announcement is transmitted only to those companies that are supposed to respond. In others, the signal is transmitted more widely, and the companies respond if the indicated alarm box is in their response area. Assigned units that are out of quarters but available are notified by radio to respond. After the units are dispatched, the status displays are updated, and additional information about the incident may be transmitted to the companies by radio. Figure 2.4 summarizes the dispatching procedure.

2.2.4 Dispatching Additional Units

When the chief officer or company officer (if a chief is not dispatched) arrives at the scene of the incident he determines how many units are needed. If too many units have been sent, the chief sends the additional units back to their firehouses. (In some instances units may be told to stand by in case they are needed.) If too few units were sent, the chief radios the communications office and asks for one or more additional

---

[4] Washington, D. C., installed a computer-assisted dispatching system early in 1978. The computer now maintains the status of all companies.

2.2 From Alarm Receipt Until Dispatch

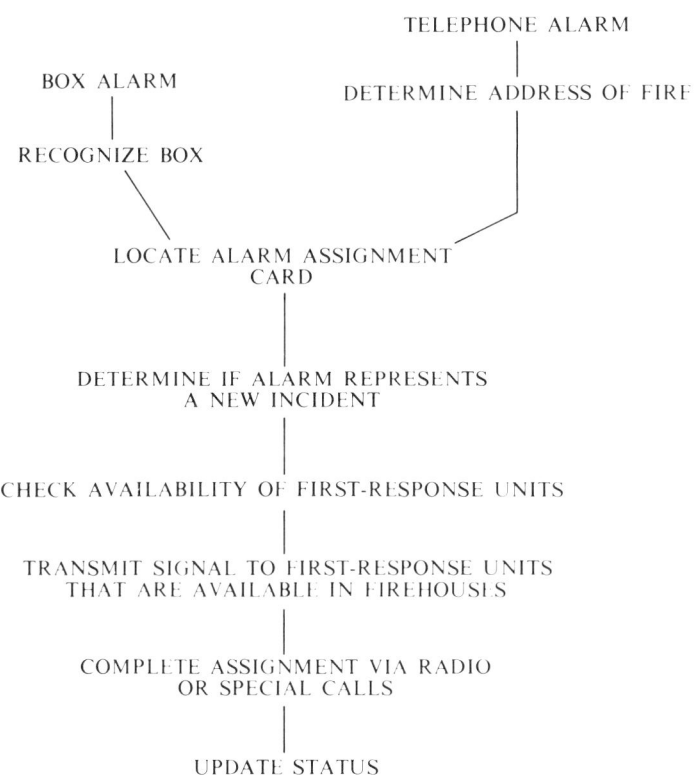

FIGURE 2.4. Steps in dispatching companies to a new alarm.

units. For more serious fires, he would order the transmission of a second alarm. For the alarm assignment card shown in Figure 2.3, such a call would result in the dispatch of the units on the second line of the card—four engine companies, two ladder companies, a rescue company, and a battalion chief. In Washington there is one deputy chief on duty at all times who would respond to the second alarm and assume command, assisted by the two battalion chiefs. As the fire progresses it may be brought under control by the companies at the scene, or it may escalate and require additional units. If more companies are needed, additional higher alarms would be transmitted. The alarm assignment card in Figure 2.3 lists the units assigned through the fifth alarm. In this case a fifth-alarm fire would involve 20 engine companies and six ladder companies. In most cities such a major fire, although extremely rare (there were no fifth-alarm fires in Washington in 1975), would severely deplete the city's firefighting resources. Most cities would react by recalling off-duty personnel to man response apparatus and by enlisting the assistance of nearby departments through mutual aid agreements.

When a serious fire breaks out (for example, when all first-alarm units are working), the area normally protected by the units working at the fire would be left with inadequate coverage. The dispatcher would, therefore, usually relocate (or "move up") some units to fill the gaps in coverage. In this case (see Figure 2.3) Engine Company 13 might be moved to the firehouse of Engine Company 2, Engine Company 9 might replace Engine Company 1, and Ladder Company 1 might replace Ladder Company 3. In some cities the relocations would be listed on the card. These preplanned changes are based on the assumption that the companies designated to relocate are available and no other serious incidents are taking place. If one or more of the designated units are unavailable, the dispatcher will usually choose a replacement. If other serious incidents are in progress, the designated relocations may be inappropriate; that is, they may create gaps in coverage that are worse than those they fill. In Chapter 12 we discuss a dynamic relocation method that overcomes the shortcomings of the traditional preplanned relocations in such situations.

2.2.5 Computer-Aided Dispatching

Most fire departments use a manual dispatching procedure similar to the one described above. But an increasing number of communities are implementing computer-aided management information and control (MICS)

2.2 From Alarm Receipt Until Dispatch

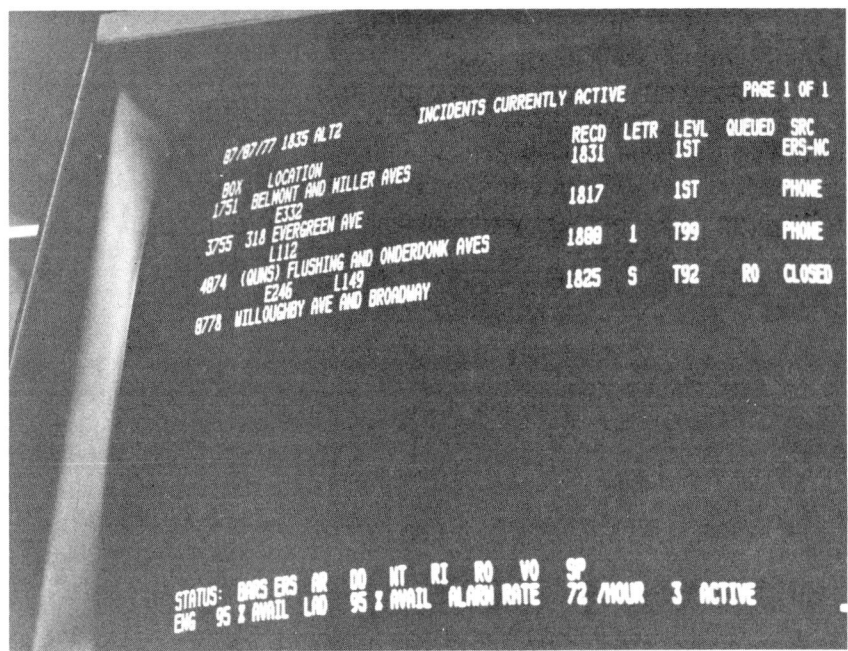

systems. For example, Huntington Beach, California has a fully operational MICS, San Francisco's computerized system was placed into operation in November 1976, and New York City implemented an MICS in one borough in 1977 and plans to extend the system citywide by 1981. Cities such as Los Angeles, Denver, Boston, Washington, D.C., and Phoenix are in various stages of implementing such systems.

The benefits of an MICS may be significant in some jurisdictions, although a well-designed manual system will operate about as fast as a computer system except in rare periods of very high demand when the computer should improve dispatching and relocation performance. The elimination of paperwork and production of timely reports is a major benefit (although not all systems provide this feature).

A department with an MICS might be able to serve as a dispatching center for surrounding communities. For example, there are about 28 small departments surrounding Denver. Because alarm rates are so low, the dispatching cost per alarm is quite high for these departments. Using a computer system, Denver could contract with these communities to provide the dispatching services at a substantially lower cost. Of course, such centralized dispatching is possible without a computer. However, the computer can make it easier by generating reports and providing data on building construction and other hazards.

Finally, a computer system may aid in improving the allocation of resources. In Chapters 11 and 12 we discuss dynamic, computer-based initial dispatch and relocation decision rules that replace the traditional alarm assignment cards.

2.3 FIGHTING THE FIRE: FROM DISPATCH UNTIL OVERHAUL

The main themes of this book are deployment and the decisions that affect the time from the dispatch of units to their arrival at the scene (i.e., fire company travel time). The sequence of company arrivals at the fire affects both fireground tactics and the growth of the fire. In the following sections we briefly describe the basic operations of engine and ladder companies at the scene of a fire. More detailed information can be found in Casey (1967) and Kimball (1966).

2.3.1 Company Operations

The flow of water and the manpower required to extinguish a fire depend on the situation at the time the companies arrive. A typical outdoor rubbish fire can be extinguished by one man within 30 seconds using a hose of 1-inch diameter or less. The effort for larger fires varies more. For example, the severity of single-room fires depends on factors such as construction, contents, window openings, and temperature. A sufficient flow of water is needed to control the fire (stop its growth); a larger flow rate is required for extinguishment. In laboratory experiments with fire completely involving 12-foot by 12-foot residential rooms, an average of about 30 seconds was required to control the fires using a 1-inch hose delivering about 20 gallons per minute (gpm) of water (Salzberg, Vodvarka, and Maatman, 1970). Other data on 40 actual fires in four cities showed that the largest flow rate used for control was about 3000 gpm in a mercantile establishment in which 1700 square feet were involved in fire (Salzberg, 1970). It took about 20 minutes to control this fire with five engine companies, two ladder companies, and a total of 45 men fighting it. Much larger fires involving a complex of buildings could require 10,000 gpm or more to control them.

Engines now commonly in use can deliver from 500 to 2000 gpm of water. Engine companies are generally equipped with hoses ranging from the 5/8-inch booster lines to 2 1/2-inch diameter lines. The booster line—a small reel of hose connected to the booster pump and water tank—can deliver between 12 and 25 gpm and is used for minor fires. Engines also carry one or more 1 1/2-inch lines preconnected to the pump and supplied initially by a water tank. These lines are used to deliver water from the tank while the pump is being attached to a fire hydrant.

A single engine company with five men including an officer should be able to deliver streams from two 1 1/2-inch lines or one 2 1/2-inch line. For example, to accomplish the latter task, three men are normally needed to extend the hose, with two of them handling the nozzle. The fourth man would assist the pump operator in connecting the line to the pump (Kimball, 1966).

Ladder companies are responsible for rescue and ventilation. In addition, they set up ladders that provide access to men and hose lines for firefighting. Also, the ladder company can supply a master stream through the ladder pipe.

A typical six-man ladder company consists of an officer, a truck operator who drives the vehicle, and four truckmen. The operator controls the power ladder and other equipment on the truck, such as generators and floodlights. Two men and the officer constitute the forcible entry team, which uses specialized tools, if necessary, to gain access to the building. The other two men are normally assigned to the roof and exterior for ventilation. Ventilation, the procedure for removing smoke, gases, and heat from the burning structure, controls the spread of fire by pulling the fire to an opening and allowing it to vent upward into the atmosphere; prevents smoke explosions, caused by a mixture of air, carbon monoxide, and other gases; improves visibility so that the exact location of the fire can be determined; and permits firefighters to enter and fight the fire.

After the fire is extinguished, the ladder company personnel perform overhaul and salvage. Overhaul is the work required to assure complete extinguishment (i.e., the search for sparks, embers, or hidden fires) and includes pulling down ceilings and cutting into walls or floors to expose concealed spaces. The related salvage activities are directed to reducing fire and water damage to buildings and their contents.

2.3.2 Firefighting Tactics

Engine and ladder companies work together: the ladder men begin ventilation as soon as the hose line is charged (i.e., water is up to the nozzle and ready to be applied). If ventilation occurs too soon, the air that is introduced will accelerate the fire.

The manner in which a fire is fought depends on the nature of the incident, the number and type of units sent to the scene and their arrival times, and the number of men assigned to each unit. As indicated earlier, the number of men assigned to each company varies from city to city. For a fixed level of resources, fewer men per company will mean more companies and, on the average, a faster response for the first-arriving company.[5] In some situations this may be an advantage: a quick response by a three-man engine company, for example, might prevent a relatively small fire from spreading. On the other hand, three men at a large, rapidly-growing fire could do little until other units arrive.

In most cities the closest available companies are dispatched to fires. This means different groups of companies work together at different fires. In some cities, several companies are grouped together and identified as a task force. The task force is generally assigned to fires as a group, sacrificing some response time but maintaining the group as a single firefighting unit, thereby improving operational efficiency.

The nature of the fire incident may present particular firefighting problems. For example, fighting fires in high-rise buildings is especially difficult for four basic reasons: (1) aerial ladders will not reach beyond about nine stories: as a result, above these levels, the fire must be fought from inside; (2) complete evacuation of occupants is not feasible (therefore, provision for safety and life support systems must be made within the buildings); (3) chimney or stack effects in tall buildings require provision for the control of smoke and products of combustion; and (4) fixed windows make ventilating the fire floor difficult.

In all types of buildings the goal is rapid rescue and evacuation and the quick and effective application of water. Communications are important: for example, one seven-man ladder company using several portable radios might accomplish as much as two six-man units without radios. Similarly, labor-saving devices such as power saws increase effectiveness.

2.4 AFTER THE FIRE: FIRE REPORTING SYSTEMS AND STATISTICS

After each incident, company officers and chief officers fill out reports describing the events that occurred. These records provide the basis for annual reports and other descriptions of fire department activity. More important, they are the data source for future analysis.

Management information systems are currently the subject of wide discussion in industry and government. The central notion is to use the computer to provide accurate, timely, and useful information. In the fire service, the Uniform Fire Incident Reporting System (UFIRS) has been the subject of much interest, while various other systems are also in use

---

[5] Because of unavailability or dispatch policy, the first-arriving company may or may not be the first-due company (the company assigned to the firehouse located closest to the fire).

at both the local and state level. The United States Fire Administration has also developed a National Fire Incident Reporting System for collecting standardized fire data nationwide.

A fire reporting system has four components: an incident reporting language, a method for systematic information collection, procedures for manipulating that information, and procedures for report generation. The National Fire Protection Association has done extensive, careful work in defining a common incident reporting language (NFPA Publication 901, 1976), and routines for the efficient manipulation of data have become standard. However, the areas of information collection and report generation are less well developed. The introduction of computers changes the the mechanics of fire reporting systems, but it does not reveal what data should be collected or how this information should be used. For example:

1. What data should be recorded about a fire?
2. Who should receive these data?
3. What should they do with them?
4. How should data on fires be aggregated and analyzed?
5. What can be learned from these data?
6. What statistical or other manipulations are appropriate for learning it?

In Chapter 8 we discuss the use of data in deployment analyses. For example, the statistical analysis of fire incidents has been used to decide how many fire companies to send to each incident, resulting in shorter response times. The choice of what to look at—in this case, the chance that an alarm received from a street box is serious—was determined by the use that could be made of the data-based prediction. The data needed were the number of street box alarms at each location, whether each represented a fire in an occupied structure, and whether each represented a serious fire. Such information needs to be routinely reported.

2.5. FIRE DEPARTMENT FIELD ORGANIZATION AND MANPOWER SCHEDULING

2.5.1 Administrative Districts

Typically, each fire company is assigned an area of the city called its "administrative district" (sometimes called its "assigned district"). A group of companies and their administrative districts make up an "administrative battalion." For example, in Washington D. C. (See Figure 2.2), Battalion 1 consists of Engine Company 6, Engine Company 12, Engine Company 17, Engine Company 26, Ladder Company 4, Ladder Company 15, and Rescue Squad 1. In the larger cities, administrative battalions may be aggregated into two or more divisions, although this is not the case in Washington.

The administrative district is used for administrative purposes (training, filing reports, etc.) and as a basis for assigning buildings to companies for inspection. A chief assigned to a particular battalion will have administrative responsibility for the companies in that battalion. He will inspect the companies and be responsible for distributing orders and other information. In most cities, each company will inspect the commercial and public buildings and the public areas of residential buildings in its district. They do so during their normal duty hours and are available by radio for dispatch to a fire incident.

2.5.2 Hours of Work and Scheduling

There are two basic schedules that prevail in almost all paid fire departments in the United States and Canada. In one, the firefighters work a 24-hour shift; in the other, there are two shifts: one of 10 hours, the other of 14 hours (8 A.M. to 6 P.M. and 6 P.M. to 8 A.M., for example). The 10 and 14-hour tours are common in the Northeast. Half of the large fire departments in the United States (including those in Chicago, Los Angeles, and Detroit) and most of the smaller (and less busy) departments use the 24-hour tour, which may entail more on-duty hours per week. Other variations also occur, such as three 8-hour tours per day. In almost all departments, schedules provide for the same number of firefighters on field duty during all times of day.[6]

2.6 FIRE PREVENTION AND OTHER FIRE DEPARTMENT ACTIVITIES

While most fire department activities are devoted to fire suppression, there has been a growing recognition that fire departments should consider the full range of alternatives available for providing fire protection. This includes fire prevention (public education and inspection), codes and standards for buildings and products, and preresponse damage limitation (installation of early detection and sprinkler devices, for example). Master planning in many departments and communities is beginning to take a broad view of fire protection alternatives and to seek least-cost solutions to the provision of fire protection.

---

[6] The actual number on duty may vary from day to day depending on the number of men sick, on leave, or otherwise absent, although many departments maintain minimum manning levels by use of overtime if necessary.

2.6.1 Fire Prevention

There are two basic fire prevention activities carried out by most fire departments: public education and inspections. The range of effort in these activities is great. Some departments carry on vigorous education and inspection programs; others give them little attention.

Most fire departments conduct a public education program aimed at reducing the number of fires and false alarms. This effort includes visits to school and community groups, posters, fire prevention week, and clean-up campaigns. Evaluating the effectiveness of such programs is difficult since they are usually not designed to permit proper statistical evaluation. The available evidence suggests that efforts directed at a particular type of fire (e.g., grease fires) are most likely to be successful.[7] However, evidence of successful programs is sparse. It is, therefore, not surprising that the amount of attention given to public education varies so widely.[8]

There is a growing recognition in the fire service that more effort needs to be devoted to public education. As more evidence of program effectiveness becomes available (through the design, implementation, and evaluation of carefully controlled experiments) it should be possible to determine the kinds and amounts of public education activities that are most beneficial. The Office of Public Education of the United States Fire Administration is attempting to identify effective programs and to establish a mechanism for distributing this information to the fire service.

The need to inspect hazardous equipment and structures is well established in the fire service. Certainly the regulations and related inspections of gasoline distribution systems have contributed to limiting the number of fires in that area. In general, fire departments are actively involved in issuing permits and inspecting hazardous products and premises. There is widespread agreement that such programs are necessary and effective (although the particular level of effectiveness may be difficult to measure). Further, permit programs produce fees that offset the costs of the inspections and record-keeping. However, the effectiveness of building inspections is much less clear. Again, as in the case of public education, inspection programs are rarely designed with statistical validation in mind. The few attempts at such validation have yet to prove the positive effect of inspections. This does not necessarily mean that building in-

---

[7] For example, the fire prevention campaign in Kileen, Texas, described in *Review of Fire Prevention Education Programs* (National Fire Prevention and Control Administration, Office of Public Education, August 1975).

[8] Several public education programs are discussed in Swersey et al. (1975).

spections are not effective; it means only that available data do not establish their effectiveness.

Schaenman et al. (1976) suggest an approach to measuring the effectiveness of inspection programs that would relate fire occurrence to inspection effort. It would measure the number of fires that were relatively preventable by inspections per 1000 occupancies. Hall et al. (1978) applied the approach using data from 17 cities and one county. They found that "cities that annually inspect all or nearly all inspectable properties appear to have substantially lower fire rates than do other cities."

2.6.2 Codes and Standards

Most fire safety regulations that apply to buildings appear in a jurisdiction's building code. A typical code specifies requirements relating to a building's size, occupancy, use, and construction. The requirements include the fire resistance of materials, protection of structural members, the existence of fire walls and partitions, and the enclosure of stairs and shafts. Extinguishing equipment regulations cover standpipe and hose systems, sprinklers, tanks, fire department connections, fire alarm systems, and fire extinguishers. The code also specifies requirements for exits, elevators, and electrical installations. However, most building codes do not contain regulations covering the storage and handling of hazardous materials such as explosives, flammable liquids, paint products, plastics, film, and combustible metals.

The provisions of most building and fire codes are drawn from technical standards developed by govermental agencies, technical societies, and trade associations. The codes used most often are produced by the National Fire Protection Association and the Underwriters' Laboratories.

2.6.3 Automatic Detection Systems

As fire department costs increase there is a growing incentive for more widespread use of automatic fire detection devices (and sprinklers). Under some circumstances it may pay to increase detector use and reduce the number of fire companies. That is, the savings in response time that would result from more rapid fire detection may be greater then the increase in fire company travel time that would result from having fewer companies.

Automatic detectors are of two general types: heat detectors that react to an increase in temperature; and smoke detectors that respond to the products of combustion. The simplest detection systems trigger a local alarm; others are connected to a central alarm.

With the recent reduction in the price of home smoke detector units (they now cost between $20 and $40 apiece), their use is increasing rapidly. The installation of individual detectors and more complete systems in homes provides data that are potentially very useful for evaluating detection effectiveness. At present, estimates of detector effectiveness are mainly subjective. For example, McGuire and Ruscoe (1962) analyzed descriptions of 342 residential fires in Ontario and estimated that smoke detectors could have saved 41 percent of the victims. As more data become available, it should be possible to estimate the effectiveness of detectors in varying circumstances.

2.6.4 Sprinklers

Sprinklers are heat-activated devices designed to control or extinguish a fire. Although they are costly,[9] some cities are passing new laws that require sprinklers in certain structures. There is little doubt that under some circumstances the benefits of sprinkler systems outweigh their cost. But additional data and careful analysis are needed to identify the appropriate situations. In one study, Simon, Shephard, and Sharp (1943) compared losses in sprinklered and unsprinklered buildings of the same type. They divided occupancies into five classes: public buildings, residential, mercantile, manufacturing, and miscellaneous buildings. They divided construction into three types: fire-resisting, masonry-walled, and wood-framed. For each of the resulting 15 building classes (and for occupancy subclasses within each class) they estimated average annual fire loss per thousand dollars of building valuation for sprinklered and unsprinklered buildings. They found, for example, that for masonry-walled manufacturing buildings in Oakland, California during the period 1935-1940, these losses were $2.38 for unsprinklered buildings and $2.05 for sprinklered buildings.

With the development of improved information systems and the collection of relevant data it should be possible to perform similar analyses in order to estimate the benefits (and costs) of sprinkler systems in a wide range of situations.

---

[9] Estimates of sprinkler installation costs in new construction in New York City, for example, are close to $1.00 per square foot. For existing buildings the rate is even higher, since installation requires walls and ceilings to be broken and then patched back together.

Chapter 3
An Introduction to Deployment Analysis

Synopsis

Some large systems, such as the system of fire department operations, contain many interacting elements. These interactions make it difficult to determine the consequences of policy changes. <u>Systems analysis</u> is a method for studying such changes in an organized, step-by-step manner. <u>Deployment analysis</u> is systems analysis applied to problems of resource deployment—firefighting resources in the present context. As such, it is one element of <u>fire protection master planning</u>, that is, systems analysis applied to the evaluation of a community's present and future fire protection and needs.

This chapter, which provides a framework for the material presented in the rest of the book, describes the eight steps in a typical systems analysis study. Each step is illustrated by examples drawn from the fire service. The steps are:

1. *Identify the problem to be studied.*
2. *Identify the objectives of the analysis.*
3. *Choose the criteria to be used in evaluating alternative policies.*
4. *Select the alternative policies to be evaluated.*
5. *Determine the consequences of implementing each alternative.*
6. *Compare the consequences of each alternative using the previously defined criteria, and choose the preferred policy.*
7. *Implement the new policy.*
8. *Monitor and evaluate the performance of the new policy to make sure that the expected results are actually being realized.*

3.1 WHAT IS DEPLOYMENT ANALYSIS?

Deployment analysis is the application of systems analysis to the problems of deploying (or allocating) firefighting resources. We use systems analysis to help make better deployment decisions because, in many cases, it provides an objective framework for comparing alternative policies. Such a framework is especially helpful in dealing with large systems, such as the system of municipal fire department operations, in which it is difficult to determine the consequences of a policy change.

Systems analysis developed after World War II as a new approach for evaluating policy options for the U. S. Department of Defense. It has recently begun to be applied to problems of local governments; in particular, to those of municipal fire departments.

Quade and Boucher (1968) define systems analysis as: "a systematic approach to helping a decision maker choose a course of action by investigating his full problem, searching out objectives and alternatives, and comparing them in the light of consequences, using an appropriate framework—insofar as possible analytic—to bring expert judgment and intuition to bear on the problem."

Thus, systems analysis is not a way of solving a specific problem, but it is a general approach to problem solving. In this book we use the approach to analyze problems related to the use of the firefighting resources of a fire department. The same general approach is used by the United States Fire Administration in the process it has developed for fire protection master planning in a community.[1] A master plan, when completed and implemented, results in a general program of action for fire prevention and control. Not only are fire suppression forces considered in a master plan, but also building codes, private fire protection systems, and other elements in a community that have an impact on its fire protection. In this context, deployment analysis can be considered as one element of master planning.

Systems analysis has also been applied to other elements of master planning. For example, Walsh and Marks (1977) have shown how the steps of systems analysis can be followed in handling tactics of suppression on the fireground. They recommend that the fire officer should develop an "action plan," which is a standardized way of thinking and acting at fires. In this way, they claim, the officer will develop decision-making skills that will result in more effective firefighting.

---

[1] See, for example, *A Basic Guide for Fire Prevention and Control Master Planning* (1978) and *Criteria for Master Planning and Resource Allocation* (1978).

Similarly, the U.S. General Services Administration (GSA) (Nelson, 1973) applies systems analysis in its procedure for evaluating and designing fire protection in buildings. Since federal buildings do not fall under the jurisdiction of local building codes, the GSA has been able to formulate its own substitute for code compliance, which is called the Goal Oriented Systems Approach. A review and elaboration of this approach by Watts (1978) shows exactly how it is related to systems analysis.

Systems analysis almost always involves performing a certain set of logical steps. The steps are so logical that they are used by most people, usually implicitly or unconsciously, in making common decisions such as what to eat for dinner, what movie to see, or where to go for a vacation. The steps, summarized in Figure 3.1, are:

1. *Identify the problem.* For example, an old firehouse must be torn

FIGURE 3.1. Steps in a systems analysis study.

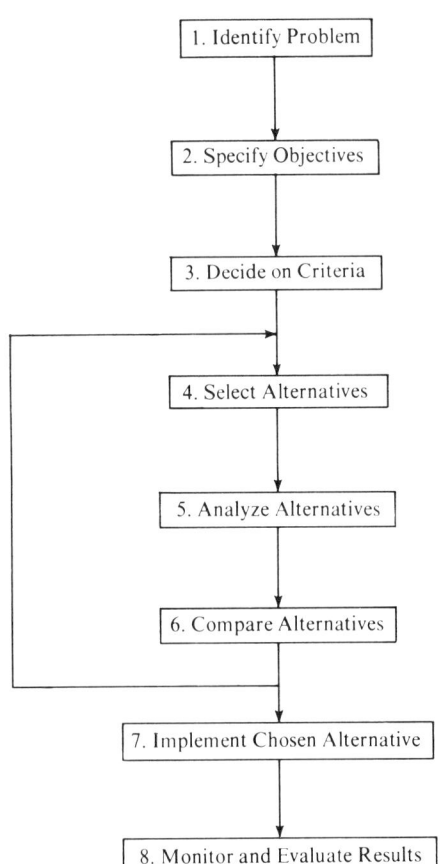

down; where should its fire companies be moved? Or, it is taking too long to process alarms in the communications office.
2. *Identify the objective of the new policy.* For example, the objective might be to obtain a more equitable distribution of firefighting resources throughout the city; or to improve the effectiveness of operations in the communications office.
3. *Decide on criteria (or measures of performance) with which to evaluate alternative policies.* For example, for company location policies, the measures may include average travel times to fires, the percentage of alarm boxes that are within one mile of the nearest firehouse, and fire company workloads. To evaluate alternative communications office policies, a reasonable performance measure would be the average elapsed time between alarm receipt and the dispatch of companies.
4. *Select alternative policies to be evaluated.* For example, should the new firehouse be placed at First and Market Streets, or at Third and Main? Should two engines and one ladder be sent to box alarms, or should three and two be dispatched?
5. *Analyze each alternative.* This means determine the consequences that are likely to follow if the alternative is actually implemented, where the consequences are measured in terms of the criteria chosen in Step 3. This step usually involves using a "model" of the system.
6. *Compare alternatives.* This step involves ranking the alternatives in order of desirability and choosing the one preferred. If none of the alternatives examined so far is good enough to be implemented (or if new aspects of the problem have been found, or the analysis has led to new alternatives), return to Step 4.
7. *Implement the chosen alternative.* This step means obtaining acceptance of the new procedures (both within and outside the government), training people to use them, and performing other tasks to put the policy into effect. The implementation process is discussed in detail in Chapter 5.
8. *Monitor and evaluate the results.* This step is necessary to make sure that the policy is actually accomplishing its intended objectives. If it is not, the policy may have to be modified or a new study performed.

Each of the above steps is important, and none is necessarily easy to perform. Each involves both objective and subjective elements, and usually many people in addition to the analyst. The steps are discussed in detail in Sections 3.2 through 3.9, where the emphasis is placed on what has to be accomplished rather than on how to accomplish it. The questions of who does the work and how it is organized and managed (which are as important as what work is performed) are discussed in Chapter 4. The question of how to perform the work to increase the chances of getting the results implemented is discussed in Chapter 5. Chapters 3, 4, and 5 together provide the analyst, mayor, or fire chief with an idea of the steps to be followed, the people to be coordinated, and the environment to be worked in when performing a deployment study. Chapters 6 through 13 provide the analytical tools for carrying out the study, and Chapter 14 illustrates how the systems analysis steps have been applied to the solution of several specific deployment problems.

3.2 STEP 1: IDENTIFYING THE PROBLEM

This step may appear to be the easiest, but it is often the hardest. Working on a "problem" that is not really a problem can be a waste of time, and can divert attention from the real problem. People in different positions will generally have different perceptions of the problem. Nevertheless, a precondition for analysis is that someone must think that a problem exists and be interested in solving it.

For a problem to exist, in the sense used here, certain conditions must be met. In particular, it must be possible to view the situation in terms of alternative courses of action that will produce different results in terms of the desired objectives (see Step 2). This may seem obvious but some situations regarded as problems—such as "human carelessness"—are too general or too vague to permit analysis to proceed without further specification.

The problem may come to the attention of the department in one of two ways. First, political or other developments outside the department may force consideration of a particular policy issue. Some examples are: the boundaries of the department's jurisdiction may change; its budget may be reduced; an existing firehouse may become unsuitable for future occupancy; a regional dispatching center may be constructed; the workload of certain companies may increase rapidly.

Second, the department's management may wish to explore the possibilities for improving operations even though no outside crisis has occurred. In this case, analysis should begin with an exploration of the policy issues that might be addressed and the likely costs and benefits of pursuing each of them.

In some cases it will not be possible to know whether a deployment problem exists or whether the assumptions behind the problem statement were correct until preliminary data collection and analysis have begun. For example, an analysis of fires by property classification might suggest a problem in code enforcement or the need for changes in the code. Statistics on false alarms by time of day and geographic area might suggest the need for a new dispatching policy. Chapter 8 covers various approaches to collecting and analyzing data for use in deployment analyses.

In identifying the problem it is most important to be very specific and

3.2 Step 1: Identifying the Problem

to limit the problem to manageable size. To increase the chances for implementation of the results of the analysis, the probable solution to the problem should lie within the jurisdiction of the department. As Wildavsky (1976) observed, "Analysis requries creative juxtaposition of resources and objectives until problems are found that decisionmakers can solve—with the variables under their control, and within the time period available."

The specific deployment problems that have been analyzed successfully using systems analysis and that are covered in later chapters generally involve the manner in which fire companies are located and dispatched. These deployment problems can be divided into *strategic* and *tactical* problems.

3.2.1 Strategic Problems

Strategic problems (which are treated in Chapters 9 and 10) involve long-range planning issues. Among the strategic problems faced by a fire department are:

1. *How many fire companies should be on duty?* There are two aspects to this question. The first is the size of the department's budget, which determines the total amount of firefighting resources available to be deployed. The second concerns possible changes in the number of companies on duty at different times of day or in different seasons of the year.
2. *How many fire companies should be allocated to each region of the jurisdiction?* For example, how many companies should be in the central business district? How many in residential areas?
3. *Where should the jurisdiction's fire companies be located?* This question is specifically about choosing sites for firehouses. To answer it, many factors must be considered that do not arise when general allocation questions are being analyzed. These include the availability of specific land parcels, the directions of one-way streets, and traffic conditions.
4. *How many firefighters should be assigned to each fire company?* This number varies from locality to locality, and may even vary from company to company within a locality. The more men assigned to a company, the more it can do once it reaches the fire. But, given the same manpower resources, assigning more men to each company means fewer companies and, therefore, longer response times.[2]

---

[2] We only treat the first three strategic problems in this book, since little research has been conducted to date on the fourth problem. When we treat the other problems we assume that the same number of firefighters are assigned to all units of the same type in the jurisdiction.

3.2.2 Tactical Problems

By "tactical," we do not mean tactics on the fireground, but rather problems that arise from moment to moment during the course of a day. Given some overall allocation of resources, the tactical questions are how to respond to incoming alarms and to changing fire situations. A department's answers to these questions are embodied in their dispatching and relocation policies.

Dispatching Policy (see Chapter 11). This encompasses all the rules and procedures used by dispatchers, including:

1. *How many fire companies of each type should be sent to an incoming alarm?* The answer may vary among departments according to the number of firefighters in each fire company. It may also depend on the availability of companies at the time of the alarm and on what is known about the nature of the incident at the time the dispatch is made. For example, more companies might be sent to a telephone report of a fire in a building than to a signal from a street alarm box.
2. *Which particular fire companies should be dispatched?* Most fire departments dispatch the units that are closest to the location of an incident. However, in localities where alarm rates are high and workloads are heavy, there may be conditions under which it is sometimes better not to send the closest units.

Relocation Policy (see Chapter 12). Multiple-alarm fires need many companies quickly, and most departments dispatch all of the closest available units. This leaves a large region unprotected, so companies further away are often moved to some of the empty firehouses for the duration of the incident. If a department uses such a relocation policy (also called a "redeployment" or "move-up"), then rules must be developed for when and how it is to be accomplished.

3.2.3 Pitfalls in Identifying the Problem

There are various pitfalls that may arise in the course of identifying a deployment problem. First, if a careful analysis of the available data is not made before a large-scale systems analysis study is begun, great effort can be wasted on a wrong interpretation of the problem, or on something that is no problem at all.

An example of misinterpretation is provided by a study of dispatching delays performed in a communications office (C.O.) of the New York City Fire Department. Both the department's administration and the dispatchers correctly perceived that there was a performance problem in the Brooklyn C.O. At high alarm rates there were sometimes long delays between alarm receipt and the dispatch of equipment. A systems analysis approach to this problem would have considered all of the activities in the C.O. to identify the source of the problem and then to develop and evaluate alternative solutions.

Instead, the administration and the dispatchers took a narrow view of the problem, deciding in advance that the problem was in the first stage of the dispatching operation: receipt of the alarm and determination of the appropriate alarm box number. It is easy to draw this conclusion because attention in the C.O. is drawn to this stage. There is a great deal of noise and activity associated with the ringing of box alarms and telephones, counting of rings, talking on the telephone, and determining the location of an incident reported by telephone. The assumption that the problem was in this stage of the dispatching process led to consideration of solutions that would expedite alarm receipt. These included installation of automatic alarm readouts to identify the alarm box number of incoming street-box alarms (instead of counting rings to determine the box number), and using a computer to determine the alarm box closest to a given street address.

However, a study of the complete C.O. system showed that the crux of the problem was not in receiving the alarms but in sending them out to companies for response. The bottleneck in the system was found to be at the decisionmaking stage, where a dispatcher had to decide which units to send to the alarm. No matter how many other dispatchers were working in the communications office or how much equipment there was to help out, dispatch decisions were being made one at a time by a single man. After this discovery, analysis could concentrate on the real problem. (See Chapter 14 for further details.)

A second typical pitfall, worrying about something that is not a serious problem, is illustrated by an examination of the "false alarm problem" in Yonkers, New York. The Yonkers Fire Department had implemented a reduced dispatch to solve what they thought was a false alarm problem. Instead of dispatching their standard two engines and two ladders to box alarms, they sent only one engine and one ladder to those box alarms occurring between noon and midnight.

But did Yonkers have a false alarm problem? At first glance, the graph in Figure 3.2 suggests that it did. False alarms grew sixfold between 1961 and 1972. In 1961 false alarms were only 10 percent of the total alarms received; in 1972 they constituted 29 percent. However, despite this drastic increase, Yonkers still averaged fewer than five false alarms per day.

Even so, the reduced response policy might have made sense if some of Yonkers' fire companies had had workload problems. But the busiest company in Yonkers made 1100 runs in 1972, an average of about three

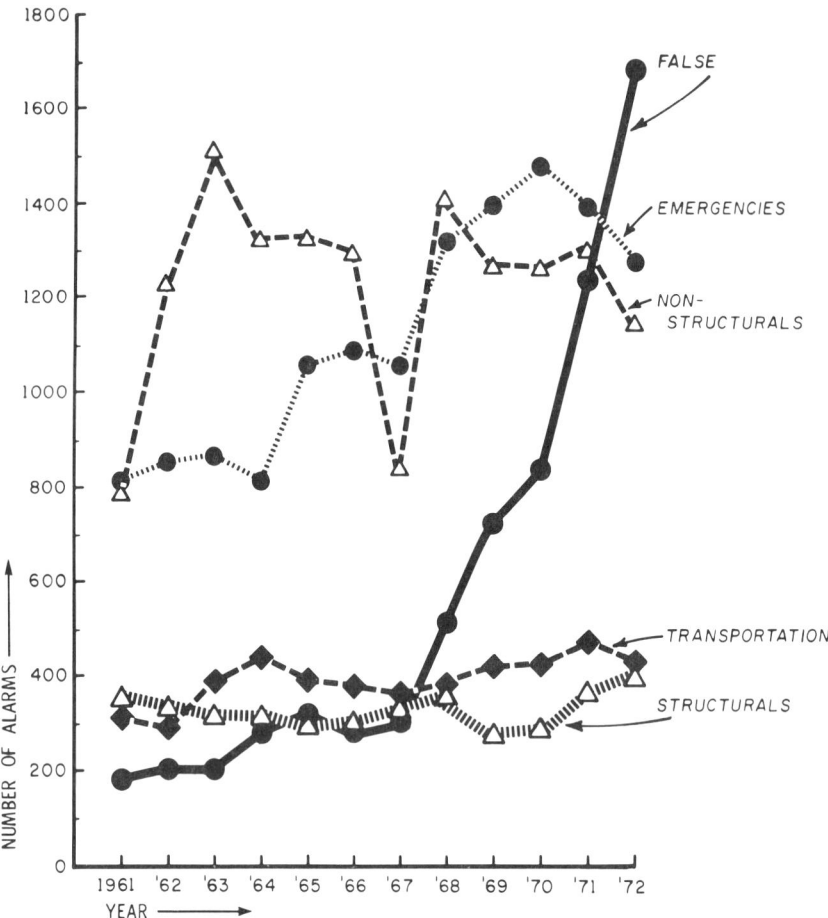

FIGURE 3.2. Yonkers alarm rates by type, 1961–1972.

responses per day. In addition, because of the relatively low alarm rate in Yonkers, there was no reason to reduce the response in the expectation that the units would be needed soon at another alarm.

Therefore, reducing the response in Yonkers (and most small cities) merely reduced fire protection. A deployment analysis of the Yonkers Fire Department (Hausner et al., 1974) showed the city that increasing the initial dispatch to two engines and two ladders between noon and midnight would give the busiest company in the city about 1400 responses per year (an average of less than one additional response per day). But more importantly, the study showed that over the course of a year, this policy would assure a better response to about 100 structural fires—the ones that would be received by street box during those hours. (See Chapter 14 for a more complete description of the Yonkers study.)

3.3 STEP 2: SPECIFYING THE OBJECTIVES

Most of the deployment problems in a fire department have many possible solutions. But some of these solutions are obviously inferior or even unacceptable. One of the most important tasks of the systems analyst is to discover and define precisely what objectives the decisionmaker is or should be trying to attain. That is, what is to be accomplished with a new policy? The options can then be compared and a solution chosen on the basis of how well they accomplish the objectives. Choosing the wrong objectives means that the solution obtained in the following stages of the analysis may be far from the most desirable solution to the problem.

However, in most public systems, the decisionmaker is often faced with several objectives. These objectives may be hard to translate into policy alternatives and will often conflict with one another. We illustrate this dilemma by considering how to distribute a given number of fire companies throughout a city. (This problem is analyzed in detail in Chapter 9.) The conflicting objectives in this case are: (1) minimizing damage at fires and (2) providing equitable protection to all parts of the city.

The objective of minimizing damage at fires is fairly straightforward to define operationally. If we assume that the smaller the travel time to a fire, the smaller the damage, the department's objective of minimizing fire damage might be achieved (approximately) by minimizing the total travel time to all fires that occur in the city.

The objective of providing "equitable" protection to all parts of the city requires further clarification. As Yin (1974) has pointed out, the equalization effects of urban service programs may be judged by at least four different criteria:

1. The amount of effort used to sustain the service (equalization of input).
2. The amount of service accomplished (equalization of output).
3. The amount of service accomplished in relation to residential needs (equalization of outcome).
4. The amount of residential satisfaction with the service (equalization of citizen perceptions).

In this example we will assume that providing equitable protection to all parts of the city means equalizing the average travel time in all parts of the city. (This corresponds to criterion 2 above.)

How do these two objectives conflict? Consider the hypothetical city shown in Figure 3.3, which has been partitioned into two regions of about equal size but with very different fire alarm rates. One region has many

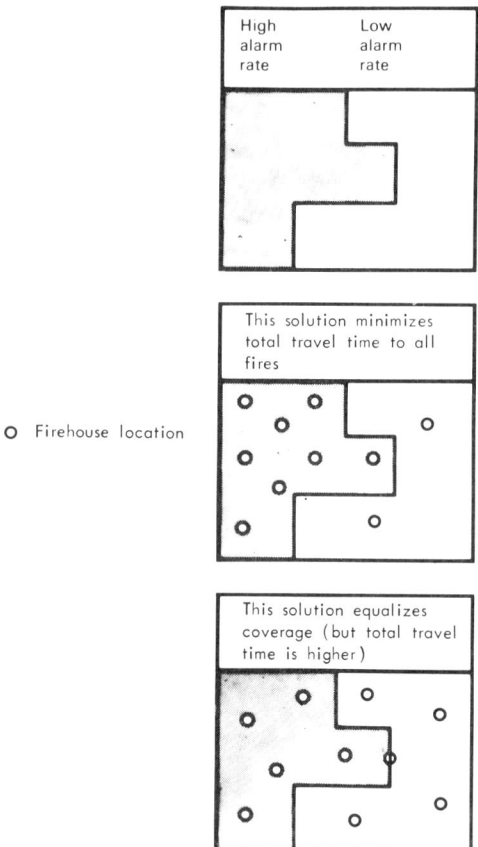

FIGURE 3.3. Conflicting objectives in the placement of firehouses.

fire alarms, the other very few. How should the city's 10 fire companies be allocated between the two regions?

Minimizing the total travel time to all fires that occur in the city can be achieved by placing the companies close to where fires are expected to occur. As a result, eight companies would be allocated to the high-demand region and only two to the other region. A problem with this solution is that when a fire does occur in the low-demand region, it may take a very long time for the fire companies to arrive. Residents of the low-demand region might claim that they are receiving substandard protection and are being penalized for being careful and having fewer fires. Minimizing travel times to actual fires also ignores the potentially high fire hazards or special dangers that may be present in the low-demand region; for example, those associated with hospitals, schools, chemical storage areas, and nursing homes.

Locating the fire companies so that the average travel time to alarms is made equal in the two regions would put approximately the same number of companies in each region[3] and may seem to be the more equitable solution. But as a result, the travel time to many fires in the high-incidence region will be increased in order to reduce those to the few fires in the low-incidence region. Moreover, the average travel time throughout the city will be larger than the minimum possible. Under this policy, therefore, it is likely that total fire losses in the city would be greater than under the minimum travel-time policy, because many fires would be getting slower responses. In addition, the companies in the high-incidence region would have a greater workload than the companies in the low-incidence region, an important consideration in some cities. Equalizing travel times in all regions of a city fails to take into account differing levels of demand in different regions; it results in the same travel time in high-hazard, high-alarm rate areas as in low-hazard, low-alarm rate areas.

So a fire department must face up to conflicting objectives in placing fire companies. In practice, departments make allocations that are compromises between these two extremes by placing more fire companies in high-demand regions, but still making sure that all regions receive an acceptable level of coverage.

A second difficulty in setting objectives is that there are many interest groups concerned with fire policy (community groups, labor unions, and good government groups, to name a few), and policy decisions must take their various, often conflicting, desires into account. In order to get a policy implemented, it is important to make sure that the concerns and interests of each group are recognized and accounted for. This aspect of deployment analysis is discussed in Chapter 5.

The analyst will usually play an important role in the definition of objectives. Just as he cannot accept the problem as given, he should not accept the objectives as given. Quade (1975) advises: "As one of his major tasks the analyst must help the decisionmakers to clarify and ultimately define the objectives they have in mind before he can do much to help them determine which alternatives to select."

3.4 STEP 3: CHOOSING THE CRITERIA

In order to evaluate alternative policies, the systems analyst needs a way of comparing two or more policies and deciding which is best. Here "best" means "comes closest to meeting the objectives." The analyst

---

[3] The number would not be exactly the same in each region because, on the average, more companies will be busy in the high-demand region. This means the high-demand region needs more companies to end up with the same average travel time as the low-demand region. See Chapter 6 for further details.

therefore defines criteria of performance that are related to the objectives. For each criterion, a measure (usually expressed as a number) is also defined.[4] The values of these measures are calculated for each alternative policy being considered. If there is only a single measure of effectiveness, then, all other things being equal (for example, cost), the policy with the best value of that measure would be recommended for implementation. (Such a policy would come closest to meeting the objectives.) If, as is more likely, there are several criteria, and it is not possible to relate them all in terms of a common measure (for example, dollars), the choice of the best policy is not so clear. But the analyst would report his results to the decisionmaker in terms of the values that a given policy would achieve on each of the criteria.

Service criteria and measures were discussed in Chapter 1 in a general way. Here we become more explicit and define the measures that will be used throughout the remainder of the book.

A fire department's primary objective is to protect lives and property from fire. Therefore, the most important measures of a fire department's performance are the number of fire-related fatalities and the value of property lost as a result of fire. However, it is not possible to use these measures as criteria in evaluating alternative deployment policies. This is because there are as yet no reliable methods for estimating the effect of changes in deployment policies on these measures. For example, if the number of fire companies on duty is doubled or halved, no one can state with any degree of certainty what will happen to the number of fire deaths or to the amount of property destroyed by fire.

In order to analyze deployment policies, it is necessary to use "proxy" measures, and they generally fall into two groups. The first group consists of departmental characteristics related to the insurance rates that the city's property owners are charged. These rates are based on the city's insurance grade, which is established periodically by the Insurance Services Office (ISO) after a survey of the city—including its water supply, fire department, and fire safety control procedures. The insurance grade depends in part on the number of companies on duty and other deployment decisions (*Grading Schedules for Municipal Fire Protection*, 1974).

Certain types of deployment changes will result in an increase or decrease in the total insurance premiums paid by the city's property owners. This is an important consideration in deciding whether or not the proposed changes should be made. However, as reported by the National League of Cities (*The Grading of Municipal Fire Protection Facilities*, 1967), calculating the effect of a change in insurance grade on

---

[4] Sometimes, especially informally, "criterion" and "measure" are used more-or-less synonymously.

3.4 Step 3: Choosing the Criteria

total premiums paid is both difficult and subject to error. In addition, since a city's insurance grade will stay fixed through a large range of deployment changes, it is usually of little assistance in choosing among certain alternative policies. We mention it here primarily because many cities still place great reliance on this method in determining their deployment policies.

The second group of proxy measures are numerical quantities that can be calculated easily and reliably, and that are related to the performance of the fire department. Use of these measures relies on the fact that some kinds of changes can be identified as desirable even if it is not known exactly how desirable. Travel time is one such measure. If a change in deployment policy that uses existing firefighting resources can reduce travel times to all incidents that are of concern to the department, this is a desirable change, all other things being equal. Or if the existing level of travel times can be achieved at lower cost, such a change is also desirable. Although such ideal changes cannot often be achieved in practice, they do show that the desirability of a specific change can often be identified without knowing its precise impact on fire protection.

Relating changes in proxy measures such as travel time to changes in the real effect of fire department activity would require gathering and analyzing vast amounts of data that have been and will continue to be unavailable. One would need accurate travel times, accurate measures of property damage, accurate accounting of injuries and loss of life, together with appraisals of whether any change in speed of response would have helped. To those data one would have to add more standard, but equally important information, such as: the type of structure; the time of day; the area of origin of the fire; and the age, sex, and prior physical condition of those injured.

Several attempts have been made to carry out such studies with the less than ideal data that is currently available. Ignall, Rider, and Urbach (1978), and Hogg (1970) have tried to relate fire severity to response distance and response time (defined below). Corman et al. (1975) have tried to relate fire fatalities to response distance. Recent work by Hogg and Morrow (1973) attempts to translate response times into monetary terms. These studies have not led to conclusive results. But it is clear that any policy that improves response time should result in less severe fires and fewer lost lives, all other things being equal. So the analyst wishing to do practical, applied fire research, while forced to accept the present lack of direct performance measures, may nevertheless do important work using proxies, such as response time.

The primary measures that we will be using throughout the book for comparing alternative deployment policies are described below. These measures are both able to be calculated and relevant for deployment analysis. We indicate in succeeding chapters which measure or measures are appropriate for each deployment issue. Additional measures of fire department performance, and the uses to which they can be put, are given by Schaenman and Swartz (1974), by Schaenman et al. (1976), and in *Evaluating the Organization of Service Delivery: Fire* (1977).

Response Time. This is the elapsed time from the moment the fire department is notified until a fire company is on the scene and ready to operate. We assume that shorter response times will lead to fewer fire fatalities and less property damage. As indicated in Figure 3.4, response time includes:

Dispatching time, the time between the receipt of an alarm and the dispatch of a unit (notifying it to respond) by the dispatcher.

Turnout time, the time required for the unit to leave its quarters and start moving once it has been dispatched.[5]

Travel time, the time between the start of the unit's trip and its arrival at the scene.

Setup time, the time required for the unit to prepare and position equipment at the scene before commencing firefighting.

The only component of response time that is affected by changing a company's location is travel time. Therefore, the analysis of company locations focuses on changes in travel times. However, in analyzing dispatching policies, response time is often the most important measure because a dispatching policy may affect dispatching time, turnout time, and travel time. Our discussion below concentrates on travel time; in most cases, the words "response time" can be substituted for "travel time" and the statements will remain correct.

Actually, there are several travel time (or response time) measures that are useful in most deployment studies. First, since different types of units (engines and ladders, for example) perform different functions at a fire, it is important to distinguish travel times for each type of equipment. In addition, since two units of the same type working together may be able to take some action that neither could take alone, the travel time of each arriving piece of equipment is important. Therefore, in evaluating alternative deployment policies it is important to consider the list (or *vector*) of travel times for engines, ladders, and other firefighting units that would respond to each incident under each policy.

The travel time list for engines, for instance, gives the time of arrival (relative to the time the unit leaves the firehouse) of the first engine,

---

[5] A unit dispatched via radio while returning from another alarm is not subject to this delay.

3.4 Step 3: Choosing the Criteria

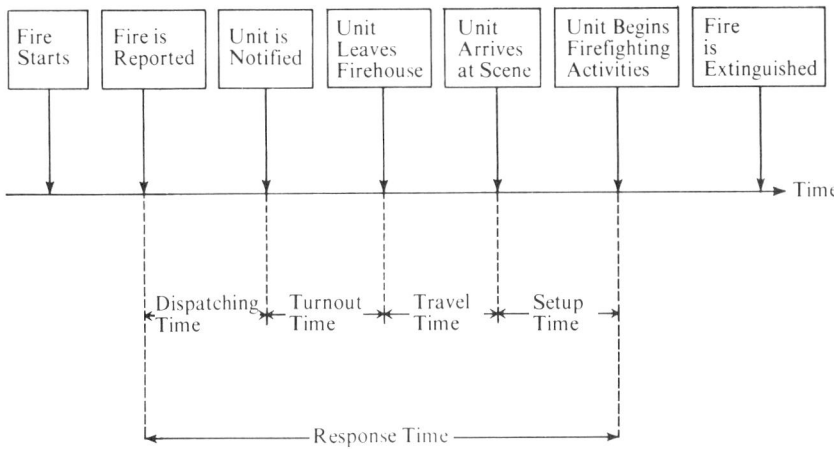

FIGURE 3.4. The components of response time.

second engine, etc. For example, at an incident to which three engines are dispatched, the travel time list might be (1,3,4), which corresponds to travel times of one, three, and four minutes for the three companies.

There are at least two reasons why it is difficult to use individual travel time or response time vectors to compare the attractiveness of alternative deployment policies:

1. There is no reliable way to rank the vectors from best to worst.
2. The vectors for all incidents or incident locations in the city must be considered, resulting in the need to compare a very large number of them.

As an example of the first difficulty suppose that one dispatching policy (Policy 1) produces (1,3) as the engine travel time vector to a certain incident location, and another dispatching policy (Policy 2) produces (2,2). Which policy is better? Policy 1 gets the first-due engine there sooner; Policy 2 gets the second-due engine there sooner. Even if we are only concerned with this one location, it is not clear which policy is preferable.

One way of comparing vectors is to calculate a single number that summarizes the information in the vector. This number is often referred to as the "utility" of the vector. One such number is the average of the numbers in the vector. In this case, the average of the first- and second-due travel times is 2 minutes for both policies, implying that the two policies are equally good. But, from a fire protection point of view, the first-engine (first-due engine) response time is usually more important than the second-engine response time. So more weight should be given to the first-engine time. But how much more weight?

Keeney (1971) determined some weights from the answers of a Deputy Chief in the New York City Fire Department to a set of questions about the chief's preferences. For example, the chief was asked, "Would you prefer the certainty that the first-due engine will arrive in 3 minutes to a 50% chance that it will arrive in 1.5 minutes and a 50% chance that it will arrive in 4 minutes?" The chief was also asked, "Would you prefer a response time vector of (2,3) to (1,4)?" From the answers to these questions Keeney learned that as far as this chief was concerned, the first-engine time should be weighted about twice as heavily as the second-engine time. (That is, getting the first engine to an incident 10 seconds sooner is worth about as much as getting the second there 20 seconds sooner.) He also found that more weight (i.e., a higher penalty) should be placed on longer responses, in order to reduce the occurrence of long travel times. (For example, the answer to the first question was that a sure 3 minutes was preferable to an average of 2.75 minutes because the 4 minute response "counts" more than the 1.5 minute response.)

The use of utility models to compare deployment policies must still be considered speculative. It is easy to challenge the meaning of the results of such a questioning process, and it is clear that responses from more than one officer are needed. It is also undoubtedly true that different utility functions would have to be developed for different communities. In addition, in reducing a vector of response times to a single number, a great deal of information is lost. It is unlikely that a fire department would choose one deployment policy over another solely on the basis of utility; that is, without looking at and comparing first-engine travel times, second-engine travel times, etc.

If utility models are not to be used, some way must be found to compare the individual components of travel time vectors. The approach that we take in this book is to perform separate analyses of travel times for first-arriving engines, first-arriving ladders, second-arriving engines, second-arriving ladders, third-arriving engines, and so on. The results are then presented to the policymaker for his evaluation. If, for example, one policy does better on first-arriving engine travel times, and another does better on second-arriving engine travel times, the policymaker will have to take these factors into consideration when making his decision.

There are a wide variety of travel time measures that may be used in different situations. First, consider how to compare the first-engine (or ladder) travel times to incident locations throughout a city or in different regions of a city under different policies. One approach is to look at the frequency with which long travel times occur. For example, suppose that under one policy 93 percent of the alarm boxes would have first-engine travel times of less than 3 minutes, while under another this would be true of only 80 percent of the alarm boxes. The first policy would be preferred. Another procedure would be to get maximum acceptable travel

3.4 Step 3: Choosing the Criteria

times to different incident locations in the city.[6] Then alternative policies could be compared on the basis of how well they satisfied the maximum travel time requirements.

Another set of travel time measures relies on the vector of average travel times to groups of incidents or incident locations. Incident locations can be grouped in many different ways—by region of the city or company response area, for example—and the travel times can be averaged in several different ways. For example, the average travel time to incidents can be found by weighting the travel time to each location by the alarm rate at that location. However, since travel times to fires at each location are far more critical than travel times to incidents that turn out to be false alarms, it might be more desirable to weight the travel time to each location by the structural fire rate at that location. This would provide the average travel time to a structural fire occurring within that group of locations.

Coverage. Most of the time fire companies are not responding to or working at alarms. In addition to district inspection and fire prevention services, fire companies provide insurance against major catastrophes and loss of life by being available and close-by should a fire occur. All locations must be covered, not only those with long histories of fires. There are certain places where fires may rarely occur (nursing homes, chemical plants, hospitals, and high-rise buildings, for example), but when one does, the resulting loss of life and property can be substantial. A measure of how well a deployment policy succeeds in providing this type of fire protection (called "coverage") is how often specific locations have nearby units available. One way of estimating coverage is to calculate the average travel time to all locations in a region of the city (where equal weight is given to each potential fire location) assuming all fire companies are always available. A more accurate estimate of coverage can be obtained by taking into account the unavailability of fire companies (see below).

Availability. It is of little comfort to know that there is a firehouse one block away if the fire company stationed there is rarely in the house. The coverage measure described above assumes that when an alarm from a specific location is received, the companies designated to respond are available. When this assumption is inappropriate, it is necessary to consider each company's *unavailability*, which is the fraction of time it is busy. This measure indicates how often alarms in the company's first-

---

[6] However, there are presently no accepted standards that can be used for setting such maximum travel times.

due area will suffer a travel-time delay because the responding companies are located in more distant firehouses, (Unavailability is also a measure of the company's workload; see below.)

More refined unavailability measures indicate not only how often the first-due company to a particular location will be unavailable, but also how often both the first-due and second-due companies will be unavailable, the first-, second-, and third-due, etc. Unavailability measures permit calculation of better estimates of coverage than the average travel time to all locations in the city. They provide a more accurate answer to the question, "What would the travel times to this location be if there were a fire here?"

Initial Response Adequacy. A simple measure that is useful in comparing dispatching policies and is related to response time is the proportion of alarms for which the initial response was appropriate. Sending *fewer* units than are needed may prevent or delay firefighting and rescue operations until the required companies are dispatched and arrive, and thus add to life and property loss. Sending *more* units than are needed means unnecessary responses for the extra companies, and their not being available for other incidents, at least until the nature of the alarm becomes known.

Fire Company Workloads. In New York City, some fire companies respond to more than 8000 alarms per year. As a result, one of the important considerations in evaluating any new deployment policy there is its effect on company workloads. Workload is not so much of a problem in most localities, where a "busy" company might respond to fewer than 1000 alarms per year. However, as fire departments begin to take over some emergency medical service functions, they are finding that many of their fire companies are busier than they used to be. Even where the absolute company workloads are not high enough to cause problems, the departments may be concerned about maintaining a reasonable balance of work among its companies. For these reasons, a workload measure is often used to compare alternative policies—for example, the average number of times per day that a fire company responds to alarms, or the average amount of time it spends working at fires.

Cost. The measures of performance discussed above can usually be improved by spending more money. Therefore, comparison of various alternative deployment policies should either be made among equal-cost alternatives, or the differences in costs should be explicitly identified.

The direct cost of an existing company's response to each new alarm is very small—gasoline plus wear and tear on the apparatus—if the alternative is having it remain in the firehouse. In contrast, the cost of creating a new company is very large, and, as shown in Chapter 1 (Section 1.3.2), the capital cost of the apparatus and the firehouse is small when compared to the cost of manning the company. For example, to field one extra fire company manned by four firemen and an officer around the clock would most likely cost over $400,000 per year. The yearly capital cost (debt service) on a $400,000 firehouse (assuming it can be used for at least 40 years) and a $70,000 piece of apparatus (assuming it has a 15-year life) would then amount to only about 12 percent of the total cost of maintaining the company. The comparison is even more dramatic if two or three companies share a single firehouse.

Consequently, the cost of a deployment policy is often adequately represented by the number of men it requires on the payroll, rather than the number of firehouses needed or the number of responses that will be made.

3.5 STEP 4: SELECTION OF ALTERNATIVES

In this step alternative policies are suggested for examination and evaluation. At this stage of the analysis it is important to specify a wide range of alternatives for consideration. Include as many as it is possible to examine. If a policy is not specified as an alternative it cannot be evaluated. If it is not evaluated there is no way of knowing just how good—or bad—it may be. The "best" policy may not be chosen by the analysis because it was never suggested as an alternative!

Alternatives should not be excluded merely because they seem impractical or run contrary to past practice. The analysis will be able to show whether the benefits to be derived from such a policy outweigh the costs of making such a radical change. On the other hand, the set of alternatives should be developed with implementation in mind. It is obviously not very useful to choose a brilliant new deployment policy that cannot be implemented. Therefore, at this stage, the interests of the various employee and public interest groups should again be kept in mind. It is useful to have representatives of unions, community groups, and the city administration involved in selecting the alternatives to be evaluated. (See Chapter 5 for a discussion of these factors.)

The generation of alternatives requires a thorough understanding of the system, as well as a good deal of creativity and imagination. The alternatives should not be restricted to changes within the limits of the existing environment. If some alternative proves very valuable, it might be worthwhile to modify the environment in order to get the alternative implemented. For example, changes in dispatching and relocation policies should not necessarily be restricted to policies that can be implemented by revising alarm assignment cards. Chapters 11 and 12 show the significant benefits that can be obtained from dispatching and relocation policies that make use of an on-line computer.

From where do the alternative policies to be tested come? Most will probably result from the informed judgment and experience of people within the fire department. They generally have a wealth of ideas for improving the deployment of their department's companies, but lack hard evidence to justify the changes. Some of the changes they have in mind might be beneficial, others might not. The availability of methods for comparing alternatives (Step 5 in the systems analysis procedure) permits these ideas to be tested and evaluated before being adopted by the city, so that no lives or property are jeopardized.

The analyst may also develop alternatives after observing the system in operation, or from approximate analytical models of the system. And the other interested groups involved may submit still further alternatives for examination. It is important to remember to include the current policy in the set of alternatives as the "base case." By comparing the effects of other policies to the base case it is possible to determine whether a proposed policy will be better, and how much of an improvement can be expected.

As Figure 3.1 shows, the generation, analysis, and comparison of alternatives will generally be performed several times. The analysis and comparison of the first group of policies may reveal problems with the alternatives—unanticipated results, factors that had not been considered, etc. To correct these problems, new alternatives are developed, which are then analyzed and compared. This process should result in better and better solutions.

3.6 STEP 5: ANALYSIS OF ALTERNATIVES

Once alternatives have been selected, each one has to be examined to determine the likely consequences of its implementation in terms of the measures of effectiveness specified in Step 3. How can alternative policies be evaluated to see which best meets the objectives? One way is to try each one in the city for some period of time, observing what happens in each case. Then, after all have been tried, the one that worked best can be implemented permanently.

The trouble is that experimenting with operating systems such as the fire protection system is likely to be impractical, expensive, or dangerous. For example, it is clearly impractical to compare alternative arrangements of firehouses by building a large number of new firehouses and choosing only the set of houses that turns out to provide the best fire protection. Similarly, no fire department is likely to consider operating a few weeks at a time with different numbers of companies on duty to determine the appropriate number to deploy. This approach is also time-consuming (it

3.6 Step 5: Analysis of Alternatives

will take a long time to collect sufficient data with which to evaluate a policy), disruptive, and confusing, since the trial policies would be continually changing.

As a result, a systems analyst usually works with a *model* of the real world. A model is an imitation of reality, on which manipulations and experiments can be performed without the real world costs or dangers. It is used to predict what would happen in the real world if a certain policy were implemented. The analyst feeds information about the policy into the model. After making various calculations using this "input data," the model produces as output predictions of what the values of one or more performance measures would be if the policy were implemented. This procedure is depicted in Figure 3.5.

Models are neither mysterious nor magical. We see and use models all the time. A road map is a model of the patterns of roads in the real world. It enables us to plan a trip in advance—finding the length and other characteristics of various routes before selecting the best one to travel. A model of an airplane is tested in a wind tunnel before a pilot tries to fly it.

These models, just like a child's model train or model airplane, look much like the systems they represent. But there are many other models that look very little like the real thing. Some models consist entirely of mathematical equations. For example, in high school algebra we are taught that the time it takes a car traveling at a certain speed to go a certain distance can be calculated as:

$$\text{time} = \text{distance/speed}.$$

This can be a very useful model. If someone planning a 100-mile trip knows that an average speed of 50 miles per hour is possible on the route, the model says that two hours should be allowed for the trip. Given the distance and speed as inputs, the model produces an estimate of the travel time as output. Of course, the predicted time is no more

FIGURE 3.5. The role of a model in policy analysis.

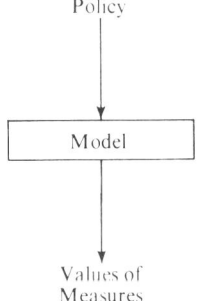

than an estimate. The actual speed and distance traveled will not be known until after the trip. But if the estimates of these inputs are reasonably accurate, the estimated travel time will also be reasonably accurate. Use of this and similar models permit people to plan for the future even if they have imperfect knowledge of the road ahead. In this case, for example, the traveler can arrange to meet someone at his destination approximately two hours after he starts out.

So while models imitate the real world, they do not have to look like the real world. The important thing is that the model must provide valid answers to the questions asked of it. The answers may not have to be extremely accurate. For purposes of choosing a policy, usually only large differences between the alternatives are important. For example, it matters little in choosing a new location for a firehouse if one policy results in an 8-second or a 10-second reduction in travel time relative to the existing policy in a region if another policy results in a one-minute reduction. It is generally the relative *differences* in the outcomes of different policies that count, not the absolute outcomes.

Because mathematical models are usually used to analyze alternative policies in a systems analysis study, systems analysis is often referred to as "quantitative analysis." If in fact, the problem being investigated could be described so faithfully by a mathematical model that a decision could be made purely on the basis of the results that are obtained from it, the analysis would be completely quantitative. This is rarely the case in deployment analysis. However, models are the heart of any deployment study.

Types of Models. A wide range of models have been developed to analyze fire deployment problems. Many of these are discussed in subsequent chapters. Sometimes several models can be used for analyzing the same problems. The choice of which model to use usually depends on a trade off between the simplicity of the model and the accuracy of the results. The more complex the model, the closer it can be made to represent the real world and the more accurate its predictions about the consequences of a policy will be. But increased realism is bought at a price. A more complex model generally costs more to operate and requires considerably more data than a simple model. Before using a complex model the analyst should try to make sure that the expected improvements that might follow from implementation of a new policy will more than offset the expense of using the model. He should also make sure that there is not a simpler model that will be just as useful for analyzing the policies being considered. The simpler the model, the easier it will be to explain it to the policymaker; and the more a policymaker knows and understands about a model, the more likely he is to accept its results in evaluating policies.

3.6 Step 5: Analysis of Alternatives

There are many ways of grouping models into classes for descriptive purposes. For example, they may be grouped by their degree of abstraction from the real world—from a scale model (of an airplane, for example), to an analog model (one using fluid flow to represent traffic flow), to a symbolic model (a mathematical equation to represent the growth of heat in a fire over time). They may be separated into deterministic models (those in which all the factors are known with certainty) and probabilistic models (those in which the behavior of some of the factors is uncertain). Or they may be classified by the manner in which they treat time, where static models are time-independent, and dynamic models account for changes in a system over time. There are many other ways to classify models. Of course, such classification schemes are not rigid. Categories may overlap and models may fit into several categories.

We will not discuss models in terms of any consistent classification system. Instead we will illustrate what models are by briefly presenting some of the models that have been developed to analyze deployment problems. All of them are discussed in more detail in the following chapters. All share two common features of models: they are partial representations of reality and they are used to approximate performance measures of a real world system. The idea is to use models to relate factors of the system that are under the control of the policymaker to the measures of performance that are being used to evaluate alternative policies.

Empirical Models. An empirical model usually relates an output or performance measure of a system to the input variables in a particularly simple fashion. Usually a linear relationship is assumed so that, whenever all other inputs are held constant, an increase of two units in the input will affect the output by twice as much as an increase of one unit of the same input. Statistical techniques are used to find the best estimate of the amount by which each unit of an input variable affects the output variable. If there is enough data, the statistics will also tell you when the effect of an input variable is so small that one may simplify the model by eliminating it. In this way, patterns in the data can be used to help shape the resulting model.

In Chapter 6 an empirical model for predicting travel times is discussed. We have already said that travel time is an important measure of the performance of a fire department. However, most departments know very little about how quickly their emergency units respond. One way to determine the travel characteristics of their units is to give them stop watches and coding forms and have them note the distance traveled and time required for each response. If the resulting data are plotted on a graph, some patterns in the data can be seen by inspection. For example, travel times are generally higher for longer response distances. But to be useful for predicting future travel times for response distances, a more precise relationship is needed.

Figure 3.6 shows the results of such an experiment in Wilmington, Delaware. Five fire companies (two engines, two ladders, and a rescue squad) recorded the distance traveled and the travel time for 243 responses. The best estimates of travel time were obtained by using the relationship:

travel time (minutes) = 0.69 + 1.69 × travel distance (miles).

This relationship (which is a model) was used in a subsequent analysis of the deployment of Wilmington's fire companies. After the distance between a firehouse and an alarm box was estimated (using another model), the time required to travel that distance was estimated using the above model. For example, if a travel distance was estimated to be one mile, the model predicts the travel time to be 2.38 minutes (0.69 + 1.69 = 2.38), or 2 minutes 23 seconds.

The purpose of most empirical models is to use data gathered in the past to make predictions about the future. For example, Chapter 8 de-

FIGURE 3.6. Wilmington: The relationship between travel time and travel distance.

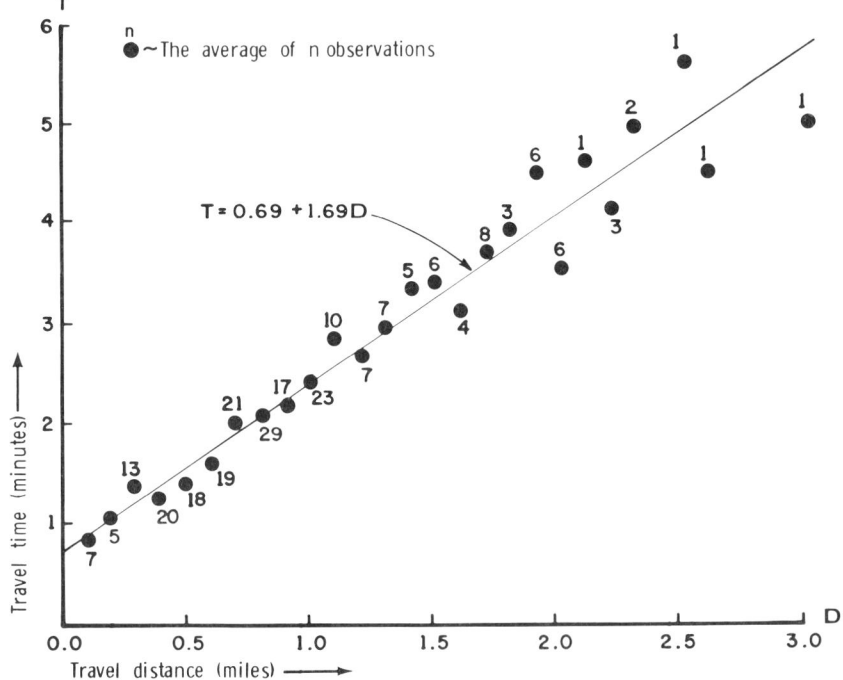

3.6 Step 5: Analysis of Alternatives   93

scribes an empirical model for predicting alarm rates (needed as input to many deployment models).

Descriptive Analytic Models. Another type of model that is useful in deployment analysis is the descriptive analytic model. This type of model deals with relationships among variables that are more complicated (in a mathematical sense) than those of empirical models. The form of the model is derived mathematically from theoretical statements of the relationships that hold in the real world. Simplifying assumptions are made so that the model is not too complex mathematically.

One such model, the "square-root law," is used to estimate the average travel distance from firehouses to fires in a region, based on a few easily determined characteristics of the region. To describe this law, which is covered in detail in Chapters 6 and 7, we consider engine companies and suppose that no more than one is located in any firehouse. If a region has area A (in square miles) and there are an average of $\bar{N}$ engine companies available in the region (the average number available is the number located in the region less the average number busy), then the square-root law states that the average travel distance (in miles) for the first-arriving engine company can be estimated using the equation:

$$\text{average travel distance} = (\text{constant}) \times \sqrt{A/\bar{N}}. \quad (3.1)$$

The constant depends on the street configuration and on how the companies are distributed in the region. However, from studies in several cities, a value of 0.55 has been found to provide good estimates. The relationship in Equation (3.1) is certainly not obvious, and much of Chapters 6 and 7 is devoted to deriving and validating it. But it is a simple and powerful relationship that is very useful in performing deployment studies.

As an example, imagine a city of 9 square miles that has, on the average, 4 engines available. Then the square-root law estimate of the average response distance $(\bar{D})$ for the first-arriving engine company to fires in this city is:

$$\bar{D} = 0.55\sqrt{9/4} = 0.55(3/2) = 0.825 \text{ miles}.$$

If we use Wilmington's empirically determined travel-time function for this city, we predict that the average travel time $(\bar{T})$ for the first-arriving engine company to fires in this city is:

$$\bar{T} = 0.69 + 1.69 \times 0.825 = 2.08 \text{ minutes} = 2 \text{ minutes 5 seconds}.$$

Using the square-root model, it is possible to answer a large number of deployment questions. For example, it would be easy to determine how average response distances in a region would change if the number of companies were changed, or if the alarm rate were to change. If regions having the same types of fire hazards and alarm patterns have very different average response distances, this might indicate that fire companies should be rearranged to bring the protection in the various regions into better balance.

Simulation Models. The square-root model was not derived empirically, but with mathematical formulas in which a large number of simplifying assumptions were made (see Chapter 6). Even though these assumptions will not be true in any real world situation, this does not mean that the model is not useful. But how could the model be tested for accuracy? It would be hard to collect the necessary test data in the field (among the many problems with this approach, it would be necessary to vary the number of units on duty in the city during the course of the data collection), so another type of model was used to verify the square-root model—a simulation model of fire department operations. A simulation model is generally a more complex and more accurate model of the real world than a descriptive analytic model. (See Chapter 13 for a detailed description of the Fire Operations Simulation Model.) The simulation imitates, inside a computer, the real world operations of a fire department. It tracks the events in each of a large number of alarms from the time it is reported to the department, through the dispatch of companies, their arrival at the scene, their work at the incident, their release, and finally their return to quarters and availability for another dispatch. Figure 3.7 shows how good the predictions of the square-root model (for

FIGURE 3.7. Validation of the square-root law using simulation. The average response distance for the first-arriving ladder company is $\bar{D}$; A is the area of the region, and $\bar{N}$ is the number of ladder companies available.

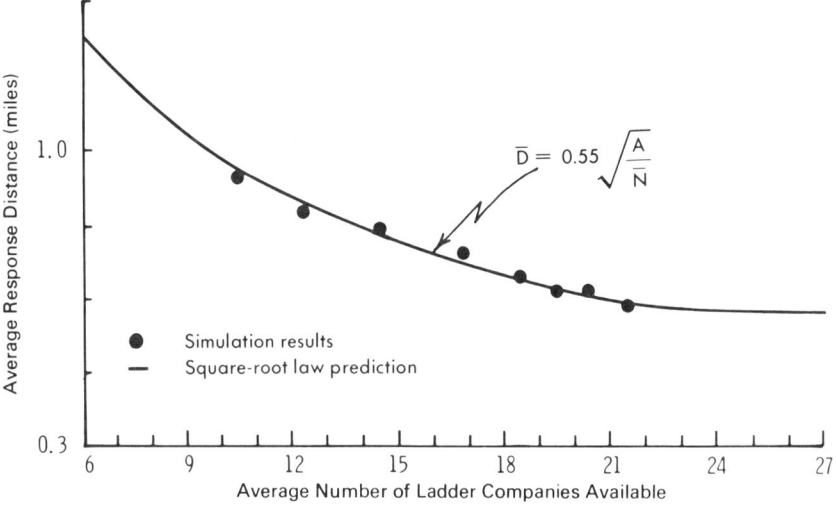

3.6 Step 5: Analysis of Alternatives

ladder companies) turned out to be when compared to results of the simulation.

A simulation model can be one of the most accurate and informative models of the real world. For example, the output reports from the Fire Operations Simulation Model include detailed information on every alarm, the number of responses made and time worked at fires by each of the companies during the course of the simulation, and the amount of time each one spent relocated in another company's firehouse.

A simulation model allows a wide range of deployment policies to be examined. The results are also more easily accepted by decisionmakers because the model is closer in its assumptions to the real world than the abstract mathematical models. These benefits are accompanied by significant costs: the computer program is large and relatively expensive to run; an experienced programmer and a moderately large computer are needed; and a substantial amount of detailed data, including a geographical representation of company and alarm locations, must be specified.

Prescriptive Models. All of the types of models discussed above are descriptive. They predict the values of various performance measures for given deployment policies (as shown in Figure 3.5). But none suggest what policies to try. In many operations research studies in business and industry, "optimization" models are employed that can determine policies that will maximize or minimize performance measures such as profits or costs. These are called *prescriptive models*. They are the most desirable type of model, and analysts try to use them whenever they are appropriate.

One example of a prescriptive model is the use of the square-root model in a prescriptive mode. Instead of predicting the average travel distance for the first arriving engine in a region from the density of engine companies, it is possible to determine the smallest number of engine companies needed to provide a given average first-arriving engine travel distance. Letting N be the number of engines needed and $\bar{B}$ the average number of engines that are busy, then from Equation (3.1) we see that:

$$\text{average travel distance} = \text{constant} \sqrt{A/(N - \bar{B})}$$

so, solving for N,

$$N = \bar{B} + A \left[\frac{\text{constant}}{\text{average travel distance}} \right]^2.$$

A prescriptive model that can be used to determine the number of firehouses to have, and where they should be located in order to meet certain travel-time requirements, is discussed in Chapter 10.

Prescriptive models can rarely be used in public policy analysis, because their use requires a clear, unambiguous objective (so a "best" solution can be identified), and a single measure of performance characteristics. These conditions are not usually found in public policy affairs. For example, a jurisdiction would usually not determine the number of engine companies it needs solely on the basis of average travel distances.

So, in performing most deployment analyses, the analyst uses descriptive models to supply quantitative information about a policy, which can then be used together with the judgment and intuition of those involved in reaching a decision. In this way, decisions can be made using the best information available, while taking all relevant constraints, judgments, and other considerations into account.

3.7 STEP 6: COMPARISON OF ALTERNATIVES

In principle, if Steps 1 through 5 of the systems-analytic process have been performed conscientiously, there should be no difficulty in comparing the performance measures resulting from each of the alternatives and choosing the best one to implement. The expected performance measures of the system under each of the policies would be tabulated, the values compared to one another, and the best policy chosen. In practice, however, qualitative factors that are difficult to build into the models—municipal politics, union interests, and various community considerations—enter the decisionmaking process. These factors must be considered, along with the quantitative information produced by the models when evaluating alternatives.

Moreover, models and mathematics are not substitutes for good judgment and common sense. Their value lies in the understanding and insight they can provide on specific questions that are not directly accessible to even the best-informed judgment. Since models are only approximations of reality, they must leave out some aspects of the real world. It is in bridging these gaps that expert judgment, guided by both experience and modeling, is most effective.[7]

The problem that usually arises in comparing alternatives is that no one of them is a clear-cut "best" policy, even if the choice is to be made purely on the basis of the quantitative criteria. One deployment policy may best distribute company workload, another produce a better average citywide travel time, and a third provide the best coverage of the central business district. It will be hard to rank these policies since each of the measures uses different units of value (responses per day, minutes per response, etc.). One approach to this problem is to assign arbitrary,

---

[7] For example, in analyzing alternative locations for a fire company, a model can be used to predict resulting travel times and the workloads of the company. But that model cannot predict the resulting reactions of the community to the various alternatives.

subjective weights to each criterion. The values of the criteria for each policy are then multiplied by the appropriate weights, and the sum over all the criteria provides a single number that is used as the "value" of the policy. However, the specification of weights requires the imposition of the value scheme of a single person or group, and it is generally difficult to explain the meaning of the resulting "value" to the policymaker.

An alternative approach is to present results in the form of scorecards on which a column of performance measures is presented for each policy alternative, with each measure expressed in natural units. Some scheme is normally used to indicate the relative rankings of the policies for each measure (e.g., colors), but the problem of direct comparison and selection is left to the decisionmaker's judgment and intuition. Removing the reliance on weights allows the analyst to present results that are relatively value-free. Different interest groups may be able to agree on a single alternative that they all prefer (perhaps for different reasons), while they would be unable to agree on weights to assign to the various performance measures.

The scorecard approach has been used to present deployment alternatives to the Chief of the New York City Fire Department. It was also used in a transportation study to present results to federal transportation policymakers, state legislators, and local planners (Chesler and Goeller, 1973), and in an evaluation of alternative ways of protecting an area of the Netherlands from floods (Goeller et al., 1977). Figure 3.8 is one of the scorecards that resulted from the latter study.

3.8 STEP 7: IMPLEMENTATION OF RESULTS

Steps 4, 5, and 6 should be performed with implementation in mind, so that this step can be carried out as easily as possible (although the implementation of new public policies is never easy). This means that all interested parties, including community groups and union representatives, should be involved as much as possible during the development and evaluation of alternatives. The costs associated with implementation (including the costs of upsetting the status quo) should be explicitly considered in the analysis, as should the development of an implementation plan.

Many factors determine whether a new policy that is developed during a deployment analysis study is actually implemented, including timing, the political environment, and the organizational structure of the fire department. There are also a number of factors associated with a policy alternative that can enhance the chances for its implementation. An extensive discussion of how to increase the chances of successful implementation is presented in Chapter 5.

IMPACTS OF ALTERNATIVE POLICIES ON RECREATION

Type of Recreation	Closed Case	SSB Case	Open Case
Sea Beaches			
Added shoreline (km)	8	0	0
Increase in attendance (annual visits, in thousands)	>338	0	0
Inland Beaches			
Added shoreline (km)	17	11	6
Increase in attendance (annual visits, in thousands)	>108	>88	>68
Boating			
Sea access restricted for large boats?	Yes	Yes	No
Added moorings due to departure of:			
fishing vessels	<240	0	0
large boats	<900	<900	0
Sportfishing			
Decrease in salt-water fish quantity (percent)	<75	0	25
Added shoreline (km)	17+	11	6+
Fresh-water fish available?	Yes	No	No
Touring			
Decrease in attractiveness of areas around dikes	None	Minor	Some
A major tourist site at mouth of Oosterschelde?	No	Yes	No

Rankings: ☐ Best ▨ Intermediate ■ Worst

FIGURE 3.8. Sample scorecard. (Source: Goeller et al., 1977.)

3.9 STEP 8: MONITORING AND EVALUATING THE RESULTS

The analysis does not end with implementation of a new policy. Recall that the techniques used during the evaluation and comparison of alternatives were only approximations of reality and provided only estimates of what would happen if any particular policy were implemented. Once a policy is implemented (and the implemented policy is rarely identical to the one that was recommended), it is important to watch its behavior closely to make sure that the anticipated benefits actually occur and that the projected costs were realistic. If not, this should be recognized as soon as possible and changes should be made.

3.9 Step 8: Monitoring and Evaluating the Results

Procedures for monitoring and evaluating the results of a new policy should be integral parts of the implementation. Data should be gathered on a regular basis to permit calculation of the same measures of performance that were used in the evaluation of alternative policies. The performance of the system before and after implementation should be compared on the basis of these measures.

Continual monitoring of the results of a new policy will also help determine when changes in the operating environment have weakened or invalidated the assumptions of the analysis. Under such circumstances a revision of the policy will be required. For example, a change in the types of alarms that a department receives or in their distribution by time of day or geographic region might require rethinking a deployment policy based on a different set of alarm patterns.

Chapter 4
Organizing for Deployment Analysis

Synopsis

For deployment analysis to be useful to a fire department, an analytical team must be assigned responsibility for conducting—or at least directing—the work. The team leader is usually a member of the fire department, but other organizational arrangements are possible and have proved successful. The team may be a permanent in-house group, a permanent consortium of individuals or organizations, or a temporary task force.

Deciding whether to organize an analytical team involves matching deployment problems with the necessary resources—primarily with skilled people. Fire departments have many problems, but only some of them are deployment problems, and even these are not necessarily susceptible to resolution by the techniques described in this book. A sober assessment must be made of the decisions likely to be faced by the fire department in the future. These should then be compared with the cost and difficulty of undertaking an analytical effort, by considering the seriousness of the problems and the chances that existing ways of operating the department will be unable to handle them. In addition, the manager must attempt to envision the results that might emerge from analysis and to evaluate the usefulness and acceptability of these results. At least one potentially feasible solution for each problem should be firmly in mind before starting analysis.

If the preliminary assessment reveals a need for an analytical team, its position in the organization should be established to reflect and assure strong, visible, continuing support of the chief executive officer. The team should have one full-time individual responsible for its leadership and should include a variety of skills—technical, managerial, and political. Often the team will draw upon outside resources, such as other units within the department, other analysis groups in local government, universities, or consulting firms. Since the ultimate goal of analysis is to change policy, potential future supporters should be identified, cultivated, and called upon for help.

The skills and resources required by the team will depend on the types of problems to be attacked. Answers to the following questions are relevant for selecting the composition of the team:

Is the problem labor or capital intensive?

Will a one-time decision resolve the problem, or must recurring decisions be made?

Will a solution, once it is selected, be readily reversible?

What kind of technology is needed?

Can the fire department itself act to solve the problem, or must other organizations be involved?

What will be the political impact of solutions?

How much is the solution likely to cost?

Analysis makes demands on a fire department that are not easy to meet. Analysts presume that organizations want to evaluate their performance, that top policymakers embrace the concept of rational decisionmaking based on quantitative information, and that appropriate data on activities and performance can be readily collected. In the fire service there are few departments that fully match these assumptions. The team leader must work actively to create consumers of analytical results within the department and a congenial climate in which analysis can proceed. Nevertheless, establishing and maintaining an analytical team is a rewarding as well as a challenging experience.

4.1 INTRODUCTION

The purpose of Chapters 4 and 5 is to provide guidelines for organizing teams to conduct the deployment analyses outlined in later chapters. These two chapters also present useful strategies for managing change in fire departments. In Chapter 4 we discuss issues surrounding the decision to use quantitative techniques and the organization of analytical teams. In Chapter 5 we concentrate on implementation of the results of analysis.

Some fire departments have existing analytical staffs. Others do not, but may draw upon other local government resources or may use outside consultants from time to time. Still other departments may not have used analytical techniques at all for deployment planning. For ease of exposition, we assume in this chapter and the next that responsibility for guiding the analysis has been placed within the fire department. However, the issues raised are applicable whether or not the analyst happens to be in the department. Fire deployment studies have been performed by teams directed from a mayor's office, a city manager's office, a budget bureau, and other governmental units. Also, the chapters are written as if the reader is the "team leader"—the individual primarily responsible for using analysis to aid in deployment planning. This individual may be a policymaker, a senior local government official, or an analyst, depending on the local circumstances. The reader whose role is different should benefit nevertheless by understanding the problems and decisions faced by the team leader.

Throughout this chapter we speak of *analytical teams* (or units). The team may be a permanent in-house group, a permanent consortium of individuals or organizations, or a temporary task force formed to solve a particular problem. Aside from the basic decision whether or not to create a permanent analytical team in the first place, most of the issues raised are relevant for the team regardless of its composition or tenure. The term "analytical team" can and should be replaced by whatever phrase best fits local circumstances.

4.2 ESTABLISHING AN ANALYTICAL TEAM

Understanding the steps in a systems analysis study as outlined in Chapter 3 is a prerequisite for successful deployment analysis. However, it is also necessary to understand how and when to carry out the required analysis. The purpose of this section is to explore questions that have to be answered to determine how to make the systems analysis approach usable in the fire department.

First of all, analysis is done by people. Moreover, the type of analysis discussed in this book is done by people with special training and skills. This means that anyone attempting to determine what strategies to follow to fully employ the more sophisticated techniques of deployment analysis should ask, "What kinds of problems do I have, and what kinds of resources, primarily skilled people, can I get to solve them?" A careful assessment of these issues is the first task in deciding how best to use deployment analysis.

Fire departments have many problems, but only a few of them are deployment problems. The specific strategic and tactical issues addressed in this book occur in all fire departments, but to varying degrees and certainly with widely varying frequencies over time. Rapidly growing communities may locate and build several new firehouses each year. Other communities locate and build a new firehouse only once every several years. While it is reasonable to argue, on the strategic issue alone, that the community that frequently locates and builds new fire stations

4.2 Establishing an Analytical Team

might reasonably employ analysts full-time to conduct the type of analysis discussed in Chapter 10, the community rarely faced with that decision should not.

One way to evaluate the need for an analytical team is to consider the interaction among the following factors: the number and size of deployment problems; the frequency with which they occur; and the amount of time that analytical skills will be needed to solve them.

Even in terms of tactical issues, such as those addressed in Chapters 11 and 12, there are towns where quantitative approaches using the computer may require more effort in data collection and analysis than the outcome is worth. A decision by an informed fire official, using common sense and experience, is likely to be perfectly satisfactory when deployment problems are small. However, notice the qualifications: informed fire official and common sense and experience. Even if there are no right and wrong decisions, there are better and worse decisions. Insights gained from understanding a particular quantitative approach to a deployment problem can contribute to the development of informed fire officials.

The first step in assessing the need for an analytical team is to identify the problems at hand and to predict the major problems to be faced by the department during the next several years. This problem analysis is probably best carried out by outlining the major *decisions* expected to be made by the department, with special reference to changes expected in the operating environment. Examples of such changes might be a large annexation of territory to be protected, imposition of severe budget constraints, large new shopping centers or highrise buildings, introduction of new services such as paramedical or ambulance service, or combining services into a single public safety department. Although it is not easy to predict what problems the fire department may be facing in the future, several assessments of the problems of the fire service exist as guides (Fyffe and Rardin, 1974; Swersey et al., 1973). If, in general, the major decisions correspond to the strategic and tactical deployment issues discussed in Chapter 3, the task becomes one of tailoring the application of analytical talent to these problems in a timely and orderly fashion.

The decision to use analytical methods in the solution of deployment problems requires substantial time and effort by analysts. More importantly, since most organizations do not easily embrace quantitative techniques, such a decision also requires a substantial commitment by others involved in fire department policymaking. The stakes are high, because the use of systems analysis comes at the expense of not using other, usually more familiar, decision procedures. Also, deployment analysis will usually begin with a couple of strikes against it. First, its utility remains to be proved to many. There are still only a few truly convincing uses of analysis as an aid to deployment planning in the country. (Some of these appear in Chapter 14.) Second, analytical approaches depend on a fundamental concept of inference that is, if not antithetical to, at least not common in the tradition of the fire service. "Every fire is different" is a cornerstone of the service lore. Searching for patterns of sameness and developing policies that are reliably replicable in most situations are goals of the analyst. In such a search, rules of probability theory are presumed to operate, and abstractions that rob the real world of some of its richness must be employed. Because the consequences of mistakes are so high—the loss of human life being the most visible—it is not easy to convey the utility of a policy based on the blatant expectation that some proportion of the cases, albeit small, have negative outcomes.

Like any other technique that involves expertise limited to only a few members of an organization, deployment analysis will never be well understood by the majority of department decisionmakers. Someone must make the translation from an analytical result to an implemented policy. Successful *use* of deployment analysis requires not only analysts, but also individuals with skill in program design, implementation, and management. Experience suggests that it takes a minimum of two to three times as many people as the number of analysts working on a problem to structure policy, develop programs, and manage implementation of even the simplest changes indicated by the analysis. Preferably, most of these people are not newly hired, but are already engaged in carrying out the processes to be changed. However, new skills in program development and implementation may be necessary to implement substantial changes in deployment; the need for these skills could represent new resource requirements for the organization.

Even when the necessary resources are available, the use of analytical techniques may not be appropriate for the department's particular problems. Sophisticated deployment analysis is not appropriate for every problem. Fire departments often face problems that are not necessarily best solved through mathematical modeling. For example, maintaining morale is an important day-to-day problem faced by fire officials. A model of morale-building may be a suitable topic for research; a complex questionnaire about firefighters' attitudes may be a useful tool in understanding the problem; but, in general, expectations that quantitative analysis techniques will solve problems of morale are unrealistic.

Since quantitative techniques are not appropriate for many problems faced by fire department administrators, it may be best for most departments to make use of analysts periodically, to draw on some communitywide pool of analysts when needed, and not to maintain an in-house capability at all. The choice of the best approach is not an easy one, but some guidelines are available.

4.2.1 Testing for Need

There are some general tests of need that can help determine whether or not an analytical team should be assembled. First, are there truly problems with the existing state of affairs? Second, are they serious? Third, are there potentially feasible solutions to the problems, given the resources available to the department? We consider each in turn.

Dissatisfaction with the Status Quo. Hardly anyone admits to liking change. Most people tend to react adversely to it. There are some situations, however, that make the introduction of change somewhat easier. This happens when some kind of change is perceived to be needed, even though just what change may not be well specified. No matter how distasteful the change, it is more likely to succeed if it is believed to be needed than if it is introduced when the existing situation is generally perceived to be satisfactory. This elementary test should not be taken lightly. Extending it to include assessment of the likely situation three to five years in the future is also important. In most cities it takes several years to transform a fire station from a gleam in the planner's eye to final occupancy, so it is important to take account of the demands and constraints likely to be placed on department decisionmakers in the future.

In short, a simple test of whether or not an analytical team is a viable investment is the current degree of dissatisfaction with the status quo. The greater the dissatisfaction, the greater the chance that the team and its approach can be used effectively.

Seriousness of Issues. Taking stock of the seriousness of issues may seem rather unrelated to what commitment to make to analysis. But deployment analysis using quantitative techniques is not worth the effort if the question is where to locate the searchlight unit. Complex, expensive methodology should not be brought to bear on small problems. This is especially the case in communities where fires, false alarms, and so forth are infrequent, where resources (engines, ladders, personnel) are few in number, or where the data needed for the models are not available or would be costly to acquire. The problems the fire department faces must be judged serious enough to warrant the investment in analytical skills.

Feasible Solutions. The third test, requiring advance knowledge of potentially feasible solutions, may seem a little like requiring the answer be known before the analysis is done. In a sense, this is not far wrong. Research cannot be conducted on the spot every time there is a problem to be solved. It is usually necessary to apply a large measure of existing knowledge and traditional lore to the solution of departmental problems.

Analytical tools provide innovative solutions in particular circumstances, but the range of potential solutions normally is known before the formal analysis begins.

In assessing whether (and to what extent) to use analytical techniques, the manager should know what kinds of results to expect and must evaluate the department's and the community's ability to use the results. No one city in this country has the resources to develop a lightweight, effective air pack, and there are only a few cities with sufficient resources to test new fire clothing effectively, although many try. The risk is high if a city tries to solve a major problem without at least one potentially feasible solution firmly in mind.

4.2.2 Staffing an Analytical Team

Given the conclusion that an analytical team should be created, it is necessary to deal with the question of how it should be organized and staffed.

Full-time Leadership. Analysis is not an avocation. It is a full-time job. At least one individual must devote full-time attention to the tasks of assessing the need for analysis, building a staff, supervising the analysis, and promoting implementation of the results.

A tradition in the fire service is to allocate staff responsibilities to officers while they retain line firefighting responsibilities. There is considerable merit to the tradition. Firefighting activities *per se* take a relatively small proportion of duty time, and the tradition gives those individuals responsible for staff activities an opportunity to keep their firefighting skills sharp. The difficulty is that in large departments the firefighting activities take precedence over staff activities, and the staff activity suffers. Moreover, the staff activity never receives exclusive attention; it is always subject to interruption.

Analysis, like certain other activities, is not easily interrupted. The requirements for dispassionate, reflective thought contrast sharply with the requirements for immediate fireground decisions. To ask an individual to be responsible for analytical tasks as well as firefighting tasks amounts to giving analysis second-class status. Given the drama and importance of the firefighting tasks, it is necessary to bring preparatory and complementary tasks such as training, prevention, and analysis into balance. If analysis is to be used successfully in the department it will have to be accorded as high a status as possible relative to firefighting.

Making the Position Attractive. There are various ways to handle the problem of mixing line and staff responsibilities for top analytical positions. First, of course, qualified personnel can be rotated through the positions, with the option to return to line duty after a period of time. A minimum period of at least one year should be specified, with two to three years designated as preferred tenure because of the high preparation and job assimilation time. Most large departments have full-time positions for training or communications, for example, that are filled by uniformed personnel moving through the ranks.

Another option is to give leadership of the analytical team to a nonuniformed employee and apply the promotional and other personnel regulations applicable to nonuniformed personnel. This approach has merit because of the increased mobility it provides analysts throughout the government, and because the motivation to succeed in the analytical leadership role is not diminished by the desire to succeed as a firefighter. The difficulty, however, is that most departments across the country have required that top positions in the department be filled by uniformed personnel. Even the most progressive departments rarely see the role of chief of department being filled by nonuniformed individuals who have risen to leadership positions based on training in, say, communications, building code regulations, chemical engineering, computer science, municipal water supply, or least of all mathematics. Until departments achieve more flexibility in matching background, training, and experience to tasks, without reference to uniformed status, it is not likely that assigning analytical positions solely or even primarily to nonuniformed personnel will be viable.

Another option is to make staff positions more attractive. For example, most cities have duty schedules based on 24-hour firefighting service. These schedules inevitably require work on some nights and weekends, but provide for time off during weekdays. Also, the schedules generally balance intensive periods of duty time with relatively long periods off duty. One drawback of staff positions, even where they have been made full-time, is that individuals must break years of acculturation to a duty chart and assume nominal 9 A.M. to 5 P.M. weekday working hours.

Analysis need not be a nine to five job. Except for moderate overlap with other department and public officials working regular weekday schedules, there is no need for analytical unit members to disrupt their familiar life style and work only during the daylight, weekday hours. Computer time is often cheaper during the evening, field visits can be made during periods of peak acitivity, distractions may be less, and most of all, a particular problem may require a pattern of intense thought or calculation that does not conform to a regular schedule. Allowing department analysts to work flexible schedules compatible with their former life style and the needs of their analytical assignments is a simple incentive that may help overcome resistance to filling staff analytical positions. There are, of course, other incentives, such as increases in pay, time off, or other benefits that can be used to make staff positions more attractive.

One Responsible Individual. Although a committee or task-force approach may be useful in the early exploration of the applicability of analysis to the department, and the team approach is useful in accomplishing the analytic tasks, it will be necessary almost without exception to assign team leadership responsibility to one individual. Fragmentation and diffusion of effort occur too easily when it is not possible to identify one responsible individual.

4.2.3 Position of the Team in the Organization

Nearly all available evidence suggests that strong, visible support by top leadership is the most important factor in successful use of analytical techniques, or for that matter, in any innovative endeavor.[1] Since quantitative analysis is not commonly used in fire departments, it is reasonable that the fire service should view its use with caution. If analysis is to be successful, the overwhelming likelihood is that the chief must embrace and actively support the analytical endeavors. This support should be highly visible, not just quiet, behind-the-scenes aid.

But all is not lost in departments whose chiefs do not embrace analysis, or in jurisdictions whose elected officials prefer people to numbers. It is just a reminder of the case in most organizational decisionmaking: you have a better chance to succeed if your boss understands and supports what you are doing. An unsympathetic boss, however, is not necessarily an insurmountable barrier to determined subordinates. Careful use of analysis by informed, dedicated staff can overcome substantial leadership barriers. Also, the environment may be more neutral than fiercely hostile. In such an environment the analyst should feel encouraged to try to provide policies sufficiently clear and useful to gain the support of the pessimists.

One visible and often important sign of top management support is the position of the analytical team within the organization. Usually, operations research units start as a staff function, reporting directly to a chief executive and, if they survive, join another functional department or become a separate unit reporting up through the management structure (Radner and Neal, 1973). Initially, it is also likely to be best for a fire department analytical team to report directly to the chief, although alternative arrangements exist which are discussed below. As the team approaches the point at which its survival does not depend on direct access, it is probably best for it to establish its own formal identity, less attached to the chief.

Temporary teams should almost invariably start and stay with the

---

[1] See, for example, Zaltman, Duncan, and Holbek (1973), and Yin et al. (1976).

4.2 Establishing an Analytical Team

status and protection provided by the chief. One purpose of reporting directly to the chief is to balance the power between the new unit and the existing units in the departments. A new unit can be more easily nurtured if it is part of the chief's staff. However, the postition alone is not sufficient. It is important that access to the chief in fact occur and be used to acquire and maintain the confidence of the chief. The team must capitalize on that access in such a way that the chief depends on and uses the advice of his analyst.

There may be situations in which reporting directly to the chief is not possible, however. Sometimes it is possible to take advantage of existing departmental resources by combining analytical teams with existing organizational units. Most fire departments have people, and sometimes units, charged with what might be termed "management information" tasks: gathering data about fire operations, keeping employment records, handling the many administrative tasks necessary to operate any public service organization. Certain aspects of each of these tasks are important to the analyst, as they frequently involve the generation of primary source data needed for analysis. Thus, the analyst is attracted naturally to such parts of the fire service organization. Moreover, individuals with skills analogous and complementary to those of the analyst are more likely to be found in units performing these tasks. The "finance" section, the "planning" section, the "research" section, the "computer services" unit, the "management services" unit, the "communications" unit, and the "training" unit are all places in the fire department where data are likely to be handled regularly, and where the foundation for an analytical team may exist. Thus, the analytical team may be able to find a home where related skills, somewhat similar tasks, and respect for careful gathering and use of data already exist.

Whether to tie analysis to an already existing unit or establish a separate unit is a matter that must be solved individually for each department. We have already discussed issues related to chain-of-command and the survival of a fledgling team. In joining an existing unit there are still other dangers that are a part of any sharing. Differing objectives, competition for scarce resources, and different workstyles and pace are examples of incompatibilities that can arise. An especially important fact is that most analysis is, in comparison to other routine fire department tasks, relatively slow moving and generally "resource-taking" for long periods of initial development before there are visible returns.

This difference in pace provides a rationale for a separate unit, one not coupled to operating units that have day-to-day responsibilities. However, there is yet another consideration: a separate analytical unit is a much easier target for critics. If indeed considerable start-up and data-gathering efforts are required, the separate analytical unit may find itself on the defensive before it has really even done any analysis. It is likely to be visible during the data-gathering stage, and as soon as that is over, it is likely to feel the pressure for results. On the other hand, if analysis is only one of several tasks assigned to a unit, the normal delivery of the unit's other outputs may tend to reduce the pressure for quick analytical results.

Suppose, for example, that the planning bureau has been collecting and publishing monthly fire statistics for years. Suppose further that the analytical team is added to the bureau and the analysts wish certain data to be collected (for analytical purposes) quite differently. If the bureau can alter its data collection procedures, but still provide the expected fire statistics as routinely as ever, then whatever procedural changes are made may be seen simply as an alteration in routine operations. What the analysts are going to do with the data and how soon results will be published need not be at issue. Alternatively, if the analytical team has to go through some more "public" lobbying (i.e., discussions involving several department units) to "change the data collection system," the expectation of and pressure for results might begin almost immediately.

The example may seem oversimplified, but the underlying choice is relatively straightforward. Either an analysis team "joins" an existing unit or "stands alone." The basic advantage of joining is resource support and diffusion of visibility. It is more likely in such circumstances to get the lead time necessary for analysis and analysts to mature. The basic disadvantage is that analysts are going to have to participate in some everyday tasks that are part of the responsibility of the unit they join. Following the example above, if the data collection methods for fire statistics are to be changed to suit the analysts' needs, then the analysts are going to have to take part in the specification, development, and implementation of that process. That means commitment to routine tasks. Once the analyst is drawn into providing daily task support, the contemplative, longer range analyses will suffer. And that means that the big payoff of analysis will suffer.

Thus, in deciding where to introduce the analytical team into the department, there is a fundamental trade off between (1) accepting and balancing a mix of "everyday" and longer range analytical tasks and (2) creating a separate unit with no everyday responsibilities. There is no correct solution; but the decision should take the following questions into account:

1. Is the climate for accepting and using analysis sufficiently good for the team to exist as a separate unit?
2. Even if acceptance is uncertain, will direct reporting to the chief provide the shelter necessary for a fair trial period?
3. Can the data necessary for analysis be acquired easily and without a high price of negotiation if the team is separate? Or would they be

easier to acquire if the analysts were engaged in the task as part of their duties?
4. If the team is set up as a separate unit, will the analysts be sufficiently aware of the department's activities to be able to perform sound analysis? Or would they be better able to grasp the policy content of the department's problems if they faced some of those problems everyday?

4.2.4 Skill Mix for the Team

Team members will need to have a variety of skills. The steps of systems analysis outlined in Chapter 3 can be collapsed into three broad tasks: (1) problem identification and goal formulation; (2) technical analysis; and (3) implementation. Each of these tasks requires the use of different skills.

Identifying the problem and formulating goals should involve at least the chief, elected officials, other policy level officials, other fire department members, and in many cases local citizens. Translating objectives into analytically useful arguments must involve the analyst, but the early stages of goal formulation should involve individuals who are not analysts, and whose skill is their ability to translate the views of the community into problem statements and concrete objectives. Generally speaking, analysts are not best suited for assessing the tenor of the community, its needs, and its likely support of different goals.

The analyst, on the other hand, has the unique skills needed to analyze the problems and to scientifically evaluate the alternative approaches to achieving the desired goals. In addition, one of the hallmarks of systems analysis is that while trying to understand the problem in an organized, quantitative fashion, the analyst may well produce information that calls for the problem to be redefined and for the original goals to be reconsidered.

The skills needed to transform an analytical solution to a policy problem into a viable program for implementation are quite different from those of the analyst. The analyst does not always have the program development and project management skills necessary for successful implementation. Even when one individual does have these skills, it is difficult to switch roles constantly while working on one problem. Consequently, when we speak of an analytical team, we mean a group of persons that must possess a wide range of skills—not simply those of the technically competent analyst. And, of course, it is an oversimplification to lump all analysts together. Scientists, just as politicians and fire chiefs, come with varying skills and perspectives.

Another skill consideration is the absolute minimal type and level of skills necessary to sustain a viable team. Most of the models discussed in Chapters 6 to 13 should be applied by an analyst with intensive analytical training. In general, the models rely on use of the computer for convenient solution. Most of them require the ability to abstract essential insights about deployment planning from the real world of firefighting and apply them to situations that may not be covered in the illustrative examples. In addition, there are many political considerations that must be accounted for in the process of implementation. Therefore, more than just a lone analyst is needed. The team must have, or be able to draw upon, political leadership, analytic and computer science skills, program development, and project management skills. It is also important to distinguish here between general management science approaches and the specific use of analysis in deployment planning. Management science skills have a wide range of applicability in any fire service organization. For example, suppose that equipment replacement, inventory, and scheduling problems occur frequently in the fire department. In such a department, relatively rare deployment analyses may complement more frequent routine applications of management science techniques.

It is safe to say that one team leader (frequently, but not always an analyst with general skills), one person skilled in data collection and computer science, one analyst, and one person skilled in program development and implementation are the minimum required to sustain an analytical team. There can, of course, be an overlap of skills, and the absolute number of people may be less than four with an unusual combination of individual talents, but these skills must be available, and should be part of the analytical team itself. Notice that in the minimal unit the analyst is only one of several individuals. This is because identifying the right problems (political responsibility) and getting results translated into practice (project management and leadership responsibility) are necessary ingredients to the long-run success of an analytical unit. Analysis alone will not do the trick.

4.2.5 Use of Resources Outside the Team

There are a variety of groups with which it is useful for the analytical team to have relationships. These include other units in the department, the local government, the fire service in general, other analytical organizations, and the many consumers of analysis. Departments in large urban areas may be able to establish good working relationships with other departments using analytical talent. A department within a jurisdiction committed to the use of analysis may be able to draw upon other analytical talent in the jurisdiction. The existence of such talent nearby is useful both in supporting a decision to develop an in-house capability (because colleagues and empathy for the approach are readily available) and, conversely, in avoiding commitment to a permanent analytical unit, because available talent can be called on as the need arises. The lack of mutually supportive analytical talent in an area is a sign that a separate in-house capability will require a unique commitment and will be more difficult to sustain than otherwise. The minimal size of the team and time needed to establish a firm foothold in the organization increase.

Help in establishing and maintaining an analytical team should be sought. We have already noted the importance of top leadership in connection with this. Additional support may be sought from eventual beneficiaries of analysis: the mayor's office; fire department units with acknowledged problems; the city manager's office; the budget bureau. In addition, national associations, local universities, the unions, and local community groups may be supporters in some cases. Building and maintaining a viable analytical team requires pragmatic political insight as well as enthusiasm.

Friends of analysis should be identified, cultivated, and called upon for help. Local circumstances will influence how best to do this. Advisory committees may be established to provide policy guidance and check the feasibility of proposed solutions. Other local officials (for example, budget bureau staff) may be ex-officio members of the team. Or the team may be composed only of department members but may follow a conscious strategy of seeking help from and informing outsiders at particular stages of analysis. The ultimate goal of analysis is to change policy. The more those who change policy and those who are most affected by changes in policy are consumers and supporters of analysis, the more likely it is that analysis will affect policy.

4.2.6 Introducing Analysis: One Example

One example of how analysis can be introduced into a fire department is the case of the New York City Fire Department during the administration of Mayor John V. Lindsay. The impetuses for analysis in this case were the Chief of Department, the Office of the Mayor, and the Bureau of the Budget. Importantly, the Fire Department had a willing, informed client in the Chief of Department.

The strategy for introducing analysis was three-fold. First, a special unit was created within the Bureau of the Budget and given responsibility for program analysis (a quasi-analytical look at the problems faced by the city agencies and the potential improvements that could be fostered through the budgeting process). This unit was staffed by young college graduates with some analytical training but little experience. They were assigned to work closely with traditional budget examiners and the individual agencies, outlining issues and helping to formulate programs based on analysis to attack these issues. Their influence derived from the well-publicized reform attitude of the Lindsay administration and the political power of the budgetary process.

Second, a new, fifth-ranking position (Assistant Commissioner) was created in the fire department itself and filled by a qualified civilian analyst who had staff experience in a large federal bureaucracy. Third, outside technical support was obtained by establishing a consulting relationship with the Rand Corporation, a California-based "think-tank."

Thus, the Mayor created three new sources of intelligence: better knowledge of issues through the budget staff, an analyst's view from the agency, and an analyst's view from the outside. This required three new resources: the program planners, the Assistant Commissioner, and Rand. These efforts, which began in 1968, have been continued in the fire department. The department maintains units devoted to analysis, with a mix of civilian and uniformed personnel involved.

Although the case of New York is admittedly unique, the principle is not. Analysis was not started by the simple introduction of an analyst to the department. A much broader approach was taken, recognizing that solutions to pressing issues included committed department personnel (the Assistant Commissioner and the Chief of Department), and that technical support had to be readily available (the budget bureau staff and Rand). This concept is applicable to much smaller fire departments than that of New York City, and variations on the theme are readily apparent. Although not stressed in the example above, it is especially important to establish early ties with other city officials, community leaders, and union officials. Depending on the locale, this can be a crucial part of the support needed to get an analysis unit underway.

4.3 PROBLEM ASSESSMENT

4.3.1 The Fire Department's View

It is important to assess problems in terms of the resources needed to solve them. Several distinctions can be made to help determine the tasks to be faced by an analytical team.

Is the Problem Labor or Capital Intensive? Problems that require manpower for their solution are quite different from those requiring substantial equipment, and sometimes the distinction is not clear. For example, fire apparatus is generally quite expensive, and the high cost of a ladder or engine is frequently a cause of concern. In some departments, engines have been replaced by personnel carriers in an effort to reduce the cost of equipment. However, it is necessary to take more into account than just the cost of the apparatus. The cost of the manpower in paid departments is so great that the relative cost of the apparatus is usually too small to forego the advantage of having the engine at the scene, even if it frequently does no more than carry personnel.[2] Despite the popular image of fancy equipment, fire service delivery is extremely labor intensive. This means that most of the problems that analysts face involve personnel as a scarce resource, but it also means that searching for solutions where capital might substitute for labor is a large part of the analytical task. Automated pumpers and "rapid water" are two examples of attempts to substitute capital for labor in the fire service. Almost all the techniques discussed in later chapters recognize the labor intensive nature of the paid fire service; their thrust is toward improved efficiency through improved use of manpower.

Is the Problem One-time or Recurring? Setting up a substantial analytical unit may not be worth the effort if the problems that have been identified are susceptible to solutions that should last for a long time. Several cities, including Wilmington, Delaware and Yonkers, New York, have used analytical teams to help determine firehouse locations without creating continuing analytical units. If the environment is changing rapidly, and certain problems such as the need to adjust response boundaries and policies can be expected to recur, the chances are greater for establishing a permanent unit. However, if the major problems do not appear to be recurring ones, then there must be large number of them to warrant the effort required to establish a permanent unit.

Are the Potential Solutions to Problems Reversible? Building a firehouse in the wrong location is pretty much irreversible—once the station is in place, it cannot easily be moved. A change in response patterns to alarms, however, can be reversed—a change from one policy to another generally does not foreclose the opportunity to return to the original policy if so desired. Purchase of equipment is somewhere in between. Changing from tractor-trailer (tiller) aerial ladders to rearmount aerials is not easily reversed, but the apparatus could be sold and other apparatus purchased, albeit at some increase in cost.

The reversibility of solutions to problems affects the importance of the problem and the stakes involved using analysis. The less reversible the potential solutions, the greater the risk. An analyst must expect to make some mistakes. Therefore, it is prudent to undertake a mix of problems so that one error does not foreclose continuing use of analysis. On the other hand, analysis may have the greatest chance for acceptance when the costs of error are high and the consequent value of analysis in contributing to solutions is clear.

---

[2] See the discussion of fire company costs in Chapter 1.

What Kind of Technology is Needed to Solve the Problem? Fire departments have always been fascinated with and plagued by technological problems. For years, many departments built or adapted their own apparatus because of needs believed to be unique. Everyone in the fire service has struggled with heavy, cumbersome, short-lived breathing apparatus. And perhaps as much has been written on standardizing hose coupling sizes for mutual aid, as on any other minor problem faced by the fire service. Foam fire suppressants, smoke and heat detectors, power saws, forcible entry equipment, and scores of small tools have been fashioned by and for the fire service. Yet when all is said and done, most experts agree that the technology of putting out fires has advanced very little in this century. Men with hoses full of water put out fires now as they did 100 years ago. Nevertheless, new technology remains an attractive possibility for the solution of many department problems. Whether any one department can or ought to take on most technological problems is unclear. Most of the capital for development of new technology will probably have to come from the federal government, or from private enterprise when it judges that there will be sufficient return to warrant the investment. Technological development spread across the fire service, with each locale devoting a small amount of resources to some particular item or part of an item, is probably not the best strategy. Yet, the new analytical team is likely to find technological improvement a major client interest. This may be of use in designing the team's work program.

What Involvement is Required of Other Organizational Units, Both Within and Outside the Fire Department? The more people involved in a decision, the more difficult it is to reach one. Similarly, the greater the number of participants, the more difficult it will be to steer analytical solutions through implementation without substantial alteration. Therefore, in planning an analytical agenda, it is important to think about how many problems have potential solutions that will affect (chiefly) only one part of the system, and how many will have a more extensive impact. The greater the impact, the higher the value of useful analysis. But to the extent that the results of the analysis frequently disrupt the system, the chances of sustaining the analytical team are lowered.

What are the Political and Legal Impacts of Solutions? Policy changes resulting from analytical solutions are likely to have political and legal consequences. It is important to understand this and plan for it. Ideally, the analytical team should seek a mix of problems—some that can be easily solved with the results unambiguously communicated to policymakers, others that require more extensive implementation and deeper understanding and support of the policymakers. If a problem has high

4.3 Problem Assessment

political visibility or significant legal constraints, steps must be taken to protect the team from easy attack. For example, mistakes in terminology or minor detail can be exploited by opponents. Some of the inevitable mistakes are not serious, and the analytical team must be prepared to overcome such obstacles.

However, to the extent that implementation of a policy change is more rather than less political, the analytical team must carry its own political weight. This can be achieved in different ways; for example, by forging a relationship with the budget bureau, by appointing a politically able individual as leader of the team, or by convincing politically powerful clients that a solution is worth their support and advocacy. In many cases it is also necessary to do considerable legal homework. Unabashed recognition of political power and salesmanship is necessary for the successful analytical team. Analysis that is to be effective in changing operating practices must be able to withstand the process by which changes are made. That process is necessarily and properly political.

The political views and personal biases of members of the team should not be overlooked. Management scientists have opinions like everyone else, and they cannot do analysis entirely free of those opinions. Although they can and ought to be scientific by explicitly stating their assumptions and by documenting the analysis so that it is replicable by other scientists, the very nature of the work implies that something individual, something creative is brought to the problem. An abstraction will invariably and inescapably bear the personal values and perspective of the individual doing the work. Understanding and facing the political involvement required for successful functioning of an analytical team is a necessary task in the initial stages of its development.

What Variation is There in Potential Solutions? No one likes to do a study if the result is a foregone conclusion. The analyst likes to think that the solution will reflect whatever the analysis suggests. However, many classes of problems are presented in terms of solutions: where to move this firehouse, when to replace this vehicle, whether to buy these voice alarm boxes. As we have seen, however, the question asked initially may not be the appropriate question. Better ones might be: (1) How many firehouses are needed and where should they be located for the next several years? (2) Under what general policy should all vehicles be replaced, and should they be rotated from busier to slower units during their useful lives? (3) What ways of reporting alarms to the fire department should be available in the first place? The more flexibility given the analyst to formulate the problem in a broad context, the higher the likelihood that analysis can have a significant impact on policy.

How Much is a Solution Likely to Cost? It is fruitless to pursue extended analyses when the resulting solutions are likely to cost more than the department or the local government can afford. It is not advisable to undertake analysis without a fair sense of the resources required for a range of likely solutions. The analytical team must be responsive to the budgetary facts of life and must try to select its work program so that analysis is not concentrated on a problem or two in which the potential solutions are likely to break the municipal bank. Thus, devoting considerable analytical resources to developing an improved breathing apparatus, for example, is inadvisable. The physical development and testing costs are enormous—unlikely to be recoverable by a local government—and the proposed changes are likely to prove costly.

It is equally fruitless to pursue a study if the cost of the analysis itself is likely to exceed the benefits of potential solutions. Some estimates of costs and benefits should, therefore, be made before making a commitment to carry out a study.

The costs of doing the analysis *per se* and costs of the solution are relatively easy to understand. There are also, however, opportunity costs and political costs associated with the choice of an analysis agenda. Opportunity costs are the costs of opportunities foregone by the choice of one problem rather than another. Especially outside the marketplace these costs are hard to measure. But they are quite significant. Solving the problem of where to locate firehouses may mean that response policies cannot be assessed fully at the same time. The analyst has made an obvious tradeoff of one problem (client) versus another. It is useful to try to assess the damage, if any, that such choices make on the chances for successful solution of the problem chosen (there could be significant interaction effects) and on the durability of the analytical team.

Opportunity costs in this sense are almost always measured in political terms. How is support from Client A affected by choosing to work on Client B's problem? What is the likely political impact of addressing one policy rather than another? What the analytical unit does not do may count as much as what it does do.

4.3.2 The View from Outside the Department

Perhaps one of the most difficult tasks facing the analyst trying to form an analytical team is understanding other people's perspectives. To an analyst in the budget bureau, delivering service at lower unit costs may be the critical (current) objective. However, the same service delivery problem may be viewed in the fire department as one of changing response policy without lowering morale. At the same time it may be seen by the mayor as a question of maintaining labor peace, and by the local Chamber of Commerce as a matter of increasing the number of fire companies available to serve industry growth. The analyst must try to predict where analysis can aid in mutually satisfactory solutions to problems, and where analysis may unavoidably become the evidence for one side or another in a political dispute.

We believe the deployment planning methodology described in this book represents sound approaches to developing fire department policy—the best approaches available. However, this view is not unanimous. Many of the abstractions required to make the models easy to use and insightful are not easily accepted by fire officials and other consumers. Also, the models provide different results depending on the data provided as input to the model and often depending on how certain key parameters are set (such as travel time, or the distribution of work at different classes of alarms). Model designers can incorporate certain judgments and mask them from view (for example, the method used to calculate distance or travel time), or they can make the model so flexible that a wide range of judgments can be made by the user (for example, the worktime allowed at simulated incidents for different classes of equipment).

Participatory modeling, in which each interested party can input data and view the results, is a relatively new approach and not widely used. However, New York City came close to it in 1969 when it negotiated a change in response policy based on the results of analysis, and used output from the modeling to define the scope of the agreement. In effect, the unions asked the city to guarantee that the analysis had been structured to account for certain rare events of concern, and that the analysis indicated the rare events would occur with a stated (low) probability. The city did so. The circumstances were much more complex than portrayed here, but the example is intended to demonstrate that implementation will take the analyst far from the mathematical model. People make and change policy, and people use and evaluate models. Sooner or later the analyst must deal with these people, not just the models. The sooner the analyst learns the objectives, motivations, backgrounds, and perspectives of those who influence fire service delivery in the community, the sooner analysis will become relevant.

Thus, setting the agenda for an analytical team is not just a problem-cataloging exercise. It demands a more complex and subtle assessment of the community into which analysis is to be introduced. Knowing whether to go it alone, to call in outside help, to use a one-shot approach, or to create a permanent unit depends not only on the problems themselves, but on the environment in which they are to be faced.

4.4 TAKING STOCK OF THE DEPARTMENT

In this section we look at the fire department as an organization, with many of the typical characteristics of organizations, and consider both the internal and community resources it can draw on. Examining these resources amounts to taking an organizational inventory.

A crucial part of this stock-taking is to estimate how well the department will respond to the demands and assumptions of analysis. The use of analysis pretty much *demands* that an organization have the necessary skills to mature and grow in the face of the disruption. Most organizations do not find it easy. Among the demands analysis places on an organization are:

Making open, explicit statements of organizational goals.

Evaluating critically the performance of tasks under analysis.

Devising (or at least reevaluating) measures of effectiveness for activities that have been performed, in many cases perhaps by rote, for many years.

Committing organizational resources to thinking introspectively.

In essence, the analyst begins by asking two philosophical questions: (1) "Why does this activity exist?"; (2) "How do I know whether or not it's being done well?"

Perhaps more importantly, strong presumptions about an organization's capacity to plan and manage its activities must be valid for the use of analysis. These include:

Top policymakers embrace the concept of decisionmaking based on quantitative assessment of problems and want to improve their ability to make rational decisions.

An internal analytical capability sufficient to deal with a wide range of economic and mathematical concepts exists.

A data collection system suitable to support analysis exists.

For most of its activities, the organization has a fair sense of the relationship between the resources used in an activity and the result of that activity.

In the fire service, there are few departments that meet these assumptions, especially the last one. In order to perform effective analysis, it would be useful, for example, to know what difference four rather than five firefighters on the back step would make in any one of several measures of department performance: loss of life, extent of property damage, proportion of fires extending beyond the original structure on fire, etc. However, as we have already seen, little research has been done on such topics.

Most of our knowledge has resulted from the trial and error decisionmaking that comes from the need to run departments whether or not research is around to support decisions. There has been little modeling of the fire response process that provides insight into the consequences of changing response policy from two engines and one ladder to one engine and one ladder, or to two engines and two ladders. Attempts to measure the consequences of such changes have only recently been made for a handful of situations. If a local official were suddenly to impose upon a department an intensified prevention inspection program and an initial response policy of one engine and one ladder, it is unlikely that any fire department would be able to provide a quantitative assessment of the resulting change in fire protection. The research has not been done.

There are, of course, many positive resources in the fire service. The basic ones, high-quality human resources, are available in all departments across the county. The average work week for firefighters in 1978 was 53 hours (Pigeon, 1979). Much of that time is devoted to work duty, but a significant portion is devoted to peripheral activities that contribute to making a better firefighter (study for promotional examinations, physical exercise, etc.), but are not required work. During this time, many firefighters also develop and pursue skills in addition to those of firefighters. Analytical capability is one such skill that could be encouraged.

Also, because of the special characteristics of the fire service, individuals originally trained as firefighters often find their way into supporting roles (computer programming, payroll supervision, dispatching). They sometimes receive only on-the-job training for their tasks, although many attend classes on their own initiative. These individuals are a valuable resource, and often are capable of absorbing training to become a part of an analytical team. Their dedication to the fire service and their experience can be valuable assets to the analytical team.

Some departments, especially those in which costs have risen faster for uniformed personnel than nonuniformed personnel, have civilian staffs assigned in nonfirefighting roles. These nonuniformed personnel represent a significant resource. They are likely to have had formal training outside the department, and to be performing tasks related to their training. The budget officer, for example, may have an accounting or business administration degree; a communications engineer may have a degree in electrical engineering. Exposure to a discipline and the need to absorb a body of knowledge in a systematic fashion constitute a useful background for any member of an analytical team.

Thus, in assessing what resources are available, the analytical team manager must look not only to the one operations research scientist (who may in any case be available only in larger cities), but to the resources at hand. Professional, highly skilled help is necessary; but most departments will not be able to and will not necessarily want to attract that on a long-term basis. Firefighters and fire officers must increasingly accept the need to analyze and solve complex deployment problems simply as another part of the fire service's tasks. This should be accepted in the same spirit as other technical tasks: the need to become technically proficient in evaluating smoke detection devices, for example, or to design safety regulations for high-rise buildings.

We have looked at some of the demands that analysis makes on an organization, and we have talked about the human resources available in departments across the county. Finding ways to use this talent, and to provide incentives for both uniformed and nonuniformed personnel to serve the fire service in analytical capacities, can encourage and support the use of analysis in fire departments.

For many years, certain kinds of institutions have recognized the importance of providing new training, retraining, or just time away to encounter new experiences (e.g., the familiar sabbatical for professors). But many corporations also send their executives to a wide variety of seminars, training courses, public service leaves of absence, and other learning situations. Police departments have long sent their outstanding officers to study at the FBI Academy. Unfortunately, there has been relatively little of such activity in the fire service, although recent establishment of the National Fire Academy should change this. Fire departments that routinely send personnel to the pumper manufacturer to learn how to operate a new pumper, do not send training personnel to seminars to learn how to teach. There are many reasons for this, money being the most prominent. But if fire departments are to absorb analysis successfully, and if they expect to use available talent and not always be dependent on consultants and other outsiders, they must accept such approaches and their costs.

So the department's ability to absorb analysis depends in an important way on the likelihood that methods can be found to create and nurture a pool of analytical talent. This means development of training or retraining opportunities, monetary or work schedule incentives, and means for personal recognition that, while they may not necessarily rival those of firefighting, are sufficiently valuable in their own right. It is relatively easy to get a few people detailed to begin an analytical unit, to establish an advisory board to discuss and evaluate the analysis agenda, and to acquire some outside expertise. But what happens after that? Incentives and support over the longer term must be provided. The long-run issues of personnel acquisition, growth, and development should be addressed early.

Up to this point we have been concentrating on departments with sufficient resources to create an internal analytical unit, and with problems susceptible to the analytical techniques described in later chapters. Less than 20 percent of the 2300 cities in the country with a population of at least 10,000 have populations greater than 50,000. Because hazard and geography are such key ingredients to any assessment of deployment of firefighting resources, there are undoubtedly locales with less than 50,000 population where full-time analytical staffs are warranted. But it is unlikely that very many cities with 50,000 or fewer people have the fire problems or the resources to sustain analytical units.

In many of these cases, and certainly in metropolitan areas where several cities face similar circumstances, the best strategy may be to join with other departments, or with local agencies such as areawide planning and development commissions, to create a common pool of analytical talent that each organization can draw upon periodically without having to absorb the costs of a full-time operation. Seeking the participation of other city governments, county governments, or the state may be the method by which smaller communities can take advantage of analysis when needed.

Alternatively, some analysts are trained more as generalists than specialists. Seeking out an individual who can perform a wide range of management science tasks, but who may not be as skilled in the more complex analytical tasks, may be the best approach for smaller departments. This individual can serve the department not only by performing some analytical tasks but also by being the broker, bringing analytical talent to the department as needed. Obviously, a combination of strategies is also possible.

The dangers of hit-and-run analysis are probably greater in small departments than in large ones. The small department, tempted to use analysis briefly and then cast it aside, should be wary of the difficulties of implementing analytical solutions when the analysts have long gone. Again we reiterate that good analysis involves the implementation of the results and incorporation of the feedback that may develop from that implementation. Attempting to reinterpret another analyst's results in the light of new information is tricky at best, even when analytical efforts are well documented. Thus, especially in the smaller cities, the user of analysis should be sensitive to the dangers of short-term, ad hoc relationships with analysts. Explore the other alternatives, including commitment of the analyst through implementation, before accepting the ad hoc approach.

4.5 SUMMARY

Deciding exactly how to approach the development of an analytical capability for deployment planning involves matching problems and circumstances to the capabilities available to solve the problems.

First, is there dissatisfaction with the status quo? Is there an active effort to identify the problems and search for solutions? The greater the dissatisfaction, the easier it is likely to be for analysis to be considered a viable tool leading to change. Second, is there a client? Will top leadership support the analytical effort? Does the mayor reward budget and program development based on analysis? There should be an identifiable client, one (or more) who will be around to use and participate in the implementation of the analysis. Third, what is to be the relationship between the analyst and the client? Is the analyst to be part of the department? To work out of the mayor's office? To be a consultant? Whatever the location of the analyst, a solid and lasting bridge to the client must be built.

Fourth, have the necessary skills been identified? Are they available in the department, or can they be developed there? Is there a plan for using the available skills, especially over the longer term? If the skills must come from outside the department or the local jurisdiction, what are the alternatives? If a relationship with a university, a management consulting firm or research firm will be needed, a substantial investigation must be made of their ability to see the work through from analysis to implementation. Before proposing the development of any analytical team, whether composed of insiders, outsiders, or both, it is imperative to identify the skills that are needed, and to develop a plan to use them. Fifth, what are the likely outcomes of the analytical effort? Is the extent of implementation tasks that are likely to be generated by the analysis understood? Has the political environment in which the analysis must be implemented been carefully considered?

Chapter 5
Managing Change In The Fire Department

Synopsis

The process of converting the results of deployment analysis into changes in fire department operations is at least as important as the process of performing the analysis. The skills required to manage change are different from analytical skills, and the change agent's task is often difficult and lengthy.

Fire service organizations pose special problems and opportunities for the manager of change. For example, the quasimilitary bureaucratic organization of fire departments is a source of resistance to changes in authority structures, tasks, and procedures; but this same organizational form can help expedite compliance with changes that have been ordered by the chief executive. The traditional single entry level into the organization is often a source of resistance to recommendations of people who have not personally experienced firefighting. Knowledge derived from unfamiliar disciplines or distant cities is not readily accepted by fire service personnel.

The change agent must also learn to deal with the crisis orientation of fire departments, which focuses rewards on action rather than on contemplation. The lengthy, sequential decisionmaking process of systems analysis contrasts sharply with the drama of decisionmaking by commanding officers at the scene of a fire. Moreover, because most fire departments have not experienced financial pressures until recent years, fire service personnel with budgeting and planning skills are few in number.

The manager of change must understand how organizations operate, and be able to view the fire department as a collection of organizations interacting with other organizations. New policies that arise from deployment analysis are likely to have impacts on other organizations— such as labor unions and community groups—whose interests must be considered.

Several strategies for change should be familiar to anyone attempting to implement the results of deployment analysis. These include reorganization, altering communications patterns, changing managerial style and methods of work performance, rearranging the relationships between the organization and its environment, altering employee incentives, and changing individual attitudes and behavior. The chances of success are enhanced by searching for and exploiting natural points of entry for change. These are routine, recurring procedures normally associated with some kind of change. Examples include collective bargaining, purchase of new equipment, and education, training, and certification programs.

Several characteristics of the proposed innovation can be assessed to predict its chance of adoption. While there are no universal rules, these are usually important factors:

Cost, complexity, and divisibility. *An expensive or complex innovation is less likely to succeed than a simple one. If it can be broken into smaller stages, its prospects for adoption are improved.*

Risk. *Risky ventures rarely return high benefits to fire departments and are difficult to implement.*

Merit. *Analytical findings can help in developing a consensus that a proposed innovation has intrinsic value.*

Communicability. *Recommendations must be readily understandable and should be easy to communicate to others.*

Visibility. *This factor has mixed implications. An open, visible decision generally has better chances of succeeding, but sometimes changes are accepted because it is difficult to notice that they have occurred.*

Compatibility. *The change should be designed to cause as little disruption as possible.*

Origin and scientific status.

In addition to characteristics of the innovation itself, organizational factors can influence implementation. Generally, change is more difficult in organizations that are low in complexity, high in centralization, and high in formalization. Fire departments conform to this description and therefore represent a special challenge to the change agent.

5.1 INTRODUCTION

In Chapter 4, we examined some of the things that should be considered when establishing an analytical team. In this chapter, we assume that a decision has been made to use analysis and that an analytical team, either permanent or temporary, has been created. We now turn to the broader process of seeing the analysis through implementation, with the emphasis on general strategies for introducing innovative ideas and practices.

The perspective taken is that of a "change agent" (i.e., a manager of change). The introduction of analysis is expected to change the end product or service delivered by the fire department. Most likely this will also mean changes in structure (the organizational system) and in process (the various methods and procedures employed to deliver the services). In turn, these changes will require members within, and perhaps outside, the organization to change their behavior. The analyst must see the issue not only in terms of solving a particular technical problem, but more importantly as the creation of circumstances that will encourage people to change their behavior. In performing this task, the analyst becomes the change agent.

Taking this view, we first review some of the aspects of fire service organizations that have important implications for the management of change. We then discuss the concepts of organization and organizational environment that may be helpful to the analyst when considering how to bring about change. Following that is a discussion of some general strategies for introducing change. We conclude the chapter with a review of some attributes of specific innovations and organizational behavior that are likely to be successful in managing change.

The material presented here stresses the importance of thinking about groups of people, their common motivations, their organizational positions, and their values as they influence decisionmaking. As the analyst moves from the model of the problem to the development of programs to achieve desired results, the importance of who makes the decisions and who influences the decisionmaking process cannot be overstated.

Sound analytical results should be able to stand alone but they do not. People who make decisions frequently find themselves in situations in which the analysis alone is not sufficient to guide decisionmaking. A broad political rationality is likely to guide an individual's decisions more often than a narrower technical rationality. If political and managerial views are to be meshed with the specific problem-solving perspective of the analyst, the analyst needs to have anticipated, understood and tried to accommodate the values and perspectives of decisionmakers and the pressures they face. It is often too late to account for these factors (solely) during implementation.

5.2 THE CHALLENGE OF CHANGE IN THE FIRE DEPARTMENT

There are several aspects of fire service organizations that pose special problems for the manager of change. We begin with a recital of some of the difficulties before turning to ways of dealing with them.

Fire departments are quasimilitary bureaucracies, with well-defined tasks, highly structured authority relationships, and formal rules and procedures. Almost any innovation will involve changes in tasks, rules, and procedures. It is also likely to alter authority relationships. One consequence of the bureaucratic nature of the fire department is that the formal reward structure is imbalanced. Failure to meet prescribed performance norms carries a penalty; performance above the prescribed norms does not carry a commensurate reward. Since any program requiring change has certain risks, and since even an excellent analytic team will experience some failures, a disincentive to change is built into most fire departments.

Most fire departments have only a single entry level into the organization. All uniformed members start as firefighters and generally must pass civil service examinations for promotion. Uniformed managers "come up through the ranks." There is no differentiation at entrance, so no one is earmarked for officer training, and no one enters the department directly as an officer. Although there usually are civilian positions in support areas, there are no parallel promotion paths. The firefighting organization is a closed, uniformed system with no lateral entry and no provision for entry, exit, and reentry at different levels.

This arrangement has its merits, but it also has its drawbacks. Among the drawbacks are the similarity of individual values that develop over time and the emphasis on the organization that is created. Members of the fire department go through a long acculturation process during which aberrant values are spotted early and discouraged. Without new perspectives on issues and procedures, and with too few mechanisms for meaningful sharing of common experiences across departments, individual department norms are developed and passed on through the generations. Most departments feel that local circumstances are truly unique, requiring in-house training and expertise best acquired only in that locality. Knowledge about firefighting performance is accepted as residing with those firefighters having many years of experience. This means that much firefighting knowledge is folklore, handed down from generation to generation by word of mouth, orders of the day, and training manuals.

Fire departments have a crisis orientation, with attention focused on fire suppression. The drama of fire itself and the firefighter's role in saving lives and extinguishing the fire dominate both firefighters' and society's images of their role. There is no question but that the drama is real. An unfortunate drawback of the crisis orientation, however, is that many other important tasks of the fire service are neglected. The nonmonetary rewards for being a firefighter are focused so keenly on firefighting that other tasks are seen at best as necessary evils, at worst as trivia to be resisted. This orientation works against a broader view of the firefighter as a public agent who is expected to provide a wide variety of

5.2 The Challenge of Change in the Fire Department

inspection, prevention, community relations, planning, training, alarm communications, and other fire protection services.

Crisis orientation also encourages the idea that staff positions in which firefighting itself is not part of the job assignment are not as valuable as those in which firefighting is clearly the primary job assignment. Partially because of this, many departments have been slow to develop the wide range of planning and support functions appropriate to their size. Perhaps more importantly, the skills required to provide these functions have, by and large, not been seen by the fire service as a legitimate part of the qualifications of a fire officer.[1] One premise of this book is that an understanding of the concepts and possibilities of deployment analysis ought to be a requirement for all executives managing fire departments.

Also troublesome for the manager of change is the lack of planning and budgeting skills in many fire departments. The drudgery of the budgetary process contrasts sharply with the drama of firefighting; but the importance of budgeting skills to fire departments should not be underestimated. For years, fire departments have commanded a relatively small portion of the municipal budget, firefighters have worked many hours per week, and fire protection capability has been designed around rare conflagration possibilities. The practical result of this arrangement has been an oversupply of firefighting service *per se*. The majority of the fire companies in this country spend substantially more time preparing for and waiting to fight fires than fighting them. Consequently, in many localities it has been possible to absorb large increases in demand without a commensurate increase in firefighting resources. Because of good public acceptance of expenditures for firefighting and a general oversupply of resources, fire departments have appeared to fare reasonably well.

However, time is catching up with the fire service. Needs for capital improvements have been neglected. Fire personnel have increased the pressure for a shorter work week and more narrowly defined firefighting roles. There have been increased demands for fire protection, caused by urban expansion in some areas and urban decay in others. All of this, combined with increasing pressures to hold down municipal budgets, has put most departments in the position of demanding more when there is less to get. As the competition for funds intensifies, planning and budgeting skills become especially important. Well thought out programs with analytical back-up and well-developed work plans become more attractive to decisionmakers who find themselves unable to satisfy all the demands for municipal service. Moreover, when departments are told

---

[1] It is important to note, however, that firefighters and officers frequently acquire such skills on their own time because they are self-motivated and because their jobs often can be performed better if they have such skills.

they must make do with what they have, deployment analysis is a valuable tool for helping to achieve a more efficient operation without having to make reductions in service.

The fire service has one of the widest ranges of employee/employer relationships in the public sector. A substantial portion of the nation's firefighters are serving in volunteer fire companies. At the other extreme, *over 90 percent of the nation's paid firefighters are represented by labor organizations,* principally the International Association of Fire Fighters (Spero and Capozzola, 1973). Firefighters are perhaps the most highly unionized labor force in the public service. Given this spectrum of relationships, the change agent must be especially sensitive to local organizational arrangements, and to the impact that any attempt to change the pattern of service delivery may have on those arrangements.

The change agent will inevitably face the challenge of how to integrate union leadership into the analysis and program design aspects of deployment planning. Participation at some point in the process is essential; on the other hand, the analyst must be sensitive not only to employee perspectives, but also to management perspectives. Management prerogatives for public sector organizations are not as well-defined as for private sector organizations, nor are rules of bargaining over managerial issues such as fire department response policy and manning practices settled. However, the resolution of almost all deployment planning issues will require the participation of union leadership.

5.3 ORGANIZATIONS

An analyst must understand organizations and how they operate. We all have an idea of what an "organization" is. Most of us work for organizations, many of us belong to professional, fraternal, or charitable groups that we regard as organizations, and all of us interact at least once a year with that pervasive organization, the federal government. In general, theorists consider an organization to be a group of individuals joined together to carry out coordinated activities to achieve some goal (Barnard, 1949; March and Simon, 1958). We consider the fire department to be such an organization.

5.3.1 Formal Organizations

One special type of organization is a bureaucracy. Most fire departments are bureaucracies. A bureaucracy is characterized by a hierarchy of authority, a division of labor, the existence of formal rules and procedures, the performance of tasks without regard to specific personal characteristics or attitudes, and the selection and promotion of organization members according to technical ability in completing an assigned task (Perrow, 1972). However, there are characteristics of organizations other than their bureaucratic ones that are important. First, since organizations consist of human beings, many theorists view organizations from the point of the individual personality, considering what effect the health of that personality might have on the organization's chance to achieve its goals, and vice versa (Perrow, 1972). Second, theorists have emphasized that just as no individual operates in a vacuum, unaffected by the behavior of friends, neighbors, and the surrounding society, no organization functions without regard to the environment in which it exists. These theorists stress that the organization operates in an "open system," that is, its actions affect (and it is itself affected by) individuals and organizations outside its direct control (Churchman, 1973).

The systems approach to understanding organizations is taken here. Each group of individuals assigned as a unit to perform a task can be seen as one element in a set of such groups. Each set can be seen as one of several combined to achieve a common goal (or alternatively, combined to advance competing goals). Whenever one looks at an organization, one must look not only at the groups that taken together are what we commonly know as the organization, but also at the many groups (organizations) that operate in the larger setting in which the organization attempts to achieve its goals.

This concept is especially important when assessing strategies and tactics for implementing change. During some phases of the process it is important to be concerned mostly with individual personalities and the relationships among them. During others, the units within an organization are the principal objects of interest. And at still others, relationships among the units and how each influences achievement of the organization's goals require the most attention. Lastly, the place of the organization in its environment, its relationships with other organizations, must be a focus of attention. A view of individuals and groups of individuals as members of a system called an organization, and a view of organizational units and organizations as elements of a larger societal system, help in thinking about change within the organizational unit, the organization, and the society.

Thus, when we think about change in the fire department, we will think sometimes about individual firefighters, other times about fire companies or the personnel bureau, other times about the "department" itself, and often, about the budget bureau, the mayor's office, the citizens of the community, and the firefighters union. In each circumstance, the description of the issue and the prescription of a tactic or strategy may be understood differently, according to the position of the eventual doer in the larger system of actors. It is vital to understand this point. Position (in the unit, organization, community) is an important determinant of perspective and action; translations must be made, from action prescriptions for one actor into prescriptions for other actors in other places or times. When we speak of the need to have top leadership support in order to achieve a certain goal, we may mean the captain if the issue is confined to the fire company, the chief if the issue is relevant to the department, the mayor if the issue affects the community, and perhaps the governor or state fire marshal if the issue is statewide.

These concepts may be illustrated with a few simple examples. Hypothetical collections of organizational units that are helpful in visualizing the fire department and its environment are shown in Figure 5.1. The smallest organizational element is the individual. Figure 5.1 (a) depicts one of the many small groups that exists in a fire department: the fire company. It is shown here as composed of four firefighters and one officer. This represents the size of the group on duty together in some fire companies. Alternatively, the company could be portrayed as many members and several officers, the total of the men required to operate the unit identified as the fire company around the clock, seven days a week.

Figure 5.1(b) depicts a portion of the total fire department organization, including fire companies, a personnel bureau, a training bureau, an arson squad, and a fire prevention bureau. Of course, several other functional units would have to be added for a more complete picture of a fire department.

Figure 5.1(c) portrays part of a local government. The fire department is seen as one of several organizations that constitute the set of units within the local government (again, many other units would have to be added to complete this picture). Finally, Figure 5.1(d) portrays one of many possible conceptions of the organizational structure of a community.

5.3.2 Interest Groups as Organizations

Figure 5.2 is another view of the fire department. Instead of seeing the department as a set of formal organizational units, one can see it as a set of different interest groups whose members have joined together to attain one or more goals. The diagram includes as examples the union leadership, an apparatus safety committee, a medical disability board, and so on. One could add to this list other groups with less formal stature; for example, a study group formed during preparation for promotional examinations, a group of "old timers" who meet infrequently to talk about and perhaps try to influence department policy, or a group of younger officers joined together to determine how to make department policy more receptive to their attitudes and desires. In the larger departments there are also many special interest groups based on religion, ethnic background, fire folklore, specific aid missions, or other common traits.

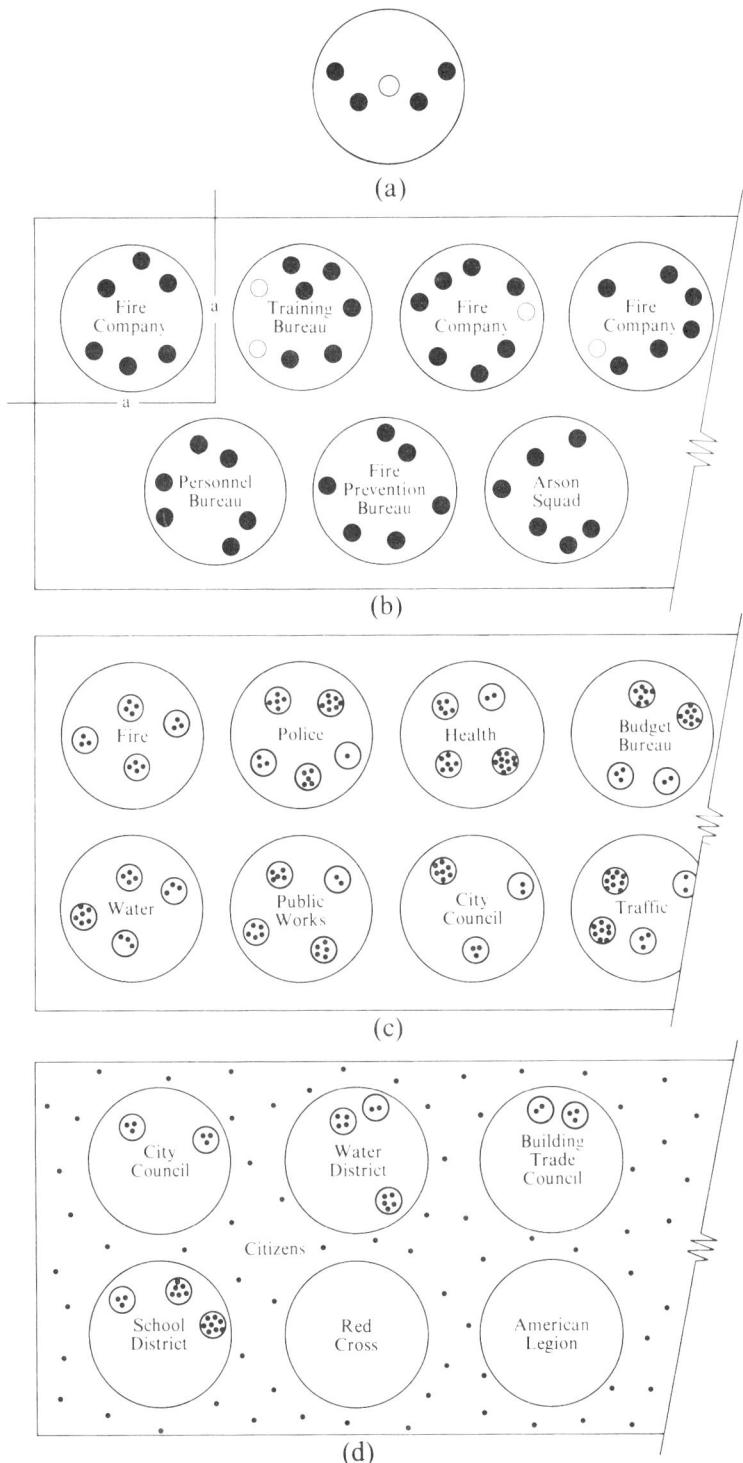

FIGURE 5.1. Systems of organization in the community: (a) A fire company; (b) A fire department; (c) A local government; (d) A community.

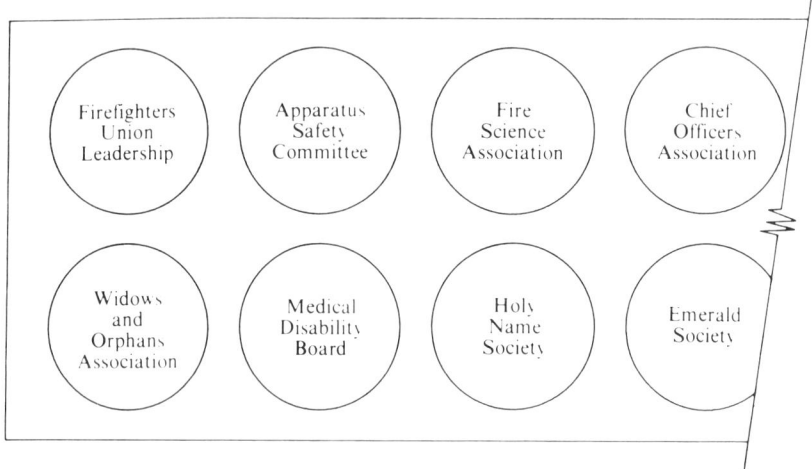

FIGURE 5.2. The fire department as a set of interest groups.

When one views the fire department from this perspective, it is not necessary that all "members" of the department be current, active employees; the concept of the department may include retired members, citizens who take an interest in the department through membership in one of the special interest organizations, or individuals from distant communities who take a special interest, for whatever reason, in department activities.

In many situations faced by department leaders, it may be more appropriate to view the department as this collection of special interest groups than as a set of formally authorized functional bureaus. For example, those attempting to change the work hours of firefighters to provide what is believed to be more efficient operations, must take into account the views of fire union leadership. Similarly, those attempting to change the standards for a promotional examination may find it necessary and appropriate to take into account the views of individuals already in the ranks as well as those who have passed an earlier promotional examination but have not yet been appointed.

Also, it is important to be able to see the fire department as one organization influencing and being influenced by a set of state, regional, and federal interest groups. Figure 5.3 shows only a handful of the organizations whose actions affect, and sometimes are affected by, the local fire department. The state may set standards for local departments, the United States Fire Administration may promote particular policies by providing matching funds, the National Fire Protection Association may influence local fire administration by publishing a new standard, the International Association of Fire Fighters may change firefighters' atti-

5.3 Organizations

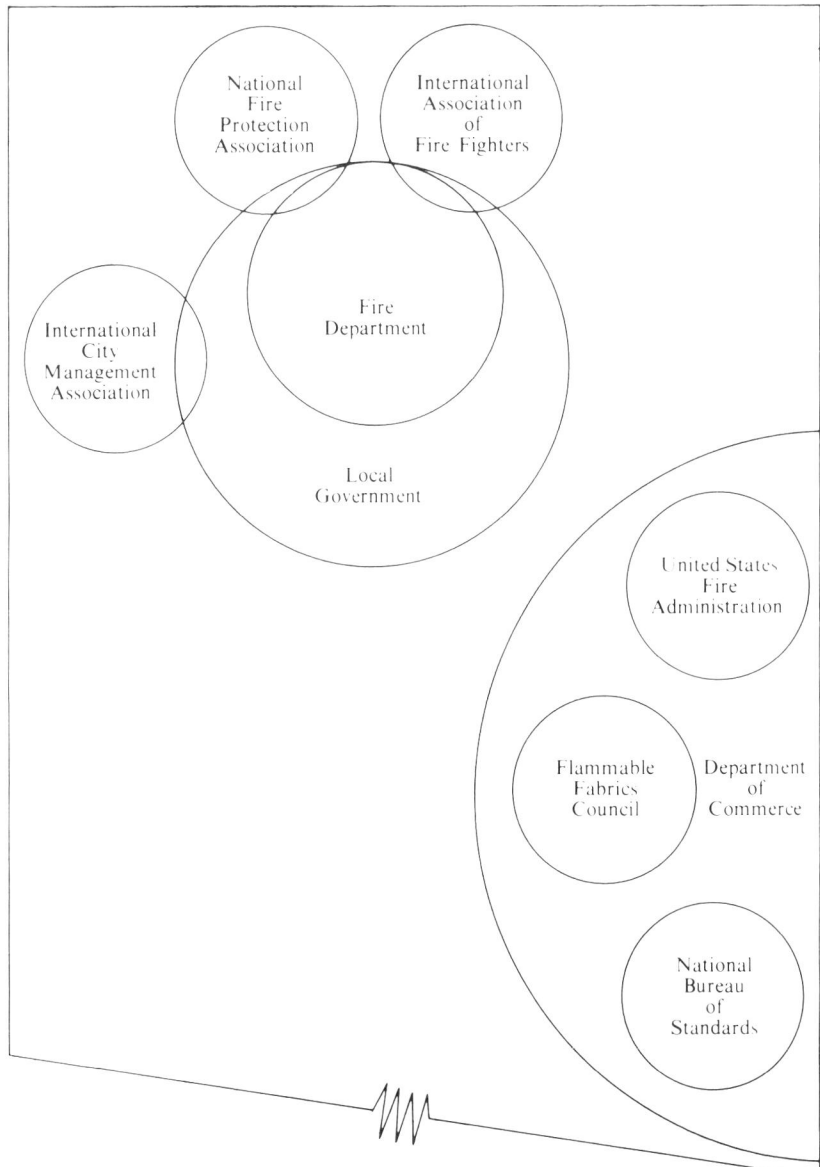

FIGURE 5.3. The fire department in the nation of special interest groups.

tudes by publishing the results of collective bargaining in different cities, or the International City Management Association may indirectly affect the future of a fire department by holding a seminar on how to combine police and fire functions into one public safety department.

Several points can be made about these oversimplified diagrams. An individual may be a member of a number of different organizations, serving jointly, for example, as a fire officer, a member of an NFPA committee on hydrant standards, a member of the department's safety committee, an officer in a local taxpayers' association, and a part-time student working toward an MBA degree. An individual's membership in one organization does not necessarily influence membership in another. For the purpose of analysis, it is often useful and convenient to think of the individual solely with respect to a particular role in one organization at any one time. Thus, we usually ignore an individual's membership in a taxpayer's association when assessing performance as a firefighter. Nonetheless, it is difficult to completely separate an individual's many roles and to argue that they never interact. Consider, for example, a fire officer who also is an official of a taxpayers' association. It is not so obvious what his most likely action will be when faced with deciding whether or not to recommend a tax increase to reduce the average life of apparatus from 25 to 20 years.

Defining the environment in which each organization operates helps distinguish among the collection of resources, attitudes, and skills that are directly controllable by the organization, and those that are not. An important aspect of an organization's environment is the extent to which it contains factors that directly or indirectly affect the organization. A key point in viewing an organization this way is that actions taken by one unit of a large organization, or by one organization in the environment of another, can have a profound effect on the ability of the organization to act. For someone concerned with the management of change, a large part of the primary task is to sort out the many relationships among organizations (often unseen), to identify patterns of influence, and to attempt to predict the forces that can be brought to bear on any organizational decision.

For example, we can imagine a boundary around a fire company, as illustrated by line a-a in Figure 5.1(b).[2] It might be quite important to understand this boundary if, for example, the department were considering abolishing the fire company, moving the company to a new location, replacing the company's apparatus, or changing the response pattern of the company. For each of these changes, it is likely that the individuals

---

[2] An organization "boundary" is the dividing line between the organization and its environment.

who constitute the fire company would join together to present a common position to management. And, in some cases, that position might be inimical to other units in the department. Thus, the agent of change would want to consider the collective opinions and possible actions of that fire company, as well as the relationship of that company to its environment. The agent would try to isolate these connections between the company and its environment. In other instances, the relevant boundary may be between officer and firefighters, or between the fire department and the budget bureau. The change agent should always try to identify the groupings of individuals who will be acting collectively to achieve a common goal, and should strive to understand group objectives, constraints, and likely patterns of interaction with the environment in which they operate.

5.4 STRATEGIES FOR CHANGE

5.4.1 Changing Organizations and People

Research does suggest some strategies for changing organizational behavior (Rogers, 1976 and Yin et al., 1976). Most of these are derived from analyses of circumstances in which favorable change occurred. Much less is known about strategies that failed.

Form a New Organization. An obvious, although extreme strategy is to destroy the organization; or to put it more positively, to create a new organization. In the fire service, this strategy is exemplified by large consolidations and creation of public safety departments. Although extreme, the concept of destruction should not be dismissed too quickly. It may well be that the existing organization cannot deliver the new type or quantity of service proposed, and that successful implementation is best achieved by creation of an entirely new organization. However, the techniques outlined in Chapters 6 to 13 do not generally lead to this extreme.

Reorganize. Another strategy, perhaps the most common one employed, is to reorganize—to change the structure of the organization. New ideas may require new or differently arranged organizational units for successful integration into the organization. A new operation or policy that requires two organizational units with traditional, well-defined missions to cooperate in achieving a new mission may create conflict and uncertainty that could be avoided by creating an entirely new organizational unit. There are, of course, many variations on this theme, and most organizations reorganize frequently, often in response to changes in leadership. Reorganization can be used to forestall real change, and it can be used to destroy a program (for example, by placing one of two units of approximately equal power subordinate to the other in order to carry out a program). However, it remains a powerful tool to be used when trying to implement change.

One variant of reorganization that may be useful is the creation of a temporary unit to carry out some particular function. An example is the formation of an analytical team solely for the time period necessary to accomplish a specific analytical task. The same strategy can be used for implementation. A temporary unit can be created whose sole task is to introduce and support a program until it is fully integrated into the organization. Another unit can assume responsibility after the integration is complete. For example, changes in a dispatch center may require establishment of a brand new unit whose life is perhaps two years, and whose sole mission is to convert from the old operation to the new operation. Another variation on this theme is the creation of test or pilot units within the organization, where the major element changed is the mission of the unit. The new mission is broader, and includes the testing and evaluation of some practice or item as a major goal, as well as continued service delivery. This may be superior to simply imposing the new policy on the existing organizational structure.

Change Communication Patterns. One aspect of reorganization that in itself is an important strategy for change is the changing of communication patterns, both formal and informal. With a change in communication come new associations, new patterns of influence, and the need to adapt to a changed situation. Thus, selective intervention in some communication channels, and the careful structuring of new or different communication channels, can help in implementing new programs.

Change the Managerial Style or Method of Working. Changing the managerial style or the method by which work is performed are also important strategies to be considered. A commonly advocated change in managerial style is to increase employee participation in decisionmaking. Especially when change and its resulting uncertainty are involved, employee participation in defining problems, establishing priorities, developing work plans, and evaluating results can be a key ingredient. Simply changing methods of work performance is also viable in some circumstances. Redefinition of tasks may provide jobs with better mixes of menial and challenging tasks, indoor and outdoor tasks, high-specificity and low-specificity tasks, and other variable job aspects. Innovations that may have been seen as undesirable without such changes may be much easier to implement with them.

Change the Relationship Between the Organization and its Environment. As we have noted, organizational behavior is closely tied to the environment in which the organization operates. If there are significant changes in the environment, it is likely that the organization will have to adapt to them. The most common example of this in the private sector is the introduction of new technology or new firms into a market. Other firms in the market must react in order to stay competitive. In the case of the fire department, if the leadership of the local government changes, the department can anticipate different interests, concerns, demands, and altered performance requirements. The environment has changed, so the department must adapt. At the national level, one can expect over time that the new United States Fire Administration will create standards of training and administration. Most departments will try to meet them, and many may be required to achieve them. A change agent wishing to implement a specific change in his community may find it best to support such a change at the national level in the expectation that it will subsequently filter down.

One can also attempt to change the demands placed on the fire department by the local community. Trying to change the behavior of members within the organization may be the wrong direction from which to approach some kinds of change. Change the community's concerns and demands for fire department service and the desired departmental behavior may follow. It appears, for example, that community pressure (including the various telephone companies) to install 911 as a general emergency number has been as important, if not more important, in generating such changes than the desire for such a change on the part of fire departments. Similarly, forces outside the fire service would probably be judged as providing the most impetus for establishing paramedical units within fire departments.

Change Individual Attitudes and Behavior. Of course, another strategy is to change individuals. Oganizations with the same general mission and organizational structure can be expected to perform differently if the background, training, attitudes, and morale of their individual members are different. Changing the way individuals feel about themselves and their work may eliminate great barriers to change. Most efforts to change individuals involve some kind of training, more participation in task-definition and goal-setting, or other programs to improve employees' understanding of their value.

Change Incentives. One direct approach to get employees to accept change is to change their incentives. This generally means increased pay for increased performance, but the approach is by no means limited to economic incentives. To the extent that nonmonetary rewards can be identified, they can be used as incentives. For example, providing time off during normal business hours may provide desired flexibility for employees to pursue their other interests. And, of course, one should never underestimate the value of praise, when deserved, from the boss.

5.4.2 Natural Points of Entry

Our objective is to see how to gain leverage for change. In seeking leverage, it is helpful to look for "natural points of entry" to introduce change (Yin et al., 1976). A natural point of entry occurs, for example, during times of low activity. Other examples are the specific points in individuals' careers when they must be trained, licensed, or are required to pass tests to be promoted. Natural points of entry also occur when major equipment and supplies must be acquired, and during periods accepted as requiring change—during labor contract negotiations, for example.

Collective Bargaining. In the future, the time to introduce change will be increasingly, and perhaps in some places exclusively, during the collective bargaining process. Public employees have long been protected by the civil service system, which promises consistent and fair application of employee entry, promotion, and termination regulations, but leaves determination of those regulations exclusively to legislators and public managers. Civil service protection remains strong in this country, but a more powerful protection has also been given to most public employees: the right to bargain collectively. This has been added to the civil service system, providing public employees with a combination of both the traditional civil service protection and the economic and political strengths of labor unions.

The legitimate scope of collective bargaining in the public sector is considered by many to include only wages, fringe benefits, and working conditions. Excluded specifically are so-called managerial prerogatives such as the organization and technology of the work. However, practice throughout the country indicates that almost any subject remotely connected to working conditions will be judged subject to bargaining in jurisdictions that have recognized public employees' right to bargain collectively (Horton, 1973). Since most paid firefighters have chosen to bargain collectively, the change agent must learn to understand and deal with labor organizations. Literally every technique of analysis discussed in later chapters can lead to proposals that the union leadership would consider proper subjects for collective bargaining. Changes in manning and response policy have been the subject of negotiation in some jurisdictions. And even if the unions do not choose to press an issue at the

5.4 Strategies for Change

bargaining table, they are becoming increasingly able users of political power. In a very real sense, the unions are partners with local government officials in delivering fire service to a community, and they must be treated as such if change is to be implemented successfully.

Because contract negotiations signal the formal renewal of the operating covenants between labor and management, expiration of a contract is an appropriate time to introduce change. And since public sector bargaining is coming to have all the trappings of long hours of caucus and debate, offer and counter offer, and eventual compromise, the analyst should expect that deployment analysis may include not just a particular study, but a series of analyses stemming from the conduct of negotiations. Some jurisdictions are now embarking on what is termed productivity bargaining, in which specific improvements in productivity are requested in exchange for pay increases. Often these productivity improvements can be the result of analysis conducted using the techniques discussed in Chapters 6 to 13.

This was the case, for example, in Wilmington, Delaware, where deployment analysis led to a proposal to reduce on-duty manning and to eliminate one engine company immediately and perhaps another in the future. A program of change was prepared and presented to the unions at the bargaining table. Several months of negotiation followed, in which the proposed program was turned down twice before finally being adopted. As part of the process, however, issues far from those originally posed were examined in an effort to reach a settlement. A reduction in the work week was proposed by the union, and the city countered with a proposal to increase the number of hours of nonfirefighting duties (including the possibility of a police-type patrol) during the shortened week. This is one example of how changes in deployment have been achieved in the collective bargaining process.[3] It is instructive because it highlights the importance of actors other than the analyst, the creative exchange at the bargaining table stimulated by analytically supported proposals, and the long time it takes for analytical results to alter practice.

It is likely that in the future, labor–management relations will be even more important than they are now in introducing change into the fire service. Therefore, it is worth taking a closer look at ways of using inputs from employee organizations. There are three general models that may be helpful. The first, less commonly practiced today than in the past, but still prevalent in many localities, is the authoritarian approach. The mayor (fire chief, city manager) is the client for analysis, and the results are

---

[3] David W. Singleton (1975) reviews the entire change process from analysis through the final implementation and includes a careful description of the contract negotiations. The analysis is reported by Warren Walker, David Singleton and Bruce Smith (1975).

withheld from circulation until a complete program is introduced by the client unilaterally. This approach may be necessary in some circumstances, but it is likely to lead to a sharp confrontation.

A diametrically opposite approach is the open, participative model. Employee organizations participate early in setting goals and formulating problems, and they maintain constant surveillance and input throughout the analysis and program design. This model is rarely used in pure form, but the realities of collective bargaining are bringing about instances in which more participation takes place than management has intended. This approach too may be necessary in some circumstances, but it makes it extraordinarily difficult to complete sound analysis, and almost impossible to get a full range of alternative programs fully evaluated in a careful, rational fashion.

A third model is the most common. The views of all participants in the system are sought, and provisions made, to vary inputs to the model, in order to provide results for the types and levels of inputs likely to be of value to others. However, the mayor (fire chief, city manager) remains the client for the analysis and assumes the advocacy role using the analytical results as supporting material. Management expects to be able to provide answers to questions that might be raised by the unions, because management counts on the analyst to have involved the unions in the analysis sufficiently that results regarding matters of interest to the unions will be available. This model potentially puts the analyst between management and labor, for in order to do "good" analysis, the analyst must understand and be able to model considerations relevant to labor. On the other hand, to serve his client (the chief executive), the analyst must face up to the reality of not having analytical results made available to all parties on the same basis. Inevitably, the agent of change can expect to face a choice between the potentially premature release of analytical results and the inability to implement change because relevant actors did not participate fully in the early stages of the analytic process.

Education and Training. In the long run, perhaps the greatest leverage for change lies in the education and training of firefighters and officers. Consideration should be given to new basic requirements for certain positions. We tend to acknowledge the need for special training for certain highly technical functions—we do not expect firefighters to repair computer terminals—but we sometimes forget the importance of special skills when introducing new programs or methods.

It is especially effective to introduce change in the course of routine in-house training, or as a part of different schooling or experience requirements for entry into a position. This is even more powerful if existing practices do not have to change simultaneously. A simple but important example is the introduction of new procedures for artificial respiration and cardio-pulmonary resuscitation into departments across the country. Training one individual does not detract from existing practice, and implementation of the technique by that individual does not have to wait until an entire department is trained. As successive individuals are trained, the department slowly changes from the previous practice to the new practice. New educational requirements and variation in experience and training requirements are usually introduced in the same way (although usually motivated by the need to give existing organizational members fair warning of new standards).

The technique is much harder to apply when there are interactions that require more than a few individuals to be knowledgeable for the program to be implemented at all. In this case, implementation may be a variation of the pilot program approach in which the program is composed of differently trained or schooled individuals, and spreads as rapidly as the training or schooling takes place.

Timing. The fire service has seasonal variation in demand, and generally some daily and weekly variation as well. A chief once told the story of a fire company that kept complaining about its meal hour being interrupted. Every evening at about 5:30 P.M. when the company sat down to eat, the meal would be interrupted by an alarm. The chief suggested this was so because the company was eating during the hour with the highest probability of an alarm, and suggested that the meal hour be changed. A skeptical company changed its dinner hour to a later time and found that it could invariably eat uninterrupted. But the story does not end there. Subsequently, a new, unpopular, mandatory exercise program was introduced. Negotiations led to its being scheduled just before the new dinner hour, precisely the time that would make it the most interrupted task of the day! The agent of change must be sensitive to the peaks and valleys of activity, and consider timing the introduction of new programs during periods with the fewest competing activities.

Routine Purchases. Obviously, when the fire department buys new equipment, it has the chance to change technology or vary some key practice, depending on what the equipment can do. Since it is natural to expect some changes when one is faced with a new piece of equipment, the burden of new practices or procedures may seem less if introduced at the same time that new equipment is provided.

5.5 CHANGE IN ORGANIZATIONS

No matter how it comes about or how it is received, change occurs all the time in organizations. Significant change involves rearrangement of power, association, status, skills, and values (Bennis, 1965). The changes of interest here are ones that are brought about or are supported by quantitative analyses, that have wide-ranging effects that may disrupt existing patterns of practice, and that have sufficient impact to require adjustments of the preferences of various department members, government officials, or other members of the community.

Fire officers carry out a wide range of managerial tasks every day, including, for example, supervising routine apparatus maintenance, and training and disciplining personnel. Most of these tasks are accomplished without the aid of formal analysis. Moreover, most of these daily tasks and decisions are not perceived by other department members, city officials, or members of the community as requiring opposition, support, or even close supervision. In short, they are routine, programmed activities (Leavitt, 1964).

In contrast to such activities are the ones that require special information to be gathered, that do not occur routinely, that are likely to generate controversy. Such decisions might include, for example, closing a firehouse, opening firefighter positions to women, or changing a traditional response policy to alarms. It is not important to specify a list of activities to be included or excluded from consideration. What is important are the circumstances under which such significant changes may be accomplished successfully.

A large body of literature exists to provide managers with guidance for everyday management. Such massive works as Bertram Gross's *The Managing of Organizations* (1964) or Peter Drucker's *Management: Tasks, Responsibilities, Practices* (1973) assemble the literature on management practice and offer guidance on nearly every phase of management. Works such as these, specific methods pamphlets, and the body of management consulting techniques provide a wealth of general guidelines for management practice. Unfortunately, this literature on management says little about the specific problems of implementing new ideas in organizations. In general, the literature on social change is not especially helpful either.

There is, however, literature on innovation in organizations that provides some useful insights. We shall draw upon it to highlight aspects of innovation that have been found to be important in implementing change. Most studies of innovation consider the process as one of social change in an organization. Social change is defined as "the process by which alteration occurs in the structure and function of a social system" (Rogers, 1969), and many authors have studied the characteristics of people and organizations undergoing change.

The need for change is motivated in two ways: (1) a change in the environment changes the expectations of organization members and leads to their perceiving a "performance gap," (and thus a need to change their behavior in some way); and (2) a change occurs somewhere within the organization which in turn either (a) has some impact on the environment (which may then influence the organization) or (b) generates perceptions of a need for change elsewhere in the organization. A performance gap occurs when individuals perceive a difference between current and possible achievement, which in turn creates a "felt need" for change.

Theorists have also speculated that change develops when something called "organizational (or managerial) slack" exists. This occurs when organizational resources are not completely absorbed by the everyday routine, and some portion is available for exploration that may generate pressure for change (Downs, 1967). Consider the fire chief who attends a national convention and is exposed to alternative approaches to fire station location. He may conclude that there is a "performance gap" between his city's approach and superior approaches available elsewhere. A difference between existing performance and what is possible is perceived. To the extent that the difference is significant, one can predict that the chief will push for change. Providing sufficient resources in the first place so the chief can attend such a convention (and presumably have his duties performed by others) is an example of organizational slack.

In Chapter 4, dissatisfaction with the status quo was identified as an advantage in attempting to introduce analytical techniques. The amount of dissatisfaction is one measure of a performance gap. An important task of the analyst throughout the process of change is to provide new or reinterpreted data that demonstrate performance gaps.

This process of change tends to be self-reinforcing. Managers who are exposed to new ideas and then generate pressure for change also tend to see that managerial or organizational slack exists and will use it to seek out additional ideas and generate more pressure for change. Although there are many research results which suggest that one or another type or style of approach may be best in certain tactical situations, a fundamental tenet for the change agent is that change works best when individuals want to change.

5.5.1 Factors Facilitating Change

There are many characteristics of an innovation that can be used to predict the chances of its adoption, although the existence of any one characteristic does not guarantee success, and the lack of any one does not doom the innovation. The purpose of reviewing them here is to provide a general checklist that can be applied to particular implementation strategies in particular settings. Every organization has its own peculiar circumstances, and individual good judgment always remains essential to the successful implementation of change.

Cost. In general, the more expensive the change, the more difficult it is to get approval to do the analysis, develop a new program, and implement the change. Cost is important in another way. Given scarce resources, the higher the cost of any particular innovation, the fewer the innovations one unit is likely to be able to develop. Thus, the analyst may be caught with all his "eggs in one basket." And since failures will occur, the more resources that are used for one particular innovation, the greater the chances that the failure will be the high-cost innovation. Costly solutions are necessary in many circumstances, but to the extent that the analyst can keep cost down, the chances for successful implementation are improved.

Risk. By definition, the riskier the innovation, the greater the chances for failure. Also, as indicated earlier in this chapter, the risk is generally likely to be one-sided. That is, the risk of failure may be high, but the potential benefits of success are not equally high. Fire departments do not operate in markets where risky ventures might return high benefits in the form of dramatically increased profits or market share. "High-risk, high pay-off" innovations are not often found in public services. Success is not measured by profit, but failure often is measured by cost, both monetary and political. The public administrator who takes on high-risk projects can rarely look forward to similarly high-valued success.

There is, of course, a large literature on bureaucratic behavior stressing the lethargy, inertia, and active opposition of bureaucrats to change. This literature is discouraging since it highlights the barriers to achieving successful implementation, but it is also instructive with respect to the riskiness of new ventures. Since the reward structure faced by most bureaucrats is so imbalanced—the punishment for failure far exceeds the reward for success—the analyst can rarely design a program that promises real opportunity for significant rewards. Too often the most visible aspect is the potential for failure.

Merit. In general, the more intrinsic value, or merit, that an innovation is perceived to have, the easier it should be to implement. This factor of merit is related to visibility and communicability. If those individuals who must approve an idea in order for it to be adopted, or who must work in the changed circumstances resulting from the idea, can see merit in the idea itself, then they may need less detailed knowledge or deep understanding of the analytical basis for the innovation. Even if the individuals only recognize that a problem exists ("there must be a better way"), the chances for successful implementation are improved. Ideas that are hard to understand, that are counterintuitive, that have benefits that are diffuse, or that do not have easily recognizable outcomes are all harder to "sell" than ideas that do not have such characteristics.

For example, to most individuals involved in the fire service, subtle changes in response policies do not have intrinsic merit. Although there is wide variation in response policy across the country, there has been only a small amount of research attempting to address scientifically the different outcomes of different response policies. In general, more is better when response policy is discussed in the fire service. The analyst who proposes to vary response policy in relation to demand (or to what might appear as a function of geography or time of day) must expect that the merits of such a policy will not be immediately obvious. Another example is provided by the model discussed in Section 7.3. The model suggests that, on the average, it is not always best to send the closest fire company to an alarm. The analyst who proposes, therefore, not to send the closest company must expect tremendous resistance. Without substantial explanation, it just does not seem reasonable. Such a policy faces more intensive scrutiny throughout the implementation process than one easily (though not necessarily correctly) seen as having merit.

Relative advantage. When two policies can be compared and one can be clearly shown to be more advantageous, its chances are enhanced. However, as indicated in Chapter 4, dissatisfaction with the status quo is a major reason for change, and proposed programs may not be easily comparable to current operations. A proposed policy with intrinsic merit is better than one without it, but an even better policy is one with merit, that can be compared favorably to a policy easily understood to be inferior. The degree of difference is important here. The greater the contrast (the greater the relative advantage), the better. A "marginally better" policy may be harder to implement than one perceived as "unambiguously better."

Communicability. Many of the decisionmakers responsible for deployment, and almost everyone carrying out deployment policies, are likely to be unfamiliar with the analytical techniques described in this book. Proposed policies should have the clarity to be easily communicated to individuals not involved in the analysis. Almost all attempts to introduce change will be accompanied by rumor, supposition, and even intrigue on the part of those affected by the change. If the rationale for a policy can be easily and quickly communicated, the chances of rumor, misinformation, and ignorance destroying successful implementation are minimized.

Complexity. The complexity of deployment planning presents particularly difficult implementation problems. Most of the techniques discussed in later chapters require differentiation of fire hazards, analysis of different types of alarms, and variation in response policy depending on circumstances that may vary dramatically by geography and time of day. Almost all the analytical techniques attempt to tailor deployment planning to very specific indicators of need. The outcomes of analysis are thus likely to be more rather than less complicated. To the extent that this is true, the analyst adds implementation burdens to his task. The simpler the idea, the simpler the proposed policy, the easier it is likely to be to implement. This is related to communicability and merit, for it is the simple, obviously useful change, which can be explained easily to others, that has the best chance for implementation.

Maintaining simplicity is also related to the concept of divisibility. It is common in program development to try to account for as many as possible of the objections to, or special circumstances that might arise from, implementation of a particular change in policy. This is a natural response to the various, often competing objectives of the groups that are affected by the policy change. However, if there is substantial conflict in objectives and the program tries to deal with many unusual circumstances, the design is likely to become too complicated to be easily comprehended. This can be overcome by breaking the program into small, easily identifiable parts to be implemented at different times, or by fashioning a selling approach that is effective in simplifying the program. In general, however, the analyst will face a natural tension between the finely tuned, extraordinarily detailed and responsive solutions that can be derived from analysis, and the simple, easy to comprehend programs that gain widespread implementation support. Even though the thrust of social science is toward the more refined, detailed analysis, and even though programs are often designed to include many parts, the purpose of which is to "take care of" one group or another, program designs that are extremely complicated are likely to be harder to implement and will certainly require more extensive communications efforts. The analyst must strike a balance between the desirable analytical goal of understanding and changing the system all at once, and the practical goal of selling and implementing the ideas.

Visibility. A visible innovation usually has a better chance of succeeding than one hidden from scrutiny, although research findings are mixed. It is desirable that debate on the issues take place during analysis, program design, and throughout implementation. Potential supporters have to be kept informed; and the visibility of an innovation can affect the perceptions of potential detractors, who may at least gain a better understanding of the support for the project and perhaps recalculate the value of opposition. We have all had the experience of complaining loudly about some project only to find out later that it is the chief executive's favorite idea. Good visibility and publicity can reduce some uncertainty about the project and improve the level of support.

On the other hand, high visibility can lead to inflated expectations of success, causing too much pressure for early, unambiguous results. It can also make an otherwise tolerable innovation too important to be left without opposition. For example, a union may be able to ignore or participate in a low-visibility pilot program aimed at improving productivity, but may find it necessary to actively oppose the same program if it is publicly and widely touted by the fire chief and mayor as the city's answer to the rising costs of local government. Of course, if the program has been designed from the beginning to include union participation, then the mayor, the fire chief, and the local union leader can participate in the publicity.

Compatibility. The more compatible an innovation is with existing norms and procedures, the more it complements rather than clashes with existing practices, the easier it is likely to be to implement. Compatibility is probably most important in large, new programs or policies that replace existing ones. It is here that the designer must try to disrupt as little as possible while still achieving the goal. An example might be introducing women as firefighters. This will be seen as a dramatic change, requiring adjustments in just about every phase of firefighting operations and lifestyle. The design of such a program will be better received if compatibility with existing norms, practices, equipment, attitudes, and values can be maintained. This example was chosen to indicate that maintaining compatibility does not mean giving up significant, visible, large-scale changes in fire service practice. It just adds to the challenge of the innovator to tailor the program so it is as little disruptive as possible to current patterns of practice.

Origin. Whether or not the innovation comes from within the department, the city, the county, or the fire service in general, can affect its likelihood of success. If the innovation has proven successful elsewhere, it may be easier to introduce. If the innovation comes from within the department, it may be easier to introduce. In general, the origin of the innovation is an indication of its worth in the eyes of those evaluating it. If the innovation has been used in what is perceived to be a reputable setting, its chances for local acceptance are improved.

Origin within the local political jurisdiction is also important. For example, while firefighters do not like to be told to "do it the way the sanitation men do it," it can be useful to endow an idea with local flavor by publicizing that it was "invented here" or "modified here," especially since the fire personnel perceive many of their problems as unique to their specific locales.

National associations and professional organizations can be useful as authoritative references for a new approach, especially when they can be cited as originators or promoters of the new idea. For example, using the NFPA as the source of a particular change may be useful in a couple of ways. First, some risk of failure is transferred outside the department of local jurisdiction. Second, the stature of the NFPA is such that its support of a particular approach can be very influential. Careful use of authoritative references can be extremely important.

Scientific status. Ideas that have been tested and developed in accordance with the highest scientific standards can be sold more easily than those that have not been subject to such scrutiny. For example, testing laboratories have a rich tradition in fire prevention. The satisfactory completion of certain tests (such as flammability) is a necessary step in the course of much product development. "How is the product rated?" is a frequent question. The deployment planning techniques discussed in this book are scientific approaches to problem solving. The results can be replicated by other scientists. When implementing changes based on these methods, the analyst may be able to improve acceptance by pointing out that these methods have been developed, reviewed, and used by scientists.

Reversibility. By reversibility we mean the degree to which it is possible to return to conditions that existed before a change if that change does not work out. Installation of a computerized dispatching center is not reversible for many years, and is reversible only at great cost. For practical purposes, such a proposal is irreversible. Changing initial response policy from three engines and two ladders to one engine and one ladder is reversible. If the policy is not satisfactory, another policy can be introduced at relatively little cost. (This is not to deny the high political cost of any reversal of policy.) Obviously, a reversible innovation is less risky than an irreversible one. If risk of failure is especially worrisome, the analyst should try to design programs that can be readily reversed.

Divisibility. One practical way to attempt to achieve reversibility is to design programs that can be implemented one step at a time; that is, programs that are divisible into several parts. Although this strategy has its dangers, it has proven successful time and again, especially where it is necessary to build credibility. Failures are easier to accept when they are small, and when they are preceded or accompanied by successes. The innovative package that can be broken into small parts to be sold incrementally is also helpful in bargaining. More may be achieved through negotiation if, when a large, comprehensive program is proposed, it is agreed that implementation be staged over time. Conceptually, the deployment planning approaches outlined in this book call for identifying and taking into account all of the relevant factors in a particular fire service region, even if those factors may be one or two steps removed from obvious connection to the problem. This does not diminish the value of staged implementation; in fact, the use of feedback to improve programs is inherent in the systems analysis process.

Adaptability. Programs can be too tightly designed, so that failure of one small element (for example, a change in the environmental influences on the program) is enough cause to scuttle an entire program. A better program design is an adaptable one, one that can survive unexpected consequences in implementation. For example, adaptability has been built into a project when individuals not intensely involved in its design can say, "They started out on the wrong foot, but now that they've made the couple of changes I suggested, the project isn't so bad." Unexpected consequences frequently occur during implementation, and new programs should be designed to accommodate change. A plan for new fire station locations that hinges on the acquisition of a specific set of parcels likely to require protracted negotiations or condemnation may make less sense than a plan incorporating a range of parcel combinations, even though some may be less effective than others.

Interpersonal relations. New programs tend to disrupt long-standing and well-developed relationships. Consequently, it is important for the program design to consciously encourage and develop new interpersonal relationships. It is necessary to deal directly with employees attitudes, their work group associations, and their established and often comfortable patterns of communication. We all use informal, as well as formal, contacts to maintain an understanding of what is expected in our work setting and what is going on around us. New programs frequently and deliberately involve a reorganization of formal lines of authority. But they can also disrupt informal contacts, leaving the employee with a major task of finding new associates and sources of information about a changed work environment. The better program design is one that accounts for the uncertainty individuals feel when placed in strange, unfamiliar circumstances, and facilitates development of reassuring and valuable interpersonal relationships.

5.5.2 Organizational Factors Affecting Implementation

People who have studied change in organizations have reached some tentative conclusions about how it is affected by the organizational structure (Zaltman et al., 1973; Burns and Stalker, 1961; Hage and Aiken, 1970). Although the results have not always been consistent, there is general agreement that the amount of complexity, centralization, and formalization in the organizational structure has an identifiable effect on prospects for change. Complexity refers to the number of different skills required in an organization, the amount of training and preparation required to exercise those skills, and the intricacy of the tasks to which those skills are applied. In a hierarchy of organizations, fire departments are considered to have relatively low complexity because the majority of their members perform one basic task that is relatively straightforward and requires only a moderate amount of training.[4] Centralization refers to the amount of decision authority delegated throughout the organization. Fire departments are said to be highly centralized, since ultimate authority rests with a single person at the top of the organization and flows down through a chain of command. Formalization refers to the degree that written rules and regulations guide the behavior of members of an organization. Fire departments are considered to be highly formal organizations.

These three concepts have been used to advance hypotheses about organizational change. An important hypothesis for fire departments is that organizations which are (1) low in complexity, (2) high in centralization, and (3) high in formalization are not likely to change to a great extent. Fire departments have, in general, conformed to this prediction.

Some investigators include other variables such as morale and job satisfaction, volume and efficiency of production, conflict resolution capability, and density of interpersonal relations when assessing the effect of organizational structure on rate of change. The higher the morale and job satisfaction, the higher the rate of change; the greater the density of interpersonal relationships, the greater the rate of change; the greater the emphasis on high volume of production and efficiency, the lower the rate of change.

Theorists have also noted that different organizational structures are important at different stages in the changes process. During the early stages when ideas are first explored, a less centralized, less hierarchical organization may be helpful; while later, at the implementation stage, the more tightly knit, hierarchical structure can faciliate efficient implementation (Zaltman et al., 1973). Highly complex organizations may facilitate generation of many ideas, but getting agreement on action may be more difficult.

Other organizational variables include the political organization and the size of the organization. Some theorists have looked at organizational change primarily as a political process, with coalitions formed and power distributed through a bargaining process. Others have noted the strong

---

[4] Many students of the fire service would take exception to this classification, and this book shows that more recognition must be given to some of the hidden tasks of the fire service. Nevertheless, using the criteria given, fire departments would be considered to have relatively low complexity.

influence of size on innovation. Larger organizations acquire sufficient resources in order to devote some of them exclusively to idea-generating assignments, whereas smaller organizations cannot afford the costs of exploration.

Authors who have studied change in public sector organizations always point to some concept of bureaucratic behavior as an important indicator of the ability to change. In a recent study of technological innovations in state and local government, Yin and his associates identified bureaucratic self-interest as one of the two most important variables affecting successful implementation of innovations in public sector organizations. They suggest that, at least in local government, bureaucratic factors may transcend other apparent organizational differences, such as type of service provided or product produced (Yin et al., 1976).

Most organizational settings are quite complex, and researchers are continuing to take new perspectives rather than replicating one approach in a series of different organizational settings. The change agent must be careful not to accept the hypotheses mentioned here as proven over a wide range of circumstances, but should regard them as suggestive of the considerations that should be made in planning for change.

5.5.3 Combined Strategies

By combining general strategies for change with an assessment of the natural points of entry into the system and the various attributes of change programs that have led to success, it is possible to fashion a general approach to managing change. The rewards are well worth the effort. While the process may require intensive public relations campaigns, legal maneuvers, political conflict, and many hours of persuasive discussion, the courage to see it through can result in a first-rate accomplishment of more effective delivery of fire protection service.

PART II
BASIC TOOLS AND TECHNIQUES

Chapter 6
Travel Time and Travel Distance Models

Synopsis

Travel time is a major component of response time, an important measure of the service provided by fire departments. The travel time from one particular point to another, for example from a specific firehouse to the location of a specific incident, can be estimated in several ways. These various procedures are described and their comparative advantages and disadvantages are discussed. This chapter also shows how the average travel distance or travel time to incidents in a region can be estimated from information about the region's area, alarm rate, number of companies stationed there, and other characteristics. The models for making these estimates can be used by themselves for quick, approximate evaluations of deployment policies, and also serve as building blocks in the models of subsequent chapters. They replace manual map measuring with computerized calculations and simple formulas.

The following is a brief summary of the procedures developed and discussed in this chapter for estimating travel distances and travel times.

ESTIMATING POINT-TO-POINT TRAVEL DISTANCES

To estimate the distance between two specific points i and j that have grid coordinates (x_i, y_i) and (x_j, y_j), respectively, assume that the coordinate system is oriented to conform with the orientation of the major streets. If the streets are laid out as a rectangular grid, the distance between i and j is $d_{ij} = |x_i - x_j| + |y_i - y_j|$. If travel is "as the crow flies," in a straight line connecting the two points, the distance between i and j is $d_{ij} = \sqrt{(x_i - x_j)^2 + (y_i - y_j)^2}$. In practice, neither of these conditions may hold exactly, so an approximation is needed. In many cities throughout the country the following formula has provided good estimates of the travel distance between point i and point j: $d_{ij} \approx 1.15 \sqrt{(x_i - x_j)^2 + (y_i - y_j)^2}$.

As an alternative approach, a model of the street network can be constructed with arcs representing (directed) street segments. Then travel distances may be computed as the shortest paths in the network connecting points i and j.

ESTIMATING AVERAGE TRAVEL DISTANCES IN A REGION

To estimate the average travel distance of the first-arriving company to alarms in a particular region, suppose that the area of the region is A square miles and $E(N)$ is the expected (average) number of firehouses in the region from which engines are available to respond. Then the expected (or average) distance traveled by the first-arriving engine ($E(D)$) is given by the square-root law

$$E(D) = k \sqrt{\frac{A}{E(N)}}.$$

The constant k depends on the geometry of the particular situation, but it varied little among regions where it was tested. It is approximately 0.55 in most situations. The area (A) can be measured in a variety of ways: for example, by counting grid squares on a map or by using a polar planimeter. The average number of firehouses with engine companies available to respond can be estimated by subtracting the average number of companies busy in the region from the number of stations housing engines. The average number of busy engine companies can be estimated from alarm rate and work time statistics (Chapter 7). The square-root law is usually applied separately for engines and ladders. Average travel distances for second-arriving units can also be estimated using the square-root law. The only change is in the value of k, which is approximately 1.0 for second-arriving units.

ESTIMATING POINT-TO-POINT TRAVEL TIMES

To estimate the time to travel between two specific points when the distance between them is known, it is necessary to relate travel time to distance traveled. The travel time depends primarily on the distance between the points, but it may also depend on the time of day, the type of apparatus, the driver, the traffic encountered, the types of roads, etc. In several cities it has been found that:

Time of day has only a small effect. Travel times between the same pair of points during daylight and darkness are almost the same. Travel times during rush hours are about 20% longer than during other hours.

Average cruising speeds are similar in different regions of the same city, and in different cities. They fall in the range of 35 to 40 mph.

Travel time increases with the square root of distance for short trips—on side streets and with a significant number of accelerations and decelerations—and increases linearly for longer trips. This can be expressed by the following mathematical model relating the travel distance, D_{ij}, between points i and j, and the expected time to travel between the two points, $E(T_{ij})$:

$$E(T_{ij}) = \begin{cases} c\sqrt{D_{ij}} & D_{ij} \leq d \\ a + bD_{ij} & D_{ij} \geq d. \end{cases}$$

The values of the parameters a, b, c, and d can be estimated from empirical data for any city or region. However, as a result of collecting such data in several cities, it has been found that the values of these parameters vary surprisingly little from city to city. Therefore, it may be possible to obtain useful travel time estimates without carrying out detailed data collection by using the following relationship:

$$E(T_{ij}) = \begin{cases} 2.10\sqrt{D_{ij}} & D_{ij} \leq 0.38 \text{ miles} \\ 0.65 + 1.70 D_{ij} & D_{ij} \geq 0.38 \text{ miles,} \end{cases}$$

where T_{ij} is given in minutes, and D_{ij} in miles.

If travel times on street segments are known, point-to-point travel times can be constructed by finding the shortest time path through the network of streets and roads.

ESTIMATING AVERAGE TRAVEL TIMES IN A REGION

One way of estimating the average travel time in a region is to average the appropriate point-to-point travel times, taking into account the proportion of regional trips that are accounted for by each point-to-point trip. This calculation can be quite tedious. A useful approximation is obtained by combining the model for estimating average regional distances and the time vs. distance function for point-to-point trips. The following formulas for estimating regional average travel times result:

In regions where average travel distances are short enough (say, ≤0.4 mile) for the square-root part of the time vs. distance function to hold, we have

$$E(T) \approx r\left(\frac{A}{E(N)}\right)^{0.25}.$$

Results from the two models suggest that $r = 1.56$ should be used.

In regions where average travel distances are longer so that the linear part of the time vs. distance function holds, we have

$$E(T) \approx q + r\left(\frac{A}{E(N)}\right)^{0.5}.$$

In this case, $q = 0.65$ and $r = 0.94$ should be used.

6.1 INTRODUCTION

This chapter is about models for estimating and predicting fire company travel times and travel distances. These models play an important role as components of nearly all the models described in succeeding chapters. As indicated in Chapter 3, difficulties in measuring the performance of a fire department force us to use response times as surrogate measures of performance, and travel time is an important component of response time. Moreover, travel time is the component of response time that is most directly affected by deployment changes.

Recall that response time is the interval between the receipt of an alarm and the moment when the firefighting unit is on the scene and ready to begin firefighting or rescue operations. It has four key components: dispatching time, turnout time, travel time, and setup time (see Figure 3.4). It is important to note that response times and travel times are random; that is, they cannot be predicted exactly in advance. Even if a fire engine traveled from a particular firehouse to the same street corner over and over again under essentially constant conditions—same apparatus, driver, weather, time of day, etc.—there would still be variations in travel time from run to run. If the conditions changed between runs there would be even greater variations. If an alarm were received over and over again from a given location, the time elapsed until the alarm was dispatched (units were notified to respond) would also vary depending on the nature of the call and what else was happening in the communications office when it was received. Similarly, the turnout time and setup time would vary from run to run. The random nature of response time must be taken into account when doing analysis using response times as a performance measure.

To get an idea of how large travel time is likely to be, compared to the other components of response time, let us make some rough estimates. Except under very high alarm rate conditions, even a manual dispatching system will be able to achieve rather short dispatching times. Thirty seconds to a minute are reasonable figures. Observations in the New York City and Denver fire departments showed that turnout times and setup times fall in the same range. However, the time required for the closest unit to travel to the scene of an alarm is typically somewhere around three minutes. Thus we have as rough estimate for the first-arriving company:

average response time = average dispatching time
+ average turnout time
+ average travel time
+ average setup time
= 1 + 1 + 3 + 1 = 6 minutes.

Thus, of the total of 6 minutes, about half is travel time. For companies that arrive on the scene second or third, travel time is an even larger fraction of the total response time than it is for first-arriving units. And travel time is the only component of response time that is affected by most of the deployment changes discussed in this book.[1] We shall see that travel times play an important role in the relocation algorithm described in Chapter 12, in the allocation and station siting analysis described in Chapters 9 and 10, and in the initial dispatch procedures described in Chapter 11.

Above all else, travel time depends on the distance the apparatus must go. Time generally increases with distance traveled. In many situations it may be inconvenient, impossible, or unnecessary to measure or estimate travel times directly and so the analyst will work with travel distances. The analysis can either use distances directly[2] or can use distances to estimate times. There is a long-standing precedent for the direct use of distances. The ISO grading of municipal fire departments is based on distance standards. Whether the analyst works with distances themselves or converts from distances to times, an understanding of travel distances is vital. In the sections that follow, estimating travel distances is discussed before travel times.

6.2 ESTIMATING POINT-TO-POINT TRAVEL DISTANCES

How travel distances are estimated depends upon how the estimates are to be used. We can identify two broad needs. The first is the need to estimate the distance from one specific location in the city to another specific location. The second is the need to estimate average fire company

---

[1] Dispatching times can be reduced in some instances, as discussed in Chapter 14. Turnout times and setup times can be affected primarily by changes in procedures, management, or equipment, rather than deployment.

[2] An advantage of direct use of distances in analysis is that they are more stable than times. They do not change with weather, time of day, etc. Another advantage is their simplicity. There is likely to be broad agreement on distances and how they are measured.

travel distances in different regions of the city; for example, in a fire company's first-due area, in the central business district, and so on.

In this section we consider the problem of determining the travel distance between two specific points, say point i and point j. (For concreteness we can think of i as the location of the closest fire company and j as the location of the alarm.) Of course, there is no way of knowing the precise distance short of riding the route or tracing it on an accurate map. (In a hilly city even a map trace might be misleading.) In a city with very curvy and complicated streets, as in Figure 6.1(a), it might be that only such direct measurements could give accurate distances. On the other hand, in many cities there are large regions where the streets run at right angles, as in Figure 6.1(b). In such cases a mathematical procedure far simpler than direct measurement would give distance estimates accurate enough for deployment analysis.

For example, consider the situation shown in Figure 6.1(b). Suppose that we know the coordinates (x_i, y_i) of point i and (x_j, y_j) of point j with respect to a right-angle coordinate system.[3] Assume that distances in both the x and y direction are measured in miles. Then the *right-angle travel distance* from i to j, r_{ij}, is the sum of the absolute values of the differences in the coordinates; that is,

$$r_{ij} = |x_i - x_j| + |y_i - y_j|. \tag{6.1}$$

If a straight road directly connected the two points, we would not want to use the right-angle distance but instead would compute the travel distance using the equation for *straight-line* (Euclidean) distances:

$$s_{ij} = \sqrt{(x_i - x_j)^2 + (y_i - y_j)^2}. \tag{6.2}$$

In most situations in actual cities neither Equation (6.1) nor (6.2) applies exactly, yet the situation is often not as extraordinary as the curvy road case, for which we might have to record actual measured distances. What options does the analyst have, short of keeping a table of point-to-point distances? We consider three possibilities, listed below in order of preference (that is, preference if they work):

1. Create a simple modification or adjustment to right-angle or straight-line distance (or both).
2. Create a more complicated distance function.
3. Compute point-to-point distances from a representation of the road system as a network by using an algorithm that finds the shortest path.

If the street network is reasonably dense (the streets are not very far

---

[3] This is the familiar standard coordinate system commonly used in geometry—often called Cartesian or (x,y) coordinates.

6.2 Estimating Point-to-point Travel Distances

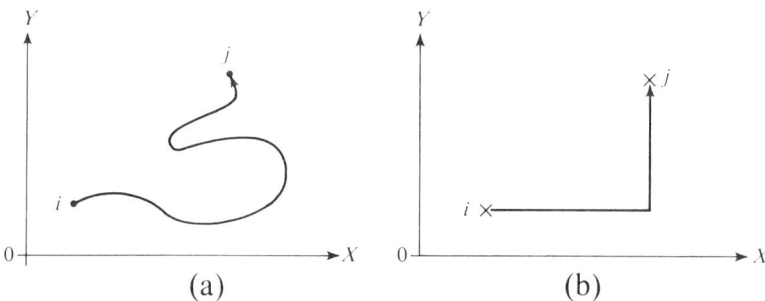

FIGURE 6.1. Some possible street patterns and their effect on distances between two points: (a) A typical route in a city with winding roads; (b) A typical route in a city with a right-angle road network.

apart) and not too irregular, common sense indicates that the actual travel distance should be very close to right-angle or straight-line distance. For right-angle distance, the coordinate system should be oriented parallel to the dominant street direction, which might vary in different parts of the city. Actual distances could then be compared to those computed from Equations (6.1) and (6.2). The comparison will typically show that actual travel distances are slightly larger than right-angle distances (because of curves, hills, or one-way streets). An adjustment to Equation (6.1) can then be made by adding a constant or multiplying by a number slightly larger than 1.0 (or both). The same approach can be used with straight-line distances. For example, if d_{ij} denotes the actual distance, an approximation to try might be $d_{ij} \simeq k \, s_{ij}$, where k is an empirically determined constant that scales the Euclidean distance. $k = 1.15$ has produced good estimates of travel distances in a number of cities. Thus a reasonable approximation of travel distances is

$$d_{ij} \approx 1.15 \sqrt{(x_i - x_j)^2 + (y_i - y_j)^2}. \qquad (6.3)$$

The second approach to estimating travel distances—creating a more complicated function—was used in The New York City–Rand Institute's Fire Operations Simulation Model (Chapter 13). In the simulation the distance between two points was computed on the following basis: If the distance traveled is short, the fire company is presumed to travel on a right-angle grid of streets oriented at a specified angle with respect to the coordinate axes. If the distance traveled is long, it is assumed that a straight line is followed. If the distances are of intermediate length, a combination of right-angle and straight-line distances is used. Carter (1974, pp. 35–44) explains the details of these computations.

The third possible approach to estimating travel distances, computation using network models of the actual streets in a city, can be quite accurate, but requires an extensive data base and time-consuming calculations.

The accuracy of the distances computed in this way is limited only by the detail with which the street network is represented. The greatest accuracy can be attained by a network model having a "node" for every intersection and an "arc" for every street segment. One-way streets could be modeled explicitly in the network by using directed arcs. Parks, lakes, railroads, highways, and other barriers to direct travel are automatically taken into account when computing travel distances using a network representation, since the permissible paths in the network would avoid these obstacles.[4]

The analyst using a network model for point-to-point distances must decide whether to compute the distances between all pairs of points at one time and store them—perhaps in advance of actual use—or to compute specific point-to-point distances when they are needed. Computation of all distances in advance reduces the amount of computer time used if it is certain that all or a very high proportion of the distances between possible pairs of points must be evaluated, or if the distance between many pairs of points will be used over and over again. The computational advantage is a result of two factors. First, a particularly efficient algorithm can be employed that evaluates the length of the shortest path between every pair of points in a network in one pass (see for example, Dreyfus, 1969, or Dreyfus and Law, 1977). Second, one would never evaluate the same distance twice. But there are also disadvantages to using this procedure. First, the table needed to store all of the distances can be very large. If there are 300 points, for instance, the distance table would contain 300 × 300 or 90,000 entries.[5] Second, one might compute many distances that would never be needed.

6.3 ESTIMATING POINT-TO-POINT TRAVEL TIMES

There are essentially three different ways that the travel time between two points can be estimated:

1. Several actual travel times for the trip can be obtained either when the fire companies happen to be responding between the locations of interest, or by having the companies make experimental trips for this purpose. Except in small communities, this method is tedious and impractical, since a large amount of data must be collected.

---

[4] The U.S. Bureau of the Census has created a file of data for computerized map generation that can be used for creating such a network. It exists for the approximately 250 Standard Metropolitan Statistical Areas (SMSA's) in the United States, and is called the Dual Independent Map Encoding (DIME) file.

[5] If only the distances between firehouses and points at which alarms occur are needed, the table can be much smaller.

6.3 Estimating Point-to-point Travel Times

2. The travel time can be estimated directly from a street network in the same way as described for travel distances. In this case, the travel time on each arc must also be determined. (This can be done approximately by measuring the distance on each arc and estimating the average travel speed.)
3. The travel distance can be estimated by any of the methods described in Section 6.2, and then the distance can be converted into a time.

Although a network can be used to estimate travel distances, after which *distance* is converted to *time*, the result will not necessarily be the same as when using a network to estimate travel time directly. The difference arises from the fact that the shortest-distance path between two points may not be the fastest path. For example, part of the trip could be made on a limited-access divided highway, which may make the trip longer but faster. When a network is used to estimate travel times, the computer program assumes that the fire companies follow the fastest route, even if some other route would have a shorter distance.

Some fire departments have constructed a street network for estimating travel times as part of their analysis of firehouse locations using the Fire Station Location Package developed by Public Technology, Inc. (see Chapter 10). The network method is especially valuable in cities that are irregularly shaped, divided by having a limited number of crossover points, or that contain large areas (parks or airports, for example) through which fire companies cannot travel. However, many cities are sufficiently regular that much simpler methods for estimating travel times are appropriate. These methods, to be described in the remainder of this section, convert estimated travel distances to travel times.

Such a conversion would be especially easy if fire companies traveled at a constant speed: time would be estimated by simply dividing the distance by the speed. But data that have been collected in several cities show that constant speed is a bad approximation. These data show that average speed is higher on longer trips, and an appropriate time–distance relation should reflect this. In fact, travel time tends to be related to travel distance according to a curve like the one shown in Figure 6.2. This curve begins as if a square-root relationship held between travel distance and travel time, and then blends into a straight line. Mathematically, if $E(T_{ij})$ denotes the time required to travel the distance between points i and j, D_{ij}, the curve has the form

$$E(T_{ij}) = \begin{cases} c\sqrt{D_{ij}} & D_{ij} \leq d \\ a + bD_{ij} & D_{ij} \geq d. \end{cases} \quad (6.4)$$

Here a, b, c, and d are parameters that can be estimated empirically for any city or part of a city, and $E(T_{ij})$ is intended to be an estimate of the average travel time for all responses having a response distance D_{ij}. For

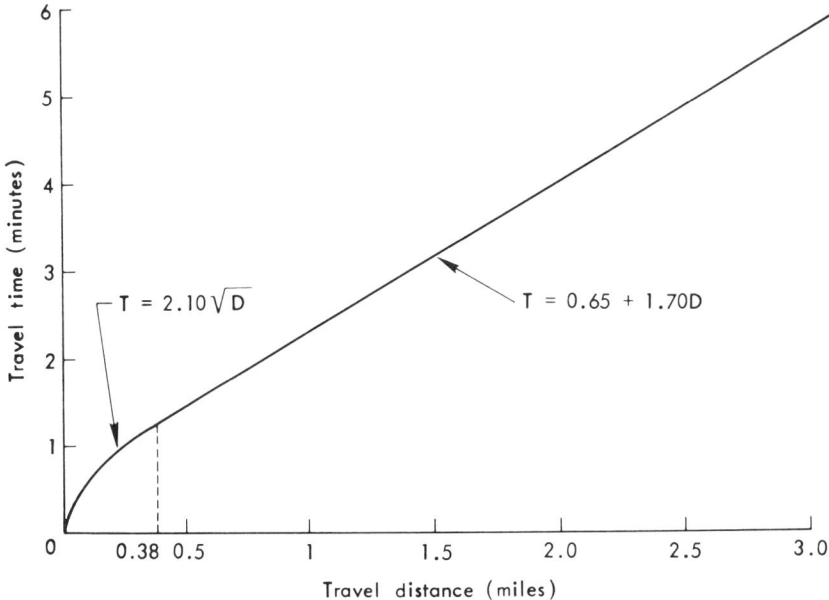

FIGURE 6.2. The relationship between travel time and travel distance. (Source: Average of empirical results from Denver, Trenton, Wilmington, and Yonkers).

the curve shown in Figure 6.2, distance is measured in miles, time is measured in minutes, and the parameters are $a = 0.65$, $b = 1.70$, $c = 2.10$, and $d = 0.38$. That is,

$$E(T_{ij}) = \begin{cases} 2.10\sqrt{D_{ij}} & D_{ij} \leq 0.38 \text{ miles} \\ 0.65 + 1.70 D_{ij} & D_{ij} \geq 0.38 \text{ miles,} \end{cases} \quad (6.5)$$

where T_{ij} is measured in minutes and D_{ij} in miles. As a result of collecting data in several cities, we have found that the parameters a, b, c, and d vary little from city to city, and that Equation (6.5) (which is based on an analysis of data from Denver, Trenton, Wilmington, and Yonkers) provides very good travel time estimates in most cases (Section 6.3.3).

An equation of this type does not provide an exact estimate of the travel time for each and every response of a fire company. Instead, some travel times will be longer than the estimate given by the equation, while others will be shorter. The typical variations to be expected are indicated by the examples given below.

The use of a network might appear to guarantee more accurate estimates of travel times than the use of Equations (6.4) or (6.5). However, this need not be so. For example, it is usually assumed, when using a network, that vehicles do not accelerate or decelerate on street segments, and that they do not stop or slow down when turning corners. These

6.3 Estimating Point-to-point Travel Times

assumptions can lead to errors in estimating travel times even if the description of the street network is very precise. No direct empirical comparison between the network method and the distance conversion method has been conducted to date, so their relative accuracy is not known.

Generally, the analyst must consider several factors when choosing an appropriate method for estimating travel times: the particular purpose for which the travel-time estimates will be used, the configuration of the city and the street network, and available data and computer processing capabilities. In some cases, it will be satisfactory to use Equation (6.5), at least temporarily, even though the parameters in the equation were fit to data in cities other than the analyst's own. In other cases he will want to use Equation (6.4), after finding the values of parameters a, b, c, and d that best fit his own data. He may also choose to use a network method. Table 6.1 present a comparison of the second and third methods to assist in making this choice.

6.3.1 A Travel-Time Experiment

The form of the relationship between travel distance and travel time, as given in Equation (6.4), was discovered by statistical analysis of empirical data from several cities. These data were collected during experiments in which selected units measured their travel times with stop watches and their travel distances with vehicle odometers. Such travel-time experiments can be conducted by any fire department. In addition to providing data for determination of the parameters a, b, c, and d in Equation (6.4), they permit analysis of other interesting questions about travel times, such as the following:

1. *How do response speeds vary by time of day?* One would presume that speeds, and hence travel times, vary considerably by time of day as a result of differences in traffic conditions, street lighting, etc. It has been found, surprisingly, that although differences do exist, they are considerably less than expected and can be ignored for many planning purposes.
2. *How do travel speeds vary within a city?* In New York City, for example, only small variations among regions were detected in the travel time versus distance relationship. This suggests that the average speed for a given travel distance is almost constant throughout the city.

In this section we discuss the general procedure for conducting a travel time experiment in some detail. In Section 6.3.2 we discuss the analysis of a travel time experiment conducted in New York City, and in Section 6.3.3 we present results from experiments in other cities.

TABLE 6.1. A comparison of two methods for estimating point-to-point travel times.

Steps in the Method	
Distance Conversion Method	Network Method
Run a travel-time experiment showing origin and destination for each response by fire companies, odometer distance traveled, and the time required for each response.	Describe the street network of the city in computer-readable form. Street intersections are identified as nodes in the network; streets are represented as connecting arcs between nodes. (It may not be necessary to consider all streets; main arterials are usually adequate.)
Fit the parameters a, b, c, and d in Equation (6.4) to data showing actual travel time versus distance.	
Determine (x,y) coordinates of the points of interest on a grid map of the city. (These would typically be existing and potential fire station sites and selected street intersections.)	Estimate distance for each arc. (This is already available on DIME files.)
	Estimate average travel speed on each arc. This may be based on experienced guesses, traffic surveys, experimental trips by fire companies, or previously collected travel-time data.
Estimate distance between points in some way; e.g., as the sum of x and y distances (right-angle distance) or as a modification of straight-line (Euclidian) distance.	Estimate the time to travel over each arc using speed and distance.
Parameters of the curve fit to the experimental points are used to estimate travel time between any two points, using estimated distance and Equation (6.4).	A computer program estimates the travel time from one point to another by finding the set of connecting arcs that form the minimum time path between the two nodes, and summing the travel times of these arcs.

Collecting the Data. To carry out a good experiment to measure travel time requires some care and effort. A primary consideration is that data collection should not interfere in any way with firefighting operations. Moreover, the accuracy of the data collected depends on the attitudes of the firefighters involved, so that good will and understanding of the aims of the experiment are necessary. Care must be taken that firefighters do not view a travel time experiment with hostility.

In order to obtain a statistically reliable picture of both citywide and regional travel characteristics, selection of the units to participate in the experiment should take into account the following factors:

Location—the primary response districts of the selected units should represent a topographical cross section of the city, and enough units should be included to cover all types of response patterns in the city.

6.3 Estimating Point-to-point Travel Times

TABLE 6.1. *(Continued)*

Why to Consider Using the Method	
Distance Conversion Method	*Network Method*
An elaborate data base and computer program are not needed to prepare input; lower cost for analysis.	If a street network has already been developed in computer-readable form (by the traffic department or Census Bureau, for example), this is the fastest way to proceed.
If a street network has not already been developed, this method is significantly quicker in beginning to produce estimates.	The street network, when developed, may be useful to other city agencies in locating other public facilities.
If travel times have already been collected, this method can be used to produce estimates very quickly.	Both permanent and temporary barriers to travel (hills, one-way streets, railroad tracks, rivers, airports) can be taken into account.
Parameters (a, b, c, and d) for fit curve have been so close to the same values for many cities that it may be possible to proceed without collecting any travel-time data.	Effects of changes in structure of road network can be analyzed in advance (new interstate highway, new bridge, closing of existing bridge).
Method has been validated against actual travel-time data and has been found to be of sufficient accuracy for site selection.	Irregularly shaped areas (peninsulas or cities with "holes" in them, for example) are handled accurately.
	Fire officials may feel more comfortable with a method that actually imitates the path followed by fire companies.

Response Frequency—the units chosen should be reasonably busy so that the experiment need not last too long. At least 50 observations should be collected for each participating unit.

Odometer Availability—Each vehicle involved in the experiment must have a working odometer capable of measuring travel distances to the nearest tenth of a mile.

Each unit participating in the travel time experiment would be supplied with a stopwatch, coding instructions, and several copies of a form on which to record data on all responses made by that unit during the course of the experiment. At least the following information should be recorded for each response: the odometer reading before departure; the odometer reading after arrival at the incident; the stopwatch reading indicating the duration of the run; and the time of occurrence. A detailed description of the data collection method is given in a report by Hausner (1975). The report includes a sample coding form and instructions for filling out the form.[6]

Editing the Data. Before doing any computer analysis, the raw data should be edited to eliminate obviously erroneous records. This is quite important and should be done early in the analysis. A number of consistency checks can be used. For example, records for which the average speeds attained are higher than 60 mph can possibly be eliminated.

Analyzing the Data. Other things being equal, the farther a fire engine travels, the longer it takes to make the trip, and many mathematical relationships that reflect this fact are candidates for use in converting travel distances to times. A simple time-distance relationship often employed by analysts assumes that a unit makes an entire trip at a constant speed, and, therefore, that travel time increases proportionally with the distance traveled.

As an alternative, we hypothesized the following: Suppose that, for short runs, the apparatus never reaches a cruising speed, but rather increases its speed for the first half of the trip (as it accelerates, gets onto main thoroughfares, and so forth); then it decelerates as it approaches its destination, gets off main thoroughfares, etc. Suppose further that, for longer runs, there is a similar initial "acceleration" phase, but that the unit then runs at cruising speed for some distance before decelerating as it nears its destination. These hypotheses can be expressed mathematically as follows:

Let
  z = acceleration
  D = distance traveled in a run
  D_c = distance required to achieve cruising speed
  v_c = cruising speed
  $E(T)$ = expected travel time for the run.

Then, assuming a constant acceleration and deceleration, z, during the initial and final phases of travel, and a constant cruising speed, v_c, during the middle phase, travel time as a function of travel distance is given by:

$$T = \begin{cases} 2\sqrt{\dfrac{D}{z}} & D \leq 2D_c \\ \dfrac{v_c}{z} + \dfrac{D}{v_c} & D \geq 2D_c. \end{cases} \quad (6.6)$$

---

[6] Data were collected by an alternate way in Denver, Colorado (see Section 6.3.3).

6.3 Estimating Point-to-point Travel Times

From this, we obtain for $E(v)$, the average speed, as a function of travel distance (average speed being defined as $E(v) = D/T$):

$$E(v) = \begin{cases} (1/2)\sqrt{zD} & D \leq D_c \\ \dfrac{zD}{v_c + \dfrac{zD}{v_c}} & D \geq D_c. \end{cases}$$

While the assumptions used in deriving these equations are not to be taken literally, they provide an intuitive explanation of why the *form* of the conversion given in Equation (6.4) might possibly be correct. In other words, Equation (6.6) is the same as Equation (6.4), except that the parameters have been given names that relate to their physical interpretation.

With these hypotheses in mind, we wrote a computer program to analyze the experimental data. The program, which has been called the Travel Time Analysis Program, can be used to analyze travel-time data from any city. It is fully documented in Hausner (1975).

The program calculates least-squares regression fits of the relationship in Equation (6.4) and of the relationships:

$$E(T) = c\sqrt{D},$$

and

$$E(T) = a + bD.$$

A regression fit determines the values of the parameters a, b, c, and d that minimize the sum of the squares of the errors between the fitted curve and the data.

Fitting Equation (6.4) to the data requires finding a square-root function for short runs and a linear function for long runs that intersect in a single point and have the same slope at that point. Mathematically the problem is:

minimize

$$\sum_{i=1}^{N_d} (T_i - c\sqrt{D_i})^2 + \sum_{i=N_d+1}^{N} (T_i - a - bD_i)^2,$$

subject to

$$c\sqrt{d} = a + bd \quad \text{(the curves intersect at point } d\text{)}$$

and

$$\dfrac{c}{2\sqrt{d}} = b \quad \text{(the curves are tangent at point } d\text{)},$$

where

(T_i, D_i) for $i = 1, \ldots, N$ are the observed travel-time, travel-distance pairs ordered by increasing distance

c is the parameter of the square-root portion of the function

a and b are the parameters of the linear portion of the function

d is the distance at which the two segments of the function are tangent

N_d (for any given d) is the number of observed distances that are less than or equal to d.

The constraints specify the tangency conditions. That is, calculations of the best values of a, b, c, and d cannot allow arbitrary values for all four parameters; rather they must assure that they are related in such a way that the two parts of the curve meet and are tangent at $D = d$.

An iterative method was developed to solve this constrained minimization problem for the estimation of the parameters (see Kolesar and Walker (1974) for details).

6.3.2 Results from the Travel Time Experiment in New York City

Fifteen units participated in the New York City experiment described here: thirteen ladder companies and two battalion chiefs' cars. Only moderately busy companies were selected, since the process of data collection would have been unduly burdensome to the very busy units, and it would have taken months to gather data on an adequate number of responses with units that were not busy enough. Each unit was provided with a stopwatch and copies of a form to keep a record of all responses made *from quarters*. Responses made when returning from an earlier run or from a position in the field were not included, because of the difficulty of accurately recording times, distances, and locations at time of dispatch.

In making the selection of units, consideration was given to obtaining a good geographical spread of the participating companies, but the need for odometers that recorded in tenths of miles limited the experiment to ladder companies and battalion chiefs. The absence of engines in the experiment may have introduced an element of bias in the results, since engines are generally smaller than ladders and may be able to maneuver more easily and faster in traffic and narrow streets.

In order to encourage cooperation in collecting data, the recording forms were kept simple and anonymous. Consequently, such information as the date, the identity of the officer recording the data, and special circumstances (such as weather or road conditions) were not recorded. As a result, the experimental design was imperfect. This is typically the case when performing policy analysis. One cannot hope for perfect experiments. One does require that they be carefully done and adequate to the end purposes of the study, as was the case here.

Regressions and related analyses were done separately for each participating company. In addition, separate regressions were done for: (1) runs (responses) to alarms to which the company was the closest ladder; (2) runs to alarms to which it was the second-closest ladder; and (3) all runs, including runs made to more distant alarms. The purpose of these separate analyses was to determine how the travel-time patterns varied among companies, and how they differed, if at all, for short runs and for longer runs. The detailed results have been described by Kolesar and Walker (1974), and Kolesar, Walker, and Hausner (1975).

The major result of this analysis was that, although the parameter values for different companies exhibit statistically significant variations, the differences are not very large, and, for many purposes, a single function can be used for all companies in the city.

The best fit of Equation (6.4) to the combined data from the 1772 responses made by the thirteen participating ladder companies produced the estimates:

$$E(T) = 2.88 \sqrt{D} \qquad D \leq 0.88 \text{ miles}$$
$$E(T) = 1.35 + 1.53D \qquad D \geq 0.88 \text{ miles.}$$

Referring to the notation used in Equation (6.6), this equation implies that the acceleration cutoff distance, D_c, is 0.44 miles, the cruising speed, v_c, is 39.2 miles per hour, and the acceleration, z, is 29.0 miles per hour per minute.

This function, fitted to the experimental data, is shown in Figure 6.3. For clarity of presentation, dots on the figure show the average travel time for all observed responses having the same distance (grouped to the nearest 0.1 mile). However, the actual data points were used as input to the regression program.[7] The goodness of fit is largely insensitive to the choice of d in the range from 0.6 to 1.2 miles. Further, for different values of d in this range, the values of the parameters are relatively stable. The reason for this is the near linearity of the square-root function in this range.

6.3.3 Results of Travel Time Experiments in Other Cities

Travel time experiments, similar to the New York City experiment, have been carried out in a number of other cities. The results have been consistent with the findings discussed above. Figure 6.4, which shows

---

[7] Exactly the same fit curve is obtained by using as input the average travel time for each travel distance and weighting each average by the number of observations it represents.

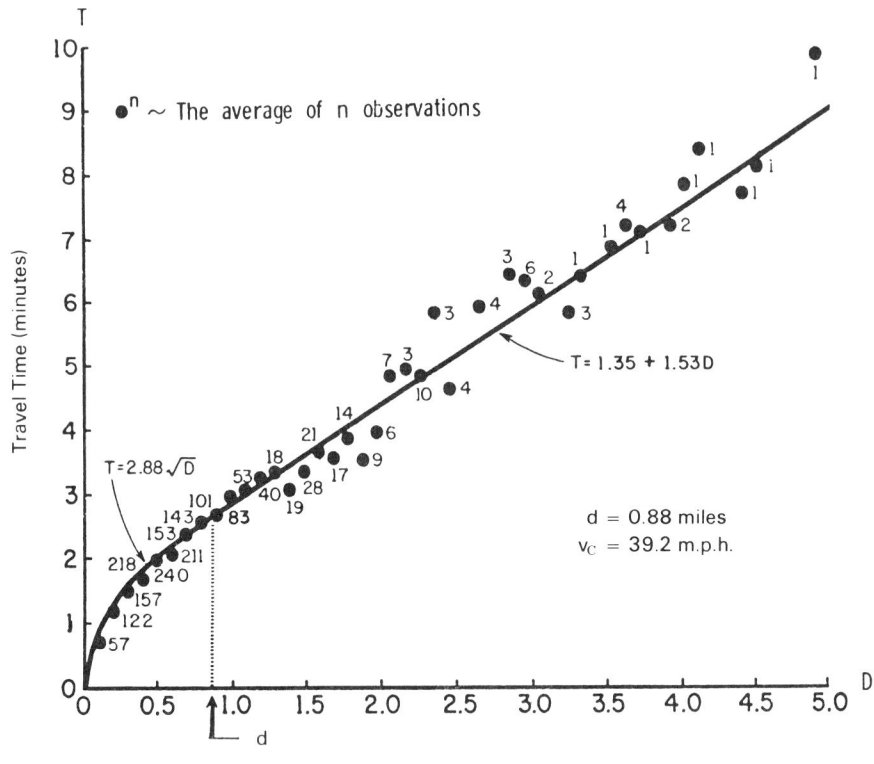

FIGURE 6.3. Travel time vs. distance: all responses, all companies, New York City.

the results for Trenton, New Jersey, is typical of the results from other cities. (In Figure 6.4 all data points are shown, not just the averages for each distance.) Among the fire departments that have performed similar experiments are those in:

Trenton, New Jersey (Hausner and Walker, 1975).
Yonkers, New York (Hausner, Walker, and Swersey, 1974).
Denver, Colorado (Hendrick et al., 1975).
Wilmington, Delaware (Walker, Singleton, and Smith, 1975).

With the exception of Denver, the experiment was performed in the same way in each city as it was performed in New York. In Denver, the travel time for each response was recorded by dispatchers at a central location (the dispatching office) using an electric timer. The timer was started as soon as the dispatcher finished announcing the incident over the voice-alarm system. It was stopped when the first vehicle announced

6.3 Estimating Point-to-point Travel Times

its arrival at the scene of the incident by radio. The time was recorded on the dispatcher's fire alarm sheet, which also recorded the address of the incident and the identity of the first vehicle to arrive. A Census Bureau address-matching program was used to assign (x, y) coordinates to the locations of all firehouses and all incidents for which travel times

FIGURE 6.4. Relationship between travel time and response distance: Trenton. All data points are shown (not just averages).

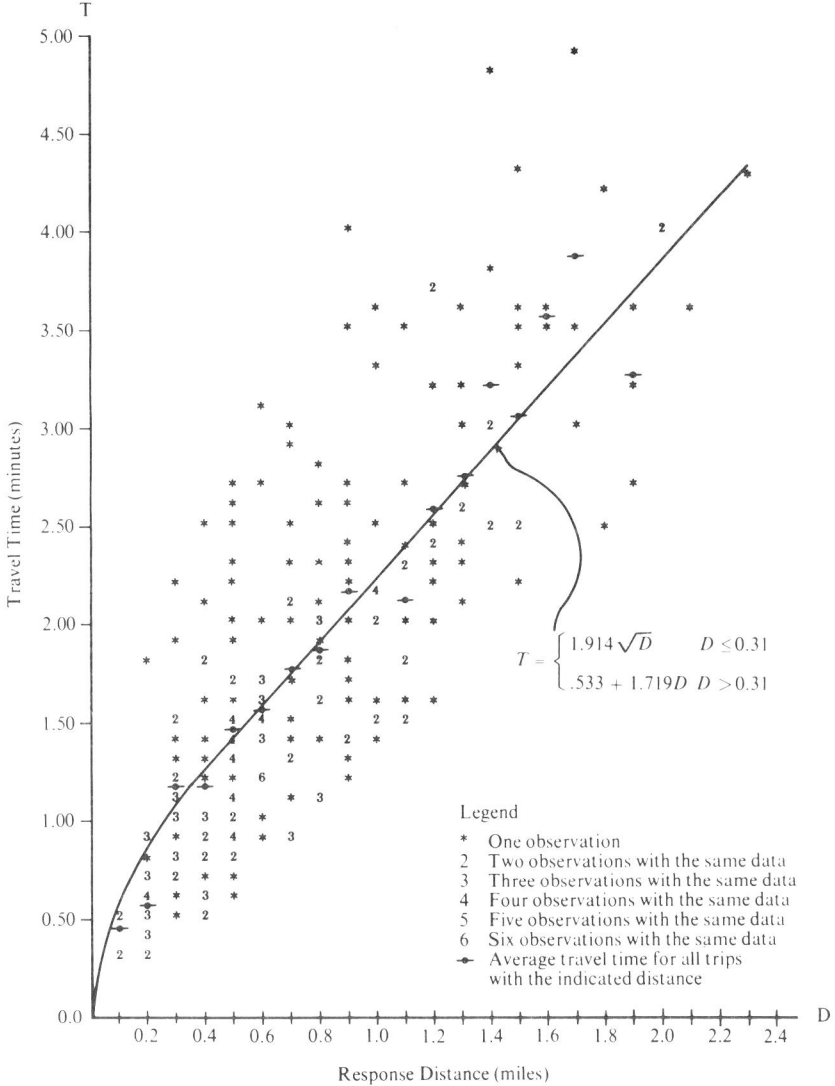

$$T = \begin{cases} 1.914\sqrt{D} & D \leq 0.31 \\ .533 + 1.719D & D > 0.31 \end{cases}$$

Legend
* One observation
2 Two observations with the same data
3 Three observations with the same data
4 Four observations with the same data
5 Five observations with the same data
6 Six observations with the same data
● Average travel time for all trips with the indicated distance

had been recorded. The travel distances for each of those responses were then estimated by calculating the right-angle distance between the firehouse and the incident location (Equation (6.1)).

The data from all four cities were processed by the same regression programs, which fit a number of different functions, including the piecewise linear/square-root function given by Equation (6.4). The values of parameters a, b, c, and d that provided the best fit to the data are given in Table 6.2.

The travel time functions for the four cities are remarkably similar to each other. In fact, they are so similar that it appears that a single function, based on combined observations in the four cities, can be used in any city—at least until a travel time experiment can be set up, run, and analyzed. The regression program was used to determine the combined parameters. The resulting function given by Equation (6.5) should provide quite good travel time estimates in most cities.

The travel speed characteristics were also quite consistent among the cities. We take as a broad measure of speed the reciprocal of the linear part of the time–distance function, and call it the cruising speed. Table 6.3 shows the cruising speeds derived from the references cited above.

6.3.4 Variation in Response Speeds by Time of Day

In each of the cities studied, an analysis was conducted to determine if fire companies travel slower at some times of day than at others. This is particularly important if a department is considering policies that vary the number of companies on duty and the number of companies dispatched to alarms at different times of the day. The questions are: (1) Do fire companies travel faster or slower in daylight than in the dark? (2) How much slower do fire companies travel during rush hours?

The results of analysis in a range of cities are simple and surprising. First, no practical differences were found between travel speeds under conditions of daylight and darkness. Second, while speeds were somewhat slower during rush hours, they were closer to speeds at other hours than anticipated. The reduction in average speed (about 20 percent) was

TABLE 6.2. Parameters of the travel time function in four cities.

City	a	b	c	d	No. of Responses
Wilmington	0.63	1.79	2.10	0.35	243
Trenton	0.53	1.72	1.91	0.31	245
Yonkers	0.62	1.79	2.12	0.35	378
Denver	0.62	1.53	1.95	0.40	1575
All Four Cities	0.65	1.70	2.10	0.38	2441

TABLE 6.3. Estimated cruising speeds in five cities.

City	Cruising Speeds (mph)
New York, New York	39.2
Trenton, New Jersey	34.9
Wilmington, Delaware	35.5
Denver, Colorado	34.0
Yonkers, New York	33.9

greatest during the 8 A.M. to 9 A.M. period. The data in Tables 6.4, 6.5, and 6.6 support these conclusions.[8]

Table 6.4 shows the average speed and the standard deviation of speed for runs by the thirteen ladders in the New York City experiment, grouped by two-hour intervals and by division of the day into the following four periods: 5 A.M. to 8 P.M. (these are taken to be daylight hours), excluding the "rush hours"; 8 P.M. to 5 A.M. (these are taken to be hours of darkness); and two rush-hour periods, 8 A.M. to 9 A.M. and 4:30 to 5:30 P.M. The results indicate that, although there are time-of-day effects, they are not strong. Table 6.5 shows the small variation in average speed over the day in Wilmington, Trenton, Yonkers and Jersey City.

Table 6.6 shows the results of additional analysis performed on the New York City data to check for possible confounding of speed and distance effects with time-of-day effects. Separate regressions were made of the square-root travel time model for hours of darkness, for daylight hours excluding rush hours, and for rush hours. The table gives the estimated values of $\hat{c}$, the square-root model parameter, as well as $\bar{v}$, the average speed, $\bar{D}$, the average response distance, and $\bar{T}$, the average travel time. The results indicate clearly that response speed does not change markedly by time of day.

6.4 THE SQUARE-ROOT LAW FOR ESTIMATING AVERAGE REGIONAL TRAVEL DISTANCES

6.4.1 Introduction

In this section we discuss a simple model for estimating the average travel *distance* in a region. (Average regional travel *time* is treated in Section 6.5.) This model is one of the major results of our research on

---

[8] One qualification about these observations must be made. Since dates were not recorded, weekends and weekdays could not be separated. A reasonable assumption is that the rush-hour effect would be stronger on weekdays. However, in the Denver analysis, weekdays were separated from weekends, and the findings were similar.

TABLE 6.4. Response speeds (miles/hour) by time of day in New York City.

	Average Speed	Standard Deviation of Speed	Number of Observations
0000–0200	19.2	7.3	136
0200–0400	17.7	6.8	104
0400–0600	18.0	7.7	62
0600–0800	17.7	7.1	45
0800–1000	16.2	6.7	61
1000–1200	18.3	7.6	117
1200–1400	18.9	6.9	165
1400–1600	18.4	7.3	205
1600–1800	17.0	7.6	200
1800–2000	18.9	7.3	216
2000–2200	18.5	7.5	239
2200–2400	18.8	7.2	272
0500–2000 (Daylight; rush hours excluded)	18.2	7.3	904
2000–0500 (Dark)	18.6	7.3	742
0800–0900 (Morning rush hour)	14.3	5.2	27
1630–1730 (Evening rush hour)	18.2	7.6	99
All hours	18.3	7.3	1772

fire company deployment. It achieves a high score on three key criteria by which a mathematical model should be judged.

First, the model is very simple. It links travel distances to the key decision variable—the number of companies in a region—via an equation that can literally be used to calculate results on the back of an envelope.

Second, the model is justified by mathematical analysis. This analysis depends only on formal mathematical logic that has been carried out under many different assumptions, which all lead to the same basic result. This mathematical justification, together with the fact that square root models for average distances are used in the physical sciences, gives one confidence in the strength of this model.

Third, the model has been tested and verified empirically. The theoretical derivations mentioned above lend an air of plausibility to the model, but each is based on simplifying assumptions that are not true in the real world. Hence empirical testing was called for before the model could be used with complete confidence. The testing used simulation data and "real world" data. It also permitted us to estimate a scale factor whose value was not completely specified by the theory.

6.4 Square-root Law for Estimating Travel Distances

TABLE 6.5. Response speeds (miles/hour) by time of day in four cities. The variables are $\bar{v}$ = average speed; n = number of observations.

Time of day	Wilmington $\bar{v}$	n	Trenton $\bar{v}$	n	Yonkers $\bar{v}$	n	Jersey City $\bar{v}$	n
0001–0200	19.9	21	27.0	28	28.4	25	21.9	29
0201–0400	23.0	14	24.0	7	25.8	18	21.3	2
0401–0600	26.6	11	25.0	6	25.8	6	20.5	7
0601–0800	21.7	6	22.6	5	24.8	6	15.1	6
0801–1000	24.5	15	27.3	8	27.8	22	21.1	9
1001–1200	30.9	17	24.5	12	25.5	29	19.3	13
1201–1400	23.5	22	26.1	21	27.4	47	18.9	25
1401–1600	24.7	27	27.4	20	23.5	36	20.6	28
1601–1800	24.5	28	23.9	25	28.5	31	20.5	31
1801–2000	23.6	43	25.1	28	26.5	53	19.4	23
2001–2200	25.1	25	25.1	49	24.4	61	20.4	22
2201–2400	25.5	14	24.9	36	24.8	44	21.1	17
All responses	24.4	243	25.4	245	26.0	378	20.2	212

Before we discuss the model's derivation and testing, a word of caution. The model is designed to estimate the average travel distance in a reasonably large region over an extended period of time. While it is true that this is an important measure of performance, such an average must be used with some caution. *It would be irresponsible to implement any significant change in deployment on the basis of a regional average, however estimated.* Computation of regional averages is the first step in a deployment analysis. Its primary purpose is to identify options that

TABLE 6.6. Regressions to isolate time-of-day effects in New York City. The symbol definitions are: $\hat{c}$ = fitted parameter of the square-root model $T = c\sqrt{D}$, which can be interpreted as the average travel time for a one-mile run in minutes; $\bar{v}$ = average response speed (mph); $\bar{D}$ = average response distance (miles); $\bar{T}$ = average travel time (minutes).

Hours	First-Due Runs $\hat{c}$	$\bar{v}$	$\bar{D}$	$\bar{T}$	Second-Due Runs $\hat{c}$	$\bar{v}$	$\bar{D}$	$\bar{T}$	All Runs $\hat{c}$	$\bar{v}$	$\bar{D}$	$\bar{T}$
0500–0200 No rush hours (Daylight)	2.73	16.1	.45	1.77	3.11	17.8	.75	2.67	2.95	16.9	.58	2.16
2000–0500 (Dark)	2.77	16.4	.48	1.85	3.08	17.6	.73	2.59	2.91	17.0	.58	2.14
Rush hours	2.61	16.0	.44	1.70	3.17	16.7	.73	2.70	2.90	16.6	.57	2.12
All hours combined	2.75	16.2	.46	1.80	3.10	17.7	.74	2.64	2.93	16.9	.58	2.15

look attractive and to eliminate obviously inferior options. Those that appear attractive must then be examined in greater spatial and temporal detail using other models that provide other measures of performance.

6.4.2 Derivation of the Square-Root Law

It is possible to calculate the average travel distance in a region by first estimating the specific point-to-point distances for each possible trip in the region and then computing a weighted average of these distances. The weight for a particular trip should be the proportion of the total number of trips made in the region that it represents. It is often possible to avoid this lengthy calculation. We present here a simple method for approximating average travel distances in a region, which is called the square-root law.

Suppose we wish to compute the average travel distance of engine companies to fires in a particular region of the city.[9] We will be computing this average over all the engines and alarm boxes in the region. If D_1 denotes the distance traveled by the closest available engine, then we denote by $E(D_1)$ the average (or expected) travel distance.

In its simplest form the square-root law states that $E(D_1)$, the expected distance between the points in the region at which fires occur and the location of the closest available engine company, is given by

$$E(D_1) = k_1 \sqrt{A/N}, \qquad (6.7)$$

where k_1 is a constant of proportionality, A is the area of the region, and N is the number of firehouses in the region that have engines available to respond.

We illustrate the origin and use of this relation by a straightforward and idealized example. Consider a mathematical model of a city having a single firehouse located at the origin (coordinates $x = 0$, $y = 0$) of a two-dimensional (x,y) coordinate system; the city boundaries form a square with corners on the x and y axes, and its streets form a dense rectangular grid parallel to the axes.[10] This defines a diamond-shaped city with a firehouse at its center, as shown in Figure 6.5. Let the city's area be A square miles. Within the city, fires are assumed to occur at random, with equal probability and severity everywhere (i.e., fire hazards and incidence are homogeneous).

In this example we also assume that the fire company is always avail-

---

[9] Of course, the same approach can be used for ladder companies but in the discussion we will consider engines as an illustration.

[10] With right-angle travel, all points on the boundary of this square are the same distance from the center.

6.4 Square-root Law for Estimating Travel Distances

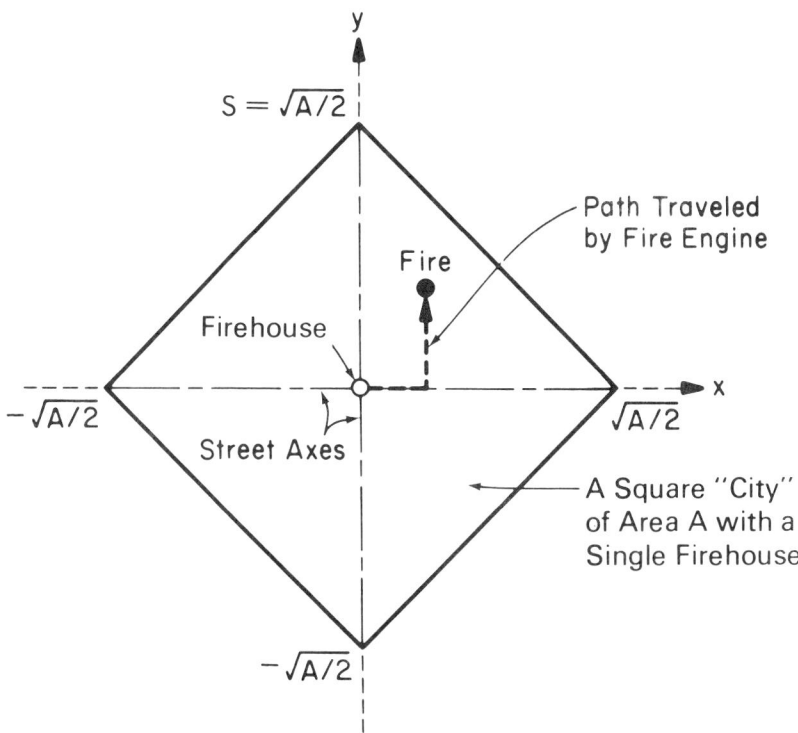

FIGURE 6.5. An idealized city with one firehouse.

able to respond when an alarm is received (we will consider the effects of unavailability later). Under these assumptions, the maximum response distance, S, in the city is the right-angle distance from the center to one of the corners, and is $\sqrt{A/2}$.[11]

We would like to determine the expected response distance for this city's fire company. We begin by answering the question "What is the chance that the fire company will have to travel less than s miles?" for any distance s that lies between 0 and $\sqrt{A/2}$. To answer the question, consider a square that is $s\sqrt{2}$ on a side, which is centered inside the original one and is oriented the same way. Every point inside this square is no further than s from the firehouse, while every point outside it is further than s from the firehouse. The chance that the company will have to travel less than s miles is, then, the probability that an alarm occurs within the smaller square. This probability is the same as the ratio of the

---

[11] In a square of area A, each side has length $\sqrt{A}$, and the distance from the origin to a corner is half of a diagonal or $\sqrt{A/2}$.

area of the small square to the area of the city. That is

$$P(\text{response distance} \leq s) = [s\sqrt{2}]^2/A.$$

The probability density of response distance, $f(s)$, can then be obtained by differentiation: $f(s) = 4s/A$. So the expected response distance is given by:

$$\begin{aligned}
E(D_1) &= \int_0^{\sqrt{A/2}} s\, f(s)\, ds = \int_0^{\sqrt{A/2}} [4s^2/A]\, ds \\
&= \tfrac{4}{3}[s^3/A]_0^{\sqrt{A/2}} \\
&= \tfrac{4}{3}[\sqrt{A/2}]^3/A \\
&= (\sqrt{2}/3)\sqrt{A}.
\end{aligned}$$

Hence, in the case of a single company ($N = 1$) in a square city, the square-root law holds with $k_1 = \sqrt{2/3} = 0.4714$.

Now suppose that four stations instead of one were located in the city, as shown in Figure 6.6. The city is now divided into four districts, each with one-fourth of the total city area and each with boundaries one-half

FIGURE 6.6. An idealized city with four firehouses.

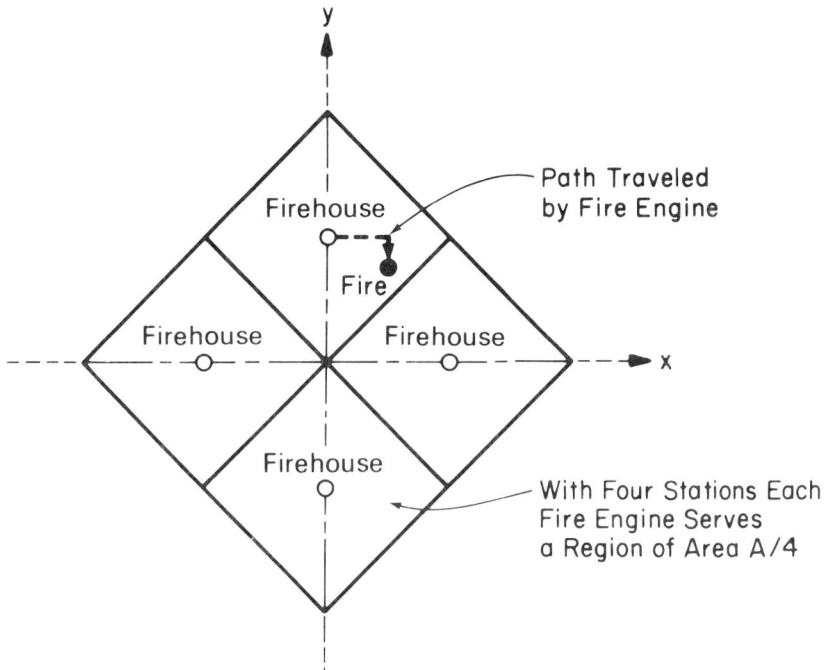

6.4 Square-root Law for Estimating Travel Distances

the length of the total city boundary. Indeed, all distances in the new districts are half the corresponding distances in the city as a whole. Hence, it follows that the average response distance is now

$$E(D_1) = \frac{1}{2}\frac{\sqrt{2}}{3}\sqrt{A} = \frac{\sqrt{2}}{3}\sqrt{A/4} = \frac{\sqrt{2}}{3}\sqrt{A/N},$$

because now $N = 4$. So for a square city with $N = 4$ companies located as shown in Figure 6.6, we have shown that

$$E(D_1) = k_1 \sqrt{A/N}.$$

This example could be further continued by dividing each of the four squares into four squares, thereby producing $N = 16$ stations and response distances that are $\frac{1}{4}$ as long as in the one-station case. Thus, we have shown that

$$E(D_1) = \frac{\sqrt{2}}{3}\sqrt{A/N},$$

for $N = 1, 4$, and 16, and it is clear that the equation is true for $N = 64$ and higher powers of four. However, the square-root law shown in Equation (6.7) is quite general, and does not simply apply to idealized square cities with right-angle travel, and a number of companies that is some power of 4. In fact, as explained by Kolesar and Blum (1973 and 1975), the square-root law actually reflects the basic dimensional relation that *area is proportional to distance squared*, which implies that *distance is proportional to the square root of area*.

When applied to other situations, the constant k_1 in Equation (6.7) will be different from 0.4714, but the basic form of the relationship remains the same. Moreover, for estimating the average travel distance D_2 for the second-closest engine, a similar relationship holds:

$$E(D_2) = k_2 \sqrt{A/N}. \tag{6.8}$$

Some of the values of k_1 and k_2 derived by Kolesar and Blum are shown in Table 6.7.

The numerical values in Table 6.7 illustrate several points. First, they suggest that—at least for regions with homogeneous fire hazards and alarm rates—the potential improvement in average response distance that can be achieved by "optimal" firehouse location or dynamic relocation of units during busy periods is limited (certainly less than 25 percent, which is the greatest difference between the completely random location and optimal location cases in Table 6.6). In practice, since actual locations are likely to lie somewhere between being optimally and randomly located, realizable gains for homogeneous regions will be less. (See Larson and Stevenson (1971) for elaboration of this point.) Second, the

TABLE 6.7. Constants for the square-root law when alarms are spatially uniform. The expected response distance for the nth closest company is obtained by multiplying k_n by $\sqrt{A/N}$, where A is the area of the region and N is the number of companies available at the time of dispatch. Optimal locations yield the lowest possible average travel distance for first-arriving company.

Metric	Companies are Randomly Located		Companies are Uniformly and Optimally Located	
	k_1	k_2	k_1	k_2
Euclidean (straight-line) travel	0.5000	0.7500	0.3772	0.7287
Right-angle travel	0.6267	0.9400	0.4714	0.9428

constants of proportionality are close enough to each other to suggest that the range of constants found in the real world would be small. If so, the square-root law would be a practical tool for estimating travel distances.

In the preceding discussion we have assumed that each firehouse has a company available and ready to respond when an alarm is received. In Chapter 7 we examine some of the effects on the square-root law of companies being unavailable for dispatch. Queuing theory is used to look at the effect on the square-root law of dynamic changes in the number of firehouses from which units are immediately available to respond.

Since the number of companies available to dispatch will vary from time to time, it is not appropriate to use the number of firehouses as the value for N if Equation (6.7) is being used to estimate the average travel distance to alarms over the course of time, say an hour, several hours, etc. However, as the discussion in Chapter 7 shows, if the average number of available engines in a region is not too small (say, more than 2.0), a reasonable approximation is to replace N in Equation (6.7) by $E(N)$, the expected (long run average) number of firehouses having at least one engine company available.[12] The equation then reads:

$$E(D_1) = k_1 \sqrt{A/E(N)}, \tag{6.9}$$

where $E(D_1)$ is the expected travel distance for the first-arriving engine, with the expectation taken with respect to the fluctuations in engine availability over time, as well as with respect to the geographical distribution of alarms. Equation (6.9), and its generalization for the nth-arriv-

---

[12] Chapter 7 also describes how $E(N)$ can be estimated from the number of firehouses, the alarm rate in the region, and average service times. In cases where one engine is located in each station, $E(N)$ is found by subtracting the product of the alarm rate and the average number of engine company hours per alarm from the total number of engine houses.

ing engine

$$E(D_n) = k_n \sqrt{A/E(N)}, \qquad (6.10)$$

are the most useful forms of the square-root law for policy purposes.

In the next section we discuss how a detailed simulation model was used to test the square-root law under conditions approximating reality. With this model it was possible to incorporate the effects of uneven distribution of alarms and firehouses in the region, boundaries of the region, fire company unavailability, and other factors.

6.4.3 Testing the Square-Root Law with Simulation and Empirical Data

In deriving the square-root law mathematically, Kolesar and Blum made a number of assumptions:

Alarms are distributed randomly but with uniform probability density throughout the region of interest

Firehouses are spread either in a regular pattern or randomly throughout the region of interest

Boundary effects are insignificant[13]

Units are always available to respond

Fire companies travel either on a straight line between two points or on a dense rectangular grid of streets.

In the real world, of course, none of these assumptions is strictly true. Complications that are not consistent with this simple model abound: a city is of finite size and irregular shape; the distribution of units is not homogeneous; several companies (in varying numbers) are dispatched to each alarm; in the event of a very serious fire, companies from other regions may be relocated into the depleted area; and responding units must follow actual street patterns that are often irregular, observe one-way streets, and route themselves around obstacles such as parks and rivers. The question is: notwithstanding such complications, does the square-root law still provide useful estimates of average response distances? We examine the validity of the square-root law using both simulation and empirical data.

Two relationships will be examined. To be precise in their specifica-

---

[13] This means that the locations near the boundary of the region do not constitute a substantial fraction of the total area. Such an assumption would be incorrect in the case of a long, thin peninsula, for example.

tions, we adopt the following notation:

n is the number of firehouses with engine companies (locations from which engines can respond) in the region being studied;

$j = 1, 2, \ldots$, indexes a particular (random) sequence of fire alarms;

T_j denotes the response distance of the closest available engine company to alarm j;

N_j denotes the (random) number of firehouses with engine companies available to respond when alarm j occurs.

(As in the earlier discussion, we will speak of engine companies, but the results apply equally well to ladder companies.) We will examine:

1. *The relationship between $E(D)$ and N_j.* We suppose that n, the number of firehouses with engine companies stationed in the region, is fixed and, thus, the random variable N_j can vary between 0 and n. We shall be interested in determining if the relation between expected response distance and the number of houses with engine companies available when the alarm comes in, is given by the square-root law; that is, if $E(D_i|N_j) = k_i \sqrt{A/N_j}$. Of course, this relationship cannot be correct when $N_j = 0$. ($N_j = 0$ means that no engine companies are available in the region, in which case a company responds from elsewhere.)

2. *The relationship between $E(D)$ and n.* We are interested in the effect that varying n (the number of firehouses with engine companies) will have on the expected response distance to alarms. The arguments and mathematics of the previous section support the hypothesis that

$$E(D_i(n)) = k_i \sqrt{\frac{A}{E(N_j)}}$$
$$= k_i \sqrt{\frac{A}{n - \text{(average number of empty engine houses)}}}.$$

Since n is a major policy variable that management can control, this relation, if valid, is of more practical use than that between $E(D)$ and N_j.

Collecting empirical data to test these relationships would be a formidable task. Consider how we might test the first of them for closest engines. Data could be gathered by posting an observer in the dispatching office who would note and record the number of fire companies available to respond at the instants when alarms are dispatched ($N_1, N_2, \ldots$). Simultaneously, each responding unit could note and record odometer readings before and after each response, so the corresponding first-arriving unit response distances could be determined ($D_1^1, D_1^2, \ldots$). By assembling this information, we would produce a set of data (D_1^1, N_1), (D_1^2, N_2), ..., etc. All this, however, is easier said than done. For

6.4 Square-root Law for Estimating Travel Distances

example, few fire companies are equipped with odometers that give distance readings except to the nearest mile! During busy periods, fire companies may be dispatched while they are returning from an earlier call before arriving at their home station, and it would be extremely difficult, and perhaps disruptive of their primary responsibilities, to record such response distances.

Formal validation of the second relationship with empirical data is literally impossible, except on the rare occasions when fire companies are added or removed in a region for other reasons. Such changes, if made, would usually be minor. A meaningful experiment would require operating with considerably different numbers of fire companies assigned to the experimental region. Cost and risk preclude such experiments. As a result, the square-root law was validated using computer simulations and historical data.

The validation experiment used the simulation model of firefighting operations discussed in Chapter 13. The conditions simulated varied over a broad range: alarm rates were varied from 5 to 30 alarms per hour and the number of active ladder companies was varied from 12 to 31. In each simulation, the number of engine companies was fixed at 37. The locations of the engine companies were the actual locations of existing companies in the Bronx at that time. The ladder company locations were chosen in the following way: In simulations with fewer than the existing 24 ladder companies, a subset of the existing locations was used that gave (intuitively) a good geographical distribution of ladders throughout the Bronx. For simulations with additional ladder companies, new locations were chosen that appeared to be good spots at which to add new companies.

Alarm locations and alarm patterns were also chosen to imitate reality. In addition, the simulation program imitated actual dispatching procedures, including the dispatch of units that were returning from other incidents. Travel distances were simulated using the method mentioned in Section 6.2 (Carter, 1974, pp. 35–44).

In each case a long time period was simulated, during which the alarm rate and number of active units were unchanged. The simulation durations were chosen so that, in each case, about 3500 alarms were handled. This sample size was selected after statistical analysis of the random variation in simulation output statistics. The results produced should be interpreted as estimates of performance of "steady state" behavior of the system under the conditions simulated.[14] Table 6.8 briefly lists the simulations carried out.

---

[14] See Section 7.1.5 for a discussion of "steady state" behavior.

TABLE 6.8. Conditions simulated.

Simulation Number	Alarm Rate (alarms/hour)	Number of Active Ladders	Number of Active Engines
1	30	31	37
2	5	31	37
3	5	24	37
4	10	20	37
5	30	20	37
6	5	12	37
7	10	12	37

The Relation Between $E(D_i)$ and N. The simulation program recorded the response distances $(D_i{}^j)$ and the number of companies available at the instant of dispatch (N_j) for each alarm, j. These data were accumulated separately for two regions of the Bronx; they were, approximately, the South Bronx and the rest of the Bronx. The data were collected for the closest engines and ladders to each alarm ($i = 1$), as well as for the second- and third-closest units for those alarms to which such units were dispatched ($i = 2$ and $i = 3$).

In order to analyze these data and determine if the square-root law was appropriate, the response distances for each value of N were averaged, and the resulting averages ($\bar{D}$'s) were plotted against the numbers of units available (N's) for each individual set of data. (By an individual set of data we mean, for example, data for second-closest ladders in the North Bronx from the simulation run with 12 active ladder companies and an alarm rate of 10 alarms per hour.) In addition, for each set of data we used the method of least-squares regression to determine the parameters of two response distance models:

$$\bar{D}_i = k_i N^{-1/2} \sqrt{A} = k_i \sqrt{A/N}; \qquad (6.11)$$

$$\bar{D}_i = \alpha_i N^{\beta_i} \sqrt{A}. \qquad (6.12)$$

We were concerned with how well these models fit the data. If square-root relations hold, Equations (6.11) and (6.12) should both fit well, and estimates of β should be "close" to $-\frac{1}{2}$. Determining the accuracy of the estimates of the parameters k_i, α_i, and β_i is not easy, since the simulation data do not satisfy the conditions requisite for classical statistical analysis. For example, the observations are not independent, and the square-root relation itself implies unequal variances. (The standard deviation of travel time also obeys a square-root law.) Examination of the sum of squared errors indicated, of course, that Equation (6.12) fit better than

6.4 Square-root Law for Estimating Travel Distances   189

Equation (6.11),[15] but the difference between the models was small, and an "eyeball" check of the graphs revealed little difference between the two.

Temporarily setting aside any reservations about standard statistical tests, approximate 95 percent confidence contours were calculated for the coefficients α_i and β_i ($i = 1, 2$). In each case, these included $\beta_i = -\frac{1}{2}$, indicating that the square-root law would provide a good fit. These data are typical of other results. They indicate that an inverse square-root relationship between the average response time and N would provide good estimates, even in realistic, complex situations.

The same analysis was done for closest and second-closest engines and ladders, for the North and South Bronx, for each simulation—a total of 28 cases. In each case, the square-root fit was good, and the parameters of the more general model were close to those of the square-root model.

There was a general consistency between the square-root law parameters for engines and ladders, and between results from the North and South Bronx. Because of this overall consistency, the analysis was repeated with the data grouped from various simulations and for engines and ladders. This grouping yielded parameter estimates in which slight differences due to the geography of the regions and to the particular company locations were averaged out, and for this reason were more appropriate for use in other regions of the city. Figures 6.7 through 6.10 display the results of these groupings, and Table 6.9 gives a summary of the results. We note that the r^2 (coefficient of determination) values for the square-root model are quite high and that the graphs show a close correspondence between the fitted functions and the data. Moreover, when both were plotted on the same graph, one could hardly see any difference between the curves for the exponential model and the square-root model.

Data from previous simulations that had been made for other purposes was analyzed in the same way and yielded similar results. Some of these results have been reported by Kolesar and Blum (1973). On the basis of all the simulation results, it was concluded that the data confirmed the validity of the square-root law relating average response distance to the number of units available at the moment of dispatch. It was also observed that, although there appear to be differences in the parameter values between the regions (due again perhaps to different company locations, alarm locations, and boundary effects), they are not so great that a single

---

[15] Equation (6.11) is simply a special case of Equation (6.12), so the latter has to fit better. Here k_i, α_i, and β_i are the parameters to be chosen for best fit to the data pairs (D_i^j, N_j).

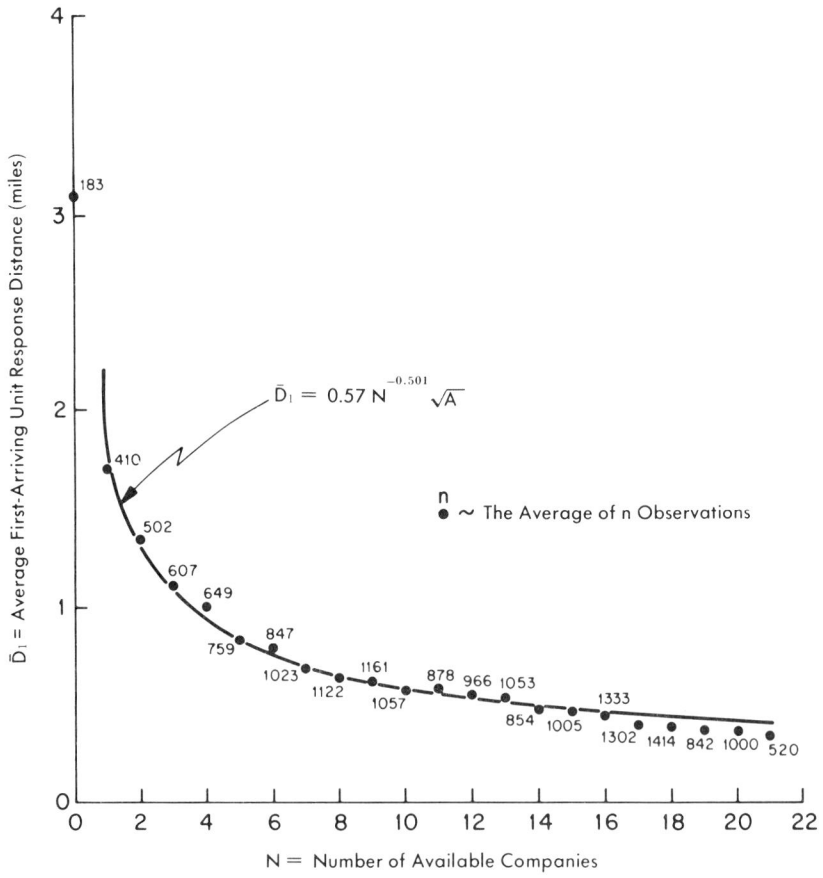

FIGURE 6.7. Simulated average response distance vs. the number of available companies (closest engine and ladder companies in the South Bronx).

average parameter value cannot generally be used. This point is important because it permits one to apply the square-root law to other regions and cities without the necessity of carrying out simulation experiments for each application.

The conclusions that can be drawn from this analysis is that the square-root laws shown in Equations (6.7) and (6.8) appear to be valid with constants k_1 and k_2 approximately equal to 0.6 and 1.2, respectively.

The Relation between $E(D_i)$ and n. We now turn attention to the validation of the relationship between long-run average response distance and n, the number of companies assigned to the region. The data and analysis just discussed indicate that a square-root law provides a good description of the relationship between average response distance and

6.4 Square-root Law for Estimating Travel Distances

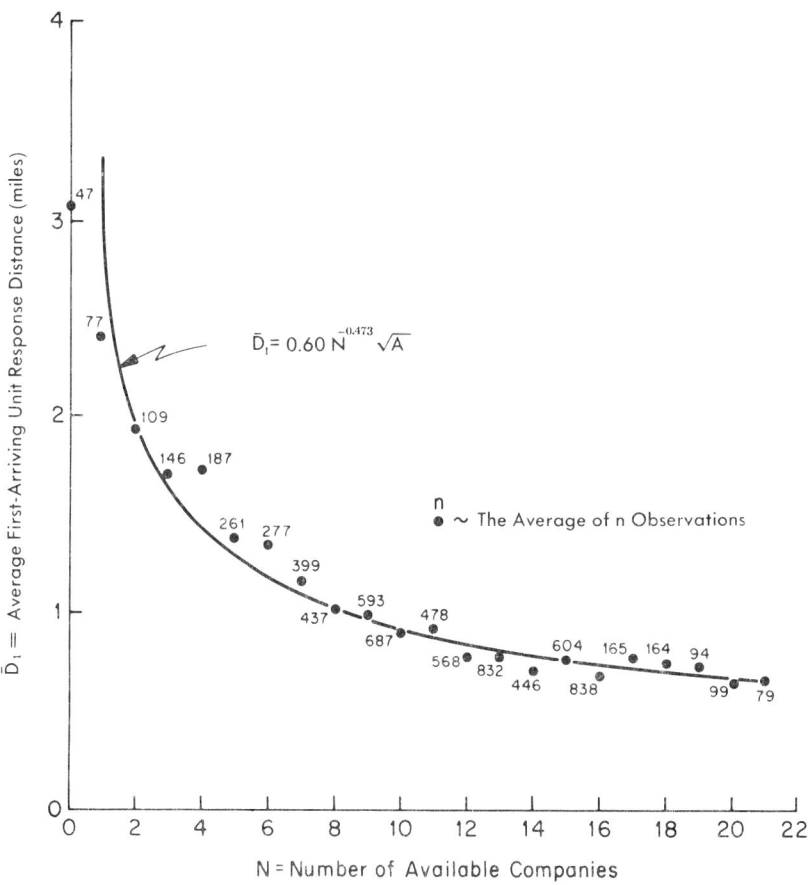

FIGURE 6.8. Simulated average response distance vs. the number of available companies (closest engine and ladder companies in the North Bronx).

the number of units available when an alarm occurs. But this does not assure that a square-root law describes the relationship between long-run average response distance and the average number of companies available to respond to an alarm. On the contrary, if a square-root law holds for the former, it cannot hold exactly for the latter since the inverse square-root function is strictly convex, and for a strictly convex function $g(\cdot)$ of a random variable X, $E(g(X)) > g(E(X))$ (Jensen's inequality).[16]

---

[16] This technicality is of some importance. The reader with a background in statistics will be aware of the fact that $E(X^2)$ is not equal to $(E(X))^2$. (Otherwise, all variances would be zero, since $\text{Var } X = E(X)^2 - (E(X))^2$.) In general, we are saying that

$$E(g(X)) = \int_{-\infty}^{\infty} g(t) dF_x(t) \neq g(E(X)) = g\left[\int_{-\infty}^{\infty} t\, dF_x(t)\right]$$

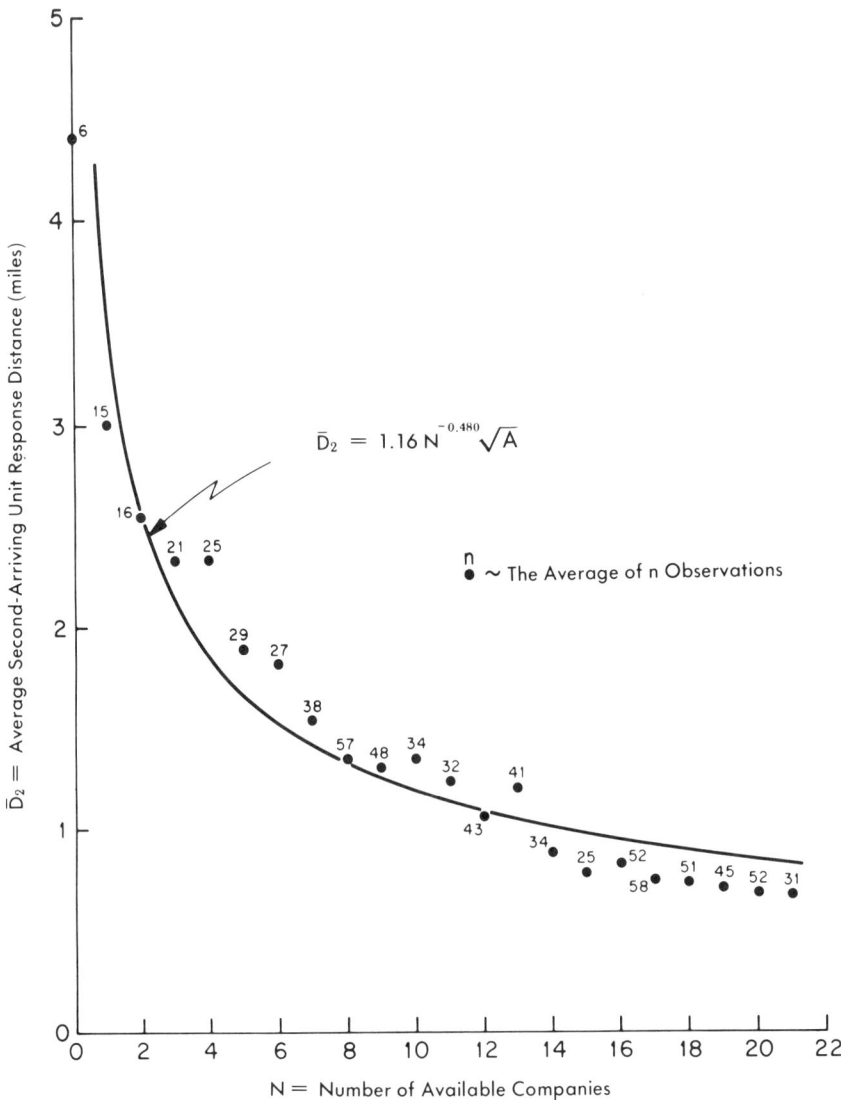

FIGURE 6.9. Simulated average response distance vs. the number of available companies (second closest engine and ladder companies in the South Bronx).

However, the errors in using $g(E(X))$ instead of the correct $E(g(x))$ are small in the range of parameters we have encountered in practice.

Figure 6.11 displays an example of simulated long-run average response distance for closest ladder versus average number of ladder companies available. (Recall that the simulations were run at different alarm rates, with 12 to 31 ladder companies assigned to the region.) Each of the

6.4 Square-root Law for Estimating Travel Distances

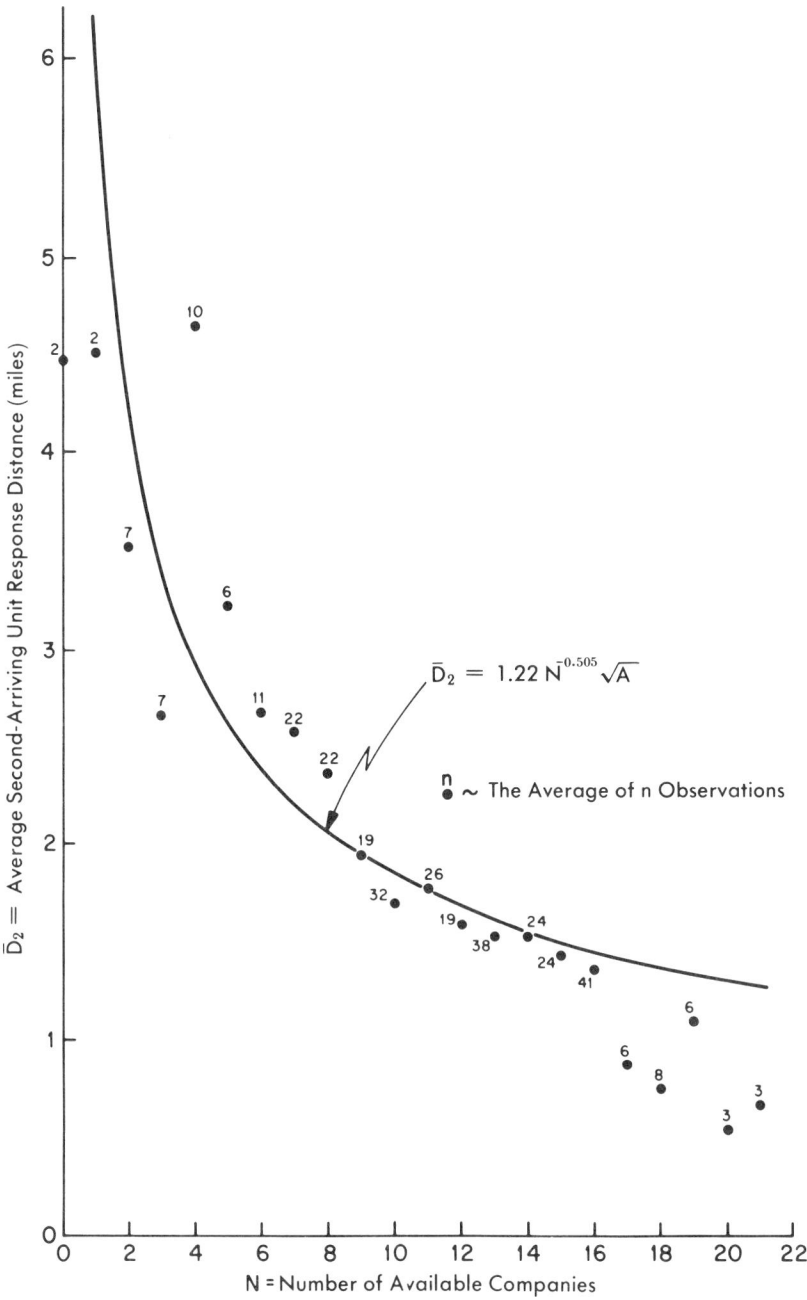

FIGURE 6.10. Simulated average response distance vs. the number of available companies (second closest engine and ladder companies in the North Bronx).

TABLE 6.9. The relation between $\bar{D}_i$ and N: results of regressions using simulation data.

Exponential model: $D_i = \alpha_i \sqrt{A}\ N^{\beta_i}$.
Square-root model: $\bar{D} = k_i \sqrt{A/N}$.
r^2 = The square of the sample correlation coefficient for the square-root model, called the coefficient of determination. This was determined from the actual data points, not from the averages shown in Figures 6.11 to 6.14.

Grouping	Parameters of Exponential Model $\hat{\alpha}_i$	$\hat{\beta}_i$	Parameter of Square-Root Model $\hat{k}_i$	r^2 for Square-Root Model
FIRST-ARRIVING ENGINES AND LADDERS ($i = 1$)				
North Bronx	0.57	−0.47	0.60	0.93
South Bronx	0.57	−0.50	0.57	0.97
SECOND-ARRIVING ENGINES AND LADDERS ($i = 2$)				
North Bronx	1.23	−0.51	1.22	0.73
South Bronx	1.13	−0.48	1.16	0.88

FIGURE 6.11. Simulated long-run average response distance vs. the average number of available companies (closest ladder companies in the Bronx).

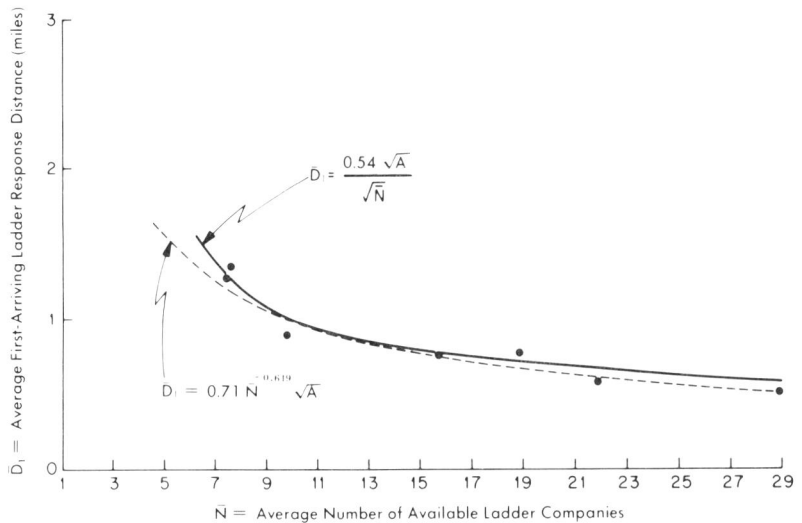

6.4 Square-root Law for Estimating Travel Distances

plotted points represents the results of an entire simulation run. In addition to the simulation data, we have also plotted regression fits of the functions

$$\bar{D}_1 = k_1 \sqrt{A/\bar{N}},$$
$$\bar{D}_1 = \alpha_1 \sqrt{A} \, (\bar{N})^{\beta_1}.$$

As before, we are concerned with how well these functions fit the data, whether β_1 is close to $-\frac{1}{2}$, and whether α_1 is close to k_1. As the figure shows, the fits are good and the two functions nearly coincide. We were also concerned with consistency of the results across the regions. Table 6.10 summarizes the results for three sets of regressions. Note the consistency with the values of k_1 given in Table 6.9. Other regressions—not shown here—were done of the standard deviation of response distance versus the average number of companies available. The theory indicates that this relationship should also be an inverse square-root function, and the analysis supports this hypothesis.

In summary, the results obtained from the simulations show that the square-root law shown in Equation (6.9) holds as a good approximation under the assumption of straight-line travel even when hazards, alarms, and unit locations are not homogeneous, when distances are computed with a complicated function, and when units may often be unavailable to respond.

Boundary Effects. In these simulations, statistics for regions near the boundaries were not specifically isolated to check the validity of the relation there, so we discuss what the boundary effects might be. Two sets of results are pertinent. Leamer (1968) considered location problems in a finite region, with homogeneous demands and distances calculated under the assumption of straight-line travel. He considered finite regions of regular shape (equilateral triangles, squares, and circles) in which the number of facilities varied. Choosing locations to minimize $E(D_1)$, he calculated $E(D_1)$ for $n = 1$ through 16. The results show that even for

TABLE 6.10. The relation between $\bar{D}_1$ and $\bar{N}$: results of regressions using simulation data. Exponential model: $\bar{D}_1 = \alpha_1 \sqrt{A} \, (\bar{N})^{\beta_1}$. Square-root model: $\bar{D}_1 = k_1 \sqrt{A/\bar{N}}$. r^2 = the square of the sample correlation coefficient for the square-root model.

Region	$\hat{\alpha}_1$	$\hat{\beta}_1$	$\hat{k}_1$	r^2
North Bronx	.50	−0.41	0.56	0.68
South Bronx	.75	−0.62	0.61	0.92
Entire Bronx	0.71	−0.62	0.54	0.86

small n, where boundary effects are greatest, the relationship between $E(D_1)$ and N could be well-approximated by an inverse square-root function. Chaiken (1973) calculated the exact distribution for travel distances in regions with randomly distributed vehicles. His results show that "the distance from points near the boundary of a finite region to the closest vehicle is large enough that the actual average distance can be substantially larger than the region-wide estimate." He still found the square-root relation valid, but cautioned against the use of a priori theoretical estimates for the proportionality constant, which may not adequately account for effects near the boundaries. Instead, he pointed out that the possibility of boundary effects indicates the desirability of using empirical estimates for k_1 that take into account the particular features of the region being examined. Thus, while boundary effects can be significant, they do not appear to affect the basic nature of the square-root relationship.

Empirical Data. We conclude this section by examining the results from two independent studies—one to determine fire station locations in Bristol, England, and the other to determine locations for ambulances in a suburban county near Washington, D.C.

Hogg (1968) examined 15 sites in Bristol, England at which fire stations could be located, drawing on data detailing the locations of 6813 fires that had occurred there between 1958 and 1964. Neither the site locations nor the fires were evenly distributed spatially, both being more dense in the center of the rectangular region under study. In Hogg's analysis, variations in the alarm pattern by time of day were considered, but possible unavailability of fire companies was ignored. She calculated travel times from knowledge of the distances involved and from estimates of travel speed, which varied by region and time of day. We are interested in analyzing Hogg's results for travel times, even though our main concern at the moment is distance, because when run lengths are long and the time-distance relation is approximately linear, her data can be used as a check on the square-root model for distances. Some of Hogg's results (replotted here in Figure 6.12) give average travel times as a function of N, the number of firehouse locations occupied, together with the least square fits of Equations (6.11) and (6.12).

Berlin and Liebman (1974) present results of a combined optimization-simulation study of emergency ambulance locations in a suburban county near Washington, D.C., with 24 potential depot locations. Using a set-covering model, they computed the relation between the *maximum* response time and the number of locations occupied. (Their computations are based on a linear relationship between time and distance; although the results are given in terms of response times, they are easily converted to or interpreted as travel distances.) Figure 6.13 shows their results and

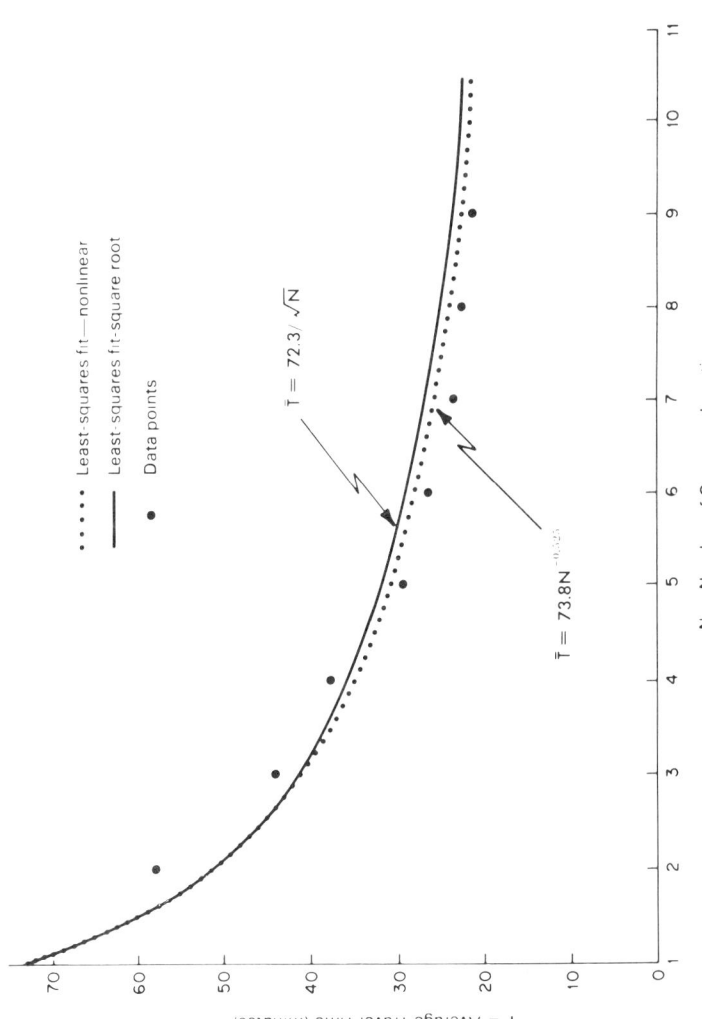

FIGURE 6.12. Average response time vs. number of fire company locations (Bristol, England). (Source: Hogg, J., 1968.)

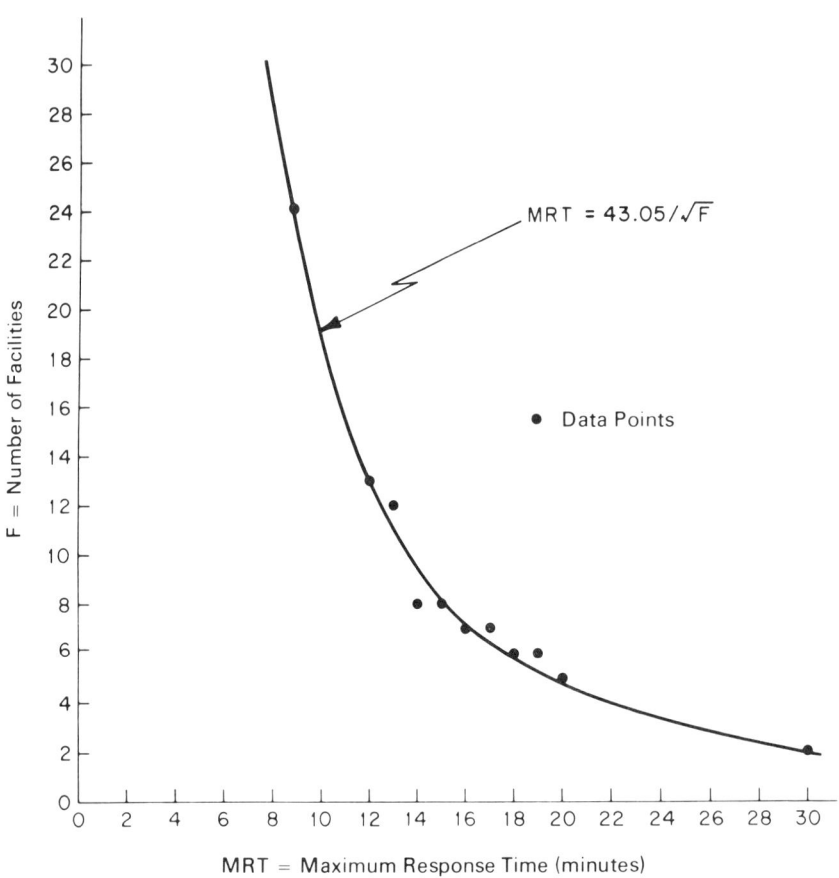

FIGURE 6.13. Maximum ambulance response time vs. number of facilities. (Source: Berlin and Liebman, 1974.)

includes the fitted equation

$$\text{maximum response time} = K/\sqrt{\text{Number of facilities}}.$$

This relation has an empirical constant, K, that is related to our k_1 and to the square root of the area of the region.[17] The square-root curve fits well the results for the 10 sets of "optimal" locations. The square-root law indicates the benefits that might be achieved from improving the depot locations. It shows that 24 better-selected locations should yield a maximum response time of approximately 8.8 minutes, compared to the

---

[17] For the rectangular city model described in Section 6.4.2, it is easy to see that the maximum response distance (S) obeys a square-root law.

11.7 minutes achieved with the current locations. Such an estimate, although an approximation, permits one to evaluate the desirability of carrying out a siting improvement study, gives a target value for which the analyst can strive, and may also highlight the local areas in which attention to better siting could have the greatest returns. The square-root law permits the analyst to extrapolate beyond the computer values and to interpolate accurately between them, both with a minimum of effort.

6.5 ESTIMATING AVERAGE TRAVEL TIMES IN A REGION

Now we consider how to compute the average travel time in a region. Such a regional travel time is the average of many point-to-point travel times. The frequency of each potential trip is determined by the frequency of alarms at each alarm box, the dispatching rules used to assign fire companies to respond, and the availability of the fire companies assigned to respond.

Consider the following way of computing such an average. One could collect actual travel time data for a series of alarms. Supposed that there are q alarms (trips) to be considered. Let T_j denote the travel time of the closest engine to alarm j for $j = 1, 2, \ldots, q$. Some of the individual trips will be repetitions of the same trip—company m traveling to alarm box b—as many times as that run was made during the period of interest. All such runs are entered into our computations. The average of all run times,

$$\bar{T}_1 = \sum_{j=1}^{q} T_j / q,$$

is a good statistical estimator of the expected regional travel time for the first-arriving engine company. Our earlier discussions of the problems encountered in carrying out travel time experiments are relevant here, for it is difficult and expensive to gather such data.

An alternative approach uses other historical data and the conversion from travel distance to time discussed in Section 6.3. Suppose that for each possible trip—company m to alarm box b—we can estimate the distance d_{mb} by one of the methods discussed earlier, and that we also know the fraction p_{mb} of all trips made by all first-arriving companies that involve company m responding to box b. We use a function for converting distance to time (for example, Equation (6.4)), and call the resulting estimate of the travel time of a trip of length d by the name $G(d_{mb})$. The average regional travel time for the first-arriving engine company can be estimated as

$$\bar{T}_1 = \sum_b \sum_m G(d_{mb}) p_{mb},$$

where the double sum goes over all relevant m-to-b combinations.

Even this computation can be quite tedious. A simple approximation is obtained by combining the square-root law for average distances (Equation (6.9)) with a function for converting travel distances into travel times (e.g., Equation (6.4)). With the resulting function, average travel times can be estimated in regions where comparatively little is known about the details of travel patterns, alarm distributions, etc.

If a city has obtained empirical estimates of k_1, a, b, c, and d, it should use them in estimating average regional travel times. The expected first-arriving engine travel time in a region whose area is A would be estimated by

$$E(T_1) = \begin{cases} c\sqrt{k_1}[A/E(N)]^{1/4} & k_1\sqrt{A/E(N)} \leq d \quad (6.13) \\ a + bk_1[A/E(N)]^{1/2} & k_1\sqrt{A/E(N)} \geq d; \quad (6.14) \end{cases}$$

where $E(N)$ is the expected number of firehouses having at least one engine company available. If a city has not obtained estimates of the various parameters, it may obtain useful initial estimates of average regional first-arriving engine travel times by using the values $k_1 = 0.55$,

FIGURE 6.14. Simulated average travel time vs. average number of available companies (closest ladder companies in the South Bronx).

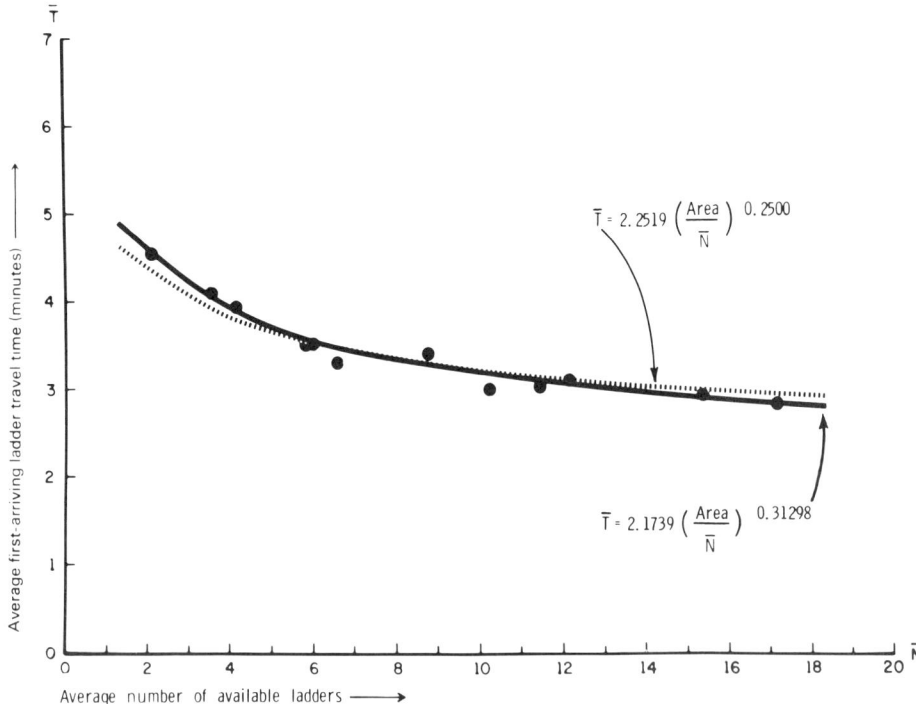

6.5 Estimating Average Travel Times in a Region

$a = 0.65$, $b = 1.70$, $c = 2.10$, and $d = 0.38$. The function to use would be:

$$E(T_1) = \begin{cases} 1.56[A/E(N)]^{1/4} & 0.55\sqrt{A/E(N)} \leq 0.38 \quad (6.15) \\ 0.65 + 0.94[A/E(N)]^{1/2} & 0.55\sqrt{A/E(N)} \geq 0.38. \quad (6.16) \end{cases}$$

It is also possible to obtain the parameters of Equations (6.13) and (6.14) directly from empirical data, instead of indirectly from Equations (6.9) and (6.4). Travel time data could be used to estimate r_1, or r_2 and r_3, in the following pair of equations:

$$E(T_1) = \begin{cases} r_1[A/E(N)]^{1/4} & \text{if } E(D_1) \text{ is ``small''} \quad (6.17) \\ r_2 + r_3[A/E(N)]^{1/2} & \text{if } E(D_1) \text{ is ``large''}. \quad (6.18) \end{cases}$$

Equations (6.17) and (6.18) suggest that the general form for the expected travel time of the first-arriving engine can be written:

$$E(T_1) = \eta + \delta [A/E(N)]^\gamma. \quad (6.19)$$

Kolesar (1975) performed regressions using simulated data from New York City to show the validity of using Equations (6.17), (6.18) and (6.19) to estimate expected travel times. He also showed that it does not matter whether one forces $\gamma = 0.25$ or 0.50 in accordance with the theoretical results, or lets the regression fit γ as a free parameter. The fit of either is very good. Figure 6.14 is typical of the results Kolesar obtained.

Chapter 7
Probabilistic Models of Fire Company Availability and Dispatching

Synopsis

The availability of fire companies to be dispatched to alarms changes from time to time as incidents occur, and as companies are released from the scene of incidents. To estimate performance characteristics such as workloads of companies and travel times to incidents, it is sometimes necessary to know how often each company will be unavailable, or how often a given number of companies will be unavailable.

Among the methods that can be used to make such estimates, the ones described in this chapter are the least complicated. By making simplifying assumptions that are approximately correct, principles of queuing theory and Markov decision theory can be applied to problems concerning unavailabilities and dispatching policy. While the results from such models are necessarily no more than rough approximations of the real world, they can be useful in several ways:

1. In some cases, a rough calculation is sufficiently accurate for choosing among alternative policies.
2. In other cases, rough calculations indicate the type of model needed for more detailed analysis. For example, the firehouse siting models described in Chapter 10 are based on the assumption that all companies are always available. Calculations based on queuing theory can indicate whether or not this is a reasonable assumption.
3. The insights derived from using simplified models often suggest how to design more complex models, or what policy options to try in more complex models.

Queuing models show how to estimate the average number of companies busy in each region of a city. This information is important not only for travel time calculations, as described in Chapter 6, but also for other aspects of deployment analysis. In addition, since the actual number of busy companies fluctuates around the average, the analyst some-

Synopsis 203

times needs to know how large the variations might be. For example, how often will it happen that all the companies in a region will be busy? The answer to this question, also provided by queuing models, helps to determine whether a region is self-sufficient in terms of fire protection.

When companies are frequently unavailable, a dispatcher's decisions about what companies to dispatch to an incoming alarm will affect not only the response times of companies sent to the current alarms, but also the response times to future alarms that occur while some of these companies are still busy. Although the dispatcher cannot know exactly when and where the future alarms will occur, probabilistic information about them can help improve his decisions. This chapter presents several simplified models of the dispatching decision; these motivate the complete treatment presented in Chapter 11.

One key finding is that dispatchers need not always send the closest available companies to every incoming alarm. Indeed, if the dispatcher has a choice between two companies that are "almost" equally close to an alarm, and the incident is unlikely to be affected by a delay of a fraction of a minute in response time, the dispatcher should, in some circumstances, choose the farther company. By sending the farther company, the dispatcher leaves the closer one available to respond to the next alarm, and this is desirable if future alarms are likely to be near the closer company.

When deciding the number of companies to send to an incoming alarm, fire department dispatchers generally take into account the reported nature of the incident. However, when no information about the incident is obtained (as with an alarm from an alarm box), models show that the past history of alarms from the same location can help determine how many companies to dispatch. If past data show that alarms from the location in question are unlikely to be serious, fewer companies should be dispatched than if the alarms often signal serious fires.

This chapter describes the characteristics of fire alarms and fire company unavailabilities that are central to many of the models presented in later chapters. Terms that will be used repeatedly, such as *Poisson process* and *service time distribution*, are defined and illustrated by examples in this chapter. In addition, principles of queuing theory and Markov decision theory are applied to several problems concerning the unavailabilities of fire companies and policies for dispatching companies.

The models described in this chapter are fairly elementary and, in many cases, are based on unrealistically simplified assumptions. However, there are several benefits to be gained from studying simplified models. First, they give a clear indication of the types of data that must be collected to analyze fire deployment options. This topic is discussed in detail in Chapter 8, so for now we shall proceed as if any needed data can be somehow collected. Second, simple models often lead to general conclusions that are true, no matter how complicated a model is used. Finally, some of the conclusions derived from simple models are useful for the insights they lend, although they are not correct except under the restrictive assumptions made in this chapter. Such conclusions motivate more detailed models or policy options that are worth trying out in other models.

The chapter begins with an introduction to queuing theory. Readers who are familiar with this subject, including the use of bubble diagrams to solve for steady-state probabilities, can skip Section 7.1 or skim it briefly to determine the terminology being used in this book.

7.1 BASIC ELEMENTS OF QUEUING THEORY

Queuing theory is a collection of mathematical techniques that apply to situations where customers arrive at some kind of service facility and may have to wait for service. A typical example would be a bank where customers may have to wait for a teller to be free. Airplanes waiting to land at an airport also constitute a queuing system; here the "customers" are the airplanes and the "servers" are the runways on which they can land.

In most applications of queuing theory to problems of the fire service, the "customers" are fire alarms (or any type of incidents requiring a response from the department), and the "servers" are dispatchers or fire companies. Some of the earliest uses of queuing theory involved telephone calls, and fire alarms have many properties in common with telephone calls (indeed, many of them *are* telephone calls). Thus, some of the important facts in this chapter were known long before anybody began to use queuing theory to analyze fire service problems.[1]

While the word "queuing" brings to mind customers waiting in a line, queuing theory can be very useful in analyzing situations where no one actually has to wait for service. For example, in most medium- and large-sized cities it has never happened that a fire alarm occurred when all the fire companies in the city were busy at previous fires, so that the new fire had to wait for a company to become available. Or, if it did happen, mutual aid agreements provided for a response from a neighboring department, in which case the new fire did not wait for a response anyway.

---

[1] Many excellent textbooks on queuing theory are available. The reader interested in an introductory approach might consult Kleinrock (1975), Lindgren and McElrath (1967), or Morse (1967). Kleinrock uses bubble diagrams.

7.1 Basic Elements of Queuing Theory

Nevertheless, queuing theory can be used to calculate important information about fire companies.

7.1.1 Describing a Queuing System

When considering a real-world problem in terms of queuing theory, some characteristics are irrelevant, while others are important. For example, the color of an airplane has no influence on whether it will be delayed in landing or not, while the time of its arrival in the vicinity of the airport is important. If it arrives when no other aircraft are nearby, it will be able to land without delay (assuming that the runways are open). But if several planes arrive at nearly the same time, some or all of them will have to wait before landing. Similarly, the length of time from the landing of an airplane until the runway is free for another landing is an important descriptor of the system. In this section, five descriptors of a queuing system are defined.

Arrival Process. The times at which airplanes will arrive in the vicinity of an airport can be predicted with reasonable accuracy, especially after they are all airborne. Not so with fire alarms. A fire department cannot state with assurance that the next fire alarm will occur between 10 and 11 minutes from now, but it can compare the relative chances of various events. For example, based on past experience it might be possible to say that the next fire alarm is more likely to occur within the next 10 minutes than it is to occur after 10 minutes have passed.

Whatever is known about the times at which future arrivals will occur is an important characteristic of a queuing system. It can be expressed mathematically in terms of the *cumulative distribution of interarrival times at time t*, which is defined as the function[2]

$A(t,T)$ = probability (no arrival will occur between t and $(t + T)$).

(7.1)

For example, if it is now 12:00 noon, and the next arrival will definitely occur between 12:10 and 12:11, then $A(12:00,T)$ will equal 1 for T less than 10 minutes and will equal 0 for T greater than 11 minutes. For values of T between 10 and 11 minutes, $A(12:00,T)$ decreases from 1 to 0. Such a distribution of interarrival times might apply to airplanes but not to fire alarms. Typical distributions for fire alarms will be discussed in Section 7.1.3.

---

[2] In most textbooks the cumulative distribution is defined as $1 - A$, but defining the cumulative distribution as A is more convenient for the particular distribution to be discussed in this chapter.

If the cumulative distribution is known, then other probabilities can be calculated from it. For example, the probability that the next arrival will occur between 5 and 6 minutes from t is $A(t,5) - A(t,6)$.

Service Time. A second important characteristic of a queuing system is the length of time during which a server will be handling a customer. This is called the "service time." If fire companies are considered the servers, the service time is the number of minutes from the moment the company is dispatched until the moment it is released and available to be dispatched to a new incident. If dispatchers are the servers, the service time might be the length of time spent determining which companies to dispatch, or the length of time they speak to the caller on the telephone, or both of these together, depending on the questions to be answered by the queuing analysis.

The service time ordinarily varies according to the nature of the incident (false alarms have shorter service times than three-alarm fires), the particular server in question (distant companies have a longer service time because their travel time is longer), the tasks assigned to the server (first-due companies may work longer than third-due companies), and perhaps other characteristics. Even when all these characteristics are known, the service time still cannot be specified exactly in advance, so it is necessary to consider a probability distribution as in the case of arrivals. The cumulative distribution of service times is

$$S(T) = \text{probability(service takes at least time } T \text{ to complete)}. \tag{7.2}$$

Although it is possible to specify one distribution of service time that applies to the totality of alarms, for many purposes it is preferable to have several distribution functions, one for each combination of characteristics, such as incident type, server, and so forth.

Number of Servers. This is an important descriptor that is readily understood. An airport with two runways has two servers from the point of view of the landing aircraft. A bank with seven tellers has seven servers. A dispatch center with five dispatchers has five servers and will perform differently from the same center with only three dispatchers on duty.

Maximum Number of Customers Who Can Wait for Service. Some systems do not permit any customers to wait; these are called *loss systems*. For example, a business firm might have 12 incoming telephone lines. When all the lines are in use, a caller gets a busy signal. He cannot wait on his telephone until one of the firm's lines is free, but must hang up and try later. This constitutes a 12-server loss system. By contrast, another firm, such as an airline company, might have a device to hold callers in queue until one of the reservation clerks is free. Such devices are also installed in many "911" systems. They have a limited capacity, so that, for example, at most 30 callers can wait in queue. The thirty-first caller will get a busy signal. In this system, the maximum number of customers who can wait is 30.

In some circumstances there is practically no limit on the number of waiting customers. For example, a dispatcher of ambulances could keep a stack of cards, each indicating a person who is waiting for an ambulance to be dispatched. There is no reason why he would have to stop accepting cards after five were in his stack, or ten, or more. In this case we say that an *infinite number of customers can wait*. This does not mean that an enormous number of customers *do* wait, simply that there is no identifiable limit on the possible number of waiting customers.

States of the System. To complete the description of a queuing system, the analyst must specify what *conditions* or *states* of the system are of interest. For example, in a telephone system one might like to know the *number* of lines in use at any time, the particular lines being of no importance. If there are N lines, this system has $N + 1$ states: no lines in use, 1 line in use, 2 lines in use, and so forth up to N lines in use.

If the servers are fire companies, one might like to know whether Company 1 is busy, rather than simply that some company is busy. One might also need to know when both Company 1 and Company 2 are busy simultaneously. To add to the complexity, one might like to know whether Company 1 is busy at an incident in its own first-due area or in some other company's first-due area. As the number of descriptions for each state increases, the total number of possible states for the system can become so enormous that even high-speed computers would require years to calculate the probability of each state occurring. For example, with only nine fire companies, if one is interested in knowing the first-due area in which each company is working (i.e., it is either available or working in one of nine first-due areas), the system has a billion states (all companies available, Company 1 busy in its own first-due area with all the others available, etc.). Thus, it is a challenge to formulate a queuing problem in such a way that the results tell the analyst what he needs to know, without overwhelming him with computational problems.

7.1.2 How Queuing Theory is Related to the Fire Service

The most common uses of queuing theory for problems related to the fire service tell the analyst *how often* a particular state of the system will occur and *how long* it will last. This information can be used in many ways: to calculate travel times, workloads, and various other performance statistics corresponding to the current operations of the department; to devise better locations for fire companies, or improved dispatching practices; and others that will be illustrated in this and subsequent chapters.

Each of the applications will be described at the appropriate place in terms of the characteristics just mentioned: interarrival time distribution, service time distribution(s), number of servers, maximum number of waiting customers, and states of the system. However, before getting into the details, we can indicate roughly the types of queuing systems that have been applied to fire deployment analysis.

Several models consider the fire companies to be the servers. In some cases the system includes all the engine companies (or ladder companies) in the city or in a large region of the city, and no distinction is made among the various engine companies. These models are used to calculate the probability that any specified number of companies are busy at once. Since the chance that all companies will be busy is typically very small, in which case it is of little value for answering policy questions, the number of servers can often be assumed to be infinite. While this results in an infinite number of states for the system, the calculations focus on the first ten, twenty, or thirty states (whatever number is relevant). The calculations are actually simplified somewhat by assuming an infinite number of servers, without any significant loss of accuracy.

In other cases, such as in considering the design of first-due areas, only two companies are of interest, or perhaps a single company plus the four or so others whose first-due areas are adjacent. For such analyses, the system of two companies, or five, or whatever, may be considered a loss system because any alarms that arrive when all of these companies are busy will be handled by some other companies. These other companies are not included in the queuing system, and so, from the point of view of the system, the extra alarms are "lost."

An example of a queuing system in which the fire companies are not the servers is given by a bank of operators who answer the emergency telephones. While few fire departments that have their own telephone numbers experience problems where callers get a busy signal or have to wait before talking to an operator, this problem can arise with centralized police-fire-ambulance numbers (such as 911). Calculating the number of telephone operators needed at different times of the day is quite easily accomplished using queuing theory. Here the telephone calls are the customers, the servers are the telephone operators, and the service time is the length of time needed to complete the conversation. The method for performing the necessary calculations has been described by Larson (1972) and will not be repeated in this book. One has to consider not only the probability that a caller will get a busy signal but also the length of time he will have to wait until his call is answered. In an emergency situation, a delay of twenty seconds can seem like many minutes to a caller.

In Section 14.5 we discuss a queuing system in which the servers are the dispatchers who must decide which companies to send to each incoming alarm. When several fires are in progress at once, the dispatcher may not be certain about the availability of particular companies, and any of the available companies may be the best choice for two or more different alarms waiting to be dispatched. This constitutes a particularly complicated queuing system, since the service time (length of time needed to make a decision) can vary according to the number of incidents in progress at the moment of dispatch. In our previous discussion, and for the remainder of this chapter, the service time has been assumed to be unrelated to the state of the system.

7.1.3 The Poisson Process

The distribution of the arrival times of fire alarms is central to any queuing analysis of the fire service. Fortunately, one family of distributions has been found to apply in every fire department that has been studied, no matter what region of the city is considered or what time of day it is. These are the *time-dependent Poisson processes*, which will be described in this section.

The Poisson process is a mathematical formulation of the observation that fire alarms are completely unpredictable, or totally random. In fact, in order to derive all the properties of time-dependent Poisson processes, it is necessary to make only two assumptions: (1) in very short intervals of time, fires or other emergency incidents occur singly, rather than in pairs or triplets; that is, two alarms do not arrive simultaneously[3]; (2) the arrival of one alarm does not affect the probability of another alarm in either the future or in other locations. In order for the second assumption to be correct, the term "alarm" must be properly defined to exclude multiple reports of the same event. Each incident requiring a response from the department (whether it is a fire, a medical emergency, or even a false alarm) corresponds to just one alarm. In the case of large fires, several telephone calls and signals from alarm boxes may be received at the dispatch center.[4] Only one of these should be considered the alarm.

---

[3] In rare disasters, such as aircraft collisions, several fires may start simultaneously, but otherwise this assumption is valid.

[4] The arrival times of telephone calls at a fire department dispatch center may not constitute a Poisson process because of this "bunching" phenomenon. However, any delays experienced by the second or third caller are unimportant, since the fire companies will have been dispatched upon first notification. For this reason, it is possible to perform many analyses of telephone calls by assuming that they constitute a Poisson process, even though this is not precisely true.

When interpreting the term alarm in this fashion, it is intuitively reasonable that fire alarms do obey the two assumptions stated, and therefore constitute a time-dependent Poisson process. However, it is not necessary to accept this conclusion on faith. We indicate here some properties of Poisson processes that can be tested for validity by statistical techniques. Then, in Chapters 8 and 14, examples will show how well actual data concerning fire alarms match the Poisson assumption.

Interarrival Time Distribution for a Poisson Process. The only characteristic of the arrival times that must be specified to describe a particular Poisson process is the average number of fire alarms per hour. This is called the *alarm rate* and is denoted by λ. The term *time-dependent* means that the alarm rate can vary over the course of the day, week, or year, in which case its value at time t is denoted $\lambda(t)$. For example, if an average of two alarms per hour occur at 3 A.M., and an average of nine at 6 P.M., we have $\lambda(0300) = 2$ per hour and $\lambda(1800) = 9$ per hour.

As defined in Section 7.1.1, the interarrival time distribution, $A(t,T)$, is the probability that no alarm will occur between t and $(t + T)$. To calculate the interarrival time distribution for a Poisson process, one must find the average alarm rate[5] between t and $(t + T)$, which is denoted $\bar{\lambda}$. Then

$$A(t,T) = e^{-\bar{\lambda}T}.$$

For short periods of time, it may be assumed that the alarm rate is a constant λ. In this case we have an ordinary (not time dependent) Poisson process with interarrival time distribution

$$A(t,T) = e^{-\lambda T}, \tag{7.3}$$

which does not depend on t. This interarrival time distribution is called an *exponential distribution*[6] and completely characterizes an ordinary Poisson process with alarm rate λ. An example is graphed in Figure 7.1. In most types of analyses it is mathematically much more complicated to assume time-dependent Poisson arrivals than to assume a constant alarm rate λ. For this reason, the analysis is performed separately for short time intervals, such as an hour.

Memoryless Property. For a Poisson process with constant rate λ, the average time until the next fire alarm is $1/\lambda$. Thus, if there are two fire alarms per hour (on the average), then the average time to the next fire alarm is $\frac{1}{2}$ hour. Remarkably enough, it does not matter when you start

---

[5] The average alarm rate is mathematically defined as $\bar{\lambda} = 1/T \, (\int_t^{t+T} \lambda(u)du)$.
[6] Or, more precisely, it is called a *negative exponential distribution*.

7.1 Basic Elements of Queuing Theory

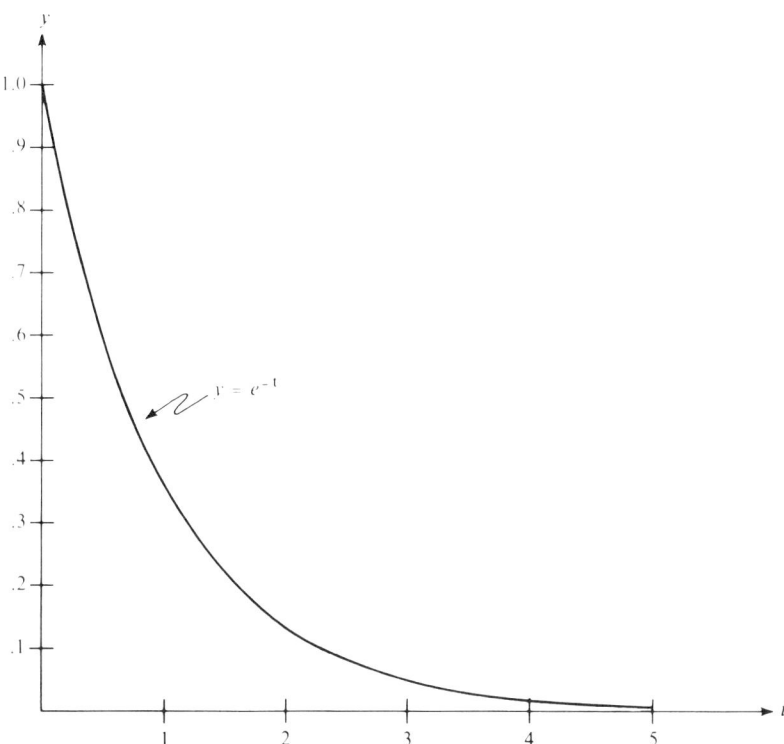

FIGURE 7.1. The exponential function. The curve shows the probability of waiting more than t hours for the next alarm when the alarm rate is one per hour.

counting the time to the next arrival; the answer is always the same. This means that you could begin at 2:00 P.M. or at the last fire alarm, and the distribution of the time until the next alarm will be the same as Equation (7.3). Stated another way, knowing when the last fire alarm occurred does not help predict when the next fire alarm will occur.

Number of Alarms in a Time Interval. If $\bar{\lambda}$ is the average alarm rate over any time interval of length T, say 15 minutes, then the average number of alarms that will occur is $\bar{\lambda}T$. For example, for a constant $\lambda = $ 4/hour, if you average the number of alarms that occur in many different 15-minute periods, the result will be that, on the average, one call occurs in 15 minutes. However, some 15-minute periods will have no alarms, others will have one alarm, others will have two, and so forth. (In principle, a 15-minute period could have 10,000 alarms, but the probability of this is so small that it can be ignored.)

In a Poisson process with average alarm rate $\bar{\lambda}$ over an interval of length T, the probability that n alarms will occur is

$$p(n,T) = \frac{(\bar{\lambda}T)^n}{n!} e^{-\bar{\lambda}T}, \qquad n = 0, 1, 2, \ldots \qquad (7.4)$$

For fixed values of T, this is called a *Poisson distribution with mean* $\bar{\lambda}T$. (The *Poisson process* refers to the arrival pattern of alarms; the *Poisson distribution* refers to counting the number of alarms that occur in some period of time.) An example of a Poisson distribution is given in Figure 7.2.

Interpretation of Randomness. An interpretation of the randomness of the Poisson process with constant alarm rate λ can be obtained by considering a long time interval of length K hours. This interval may be divided into consecutive subintervals of length T, as shown in Figure 7.3. (We assume that K is some integer times T.) Suppose that we know exactly how many alarms occurred in the whole interval of length K. Call this N. If the precise arrival time of each of these N alarms is determined completely randomly (for example, by throwing darts at the line without favoring one location over another), the number of alarms falling in the various intervals of length T will be distributed approxi-

FIGURE 7.2. The Poisson distribution, with mean 6.2.

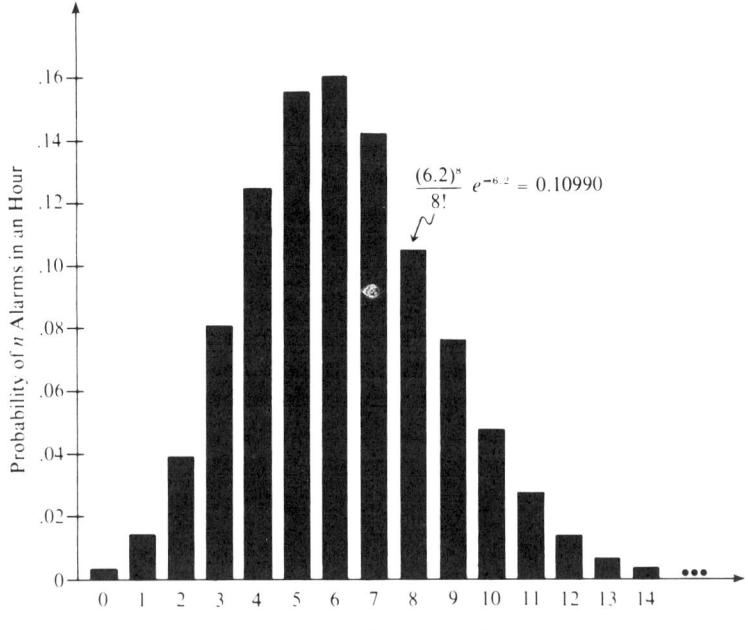

7.1 Basic Elements of Queuing Theory

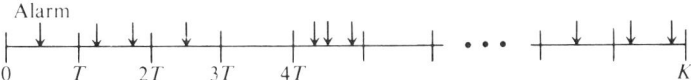

FIGURE 7.3. An interval of length K divided into subintervals of length T.

mately as in Equation (7.4).[7] This fact corresponds to our intuitive feeling about the unpredictability of fire alarms, and adds strength to our assumption that the Poisson process is a good mathematical representation of the arrival times of fire alarms.

Additive Property. When you add together two or more Poisson processes, the result is a Poisson process where the alarm rate is the sum of the two original rates. For example, suppose a city is divided into two regions. If the alarms coming from Region 1 constitute a Poisson process with alarm rate $\lambda_1(t)$, and the alarms from Region 2 constitute a Poisson process with alarm rate $\lambda_2(t)$, then the alarms from the whole city constitute a Poisson process with alarm rate $\lambda(t) = \lambda_1(t) + \lambda_2(t)$. This mathematical property makes Poisson processes easy to work with.

7.1.4 Service Times

Some types of queuing systems, such as those involving telephone calls, have an exponential service time distribution, exactly like the distribution of interarrival times for the ordinary Poisson process. This means that there is a number μ (called the service rate), such that the cumulative distribution of service times is

$$S(T) = e^{-\mu T}.$$

In this case the average service time is $1/\mu$.

The service times for fire companies do not match an exponential distribution. In fact, for a small fire, the distribution is likely to look something like Figure 7.4. This shows that the probability of the service time lasting more than 10 minutes is nearly 1. We are assuming that the company must travel to the scene of the fire, connect a hose, extinguish a fire, and return the hose to the apparatus before its service time is completed. Accomplishing all these tasks in less than 10 minutes is nearly impossible, while in half of all fires of this type it can be accomplished

---

[7] More precisely, each of the N alarms is assumed to be uniformly distributed over the interval $(0, K)$, independent of the other alarms. Calculate the probability that n alarms fall in any specified subinterval, $n = 0, 1, \ldots, N$. This is a binomial distribution. Take the limit as N and K go to infinity in such a way that N/K approaches λ. The result is Equation (7.4), with $\bar{\lambda}$ replaced by λ.

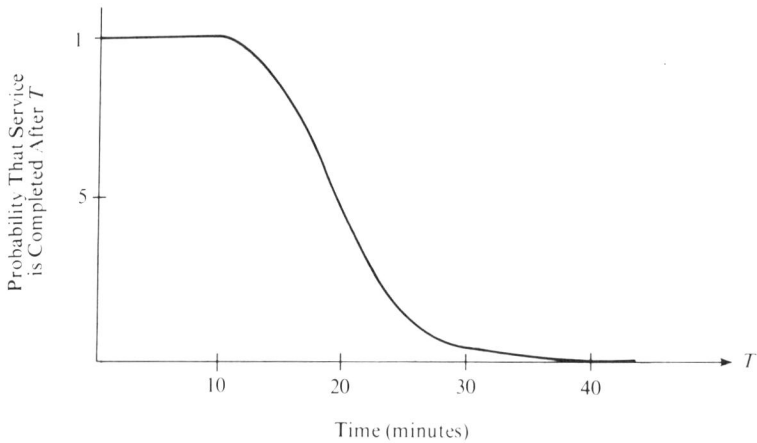

FIGURE 7.4. Typical distribution of service time for a small fire.

within 20 minutes. The distribution in Figure 7.4 does not look at all like Figure 7.1, which is an exponential distribution.

Despite the failure of the exponential service time distribution to match reality, it is often used in queuing analyses related to the fire service. The analyst assumes an exponential service time because it simplifies his calculations, not because it is correct. When his findings are obtained, he may be able to prove that they are correct for any service time distribution, even though he began with the assumption of exponential service times. More commonly, he will be able to show that his calculations are *approximately* correct for several examples of "real" service time distributions. For example, the calculation using exponential service times may show that Company 1 is busy 17.7 percent of the time, when the true value is 17.1 percent. These numbers are sufficiently close that ordinarily either one could be used for policy decisions.

7.1.5 Steady-State Solutions

Suppose that, on the average, two fire companies are busy in a city. At a particular moment, however, it could happen that ten fire companies are busy at fires. If a calculation is made for the number of companies expected to be busy, starting at that moment, it will show that this expected number of busy companies gradually decreases from 10 to 2 over the course of several hours. The formula that expresses the number of busy companies as a function of time is called a *transient solution* to the queuing problem. The transient solution depends on the state of the system at the initial moment.

No matter how many companies are present at the start, all calculations will show that after many hours have passed, two companies are expected to be busy. This part of the solution, which is independent of the situation at the start and does not vary with time, is called the *steady-state* solution.

In many types of analyses, such as planning the locations of fire stations, the situation at the time of analysis is considered unimportant, so steady-state solutions are used. In other cases, such as deciding the number of companies to dispatch to incoming alarms, the transient solution may be needed.

7.1.6 A Graphical Method for Performing Queuing Calculations

An extraordinarily useful graphical method can be used to perform queuing calculations when three assumptions are made: (1) arrivals constitute a Poisson process with constant alarm rate; (2) service times have an exponential distribution; and (3) steady-state solutions are desired. This method consists of drawing a "bubble" for each state of the system and showing by arrows the states that will be reached if a single alarm arrives or a single service is completed. On each arrow, one writes the rate at which the arrivals or service-completions occur.

Figure 7.5 shows a "bubble diagram" (also called a state diagram) for a simple example with three states. It describes a small city with two engine companies. The bubble with "0" in it represents the state with no busy engine companies. The bubble with a "1" means one company is busy, and the bubble with a "2" means two companies are busy. If an alarm arrives when both companies are busy, it is handled by another department under mutual aid.

We assume (for this example) that alarms arrive according to a Poisson process with rate λ, that each has an exponential service time with mean $1/\mu$, and that one engine company responds to each alarm. Therefore, there is an arrow from state 0 to state 1 with a λ written on it, and an arrow from state 1 to state 2 with a λ written on it. These mean that if an alarm arrives when no company is busy, immediately afterward one will be busy, and if an alarm arrives when one company is busy, immediately afterward two will be busy. Similarly, if a service is completed when one company is busy, immediately afterward no companies will be

FIGURE 7.5. Example of a bubble diagram; alarms require one engine company.

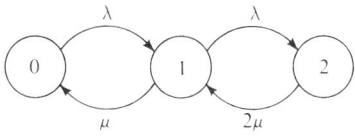

busy; and if one service time is completed when two companies are busy, immediately afterward one company will be busy. The arrow from state 2 to state 1 has 2μ written on it because either one of two companies could finish service at rate μ. In other words, the rate at which state 2 converts to state 1 is twice as fast as the rate at which state 1 converts to state 0.

The diagram is used to calculate the steady-state probability that each state occurs. We use the symbol $p(0)$ to represent the probability of state 0, $p(1)$ the probability of state 1, and $p(2)$ the probability of state 2. The meaning of these probabilities is that if every minute (or second) you wrote down what state the system was in at that point, then in the long run a fraction of $p(0)$ of all the observations would find the system with no companies busy, and so forth.

To convert the bubble diagram into equations, one considers the diagram as if it represented a flow of water through pipes. The probability of state 0 can be thought of as the amount of water in bubble 0. The diagram shows that a fraction λ flows out of state 0, so we have

$$\text{flow out of state } 0 = \lambda p(0).$$

Similarly, the arrow from state 1 to state 0 shows that

$$\text{flow into state } 0 = \mu p(1),$$

since $p(1)$ is the probability of state 1.

In the steady state the flow out must equal the flow in, so we have

$$\lambda p(0) = \mu p(1).$$

Similarly, by considering the flows in and out of state 1 we find

$$\lambda p(1) + \mu p(1) = \lambda p(0) + 2\mu p(2),$$

and by considering state 2 we have

$$\lambda p(1) = 2\mu p(2).$$

It turns out that any two of these equations tell us as much as all three of them, so we solve the first and third to get

$$p(1) = \frac{\lambda}{\mu} p(0)$$

$$p(2) = \frac{1}{2} \frac{\lambda}{\mu} p(1) = \frac{1}{2}\left(\frac{\lambda}{\mu}\right)^2 p(0).$$

To find $p(0)$ we have to realize that *the sum of all probabilities equals 1*, thus

$$p(0) + p(1) + p(2) = 1$$

7.1 Basic Elements of Queuing Theory

or

$$p(0) + \frac{\lambda}{\mu} p(0) + \frac{1}{2}\left(\frac{\lambda}{\mu}\right)^2 p(0) = 1$$

or

$$p(0)\left[1 + \frac{\lambda}{\mu} + \frac{1}{2}\left(\frac{\lambda}{\mu}\right)^2\right] = 1$$

or

$$p(0) = 1 \bigg/ \left[1 + \frac{\lambda}{\mu} + \frac{1}{2}\left(\frac{\lambda}{\mu}\right)^2\right].$$

Thus we have expressed $p(0)$ in terms of λ and μ, and so we also know $p(1)$ and $p(2)$ in terms of λ and μ. This is the solution to the problem, because the probabilities of each state can be determined for any given λ and μ, and once the probability of each state is known, any other numbers that could be calculated for this system are also known.

To summarize the method:

1. Draw the states as a bubble diagram.
2. Show changes of states by arrows with rates.
3. Set flow out = flow in for every state.
4. Solve the equations.

Another example is given in Figure 7.6. Here some alarms arrive at rate λ_1 and require one engine company. Others arrive at rate λ_2 and require two companies. All companies have the same exponentially distributed service time, namely the one with mean $1/\mu$, regardless of whether they have responded to a one-company fire or a two-company fire. (When one company is busy, and a two-engine alarm is received, the available company responds, along with a mutual aid company that is not being considered as part of the system.) The reader who was not previously familiar with bubble diagrams should find for himself the probabilities of each state in Figure 7.6, using the method illustrated above. The results are given in the Appendix to this chapter (Section A7.1).

FIGURE 7.6. Example of a bubble diagram; some alarms require two engines.

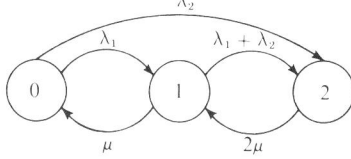

7.2 NUMBER OF COMPANIES BUSY IN A REGION

Here we apply the queuing techniques described in Section 7.1 to determine the number of fire companies busy in any region of a city. The fire alarms arising from the region are assumed to constitute a Poisson process with constant rate λ. As we have noted, this is a correct assumption for short periods of time. To apply the results of this section for policy analysis, it would be necessary to find the correct values of λ for various times of the day or week, and calculate numerical results separately for each time period of interest. Methods for estimating the alarm rate are discussed in Chapter 8.

Since ordinarily the number of companies in a region of a city is substantially less than the total number of companies in the city (although it may sometimes be greater than the number of companies stationed in the region), it is convenient to consider the system as having an infinite number of servers. This assumption avoids some mathematical complications that arise when the maximum number of servers is specified, without affecting the accuracy of the results substantially.

The results to be derived in this section include formulas for calculating the *distribution* of the number of busy companies (that is, the probability that no companies are busy, the probability that one company is busy, and so forth) and the *average* number of companies busy. The most important result is that the average number of busy companies is λ times the average number of company-hours per alarm. Numerical examples are given to illustrate how these calculations are performed. For example, the number of company-hours at an alarm is obtained by adding together all the service times (in hours) of all the companies that work at the alarm. Applications are given in this section, as well as in later chapters.

We begin with a calculation of the number of *incidents in progress* (or the number of *alarms in progress*). This is identical to the number of companies busy if only one company responds to each alarm, which might be the case for emergency medical services. If several companies respond to an alarm, then for purposes of calculating the number of alarms in progress, the service time is defined to be the length of time from the dispatch of the first company until the last company is released from the incident. Considering this special case permits us to ignore some of the complexities at the start.

7.2.1 Number of Alarms in Progress

We consider an infinite-server system in which state "0" is the situation in which no alarms are in progress (i.e., all companies are available), state "1" means that one alarm is in progress, and so forth. If we assume that alarms arrive according to a Poisson process with rate λ and have

7.2 Number of Companies Busy in a Region

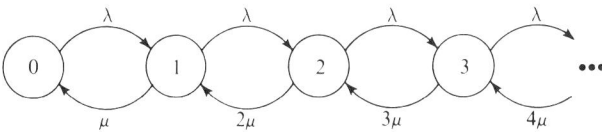

FIGURE 7.7. Bubble diagram for the number of alarms in progress.

an exponential service time with mean $\tau = 1/\mu$, the graphical method of Section 7.1.6 can be used, with Figure 7.7 representing the queuing system. In this case, the average service time (τ) is the duration of an average alarm, from the dispatch of the first company until the last company leaves the scene.

This approach provides an example of the value of the graphical method, because it can be proved (Khintchine, 1960) that the equations we will derive under the assumption of exponential service times are correct, no matter what the service-time distribution is.[8] In fact, a single service-time distribution can represent a mixture of different types of alarms, each with its own service-time distribution, so the model is a very realistic representation of the real world. The only feature of the real world that is ignored in Figure 7.7 is the possibility that alarm durations will increase as the number of alarms in progress increases. (This can happen because travel times increase as the number of available companies decreases, as explained in Chapter 6. Travel time is part of service time, and, in addition, a long travel time may permit the fire to escalate, resulting in a long on-scene service time for extinguishment and overhaul.)

The steady-state queuing equations corresponding to Figure 7.7 are

$$\lambda p(0) = \mu p(1),$$
$$(\lambda + \mu)p(1) = \lambda p(0) + 2\mu p(2),$$
$$(\lambda + 2\mu)p(2) = \lambda p(1) + 3\mu p(3),$$

and so forth. Here $p(n)$ is the probability that n alarms are in progress. These equations can be expressed in general form as

$$(\lambda + n\mu)p(n) = \lambda p(n-1) + (n+1)\mu p(n+1), \; n = 0, 1, 2, \ldots,$$

if we interpret $p(-1)$ as zero.

The equations are solved by expressing $p(1)$ in terms of $p(0)$ from the first equation, $p(2)$ in terms of $p(0)$ from the second equation, and so

---

[8] The service times may be assumed to be independently identically distributed, with a finite mean.

forth. The result is

$$p(n) = \frac{(\lambda/\mu)^n}{n!} p(0), \quad n = 1, 2, 3, \ldots.$$

Using the fact that $\tau = 1/\mu$, the equation stating that the sum of all probabilities equals 1 is as follows:

$$\left(1 + \lambda\tau + \frac{(\lambda\tau)^2}{2!} + \frac{(\lambda\tau)^3}{3!} + \cdots\right) p(0) = 1.$$

The sum multiplying $p(0)$ can be written as $\Sigma_{n=0}^{\infty} (\lambda\tau)^n/n!$, which equals $e^{\lambda\tau}$. Since $1/e^{\lambda\tau} = e^{-\lambda\tau}$, we know that $p(0) = e^{-\lambda\tau}$. Therefore, the final result for the probability that n alarms are in progress is

$$p(n) = \frac{(\lambda\tau)^n}{n!} e^{-\lambda\tau} \quad n = 0, 1, 2, \ldots. \tag{7.5}$$

This equation is identical to Equation (7.4), except that T has been replaced by τ. Therefore, the *number of alarms in progress has a Poisson distribution with mean* $\lambda\tau$, where λ is the arrival rate and τ is the average duration of an alarm. To say that the mean of this distribution is $\lambda\tau$ is the same as saying that the *average number of alarms in progress is* $\lambda\tau$.

Example. *Suppose that in some city the alarm rate is 4 per hour ($\lambda = 4$) and the average duration of an alarm is 45 minutes ($\tau = \frac{3}{4}$ hour). If the dispatcher on duty wrote down every 15 minutes (1) the number of alarms that occurred in the past 15 minutes, and (2) the number of alarms in progress, he might get a table like Table 7.1. (Note that $T = 15$ minutes $= \frac{1}{4}$ hour.) We will imagine that the dispatchers collect data for 250 hours, or one thousand 15-minute periods.*[9]

Equation (7.4) states that a fraction $e^{-1} = 0.368$ of the entries should have no alarms occurring in the past 15 minutes (because $\lambda = 4$ and $T = \frac{1}{4}$). Thus, approximately 368 of the lines on the table will show no alarms having occurred. Similarly, Equation (7.5) states that a fraction $e^{-3} = 0.050$ of the entries should have no alarms in progress (because $\lambda = 4$ and $\tau = \frac{3}{4}$). Thus, approximately 50 of the lines in the table will show no alarms in progress.

Continuing, approximately $1000 \times 1 \times e^{-1} = 368$ lines will show that one alarm occurred in the past 15 minutes (this is the same as the number of lines where no alarms occurred), and approximately $1000 \times 3 \times e^{-3} = 149$ lines will show 1 alarm in progress.

---

[9] This example ignores the fact that alarm rates vary by the time of day. The purpose of the example is to illustrate the equations.

TABLE 7.1. Number of alarms received and in progress. The city in the example has an alarm rate of 4/hour and average alarm duration of 45 minutes.

Time: March 1	Number of Alarms in the Past 15 Minutes	Number of Alarms Now in Progress
0015	1	1
0030	0	1
0045	0	0
0100	2	2
0115	0	1
0130	1	2
0145	2	4
.	.	.
.	.	.
.	.	.

If the dispatcher averaged all 1000 numbers in the column labeled "number of alarms in the past 15 minutes," he should get approximately 1.0 (= λT). If he averaged all the numbers in the next column, he should get approximately 3.0 (= $\lambda \tau$).

In the example, dispatchers have spent time writing down data that they do not need for their own work. An analyst who needed to know the number of alarms that might be in progress simultaneously could reconstruct Table 7.1 if the dispatcher simply recorded the time at which each alarm arrived, and the time at which the last company at the incident became available. But the analyst does not have to reconstruct the table from the data. He can simply calculate the average duration of an incident, which is τ, and use Equation (7.5).

Why would he need to know the distribution of the number of alarms in progress? One possible application might be for designing a computer-assisted dispatch (CAD) system. Suppose that the information to be stored in the CAD system concerning each alarm in progress requires a certain amount of computer memory space. The analyst wants to be sure that the CAD will not fail at a critical moment when there are many fires. He might feel that allowing enough space to have one alarm in progress for every company in the city, plus perhaps 10 more for mutual aid companies, gives a satisfactory safety margin. But such a specification might lead to an unnecessarily expensive CAD system.

To determine whether a less expensive system might be adequate, the analyst could ask, "How much memory space is needed so that the probability of running out of space is less than 1 in 10,000?" In other words, he wants to find a number of alarms, M, such that $p(0) + p(1) + p(2) + \cdots + p(M)$ is greater than 0.99999. This can be accomplished by calculating the value of $p(n)$ from Equation (7.5) for $n = 0, 1, 2, \ldots$ and stopping when the sum exceeds 0.99999.

The analyst will want to allow for the possibility that alarm rates will increase in the future. So, if a "busy night" currently has about 4 alarms per hour, the analyst might use $\lambda = 8$ per hour in Equation (7.5). The result of his calculations, with $\tau = 45$ minutes, is shown in Table 7.2. From this table, it can be seen that the CAD needs enough space for 19 alarms to meet the standard set by the analyst.

7.2.2 Number of Busy Companies

Calculating the distribution of the number of busy companies is similar to calculating the number of alarms in progress, except that the description of the queuing system must account for the fact that several companies may respond to a single alarm. The method applies to engine companies, to ladder companies, or to all companies together, but we illustrate it by discussing engine companies. One possible approach is to

TABLE 7.2. Distribution of alarms in progress when the alarm rate is 8 per hour and the average duration of an alarm is 45 minutes.

n = Number of Alarms	$p(n)$ = Probability that n Alarms are in Progress	Probability that n or Fewer Alarms are in Progress
0	.00248	.00248
1	.01487	.01735
2	.04462	.06197
3	.08924	.15120
4	.13385	.28506
5	.16062	.44568
6	.16062	.60630
7	.13768	.74398
8	.10326	.84724
9	.06884	.91608
10	.04130	.95738
11	.02253	.97991
12	.01126	.99117
13	.00520	.99637
14	.00223	.99860
15	.00089	.99949
16	.00033	.99982
17	.00012	.99994
18	.00004	.99998
19	.00001	.99999+

replace each alarm by several imaginary alarms that arrive simultaneously, each imaginary alarm representing an engine company that responds to the incident. This is called a "bulk arrival" model. Its bubble diagram would look like an extended version of Figure 7.6, with some arrows skipping over two or more states (representing alarms that involve three or more engine companies).

However, a bulk arrival model does not give accurate estimates of the probability that a large number of engine companies are busy. In the model, contrary to reality, each engine's service time is assumed to be independent of the service times of the other engines at the same fire. Thus, shortly after the start of a fire that requires 12 engines, the model envisions that there will be only 11 or 10 engines busy, whereas actually, the 12 engines could be busy together for a lengthy period.

To create a better representation of actual operations, Chaiken (1971) proposed a queuing model in which alarms pass through *stages*. A stage is a period of time during which a fixed number of engine companies are busy. For example, when a small fire occurs, three engines might be dispatched, and then two could be released as soon as the first one arrives at the scene. Such an incident has two stages. The first stage represents the time until the first engine arrives; in this stage three engines are busy. The second stage represents the remainder of the incident and has one busy engine. Table 7.3 shows a different kind of three-engine incident which has five stages. A large fire can have many stages. For example, there could be an eight-stage fire in which the successive numbers of busy engine companies are 3, 7, 9, and 11 (representing separate dispatches of groups of engines), and then 8, 5, 3, and 2 (representing engines being released in groups).

The results of the model are formulas for the average number of busy engine companies and for $p(n)$, the probability that n engines are busy, $n = 0, 1, 2, \ldots$. These are given in the Appendix to this chapter (Section A7.2). As mentioned earlier, the average number of busy engine companies turns out to be $E(B) = \lambda E(S)$, where λ is the number of alarms per hour and $E(S)$ is the average number of company hours per alarm. The formula for $p(n)$ is more complicated but depends only on the

TABLE 7.3. Number of engine companies working at each stage of an alarm that requires three engines.

	Stage number				
	1	2	3	4	5
Number of companies working	1	2	3	2	1

products $\lambda\tau_k$, $k = 1, 2, \ldots$, where τ_k is the average length of time that exactly k engines are busy. If two stages have the same number of busy engines, e.g., Stages 1 and 5 in Table 7.3, their durations are added together to calculate the associated τ_k. The formula for $p(n)$ is very easy to program on a computer,[10] and the numbers from the formula have been found to be close to the numbers obtained from the simulation model described in Chapter 13, which is a much more detailed model (Ignall, Kolesar, and Walker, 1975).

The essential idea of the queuing model is displayed in Figure 7.8, which represents the special case of an alarm type with only two stages. The states are described by pairs (j,k), where j is the number of alarms in stage 1 and k is the number of alarms in stage 2. The average duration of stage i is $1/\mu_i$, $i = 1, 2$. The diagram can be used to write equations for the steady-state values of the probability of State (j,k), as described in Section 7.6.1. While these equations are correct only for exponentially distributed service times, Chaiken (1971) showed that the results are valid for any distributions with finite means. Once the state probabilities are found, $p(n)$ is the sum of the probabilities of all states that have n busy companies.

To use the computer program that calculates the values of $p(0)$, $p(1)$, $p(2)$, ..., one must provide input data for $\lambda\tau_1$, $\lambda\tau_2$, $\lambda\tau_3$, ... An example showing how these numbers can be estimated will be given in the next section.

7.2.3 Application to Estimating Travel Distances

In Chapter 6, the square-root law for travel distances was presented. If N, the number of firehouses with at least one available company in a region of area A, is known, one version of this law states that the average travel distance D_1 for the first-arriving engine company at alarms in the region will be approximately

$$E(D_1) = k_1\sqrt{A/N}, \qquad (7.6)$$

where k_1 is a constant.[11] (This is the same as Equation (6.7).) Chapter 6 also mentioned that a reasonable approximation to the average travel distance to alarms over a period of time when the number of available companies changes, can be found by replacing N in Equation (7.6) with $E(N)$, the *average* number of stations with at least one engine company

---

[10] A FORTRAN program that calculates $p(n)$ and also $E(B) = \lambda E(S)$ is given in Appendix A7.3.

[11] Again, we illustrate the model for engine companies, but it can be applied equally well to ladder companies.

7.2 Number of Companies Busy in a Region

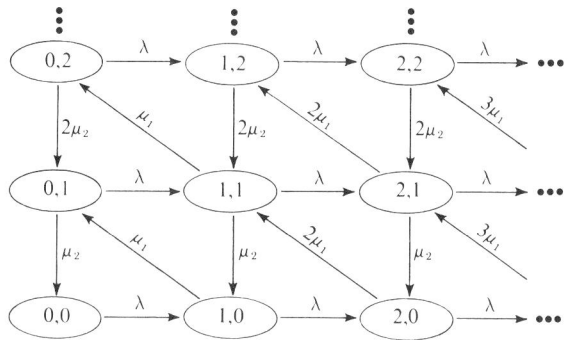

Legend

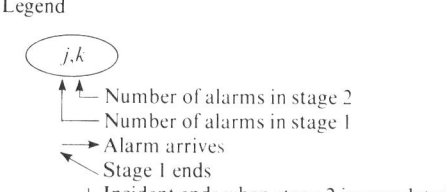

— Number of alarms in stage 2
— Number of alarms in stage 1
→ Alarm arrives
↘ Stage 1 ends
↓ Incident ends when stage 2 is completed

FIGURE 7.8. Bubble diagram for two-stage alarms.

available. In this section we illustrate why the approximation is a good one and tell how to calculate $E(N)$. We begin with the assumption that each firehouse has one engine company; in this case N is the number of engine companies and $E(N)$ is the average number of available engine companies.

We have seen, in Section 7.2.2, how to calculate the average number of *busy* engine companies, $E(B)$; and so it appears easy to calculate the average number of *available* engine companies: subtract $E(B)$ from the number of engine companies stationed in the region. However, a little reflection will reveal that this subtraction cannot be exactly correct because some companies might respond from outside the region to work at incidents in the region, and other companies might be relocated into the region. In this section we show how a somewhat more accurate calculation can be performed with the square-root law. While the discussion focuses on travel *distances*, the method can also be applied to travel *times* by using the conversion discussed in Section 6.5. The conclusion drawn from the more accurate calculation is that in most applications, the error in an approximate calculation of the average travel distance is only a few percent.

The more accurate calculation is based on using Equation (7.6) together with the probability $p(b)$ that b engine companies are busy, which was derived in Section 7.2.2. If n^* engine companies are stationed in the region, and the number busy is small compared to n^*, say $b = 0, 1$, or 2, then it will nearly always be true that the number available is $N = n^* - b$. In this case, we assume that $q(N)$, the probability that N engine companies are available, is given by the formula

$$q(N) = p(n^* - N). \tag{7.7}$$

However, if many units are busy in the region, the equation $N = n^* - b$ cannot be correct. Indeed, b could possibly be larger than n^*, leading to a negative value for N. Various assumptions can be made about the relationship between N and b when b is large compared to n^*. These would depend on the size of the region and the department's relocation practices. For example, we might assume $N = 0$ whenever $b \geq n^*$. Or, we might assume that the department will always relocate enough companies into the region to keep $N \geq 2$. (If the probability is very small that b is greater than $n^* - 2$, it will not matter exactly what assumption we make.)

Let us suppose that the number of available engine companies is always at least two. Then we can use Equation (7.7) for $q(N)$ when $N \geq 3$, and we set

$$\begin{aligned} q(2) &= p(n^* - 2) + p(n^* - 1) + p(n^*) + p(n^* + 1) + \cdots \\ q(1) &= q(0) = 0. \end{aligned} \tag{7.8}$$

The average of D_1 over time can be obtained by multiplying the probability $q(N)$ that N engine companies are available by $k_1\sqrt{A/N}$ and summing over the various values of N:

$$E(D_1) = \sum_{N=2}^{n^*} k_1 q(N) \sqrt{A/N}. \tag{7.9}$$

Example. *We will use Equation (7.9) to estimate the average travel distance for the first-arriving engine in a region having area $A = 20$ square miles and $n^* = 12$ engine companies stationed in the region, one in each of 12 firehouses. Let us assume that the constant for the region has been determined to be $k_1 = 0.6$, as suggested in Section 6.4.2.*

To calculate the probabilities $p(b)$, the analyst needs to know the average length of time τ_k that exactly k engine companies work at an alarm in the region ($k = 1, 2, 3, \ldots$). Ordinarily these data are not readily available to a fire department (although they could be calculated if the department's records show the time of arrival and departure for each company at each alarm). To obtain a reasonable estimate, alarms could be divided into types, and for each type the analyst could make

7.2 Number of Companies Busy in a Region

reasonable guesses at the service times or he could collect the required data for a sample of alarms.

The types might be:

Type 1, false alarms, or no work to do.
Type 2, phone alarms to which one engine is dispatched.
Type 3, alarms other than type 1 or 2 at which only one engine works.
Type 4, one type of alarms at which 3 engines work.
Type 5, another (more serious) type of alarms at which 3 engines work.
Type 6, alarms at which 4-7 engines work.
Type 7, alarms at which 8 or more engines work.

No matter how the types are defined, they should be related to the number of engines that will respond to and work at the incident. For the example we will assume that the initial dispatch to every alarm other than Type 2 is three engine companies.

After collecting data or making estimates, the analyst could prepare the required data in a form like Table 7.4. Next, he needs to calculate $\lambda\tau_1, \lambda\tau_2, \ldots, \lambda\tau_{11}$. This is accomplished by converting service times to hours, multiplying each one by the alarm rate for its type of alarm, and adding down the columns. This calculation is shown in Table 7.5.

The results at the bottom of Table 7.5 must be entered into a computer program, such as the one listed in Section A7.3, that will calculate all

TABLE 7.4. Average time spent by k engine companies at an alarm. Entries are time spent (in minutes), and blank entries are zero. For example, at a Type 1 alarm, all three engine companies work for an average of 8 minutes; at a Type 3 alarm, all three companies work together for 8 minutes and then one of them remains for another 12 minutes, on the average.

Type of Alarm	Alarm Rate (alarms/hour)	k = Number of Engines Working										
		1	2	3	4	5	6	7	8	9	10	11
Type 1	1.00	0	0	8								
Type 2	2.15	20										
Type 3	0.35	12	0	8								
Type 4	0.04	15	30	15								
Type 5	0.01	50	40	60								
Type 6	0.003	60	60	30	0	30	0	60				
Type 7	0.001	60	30	30	0	60	30	30	0	30	0	90

TABLE 7.5. Alarm rates multiplied by service times, for the example.

Type of Alarms	k = Number of Companies Working										
	1	2	3	4	5	6	7	8	9	10	11
Type 1			0.1333								
Type 2	0.7167										
Type 3	0.0700		0.0467								
Type 4	0.01	0.02	0.01								
Type 5	0.0083	0.0067	0.01								
Type 6	0.003	0.003	0.0015	0	0.0015	0	0.003				
Type 7	0.001	0.0005	0.0005	0	0.001	0.0005	0.0005	0	0.0005	0	0.0015
Total ($\lambda \tau_k$)	0.8090	0.0302	0.2020	0	0.0025	0.0005	0.0035	0	0.0005	0	0.0015

the $p(b)$ values from which the values of $q(N)$ can be determined. The $q(N)$ values corresponding to the numbers in Table 7.5 are:

$q(2) = 0.0038$

$q(3) = 0.0022$

$q(4) = 0.0043$

$q(5) = 0.0095$

$q(6) = 0.0164$

$q(7) = 0.0282$

$q(8) = 0.0671$

$q(9) = 0.1102$

$q(10) = 0.1251$

$q(11) = 0.2832$

$q(12) = 0.3500$.

These are entered in Equation (7.9) to obtain the average travel distance. Since $A = 20$, we have $\sqrt{A} = 4.47$ and therefore $k_1\sqrt{A} = 2.68$ (using $k_1 = 0.6$). Equation (7.9) becomes

$$\bar{D}_1 = 2.68[0.0038\sqrt{\tfrac{1}{2}} + 0.0022\sqrt{\tfrac{1}{3}} + \cdots + 0.3500\sqrt{\tfrac{1}{12}}]$$
$$= 0.843 \text{ miles}.$$

This is the estimated average travel distance for the first-arriving engine in the region. Of course, to perform these calculations repeatedly for different alarm rates and regions, and to calculate the average first-arriving distance for ladders as well as for engines, the analyst will want to have a computer program written to perform all the steps described in this example.

7.2 Number of Companies Busy in a Region

The example has shown that using Equation (7.9) to estimate the average travel distance is fairly complicated. It requires detailed data about the lengths of time that companies spend at different types of alarms, as well as a computer program to calculate the probability $q(N)$ that N companies are available. For this reason, the approximation to the square-root law based on the average number of companies available, $E(N)$, is much more convenient when it is sufficiently accurate. This approximation is

$$E(D_1) = k_1\sqrt{A/E(N)}. \tag{7.10}$$

As a rule of thumb, Equation (7.10) is sufficiently accurate when the average number of available companies is at least two; i.e., when $E(N) \geq 2$. Here we shall show how well it works for the 12-company example given above.

The most accurate way to calculate $E(N)$ is from the equation

$$E(N) = \sum_{N=0}^{n*} Nq(N), \tag{7.11}$$

which is simply the definition of the average. Using Equations (7.7) and (7.8), this sum can be calculated for the example as

$$E(N) = (2 \times 0.0038) + (3 \times 0.0022) + \cdots + (12 \times 0.35)$$
$$= 10.470.$$

However, we have not saved any effort, because all the probabilities $q(N)$ must be known in order to use Equation (7.11). The only way that Equation (7.10) can be a simplification is if there is a quick way to estimate $E(N)$. We have seen in Section 7.2.2 that the average number of busy engine companies is $E(B) = \lambda E(S)$, where $E(S)$ is the average number of engine company-hours per alarm, so an approximation to $E(N)$ is $E(N) = n^* - E(B) = n^* - \lambda E(S)$.

For our example, $\lambda E(S)$ can be determined by multiplying the numbers in the last row of Table 7.5 by 1, 2, 3, ..., 11 and adding the products; it turns out to be 1.536. Thus, $n^* - \lambda E(S) = 12 - 1.536 = 10.464$, which is practically identical to the more exact calculation done, 10.470. Thus, when the average number of companies busy is small compared to n^*, the approximation $E(N) = n^* - \lambda E(S)$ is excellent. Since $\lambda E(S)$ can be estimated directly from data showing the length of time companies work at incidents, without going through all the calculations shown in Tables 7.4 and 7.5, this constitutes a substantial simplification.[12]

---

[12] The computer program listed in Appendix A7.3 also prints out the value of $\lambda E(S)$.

Entering the value $E(N) = 10.47$ into Equation (7.10) gives $\bar{D}_1 = 0.829$ miles. Comparing this with the more accurate answer derived earlier, $D_1 = 0.843$ miles, we see that for our 12-company example the error is only 1.7 percent. Since the square-root law is itself an approximation that can lead to errors of a few percent, the use of Equation (7.10) is fully justified as a good approximation.

7.2.4 Adjustment when Two Companies Occupy a Single Firehouse

In most fire departments, some or all of the fire stations house more than one company. If these companies are of different types (e.g., an engine company, a ladder company, and perhaps an emergency medical unit), there is no need to adjust the calculations of average travel distance that are described in Section 7.2.3. The analyst simply calculates the average travel distance for engine companies separately from the average travel distance for ladder companies. For example, when using Equation (7.9) to calculate the average travel distance for first-arriving engine companies, $q(N)$ is the probability that N *engines* are available. When using Equation (7.10), $E(N)$ is the average number of *engines* available. Similarly, either equation can be used for ladder companies.

However, when two or more companies of the same type occupy a single firehouse, we must adjust the square-root law. For specificity, we will discuss the situation for engine companies, although the calculations are identical for ladder companies. In addition, we assume that, at most, two engine companies occupy a single firehouse. Suppose that there are M engine companies, and they are located in R firehouses, where $R < M$. We will show that the average travel distance for the first-arriving engine company at an alarm will be higher than if the M companies were dispersed, one to a firehouse. Thus, a fire department that has consolidated firehouses suffers a penalty in its average first-arriving travel distance. However, the average travel distance for the second- or third-arriving engine company may be higher or lower than if the M companies were dispersed, depending on the department's dispatching policy and the relationship between M and R.

When All Engine Companies are Available. Consider the situation when all engines are available. In this case the average travel distance for first-arriving engines will be $E(D_1) = k_1\sqrt{A/R}$, as compared to $k_1\sqrt{A/M}$ if the engines were dispersed. Since $R < M$, $\sqrt{A/R}$ is larger than $\sqrt{A/M}$. As an example, suppose that every firehouse has two engine companies, so that $M = 2R$. The average travel distance for first-arriving engines is $k_1\sqrt{2A/M} = \sqrt{2}k_1\sqrt{A/M}$, when all the engines are available. Thus the average travel distance is larger by a factor of $\sqrt{2}$, or 1.414 (41.4 percent), than it would have been if all the engines were dispersed, one to a firehouse.

To estimate the average travel distance for second-arriving companies, we need to know the department's dispatching policy. If the department dispatches two engines from the same firehouse, then of course the second-arriving travel distance is exactly the same as the first-arriving travel distance at all alarms that are near a firehouse having two or more engines. For simplicity, assume that every firehouse has either one or two engines. If R_1 stations have one engine and R_2 stations have two engines ($R_1 + R_2 = R$), then roughly a fraction R_2/R of all the alarms will have their second-arriving engine housed in the same station as their first-arriving engine.[13] Hence the average travel distance for the second-arriving engine will be approximately

$$E(D_2) = \frac{R_2}{R} k_1 \sqrt{A/R} + \frac{R_1}{R} k_2 \sqrt{A/R}.$$

Continuing the example, suppose that all the stations house two engine companies. Then $R_1 = 0$ and $R_2 = R$, so

$$E(D_2) = k_1 \sqrt{A/R} = \sqrt{2} k_1 \sqrt{A/M}.$$

Since $\sqrt{2} k_1$ is smaller than k_2, the average travel distance for the second-arriving engine is lower than it would have been if all the engine companies had been dispersed, one to a firehouse. (In Section 6.4.2, we saw that k_1 is approximately 0.6, so $\sqrt{2} k_1$ is approximately 0.84; but $k_2 = 1.2$, which is larger.)

If, on the other hand, the fire department never dispatches two engines from the same firehouse to the same alarm, then the average travel distance for the second-arriving engine is $k_2 \sqrt{A/R}$ when all engines are available. This, of course, is larger than $k_2 \sqrt{A/M}$. With this dispatching policy, both first-due and second-due travel times will be higher than if the engines were dispersed.

When Some Engine Companies Are Busy. We now turn to calculating estimates of average travel distances that take into account the unavailabilities of engine companies. To obtain accurate estimates one must use fairly complicated models, such as the Hypercube Queuing Model[14] or the simulation model described in Chapter 13. However, it is not too difficult to obtain a useful approximation for the average travel distance

---

[13] This assumes that the two-engine houses are not concentrated in the areas with the highest alarm rates. Since this assumption may be incorrect, the resulting calculation is only an approximation.

[14] This model, which was designed by Larson (1975), will be briefly described in Section 7.3.2. An overview of the model's design and capabilities is given by Chaiken (1975).

of the first-arriving engine. We begin with Equation (7.10), which gives the approximation

$$E(D_1) = k_1\sqrt{A/E(R)},$$

where $E(R)$ is the average number of stations with an available engine company. Our task is to estimate $E(R)$. We found that when there is only one engine in each firehouse, $E(R)$ is approximately $R - E(B)$, where $E(B)$ is the average number of busy engine companies. This approximation is unsatisfactory when several engines share a station. For example, it is possible that three engines might be busy and yet every firehouse might have an available engine present.

In fact, the average number of stations with an available engine will depend on the method used by dispatchers in selecting engines to dispatch. To simplify matters, we assume here that all firehouses that contain any engines are equally likely to be chosen for dispatch of the next engine. In other words, at any particular moment there may be r_1 stations having one engine and r_2 stations having two engines. If $r = r_1 + r_2$, we assume that the chance of choosing any one of these stations is $1/r$. Such an assumption is not entirely realistic, since it ignores the fact that alarms are more likely to occur near some stations than near others, but it is accurate enough for deriving an approximate square-root law.

Let us say that R_1 of the R stations house one engine and the remaining R_2 stations each house two engines. As a rough approximation, one might guess that the average number of empty stations is $E(R_E) = R_1 E(B)/R$. In fact, this is exactly right when $R_1 = R - 1$—that is, when only one station houses two engines and all the rest house one engine. It is also a moderately good approximation when R_1/R is large, but it is an underestimate. A better estimate for the average number of empty stations is

$$E(R_E) = \frac{R_1}{R} E(B) + \frac{1}{2} \frac{R_2(R_2 - 1)}{R^2(R - 1)} [E(B)]^2. \qquad (7.12)$$

This approximation is very accurate whenever $E(B)$ is small compared to R (say, $E(B) < 0.3R$), which is nearly always true in practical applications. One simply enters $E(B) = \lambda E(S)$ in Equation (7.12) and subtracts the result from R to obtain a value of $E(R)$ for the square-root law.

The remainder of this section is devoted to a derivation of Equation (7.12) and can be skipped by the reader who is willing to accept the estimate as satisfactory. The result is obtained by writing $R_E(b)$, the average number of empty stations when b engines are busy, in the form

$$R_E(b) = c_1 b + c_2 b(b - 1) + c_3 b(b - 1)(b - 2)$$
$$+ \cdots + c_b b!, \quad b = 1, 2, \ldots$$

7.2 Number of Companies Busy in a Region

and then ignoring all terms after the second to get

$$R_E(b) \doteq c_1 b + c_2 b(b - 1), \qquad b = 1, 2, \ldots \quad (7.13)$$

We shall show that $c_1 = R_1/R$ and

$$c_2 = \frac{1}{2} \frac{R_2(R_2 - 1)}{R^2(R - 1)}.$$

With these values of c_1 and c_2, Equation (7.12) is a direct consequence of Equation (7.13) when the number of busy engines has a Poisson distribution with mean $E(B)$. Since the number of busy engines typically has a distribution which is close to a Poisson distribution, Equation (7.12) is a reasonable approximation.

To find the values of c_1 and c_2 in Equation (7.13), we only have to consider the cases $b = 1$ and $b = 2$. However, the method we shall follow can be iterated to higher values of b, thereby verifying that the coefficients $c_3, c_4, \ldots$ can be ignored in comparison to c_1 and c_2.

Denote by $p_b(j, k)$ the probability that, when b engines are busy, there are j empty one-engine houses and k empty two-engine houses. When $b = 1$, there is one busy engine. Then $p_1(1, 0)$ is the probability that the engine comes from a one-engine house, which, according to our assumption about the dispatching practice, is R_1/R. Similarly, $p_1(0, 0)$ is the probability that the engine comes from a two-engine house. (No houses are empty because it is impossible to have an empty two-engine house when only one engine is busy.) Thus $p_1(0, 0) = R_2/R$. Multiplying the probabilities by the number of empty stations and adding gives us $R_E(1) = p_1(1, 0) = R_1/R$ for the average number of empty stations when $b = 1$. Thus the approximate formula $R_E(b) \doteq R_1 b/R$ is in fact exactly correct when $b = 1$, and we have shown that $c_1 = R_1/R$, as desired.

The formulas for $p_2(j, k)$ can be calculated similarly. For example, $p_2(2, 0)$ is determined by starting with the state in which one one-engine house is empty, and noting that the chances are $R_1 - 1$ out of $R - 1$ that the next busy engine also comes from a single-engine house. Hence, $p_2(2, 0) = R_1(R_1 - 1)/R(R - 1)$. After finding all the $p_2(j, k)$, the average number of empty stations is then

$$R_E(2) = 2p_2(2, 0) + p_2(0, 1) + p_2(1, 0),$$

which turns out to be

$$R_E(2) = 2 \frac{R_1}{R} + \frac{R_2(R_2 - 1)}{R^2(R - 1)}.$$

Comparing this with Equation (7.13), with $b = 2$, shows that

$$c_2 = \frac{1}{2} \frac{R_2(R_2 - 1)}{R^2(R - 1)},$$

which is the desired result.

Note that $c_1 \leq 1$ and $c_2 \leq 1/R$. By iteration of the derivation one can find $c_3, c_4, \ldots$ and show that $|c_3| \leq 1/R^2$, $|c_4| \leq 1/R^3, \ldots$. That is why Equation (7.13) is a good approximation when b/R is small. Attempting to obtain a more accurate estimate of $E(R_E)$ is not warranted, because the square-root law is itself an approximation.

7.3 DECIDING WHICH COMPANIES TO DISPATCH

Upon the initial receipt of an alarm, most fire departments determine how many engine companies and ladder companies to dispatch according to the location of the incident and its apparent nature. For example, four engines and two ladders might be dispatched in response to a telephone report of a structural fire in a downtown area, while only one engine would be dispatched to an automobile on fire at the same location. Once the *number* of companies to be dispatched has been determined (a matter which will be discussed in Section 7.4), standard practice is to dispatch the *closest available* units. In this section we will see that such a practice is not always the best policy.

The idea behind dispatching the closest available companies is to ensure the lowest possible response times. However, in some cases the incident may be of such a type that waiting an extra 30 seconds or so for the arrival of the second-closest company will not make any difference in the outcome. In such cases, one should think about the effect that the current dispatch will have on response times to future alarms that may occur while the dispatched companies are busy. In fact, we will see that the average of response times over a period of several hours can be reduced by making occasional exceptions to the closest-company dispatch rule.

The simplified example in Figure 7.9 illustrates the possible value of dispatching a company other than the closest one. In this figure, Com-

FIGURE 7.9. An example of when dispatching the closest company is not the best policy. (Company 1 is located in an area of high alarm rate.)

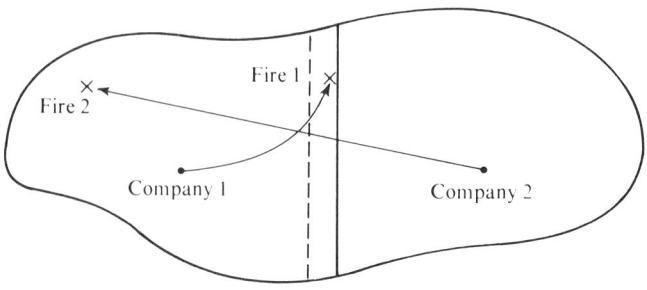

pany 1 is assumed to be in an area of high alarm rate. The solid vertical line represents all points that are equally distant from both Company 1 and Company 2. If a fire occurs at the location marked Fire 1, and one company is needed, Company 1 will be dispatched. If the alarm rate is high enough that a second fire is likely to occur while Company 1 is busy, then the fire is more likely to be near Company 1 than Company 2. Suppose it occurs at the point marked Fire 2. Then Company 2 will be dispatched.

The average travel distance for these two responses is one-half the sum of the two distances shown by arrows in Figure 7.9. Clearly the average would have been lower if Company 2 had been dispatched to Fire 1, and Company 1 to Fire 2. One way such a pattern of responses could be achieved is to divide the response areas for the two companies according to the dotted vertical line rather than the solid vertical line. In this case, Company 2 would have been dispatched to Fire 1. Such a division of response areas not only reduces the average travel distance (and thus the average travel time), but also reduces the workload of Company 1, bringing it closer to the workload of Company 2.

This example illustrates a general phenomenon that occurs when decisions are to be made in advance of an unpredictable future. It is sometimes best in the long run to make a decision that does not appear optimal at the moment it is made. Instead, the decision is made in such a way as to leave the system in a state that best anticipates future demands. Thus, dispatching Company 2 to Fire 1 leaves Company 1 in a position that is favorable for the next fire.

The problem of finding the "best" dispatching policy can be viewed in terms of finding the "best" dividing lines between pairs of companies. In general, these dividing lines can depend on the nature of the incident and on what other companies are available. Only in simple cases, such as dispatching one of two companies to each incident, is it possible to develop mathematical formulas telling where the dividing lines should be. However, analysis of these simple cases leads to insights that are helpful in thinking about this rather complex problem. Practical dispatching policies based on these insights are discussed in Chapter 11.

7.3.1 The Two-Company Case

Consider an imaginary city with only two fire companies, one of which is dispatched to each alarm. (This is the same as Figure 7.9.) We begin with the assumption that the dispatcher cannot distinguish among types of alarms, and therefore the city is to be divided into two regions. Region 1 will be the first-due area of Company 1, meaning that if available, Company 1 will respond to all alarms in Region 1. If an alarm occurs in Region 1 while Company 1 is busy, Company 2 will be dispatched if available. If both companies are unavailable, the alarm is "lost," meaning that some company from outside the city responds. Similarly, Region 2 (the rest of the city) will be the first-due area for Company 2.

The problem is to select the "best" dividing line between Region 1 and Region 2. This problem was first proposed and solved by Carter, Chaiken, and Ignall (1971). To simplify the discussion, we suppose that the service time for either company is exponentially distributed with mean $1/\mu$, no matter where in the city it responds. Chaiken and Ignall (1971) showed that the results obtained under this assumption are correct for any service-time distribution with mean $1/\mu$, so long as both companies have the same distribution. Alarms are assumed to arise from Region 1 according to a Poisson process with rate λ_1 and from Region 2 according to a Poisson process with rate λ_2. Note that although the total alarm rate in the region, given by $\lambda = \lambda_1 + \lambda_2$, is known, λ_1 and λ_2 are not known at the start, since they depend on the design of the regions.

The bubble diagram for this system is as shown in Figure 7.10. The states are defined as follows:

(0,0) = both companies available

(0,1) = Company 1 available, Company 2 busy

(1,0) = Company 1 busy, Company 2 available

(1,1) = both companies busy.

Note that the state diagram is a *square*, and the states can be interpreted as having two coordinates, the first indicating whether Company 1 is busy, and the second indicating whether Company 2 is busy. All the

FIGURE 7.10. Bubble diagram for two companies distinguished according to the region they serve.

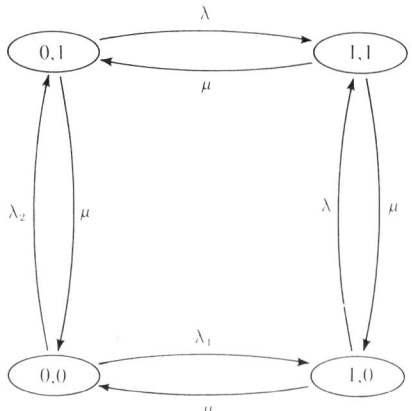

7.3 Deciding Which Companies To Dispatch

arrows in the diagram follow the sides of the square. (That is, there are no diagonal arrows.)

The steady-state equations for $p(j,k)$, the probability of state (j,k), can be read from Figure 7.10 as follows:

$$\lambda p(0,0) = \mu\{p(1,0) + p(0,1)\}$$
$$(\lambda + \mu)p(1,0) = \lambda_1 p(0,0) + \mu p(1,1)$$
$$(\lambda + \mu)p(0,1) = \lambda_2 p(0,0) + \mu p(1,1)$$
$$2\mu p(1,1) = \lambda\{p(1,0) + p(0,1)\}.$$

These can be solved (again, setting the sum of all four probabilities equal to 1) to give

$$p(0,0) = 1/(1 + \rho + \rho^2/2)$$
$$p(0,1) = p(0,0)(\rho_2 + \rho^2/2)/(1 + \rho)$$
$$p(1,0) = p(0,0)(\rho_1 + \rho^2/2)/(1 + \rho)$$
$$p(1,1) = p(0,0)\rho^2/2,$$

where $\rho = \lambda/\mu$, $\rho_1 = \lambda_1/\mu$, and $\rho_2 = \lambda_2/\mu$.

To find the optimal design of Regions 1 and 2, it is necessary to decide what performance measure is to be minimized by the design. As has been discussed in Chapter 3, selecting a suitable performance measure is difficult, but since the analysis to follow will work for any choice, we will simply call the function to be minimized the "damage function." In applications of this model, travel time has usually been chosen as the damage function. In any case, we suppose that it is possible to estimate $c_1(x)$, the expected damage if Company 1 responds to any point x in the city, and $c_2(x)$, the expected damage if Company 2 responds to point x. From these functions, the following averages can be calculated:

C_1 = average damage if Company 1 responds to all alarms in the city;

C_2 = average damage if Company 2 responds to all alarms in the city.

Example. To see how these average damages are calculated, suppose that the city has only five alarm boxes, and the damages when each company responds are as shown in Table 7.6. Evidently, Company 1 is closer to Boxes 1 and 2 than Company 2, both are equally distant from Box 3, and Company 2 is closer to Boxes 4 and 5 than Company 1. The average damage if Company 1 responds to all boxes is found by multiplying each damage by the associated alarm rate, adding for all the

TABLE 7.6. Damages in a hypothetical city with five alarm boxes.

Alarm Box Number	Alarm Rate at Box	Damage if Company 1 Responds	Damage if Company 2 Responds
1	2	3	8
2	1	4	7
3	1	5	5
4	2	7	4
5	2	8	3
Total	8		

boxes, and dividing by the total alarm rate:

$$C_1 = \frac{2 \times 3 + 1 \times 4 + 1 \times 5 + 2 \times 7 + 2 \times 8}{8}$$

$$= 45/8$$

Similarly,

$$C_2 = 42/8.$$

Carter, Chaiken, and Ignall (1971) showed how the average damage for all alarms, $E(C)$, can be expressed in terms of c_1 and c_2. Their results are reproduced in Section A7.4. They found that $E(C)$ can be minimized by calculating the number $s = \rho(C_1 - C_2)/(1 + \rho)$ and then selecting Region 1 to consist of all points x such that $c_1(x) - c_2(x) < s$, together with any or all points x such that $c_1(x) - c_2(x) = s$. (Region 2 is the rest of the imaginary city.)

Note that if $C_1 = C_2$, then the dividing line is located where $c_1(x) = c_2(x)$. Interpreting c_1 and c_2 as travel times, this dividing line means "dispatch the closest company." In other words, when $c_1 = c_2$, the queuing model prescribes the same dispatch policy that most fire departments now use. Also, if ρ is very small (i.e., the companies are busy a small fraction of the time), then s is close to zero, and we come to the same conclusion: dispatch the closest company.

However, when most of the alarms are closer to Company 1 than to Company 2, as in Figure 7.9, then $C_2 > C_1$, so s is negative. In this case points x on the optimal dividing line will have $c_2(x) > c_1(x)$. In other words, the dividing line is farther from Company 2 than from Company 1, as illustrated by the dotted line if Figure 7.9.

Example. *To give a numerical example of the variations in the average damage function as the dividing line between Region 1 and Region 2*

7.3 Deciding Which Companies To Dispatch

moves, consider the simplified geography shown in Figure 7.11. This is a rectangular city with Company 1 located at its center. We assume that any point (x, y) in the city is as likely as any other point to be the location of a fire alarm.

For this example we assume that damage is proportional to travel time, so we select the location of the dividing line to minimize average travel time. The companies are assumed to travel right-angle paths as shown in the figure, and the travel time t is assumed to be related to the travel distance d by the equation

$$t = 0.65 + 1.70 d.$$

Thus, for example, the travel time from Company 1, which is located at coordinates $(2,1)$, to the point (x, y) is

$$t_1(x, y) = 0.65 + 1.70(|x - 2| + |y - 1|).$$

We also assume that the average travel time if a company responds from outside the city, is 5 minutes.

With this information, it is possible to calculate the average travel time $E(T)$ as a function of k, which is the x-coordinate of the dividing line between Region 1 and Region 2. (The dividing line is vertical.) The results are graphed in Figure 7.12. From the graph it can be seen that the optimal dividing line (that is, the one that minimizes average travel time) is somewhat closer to Company 1 than to Company 2. This was to be expected, since more than half of the alarms are closer to Company 1 than to Company 2.

Figure 7.12 shows that the location of the optimal dividing line ($k =$

FIGURE 7.11. Example city with alarm rate $\lambda = 2$ per hour and service time $1/\mu = 30$ minutes.

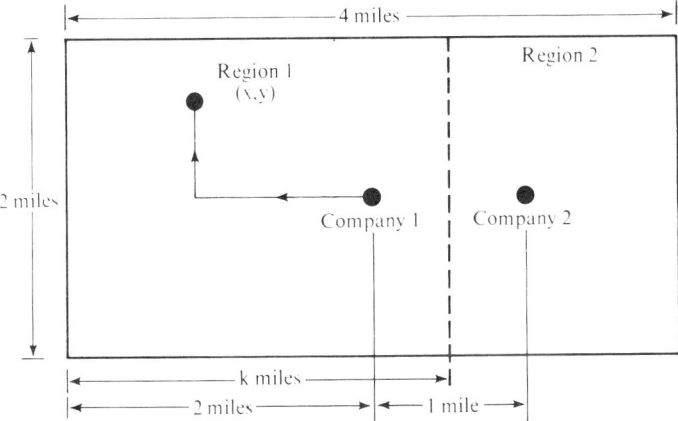

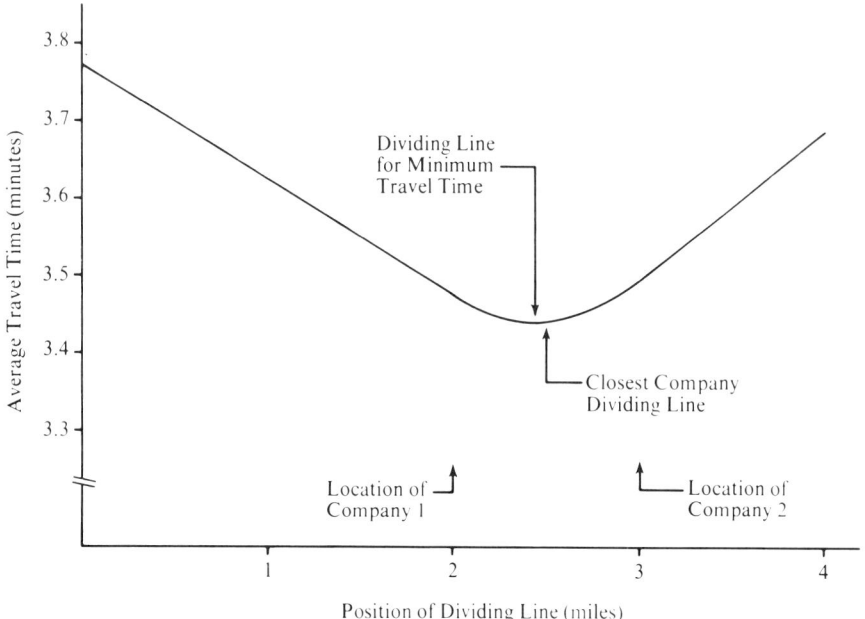

FIGURE 7.12. Relationship between average travel time and the location of the dividing line between Region 1 and Region 2 in Figure 7.11.

2.475 miles) is very close to the closest-company dividing line ($k = 2.5$ miles). Moreover, the average travel time does not vary by very much near the closest-company line. In fact, as long as the dividing line is chosen somewhere between Company 1 and Company 2, the average travel time lies between 3.44 minutes and 3.5 minutes, a difference of less than 2 percent. Thus, the point of the example is that fire departments have some freedom to move the dividing line toward the busier company (Company 1) so as to make the workloads more equal, without substantially affecting travel time.

The accuracy of this model can be improved in several ways. First, it is easy to write and solve equations when Company 1 has a service time that differs from the service time of Company 2. This is accomplished by replacing the rate μ in Figure 7.10 by μ_1 and μ_2. In this case, the results will be correct for exponentially distributed service times only, although they are good approximations for other service-time distributions.

Second, and more interesting, the service time for Company 1 can differ according to whether it responds into Region 1 or Region 2. (This takes into account the fact that travel time is part of the service time.) To accomplish this change, a larger state space (i.e., larger number of states in the bubble diagram) is required.

7.3 Deciding Which Companies To Dispatch 241

Third, one can allow for different types of alarms at each location x. Suppose there are K different types of alarms. Then it is necessary to specify the damage $c_j(x,m)$ if company j responds to a type m alarm at x ($j = 1, 2$) and the alarm rate $\lambda(x,m)$ for type m alarms at x ($m = 1, 2, \ldots, K$). Moreover, Company 1 can have different response areas A_1, $A_2, \ldots, A_K$ corresponding to the different alarm types. In this case the average damage is minimized in a similar way: let A_m be all points x such that $c_1(x,m) - c_2(x,m) < s$, together with some or all points x such that $c_1(x,m) - c_2(x,m) = s$. While it may appear that this result makes all the regions $A_1, A_2, \ldots, A_k$ the same, in fact it does not because the functions $c_j(x,m)$ are different for different values of m.

As an example, suppose there are only two types of alarms. Type 1 is "serious" and Type 2 is "not serious." Assume that for Type 2 alarms it doesn't matter which company responds. In other words, $c_1(x,2) = c_2(x,2)$ for all locations x. Then if $C_1 > C_2$, the average damage is minimized with the following dispatch policy: (1) Send Company 1 to all serious alarms at locations x such that $c_1(x,1) - c_2(x,1) \le s$, and (2) send Company 1 to *all* nonserious alarms! In this example, the assumption that $C_1 > C_2$ means that Company 1 is farther from serious alarms, on the average, than Company 2. If the alarm is Type 2, so that it does not matter which company is dispatched, it is better to send Company 1 so that Company 2 will be left to respond if a serious alarm occurs.

The example is peculiar because we have assumed that the dispatcher *knows* which alarms are serious. If the alarm types were defined so that Type 2 alarms were *less likely* to be serious than Type 1, then the model would not suggest sending Company 1 to all Type 2 alarms. However, the dispatching policy that minimizes $E(C)$ *would* send Company 1 farther to Type 2 alarms than to Type 1 alarms. A general principle arising from this model is that one should find out which company would yield the largest average damage if it were dispatched to *all* alarms, and should then dispatch that company past the closest-company dividing line, especially for alarms that are unlikely to be serious.

It is also possible, in this case where there are K different types of alarms, to allow each type to have its own service time distribution. In this instance, $s = (C_1 - C_2)\rho/(\rho + 1)$ is replaced by $s_m = (C_1 - C_2)\lambda E(S_m)/(\rho + 1)$ for a Type m alarm, where $E(S_m)$ is the expected service time for a Type m alarm. See Wrightson (1976) and Winston (1978) for details.

7.3.2 Extensions to Several Companies

The insights into dispatching policy gained in Section 7.3.1 apply only to the limited case of a city having two companies. To make further progress, we must consider more realistic examples. In this section, we

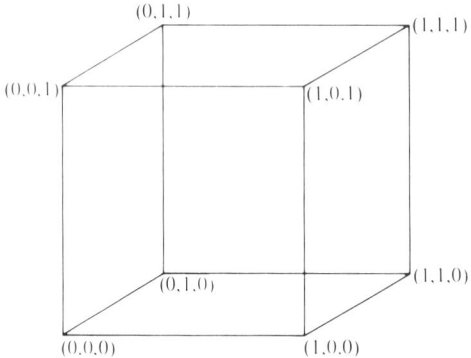

FIGURE 7.13. State space for three distinguishable companies.

continue to assume that only one company is dispatched to each alarm, leaving the multiple-dispatch case for Section 7.4.

We have seen that the state space for a city with two companies can be envisioned as a square. For three companies, the state space becomes a cube, as shown in Figure 7.13. Again, all the arrows representing transitions between states follow the edges of the cube if only one company is dispatched in response to each alarm. (These arrows are not shown in the figure.)

For more than three companies, the state space becomes a multidimensional analog of a cube and is called a *hypercube*. Larson (1973) devised a computer program to solve for the steady-state probabilities for this hypercube model, which retains the assumption that only one company is dispatched for each alarm.[15] If there are more than 15 companies, even high-speed computers cannot solve the equations of the hypercube model fast enough to be practical, so Larson (1974) developed an approximation for the hypercube model. Both the exact and the approximate hypercube models have been incorporated in a single computer program (Chaiken, 1975 and Larson, 1975).

These models can be used to find dispatch strategies that minimize the average damage function. Jarvis (1975) showed that the optimal dispatching policy is a direct generalization of the result given in Section 7.3.1 for two companies. First, at the time of dispatch one must know which companies are available. For every pair of available companies, say Company m and Company n, there is a constant K_{mn} such that the

---

[15] For three or more companies, the solution for exponentially distributed service times is no longer correct for other service-time distributions, even when all companies have the same distribution (Jarvis, 1975).

optimal policy prefers Company m over Company n at all points $\mathbf{x}$ with $c_m(\mathbf{x}) - c_n(\mathbf{x}) < K_{mn}$. Here $c_m(\mathbf{x})$ is the expected damage if Company m responds to point $\mathbf{x}$.

This policy can be envisioned as consisting of a large collection of maps. One map refers to the situation where all companies are available and shows the optimal response area for each company. The optimal response area looks like the usual first-due area for the company, except that the dividing lines are not necessarily halfway between companies. A second map refers to the situation where Company 1 is busy and all the others are available. It too shows response areas for all the companies.

There must be one map for each possible combination of available and busy companies. If there are n companies in the city, this means that there must be 2^n maps. The number 2^n can be very large even when n is moderate in size. For example, with $n = 17$ companies there must be 131,072 maps. Clearly, such a dispatch policy is impractical for manual dispatching systems and is not even sensible for use in a computer-assisted dispatch system. We can see that practical dispatching policies will have to be based on approximations to the optimal policies discussed here.

The next natural step in analyzing response areas is to consider the case where several companies can be dispatched to each alarm. However, it is not a good idea to assume that the dispatcher knows, in the first instance, *how many* companies he will dispatch and then decides *which ones*. In fact, these two questions are intertwined and must be answered together.

So for now we will discontinue analysis of the decision concerning *which* companies to dispatch and turn our attention to the decision concerning *how many* should be dispatched. A full discussion of both questions together appears in Chapter 11.

7.4 DECIDING HOW MANY COMPANIES TO DISPATCH

Our approach to deciding how many companies to dispatch is similar to the one taken in Section 7.3. We will consider an unrealistically simplified model so as to see what insights it provides. In the model discussed in this section, which was developed by Swersey (1972), the dispatcher has only one choice for each incoming alarm: he can dispatch either one company or two companies. Incidents occur according to a Poisson process at rate λ and are of two types. Type 1 is "serious" and requires two companies in order for the fire to be extinguished. Type 2 is "not serious" and requires only one company. However, when the dispatcher receives a report of an incident, he does not know for sure which type it is. Instead, he knows the *probability* that it is serious. This probability can be determined from information provided to the dispatcher by whoever reported the incident, or by analysis of past experience at the location of the incident, as discussed in Chapter 8.

Swersey made the following simplifying assumptions in order to analyze this problem. First, at every incident (no matter what type it is), the first-arriving company works for an exponentially distributed length of time with mean $1/\mu_1$, and the second company (if dispatched) is busy for an exponentially distributed time with mean $1/\mu_2$. The time $1/\mu_2$ is intended to represent only the length of time that the second company is unavailable because it is responding to an incident of unknown type. In this model, the second company never actually stays at a fire, whether it is needed or not. Instead, it is "magically" replaced by another company from outside the region of interest. (This "magic company" can be imagined to relocate into the station of the second company.) The purpose of this assumption is to arrange for transitions, from one state of the system to another, to depend only on the dispatcher's decision and not on the incident type.

The second assumption is that the damage function for nonserious (Type 2) incidents is zero, while the damage function for serious incidents is the following linear combination of the response times of the two companies needed at the incident:

$$C = R_1 + \beta R_2,$$

where

C is the damage

R_1 is the response time of the first-arriving unit

R_2 is the response time of the second-arriving unit

β is a constant that is less than one.

The response time of the second-arriving company varies according to whether or not it is dispatched when the alarm is received. Suppose that T_2 is the response time for the second-arriving company if it is dispatched at receipt of the alarm. The response time is assumed to be $T_2 + R_1$ if the second company is not dispatched. This means that the second company waits until the first company arrives before beginning its trip (i.e., the first company requests a second company the moment it arrives at the scene).

The model can be used to find the dispatch policy that minimizes the average damage per unit time. A *policy* consists of instructions to the dispatcher telling him whether to dispatch one company or two companies depending on (1) the state of the system and (2) the probability that the incoming alarm is serious. The states of the system are described by pairs (i,j), where i is the number of first-arriving companies busy at

7.4 Deciding How Many Companies To Dispatch

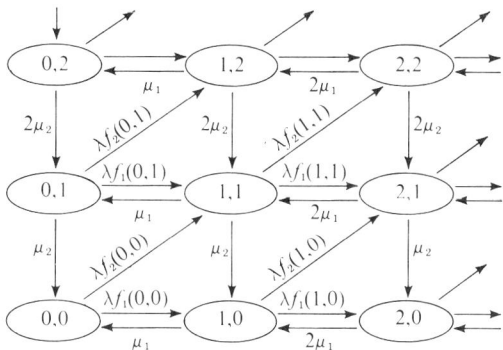

Legend

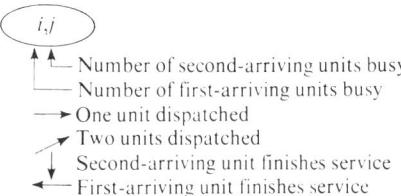

FIGURE 7.14. State diagram for choosing between "dispatch one" and "dispatch two."

incidents and j is the number of second-arriving companies busy. Once a policy is selected, there will be a certain fraction $f_1(i,j)$ of alarms to which the dispatcher sends one company in State (i,j), and another fraction $f_2(i,j)$ to which he sends two.[16] Thus, the bubble diagram for the system is as shown in Figure 7.14.

Using techniques of Markov decision theory, Swersey (1972) showed that the optimal policy for this problem has the following form: If the state is (i,j), all incidents whose probability of being serious is larger than a certain number $s^*(i,j)$ should be sent two companies, while only one company should be sent to all other incidents. The trick is to find the numbers $s^*(i,j)$. Although this can be accomplished by linear programming, the problem is often too complicated to be solved sufficiently rapidly on typical computer systems. However, by solving the problem for several examples, Swersey found suitable ways to simplify the calculations and obtain reasonably accurate approximations. For example, the value of $s^*(i,j)$ is nearly the same for all states (i,j) having the same

---

[16] $f_2(i,j) = 1 - f_1(i,j)$.

total number of companies busy. In addition, s^* increases as λ increases, or as the number of busy companies increases.

Rather than consider this model in greater detail, it is preferable to ask: what implications for dispatch policy can be guessed from the results of the model? The answer is that even if one chooses only a single cutoff number s^* (independent of the system state) and dispatches two companies to incidents whose probability of being serious is greater than s^*, the resulting policy is likely to be a good one. If the dispatcher sometimes has to choose between sending two companies and sending three companies, a similar cutoff probability should be useful for this decision. These notions are explored further in Chapter 11.

APPENDIX A7.1

Long-run State Probabilities for Figure 7.6

The equations corresponding to Figure 7.6 are as follows:

$$(\lambda_1 + \lambda_2)p(0) = \mu p(1)$$
$$(\lambda_1 + \lambda_2 + \mu)p(1) = \lambda_1 p(0) + 2\mu p(2)$$
$$\lambda_2 p(0) + (\lambda_1 + \lambda_2)p(1) = 2\mu p(2).$$

From the first of these we have

$$p(1) = \lambda/\mu\, p(0),$$

where $\lambda = \lambda_1 + \lambda_2$. From the third equation we have

$$\lambda_2 p(0) + \lambda^2/\mu\, p(0) = 2\mu p(2)$$

$$p(2) = \left(\frac{\lambda_2}{2\mu} + \frac{\lambda^2}{2\mu^2}\right) p(0).$$

Then, from $p(0) + p(1) + p(2) = 1$, we obtain

$$p(0) = 1 \bigg/ \left[1 + \frac{\lambda}{\mu} + \frac{\lambda_2}{2\mu} + \frac{\lambda^2}{2\mu^2}\right].$$

Hence,

$$p(1) = \lambda/\mu \bigg/ \left[1 + \frac{\lambda}{\mu} + \frac{\lambda_2}{2\mu} + \frac{\lambda^2}{2\mu^2}\right]$$

and

$$p(2) = \left[\frac{\lambda_2}{2\mu} + \frac{\lambda^2}{2\mu^2}\right] \bigg/ \left[1 + \frac{\lambda}{\mu} + \frac{\lambda_2}{2\mu} + \frac{\lambda^2}{2\mu^2}\right].$$

APPENDIX A7.2

Multistage Queuing Model

Suppose that alarms are of various types (Type 1, Type 2, . . .) and that alarms of Type i occur according to a Poisson process with rate λ_i and arrive at an infinite-server queue. Alarms of Type i are served in n_i independent sequential stages, with the jth stage requiring ν_{ij} servers. Let T_{ik} be the average length of time that exactly k servers are busy at an alarm of Type i. (In other words, T_{ik} is the sum over j of the service times for all stages having $\nu_{ik} = k$.)

We assume that $r = \Sigma_{ik} \lambda_i T_{ik} < \infty$. Define $\rho(k) = \Sigma_i \lambda_i T_{ik}$, and define convolutions $\rho^N(m)$ iteratively as follows:

$$\rho^{*2}(m) = \rho * \rho(m) = \sum_{k=1}^{m-1} \rho(k)\rho(m-k)$$

$$\rho^N(m) = \rho * \rho^{N-1}(m).$$

Then the steady-state probability that m servers are busy is

$$P(m) = \begin{cases} e^{-r} \text{ for } m = 0 \\ e^{-r}\left(\rho(m) + \frac{1}{2!}\rho^{*2}(m) + \frac{1}{3!}\rho^{*3}(m) + \cdots\right) \text{ for } m > 0. \end{cases} \quad (A7.1)$$

PROOF. We give the proof under the assumption that each stage has an exponentially distributed service time with mean $1/\mu_{ij}$ for Stage j of Type i alarms. Chaiken (1971) has proved the result for arbitrary service time distributions that satisfy the condition $r < \infty$.

Consider Type i alarms, and let $q_i(k_1, k_2, \ldots, k_{n_i})$ be the steady-state probability that k_1 alarms of Type i are in Stage 1 of service, k_2 alarms of Type i are in Stage 2, etc. Then the equations for the q_i probabilities are

$$\left(\lambda_i + \sum_{j=1}^{n_i} k_j \mu_{ij}\right) q_i(k_1, \ldots, k_{n_i})$$

$$= \lambda_i q_i(k_1 - 1, k_2, \ldots, k_{n_1})$$

$$+ (k_1 + 1)\mu_{i1} q_i(k_1 + 1, k_2 - 1, k_3, \ldots, k_{n_i})$$

$$+ (k_2 + 1)\mu_{i2} q_i(k_1, k_2 + 1, k_3 - 1, k_4, \ldots, k_{n_i})$$

$$+ \cdots$$

$$+ (k_{n_i} + 1)\mu_{in_i} q_i(k_1, k_2, \ldots, k_{n_i} + 1),$$

where any q_i with a negative argument is interpreted as zero. The solution to these equations having the total probability equal 1 is

$$q_i(k_1, \ldots, k_{n_i}) = \prod_{j=1}^{n_i} \frac{(\lambda_i/\mu_{ij})^{k_j}}{k_j!} e^{-\lambda_i/\mu_{ij}}. \qquad (A7.2)$$

This equation has the form of a product of independent Poisson distributions, as if each stage of service occurred according to a Poisson process at rate λ_i, independent of the other stages. This multiplicative property is common to many types of queuing systems and is known as Burke's Theorem (Burke, 1958). Multiplying together all the equations of form (A7.2) for different values of i and summing over stages having the same number of servers, it follows that the probability $p(\ell_1, \ell_2, \ell_3, \ldots)$ of finding ℓ_1 alarms with one server busy, ℓ_2 alarms with two servers busy, etc., is

$$p(\ell_1, \ell_2, \ldots) = \prod_{k=1}^{\infty} \frac{\left(\sum_i \lambda_i T_{ik}\right)^{\ell_k}}{\ell_k!} e^{-\sum_i \lambda_i T_{ik}}.$$

Now $P(m)$, the probability that m servers are busy, is the sum of all $p(\ell_1, \ell_2, \ldots)$ such that $\ell_1 + 2\ell_2 + 3\ell_3 + \cdots = m$. However, this is simply the coefficient of s^m in the generating function

$$\Psi(s) = \sum_{\ell_1, \ell_2, \ldots} p(\ell_1, \ell_2, \ldots) s^{\ell_1} s^{2\ell_2} s^{3\ell_3} \cdots$$

$$= \sum_{\ell_1, \ell_2, \ldots} \prod_{k=1}^{\infty} \frac{\left(\sum_i \lambda_i s^k T_{ik}\right)^{\ell_k}}{\ell_k!} e^{-\sum_i \lambda_i T_{ik}}$$

$$= \exp\left(-r + \sum_{k=1}^{\infty} \left(\sum_i \lambda_i T_{ik}\right) s^k\right)$$

$$= \exp\left(-r + \sum_{k=1}^{\infty} \rho(k) s^k\right)$$

$$= e^{-r}\left(1 + \sum \rho(k) s^k + \frac{1}{2!}\left(\sum \rho(k) s^k\right)^2 + \cdots\right).$$

Since the coefficient of s^m in the term $(\Sigma \rho(k) s^k)^N$ is, by definition of the convolution, $\rho^{*N}(m)$, the coefficient of s^m in $\Psi(s)$ is

$$e^{-r}\left(\rho(m) + \frac{1}{2!} \rho^{*2}(m) + \frac{1}{3!} \rho^{*3}(m) + \cdots\right),$$

which proves Equation (A7.1). Note that although the sum appears to be infinite, it is actually finite, since $\rho^{*N}(m) = 0$ where $N > m$.

For ease of calculation, it is convenient to note that $\rho(k)$ is λ times the average time that exactly k servers work at an alarm, where $\lambda = \Sigma_i \lambda_i$. This can be seen from the equation

$$\rho(k) = \sum_i \lambda_i T_{ik} = \lambda \sum_i \frac{\lambda_i}{\lambda} T_{ik}.$$

APPENDIX A7.3

Fortran Program to Calculate the Probability That N Companies Are Busy

```
      C     THIS PROGRAM CALCULATES THE PROBABILITY THAT N COMPANIES
      C     ARE BUSY FROM A MULTISTAGE INFINITE-SERVER QUEUING MODEL
      C
0001        DIMENSION F(51),P(50),Q(50),RHOSTR(50,50),RHO(50),TITLE(15)
      C     F(N+1) IS N FACTORIAL
      C     P(N+1) IS THE PROBABILITY THAT N COMPANIES ARE BUSY
      C     Q(N+1) IS THE PROBABILITY THAT GREATER THAN N COMPANIES ARE BUSY
      C     RHO(I) IS LAMBDA TIMES THE AVERAGE TIME EXACTLY I COMPANIES
      C          SPEND AT AN ALARM
      C     RHOSTR (RHOSTAR) IS THE CONVOLUTION MATRIX
      C     AVG IS THE AVERAGE NUMBER OF BUSY COMPANIES
      C     SYSOUT IS THE PRINTER
      C
0002        INTEGER SYSOUT,ZERO
0003        DATA SYSOUT/6/,ZERO/0/
      C
      C     DATA ARE READ FROM INPUT FILE ON FORTRAN UNIT 19.
      C     THE FIRST 80-COLUMN CARD CONTAINS THE LENGTH OF THE VECTOR
      C     RHO (IMAX), THE NUMBER OF LINES OF PRINTOUT (NPRINT),
      C     AND A TITLE FOR THE RUN. THE NEXT CARD(S) CONTAIN THE VALUES
      C     OF RHO(I), TEN TO A CARD. THE NEXT CARD BEGINS A NEW RUN.
0004  5     READ(19,110,END=100)IMAX,NPRINT,TITLE
0005        WRITE(SYSOUT,115)TITLE
```

```
0006   C
0007   C      INITIALIZE
0008   C
0006          F(1)=1.
0007          RHOSUM=0.
0008          AVG=0.
0009          DO 20 I= 1,50
0010          RHO(I)=0.
0011          F(I+1)=I*F(I)
0012          P(I)=0.
0013          Q(I)=0.
0014          DO 15 J=1,50
0015          RHOSTR(I,J)=0.
0016    15    CONTINUE
0017    20    CONTINUE
       C
0018          READ(19,120)  (RHO(I),I=1,IMAX)
       C
       C
       C      CALCULATE AVERAGE AND FIRST LINE OF PRINTOUT (ZERO COMPANIES BUSY)
       C
0019          DO 30 I=1,IMAX
0020          WRITE(SYSOUT,125)I,RHO(I)
0021          AVG=AVG+I*RHO(I)
0022          RHOSTR(1,I)=RHO(I)
0023          RHOSUM=RHOSUM+RHO(I)
0024    30    CONTINUE
0025          P(1)=EXP(-RHOSUM)
0026          Q(1)=1.-P(1)
0027          WRITE(SYSOUT,130)
0028          WRITE(SYSOUT,140)ZERO,P(1),Q(1)
```

```
0029      C
0030      C
0031      C    CALCULATE REMAINING LINES OF PRINTOUT
0032      C
0033                DO 55 N=1,NPRINT
0034                NMIN1=N−1
0035                IF (N .EQ. 1) GO TO 45
0036                DO 40 J=N,NPRINT
0037                JMIN1=J−1
0038                DO 35 I=NMIN1,JMIN1
0039                RHOSTR(N,J)=RHOSTR(N,J)+RHOSTR(1,J−I)*RHOSTR(N−1,I)
0040     35         CONTINUE
0041     40         CONTINUE
0042     45         DO 50 I=1,N
0043                P(N+1)=P(N+1)+P(1)*RHOSTR(I,N)/F(I+1)
0044     50         CONTINUE
0045                Q(N+1)=Q(N)−P(N+1)
0046                WRITE(SYSOUT,150) N,P(N+1),Q(N+1)
0047     55         CONTINUE
0048      C
0049      C
0050                WRITE(SYSOUT,160)AVG
0051                GO TO 5
0052                CALL EXIT
0053    100         FORMAT(2I5,15A4)
0054    110         FORMAT('1',5X,15A4,/)
0055    115         FORMAT(10F8.6)
        120         FORMAT('  RHO(',I2,')=',F8.5)
        125         FORMAT('0  N  PROB(N)    PROB(>N)')
        130         FORMAT('0',I6,2(6X,F6.4))
        140         FORMAT('  ',I6,2(6X,F6.4))
        150         FORMAT('0 AVERAGE=',F8.4)
        160         END
```

APPENDIX A7.4

Calculation of the Optimal Response Boundary Between Two Companies

In Section 7.3.1, a formula is given for the dividing line between two companies that minimizes an average damage function. This Appendix presents the mathematical derivation of that formula. The discussion is based on the work of Carter, Chaiken, and Ignall (1971). However, here we assume that alarms arise from a finite number of points in the city, rather than allow the more general geographical distribution of alarms permitted by the original authors.

The assumptions of the model described in Section 7.3.1 are as follows. The imaginary city has two companies, Company 1 and Company 2. There is a finite set of points A in the city at which alarms may occur. We denote by $\lambda(x)$ the alarm rate at point x in A (assumed to be positive), and by $c_j(x)$ the average damage if Company j ($= 1, 2$) responds to x. The alarms arising at point x constitute a Poisson process with rate $\lambda(x)$, independent of the process at any other point y. The service time distribution is the same at every point, independent of which company responds, and has finite mean $1/\mu$.

The city is to be divided into two disjoint regions, A_1 and A_2, and Company j will be the dispatcher's first choice to respond into region A_j, $j = 1, 2$. Define

$$\lambda = \sum_{x \in A} \lambda(x)$$

$$\lambda_j = \sum_{x \in A_j} \lambda(x), \quad j = 1, 2.$$

The states of the system are:

(0,0) = both companies available
(0,1) = Company 1 available, Company 2 busy
(1,0) = Company 1 busy, Company 2 available
(1,1) = both companies busy.

As shown in Section 7.3.1, the steady-state probabilities for each state are

$$p(0,0) = 1/(1 + \rho + \rho^2/2)$$
$$p(0,1) = p(0,0)(\rho_2 + \rho^2/2)/(1 + \rho)$$
$$p(1,0) = p(0,0)(\rho_1 + \rho^2/2)/(1 + \rho) \quad \text{(A7.3)}$$
$$p(1,1) = p(0,0)\rho^2/2,$$

where $\rho = \lambda/\mu$ and $\rho_j = \lambda_j/\mu$, $j = 1, 2$.

We also define

C_j = average damage if Company j responds to all alarms
$$= \sum_{x \in A} c_j(x)\lambda(x)/\lambda, \quad j = 1, 2$$

C_{jj} = average damage if Company j responds in Region j
$$= \sum_{x \in A_j} c_j(x)\lambda(x)/\lambda_j, \quad j = 1, 2.$$

Appendix A7.4

If the state is (0,0), Company j responds to a fraction λ_j/λ of all alarms and incurs average damage C_{jj}, so the average damage is

$$C_{11}\frac{\lambda_1}{\lambda} + C_{22}\frac{\lambda_2}{\lambda}.$$

If the state is (0,1), Company 1 responds to all alarms, so the average damage is C_1. Similarly, if the state is (1,0), the average damage is C_2. When the state is (1,1), some other company responds, and we call the average damage C_3.

Thus, the steady-state average damage to all alarms is

$$E(C) = p(0,0)\left(C_{11}\frac{\lambda_1}{\lambda} + C_{22}\frac{\lambda_2}{\lambda}\right)$$
$$+ p(0,1)C_1 + p(1,0)C_2 + p(1,1)C_3. \quad (A7.4)$$

This can be rewritten.

$$E(C) = \frac{p(0,0)}{\lambda}\left(\sum_{x \in A_1} c_1(x)\lambda(x) + \sum_{x \in A_2} c_2(x)\lambda(x)\right)$$
$$+ p(0,1)C_1 + p(1,0)C_2 + p(1,1)C_3$$
$$= \frac{p(0,0)}{\lambda}\sum_{x \in A}[c_1(x) - c_2(x)]\lambda(x)$$
$$+ p(0,1)C_1 + [p(1,0) + p(0,0)]C_2 + p(1,1)C_3.$$

Using Equations (A7.3) for the probabilities $p(i,j)$ and performing some algebra, this becomes

$$E(C) = \frac{p(0,0)}{\lambda}\left[\sum_{x \in A_1}(c_1(x) - c_2(x))\lambda(x) - \frac{\rho}{1+\rho}\lambda_1(C_1 - C_2)\right] + \alpha,$$

where

$$\alpha = p(0,0)\left[\frac{\rho + \rho^2/2}{1+\rho}C_1 + \frac{1+\rho+\rho^2/2}{1+\rho}C_2 + \frac{\rho^2}{2}C_3\right],$$

and thus α is a constant that does not depend on how Region A_1 and Region A_2 are chosen.

Setting $s = \rho(C_1 - C_2)/(1 + \rho)$, we have the final result for $E(C)$:

$$E(C) = \frac{p(0,0)}{\lambda}\sum_{x \in A_1}(c_1(x) - c_2(x) - s)\lambda(x) + \alpha. \quad (A7.5)$$

From this form, it follows that $E(C)$ will be minimized if A_1 is chosen to be the set

$$X = \{x \in A: c_1(x) - c_2(x) < s\}.$$

In addition, if there are any points x such that $c_1(x) - c_2(x) = s$, they can be chosen to lie in either A_1 or A_2 without affecting the value of $E(C)$, as is apparent from Equation (A7.5).

The model can be elaborated to allow different types of alarms at each point x. If there are K different alarm types, then $c_j(x,m)$ denotes the average damage if Company j responds to a Type m alarm at x, $j = 1, 2$; $m = 1, 2, \ldots, K$. In this case, Company j can have K different response areas $A_{j1}, A_{j2}, \ldots, A_{jK}$, corresponding to the different types of alarms. Following the calculation presented above, one finds that the average damage is

$$E(C) = \frac{p(0,0)}{\lambda} \sum_{m=1}^{K} \sum_{\text{x} \in A_{1m}} (c_1(\text{x},m) - c_2(\text{x},m) - s)\lambda(\text{x},m) + \alpha,$$

where $\lambda(\text{x},m)$ is the alarm rate for Type m alarms at x. This is a sum of terms, each of which is similar to Equation (A7.5), and therefore it is minimized in a similar way: choose A_{1m} to be the set

$$X_m = \{\text{x} \in A: c_1(\text{x},m) - c_2(\text{x},m) < s\}$$

together with part or all of the set

$$Y_m = \{\text{x} \in A: c_1(\text{x},m) - c_2(\text{x},m) = s\}.$$

Chapter 8
Analyzing the Demand for Fire Department Services

Synopsis

Estimates of the number of alarms that will occur during future time periods are needed to evaluate deployment options. Depending on the particular deployment questions being addressed, separate estimates of alarm rates may be needed for different geographical areas, for alarms signaling different types of incidents, for alarms reported in different ways, and for various time periods.

These estimates may be derived from data describing the number of alarms that have occurred in the past. The data that must be collected depend on the needs of the deployment models. In general, for each alarm one needs to know at least the following: its time of occurrence; how it was reported; the location; and the type of incident it was. Both the Uniform Fire Incident Reporting System (UFIRS) and the National Fire Data System (NFDS) provide for the collection of data required for analyzing alarm rates in formats that are relatively easy to use. UFIRS is a complete computer-based information system that aggregates incident data and generates reports that can be used for management, planning, and analysis. If incident data are recorded on NFDS forms, they may be fed into a national data bank and analyzed to detect national trends in the demand for fire service.

Examining historical incident data provides the starting point for estimating alarm rates. To be most useful, the incident data should generally be aggregated by categories, which will depend on the deployment problems being considered. There are three very important categories:

Type of Alarm. There are several ways that alarms may be categorized by type, including: amount of damage (e.g., light, medium, or heavy); how the alarm was reported (e.g., by box or by telephone); and the amount of time fire units are unavailable because of the alarm. These *categorizations provide more useful ways of defining alarm types for deployment than descriptions of what is burning.*

Geographical Region. *The geographical distribution of alarms is one of the primary determinants of the location of fire companies. "Demand regions" comprising the administrative districts of several fire units can be defined so that the alarm rates are relatively similar at locations within each region. In the Parametric Allocation Model (see Chapter 9), alarm rates within these demand regions are combined with judgments concerning the relative hazards in the regions, to determine the number of fire companies to station in each region. Alarm rates in smaller regions, which are needed for choosing specific sites for firehouses (Chapter 10), are easily derived from the alarm rates in demand regions.*

Time of Day. *Rules for initial dispatch and relocation decisions discussed in Chapters 11 and 12 require estimates of hourly alarm rates. These alarm rates vary by time of day, day of week, and season. Analysis of alarms over a period of several years is needed to estimate trends (i.e., the annual rate of increase or decrease in alarms).*

The simplest way to predict future alarms is to assume that the alarm rate will be identical to the rates that occurred in the past. However, this procedure is appropriate only if: (1) the year-to-year variation in alarm rates is small; and (2) the type of alarms whose rate one is trying to estimate occurs frequently. If either of these assumptions fails to hold, it is necessary to make additional assumptions about how the future will be related to the past. For example, for firehouse siting models, one needs to estimate the annual number of alarms that will occur in a very small area—a few alarm boxes at most. Since alarms occur only infrequently at each alarm box, one can usually produce better estimates of alarm rates in small areas by assuming that the alarm rate in several adjacent small areas will be the same, and using the average alarm rate as the estimate for each location.

A useful way of estimating how alarm rates vary over time is to assume that alarm rates are functions of known variables that describe the time of day, season, year, etc. For long-range predictions of the annual number of alarms, demographic variables, such as population and housing stock, can also be used in the functions. The parameters of the functions are estimated by regression analysis. This makes sure that the values of the functions, using known historical values of the variables, are as close as possible to the alarm rates that occurred in the past. It is also possible to derive confidence limits on the range of alarm rates that will occur; i.e., statements of the form "there is a 95 percent chance that there will be between 1500 and 2000 alarms next year."

A computer is essential for the estimation of alarm rates by regression.

Widely available computer program packages make regression relatively easy to use.

We cannot specify the exact form of alarm rate prediction models that will work best in all cities (although two specific models are developed in the last two sections of the chapter). However, there are some principles that should apply to developing any alarm prediction model. In particular:

1. Use the fact that alarms generally occur according to a Poisson process.
2. Use the smallest number of explanatory variables that is consistent with producing accurate estimates.
3. Properly chosen continuous variables are usually superior to categorical variables.
4. Assess the accuracy of the predictions by testing the model with a different set of data than that used for deriving the parameters of the model.

8.1 INTRODUCTION

Estimates of alarm rates, service times, and travel times are needed to use the methods and models described in this book. Solving strategic and tactical deployment problems requires knowing something about when and where alarms can be expected, and what this implies in the way of work by fire companies. In particular, it is necessary to know or have reasonable estimates of at least the following:

1. The rates at which serious fires and other types of alarms occur in different regions at different times of the day.
2. The average length of time a company in a particular region spends working at different times of day.
3. The constants in the square-root law.
4. The constants in the relationship between travel time and travel distance.

We have specified "in different regions at different times of day" because citywide year-round averages for the performance measures can conceal inequalities and problems. For example, despite a reasonable citywide value for average travel time, there can be unacceptably long travel times in some parts of the city. Similarly, a reasonable average daily workload may arise from a very heavy workload during the busy times of day, and little work at other times.

Chapter 6 describes how to estimate travel distances (item 3, above) and travel times (item 4). Average company work time (item 2) depends on the mix of different types of alarms to which the company responds. It will usually be sufficient to produce work time estimates for three classes of alarms: false alarms, structural fires, and all other incidents. Reasonable estimates of how long companies spend at these three types of incidents can be based on citywide figures because it is unlikely that company-to-company or time-of-day variation is appreciable. If fire companies routinely report monthly or yearly work time separately for each type of alarm, these numbers can be used directly. Otherwise, one can take a small sample from company journals, dispatcher's logs, and chief officers' reports, and compute the average work time at each type of alarm. The average number of company-hours per alarm for a particular region and a particular time of day is then computed as a weighted average of the average work times for each of the incident types. The weights are the fraction of each type of alarms for that region and that time of day. Thus, with estimates of alarm rates by region and time of day, average company workloads are straightforward to calculate.

The emphasis in this chapter is on estimating alarm rates. Besides needing alarm rate predictions for several types of incidents to estimate average company work times as described above, alarm rate predictions are needed to address both the strategic and tactical issues described in Chapter 3. Strategic or long-range planning issues include the siting of firehouses (Chapter 10) and the allocation of companies to regions (Chapter 9). They require yearly total alarm rate predictions, for a number of years into the future, for relatively large regions. The alarm rate prediction needs for strategic models are usually met by relatively straightforward projection of annual citywide total alarms. However, since strategic decisions should be based on predictions of events up to 20 or 40 years in the future, it may be helpful to use local demographic information in making longer range alarm predictions. This will be the case if the likely long-term changes or lack thereof in building composition and population are fairly well understood; for example, if urban renewal is planned for a region, or if a vacant area is zoned for a large shopping center. Section 1 of Chapter 14 describes how such considerations were used in recommending fire company locations in the city of Yonkers. Also, Section 8.4.1 describes how demographic factors were used to make 15-year projections of New York City fire alarm rates.

Tactical models, such as relocation algorithms (Chapter 12) and initial dispatch rules (Chapter 11), require more detailed and shorter-term predictions than the strategic models. Relocation rules require hour-by-hour prediction of total alarms for first-due areas, while initial dispatch rules require predictions broken down by alarm type for even smaller areas.

8.1 Introduction

It is to these more exacting requirements that most of this chapter is devoted.

Whether or not the task of estimating alarm rates presents conceptual or practical difficulties depends on (1) whether the alarms in question are common occurrences and (2) how the city currently collects and aggregates alarm records. When there are many alarms, more or less straightforward use of historical data may give good estimates of gross alarm rates. For example, to predict citywide total alarms for next year, the following approach should provide a good estimate. Look at the citywide totals over the past few years. If the total has shown little change over this period, average the yearly totals. If, as is more likely, the total has been rising, compute the annual percentage increase, and increase this year's total number of alarms by that percent. Even though this provides only a rough estimate and may not prove very accurate, it is good enough for some aspects of deployment analysis.

On the other hand, when the alarms in question are not frequent, it is often desirable to use the more sophisticated statistical models and techniques described in Section 8.4. For example, suppose that, for initial dispatch planning, you need to predict the chance that a box alarm from a particular street corner at a particular time is a serious fire. (The term "box alarm" refers to an alarm reported by someone pulling a fire alarm box as distinguished from an alarm reported by telephone or other means.) The chance that an alarm signals a serious fire may be very different for different alarm boxes. It also varies considerably by time of day. (There is a much lower chance that a box alarm signals a serious fire if it is received from a box near a school just after school lets out.)

In light of this information, it might seem that the seriousness of an incoming alarm could be predicted by considering the history of alarms at the location and the time of its receipt. But many locations have few box alarms and even fewer serious fires in a year. When the time period is also restricted—for example, between midnight and 8 A.M.—cases like the following occur: Box A had three box alarms, none serious; Box B had one box alarm, and it signaled a serious fire. It would not be sensible to conclude that future late night alarms from Box A are not serious and those from Box B are surely serious, although that would be the effect of using the historical data without modification.

This example illustrates the difference between straightforward extrapolation of historical data on the one hand, and the need for formal statistical inference on the other. For many situations, straightforward extrapolation is sufficient. For problems like predicting whether an alarm is serious, explicit probabilistic assumptions must be made about how the future will be related to the past. Then the methods of statistical inference will yield confidence statements about the future occurrence of various events. Before embarking on an effort to develop complicated predictive models, however, the fire department should be certain that it really needs such predictions to answer policy questions.

To answer many of the deployment questions arising in both tactical and strategic models, it is sufficient to consider the demand during the peak hours of the day and/or the peak day of the week or season, rather than understand the whole pattern in detail. The idea is to capture the significant patterns. For example, in many cities there are wide time-of-day variations (typically 2.5 times as many alarms from 4 P.M. to midnight as from midnight to 8 A.M.) and minor seasonal and day-to-day variations (there may be 1.2 times as many alarms on Friday as on Monday, and there may be 1.2 times as many in December as in April). The seasonal variation is more pronounced in specific kinds of incidents—for example, brush fires—but it may be reasonable to neglect seasonal and day-of-the-week differences entirely, especially if the deployment of fire companies cannot be easily changed by season or day of the week. Section 8.3 discusses the causes of variation and presents methods of tabulating data in order to examine these patterns.

For large cities, where alarm patterns differ in different parts of the city, it may require considerable analysis to discover satisfactory ways of characterizing year-to-year trends, seasonal patterns, day-of-the-week differences, hourly patterns, and how they vary from location to location. Sections 8.5 and 8.6 present two case studies of such exercises for the borough of the Bronx in New York City.

Predicting fire alarms requires models. The process of building a prediction model may begin with constructing a statement of the problem that includes the specification of the variables of interest (numbers of different types of fire alarms), and a list of potential explanatory variables (geographic factors, time, land use, weather). Section 8.4 describes some general principles to follow in developing models for predicting fire alarms. Although we use a priori mathematical considerations, such as alarms arriving in a time-varying Poisson process (see Chapter 7, Section 7.1.3), to restrict the range of possible prediction models to manageable proportion, our emphasis here is on how to determine alarm rate models that appear to underlie a body of data.

Several general points will emerge. First, parameters (constants to be estimated from the data) should be used sparingly. The goal should be achieving the maximum amount of "explanation" for each new parameter that is introduced. The second point concerns assessing how accurate predictions are for policy purposes. We recommend setting aside the last (most recent) year of data as a "calibration set." Data for the initial years should be used to select the model. The model may then be calibrated by calculating the average distance between the predicted values and the final year's data points. The common practice of using the same data set both to select and to calibrate the model will usually yield an unduly low estimate of the prediction error due to what is usually called the *selection effect*. These principles and a number of others are treated in some detail in Section 8.4 and are illustrated in the case studies of Sections 8.5 and 8.6.

After a satisfactory method of predicting alarms is found, there will inevitably be individual hours, days, and regions in which the observed number of alarms is substantially different from (usually, larger than) the prediction. Before becoming worried by large errors, some effort should be devoted to looking for the causes. Causes may range from the nonrepeatable and hence completely unpredictable, such as a garbage collectors' strike, civil disorder, or an electricity blackout, to the predictable but rare, like New Year's Eve or the Fourth of July. For unpredictable events, prediction errors can and should be ignored and the predictions should be calculated again after deleting data distorted by these events. Rare but periodic predictable events, especially holidays, should be taken into account by allowing a jump in the predicted value for just that day or hour. Events like heavy rain or snow, the effects of which are predictable over the short term, can be accounted for using an updating procedure as described in the case study in Section 8.5. Only large consistent errors with no apparent cause should lead to concern about the accuracy and appropriateness of the prediction method.

Section 8.2 covers data collection and contains a discussion of what data are needed for each of the strategic and tactical models presented in this book. Section 8.3 presents methods for summarizing and displaying the information collected on a large number of alarms that yield insight into patterns of past alarms. Section 8.4 describes how to draw inferences about the future from explicit assumptions about the similarity of the future to the past. It covers a number of general principles that should be followed when building statistical models. The final two sections of the chapter require more technical background than the rest. They describe, in detail, two case studies of predictions developed for initial dispatch policies in New York City. Section 8.5 develops a statistical model for predicting alarm rates in the Bronx, while Section 8.6 develops a model for estimating the probability that an incoming alarm signals a serious fire.

8.2 DATA COLLECTION

Some data describing the services performed by the fire department are collected routinely in all cities. They are usually published in the department's annual report. However, these data are not adequate for use in deployment analysis unless they provide information that can be used to estimate the rates at which different types of fires occur in different regions of the city at different times of day.

The analyst's role in data collection must begin with the definition of the data to be gathered. The form in which the current fire department data is gathered should be examined to determine if it contains all the information necessary for the deployment analyses being planned. If a change in data collection is needed, planning and organizing it may take considerable effort. Such a change may be the first visible step taken by the study team; if so, the considerations discussed in Chapter 5 are very important. If a limited amount of data is needed for some purpose (Section 8.2.1), collect it for a specific period of time rather than routinely. Additional required data should be added in a way that minimizes the reporting burden on the staff. Considerable thought should be given to the manner of instructing and motivating the personnel who will record the data, to encourage accurate reporting.

A method for monitoring the accuracy of the reported data should be devised and used. Validating the data is of the utmost importance. Members of the study team should talk directly to the personnel who collect the data, to make sure that all parties understand what the data mean. Editing the data to detect errors prior to any data analysis will save an enormous amount of effort and will avoid drawing conclusions based on erroneous data.

8.2.1 Incident Records

Most cities record a description of each incident that is reported to the department. The simplest way to get the incident data required for deployment analysis is to routinely put some of the information about each alarm into a file that can be processed by a computer. The file can then be processed periodically to provide summaries of current alarm characteristics for fire department management. In addition, since the characteristics of alarms change over time, it will be possible to reexamine deployment policies in the light of changing circumstances. However, such routine collection and use of data comes at a cost to personnel and computer resources. In a small city, with minimal management needs for data collection and minimal manpower and computer resources, a one-time coding of all the incidents that occurred in some recent period—say, in the last year or two—would enable one to use the deployment models described in this book. A computer file of alarm records is superior to a tabulation of alarm rates from written records, because of the greater accuracy of computation and the more flexible analyses possible whenever there is a sizable number of incidents to process.

Careful specification of the content of the incident file is necessary whether it is continually updated or limited to a single historical period.

The National Fire Protection Association has developed a Uniform Fire Incident Reporting System (UFIRS) that includes incident records as well as other management information, such as investigation and casualty reports (*UFIRS—Management Guide*, 1977). This system has several advantages. Computer programs are provided that produce summaries of the data for management purposes. Also, using a nationally accepted coding system makes it possible to compare local data to nationally reported statistics.

Separate reports enter the UFIRS system from the dispatcher, the officer in charge at the scene (or each company commander if preferred), and the city's Fire Prevention Bureau. The system collects these reports to produce a single incident record that describes the actions of the dispatcher, the location of the incident, the type of incident, the kind of property involved, the area of origin, the cause of the fire, fire spread, casualties, damage estimates, resource utilization, actions taken on the fireground, and the results of the investigation. The coding system now used by UFIRS is NFPA Standard 901-1976. A complete description of the system is found in *Uniform Coding for Fire Protection* (1976).

Some cities may find the UFIRS system too costly to use, since so much information must be collected and coded, and a computer is needed for processing the data. The United States Fire Administration has developed a simplified system for recording and reporting information on alarms. A single form (Figure 8.1) is filled out for each incident. (An additional form is filled out for fire casualties.) This system (called the National Fire Information Reporting System or NFIRS) uses the same coding system as UFIRS (NFPA Standard 901-1976). Data from NFIRS is fed into a national data bank, which permits national trends in the demand for fire service to be analyzed. In this way, new hazards such as dangerous new building materials can be detected much more quickly. A complete description of NFIRS can be found in *National Fire Incident Reporting System Handbook* (1976).

No matter how the incident data are gathered, the coding system used for type of alarm must at least distinguish the three classes of alarms: structural, false, and other. (Most cities would do well to consider adding additional types of incidents that are of interest for management purposes. More on defining the types of incidents used in deployment analysis is found in Section 8.3.)

On the form in Figure 8.1, the location of the incident is given by the census tract. If NFIRS is not used, some other coding system for location—alarm box, census tract, block number, coordinates, etc.—will do. Using census tracts has a special advantage in that socioeconomic data can then be easily related to alarm rates (see Section 8.4.1). However it is done, the location information must identify a geographic area small enough to use in siting models. Other deployment models require alarm

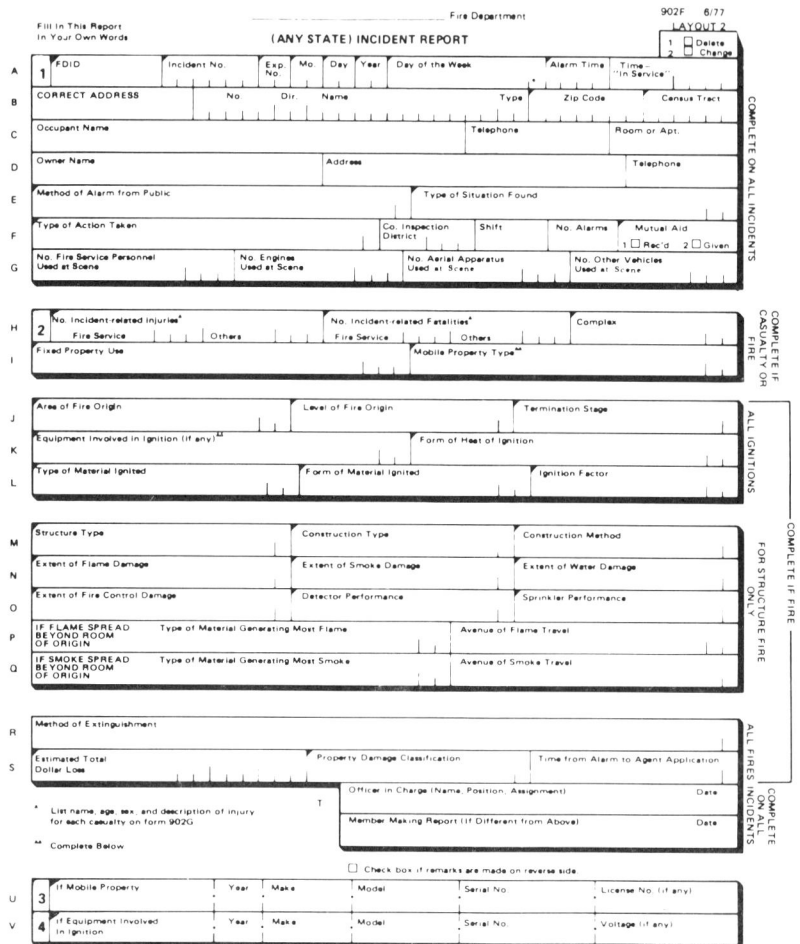

FIGURE 8.1. NFIRS Incident Report Form.

rates in larger areas, so there must be a convenient way to go from incidents in small areas to incidents in larger areas. A particularly useful way is to provide a set of coordinates for each small area. The use of street addresses may lead to serious problems in identifying the geographic area that contained the incident. Computerized address-matching programs typically fail in 20 percent of the cases due to misspelling of street names, special locations (e.g., City Hall, Mercy Hospital) and incomplete addresses. When incorrect matches are more frequent in some areas than in others, it can seriously bias a deployment analysis.

8.2.2 Special Purpose Data Collection

Many of the deployment models described in this book require information in addition to alarm rates. For example, many models require a description of the time spent working on fires of different types. Others require the relationship between travel distance and travel time to incidents.

It is necessary to collect data to determine these relationships only if the specific models requiring this information are to be used in the deployment analysis. These data also have the property that they are unlikely to change much over time—the travel time between points will change only slowly unless major changes are made in the road network. The average length of time spent at a structural fire is likely to be about the same next year as it is this year. Consequently, it is possible to collect this data only once for a period of time long enough to produce statistically reliable estimates of the parameters of the model. Data need be collected again only if the underlying process has changed.

8.3 DISPLAYS OF FIRE DATA

Having collected fire incidence data for some historical period, one is ready to perform exploratory data analysis. In this section the emphasis is on summarizing the information collected on a large number of alarms. The purpose of the summary is to better understand the patterns of alarms that have occurred in the past and the factors that can be used to describe those patterns. We discuss here the three most important sources of variation in alarm data: the type of alarm, the geographical region, and the time of occurrence. In each case, we display data taken from actual deployment studies to show what typical patterns look like.

Displays of fire data that show how alarms have varied in the past can suggest how they may vary in the future. If only rough estimates of how alarms will occur in the future are needed, data taken directly from the display may be used. If better estimates are required, these displays can guide the model builder in specifying a model.

8.3.1 Types of Alarms

The definitions of different types of alarms should be based on the questions that the deployment analysis is meant to answer. If the answers to any of the following questions are different for any two alarms, those alarms may be considered different types of alarms.

1. *How important is a fast response to this incident?* We define a serious

alarm as one in which a deployment decision might affect the outcome. Clearly, false alarms and rubbish fires that do not involve risk of spread are not serious fires. Also, fires in which a few extra minutes of response time could prevent the rescue of people trapped in the building, or could allow damage to increase, are serious. Unfortunately, current research is not adequate to specify exactly what kinds of alarms are serious. Therefore, the analyst must decide what serious means. The simplest definition to use is: all structural fires and medical emergencies. Another approach is to define seriousness in terms of resources used; for example, all fires at which at least two engines and one ladder work might be considered serious.

2. *How large a commitment of resources is required for this alarm?* The availability of units does not depend on what is burning, but rather on the number of units and the length of time for which they are required. One type of alarm might be all incidents that need only a single engine company, whether the incident is a rubbish fire, an automobile fire, or a cat up a tree. Another type of alarm might consist of all incidents requiring one engine plus one ladder, etc.

3. *How is the incident reported?* This is important for the initial dispatch decision because it determines how much the dispatcher knows about the incident. This can affect his dispatching decision. Telephone alarms and verbal call box alarms might be grouped as one type of alarm, and telegraphic box alarms as another.

The number of types of alarms of possible interest is thus quite large. If just two levels of seriousness, seven types of resource use, and two ways of reporting are defined, the result is 28 different alarm types. However, to answer any one deployment question, only some—not all—of these types need be considered. Table 8.1 shows the types of alarms that are required to use each of the deployment models discussed in this book. If only one or two of the models are to be used, this table shows which types of alarms must be analyzed. For example, to estimate the number of busy companies, alarm type need be differentiated only by the number of companies needed and the length of time they are required. However, if an ongoing program of deployment analysis is planned, then it would be worthwhile to ensure that the data collection system contains enough detail to answer each of the three questions in this section and thus define all the types of fires that might eventually be of use.

8.3.2 Geographic Variation

The size of the geographic region in which one wishes to describe the demand for fire services also depends on the deployment question being studied. As summarized in Table 8.1, the questions of firehouse siting and initial dispatch depend on demand in very small areas—the area

8.3 Displays of Fire Data

TABLE 8.1. Requirements for incident data by deployment models.

Type of Model	Chapter	Type of Alarms Defined by	Geographic Region	Time Period
Number of companies busy	7	Resource utilization	Demand region	Any[a]
Parametric allocation	9	Resource utilization	Demand region	Yearly
Firehouse siting	10	Structural, nonstructural	Small area	Yearly
Initial dispatch	11	Seriousness, how reported	Small area	Hourly
		Total	First-due area	Hourly
Relocation	12	Total	First-due area	Hourly
Simulation[b]	13	Resource utilization, seriousness, how reported	Small area	Hourly

[a] The model may be used to look at the distribution of availability over any time period, such as peak hours or an entire year.

[b] The types of alarms used in the simulation, as well as the size of the area for which alarm rates are required, may be tailored to answer specific deployment questions.

covered by one to five alarm boxes, or several city blocks. The largest area considered by the models is called a "demand region" and is composed of the first-due areas of several—at least two and sometimes (in big cities) five or more—companies.

The alarm rate and the distribution of alarm types will differ in the various regions being considered. If coordinates have been used to record the location of alarm incidents in the data file, it is easy to produce computer maps, such as those shown in Figures 8.2 and 8.3, that graphically display the geographic pattern of the alarms. A small rectangular space on the printout is used to describe one or a group of locations that cover an equal area of the city. If census tracts or some other geographic unit have been used to record the location of incidents on the file, one can produce such maps by assigning coordinates to each geographical unit, and by calculating an approximation to the area of the unit so that alarm densities can be calculated.

Hazards. In addition to differing alarm rates, regions have differing requirements for fire protection. If there were a delayed response to a fire in a crowded theatre, the resulting loss of life would be likely to far exceed the loss that would occur in a fire in a residential area. In considering the ways in which demand for fire services varies geographically, it is necessary to consider not only the rate at which alarms occur (called *realized demand*), but also the hazards posed by the fires that might occur (called *latent* or *potential demand*). For small regions, the simplest way to handle the problem of potential demand is to identify the particular

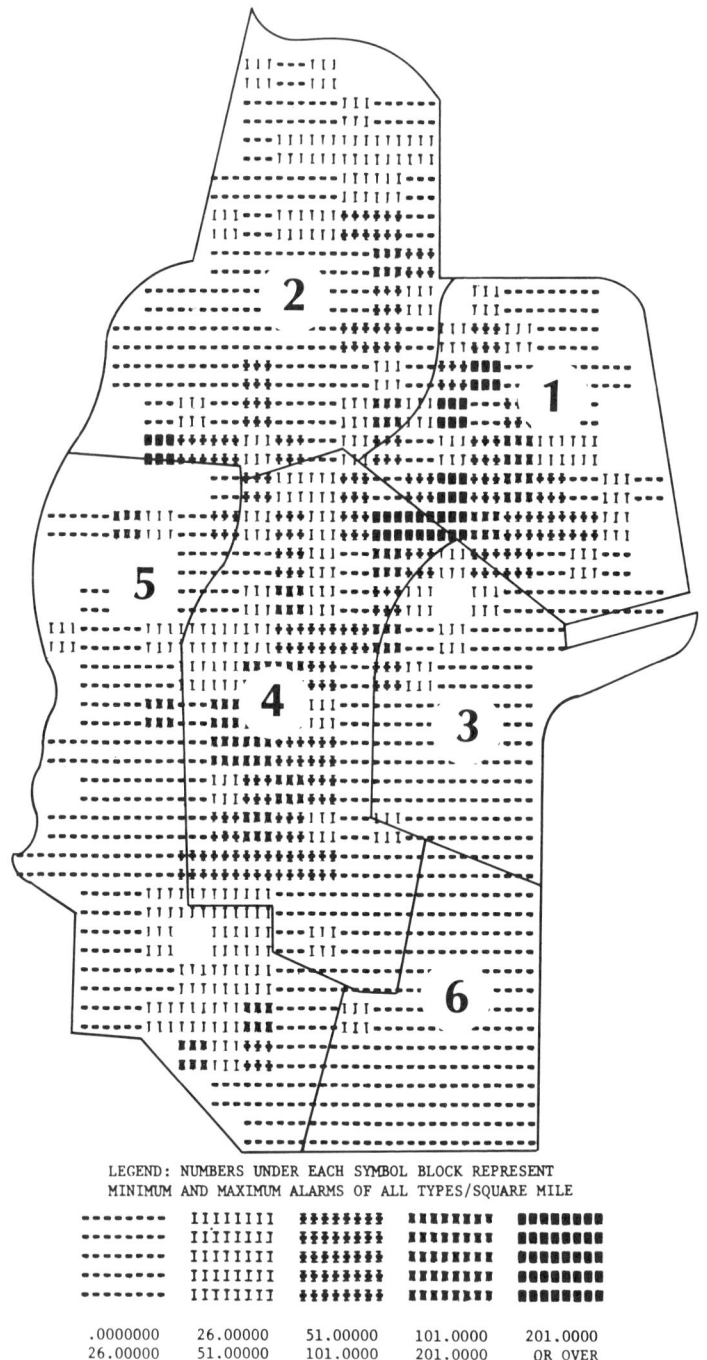

FIGURE 8.2. Geographic density of total alarms, Jersey City, 1973.

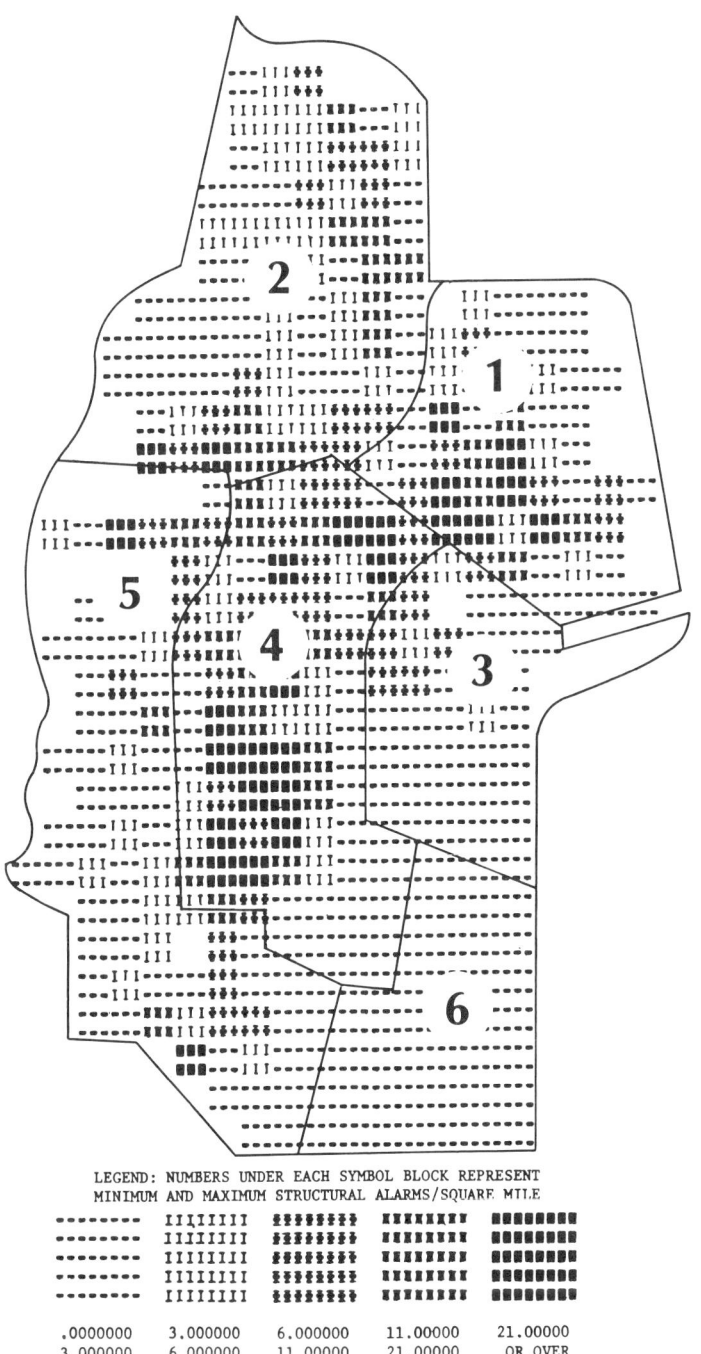

FIGURE 8.3. Geographic density of structural alarms, Jersey City, 1973.

locations that pose a special hazard—hospitals, nursing homes, and lumberyards, for example. This information can then be used in, say, the siting model, to make sure adequate coverage is provided for these special locations. Alternatively, one might attempt to classify every location in the city according to the hazards present. This would include a description of the type of land use (residential, public assembly, factory, warehouse, stores), the type of construction (woodframe, fireproof, highrise), and the population density.

The hazards present in larger regions may be identified either on the basis of the predominant type of hazard present (a region might be predominantly commercial, for instance, or predominantly multi-family residential), or from the composite of the hazards present in the region built up from the detailed data.

One of the primary reasons that geographic variation is important is the need to provide equitable service for all the citizens of the city. Although defining equity among regions that differ substantially poses severe problems, there is no problem when regions are similar. Two regions with similar potential and realized demand should receive similar service. Chapter 9 discusses the Parametric Allocation Model, which allocates companies to demand regions based on a specified tradeoff between realized and potential demand. Another clear demand of equity is that two alarms possessing the same probability of being serious and coming from regions of similar hazards should also receive the same amount of firefighting equipment on the initial dispatch. Section 8.6 describes a method for estimating the probability that alarms in such small geographic areas signal a serious fire.

Defining Demand Regions. Demand regions are the primary unit of analysis in the Parametric Allocation Model. Several tactical models require an estimate of the number of alarms that will occur in a given hour in a smaller region. For reasons discussed later in this chapter, the best way to estimate these alarm rates is to first estimate the number of alarms that will occur in that hour in an entire demand region, and then apportion these alarms among the smaller regions that constitute the demand region. Thus, the demand region is also the basic unit of analysis of the realized demand for fire services.

The demand regions are used in demand analysis by assuming that other factors (such as time of day) affect each part of the region in the same way. The distribution of the type of alarm is assumed to be the

---

[1] The one exception to this statement is covered in Section 8.6, where the probability that a box-reported alarm signals a serious fire is allowed to vary from alarm box to alarm box.

8.3 Displays of Fire Data

same throughout the demand region.[1] To use demand regions in deployment analysis, the regions should be homogeneous with respect to the hazards present. Demand regions should also be large enough to contain several companies (at least two) so that meaningful evaluations of deployment alternatives can be considered.

How are these regions to be defined? Ideally, an individual region would be a geographically compact area of the city, all parts of which have the same land use, type of structure, life hazard, alarm mix, and so forth. That is, the region would have the same fire protection problems and needs throughout. Locations with different needs would then be in different regions.

Of course, meeting this ideal is impossible. It is not likely that the existing divisions of the city into departmental administrative districts come close to this ideal. A new division of the city can be constructed that is a compromise between the alternative (and sometimes conflicting) criteria. In most small-to-medium sized cities, the number of regions to be defined can usually be settled either on the basis of the needs of deployment models, or based on a "natural" division of the city into commercial, industrial, and residential neighborhoods. The detailed definitions of the demand regions can be produced by choosing several engine company first-due areas[2] with different fire protection needs as starting points for the regions. Each starting point is expanded by adding adjacent engine company first-due areas with similar alarm characteristics and hazards until every area of the city has been assigned to a region. Computer produced maps such as those shown in Figures 8.2 and 8.3 can aid in this process. If the resulting demand regions do not appear satisfactory, then the process can be repeated using different starting points (and perhaps a different number of starting points).

Figure 8.2 shows the demand regions used for deployment analysis in Jersey City, New Jersey. As the map shows, the alarm rates within each region are not completely homogeneous, but they are reasonably so. Also, they separate the high-rise, industrial, and residential areas of the city. Moreover, as can be seen from Table 8.2, the division also distinguishes Region 1, which has the highest local alarm density, from Region 4, which has the highest structural-alarm density. This allows an assessment of the different risks present in an alarm from each region.

Demand regions are roughly comparable to the Fire Management Areas (FMAs) used as the analysis regions in the literature describing fire protection master planning. See for example page 22 of Master Planning Community Fire Protection (1976).

---

[2] It could just as well be ladder company first-due areas or company administrative districts.

TABLE 8.2. Incidence by demand region, Jersey City, 1973.

Demand Region	Number of Incidents		Incidents/Square Mile	
	Total	Structural	Total	Structural
1	3,308	395	2,176	260
2	2,459	390	872	138
3	838	113	986	133
4	3,366	840	1,700	424
5	1,599	279	617	108
6[a]	0	0	0	0
Citywide	11,570	2,107	1,185	207

[a] Demand Region 6 is an empty waterfront area being developed as a new industrial park.

8.3.3 Temporal Variation

Figures 8.4 and 8.5 show how the total number of alarms has changed over time in two cities—Trenton, New Jersey, and Wilmington, Delaware. In Trenton, the total alarm rate appears to have reached at least a temporary plateau in the last four years of the data. In Wilmington, the number of alarms increased almost continuously in the decade plotted. Strategic planning requires estimates of the number of alarms that will occur next year or several years from now. The Yonkers case study presented in Chapter 14 shows how these predictions were used in a deployment analysis.

In order to choose a method of estimation for future alarms, one must make an assumption about how the future will be related to the past. One possible assumption is that the number of alarms will be pretty much the same as it has been in the last n years; i.e., that no predictable changes in the total alarm rate are occurring. In this case, the prediction for the next year is the average number of alarms that have occurred in the last n years; i.e., $P = \Sigma A_t/n$, where A_t is the total number of alarms that occurred in year t. An alternative assumption is that the number of alarms has been increasing in the last n years and will continue to increase in the future. It is evident that alarms increased during the period of the data shown in Figure 8.5. However, in order to choose between these hypotheses for a city whose data resembles the data in Figure 8.4, one must go beyond the alarm data. For the last few years of data, the hypothesis of constant alarm rate seems reasonable, while the number of alarms grew substantially over the entire period of the data. If there is reason to believe that the causes of the growth in alarms in the earlier period have been removed—for example, by an end to the population growth of the city—then the constant hypothesis can be used and recent annual data ($n = 3$ or 4) may be averaged. If, on the other hand, the recent period is believed to be an aberration in a pattern of continual

8.3 Displays of Fire Data

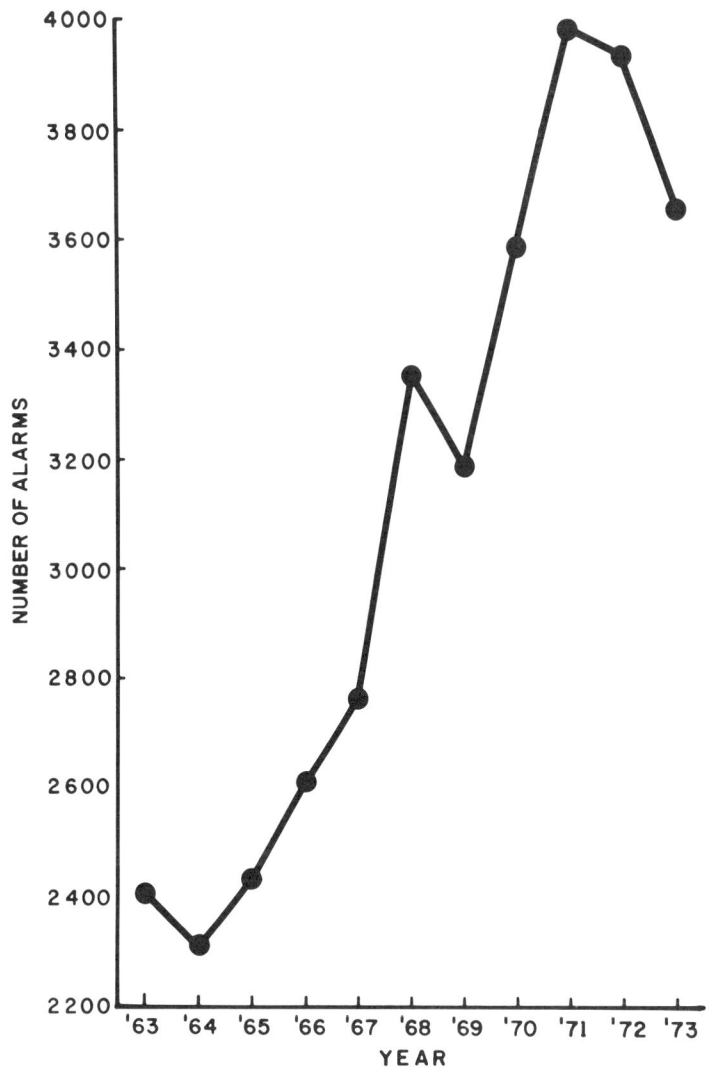

FIGURE 8.4. Total number of fire alarms, Trenton, New Jersey, 1963–1973.

growth, then an attempt should be made to estimate the increase in alarms over the longer period. As in the creation of all statistical models, knowledge about the underlying forces that govern the process being modeled is essential to making good predictions.

If an assumption of continual growth is made, one must decide on the form of the growth. One possibility is that growth is occurring linearly

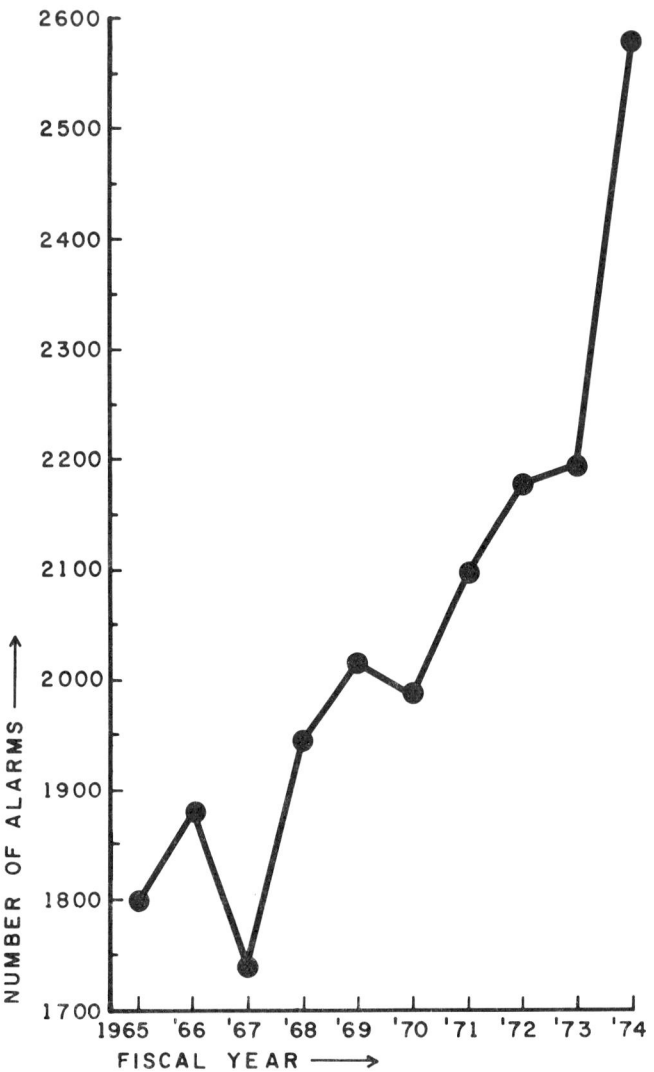

FIGURE 8.5. Total number of fire alarms, Wilmington, Delaware, 1965–1974.

with time. That is, on the average, b_1 more alarms occur each year:

$$A_t = A_{t-1} + b_1 = A_0 + b_1(t - t_0), \tag{8.1}$$

where t_0 is the first year of data to be used and there were A_0 alarms in year t_0. Under this assumption, a prediction for the future may be made by plotting a line that comes as close as possible to the data points, and then reading the predicted number of alarms directly from the graph. An

8.3 Displays of Fire Data

alternative assumption is that alarms are growing proportionally with time; i.e., on the average, an additional fraction b_2 of alarms occur each year:

$$A_t = (1 + b_2)A_{t-1} = (1 + b_2)^{t-t_0}A_0. \qquad (8.2)$$

This assumption is usually called exponential growth. The logarithm function provides a simple way of dealing with proportional increase, since:

$$\log(A_t) = \log\left[(1 + b_2)^{t-t_0}A_0\right] = \log(A_0) + (t - t_0)\log(1 + b_2).$$

Thus, when we plot the number of alarms against time on log paper, as in Figure 8.6, we can use a straight line (the dotted line in Figure 8.6) to estimate the number of alarms that will occur in the future.

The data plotted in Figure 8.6 are exactly the same data points as those plotted in Figure 8.5. A comparison of these two figures is one way to choose between the assumptions of constant and proportional increase. Since the points plotted in Figure 8.6 lie more nearly on a straight line than those in Figure 8.5, the assumption of proportional increases over time is more consistent with the data.

We will mention one other possible assumption about the growth rate. If alarms are growing at a greater rate each year, but the proportional model does not seem to fit, using a square-root transformation may

FIGURE 8.6. Total number of alarms, Wilmington, Delaware, 1965-1974. Alarms are plotted on a log scale.

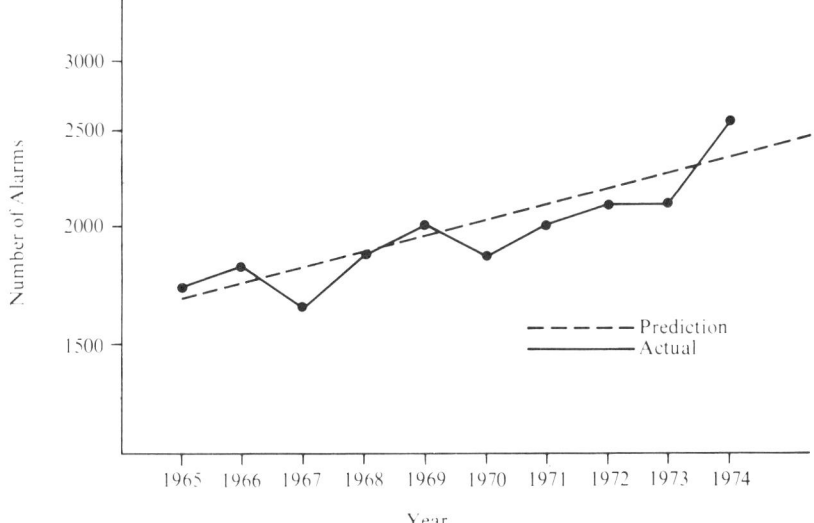

produce a good fit. More details on the square-root transformation are in Section 8.5.

In any one city, different types of alarms may display different trends over time. It is easier to compare these trends if each type is plotted on the same graph, as in Figure 8.7, which shows false, structural, and other types of alarms in Jersey City. In that city, structural alarms showed

FIGURE 8.7. Fire alarms by type of incident, Jersey City, New Jersey, 1963–1973.

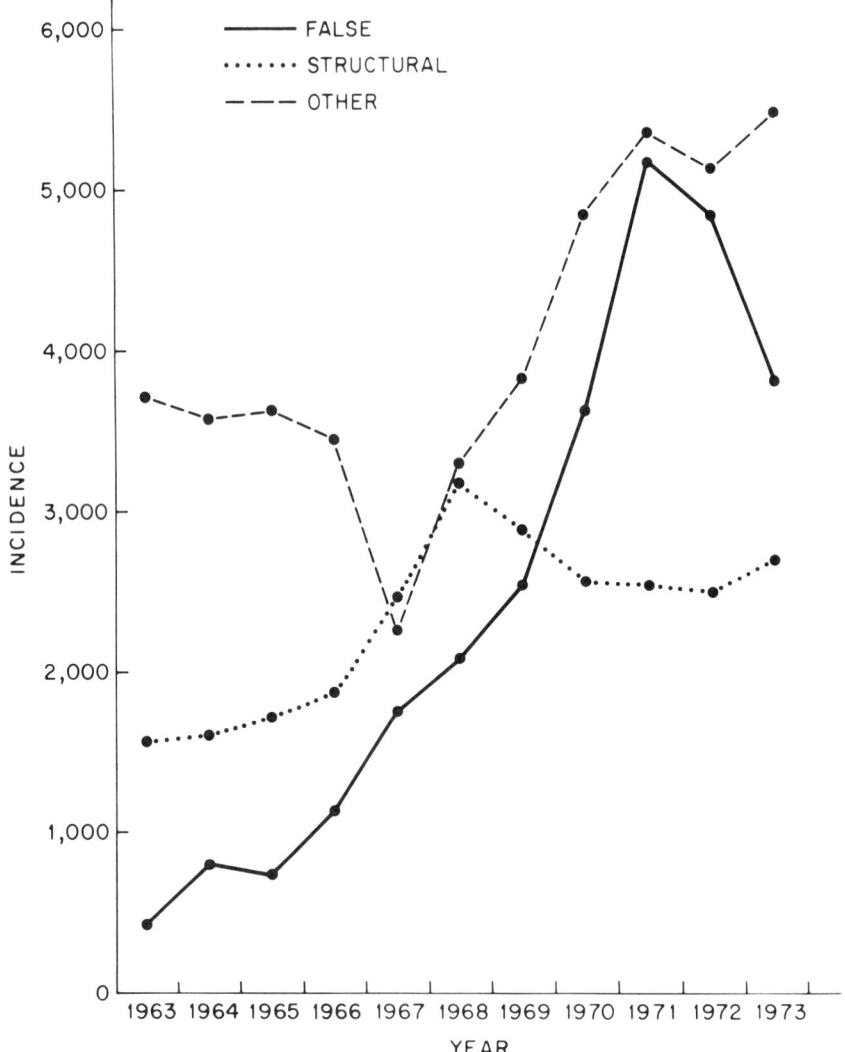

little growth between 1967 and 1973, while false alarms increased exponentially between 1963 and 1970 before beginning to decline, and other alarms increased approximately linearly between 1963 and 1973.

Alarms also exhibit consistent variation within smaller time periods than a whole year. Figures 8.8, 8.9, and 8.10 show the number of alarms in Jersey City in each two-hour period of the day over an entire year. As is true in other cities, most alarms occur in the late afternoon and early evening from 4 P.M. to 9 P.M., and a much higher proportion of structural alarms than other alarms occur during the deepest part of the night. For these data, 11.7 percent of structural fires occur between midnight and 4 A.M., versus 3.8 percent of false alarms, and 8.1 percent of other alarms.

Consistent patterns in alarms, depending on the day of the week, are usually also apparent. In the region for which data are shown in Figure 8.11, many more false alarms occur on Friday, Saturday, and Sunday,

FIGURE 8.8. Total alarms by time of day, Jersey City, New Jersey, 1973.

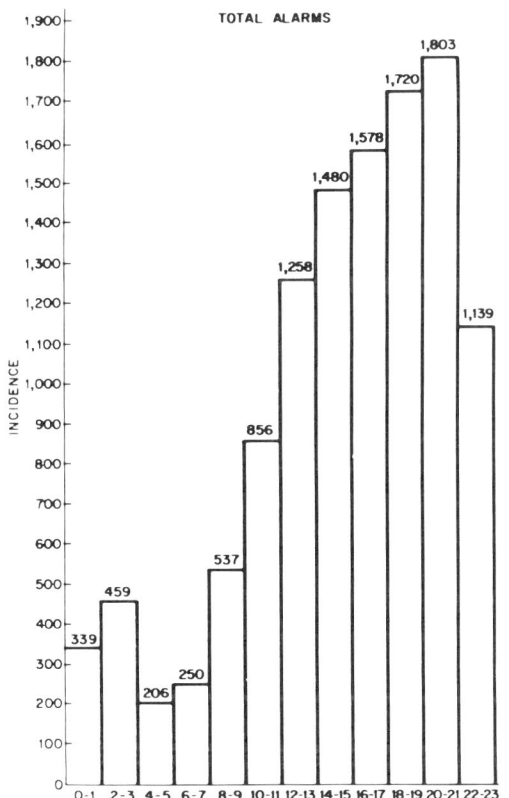

than on weekdays. The number of alarms occurring on each of the remaining weekdays is very similar, and in further analysis, could be considered to be identical without introducing error.

There may also be a consistent seasonal variation in the rate at which alarms occur. Figure 8.12 compares the number of structural and false alarms that occurred each month in New York City during 1970 and 1971. It shows that the incidence of false alarms increased dramatically in the summer months. Although there is a seasonal pattern in the occurrence of structural fires, the amount of variation is much smaller than it is for false alarms. The data from many cities exhibit only small or no seasonal variations for all alarm types.

8.3.4 Peak Demand

Because of the importance of having fire protection at all times, the magnitude of the largest simultaneous demand that will be made on fire

FIGURE 8.9. Structural alarms by time of day, Jersey City, New Jersey, 1973.

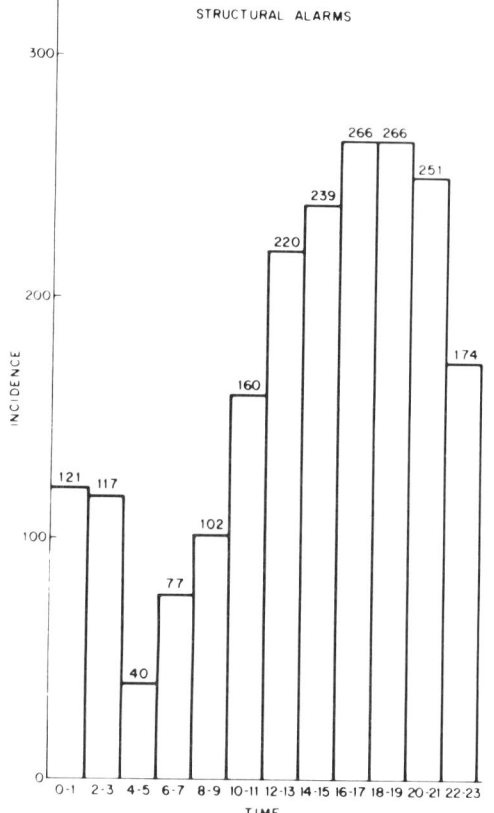

8.3 Displays of Fire Data

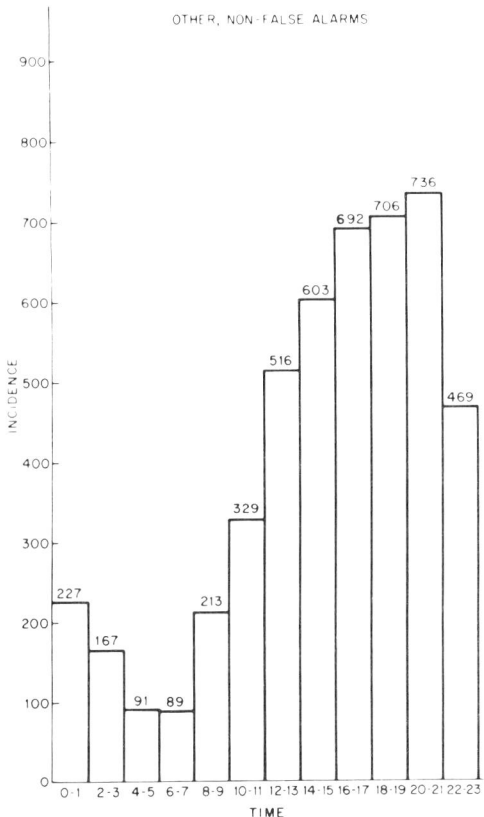

FIGURE 8.10. Other, nonfalse alarms by time of day, Jersey City, New Jersey, 1973.

services is important. The analyst should prepare curves such as those we have examined in Figures 8.8–8.12 to help identify when the peak demand for fire services is occurring. For example, this might identify a five-hour period (typically 4 P.M. to 9 P.M.) on Friday and Saturday nights as the peak period. If local incidents exhibit marked seasonal variation, the analyst might restrict the peak period to several months in the year. The easiest way to estimate the distribution of the level of demand for firefighting resources during the peak period, is to use the model described in Chapter 7 to estimate the number of companies busy in a region. In order to use this model, it is only necessary to calculate the *average number* of alarms of each type (based on resource utilization) that occur during the peak period, and the average length of time that companies were used at each type of alarm. Because the length of time for which companies were busy at any one type of alarm is not likely to change during peak periods, this can be estimated from a sample of alarms that occurred at any time of the day or year.

8.4 STATISTICAL INFERENCE

The preceding section describes how to analyze and display past fire alarm data in ways that give insight into alarm patterns. But our objective in analyzing fire alarm incidence data (and all other data described in this book) is to make inferences about the future, on the assumption that the future will be similar to the past. When year-to-year variation is very small relative to other variations (such as regional or hourly variations), decisions may be based on the assumption that the future will be identical to the past. When it appears that year-to-year change may be large enough relative to other variations to change deployment decisions, we must turn to statistical inference. That is, we make explicit assumptions about the similarity between past and future in order to use the past to reach probabilistic conclusions about what might happen in the future.

FIGURE 8.11. Percent of box-reported false alarms that occur each day of the week. The data come from one of the demand regions in the Bronx and are for 1964–1969.

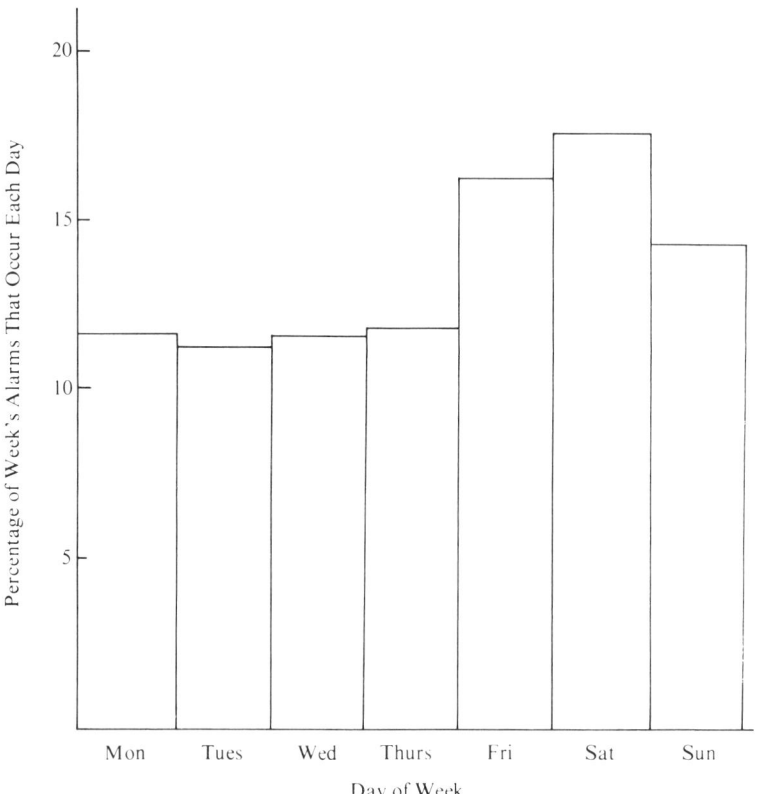

8.4 Statistical Inference

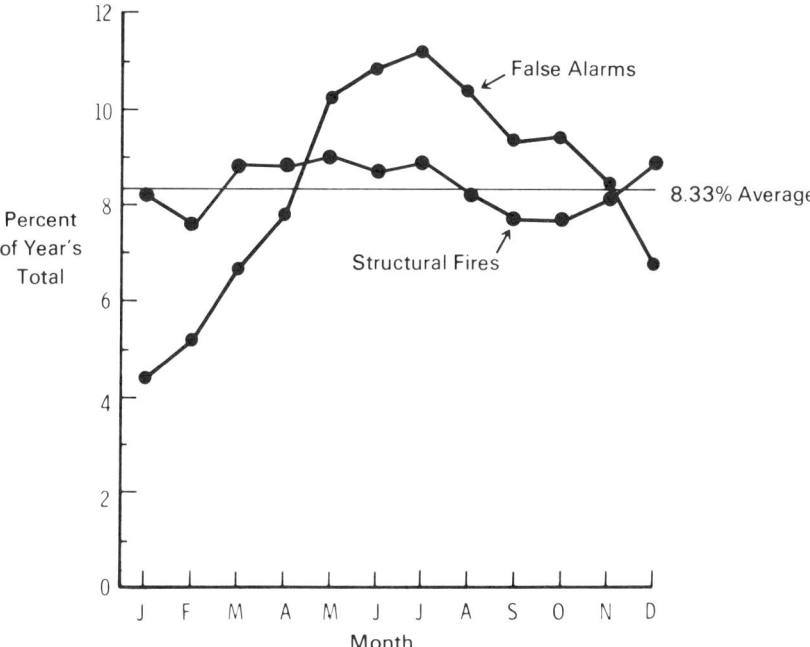

FIGURE 8.12. Monthly pattern of alarms in New York City, 1970–1971.

This section describes statistical inference for use when it is questionable whether or not the future will be approximately the same as the past. Although data from New York City and other specific cities are often used for illustration, the points being made in this section should apply to making statistical inferences about fire alarms in any jurisdiction.

8.4.1 Predictions

In predicting the future number of fire alarms, there are at least three issues of interest:

1. What is the trend or the pattern of change? That is, aside from random fluctuations, how is the number changing systematically from year to year, if at all?
2. Other than purely random fluctuations, how does the number of alarms during the year vary with region, season, day of the week, hour of the day?
3. Once a model for the *expected* number of alarms is chosen, what is the variation around this expected number? Can some limits on the future number of alarms be given with confidence?

Trends: One of the first and simplest computations, usually done with several years of data, is calculating a trend. As described in Section 8.3, it might be linear, exponential (proportional increase), or something in between. Trend lines that fit historical data nearly equally well can result in quite different predictions. For example, between 1959 and 1968, annual fire alarms in New York City went from 83,373 to 227,384. If in 1968 one were asked to predict the annual total for 1975, either of two calculations might be done. Since the number of alarms increased by 144,000 in 10 years (or 14,400 per year), one might expect an increase of 70 percent of that amount, or a total of 326,000 alarms by 1975. More precisely, the line shown in Figure 8.13 would be used to predict the 1975 total. On the other hand, since the yearly number of alarms increased more than two and a half times in ten years, one might expect a corresponding seven-year increase of about twice the total, or 434,000. The exact number is given by the exponential curve in Figure 8.13. Thus, these two methods yield a difference of 106,000 alarms as a 1975 prediction. (The actual number of alarms in 1975 was 399,000.) From this example, we see that different methods can give quite different predictions for five years into the future.

New York City from 1959 to 1968 is an extreme case in that numbers of alarms and percentage growth rates are large compared to other cities.

FIGURE 8.13. Annual alarm projections for New York City.

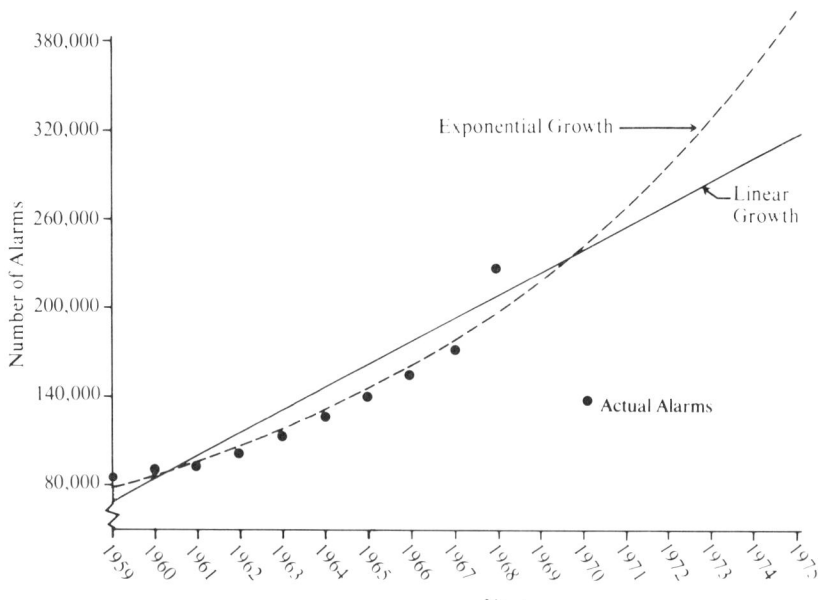

The difference in predictions between linear and exponential growth rates for a smaller city can be illustrated by Wilmington, where the 1965-1974 alarm totals were as shown in Figure 8.5. Suppose the problem is to predict the number of alarms in Wilmington in 1984 from the 1965-1974 data. Wilmington alarms grew from 1798 to 2578, or 44 percent, in the nine-year period between 1965 and 1974. A linear extrapolation yields a 1984 prediction of 3445 alarms, and an exponential extrapolation gives a 1984 prediction of 4107. In this case, the ten-year exponential extrapolation is 19 percent higher than the linear extrapolation; a modest but significant difference.

Extrapolation works best when it is used to predict only a year or two ahead. Using a proportionate increase (the exponential curve) is particularly risky for longer periods because of the assumption that alarms can grow from 10,000 per year to 20,000 per year as rapidly as they grow from 1000 to 2000 per year.

If the assumed form of the trend line is correct, statistical methods can be used to calculate a confidence interval on the number of alarms in any given year. For example, the interpretation of a 95 percent confidence interval for alarms in Wilmington in 1984 is that there is a probability of .95 that the actual total for 1984 will fall within the interval. The width of the confidence interval increases as one predicts further into the future. Reporting confidence intervals along with predictions helps to specify the reliability of the prediction. But if the assumed form of the trend line is incorrect, even confidence intervals will not prevent mistakes, particularly for longer-term predictions. Thus, the standard extrapolation methods should be used with caution when predictions for more than a year or so in the future are needed.

Long-Range Predictions. To get more accurate long-term predictions, it would be useful to collect information bearing on the underlying cause of fire alarms—land use, weather, etc. Then, if long-term changes in these variables are anticipated, this information can be used to improve long-term predictions. An extrapolation of a region's fire alarm rate ten years into the future is irrelevant if the region is a slum that will be razed for urban renewal during the period.

Rider and Walker (unpublished) used demographic information to project four different types of New York City alarms 15 years into the future. The results were designed to be used in the New York City Fire Department's long-range planning process. Their approach combined historical relationships between fire alarm incidence and social and demographic factors with assumptions about how these factors would change over time. A good reason for using this approach is that social and demographic factors frequently can be projected with some confidence, and the assumption that their relationship with fire alarm incidence remains constant is often quite reasonable. Even if this assumption is not a good one, the relationship between social and demographic factors and fire alarm incidence can be varied, and the consequences observed.

Rider and Walker used three changing aspects of New York that are relevant to fire prediction: (1) the racial composition of the population; (2) the age structure of the population; and (3) the composition of the housing stock. An additional, less predictable factor, social conditions, is used to provide upper and lower bounds to their alarm projections. The idea is to develop regression equations[3] relating these factors to alarm rates for different types of fires. Demographic information and "informed intuition" are then used to estimate future values of these factors. The regression equations, with these "future values" as explanatory variables, are used to estimate future alarm rates. By choosing a range of plausible values of the social and demographic factors for the future, upper and lower bounds for future alarm rates can be established with reasonable certainty. For accurate *long-term predictions* we recommend this approach over pure extrapolation of past fire alarms, but it does involve additional effort: gathering demographic data; fitting models that relate demographic factors to fire alarm incidence; and projecting future values of demographic factors. We reemphasize that either method for making long-term projections depends critically on current expectations.

The reader interested in regression equations relating socioeconomic and building characteristics to fire alarm rates in different cities and in different areas of the same city should see Chapter 5 of Schaenman et al. (1976). Although the emphasis there is on geographic rather than temporal variation of fire alarm rates, useful relationships are developed between alarm rates and population characteristics including family stability, poverty level, and education.

Patterns within the Year. For initial dispatch (Chapter 11), relocation (Chapter 12), and the simulation model (Chapter 13), it is necessary to predict the variation in alarm rates from season to season, from region to region, from day to day, and from early morning to early evening. In Section 8.3 we described how these dimensions contribute to defining "peak demand" periods. For predicting the number of false alarms, structural fires, or other alarms for a one-hour period in the vicinity of a particular alarm box, one must decide on the level of detail necessary for defining alarm types, geographic regions, and the time scale. Since

---

[3] Fitting regression equations is a statistical method for seeing how some variable that you want to explain varies as certain other characteristics change. Regression analysis is discussed at some length in Section 8.5.2.

there must be a sufficient number of alarms in each category for statistically accurate estimation, the fitting of parameters can be done in stages to make some of the tradeoffs between level of detail and amount of interaction along each dimension. This process of constructing empirical models is described in some detail in Section 8.4.2. An example of a fit done in stages is to use small areas (10–20 alarm boxes) to estimate for trend; then demand regions (about 1000 alarm boxes) may be used to estimate seasonal patterns, day-of-the-week patterns, and hour-of-the-day patterns for each alarm type separately.

Choosing the stages requires deciding what interactions there are between time patterns and different regions. For example, an analysis of daily box-reported false alarms in the Bronx concluded that: (1) the hour-of-the-day patterns of the four weekdays (Monday through Thursday) are the same, while Friday, Saturday, and Sunday are different from one another and from weekdays (Figure 8.14); (2) the same trend could be used for all seven days of the week; and (3) each demand region should be analyzed separately when predicting daily alarms (Figure 8.15). As indicated in Section 8.3, some of the deployment models required this detailed specification of how alarm rates vary with time, geography, and alarm type. In smaller cities this level of disaggregation is neither possible

FIGURE 8.14. Hour-of-the-day pattern by day of the week, Region 2, the Bronx, New York City, 1964–1969. (Region 2 as defined in Figure 8.17.)

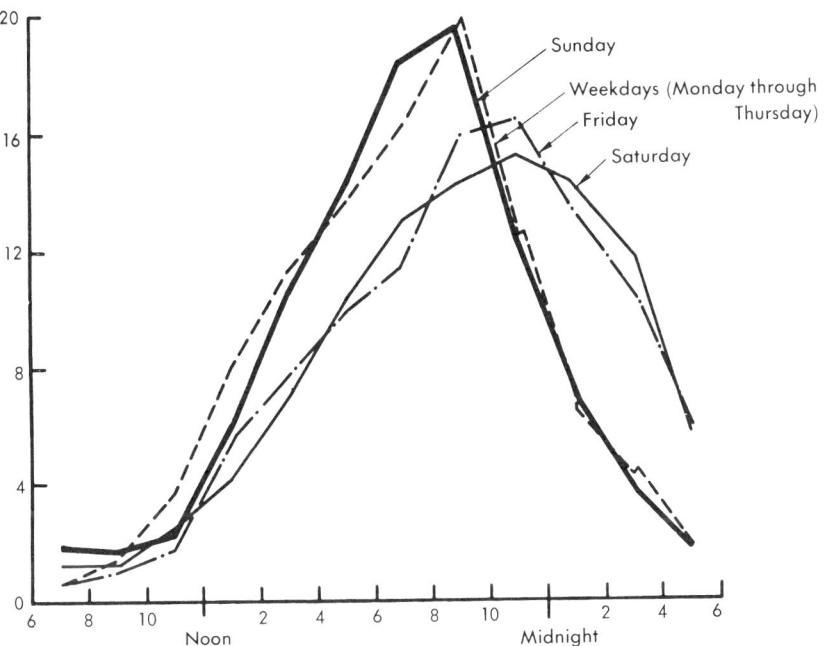

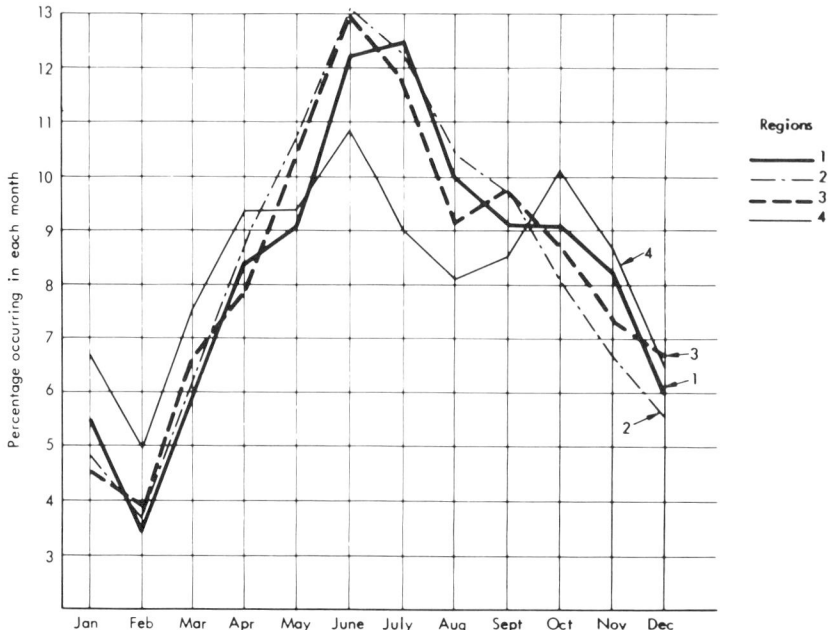

FIGURE 8.15. Box-reported false alarms, yearly patterns, the Bronx, New York City, 1964–1969. (Regions defined in Figure 8.17.)

nor needed because of the smaller numbers of alarms. Hence the task is much simplified.

Once it is determined how alarms vary from year to year and what systematic variation there is within the year, predictions can be made for next year. Many cities are changing fairly rapidly. In such cities it is important to continue to collect alarm data routinely, and to fit the models to the new data periodically. Substantial changes in the fitted coefficients (e.g., the trend) signal changing circumstances that should be examined in detail.

8.4.2 Some Principles of Modeling

In this section we describe some of the general principles of modeling fire alarm processes. To illustrate the points made here, the two case studies of Sections 8.5 and 8.6 are frequently referred to.

Building models based on data has many facets—we cover some of them in this chapter. The model-building process may begin by constructing a statement of the problem that includes the specification of the variables of interest (number of fire alarms) and a list of potential explanatory variables. Some of these cannot be directly measured, so sub-

8.4 Statistical Inference

stitutes (proxies) must be found. The costs and possible benefits of measuring different variables must be weighed. For example, is it worth gathering weather data? After data are gathered, decisions must be made about which variables to include in the model and what functional form of model to use. In this section we mention some principles that should be used in developing predictive models.

Use Available Theory. In constructing a method for predicting the number of fire alarms from potential explanatory variables, a priori knowledge can help restrict the range of possibilities to manageable proportions. As discussed in Chapter 7, theoretical considerations tell us that alarms follow a *time-varying Poisson process*. In Section 8.5.1, we show that observable fire alarm data are indeed consistent with generation by a time-varying Poisson process. Alarms following a time-varying Poisson process implies that the number of alarms are Poisson distributed with a parameter that varies over time and by region. Data are needed to estimate how the average alarm rate varies as a function of time and region, but the assumption will be made that alarms occur according to a Poisson process. This mixture of theory and data analysis is typical in modeling work.

Use Simple Models. The goal of building a predictive alarm model is to determine the average alarm rate that appears to underlie a body of data. There are two kinds of risks in attempting to relate data to a model. The first is that we may force the data into a model that is too simple to fit them well. Or, second, we might construct a model with so many parameters that the analysis is unnecessarily complex.

For our purposes, the simplest model that will give sufficiently accurate predictions for policy purposes is to be preferred. In some cases this may mean "no model at all." For example, in Tacoma, Washington, Thursdays typically have the fewest alarms of any day of the week. Because Thursdays are so slow, a reasonable deployment policy would have to be based on alarm rates on other days of the week. Thus, modeling the hour-of-the-day pattern for Thursdays serves no purpose in affecting deployment policy—one may as well assume a constant (low) number of alarms each hour.

In situations where a predictive model is needed, parameters should be used sparingly. Tukey (1961) states the "parsimony in parameters" principle: "Parameters should be introduced sparingly in such a way that the maximum amount of resolution is achieved for each parameter introduced." That is, each additional parameter should be required to improve the prediction significantly. An example of this approach is given in Section 8.5.2, which describes the modeling necessary to predict daily alarm rates in the Bronx. When modeling the seasonal pattern, only eight parameters were included because more parameters would only have served to explain relatively rare events like the annual false alarm increases on the Fourth of July or New Year's Eve.

Assess the Accuracy of the Predictions. Besides producing a prediction for the number of alarms in a given time period, some assessment of how accurate the predictions are is usually needed for policy purposes. This assessment of accuracy is called "calibration." It is tempting (and convenient) to use the same data set for both selecting and calibrating a model. We recommend that, if possible, the last year of available data be reserved for use as a calibration set. After a model has been selected by analyzing all but the last year of data, the average squared error of prediction of the last year of data should be reported as the precision. Assessing the accuracy of the prediction by predicting the same data points as were used to fit the model will yield too low an estimate of the prediction error. This low estimate is due to the *selection effect* reflecting the fact that the model has been selected to best fit that particular data set. The model may in fact do poorly in predicting future values. This effect is largest when much exploratory analysis has been performed in choosing the prediction model.

For example, Section 8.5.2 gives a prediction model for hourly alarm rates for two regions in the Bronx, developed from 1964–1969 data. The standard error of prediction of hourly total alarms for 1969 (without smoothing) was 3.34, while the corresponding standard error for 1970 was 3.65. The corresponding values of R^2 were .65 and .59. As is typically the case, the model predicts the data used for fitting (1969) more accurately than it predicts the future (1970). The above numbers motivate the setting aside of the last year of available data, in this case 1970, as a "calibration set." The 1964–1969 data should be used as a "selection set" to do all the exploratory analysis and fitting of models. When a final model is decided on, the last year of data (1970) is used to assess the accuracy of the resulting prediction, thus calibrating the model. We recommend this practice whenever there are more than three or four years of data available.[4] When actually making predictions (say, for 1978), all the data available (including 1977) should be used. But the assessment of the accuracy of the prediction for 1978 should be made using the above method.

Data Aggregation is Desirable. In selecting a prediction model, the analyst must make tradeoffs among the number of alarm types analyzed,

---

[4] For an excellent account of the theory and practice underlying selection and calibration data sets, see F. Mosteller and D. Wallace, *The Federalist Papers: Inference in Disputed Authorship* (Reading, Mass.: Addison-Wesley, 1965).

the number of geographical regions, and the level of detail in the time scale. Typically there will be differences in alarm-rate characteristics for areas as close to each other as adjacent alarm boxes, and for adjacent days (Saturday and Sunday). There will never be enough data to allow the analyst to construct a separate prediction model with all of its own parameters for each alarm box (or other small location) since an alarm box will typically have fewer than 50 alarms a year. Inevitably there will be differences in alarm rates within units of aggregation, i.e., between geographical areas, sets of alarm types, or periods of time. The analyst needs to aggregate alarms in such a way as to get the best predictions possible. It is not always obvious how to do this; decisions should be based on exploratory data analyses rather than purely a priori considerations. For example, in estimating the probability that an incoming alarm signals a serious fire, one might be tempted to group alarm boxes together into neighborhoods and use the neighborhood proportion of alarms that are serious fires as the estimate for each alarm box's probability. But Section 8.6 gives an example of two alarm boxes only three blocks apart that have very different alarm patterns. In 1970, one box had no serious fires out of 96 incoming box-reported alarms while the other had 25 serious fires out of 94 incoming box-reported alarms. In Sections 8.5 and 8.6 we present two case studies that illustrate good methods for making tradeoffs between using aggregated and detailed data.

Smooth Parameterization is Preferred to Categorization. Models may be constructed using "categorization" or "smooth parameterization" of the explanatory variables. For example, as part of the work in modeling Bronx alarm rates (described in Section 8.5) we analyzed box-reported false alarms. Suppose we wish to predict the fraction of each day's box-reported false alarms during each hour, and we fix on a lunar month (a four-week period), a single day of the week, and a region of the Bronx. Consider the following two ways of predicting the fraction of the day's alarms in each hour: (1) Predict the fraction for each hour of the day by the observed fraction in that hour over a several year period (This is the *categorization* approach.); (2) Assume the fraction in each hour varies smoothly throughout the day so that a smooth curve can be used to represent the alarm rate over the day. (This is the *smooth parameterization* approach. See Section 8.5 for details about how such curves—in this case, linear functions of sines and cosines—are fit to data.)

The latter procedure is advisable when there is reason to believe that the underlying process is varying smoothly. With smooth parameterization, random fluctuation of alarms does not seriously distort the predictions. The method uses the information about alarms in the preceding hour and following hour to adjust the estimates for any given hour, producing a smoothly changing prediction. On the other hand, if real discontinuities exist in the underlying process (such as the end of the school day sharply increasing false alarms), they will not be picked up by a smooth parameterization. The choice between smooth parameterization and categorization is best made by matching the resulting predictions with a calibration data set. It is generally true that the less data there are, the more desirable it is to use smooth curves rather than many categories. In the Bronx study, with about 50,000 alarms from 1964 to 1969 available in the selection set, both types of model were fit, and their performances compared. The table below shows the average error in the two predictions of the number of box-reported false alarms per hour (i.e., the hourly fraction multiplied by the number of daily alarms) for the following year, 1970.

	Regions 1-3-4 Combined	Region 2
	Standard Error	Standard Error
Observed fraction	1.182	1.467
Smooth curve	1.187	1.438

The above standard errors show the two predictions to be about equally good for both Region 1-3-4 and Region 2. The smooth model is to be preferred since it uses only four parameters per lunar month as compared to 23 for the observed fraction model. Usually it is more convenient and may be more accurate to use the smooth curves rather than observed averages when there are many categories. Fortunately, when predicting the fraction of box-reported false alarms in each hour, it turned out that there was no loss in the accuracy of predictions using smooth curves. For smaller selection sets, smooth parameters can be expected to be more accurate.

Update the Estimates. In some situations there are a number of factors not included in the prediction model that nonetheless affect the occurrence of fire alarms. Section 8.5 describes modeling the effect of two factors that affect fire alarm incidence in New York City—location and time. There are other readily observable factors, such as weather, for which good historical data are available and which can be used in predicting fire alarm rates. There are many other factors affecting fire alarm rates that cannot be included because they are unpredictable, lack an historical data base, or are not easily observable. Examples of such factors are strikes, riots, World Series victories, flu epidemics, and electric power failures. In Section 8.5 we describe a method for capturing all such effects. The method is called "exponential smoothing." It is an updating procedure that changes present predictions as a function of how much they have erred recently. This and other short-term updating procedures are frequently useful as a simple method for adjusting "less than perfect" prediction models.

In addition, the coefficients of the equations used in predicting alarm rates should be reevaluated periodically (at least annually) to detect changes that may occur in the trend or pattern of alarm rates. Exponential smoothing can be used to constantly update the predictions based on the accuracy of recent predictions, and thus detect short-term shifts in the alarm rates.

8.5 A MODEL FOR PREDICTING ALARM RATES

We now turn to a case study by Carter and Rolph (1975) predicting alarm rates in the Bronx. A number of the methods described in Section 8.4 will be illustrated here. Since this section is more technical than the preceding ones, some readers may wish to defer reading it until they are actually faced with the problem of predicting alarm rates in their city. In any event, this case study of the Bronx should be viewed as an example of one way to go about predicting alarm rates, rather than as a prescription of exactly how to predict alarm rates in the reader's city.

We begin by describing some relevant properties of the Poisson process and showing how to test whether a sequence of incoming alarms is consistent with generation by a Poisson process. We then describe how to estimate the average number of alarms arriving per unit time, and how this number varies by geography, by year, by season, by day of the week, and by time of day. Putting these two steps together gives us an estimate of the probability distribution of incoming alarms for company size (response) areas for any time period, as required for initial dispatch decisions.

8.5.1 The Poisson Process

Incoming Alarms as a Poisson Process. In Chapter 7, a derivation of the Poisson process and its applications to incoming fire alarms was presented. It was shown that if alarms in a given hour in a particular region arrive according to a Poisson process with rate λ, the number of alarms arriving during that hour will have a Poisson probability distribution with mean λ. Similarly, the number of alarms arriving during the first half hour will have a Poisson distribution with mean $\lambda/2$, etc. An important verifiable assumption that we make is that the incoming alarms arrive according to a Poisson process whose parameter (the average alarm rate) varies across both time and geography. If the alarm arrival rates during hours 1 and 2 for region A are $\lambda(1,A)$ and $\lambda(2,A)$ and the alarm arrival rates during hours 1 and 2 for another region B are $\lambda(1,B)$ and $\lambda(2,B)$, then by the additive property of Poisson processes, the number of alarms arriving from the region composed of areas A and B during the two-hour period has a Poisson distribution with mean λ^* where

$$\lambda^* = \lambda(1,A) + \lambda(2,A) + \lambda(1,B) + \lambda(2,B).$$

That is, the probability that k alarms will be received from the larger region during the two-hour period is

$$P(k) = \frac{(\lambda^*)^k}{k!} e^{-\lambda^*}.$$

Do the Data Fit a Poisson Process? Chapter 7 gave the theoretical grounds for the Poisson process as a model for incoming sequences of fire alarms. Alarms in cities as diverse as Monterey, California, and New York City appear to be consistent with a Poisson process (see Carter and Rolph (1975) and Finnerty (1977)). In any new situation this assumption can and should be tested before proceeding to use a prediction that assumes Poisson alarm arrivals. We now describe two different methods for testing the Poisson assumption. The arrival of incoming alarms can be characterized by either the probability distribution of the number of incoming alarms per convenient period (say 15 minutes), or by the probability distribution of the length of time between one alarm arriving and the next one arriving. Each of these characterizations leads to a different method of testing whether the incoming alarms are from a Poisson process.

Table 8.3 gives the arrival times of alarms on five successive Friday summer evenings between 8 P.M. and 9 P.M. for a particular region in the Bronx. The seasonal variation over a span of five weeks is small enough that the Poisson process can be safely assumed to have the same parameter (arrival rate) for the entire five hours of data. Therefore, the number of alarms arriving in a 15-minute period should have a Poisson probability distribution. (A discussion of the length of the time period to use follows.) Table 8.4 gives the number of alarms in each of the 15-minute periods. The chi-square goodness-of-fit test can be used to test whether the data are consistent with a Poisson distribution. Let O_k be the observed number of periods with exactly k alarms, as given in Table 8.4. If the number of alarms per period has a Poisson distribution, the expected number of periods with k alarms, $E_k(\lambda)$, is

$$E_k(\lambda) = nP(k) = n \frac{\lambda^k}{k!} e^{-\lambda},$$

where n is the number of periods observed, 20 in our example. Since λ is unknown, it can be estimated by $\hat{\lambda}$, the average number of alarms per

8.5 A Model for Predicting Alarm Rates

TABLE 8.3. Arrival times of fire alarms on five successive Friday evenings between 8 and 9 P.M.

Evening 1	Evening 2	Evening 3	Evening 4	Evening 5
805	800	803	807	801
805	804	804	815	803
809	806	824	815	807
841	808	845	819	813
844	810	854	821	814
859	822	855	822	818
859	823		834	820
	831		834	822
	834		842	824
	834		846	829
	836		848	829
	846		858	831
	854			837
				840
				842
				843
				847

period, so that

$$\hat{\lambda} = \frac{1}{n}\sum_{k=0}^{\infty} kO_k = 2.75 \text{ alarms per 15 minute period.}$$

Note that $\hat{\lambda}$ can also be calculated by observing that there were twenty 15-minute periods and 55 alarms in the five-week span: $\hat{\lambda} = 55/20 = 2.75$. The theory underlying the chi-square goodness-of-fit test requires

TABLE 8.4. Counts of arriving alarms in 15-minute intervals on five successive Friday evenings.

UNGROUPED								
Number of alarms in 15-minute intervals	0	1	2	3	4	5	6	≥ 7
Number of occurrences O_k	2	3	5	4	1	4	1	0
Expected number of occurrences $E_k(\hat{\lambda})$	1.28	3.52	4.83	4.43	3.05	1.68	.768	.442
GROUPED								
Number of alarms in 15-minute intervals	0-1	2	3	≥ 4				
Number of occurrences O_k^*	5	5	4	6				
Expected number of occurrences $E_k(\hat{\lambda})$	4.80	4.83	4.43	5.94				

grouping the data so that the expected number of periods $E_k(\hat{\lambda})$ having a given number (or range) of alarms is not too small; $E_k(\hat{\lambda}) \geq 5$ is one rule of thumb. Stretching this rule slightly gives the four categories in Table 8.5. This chi-square statistic is defined as

$$\chi^2 = \sum_{k=1}^{4} \frac{(O_k^* - E_k^*(\hat{\lambda}))^2}{E_k^*(\hat{\lambda})} = \frac{(5 - 4.80)^2}{4.80} + \frac{(5 - 4.83)^2}{4.83} + \cdots$$
$$= .021,$$

where * indicates the groupings described above. Large values of χ^2 indicate that the data are *not* consistent with a Poisson distribution. Formally, the customary procedure is to look up the 0.05 significance level cutoff point of the chi-square distribution with $k - 2$ (= $4 - 2 = 2$) degrees of freedom where k is the number of categories, and declare the Poisson assumption incorrect if χ^2 exceeds it. (See Chapter 30 in Cramer (1946) or Chapter 11 in Morris and Rolph (1978).) For our situation the 0.05 cutoff point is 5.99 while $\chi^2 = .021$. Thus the data *are* consistent at the 0.05 significance level with a Poisson distribution.

This particular data set was chosen to make explanation of the test procedure easy and allow display of the steps and results. It has only 55 alarms over a span of five hours, too few alarms for an adequate test. In general, the more data the better. The total time span should include at least several hours of alarms. The 15-minute periods were chosen so as to get 20 periods and the resulting four categories for the chi-square test.

TABLE 8.5a. Interarrival times of 55 fire alarms on five successive Friday evenings.

Evening 1	Evening 2	Evening 3	Evening 4	Evening 5
0	1	9	12	3
4	4	1	8	2
32	2	20	0	4
3	2	21	4	4
15	2	9	2	1
0	12	1	1	4
	1		12	2
	8		0	2
	3		8	2
	0		4	5
	2		2	0
	10		10	2
	8			6
				3
				2
				1
				4

8.5 A Model for Predicting Alarm Rates

TABLE 8.5b. Ordered interarrival times of the same 55 fire alarms ($X_{(1)} \leq \cdots \leq X_{(54)}$).

$X_{(1)}-X_{(11)}$	$X_{(12)}-X_{(22)}$	$X_{(23)}-X_{(33)}$	$X_{(34)}-X_{(44)}$	$X_{(45)}-X_{(54)}$
0	1	2	4	9
0	1	2	4	10
0	2	2	4	10
0	2	3	4	12
0	2	3	5	12
0	2	3	6	12
1	2	3	6	15
1	2	4	8	20
1	2	4	8	21
1	2	4	8	32
1	2	4	9	

If there is a choice of the period for counting alarms, it should be as long as possible consistent with doing little or no grouping for small values of k.

The chi-square test as described above is valid only for data from a single area generated during periods that have approximately the same average alarm rate—data from the early evening usually should not be aggregated with data from the early morning.

An alternative and frequently more sensitive method for checking whether alarms can be assumed to come from a Poisson process is based on the time between arrivals of successive alarms. In Chapter 7 it is shown that if alarms are generated according to a Poisson process, the interarrival times have a negative exponential distribution. That is, the probability of the next alarm arriving after at least t minutes is $e^{-\lambda t}$. Probability plots can be used to see whether the interarrival times have an exponential distribution. Let $X_{(1)} \leq \cdots \leq X_{(N)}$ be the N ordered interarrival times. For example, Table 8.5a gives the 54 interarrival times for the 55 alarms in Table 8.3. (Because of the "memoryless" property of the negative exponential distribution, the five evenings could be strung together resulting in an interarrival time of nine minutes between the alarm at 8:54 on Evening 2 and the one at 8:03 on Evening 3.) The ordered values of the $N = 54$ interarrival times are given in Table 8.5b.

If these points are plotted with $X_{(i)}$ on the vertical axis and log $[n/(n - i + \frac{1}{2})]$ on the horizontal axis they should fall on a straight line with slope $1/\lambda$. "Semilog" paper can be used for this purpose; plot $n/(n - i + \frac{1}{2})$ on the horizontal (log) scale and $X_{(i)}$ on the vertical scale. Figure 8.16 is a probability plot of the Bronx fire alarm data from Table 8.5. It appears to fall roughly on a straight line, which is consistent with the Poisson assumption. The slope is about $1/\hat{\lambda} = 5$ or $\hat{\lambda} = .2$ alarms per minute, roughly consistent with 2.75 alarms per 15-minute period. If the

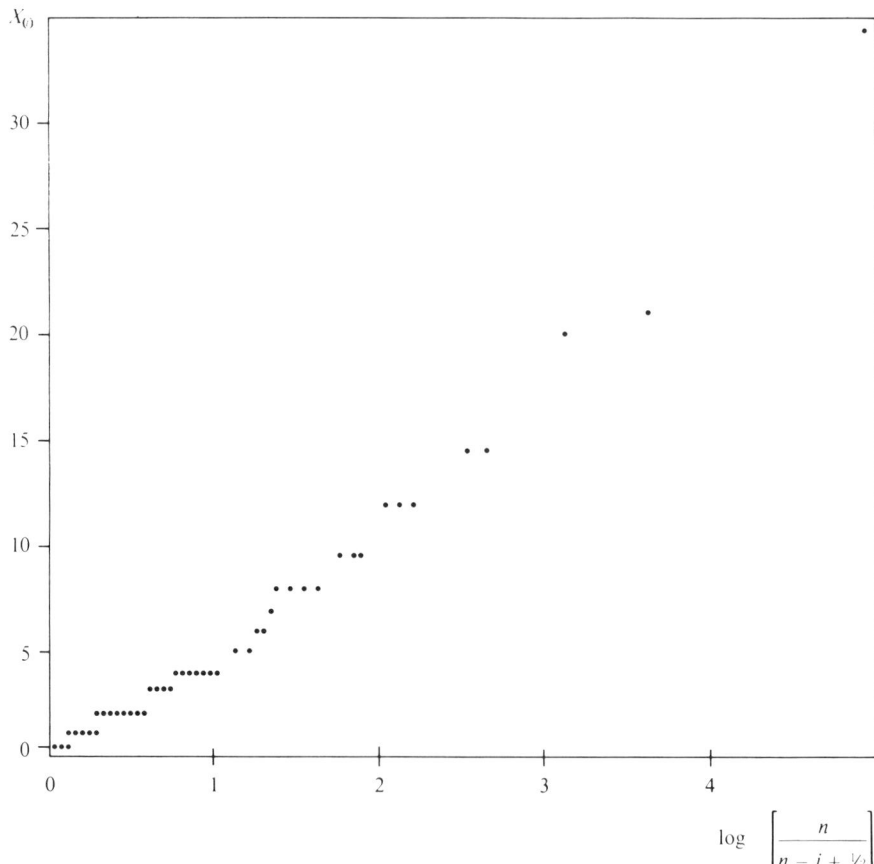

FIGURE 8.16. Probability plot for exponential distribution.

interarrival times are easily available, we recommend using this method rather than grouping and using a chi-square test of the Poisson distribution. See Chapter 9 of Morris and Rolph (1978) for a description of the limitations in using chi-square tests as compared to probability plotting.

8.5.2 Modeling Hourly Average Alarm Rates in the Bronx

In this section we describe the development by Carter and Rolph (1975) of a prediction model for forecasting hourly fire alarm rates in the Bronx. As has been pointed out before, many deployment models require good predictions of fire alarm rates. They are needed for making initial dispatch and relocation decisions. For example, one of the initial dispatch policies described in Chapter 11 requires a prediction of current alarm rates in

8.5 A Model for Predicting Alarm Rates

each first-due area in a city. The relocation algorithm described in Chapter 12 requires alarm rate predictions for larger areas over periods of several hours.

Briefly, the prediction model for alarm rates works as follows. The sequence of fire alarms is regarded as a Poisson process. Alarms are divided into several types. A sequence of alarms of a particular type is assumed to come from a Poisson process with a rate that varies by geography, time, and weather. The Poisson processes generating each of the several alarm types are assumed to be independent. We first estimate how alarm rates vary with time (year, season, day of the week, time of day). Then, by using an updating method, we estimate any additional effects, such as weather.

The alarm estimates are based solely on historical data; in particular, no information on neighborhood demographic characteristics is incorporated. Developing the model for predicting the rate of each type of alarm involves several steps:

1. Daily alarm rates are estimated for large regions.
2. For large regions, the fraction of daily alarms occurring in each hour of the day is estimated as a function of the region, season, and day of the week.
3. Exponential smoothing is used to capture some of the effects of additional variables, such as weather.
4. Large region predictions are modified to produce hourly alarm predictions for small areas.

A model for predicting alarms should be chosen both on the basis of the data and on conceptual grounds. Considerable data analysis was done before dividing the Bronx into demand regions and before specifying a parametric structure relating alarm rates to time. The rest of this section describes this analysis.

Since alarm rates vary both by geography and time, the Bronx was divided into demand regions (Figure 8.17), each being as homogeneous as possible in its incidence patterns. The criteria for grouping the neighborhoods into regions included geographic proximity as well as similarity of alarm incidence statistics. Roughly, Region 2 is high incidence, Region 4 is low incidence, and Regions 1 and 3 are in between.

Theoretical Considerations. An important early consideration is what predictor variables to include in the model. For example, exploratory data analysis reveals whether a single time pattern is appropriate for all demand regions or—as was the case in the Bronx—the model must include separate time patterns for different regions.

To predict the expected number of alarms on a given day in a particular region, it is necessary to model how the alarm process depends on the

FIGURE 8.17. Bronx demand regions.

year, the season, and the day of the week. It is important that estimates of the model's parameters be easy to compute. Also, the ability to make statistical inferences from the fitted model is essential. A linear regression model meets both criteria. Regression models require assumptions of linearity and additivity in the variables. That is, the true relationship between the dependent variable y and the independent variables $x_1, x_2, \ldots, x_k$ should be

$$y = b_0 + b_1 x_1 + \cdots + b_k x_k + \text{error}.$$

To make statistical inferences from a least-squares fit of the model, it must be assumed that the errors are independent and have equal variances. Although one may begin with a particular set of dependent and independent variables (numbers of alarms by day, year, season, day of

8.5 A Model for Predicting Alarm Rates

the week) that do not satisfy these assumptions, it may be possible to construct a set of variables that do. Transformations can be made on both the dependent and independent variables. New independent variables can be created by taking (nonlinear) functions of other independent variables.

A primary consideration in constructing daily alarm predictions is the Poisson nature of the alarm process. As mentioned earlier, one helpful property of a Poisson process with a time-varying rate $\lambda(t)$ is that the number of alarms between t_1 and t_2 is Poisson distributed with mean $\bar{\lambda}(t_2 - t_1)$, where $\bar{\lambda}$ is the average rate over the interval (t_1, t_2). Thus, the number of alarms in a given day has a Poisson distribution, although the parameter may differ from day to day. Since the variance of a Poisson distribution is the same as its mean, and the daily alarm counts in general have different means, the usual regression model assumption of equal error variances is violated. Theory tells us, however, that the square root (or possibly the logarithm) of the daily counts has approximately equal variance (Cox and Lewis, 1966).

Choosing a Good Predictor of Daily Alarms. Carter and Rolph (1975) give a detailed account of the analysis that led them to a model of daily alarms for the Bronx. They tried estimating box-reported false alarms using both the square-root transformation and logarithmic transformation. Comparisons of the standard error of estimates revealed little difference in the predictive power. The square root of box-reported false alarms was chosen because it is easier to retransform, and because the square root is the most commonly used variance stabilizing transformation for the Poisson distribution. To choose the form of the trend, Bronx-wide total alarm counts for each year from 1956 to 1970 were used. These data are plotted in Figure 8.18, which clearly shows a discontinuity in 1968—the year of the Robert Kennedy and Martin Luther King assassinations and the long sanitation workers strike in New York City. It appears that a permanent jump in alarm rates occurred in 1968 and that growth continued at the same rate in subsequent years. A number of different trend specifications for the growth of the square root of the number of alarms were tried before choosing a single linear trend with a jump in 1968 for the entire Bronx. Most cities probably do not have peculiarities like the 1968 jump, but the data should be studied carefully for such anomalies.

Displays like those in Section 8.3 revealed the interactions among region, day of the week, and season. It is clear that the four regions have differing day of the week and seasonal effects and that these effects interact. This exploratory analysis of daily alarm counts helped in choosing a smooth parameterization of seasonal patterns.

A day is defined as starting and ending at 6 A.M., rather than using the

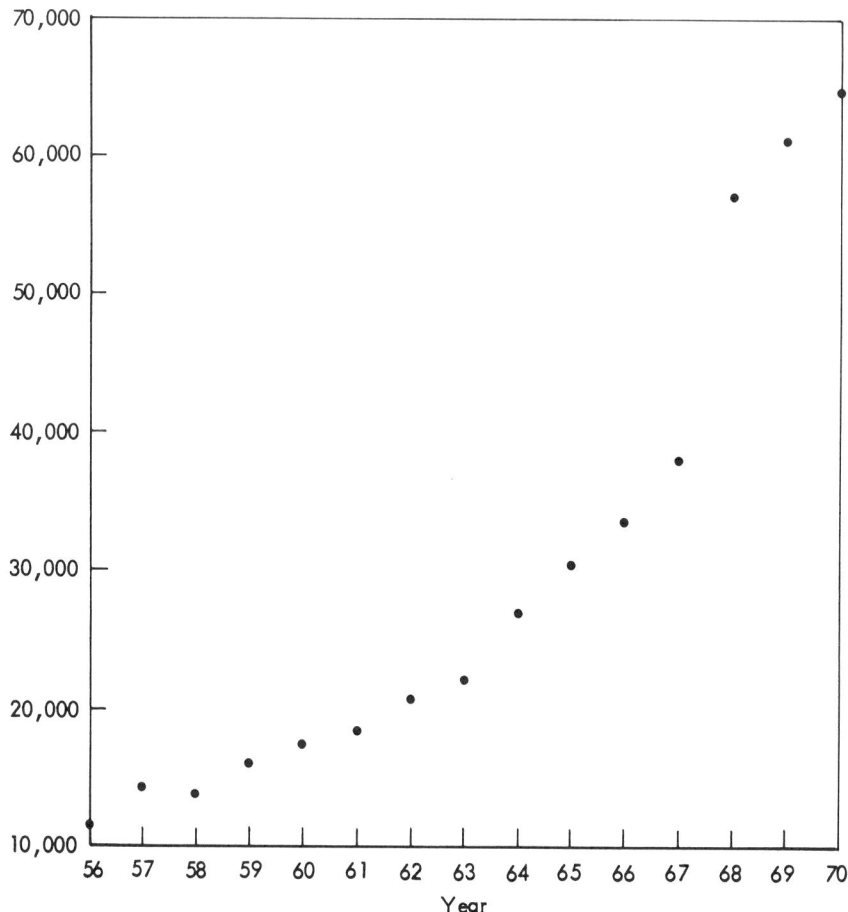

FIGURE 8.18. Annual alarm counts in the Bronx, 1956–1970.

usual midnight-to-midnight definition. Since alarms reflect ongoing social activity, dividing the days at a time when the alarm rate is low seemed desirable. The equations using 6 A.M. to 6 A.M. days also result in better hourly predictions.

To find a functional form that satisfactorily captures the seasonal pattern, an exploratory analysis was done with weekly counts of alarms. Regressions were tried, using from one to nine harmonics as independent variables. More than four harmonics only improved the fit for spikes such as the annual New Year's Eve increase in false alarms.

We will see that the final regression equation (Equation 8.4) forces

8.5 A Model for Predicting Alarm Rates

each of the four "days of the week" (Sunday, Monday through Thursday, Friday, and Saturday)[5] to have the same trend and the same higher-order harmonics, with each having its own first- and second-order harmonics. To arrive at this final equation, four separate regression equations were also tried, one for each of the four "days of the week." The difference between the regression coefficients of each day's equations and the regression coefficients in the equation using all the days together is consistent, with the trend and higher order harmonics being the same for each day. The quality of the fit obtained for each functional form and transformation was checked by making various plots, diagnostic testing, and refitting after removing extreme observations from the data.

The resulting regression model provides a good prediction of the square root of the number of alarms on a given day, but predicting the *actual* number of alarms on a given day is the problem of interest. The following technical argument shows how to make this prediction. If X is a random variable with a mean $E(X)$, and $P = \sqrt{X}$, then

$$\text{Var}(P) = E(P^2) - E^2(P),$$
$$E(X) = E(P^2) = E^2(P) + \text{Var}(P).$$

If $\hat{p}$ is an unbiased estimator of $E(P)$, then $\hat{p}^2 + \text{Var}(P)$ is an unbiased estimator of $E(X)$. In our case, the value $\hat{P}_{ij}$ from the regression equation is an unbiased estimator of $E(\sqrt{X_{ij}})$, where X_{ij} is the alarm count on day i in week j. If i is a "weekday"—Monday through Thursday—then X_{ij} is the average of those four days of alarms in week j. If S_i^2 is the estimated variance of the estimator P_{ij} for day i, then the prediction of the daily number of alarms can be obtained from:

$$\hat{X}_{ij} = \hat{P}_{ij}^2 + S_i^2. \tag{8.3}$$

This is the actual prediction of alarms used. We give the formula for $\hat{P}_{ij}$ in the next section.

The Predictor of Daily Alarms. We now give the equation for predicting daily alarms in demand regions. Let X_{ijk} = the total number of alarms

---

[5] For daily box-reported false alarms for 1964–1969, the seasonal patterns of Mondays, Tuesdays, Wednesdays, and Thursdays did not differ in a statistically significant way for any of the four regions. Thus, we assume that these "weekdays" have the same seasonal pattern for total alarms.

occurring on day i of week j in region k. The ranges are:

i: = 1(Average weekday)
= 2(Friday)
= 3(Saturday)
= 4(Sunday).
j: = Weeks sequentially numbered beginning January 1964 ($j = 1,2,\ldots,312$).
k: = Regions ($k=1,2,3,4$).

The predictions are derived separately for each region. Suppressing the subscript k on each coefficient, the prediction equation for P_{ij}, the square-root of X_{ij}, is given in Equation (8.4):

$$\hat{P}_{ij} = \beta_1 j + \beta_2 G(j) + \sum_{\ell=2}^{4}\left\{a_\ell \sin\frac{\ell\pi j}{26} + b_\ell \cos\frac{\ell\pi j}{26}\right\} \\ + \sum_{m=1}^{4} D_{im}\left\{C_m + A_m \sin\frac{\pi j}{26} + B_m \cos\frac{\pi j}{26}\right\}, \quad (8.4)$$

where the indicator variables G and D are defined as:

$$G(j) = \begin{array}{l} 1 \text{ if } j \geq 209 \text{ (i.e., in 1968 or later)} \\ 0 \text{ otherwise} \end{array}$$

$$D_{im} = \begin{array}{l} 1 \text{ if } m = i \\ 0 \text{ if } m \neq i. \end{array}$$

Looking at the prediction piece by piece we see that the first two terms give the trend, the first summation gives the overall seasonal fluctuation, and the last summation gives the part of the seasonal fluctuation that differs for each day of the week. The regression coefficients (β_1, β_2, a_ℓ, b_ℓ, C_m, A_m, and B_m) are fit to the data. After the $\hat{P}_{ij}$ are obtained by fitting the linear regression Equation (8.4) by least squares, the prediction of the daily number of alarms (x_{ij}) is obtained from Equation (8.3). The coefficients of the equation are given in Table 8.6.

This model has 22 coefficients and $4 \times 312 = 1248$ observations, so there are not too many coefficients relative to the observations. It is a parsimonious model. For example, suppose we had modeled each day of the week separately and used categorization for week-to-week seasonal differences, rather than the smooth parameterization of the sines and cosines in Equation (8.4). Then each regression equation would have had 53 coefficients—two for trend, 51 for the weeks—and 312 observations. This is too many coefficients; a rough rule of thumb is no more coefficients than the square root of the number of observations ($\sqrt{312} = 18$).

TABLE 8.6. Regression of the Square-root of Daily Total Alarms, 1964–1969.[a]

Regression Result	Region			
	1	2	3	4
R^2	0.3453	0.7356	0.6460	0.2727
Standard Error of Estimate	0.6243	1.007	0.6042	0.8303
β_1[b]	0.1508E-02	0.1066E-01	0.4696E-02	−0.2319E-04
	(5.65)[c]	(24.77)	(18.19)	(0.07)
β_2	0.4283	1.257	0.7774	0.7015
	(8.51)	(15.47)	(15.95)	(10.48)
a_2	−0.1342	−0.2343	−0.1551	−0.2560
	(7.05)	(7.64)	(8.43)	(10.12)
b_2	−0.3195E-01	0.8245E-01	0.1240	−0.1259
	(1.69)	(2.71)	(6.78)	(5.01)
a_3	−0.1376E-01	0.7695E-01	0.6139E-01	−0.4369E-01
	(0.73)	(2.52)	(3.35)	(1.73)
b_3	−0.3465E-01	−0.4403E-02	−0.1956E-01	−0.1186
	(1.83)	(0.14)	(1.07)	(4.72)
a_4	−0.3535E-01	−0.5231E-01	−0.5247E-01	−0.3659E-02
	(1.87)	(1.71)	(2.87)	(0.15)
b_4	0.5320E-01	0.1309	0.8027E-01	0.1392
	(2.82)	(4.29)	(4.39)	(5.54)
C_1 (Sunday)	2.661	5.389	3.631	4.246
	(57.87)	(72.62)	(81.58)	(69.42)
A_1	0.5689E-01	−0.7979E-01	−0.5097E-01	0.7416E-01
	(1.13)	(0.99)	(1.05)	(1.11)
B_1	−0.4432	−0.9627	−0.2900	−0.4724
	(8.87)	(11.94)	(6.00)	(7.11)
C_2 (Weekday)	2.584	4.955	3.441	4.250
	(75.26)	(89.46)	(103.6)	(93.08)
A_2	0.1226E-01	−0.1484E-01	0.3020E-01	0.3981E-01
	(0.4832)	(0.36)	(1.23)	(1.18)
B_2	−0.3486	−0.7705	−0.1968	−0.3245
	(13.95)	(19.11)	(8.14)	(9.763)
C_3 (Friday)	2.736	5.528	3.763	4.553
	(59.50)	(74.50)	(84.53)	(74.43)
A_3	−0.2599E-01	0.1145	−0.7764E-02	0.2695E-01
	(0.52)	(1.415)	(0.16)	(0.40)
B_3	−0.3377	−0.8610	−0.2354	−0.3075
	(6.76)	(10.68)	(4.87)	(4.63)
C_4 (Saturday)	2.987	6.090	3.990	4.677
	(64.94)	(82.07)	(89.64)	(76.46)
A_4	−0.2186E-01	0.5455E-01	0.5565E-01	0.1689
	(0.4357)	(0.67)	(1.15)	(2.53)
B_4	−0.3481	−1.01	−0.1440	−0.2760
	(6.97)	(12.53)	(2.98)	(4.15)

[a] See Equation 8.4.

[b] The exponential notation is read as follows: The value of β_1 in Region 4 is −.00002319.

[c] t-statistics are in parentheses.

Predicting Hourly Alarm Rates. Hourly alarm rates can be predicted by using a model that predicts the fraction of each day's alarms that will occur in each hour of the day. Preliminary analyses revealed that the number of alarms per hour in Regions 1, 3, and 4 were too small to develop reliable estimates of the hourly alarm pattern for each region separately. Therefore, to examine geographic variation, the Bronx was divided into two regions: Region 2, which was renamed Super Region 2 (this is the South Bronx, which has a much higher alarm density than the rest of the borough); and Regions 1, 3, and 4 combined, which was designated Super Region 1.

Exploratory data analysis of the hourly totals for each region showed that the hourly alarm totals have different patterns for different days of the week. On weekend nights, a much higher fraction of the day's alarms occurs after 9 P.M. than on other nights. Also, the peaks for weekdays and Sundays are much higher than for Fridays or Saturdays. The two regions exhibit different hourly patterns for the same day of the week. Super Region 2 has fewer sharp peaks on Sundays and weekdays, and sharper peaks on Fridays and Saturdays than Super Region 1, which is a lower-incidence region. The hour of the day patterns differ seasonally as well as regionally: the peak hour is later in the day in the summer than in winter.

Harmonic regression is a natural way to model cyclic phenomena—in this case, the cycle would be 24 hours. With this approach, the question for the analyst is how many terms to use. Analysis suggests that the variation in the fraction of alarms in each hour within a single day could be captured by using two harmonics of the 24 hours, and that seasonal variation in this pattern could be adequately captured by allowing the coefficients of the harmonic terms to vary smoothly with the week of the year. The four weekdays, Monday through Thursday, have the same hourly pattern of box-reported false alarms and so are assumed to have identical hourly patterns for other alarm types. The patterns of the other days of the week differ enough to justify fitting separate equations to each day's data. A further assumption is that the hourly pattern of alarms remains stable from year to year. The specification of the regression equation for predicting Y_{rijh} (the proportion of the alarms on day i ($i = 1, 2, 3, 4$) in week j ($j = 1, 2, \ldots, 52$) that occurs in hour h ($h = 1, 2, \ldots, 24$) in Super Region r ($r = 1, 2$) is given by:

$$E(Y_{rijh}) = c + \sum_{\ell=1}^{2} \left\{ \left[a_{0\ell} + a_{1\ell}(j^2 - 52j) \right.\right.$$

$$\left. + a_{2\ell}(j^3 - (52)^2 j) \right] \sin\left(\frac{\pi \ell h}{12}\right)$$

$$\left. + \left[b_{0\ell} + b_{1\ell}(j^2 - 52j) + b_{2\ell}(j^3 - (52)^2 j) \right] \cos\left(\frac{\pi \ell h}{12}\right) \right\}.$$

(8.5)

8.5 A Model for Predicting Alarm Rates

The 13 parameters—c, a_{01}, a_{02}, a_{11}, ..., b_{12}, ...—should be fit separately for each region r and each day of the week i. There are $24 \times 312 = 7596$ observations in each instance, more than enough for estimating 13 coefficients. The coefficients of each sine and cosine in Equation (8.5) are cubic equations in the week of the year, constrained so that the coefficient of week 52 is the same as the coefficient of week 0 (to ensure the continuity of the prediction).

In order to predict the hourly fraction of the daily total for each of the two regions, it is not clear a priori whether to use the same hourly fractions from the model fitted to all the Bronx data, or to use the same hourly fractions from the model fitted to each region's data separately. The fit to 1964-1969 data suggested that the two methods give somewhat different predictions.

The separate hourly models for each region should give better fits (lower mean square error) because the fitted coefficients for the two regions are quite different. However, the region-specific estimates of these parameters may have such large standard errors that using Bronxwide parameter estimates may decrease the standard error of the estimate more than enough to offset the bias of the estimate for each region. This kind of reasoning resulted in fitting 1964-1969 data by both methods, and comparing the 1970 prediction given by each method to what actually happened in 1970. Because the purpose in making the 1970 prediction here is choosing between hourly fraction models, the 1970 daily totals for each region were taken as given and the product of the predicted hourly fraction and the actual daily alarm total was compared to the actual hourly totals. The difference between the two models in the quality of the fit was not large in either region. Since the "parsimony of parameters" principle says that is is better to use one model than two, Equation (8.5) was used with parameters estimated from Bronxwide data to predict the hourly fraction of daily alarms.

Short-run Adjustments in Predictions (Exponential Smoothing). Since there are a number of factors, such as weather, that affect the occurrence of alarms but have not been accounted for, there may be room for improvement in the prediction method just described. Explicit modeling of the effect of weather on fire alarm rates in the Bronx showed that weather has a measurable effect from noon to midnight, but little effect in the morning. The main effect is that alarm rates decrease significantly in hours when precipitation occurs. Because weather tends to remain constant over periods of several hours, Carter and Rolph (1975) found that exponential smoothing on the residual of the hourly prediction (observed alarm count in the hour − hourly prediction for that hour) excluding weather captures the effect of weather just as well as using simple exponential smoothing on the residual of a prediction that includes weather explicitly.

There are problems in using the hourly residuals without transforming them, because there is such large variation in the expected magnitude of the residuals during a day. Residuals that are of reasonable size for peak hours will be much too large in absolute value if projected into the quieter hours of the morning when alarm rates are low. To avoid this difficulty, the smoothing is done on R_h, the difference between the square root of the observed hourly count and the square root of the predicted hourly count:

$$R_h = \sqrt{Y_h} - \sqrt{\hat{z}_h},$$

where $\hat{z}_h$ is the predicted hourly count. Thus, a revised prediction is based on using exponential smoothing of the past values of R_h, using a smoothing constant, α, that indexes the age of the data. The estimate, $\hat{R}_h$, of R_h is given by[6]

$$\hat{R}_h = \frac{1 - \alpha^h}{1 - \alpha} \sum_{t=0}^{h-1} \alpha^{h-1-t} R_t$$
$$= \alpha R_{h-1} + (1 - \alpha) \hat{R}_{h-1}. \qquad (8.6)$$

A revised prediction of the alarm count in h, $\hat{v}_h$, is based on $\hat{R}_h = \sqrt{\hat{v}_h} - \sqrt{\hat{z}_h}$, so that solving for $\hat{v}_h$ and estimating R_h and R_h^2, we get

$$\hat{v}_h = \hat{z}_h + \widehat{R_h^2} + 2\hat{R}_h \sqrt{\hat{z}_h} \qquad (8.7)$$

where

$$\widehat{R_h^2} = (\hat{R}_h)^2 + \frac{2(1 - \alpha)}{4(2 - \alpha)}.$$

Here α was taken to be between 0.01 and 0.5 by Carter and Rolph (1975). The quality of the smoothed prediction is insensitive to the exact choice of the smoothing constant, and any parameter in a wide range performs satisfactorily. This parameter range corresponds to the average age of the data used for updating: between 6 and 24 hours.

Brown (1962) gives a comprehensive treatment of smoothing and prediction. While exponential smoothing (or any updating method) can substantially improve prediction, it should not be used as a substitute for periodic refitting of the entire model.

Small Area Alarm Rates. Alarm rate predictions in regions the size of first-due areas are needed for some of the deployment models. For illus-

---

[6] The reader interested in the derivations of the following formulas is referred to Brown (1962) for a general treatment of exponential smoothing, and to Carter and Rolph (1975) for the application to fire alarm counts.

8.5 A Model for Predicting Alarm Rates

trative purposes, think of ladder companies, although the analysis could easily be repeated for engine companies. For example, to decide whether to dispatch one or two ladders to a particular alarm, one needs to know the alarm rate in a region consisting of first-due areas of the N ladder companies that are closest to the one that would respond second-due to the alarm. If known, the alarm rates in each of the first-due areas could be aggregated to produce the alarm rates required by the initial dispatch algorithm.

The starting points for small area predictions are the hourly alarm rates in each of the four demand regions. We assume that each smaller area possesses exactly the same seasonal and hourly alarm patterns as the region in which it is contained; therefore, we assign to each area the proportion of the region's alarms that occurred in that region over the preceding n years. The only question remaining is how many years of data to use for this calculation. As small a value of n as possible should be used to capture the effects of changing neighborhoods, while at the same time keeping n large enough to estimate the proportions adequately. Formal statistical tests showed that the prediction using 1968 and 1969 Bronx data was superior to the prediction using only 1969 data.

Summary of Procedures. We conclude this section with a brief summary of the procedures for estimating alarm rates.

1. To estimate daily alarm rates, the city should be divided into demand regions (Section 8.2). Alarm rates are estimated separately for each region.
2. For each region, the estimate of the square-root of the total number of alarms that occurred on day i of week j in region k is computed by ordinary regression using Equation (8.4).
3. The estimate of the actual alarm count ($\hat{x}_{ijk}$) is obtained by retransformation using Equation (8.3).
4. To estimate the fraction of each day's alarms that occur hourly, the demand regions are the smallest that can be used, and regions as large as an entire borough or small city may be used. The estimate $\hat{y}_{rijh}$, the fraction of alarms on day i of week j in region r (possibly with a different region definition than in (2)) that occurred in hour h, is obtained from Equation (8.5). Separate regressions are run for Friday, Saturday, Sunday, and weekdays to allow the "days of the week" to have different patterns.
5. The hourly and daily equations can be combined to estimate $\hat{z}_{rijh}$, the number of alarms in region r in hour h of day i of week j:

$$\hat{z}_{rijh} = \hat{y}_{rijh} \sum_k \hat{x}_{ijk}, \qquad (8.8)$$

where the summation is over all the "daily alarm regions," k, that make up the "hourly alarm region," r.

6. Equation (8.8) gives alarm rate predictions based on geographic location and time only. In a dynamic prediction situation, as in a real-time computerized system for dispatching and relocation, z can be improved by means of an exponential smoothing algorithm (Equation (8.7)) to capture some of the effect of weather and other unanalyzed events on alarm incidence.
7. Hourly alarm rate predictions for a small area a, which is part of demand region r, can be obtained by assigning a fraction of the predicted hourly total alarms for region r to area a. The fraction to be assigned is the proportion of the region's total alarms that occurred in area a in the most recent two-year period.

8.6 PREDICTING THE PROBABILITY THAT AN ALARM SIGNALS A SERIOUS FIRE

The policy governing initial dispatch to alarms can often be improved by knowing the probability that each alarm signals a serious fire. If this probability is high, a large number of units can be dispatched, thereby minimizing the time until a number of men and equipment sufficient to control the fire are at the scene. If this probability is low, fewer companies can be sent, leaving the additional companies available to respond to future alarms, and reducing the strain of responding on the firefighters. In this section we present a method for producing estimates of the probability that an alarm signals a serious fire, and we evaluate the method using data from New York City. Further discussion of the methodology and the case study on which this section is based may be found in Carter and Rolph (1973).

Because the main use of the estimates is in initial dispatch, we define as serious fires only those fires in occupied structures that require at least four fire companies of any type, or at least one engine company and two ladder companies. The validity of the method is not sensitive to this particular definition of seriousness and could be used just as effectively with other definitions. Chapter 11 discusses alternative definitions of serious fires and ways of using estimates of the probability that an alarm is serious to improve initial dispatch policies.

8.6.1 Partitioning the Problem

For most telephone or voice-box alarms, the caller provides the dispatcher with enough information to determine the amount of equipment needed at the incident. Although the caller may misinform the dispatcher,

8.6 Predicting the Probability an Alarm Signals a Serious Fire 309

in New York City the percentage of serious-sounding cases that turn out to be serious is sufficiently high that it pays to send a full turnout to such incidents under almost all conditions. Information about the kind of incident is not available from the person who pulls a street box alarm. Street box alarms accounted for 60 percent of all alarms and 43 percent of all structural fires in New York City in 1970. Since dispatches to these alarms engendered the greatest opportunity to improve initial dispatch decisions, only the probability that an alarm from a street box signaled a serious fire was analyzed, although the methods could be used for other types of reporting.

A model for the probability that an alarm from a street box signals a serious fire should depend only on what the dispatcher knows about the alarm: the location of the box, time of day, day of the week, and season of the year. (For example, for a given location, the probability is higher in the middle of the night than in the early evening, higher in winter than in summer.) The model should take into account the possibility that the probability may be declining over time if the number of nonserious alarms is rising faster than the number of serious fires. The development of this model follows the principle of parsimony of parameters discussed earlier in this chapter. In principle, one should be able to determine the changes in the probability at each location due to time of day, season, etc., by examining the alarm history at that location. In fact, there simply is not enough information (i.e., alarms) at each location to give reliable estimates.

Analysis showed that in New York City, the probability of an alarm signaling a fire in an occupied structure varied widely among neighboring locations within the same demand region. In Table 8.7, we show 1970

TABLE 8.7. Structural fire predictions for two alarm boxes. Using 1967–1969 data, the expected proportion of serious fires was predicted for each alarm box in the Bronx. These predictions were compared to actual 1970 data. For example, it was predicted for Box 2277 that 0.4 percent of all alarms would be structural fires, while the prediction for Box 2209 was 31.8 percent. In 1970, both of these boxes had about the same number of alarms. In both cases, the predictions were quite close to the actual results. Box 2277 had no structural fires, while Box 2209 had 25 structural fires. Further, these alarm boxes are only three blocks apart.

		Actual 1970 Data		
			Structural Fires	
Bronx Box Number	Predicted Percent Structural (1967–1969 data)	Alarms	Number	Percent
2277	0.4	96	0	0
2209	31.8	94	25	26.6

data for two alarm boxes, located only three blocks apart, with similar numbers of alarms. One had no structural fires in 1970 while 26 percent of the alarms from the other were for structural fires. However, it was also found that given a fire in an occupied structure, the probability of it being serious did not vary much by location within the region.[7] Since fires in occupied structures are far more common than serious fires, we can estimate the probability that an alarm from a given location is for an occupied structure fire with reasonable accuracy, and then estimate the probability that an occupied structure fire is a serious fire from data for the entire demand region. The steps in the analysis are:

1. Estimate the probability that an alarm at a particular location will be for a fire in an occupied structure, without regard to when the alarm occurs.
2. Model the effect of the time of day, season, and trend on the probability that an alarm is serious for all alarms in a demand region, assuming that these effects will be the same for all locations in the region.
3. Combine these two models to obtain an estimate that an alarm at a given location and time period is serious.

The data that were used in this study covered all alarms from 1967 to 1970 in the Bronx. Only the data for 1967 to 1969 were used to develop estimates, and the methodology was tested by comparing the predictions to what actually happened in 1970. Of course, when the predictions are actually used for initial dispatch decisions, the latest available data should be included in the estimates.

8.6.2 Estimating the Probability that an Alarm from a Box Signals a Fire in an Occupied Structure

Our first task is to develop, for each alarm box in the Bronx, an estimate of $p(O|i)$, the probability that an alarm from box i signals a fire in an occupied structure. The obvious approach is to determine the proportion of alarms at that box that were for fires in an occupied structure. Since many alarm boxes have only a few alarms per year, this method will not give us reliable estimates for these boxes. An alternative is to group the boxes into small neighborhoods that have, say, 100 alarms over the data period, and use the proportion for the neighborhood as the estimate for

---

[7] Space precludes us from describing the analysis here. The reader interested in applying this methodology to a different city, but who feels that this crucial assumption may not be true, is referred to Carter and Rolph (1973) for ways of determining whether or not it holds and what to do if it does not.

8.6 Predicting the Probability an Alarm Signals a Serious Fire

each box; but as we have seen, boxes only a few blocks apart may have radically different proportions of structural fires. A third estimate (called an *empirical Bayes* estimate) offers a compromise between the proportion from the alarm history of a particular box and the overall neighborhood proportion. If the data indicate that all boxes in the neighborhood are similar, all empirical Bayes estimates will be close to the neighborhood average (and the neighborhood estimates have smaller standard errors than estimates based on only alarms from the single alarm box, since there are more alarms for the neighborhood). If the data give little indication that boxes in the neighborhood are homogeneous, the empirical Bayes estimate for a box will be close to the box history proportion. This method of estimation produces more reliable estimates than either box history or neighborhood averages.

The first step in using the empirical Bayes estimator is to group the alarm boxes into small neighborhoods having alarm rates as homogeneous as possible. A map of the Bronx and a computer printout showing the number of box-reported alarms and box-reported structural fires at each of the 2500 boxes were used in the grouping. The boxes were grouped into "neighborhoods" according to the following criteria:

1. Neighborhoods should be geographically connected.
2. Boxes with obvious geographical properties (those around parks, or on highways) should be grouped together.
3. Each neighborhood should have at least 100 alarms in the period 1967–1969.
4. Each neighborhood should have at least four boxes, unless it contains one box with such a large number of alarms that that box alone could be used to estimate the probability that an alarm signals a structural fire.

Keeping these criteria in mind, we grouped boxes with similar numbers of alarms and proportions of structural fires into a set of 216 neighborhoods.

Estimates of the probability of a box alarm signaling a fire in an occupied structure were then calculated separately for each neighborhood. Let

k = number of boxes in the neighborhood.

n_i = number of alarms reported from box i ($i = 1, 2, \ldots, k$).

Y_i = number of fires in occupied structures reported from box i ($i = 1, 2, \ldots, k$).

$X_i = Y_i/n_i$ = proportion of alarms from box i that are for fires in occupied structures.

$\bar{X} = \sum_{i=1}^{k} Y_i / \sum_{i=1}^{k} n_i$ = proportion of alarms in the neighborhood that are for fires in occupied structures.

In order to combine the information from the box with the information from the neighborhood, we use for our estimates:

$$\hat{p}(O|i) = (1 - \hat{B}_i)X_i + \hat{B}_i\bar{X}$$

and choose $\hat{B}_i$ between 0 and 1. If $\hat{B}_i$ is small, we get an estimate close to the box proportion; if $\hat{B}_i$ is close to 1, we get an estimate close to the neighborhood proportion. We let the data determine what value of $\hat{B}_i$ to use. The Appendix to this chapter gives one method of calculating $\hat{B}_i$.

8.6.3 The Probability That an Alarm Is for a Serious Fire

The problem of estimating the probability that an alarm signals a serious fire as a function of the time of day, season, etc., is similar to the problem of estimating alarm rates by the time of day, season, etc., which was discussed in Section 8.5. However, there is one important difference. It is not appropriate to use a probability as the dependent variable in a linear regression model for several reasons. Most important, a probability must necessarily be between 0 and 1, while the estimates drawn from a linear model can lie outside this range.[8] A better model uses a transformation of the probability, usually the logit function, and estimates the quantity

$$\text{logit}(p) = \log\left(\frac{p}{1-p}\right) = a_0 + a_1 x_1 + a_2 x_2 + \cdots$$

where p is the probability that an alarm signals a serious fire and x_1, x_2, . . . describe the time effects that one wishes to use as explanatory variables. The earlier discussion about the choice of variables remains applicable here. If the independent variables are continuous, then coefficients cannot be calculated using most readily available program packages.[9] This complication can be avoided by using only discrete explanatory variables: for example, Carter and Rolph (1973) used three time-of-day intervals, three seasons[10] of the year, and year-to-year trend. For each year of data there were nine categories: one for each time period and season. Table 8.8 shows the proportion of box-reported alarms that were serious by time of day and season, aggregated over a seven-year period. Thus, it was possible to calculate $p(s|t)$, the proportion of box-reported alarms in time interval t that were serious fires. Then logit

---

[8] Other reasons why it is not appropriate include the fact that the errors do not follow a normal distribution, see Cox (1970).
[9] The method of maximum likelihood allows the coefficients of such a model to be calculated. See Nerlove and Press (1973) for a description and algorithm to do so.
[10] Combining spring and fall into a single season.

TABLE 8.8 Proportion of box-reported alarms that were serious fires[a] by season and time of day (Bronx data for 1964–1970).

Time of Day	Winter		Spring and Fall[b]		Summer		Total	
	Number of Serious Fires	Proportion	Number of Serious Fires	Proportion	Number of Serious Fires	Proportion	Number of Serious Fires	Proportion
0000–0800	398	0.057	401	0.042	350	0.026	1149	0.038
0800–1600	548	0.044	450	0.025	359	0.018	1357	0.027
1600–2400	623	0.025	587	0.015	516	0.011	1726	0.016
Total	1569	0.031	1438	0.021	1225	0.016	4232	0.022

[a] One that used at least four fire companies, or one engine company and two ladder companies.
[b] April, May, October, and November.

($p(s|t)$) was used as a dependent variable in a weighted least-squares regression[11] on variables giving the time of day, season, and year. If $\hat{L}_t$ is the estimate of logit ($p(s|t)$) derived from the regression, then the estimate of $p(s|t)$ is given by:

$$\hat{p}(s|t) = \exp(\hat{L}_t)/(1 + \exp(\hat{L}_t)).$$

8.6.4 Combining the Estimates

The goal of this work was to estimate $p(s|i,t)$, the probability that an alarm from box i in time period t signals a serious fire. In Section 8.6.2 we discussed ways of estimating $p(O|t)$ (the probability that an alarm from box i signals a fire in an occupied structure), and in Section 8.6.3, we discussed how to estimate $p(s|t)$ (the probability that a box-reported alarm in time interval t signals a serious fire). Then, after calculating $\hat{p}(O)$ = proportion of all alarms in the demand region that signal occupied structure fires (an estimate of the probability of an occupied structure fire), and combining our estimates, we obtain

$$\hat{p}(s|i,t) = \hat{p}(O|i)\hat{p}(s|t)/\hat{p}(O), \qquad (8.7)$$

where the "hats" denote estimated values.

8.6.5 Validating the Estimates

A good estimating procedure (and the dispatch policy based on it) should satisfy at least three criteria:

1. The policy should minimize an operationally important loss function, such as the number of underresponses to serious fires.
2. The procedure should be as accurate as possible in estimating underlying parameters of the alarm process.
3. The response dispatched to boxes should not treat the boxes inequitably. That is, there should be a sound reason if one box gets a lower response than another.

In order to validate the modeling techniques, the estimate of probability serious that resulted from use of Equation (8.7) was compared to the

---

[11] Let s_t be the number of serious alarms in time t and n_t be the total number of alarms. Then the variance of the logit of s_t/n_t is

$$V_t = \frac{(n_t + 2)(n_t + 1)}{n_t(s_t + 1)(n_t - s_t + 1)}$$

and the weight for data point t should be proportional to $1/V_t$. See Cox (1970) for a description of weighted least-squares estimation in this situation.

traditional estimate: the number of serious fires at the box divided by the total number of alarms at that box.

From the point of view of making equitable response to different boxes, dispatch rules based on box-history have some drawbacks. Consider a person who lives in the vicinity of a low alarm-rate box, say with no more than 20 alarms in 1967–1969 (63.3% of all boxes). If his residence catches fire and the alarm is reported by street box, deciding whether he gets a small response or a large response based on a box-history rule would be like deciding on the basis of a toss of a coin. The reasoning behind this assertion is as follows. Since between 1967 and 1969 there were only 782 serious fires spread among the approximately 2500 boxes, typically a box had either no serious fires or one serious fire. Thus, under a box-history rule, a box will unambiguously get a full response if and only if it has one of the serious fires, that is, one of the n "tosses comes up heads." Clearly, estimates of $p(s|i)$ based on data of the form 0 out of n_i, or 1 out of n_i, are not very good, especially for small n_i.

Since our two-stage empirical Bayes estimates are based on the much larger amount of information contained in structural fires within a neighborhood, they should provide more reliable estimates and thus avoid inequitable discrimination among boxes.

In order to verify that they were accurately estimating the underlying process, Carter and Rolph used a standard statistical procedure called a "likelihood ratio test" to verify that the estimates produced from the 1967 to 1969 data were consistent with the alarm process that occurred in 1970. Likelihood ratio tests are used to test whether data are consistent with a particular set of assumptions or hypotheses. Here we test whether the 1970 data are consistent with the assumption that they are generated by a probability distribution whose parameters for each box in the Bronx are the values of $\hat{p}(s|i)$ estimated from earlier data. Although a description of this test[12] is beyond the scope of this book, it was found that the 1970 data were consistent with this assumption. A similar test of the box-history estimates showed that it was virtually impossible for the 1970 data to have been generated from true parameters equal to the box-history estimates.

In order to examine the effect that the estimates would have on a dispatch policy, consider the class of initial dispatch policies that use a specified number, P^*, such that if for box i the estimated probability that an alarm signals a serious fire is less than P^*, a reduced response would be sent to the box; otherwise, a larger response would be sent. For example, if for box i, $\hat{p}(s|i)$ is greater than P^*, dispatch two ladders to

---

[12] The likelihood ratio test is described in any standard statistical text. (For example, Kendall and Stuart (1961).) See Carter and Rolph (1973) for the exact formulas to use in this situation.

a box-reported alarm; otherwise, send only one ladder. To compare the empirical Bayes estimator to the traditional box-history estimator (number of serious fires/number of alarms), we evaluate what would have happened in 1970 if the above dispatch policy had been used with each set of estimators.

We can measure the performance of each dispatch policy in two dimensions: (1) the savings in the number of responses to alarms, and (2) the number of serious fires that received a delayed response because more equipment was required than was initially dispatched. The penalty for delayed response has not been successfully quantified in terms of injury, loss of life, or property damage. The value of runs saved and not needed includes both a reduction in the workload of fire companies, and improved fire company availability.

The effects of the dispatch policies will change over time, depending on the arrival rate of alarms and the number of fire companies that are deployed (which depends on budget considerations). Rather than attempt to determine the "optimal" tradeoff between runs saved and serious fires that receive a reduced response, we explore the behavior of the estimates in a series of dispatch policies that span the entire range of possible tradeoffs. Each dispatch policy is defined by fixing the number of alarms that receive a reduced response. We then compare the number of serious fires that receive a reduced response, using each of the estimators.

Each of the two estimators results in an ordering that ranks the alarm boxes in the Bronx according to each box's estimated probability that an alarm signals a serious fire. Table 8.9 reproduces the results of decision policies that result in a reduced response to the minimum number of boxes for cut-off values in increments of 2000 "runs" saved. For example, if our goal is to send one ladder to a total of 4000 alarms and to send two ladders to the rest, the box history estimates result in sending only one ladder to 43 serious fires, versus sending only one ladder to 22 serious fires for the empirical Bayes estimate. For the 4000 alarm goal, the cut-off points P^* for the two policies are 0.0 and 0.0046, respectively. The actual number of alarms receiving a one-ladder response is usually above 4000 because we include as many boxes as needed to achieve 4000, and since boxes usually each have more than one alarm, we tend to overshoot. From Table 8.8 the actual number of one-ladder responses are 4010, and 4019 for the two policies, yielding proportions of one-ladder responses that are serious fires of 0.0107 and 0.0055, respectively. We see that, except for goals that give almost all boxes a reduced response (above 32,000), the empirical Bayes procedure appears to be superior.

It is necessary to decide by statistical means whether the difference between the two policies can be accounted for by random variation in the 1970 data, or whether the empirical Bayes policy would in fact perform better than the box-history policy over the long run.

TABLE 8.9. Performance of estimates of probability serious in hypothetical dispatch policy.

Runs to be Saved (Goal)	Number of Alarms		Number of Serious Fires with Reduced Response		Proportion Serious		Number of Alarm Boxes		"Test Statistic"
	Box History	Empirical Bayes	Box History	Empirical Bayes	Box History	Empirical Bayes	Box History	Empirical Bayes	
2000	2009	2003	28	12	0.0139	0.0060	119	158	3.14[a]
4000	4010	4019	43	22	0.0107	0.0055	250	296	3.03[a]
6000	6007	6008	71	41	0.0118	0.0068	420	492	3.26[a]
8000	8001	8010	105	57	0.0131	0.0071	732	599	4.35[a]
10000	10002	10089	125	84	0.0125	0.0083	1180	703	3.53[a]
12000	12024	12022	152	106	0.0126	0.0088	1521	799	3.70[a]
14000	14027	14050	167	139	0.0119	0.0099	1537	887	2.29[b]
16000	16061	16010	198	172	0.0123	0.0107	1557	985	1.86[b]
18000	18060	18244	232	206	0.0128	0.0113	1582	1100	2.10[b]
20000	20045	20003	254	224	0.0127	0.0112	1606	1224	2.10[b]
22000	22035	22086	279	259	0.0127	0.0117	1634	1304	1.47
24000	24080	24123	317	291	0.0132	0.0121	1671	1374	1.85[b]
26000	26064	26017	362	340	0.0139	0.0131	1836	1451	1.48[b]
28000	28024	28034	407	400	0.0145	0.0143	1865	1566	0.47
30000	30010	30040	462	449	0.0154	0.0149	1906	1652	0.90
32000	32062	32001	502	502	0.0157	0.0157	1940	1765	−0.11
34000	34006	34012	549	546	0.0161	0.0161	1983	1846	0.24
36000	36011	36022	593	597	0.0165	0.0166	2025	1926	−0.28
38000	38006	38238	647	649	0.0170	0.0170	2086	2098	0.49
40000	40097	40002	713	709	0.0178	0.0177	2186	2236	0.09
42000	42000	42005	778	777	0.0185	0.0185	2402	2417	0.40
44000	42140	42140	782	782	0.0186	0.0186	2451	2451	0.0

[a] Significant at 1 percent level (one-sided).
[b] Significant at 5 percent level.

The test statistic reported in the final column of Table 8.9 has an expected value that is proportional to the probability that an alarm that receives a reduced response is for a serious fire under the box history, minus the similar probability for the empirical Bayes model. This test statistic is approximately normally distributed and has standard deviation 1.[13]

We see that the two-stage empirical Bayes procedure results in a smaller proportion of serious fires receiving a reduced response for all goals of runs saved, except the two that send a reduced response to 32,000 or 36,000 alarms. For these two cases, the values of the test statistic are so small in absolute magnitude that they are not statistically significant. No statistical significance means that the observed differences in the number of 1970 serious fires receiving a reduced response are consistent with the two-stage and box-history estimators being equally good. For the policies where the empirical Bayes estimators are better, the differences are significant at the one percent level in six cases, at the five percent level in twelve cases, and not significant in seven cases using a one-tailed test.

We conclude the two-stage empirical Bayes procedure produced estimates that are superior to box-history estimates on all three counts.

APPENDIX A8.1

Empirical Bayes Estimators

Let θ be the true, unknown probability that an alarm from box i signals a fire in an occupied structure. Using the same notation as in Section 8.6, let $k = $ the number of boxes in the neighborhood, $n_i = $ the number of alarms from box i, and $X_i = $ the observed proportion of these alarms that are for fire in an occupied structure. The observations $\{X_i: i = 1, \ldots, k\}$ are independent and normally distributed with unknown mean θ_i and variances D_i. We estimate D_i by $\bar{X}(1 - \bar{X})/n_i$.

Conditional on θ_i, we write

$$X_i | \theta_i \overset{\text{ind}}{\sim} N(\theta_i, D_i).$$

Under the Bayes assumption,[14] the θ_i are independent, normally distributed

$$\theta_i \sim N(\nu, A),$$

where ν and A are unknown. Thus,

$$X_i \sim N(\nu, A + D_i)$$

---

[13] See Carter and Rolph (1973) for the calculation of this statistic.
[14] Alternative Bayes assumptions are discussed in Carter and Rolph (1973).

and
$$\theta_i | X_i \sim N((1 - B_i)X_i + B_i\nu, D_i(1 - B_i)),$$
where $B_i = D_i/(A + D_i)$.

The Bayes estimate for θ_i is $\hat{\theta}_i = (1 - B_i)X_i + B_i\nu$. To get an empirical Bayes estimate, define $\alpha = (\alpha_1, \ldots, \alpha_k)$, $\gamma = (\gamma_1, \ldots, \gamma_k)$, $\Sigma\gamma_i = 1$, and
$$S(\alpha,\gamma) = \sum_{i=1}^{k} \alpha_i(X_i - \bar{X}(\gamma))^2 \qquad \bar{X}(\gamma) = \sum_{i=1}^{k} \gamma_i X_i.$$
Then
$$E(S(\alpha, \gamma)) = \sum_{i=1}^{k} [(A + D_i)\alpha_i - 2(A + D_i)\alpha_i\gamma_i + \sum_{j} (A + D_j)\gamma_j^2]. \quad (A8.1)$$

Using values of $\alpha_i \equiv 1$, $\gamma_i \equiv 1/k$ in Equation (A8.1) yields an unbiased estimator of $(k - 1)(A + \bar{D})$ where $\bar{D} = (1/k)\Sigma D_i$ and thus allows the estimation of A and the use of the empirical Bayes estimates. However, the minimum variance unbiased estimator of $(k - 1)(A + \bar{D})$ is obtained by using α_A, γ_A where $\alpha_{A,i} = (A + \bar{D})/(A + D_i)$ and $\gamma_{A,i} = \alpha_{A,i}/\Sigma_{j=1}^{k} \alpha_{A,j}$, so that
$$S(\alpha_A, \gamma_A) \sim (A + \bar{D})\chi^2_{k-1},$$
where χ^2_{k-1} is the chi-square distribution with $k - 1$ degrees of freedom. Since A is unknown, we estimate A, and thus α and γ, from the data. Define $\hat{A}$ to be the solution to the equation
$$S(\alpha_{\hat{A}}, \gamma_{\hat{A}}) = (k - 1)(\hat{A} + \bar{D}) \quad (A8.2)$$
if the solution is positive, and let $\hat{A} = 0$ otherwise. A method for computing $\hat{A}$ is given in Carter and Rolph (1973). Letting $S \equiv S(\alpha_{\hat{A}}, \gamma_{\hat{A}})$, an estimate of $\bar{B} = \bar{D}/(A + \bar{D})$ is $(k - 3)\bar{D}/S$. Thus from the definition of B_i,
$$\hat{B}_i = \min\left(1, \frac{(k - 3)D_i}{S + (k - 3)(D_i - \bar{D})}\right)$$
and $\quad (A8.3)$
$$\hat{\theta}_i = (1 - \hat{B}_i)X_i + \hat{B}_i\bar{X}(\gamma_{\hat{A}}).$$

The rationale for using $\bar{X}(\gamma_{\hat{A}})$ is that $\bar{X}(\gamma_A)$ is the minimum variance unbiased estimator of ν.

PART III
APPLICATIONS TO FIRE DEPARTMENT PROBLEMS

Chapter 9
Allocating Fire Companies

Synopsis

The present arrangement (configuration) of firehouses in many cities is more the product of historical factors than the result of a plan to meet current needs. In the oldest parts of town, the spacing among firehouses may reflect siting decisions made for volunteer companies in the days of horse-drawn vehicles, while in successively newer parts of town the spacing reflects the gradually changing requirements of the insurance industry.

A systems analysis approach to determining an arrangement of firehouses for a city, and to the assignment of fire companies to those houses, involves obtaining the answers to two questions:

1. How many fire companies does the city need in order to provide a certain level of fire protection?
2. Where should the fire companies be located?

Answering these questions involves making subjective judgments and trade offs among competing objectives. Many factors must be considered at the same time: hazards, alarm rates, costs, and the future growth of the city, to name a few. In most cities question (1) does not get asked directly. Instead, the firehouse location problem hinges on the fire department's budget level. The city has x dollars to spend on the fire department; given this figure, how many companies should it have and where should they be located?

The budget level determines the number of firefighters on the payroll and, for a specified company manning level, the number of firefighters determines the number of fire companies that the city can maintain. The analysis concentrates on determining the best deployment of this fixed number of companies.

Several computer-based models are available to help a fire department perform this analysis. In larger cities the Parametric Allocation Model discussed in this chapter could be used first, to determine how to allocate the given number of fire companies to regions of the city. Then a more detailed descriptive model of the type discussed in Chapter 10 would be used to select specific sites for each of the companies. In smaller cities— those with fewer than ten engine companies—it is usually possible to skip the first step and use the descriptive model immediately.

A "break-even" analysis might be the most obvious framework to use in determining an allocation of fire companies. In theory, a city should add fire companies to a region as long as the "improvement in fire protection" from the addition of one more company is more than the cost of adding that company. A major problem with this approach is that researchers have been unable to accurately estimate the relationship between the number of fire companies in a region and the "benefits" derived from them. For example, it will probably never be possible to place a dollar value on human life. Therefore, a strict cost-benefit approach is difficult to pursue. One must use a service measure that can be calculated, and objectives must be stated in terms of that measure. For fire protection, the most often-used measure is travel time.

Once an allocation objective using travel time as the performance measure is decided on, an allocation that satisfies the objective limits of a budget can readily be calculated. The key question is how to formulate the objective.

One possible objective is to minimize the total travel time to all fires in a city. An allocation meeting this objective would place many companies in regions of high fire incidence. The problem is that when a fire does occur in a low-demand region, it may take a very long time for the fire companies to arrive. Another objective might be to provide an "equitable" distribution of companies by equalizing the average travel time in all regions, but this would tend to increase travel times and workloads in high-incidence areas.

The Parametric Allocation Model was developed to compute fire company allocations for a wide range of objectives and to permit them to be evaluated in terms of average regional travel times, average citywide travel times, and company workload. The model incorporates a simple formula that specifies the number of companies that should be allocated to each region, given the total number of companies to be deployed in the city.

The formula first makes sure that enough companies are allocated to each region to meet the region's average firefighting workload. The remaining companies are then allocated in proportion to a combination of each region's realized and potential demand. Realized demand is related to the actual workload in a region. Potential demand is related to the chance that a fire in a region will escalate rapidly. A run-down residential area might have a large realized demand because of a high structural alarm rate, but a moderate potential demand because the buildings are all brick. An industrial area, on the other hand, might have a low alarm rate but a high potential demand. The formula incorporates a "tradeoff" parameter that allows the user to determine how much emphasis to place on either type of demand.

The model is constructed in such a way that there are values of the tradeoff parameter giving allocations that satisfy three specific objectives. One parameter value will equalize workloads in all regions; another will minimize the average citywide travel time; and a third will equalize average travel times for all regions.

The user is free to choose one of these three parameter values to obtain an allocation that satisfies one of the three explicit objectives; or the user can choose some other value in order to effect a compromise among these objectives. Thus, without specifically embracing a given objective, the manager can generate a variety of allocations and choose the one that he likes best based on his intuition and experience, and on the resulting measures of performance in each region. The model ensures that each allocation is the best one that could be obtained for each compromise.

Experience with this model has indicated that managers find it easy to use and, most importantly, that it produces "reasonable" allocations. It has been applied to fire company allocation problems in several cities throughout the country, and has also been used in Florida to allocate emergency medical service vehicles.

The computer program requires only a small amount of data and can be used without special programming or statistical skills. The effort required to prepare the data for the program has been as low as two or three person-days in some communities, but more typically it ranges from one to four person-weeks. Usually the computer costs for running the model and storing its data files as part of a deployment study are about $100. The highest reported total cost for performing a study using the Parametric Allocation Model has been $5000. This included all personnel time for analysis of the output, writing a report on the findings, etc. Thus, the model is a good choice for a first step in a study of station locations.

9.1 INTRODUCTION

The construction of a new firehouse is a costly project. A site must be found and cleared, designs for the new house prepared, and contracts let for construction—all paid out of limited municipal budgets. Under what circumstances would a municipality undertake this expense?

Firehouses, when they are built, are located in areas where their need is perceived. But many houses are decades old. Some have been built on sites of old volunteer companies that were organized over a century ago. As a city's characteristics change, older areas may become run-down and newer areas built-up. Urban renewal projects may radically change the nature of a region of a city. With these changes, fire incidence and hazards also change. But, because the firehouses are still in the same places, the configuration of fire companies in the city will become obsolete in time. The city is then faced with the question: What should the new configuration of fire companies be?

When a firehouse becomes so old that it must be replaced, the question is the same. It may not be appropriate to rebuild the firehouse on its old site if it is no longer needed there, or if there is a greater need for it elsewhere. The city must determine where the new house should be located. The allocation model described in this chapter and the siting model described in Chapter 10 are designed to help municipal decisionmakers determine an appropriate configuration of fire companies for their city.

9.2 APPROACHES TO DETERMINING THE NUMBER AND LOCATION OF FIRE COMPANIES

9.2.1 Cost-Benefit Approaches

An economist would say that, in theory, there is no difficulty in determining the number of fire companies a city should have. If a cost-benefit approach were used, a city would add fire companies as long as the improvement in fire protection from adding one more company (the marginal benefit) is more than the cost of adding the company (the marginal cost).

The problem with this approach is that, while the severity of the consequences of fires clearly depends on the time it takes fire companies to reach them, researchers have been unable to estimate the relationship accurately enough for it to be of use in determining the number of fire companies a city should have. In addition, the relationship is probably a function of many different variables (types of housing, population at risk, etc.), so that even if the relationship could be determined for one area of the city, it would be unlikely to apply to other areas of the same city, much less to other cities. In addition, in order to compare costs to benefits, a monetary value must be placed on human life. Although one can argue that city decisionmakers do this implicitly when making budgetary decisions, it would be difficult for them to do so explicitly.

Researchers are developing models for relating fire losses to travel time. This work is interesting, but still must be considered speculative. For example, Hogg (1970) has developed relationships for the United

9.2 Determining the Number and Location of Fire Companies

Kingdom as a whole, but it has not yet been established that it is safe to apply results from these aggregate data to individual communities. Further, her model does not easily lend itself to statistical verification.

9.2.2 Response Distance Standards

Another approach to the determination of the number of fire companies a city should maintain and where they should be located is to establish maximum response distance standards. For example, the *Grading Schedule for Municipal Fire Protection* (1974) is used in most United States cities to establish fire insurance rates. As a rule, cities will attempt to meet as many standards in the schedule as possible, so as not to have a lower rating than necessary.

The only criteria provided by the schedule for the number of engines and ladders to be located in each part of the city are guidelines for maximum travel distances for each type of company. For engines, these guidelines are based on estimated fire flow (gallons of water per minute) required for different buildings; on knowledge of the number of gallons per minute each engine company can deliver; and, implicitly, on judgments of the response times needed to ensure timely delivery of the water required. For ladder companies, the guidelines are based on judgments of fire risks as determined by the Insurance Services Office (ISO).

For example, in districts with a high required fire flow (over 9000 gpm), the schedule requires every point to be no further than $\frac{3}{4}$ mile from an engine company, and no further than 1 mile from a ladder company. Moreover, within $1\frac{1}{2}$ miles of any point there must be at least three engine companies, and within 2 miles, at least two ladders. In districts with a lower required fire flow (less than 5000 gpm), the distance requirements are $1\frac{1}{2}$ miles maximum to the closest engine company and 2 miles maximum to the closest ladder company. In addition, there must be two engine companies within $2\frac{1}{2}$ miles.

Let us examine the high fire flow case in more detail. Theoretically, the optimum way to locate fire companies uniformly, if all distances could be spanned by a straight line, would be to place them on a regular grid, so that the region for which each unit is closest is a hexagon (Figure 9.1). The ISO requirements for maximum travel distances could be met by spacing the engine companies 1.3 miles apart, and the ladder companies 1.73 miles apart. The "first-alarm" requirements for three engines and two ladders would simultaneously be satisfied. The average travel distance for engines would be 0.41 miles; for ladders, 0.61 miles. The density of companies per square mile would be 0.68 for engines and 0.38 for ladders.

This example is highly simplified—straight-line distances are only a lower bound, fire companies can almost never be located uniformly, the

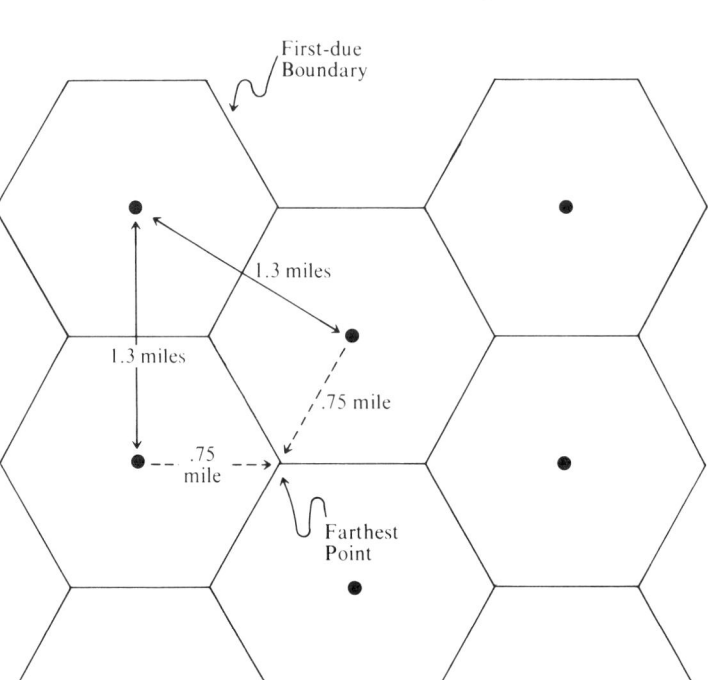

FIGURE 9.1. Uniform engine locations.

boundaries of regions will affect company location, and so on. Nevertheless, the same general results are obtained for more realistic situations. The specification of maximum travel distances results in a predetermination of average travel distances and the number of companies per unit area.

A major argument against using the guidelines to determine the number and location of fire companies is that they were not designed for that purpose. They lack the strong scientific or empirical foundations of standards in other fields. A similar argument may be made against using any other preset standard. Conditions vary greatly from city to city, making an a priori determination of the number of fire companies needed, or of maximum travel distances, impossible. A fixed schedule of standards will almost certainly be too stringent for some cities and too weak for others, because of factors not contemplated when the standards were established.

It is almost equally difficult for local decisionmakers to establish standards for their own cities. Without a firm basis for determining how much better, say, a 0.4-mile travel distance is than a 0.5-mile travel distance, any choice of standards will be largely arbitrary. In addition, it is likely that once the consequences of a standard are realized, in terms of workload, cost, or other factors important at the time, they will need to be modified. Therefore, most recently developed approaches ask fire officials to look directly at the travel distances and times implied by different allocations of companies, rather than relying on whether the allocations meet ISO (or any other preset) standards.

9.2.3 A Two-Stage Approach

We turn now to a two-stage approach to determining the number and location of fire companies in a city. The approach relies heavily on the judgment of officials responsible for fire protection in their city. It gives them the tools they need to quickly develop reasonable configurations of fire companies, and sufficient information to evaluate them.

The approach assumes that the fire department's budget level is already determined. This is a reasonable assumption because fire department budgets are most often dependent on political and fiscal considerations, rather than on objective analysis (see *America Burning*, 1973, p. 151). How many companies should a department have and where should they be located? The budget level determines the number of firefighters on the payroll, and, given a company manning level, the number of firefighters determines the number of fire companies that can be deployed.

The analysis then concentrates on determining the best way to deploy this fixed amount of resources. Mathematical models are used to predict the values of a number of performance measures that would result from various arrangements of fire companies. Then the assumed department budget level is varied, and the analysis is repeated. After looking at the results for several different budget levels, the decisionmakers can compare costs and benefits to choose the best policy for the city, taking into account factors that are not directly considered by the models, such as political constraints.

The analysis of how to deploy the fixed amount of resources is done in two stages: allocation and location. First, the best way is found to allocate the given number of fire companies to regions of the city. (See Chapter 8 for a discussion of demand regions.) Then specific sites are found for each of the companies. There are two reasons for performing the analysis in two stages. First, in any city with more than about ten engine or ladder companies, there are a great many ways to arrange the companies. Considering them all would be very costly. Allocating the companies to regions at the beginning of the study reduces the number of alternative arrangements to be evaluated. Second, the allocation stage permits a quick and inexpensive estimate of the improvement in fire protection that can be expected if the locations of the city's fire companies are changed.

The Parametric Allocation Model, used in the first stage, provides a general picture of the number of fire companies to be assigned to different regions of the city. This will help determine whether or not the current distribution of fire companies is satisfactory. If sizable imbalances are found, the model can be used to determine how to reallocate the existing units among the regions so that the balance of fire protection is improved. If changes in the number of fire companies to maintain are being considered, the model can also be used to determine the regions that should gain or lose them.

The allocation model cannot, however, be used to determine specific locations for firehouses. Once a fire department has chosen the number of companies to be assigned to each region of the city, alternative configurations of station sites within each region can be evaluated in detail in the second stage, by using a siting model. It is not difficult to develop several alternative configurations of station sites that might lead to the desired levels of performance. These can then be compared by using one of the descriptive siting models. The models show what would happen to travel times and company workloads if a given arrangement of fire companies were to be used. Although these models do not suggest arrangements to be tried, experience indicates that examination of their output makes it easy to eliminate poor arrangements and to focus on good ones. Siting models are discussed in detail in Chapter 10.

9.3 THE PARAMETRIC ALLOCATION MODEL[1]

If fire incidence and fire hazards were the same throughout a city, the allocation problem would be simple. Fire companies could be uniformly distributed throughout the city so that each region would have the same average travel time. There would be no reason to favor one region over another. In reality, however, regions have different fire incidence and hazards. Fire departments are therefore faced with the conflicting objectives discussed in Chapter 3.

9.3.1 An Approach to Conflicting Objectives

Let us reconsider the example of allocating ten fire companies between two regions, discussed in Chapter 3. Assume that in Figure 9.2, the two regions each have an area of 3 square miles, but Region 1 (the one on the

---

[1] Three versions of the Parametric Allocation Model have been developed: BASIC and FORTRAN versions for use in a time-sharing environment, and a PL/I version for use in a batch environment. The BASIC version is documented in Rider (1975), which provides details on the data requirements, output reports, and other considerations not discussed here. Copies of the programs and their documentation are available from the Rand Corporation.

9.3 The Parametric Allocation Model

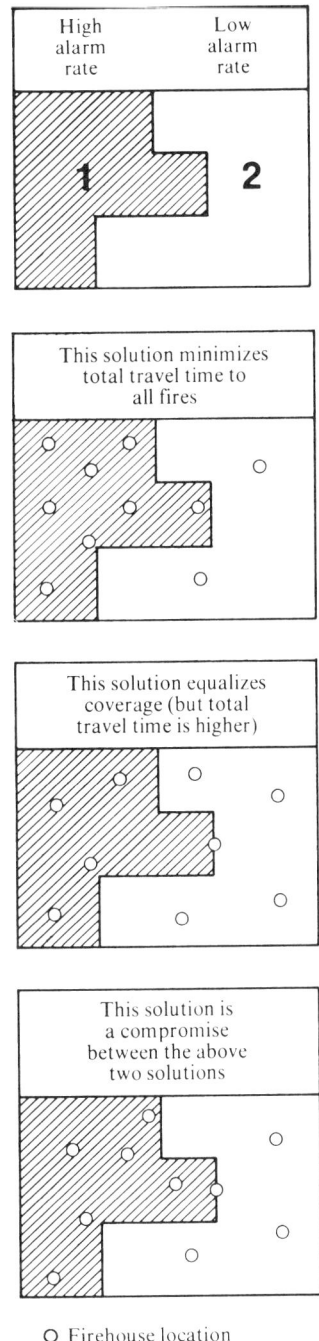

FIGURE 9.2. Three allocation strategies for fire companies.

left) has an average alarm rate of 3.7 alarms per hour while Region 2 has an alarm rate of 0.7 alarms per hour. If an average alarm keeps one company busy for 20 minutes, Region 1 will have an average of 1.23 companies busy and Region 2 will have an average of 0.23 companies busy.

Chapter 6 discussed some simple ways of relating the number of available companies in a region to the expected travel distance and of relating expected travel distance to expected travel time. For illustrative purposes we pick the following form of these relationships:

$$E(D) = 0.6 \sqrt{\frac{A}{n - E(B)}}$$
$$E(T) = 3 \sqrt{E(D)},$$

where

$E(D)$ = expected travel distance in the region (in miles)

A = area of the region

n = number of units in the region

$E(B)$ = average number of companies busy in the region

$E(T)$ = expected travel time in the region (in minutes).

It is easy to calculate an allocation that equalizes the average travel times in Regions 1 and 2. We can see from the square-root law that this condition will be satisfied if the average number of available companies in both regions is equal (since the areas are equal). Simple algebra shows that $5\frac{1}{2}$ companies should be allocated to Region 1 and $4\frac{1}{2}$ companies to Region 2. (Figure 9.2 shows how a company can be split between two regions by placing it on a region boundary.) With this allocation, the average number of available companies in each region is 4.27. We can calculate the average travel distances and times in both regions by using the two equations given in this section:

$$E(D) = 0.6 \sqrt{\frac{3}{4.27}} = 0.50 \text{ mile},$$
$$E(T) = 3 \sqrt{0.50} = 2.12 \text{ minutes}.$$

The determination of a minimum average travel time allocation is more complicated. In the following sections we present a formula for doing this. It turns out that the allocation of eight companies to Region 1 and two companies to Region 2 will minimize the average travel time over both regions. For Region 1 we can calculate the average travel distance

9.3 The Parametric Allocation Model

and average travel time with this allocation as follows:

$$E(D) = 0.6 \sqrt{\frac{3}{8 - 1.23}} = 0.40 \text{ mile}$$

$$E(T) = 3 \sqrt{0.40} = 1.90 \text{ minutes}.$$

A similar calculation shows that the average travel distance in Region 2 is 0.78 mile and the average travel time is 2.65 minutes. The average travel time over both regions, weighted by alarm rates, is

$$\frac{1.90 \times 3.7 + 2.65 \times 0.7}{4.4} = 2.02 \text{ minutes}.$$

Note that if nine companies had been allocated to Region 1 and one to Region 2, the average travel time over both regions would have been 2.06 minutes. If the allocation had been seven and three, the average travel time would have been 2.03 minutes.

We have been able to reduce the average travel time over both regions by 0.1 minute, but the average travel time in Region 2 has been increased by over 0.5 minute. This suggests that we ask if there is some allocation that combines the benefits of a low average travel time with more similar average travel times in both regions. If we allocated 6.5 companies to Region 1 and 3.5 companies to Region 2, we would find that the average regional travel times were 2.02 minutes and 2.27 minutes. This "compromise" allocation (producing an average travel time of 2.06 minutes over both regions) succeeds in combining many of the benefits of both equal and minimum travel time allocations. The principle of compromise is basic to the Parametric Allocation Model. (The allocations just discussed are illustrated in Figure 9.2.)

Even if it were known precisely how the location of fire companies affected fire fatalities and property loss, the need for a compromise allocation would still exist. For example, is the total yearly fire loss in the city to be minimized, or is the risk of loss to be spread evenly over the city? If regions have differing risks to life and to property, should the risk of fatality be weighed equally with the risk of monetary loss, or should it be given sole consideration?

The two conflicting objectives—minimizing a loss function and equalizing the loss across regions—must somehow be balanced, but in a way that is not easy to specify in advance. The loss function may simply be the average travel time to alarms, as illustrated in the last example; or, it may be a more complex function that takes into account the variations in types of alarms and relative hazards among the regions (Section 9.4.2).

The philosophy behind the Parametric Allocation Model is that any preference for one allocation criterion (compromise) over another is in effect a managerial decision based on an analysis of all the consequences of employing that criterion. Typically, all but a small subset of allocation criteria will result in allocations unacceptable to fire department management for reasons that cannot be captured by a mathematical model. Managerial acceptability imposes "hidden" constraints that may severely constrict the reasonable and possible set of allocations, and may make the detailed justification of a "best" or "most equitable" compromise superfluous. Therefore, we identify a "tradeoff parameter" (hence the name *Parametric* Allocation Model) that indicates the emphasis to be placed on satisfying each objective. The Parametric Allocation Model allows a range of values to be tried for the parameter, and finds an appropriate allocation of companies for each. For each allocation, the average travel time and company workload (percentage of time that an average company is busy) in each region of the city are displayed, along with the citywide average travel time. Fire department personnel can then compare these workloads and travel times. Based on the results, the department can decide which allocation of fire companies to regions of the city would be most desirable.

This approach is different from one requiring prior specification of performance levels to be achieved in each region. Such an approach would determine the total number of companies required to achieve the given performance levels. The allocation model, on the other hand, tells the user what performance levels can be achieved with any given amount of resources. This is often a more useful approach because the number of fire companies that a city can maintain is usually predetermined by budgetary and other considerations.

9.3.2 How the Parametric Allocation Model Works

The Parametric Allocation Model is designed to take both firefighting and protective coverage into account when it produces allocations. The general procedure for using the model is shown in Figure 9.3. First, the computer program that implements the model reads a previously created file containing data on various types of fire alarms in each region of the city. The user then provides two input quantities: the total number of companies to be allocated and the value of the tradeoff parameter. The program begins its calculations by assigning the minimum number of companies required to respond to and work at the average number of incidents that occur in each region. Generally, this average number is based on experience during the busiest time of the day (e.g., 4 P.M. to midnight). If a city had only this number of companies assigned, there would be no companies available to respond to a greater than average number of incidents, the workload of the assigned companies would be unreasonably large, and travel times to fires would be too long. There-

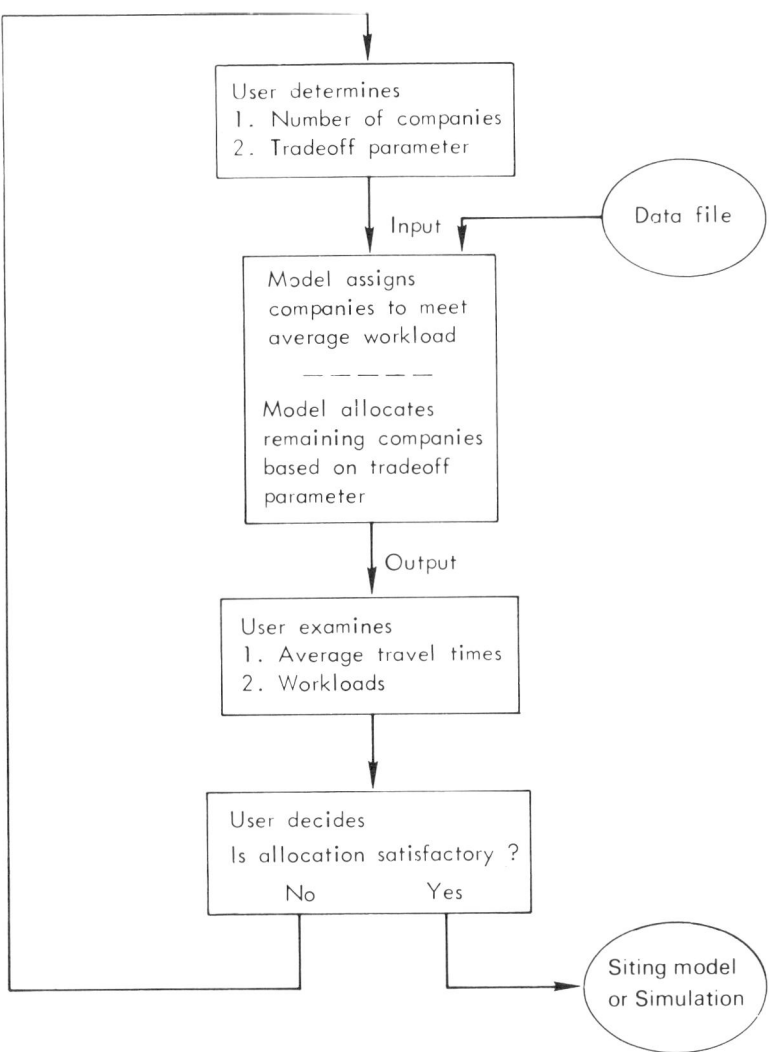

FIGURE 9.3. Steps in the use of the Parametric Allocation Model.

fore, additional companies are needed in each region to provide coverage by being available to respond quickly to alarms and share the burden of fighting fires.

Coverage is provided in the next step of the allocation procedure. Because the number of companies maintained by a city is usually much greater than the average number of companies needed to fight fires, a large number of companies will remain to be assigned in this step. These companies are allocated according to the specified value of the tradeoff parameter that balances the two types of demand for fire protection discussed in Chapter 8: potential demand and realized demand.

The user of the allocation model chooses the relative amount of emphasis to be placed on each type of demand by specifying an input parameter to the computer program. If this parameter is set equal to 1, more emphasis is placed on realized demand than on potential demand, and the busier regions of the city will be allocated a larger proportion of the remaining fire companies than the less busy regions. On the other hand, if the parameter is set equal to 0, the remaining companies are allocated in proportion to the potential demand of each region. Parameter values between 0 and 1 can be used to produce allocations that trade off realized and potential demand in various proportions. In addition, if a large value of the parameter (e.g., 50) is used, only realized demand is used in the allocation process, and the allocation of the remaining companies is in proportion to the workload of each region.

Figure 9.4 shows how the number of fire engines allocated to two regions of similar size, but with different alarm patterns and types of hazards, will change as the parameter is varied. These allocations resulted when engines were assigned to all of New York City. "Downtown" is densely packed with hazardous high-rise buildings, but it has few fires. Therefore, its potential demand is large and its realized demand is relatively low. The "Lower East Side," on the other hand, has a lower potential demand because it is a residential region, but its realized demand is larger because it is an area that experiences many fires. As the tradeoff parameter is varied from 0 to 1, more emphasis is placed on realized demand and less on potential demand. Therefore, the number of engines allocated to the Lower East Side increases while the allocation to Downtown decreases.

Figure 9.5 shows how the average travel times for the first-arriving engine citywide and in four demand regions change with the tradeoff parameter for a given total number of engine companies to be allocated. The "equal coverage" (or "equal loss") allocation (parameter $p = 0$) yields a lower travel time for Downtown than for the Lower East Side because Downtown's potential demand is higher. The average travel times for the Lower East Side and for Staten Island, a residential region that has a low realized demand, are the same because their potential

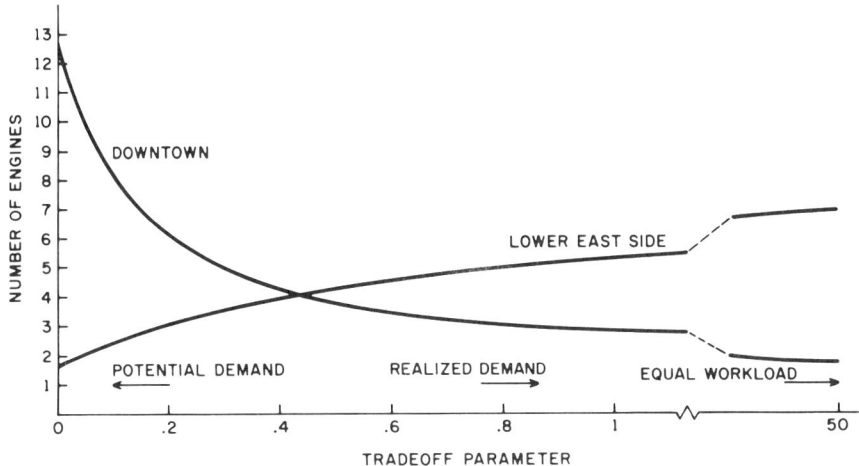

FIGURE 9.4. The effect of the tradeoff parameter on the allocation of companies.

FIGURE 9.5. The effect of the tradeoff parameter on travel times.

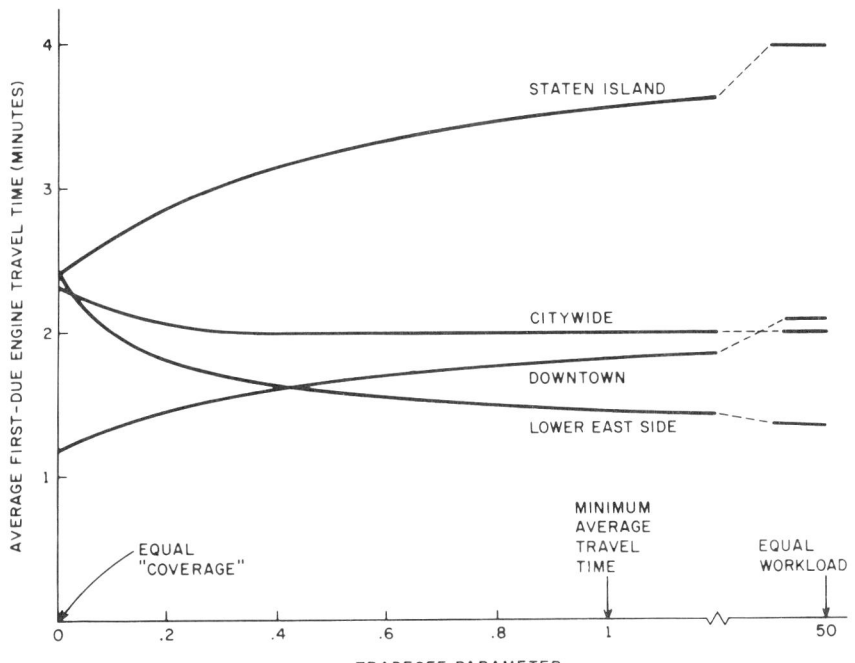

demands are the same. As the tradeoff parameter is increased to 1, the travel time for Staten Island increases while that for the Lower East Side decreases. This happens because the realized demand of Staten Island is low compared to that of the Lower East Side. At the same time, the average citywide travel time reaches a minimum when the parameter equals 1, but shows very little change past a parameter value of 0.25.

To use the program most effectively, the department's planners should identify and summarize the output of several runs so that the relative rankings of the various allocations (resulting from different values of the tradeoff parameter) can be compared. In some cases, an allocation may prove to be obviously unacceptable. For example, a low-density region might be found to have an average travel time that is disproportionately long. A new value of the parameter may then be chosen and a new allocation produced. The new output from the model should then be examined to determine whether an adequate improvement has been made. Ultimately, an administrator who understands the entire operational and political context of the department must decide which of the allocations appears best, all things considered, or whether still more allocations should be analyzed.

While any value of the tradeoff parameter can be chosen for making allocations, it is likely that only a small range of values will prove reasonable to use. It has been found in several cities that values of the parameter close to 0.25 yield allocations that are either similar to existing allocations, or ones that are acceptable to fire department management. For example, in New York, a value of 0.3 for the parameter yielded both engine and ladder allocations that corresponded fairly closely to the existing allocation. With this value the average travel time over all regions was almost a minimum, while the maximum average travel time over all regions was substantially lower than for a parameter value of 1. Also, the maximum workload was much lower for this allocation than it was for a parameter value of 0. This indicates that current New York policy is a good compromise with respect to workloads and travel times. This lends confidence to the belief that the model accurately captures most of the factors significant in allocating fire companies.

In the remainder of this chapter, we discuss the Parametric Allocation Model in the context of determining a city's long-range needs for firefighting resources. The discussion assumes that fire companies will be assigned to the same firehouses 24 hours per day. Using fixed fire company locations, however sanctioned by tradition, is not necessarily the most effective way to deploy firefighting resources. Cities with a central business district and surrounding residential areas typically experience demands that shift geographically during the day. The business district may have a large daytime population in need of fire protection, while the residential areas will experience the greatest risks to life during the night.

The Parametric Allocation Model can be used to determine how fire companies can be redeployed throughout the day to match fire protection to geographic need. This may be done by running the model with several sets of data, each reflecting the city's fire experience during a different time of day. The model will then indicate, for each time of day, the most desirable allocation of fire companies.

9.3.3 Data and Resources Needed for the Parametric Allocation Model

To use the Parametric Allocation Model, the city to be studied must be divided into demand regions as discussed in Chapter 8. The area of each demand region must be measured and the alarm rate in each region must be estimated by the user (in most instances from past data) for different types of alarms (structural fires, false alarms, etc.). Data on the existing number of fire engines and ladders in each region must also be supplied to the program. In addition, estimates of potential demand must be supplied. These estimates, called hazard factors, are discussed in the next section and in the Appendix to this chapter.

To run the allocation model on an IBM 360/370 computer requires 16K bytes of core storage. A single run using the model usually costs less than one dollar, although the cost of a run will vary from installation to installation, depending upon the price structure.

The time and effort required to create input data needed by the allocation model for use in a particular city will depend on: (a) whether or not computerized files of incident reports have been maintained, and (b) whether or not the city has already been divided into regions of similar firefighting demands. In Dade County, Florida, and Tacoma, Washington, where these conditions were met, it took two to three person-days to prepare the data file. More typically, one to four person-weeks are required to collect and process the data. (This was the case in Allentown, Pennsylvania, Wilmington, Delaware, and New York City.)

The computer costs for running the model and storing its data files during the course of a study are usually about $100. The highest reported total cost for using the model has been $5000. This included all personnel time for data collection, analysis of output, and writing a report on the findings.

9.3.4 History of Use

The Parametric Allocation Model was used in five cities with direct assistance from members of the staff of The New York City-Rand Institute: Jersey City (Rider et al., 1975 and Section 9.5 of this book), New York City (Rider, 1975); Tacoma (Section 14.2 of this book); Wilmington (Walker et al., 1975); and Yonkers (Hausner, Walker, and Swersey, 1974). After the model was documented, nine individuals or government agencies acquired copies of the program. One of the recipients modified the model slightly and used it for an evaluation of emergency medical services in Dade County, Florida (Meredith and Shershin, 1975). The study led to changes in the locations of some vehicles. The Maryland-National Capitol Park and Planning Commission operated the model interactively in a study of the Prince George's County Fire Department. In Allentown, Pennsylvania, the program was translated into FORTRAN by a professor at Lehigh University. The model was then used to determine whether it would be worthwhile to reallocate fire companies among the various regions of the city, and what the effect would be of adding or subtracting one engine company from the eleven in service in the city (Groover and Fagan, 1977).

A complete listing of all the users of the allocation model as of May 1977 is given by Chaiken (1977).

9.4 FORMAL DESCRIPTION OF THE PARAMETRIC ALLOCATION MODEL

9.4.1 Mathematical Formulation

The Parametric Allocation Model uses an objective function that encompasses, by the change of the value of a single parameter, a minimum average travel time criterion, an equal average travel time criterion, and intermediate criteria. The function contains average regional travel times raised to a power and weighted by factors reflecting the relative hazards and alarm rates in the region. The general form of the allocation model is:

minimize
$$\sum_i w_i \{\tau_i(n_i)\}^{1/p}$$

subject to
$$\sum_i n_i = m,$$

where

m = total number of companies to be allocated

n_i = number of companies to be assigned to region i

$\tau_i(n_i)$ = expected travel time in region i if n_i companies are assigned to it

w_i = weight for region i

p = tradeoff parameter ($p \geq 0$),

and the summation is taken over all regions.

To motivate this formulation, we observe that when $p = 1$, the weighted average travel times over the city are minimized. As $p \to 0$, the longer travel times dominate the objective function and the minimization serves to equalize the average travel times across the regions. When p is between 0 and 1, intermediate allocations are generated. The parameter p therefore represents the degree of tradeoff between the criterion of equal average travel time and that of minimum citywide average travel time. A further justification of this formulation, as discussed in Section 9.3, is that this model is capable of providing a good description of actual fire department strategies.

Besides the close correspondence to actual fire department allocations that the model yields, there are several other reasons for choosing this particular form of objective function. One of the most important is that the resulting allocations do not depend on the way in which the city is divided into regions. If two similar regions are combined, the allocation to the new region will be the sum of the allocations to the two former regions. (This is demonstrated in the next section.) Also, the problem in this form is analytically tractable. This is very helpful in aiding the examination of the properties of the solution and interpreting the allocations. Finally, the objective function is convex for $p > 0$, so the minimization of this function presents no special problems.

The model uses the relationship between average travel times in region, and alarm rate, area, companies allocated, and street configuration, that was developed in Chapter 6. The following form of the relation is used.

$$E(T) = \alpha \left[\frac{A}{n - E(B)} \right]^{\beta}, \tag{9.1}$$

where $E(T)$ is the expected regional travel time, A is the area of the region, n is the number of companies allocated to the region, $E(B)$ is the average number of companies busy in the region, and α and β are empirical constants that depend on the street configuration, the company placement in the region, and the travel characteristics of the companies.

9.4.2 Regional Weights

Before proceeding to a solution of the minimization problem, we discuss the weight that should be applied to each region's average travel time. These weights reflect the realized and the potential demands of the regions. They have the general form

$$w_i = \bar{\lambda}_i H_i^{1/p},$$

where

w_i = weight for region i

$\bar{\lambda}_i$ = alarm factor in region i

H_i = hazard factor for region i

The alarm factor is a measure of realized demand, while the hazard factor is a measure of potential demand.

Alarm Factor. In measuring demand in a region, it would not be reasonable to treat false alarms, for example, as if they were as important as structural alarms (that is, alarms signaling structural fires). Two regions with identical alarm rates—one with a high false-alarm incidence, the other with a high structural-alarm incidence—would certainly pose different problems for a fire department. The amount of work to be done in the region with the high structural-alarm incidence, as well as the risk to life and property, would be much greater than in the other region. We would like the alarm factor to reflect this difference. A scheme that has proved useful in practice is to weight the rate of each type of alarm in a region by the average total work time for that type. That is, let

$$\bar{\lambda}_i = \sum_j \lambda_{ij} s_j,$$

where

$\bar{\lambda}_i$ = alarm factor (hourly work content) in region i

λ_{ij} = rate at which type j alarms occur in region i

s_j = total engine or ladder work time at a type j incident.

The alarm factor $\bar{\lambda}_i$ recognizes work time as a measure of the demands on the fire department. While many other reasonable weighting schemes might be established, the end results should be about the same for all. Regions with a high incidence of structural alarms should have higher alarm factors than regions with a lower structural alarm incidence.

Hazard Factor. The term "hazard" has been used traditionally to signify three different things:
1. Anything that can cause injury, damage or loss by burning.
2. The chance of a fire at a particular place.
3. The extent to which injury, damage, or loss will occur if there is a fire that is not promptly extinguished at a particular place.

The alarm factor reflects the second meaning of hazard, which translates into realized demand when aggregated on a regional basis. The hazard factor reflects the third meaning, which translates into potential demand when aggregated on a regional basis. The following two examples illustrate the distinction between the two meanings and their operational significance to a fire department.

Consider two regions containing single-family detached houses occupied by middle-class families. In Region A, the number of houses per square mile is twice that of Region B.

9.4 Formal Description of the Parametric Allocation Model

Clearly, Region A will have an alarm rate about twice as great as that of Region B, and the fire department will be kept twice as busy in that region. However, fires will require similar suppression activities in both regions. If the fire department chooses to provide equal service in both regions, it would make sure that the same number of fire companies per square mile were *available* (not working at fires) in each region so that the time from the receipt of an alarm to the arrival of fire companies would, on the average, be the same in the two regions. It might want to do this because the chance that a fire would escalate rapidly once it occurred is the same in each region. On the other hand, if the fire department wishes to make the most efficient use of its resources, it would have more companies *available* per square mile in the more densely built region. With this allocation, more fires would, on the average, experience a shorter response time. Such an allocation would emphasize the different alarm rates, instead of the same potential demands, in the two regions.

Now consider two regions of the same building density. Region C contains fireproof apartment buildings and Region C contains old tenement buildings. Both regions have the same alarm rates. For simplicity, let us assume that on the average, tenement fires escalate twice as fast as fireproof apartment fires. In the first example (Regions A and B), equal coverage could be provided by assigning the same number of available fire companies per square mile to each region, since the potential demands were the same. Since tenement fires, however, are assumed to escalate twice as fast as apartment fires in this example, fire companies would have to arrive at the scene twice as fast to provide service in Region D equal to that in Region C. In this case, equal coverage in both regions is not the same as equal travel time or an equal number of available companies per square mile. Regions with a higher potential demand require smaller average travel times if they are to receive the same coverage as regions with a low potential demand. Figure 9.6 illustrates the points made above.

The rate at which an average fire escalates is called the *hazard factor* and is a measure of a region's potential demand. The hazard factor times the average travel time in a region yields the average escalation of fires, or what we call the "risk" in the region:

$$R_i = H_i E(T_i),$$

where

R_i = average risk in region i

H_i = hazard factor in region i

$E(T_i)$ = expected travel time in region i.

Therefore, if Region D has a hazard factor twice as large as that of

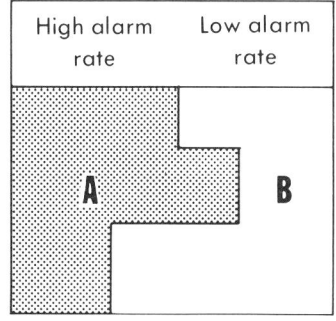
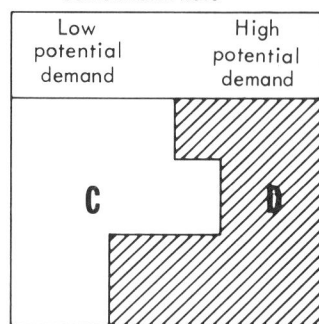
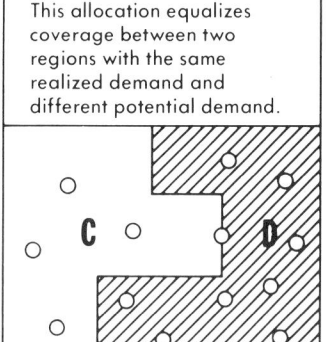

○ Firehouse location

FIGURE 9.6. Allocating companies for equal coverage.

Region C, the same average travel times in both regions would imply that the average risk at a given fire in Region D is twice that at a given fire in Region C. Conversely, if fires in both regions were to have the same risk, the average travel time in Region D would have to be half that of Region C.

There are many ways that the risk of a fire, defined in this way, can be measured. In this chapter, we take the risk at a fire to be the probability that it will require two or more hose streams for extinguishment. This probability is usually very small, and the linear relation between risk and travel time has been found to be a reasonable approximation (Ignall et al., 1975).

The concept of risk is general and may include the probability of loss

9.4 Formal Description of the Parametric Allocation Model

of life. We will not discuss the relative weights that a fire department should put on property and life. However, we emphasize that the choice is a significant one. We could just as well have taken the risk to be the probability that a fire will be fatal. In this case, escalation would mean the increasing danger to life rather than the increasing amount of property loss.

Risk to property and risk to life usually increase or decrease together. It is likely, however, that different allocations would be used if a fire department considered one risk to the exclusion of the other.

The hazard factor is independent of the alarm factor. It may be the case that some regions with an above average alarm factor will also have a greater than average hazard factor, but this is not necessarily so. For example, a central business district in a city might have a relatively large hazard factor with a low alarm factor. It will be important to keep in mind, therefore, that the hazard factor measures the *rate* of escalation of an average fire in a region. It does not measure the chance that a fire will occur. The Appendix to this chapter discusses the calculation of hazard factors.

Although residential regions vary substantially in character, most residential fires are confined to an apartment or living area and have many characteristics in common. While the average loss or the average work time per alarm may vary from region to region, these average differences will be reflected in the alarm factor. The hazard factor measures only the rate of increase of loss. Because there is little reason to believe that this rate differs substantially from region to region for the bulk of fires in residences, it is a reasonable procedure to set the hazard factors for all residential regions approximately equal. Hazard factors for commercial regions may be different from one another depending on the types of structures in the region. The Appendix shows that the values for hazard factors should generally fall between 0.8 and 1.2.

9.4.3 Solution

In this section, the minimization problem is solved analytically to find the optimal allocation of companies to each region of the city as a function of p, the tradeoff parameter. A simple interpretation of the solution is given and some of the properties of the solution are discussed.

Using Equation (9.1) and the formula for the regional weight, the problem can be written in the following form:

minimize

$$Z = \sum_i \bar{\lambda}_i \left[H_i \alpha \left\{ \frac{A_i}{n_i - E(B_i)} \right\}^\beta \right]^{1/p}$$

subject to

$$\sum_i n_i = m,$$

where

$\bar{\lambda}_i$ = alarm factor in region i
H_i = hazard factor in region i
A_i = area of region i
n_i = number of companies to be allocated in region i
$E(B_i)$ = average number of companies busy in region i
m = total number of companies to be allocated ($> \Sigma_i E(B_i)$)
α, β = travel coefficients
p = tradeoff parameter.

By using Lagrange multipliers, this can be converted from a constrained minimization problem into the following unconstrained problem:

$$\min \hat{Z} = \sum_i \bar{\lambda}_i \left[H_i \alpha \left\{ \frac{A_i}{n_i - E(B_i)} \right\}^\beta \right]^{1/p} + \xi \left(\sum_i n_i - m \right),$$

where ξ is an undetermined multiplier. This unconstrained problem is solved by finding the values of n_k that satisfy the condition:

$$\frac{\partial \hat{Z}}{\partial n_k} = 0.$$

The solution is:

$$n_k^* = \bar{\lambda}_k^\nu H_k^{\nu/p} \alpha^{\nu/p} \left(\frac{p\xi}{\beta} \right)^{-\nu} A_k^{1-\nu} + E(B_k),$$

where

$$\nu = \frac{p}{\beta + p}.$$

The constraint in the original problem, $m = \Sigma n_i$, can be used to solve for the term $(p\xi/\beta)^{-\nu}$ in order to eliminate ξ from the solution. Summing over the n_k^* and rearranging terms yields

$$\left(\frac{p\xi}{\beta} \right)^{-\nu} = \left(\sum_i \bar{\lambda}_i^\nu H_i^{\nu/p} \alpha^{\nu/p} A_i^{1-\nu} \right)^{-1} \left(m - \sum_i E(B_i) \right).$$

9.4 Formal Description of the Parametric Allocation Model

This term is a normalizing factor that ensures that the sum of the allocations adds up to m total companies. The solution can be simplified by canceling $\alpha^{\nu/p}$, which appears in the numerator of the solution and in the denominator of the normalizing factor.

Defining the resulting normalizing factor by

$$F(\nu) = \left(\sum_i \bar{\lambda}_i^{\nu} H_i^{\nu/p} A_i^{1-\nu} \right)^{-1} \left(m - \sum_i E(B_i) \right)$$

yields the final form of the solution

$$n_k^* = \bar{\lambda}_k^{\nu} H_k^{\nu/p} A_k^{1-\nu} F(\nu) + E(B_k).$$

Notice that the solution is the sum of two terms. The second term ensures that each region is allocated at least the average number of companies busy at any one time in the region. The first term represents an allocation of the companies that remain after all the busy companies are allocated.

In general, the solutions will not be integral. This is not a formidable difficulty because the region boundaries used by the model are artificial. When companies are dispatched to alarms, other boundaries, defined by the alarm assignment cards (running cards), are used. An allocation of half a company to one region and half to another would therefore mean that the company is to be situated near the region boundary, and so would have its responses divided roughly between the two regions.

Because of the way the alarm factor has been defined, the case $p \to \infty$ has a meaningful interpretation. For this case $\nu = 1$ and the solution is:

$$n_k^* = \bar{\lambda}_k F(1) + E(B_k),$$

independent of the hazard factor. The particular form for the alarm factor chosen,

$$\bar{\lambda}_i = \sum_j \lambda_{ij} s_j,$$

is the expected number of companies busy in a region $E(B_i)$. Substituting $E(B_k)$ for $\bar{\lambda}_k$, the solution becomes

$$n_k^* = E(B_k)\{1 + F(1)\},$$

and the allocations are proportional to the number of companies busy in a region. This equalizes the average workload over all regions in a city. Therefore, the allocation model, with $p \to \infty$, encompasses a third basic fire company allocation solution.

9.4.4 Interpretation of the Solution

A simple interpretation can be given to the above solution if some new variables are defined.

$$\mu_k = \frac{n_k - E(B_k)}{A_k} = \text{availability density (number of available companies per unit area).}$$

$$\eta_k = H_k^{1/\beta} = \text{redefined hazard factor.}$$

$$\rho_k = \bar{\lambda}_k / A_k = \text{busy density (number of busy companies per unit area).}$$

Using these variables, the solution can be written as

$$\mu_k^* = \rho_k^\nu \, \eta_k^{1-\nu} \, F(\nu). \tag{9.2}$$

The solution can now be seen more clearly as a result of a tradeoff between the realized demands represented by the ρ_k and the potential demands represented by the η_k. From the preceding work, the ρ_k will be composed of such factors as the total company time it takes to put out a fire, the number of fires per hour in the region, and the average loss per fire. The η_k will be composed of travel rates, the rate of possible fire spread, etc. And the parameter ν expresses the tradeoff of consideration between the two types of demand. In practice, fire department management will determine the degree of tradeoff by examining the resulting allocations. It is rare that a prior determination of ν can be made.

It should also be emphasized that the rewritten solution contains only intensive variables, that is, variables that do not depend on area. One consequence of this is that, for two regions of identical busy density and hazard factor, the allocation of available companies is in proportion to area *regardless of the value of* ν. This means that to allocate companies between regions with identical ρ and η, no choice of the tradeoff parameter need be made. An allocation of available companies in proportion to the areas of the regions will satisfy the requirements of equal coverage, equal workload, and minimum average travel time simultaneously. This result is not trivial since the two regions might differ greatly in total alarm rate per unit area. For example, one region might have a high alarm rate per unit area with a large proportion of false alarms, while the other, of similar hazard, has fewer but more serious alarms per unit area. Furthermore, if these two regions are combined and their areas added together, the resulting allocation to the new region will merely be the sum of the allocations to the old regions. In general, a homogeneous region can be split into several parts without changing the total allocation or the allocation to any sector of the region.

If two areas of unequal busy density are combined, the resulting allocation will be greater than if the allocation were made to these areas separately. Consider two regions with busy densitities ρ_1 and ρ_2 and equal hazard factors. The busy density of the combined region will be given by

$$\rho = a\rho_1 + (1 - a)\rho_2$$

where

$$a = \frac{A_1}{A_1 + A_2}$$

If the normalizing factor $F(\nu)$ is held fixed, when ν is less than 1 the second derivative of μ with respect to ρ in Equation (9.2) is negative. This implies that the optimal availability density with $F(\nu)$ fixed is a concave function of busy density for $0 < \nu < 1$. Thus,

$$a\mu(\rho_1) + (1 - a)\mu(\rho_2) \le \mu(\rho)$$

when $0 < \nu < 1$. If $F(\nu)$ is allowed to vary, the extra allocation to the combined region will cause a compensating change in $F(\nu)$. This change, however, can never be great enough to change the direction of the inequality.

9.5 USING THE ALLOCATION MODEL TO REALLOCATE FIRE COMPANIES IN JERSEY CITY, NEW JERSEY

We will use a specific example, the reallocation of fire companies in Jersey City, New Jersey, to illustrate how the Parametric Allocation Model can be used to produce new allocations of fire companies in a city.[2] A similar example for New York City is discussed in Rider (1976).

Jersey City had been changing rapidly. Large areas of the city were being redeveloped and new construction was increasing the city's built-up area. These changes made the existing locations of some fire companies inappropriate. In addition, many of the city's firehouses were old and in need of replacement. These factors led the city to recognize the need for a careful analysis of the deployment policies of the fire department. In particular, the objective of the portion of the study described here was to develop a plan for reallocating fire companies in the city over the ten-year period from 1973 to 1983.

---

[2] A complete description of the Jersey City study is presented in Rider and Hausner (1975).

9.5.1 Situation at the Start of the Study

In order to facilitate the analysis of the deployment of fire companies in Jersey City, the city was divided into six demand regions by aggregating first-due areas of engine companies. The basis of the division was the homogeneity of fire hazard and potential firefighting problems within each region. Population density, land use, housing stock, and alarm rates were all taken into consideration in determining these boundaries. Figure 9.7 is a map of Jersey City, showing the boundaries of the six demand regions and the locations of all firefighting equipment deployed in the city at the start of the study. A land use map appears in Figure 9.8.

Table 9.1 summarizes some of the demographic characteristics of five of the regions. The areas of the demand regions were measured on a map, using a polar planimeter. Parks, railroad yards, and vacant land were excluded from the measurements. Population and housing data were obtained from the 1970 census. Region 6, a "new" area of the city, will be discussed later.

Region 4 is the most densely populated part of Jersey City. It has a large proportion of buildings of wood frame construction and a central shopping street lined with small businesses. Region 1 encompasses high-rise dwellings, converted townhouses of brick construction, and a secondary commercial area. The southern part of Region 2 contains primarily the Journal Square commercial area. This area has a large daytime population. The northern part of this region has occupancies that are more typical of Region 4. The occupied area of Region 3 is primarily industrial with a mixture of residences. The bulk of this region consists of vacant land once occupied by railroad yards. Region 5 is primarily residential with relatively low population density. Buildings are well spaced and in good condition. The western part of this region has a number of chemical plants and other industrial occupancies. Region 6 (not shown in the table) consists chiefly of landfill being developed for industrial use. There are several industries in this area.

The incidence of alarms in Regions 1–5 in 1973 is shown in Table 9.2. The number of structural alarms in a region depends on several factors: the area of the region, the mix of residential and commercial properties in the region, the population density of the region, and the number of alarms per capita in that region. Where there is a high proportion of commercial fires, we may expect an artificially high ratio of fires per capita, since there is probably a relatively small number of people actually living in the region. This effect can be seen most clearly in Regions 1 and 3. A more accurate indicator of building and social problems in an area is the number of fires per capita in residences. A comparison of Regions 2 and 4 illustrates the effect of socio-economic conditions on the fire problem. Since these regions contain essentially similar occupancies, one

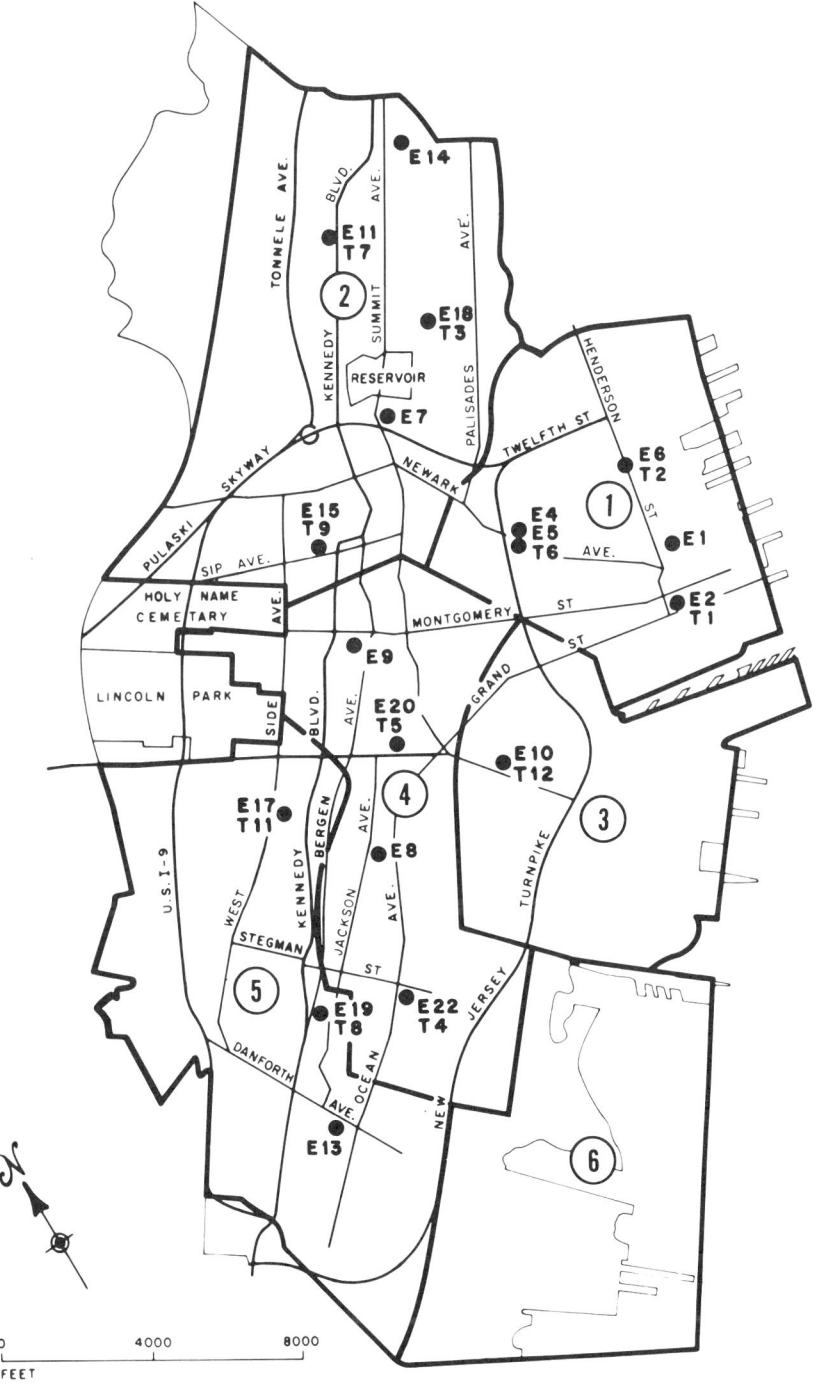

FIGURE 9.7. Map of demand regions and fire company locations in Jersey City, New Jersey.

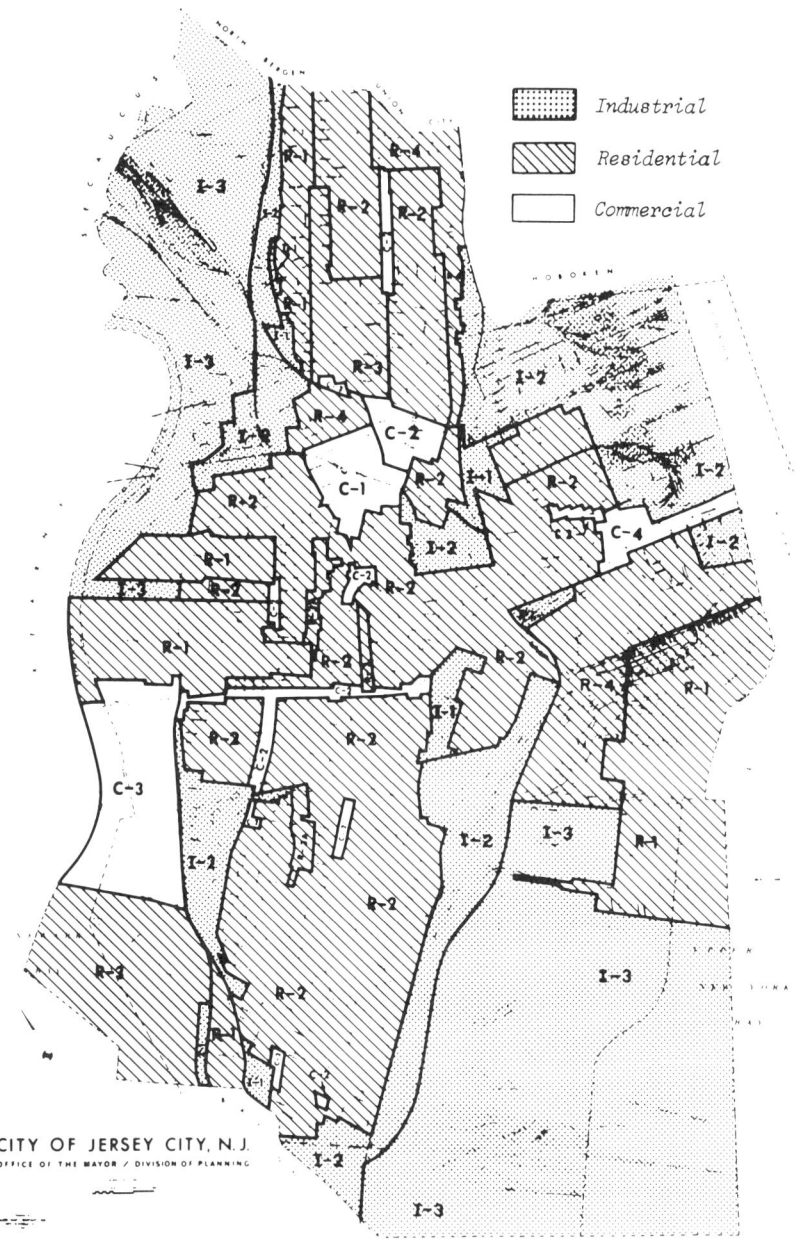

FIGURE 9.8. Jersey City land use map.

TABLE 9.1. Demand region demography.

Demand Region	Name	Built-up Area (square miles)	Population 1970	Population per square mile (thousands)	Housing Units	1-2 Family Dwelling Number	%	Vacant Units Number	%	Basic Characteristics
1	Downtown	1.52	34,876	22.9	12,512	1,830	14.6	936	7.5	Secondary downtown area, high-rise multiple dwellings, waterfront
2	Heights	2.82	82,060	29.1	30,447	11,965	39.3	1,050	3.4	Primary downtown area, semidense residential
3	Lafayette; Liberty Harbor	0.85	11,721	13.8	3,857	954	24.7	245	6.4	Mainly industrial, some residences
4	Bergen	1.98	76,019	38.4	26,589	12,651	47.6	1,390	5.2	Dense residential area, small businesses
5	Westside; Greenville	2.59	54,937	21.2	18,339	10,806	58.9	474	2.3	Less dense residential, some industry
Citywide[a]		9.76	259,613	26.6	91,744	38,206	41.6	4,095	4.5	

[a] Region 6 had no built-up area in 1973.

TABLE 9.2. Demand region alarm incidence, 1973.

Demand Region	Number		Alarms/square mile		Alarms/Capita		Fires in Residences		
	Total	Structural	Total	Structural	Total	Structural	Number	% of All Structural	Per Capita
1	3,308	395	2,176	260	0.0949	0.0113	305	77.2	0.0088
2	2,459	390	872	138	0.0300	0.0048	326	83.6	0.0040
3	838	113	986	133	0.0715	0.0096	110	97.3	0.0094
4	3,366	840	1,700	424	0.0442	0.0111	698	83.1	0.0092
5	1,599	279	617	108	0.0291	0.0051	244	87.5	0.0044
Citywide[a]	11,570	2,017	1,185	207	0.0446	0.0078	1,683	83.4	0.0065

[a] Excluding Region 6.

might expect similar levels of fire incidence. This is not the case. Therefore, in considering long-range plans for firefighting resource deployment, it was necessary to evaluate the effects of social conditions as well as those of building construction.

Ten-Year Projection. While a study of 1973 alarm incidence sheds light on the characteristics of the fire protection problem in Jersey City and on the needs for fire protection resources at that time, the future needs of the city must also be considered. It would be pointless to plan new firehouses in this area if it can be predicted that within ten years a worsening fire situation elsewhere in the city would require their removal.

In order to determine the future needs of Jersey City, therefore, ten-year projections of land use and alarm incidence for each demand region in the city were made. A sixth demand region was added to encompass a new industrial park in the southeast of the city (Port Jersey). Table 9.3 shows alarm rate data for the peak alarm hours of 4 P.M. to midnight for Regions 1 through 5, based on data from July 1972 to June 1973. Serious fires were defined as those structural fires requiring two or more engine streams. Using these data, the alarm rate per square mile was calculated. Then several assumptions about the future prospects for individual demand regions were made, and used to project average 4 P.M. to midnight alarm rates for 1983. The resulting alarm rate and land use projections are shown in Table 9.4.

While it can hardly be expected that the alarm projections will be absolutely accurate, the projections for one region relative to another should be reasonably close. In order to perform an allocation of resources under a fixed budget, the relative needs of the various regions are more important than their absolute needs. Therefore, the projections presented in Table 9.4 were expected to prove useful in considering the relative fire protection requirements of the various regions in Jersey City in 1983. We also note that since commercial and industrial property are scattered throughout the city, it was appropriate to use the same hazard factor for each region.

TABLE 9.3. Jersey City 1972–1973 alarm rates.

		Alarms per Hour from 4 P.M. to Midnight			
Region	Area (square miles)	All	False	Nonserious Structural	Serious Structural
1	1.52	.722	.403	.040	.015
2	2.82	.444	.137	.047	.009
3	0.85	.202	.088	.027	.003
4	1.98	.630	.290	.094	.013
5	2.59	.330	.127	.039	.007

TABLE 9.4. Jersey City alarm rate projections for 1983.

		Alarms per Hour from 4 P.M. to Midnight			
Region	Area (square miles)	All	False	Nonserious Structural	Serious Structural
1	1.52	.49	.20	.04	.014
2	3.20	.76	.23	.14	.020
3	1.70	.27	.06	.05	.006
4	2.08	.49	.15	.09	.013
5	2.59	.31	.06	.05	.008
6	1.47	.07	.01	.01	.002

9.5.2 Protection Levels at the Start of the Study

Table 9.5 shows that at the start of the study the average first-arriving engine travel time in Jersey City was 1.63 minutes. This average is low compared to that in some similar cities. But the travel times in some of the regions are not consistent with the fire experience in the regions. For example, the number of alarms per square mile and the population density is much larger in Region 4 than in Region 1. However, Region 4 has an average first-arriving engine travel time of 1.60 minutes, while Region 1 has an average first-arriving engine travel time of 1.48 minutes. Therefore, in order to match the supply of fire companies more closely to the demand, it was felt that any redeployment of fire companies should first try to reduce engine travel time in Region 4 relative to that in Region 1.

The citywide second-arriving engine travel time is 2.12 minutes, also low compared to other cities. By region, average second-arriving engine travel times range from 1.83 minutes in Region 1 to 2.48 minutes in Region 3. This range is not large compared to differences in second-arriving travel times found elsewhere.

An examination of ladder company travel times reveals that the average citywide first-arriving ladder travel time is 1.89 minutes. As was found for engine companies, the travel times in some of the regions are not consistent with the fire experience in the region. For example, Region 1 has an average first-arriving ladder travel time of 1.63 minutes, while Region 4 has an average first-arriving ladder travel time of 2.00 minutes. Therefore, it was felt that any redeployment of ladder companies should try to reduce the first-arriving ladder travel time in Region 4 relative to the time in Region 1.

The average citywide second-arriving ladder travel time is 2.56 minutes. By region, average second-arriving ladder travel times range from 2.22 to 2.88 minutes. The same problems mentioned for average first-arriving ladder travel times are also found for average second-arriving

TABLE 9.5. Estimated first- and second-arriving travel times (4 p.m.—12 midnight), Jersey City, 1974.

Demand Region	Engines					Ladders				
				Average Travel Time (Minutes)					Average Travel Time (Minutes)	
	Number	Average Busy	Percent Busy	First-Arriving	Second-Arriving	Number	Average Busy	Perent Busy	First-Arriving	Second-Arriving
1	5	0.36	7.2	1.48	1.83	3	0.21	7.0	1.63	2.22
2	5	0.23	4.6	1.64	2.17	3	0.15	5.0	1.93	2.62
3	1	0.10	10.0	1.87	2.48	1	0.06	6.0	1.89	2.56
4	4	0.34	8.5	1.60	2112	2	0.21	10.5	2.00	2.71
5	3	0.18	6.0	1.86	2.46	2	0.11	5.5	2.12	2.88
Citywide	18	1.20	6.7	1.63	2.12	11	0.74	6.7	1.89	2.56

travel times, although in this case the range is small and the travel times compare favorably to those in other cities.

Using the Allocation Model to Evaluate Fire Company Redeployment. In this section, we consider how fire companies in Jersey City could be redeployed to improve fire protection levels and make them more consistent with the regional fire hazards and demands expected over the ten-year period 1974–1983. We begin by deducing the allocation policy implicit in the Fire Department's 1974 configuration of fire companies. We then use this policy to reallocate the existing number of fire companies over the demand regions of the city, based on the ten-year period projections of fire protection needs. The final step is to consider the effects of changing the number of fire companies deployed by the city.[3]

Deducing the Existing Allocation Policy. In Section 9.2 we discussed the problems of subjective judgment inherent in allocating companies among the regions of a city. Fire department management must determine the degree of tradeoff desirable between equalizing travel times and minimizing travel times. In practice, any operating fire department will already have implicitly made that choice. Except for some imbalances that have been caused by changing conditions, we have seen that the allocation of fire companies that existed in Jersey City in 1974 bears a reasonable relation to the fire protection demands of the various regions. We can use the Parametric Allocation Model to determine explicitly the policy implied by the allocation of fire companies that existed then.

The model makes it possible to examine allocations that result from a wide range of criteria obtained by varying a single parameter. If we can find a value of this parameter that yields an allocation similar to the one in current use, then we have effectively determined the department's allocation policy. This parameter can then be used to generate new allocations appropriate to changing conditions of the city.

Table 9.6 compares the 1974 allocation of trucks in Jersey City to the allocations generated by a variety of values of the tradeoff parameter. When the parameter is 50 or more, an allocation that equalizes workload is calculated. When the parameter is 1, the allocation minimizes the average citywide travel time. A parameter value of 0 produces an allocation that equalizes the average travel time in each region. Values of the parameter between 1 and 0 are used to generate allocations for policies that are compromises between equalizing and minimizing average

---

[3] See Rider (1975) for a complete description of the computer program used to implement the Parametric Allocation Model.

9.5 Using the Allocation Model to Reallocate Fire Companies

TABLE 9.6. Alternative allocations of ladder companies to demand regions, Jersey City.

Region	Existing (1974)	50 Equal Workload	1 Minimize Average Travel Time	0.5 Compromise Strategies	0.25	0.10	0 Equalize Average Travel Time
1	3	3.14	2.82	2.62	2.39	2.12	1.81
2	3	2.19	2.41	2.54	2.70	2.89	3.11
3	1	0.91	0.94	0.95	0.96	0.96	0.96
4	2	3.11	2.96	2.85	2.71	2.53	2.29
5	2	1.64	1.87	2.04	2.24	2.50	2.83

travel times. Fractional allocations mean that the first-due area of a company cuts across the boundary between two regions.

It can be seen that while none of the allocations generated by the model correspond exactly to the 1974 one, a parameter value of 0.25 yields an allocation that is quite similar. The major difference between the 1974 allocation and the one generated by the model with parameter 0.25 is the underprediction of the number of ladders in Region 1 and the overprediction of the number of ladders in Region 4. This discrepancy can be explained by the changes in the alarm incidence in these two areas in the late 1960's and early 1970's.

Table 9.7 gives similar results for engines. The calculations had to be modified for Region 1 because in this region there are two engine companies in one house. For the purpose of calculating travel time, this consolidation effectively reduces the number of engine companies in the region by one (see Chapter 7). Except for Region 2, the correspondence between the current allocation and that for a parameter value of 0.25 seems adequate.

TABLE 9.7 Alternative allocations of engine companies to demand regions, Jersey City.

Region	Existing (1974)	50 Equal Workload	1 Minimum Average Travel Time	0.5 Compromise Strategies	0.25	0.10	0 Equal Average Travel Time
1	5	5.32	5.50	5.16	4.78	4.33	3.82
2	5	3.50	3.65	3.87	4.13	4.44	4.79
3	1	1.43	1.41	1.43	1.46	1.47	1.48
4	4	5.08	4.57	4.40	4.19	3.91	3.54
5	3	2.66	2.88	3.13	3.45	3.85	4.36

It would seem reasonable from the above results to take the department's 1974 deployment policy to be given by a tradeoff parameter value of 0.25. This value has been found to approximately represent the implicit deployment policies of the New York City Fire Department as well as those of several other cities.

9.5.3 Planning for 1983 Fire Protection Needs

In the preceding section we made projections of land use and alarm incidence in Jersey City for 1983. We now use these data, together with what we have learned about fire department policy, to see how the existing resources of the department can be allocated among demand regions to meet the projected needs. The purpose is to show how, even if the existing policy should remain unchanged, the city would have had to redeploy its resources because of a changing environment. The resulting travel times will serve as a basic reference against which different deployment strategies may be evaluated.

Table 9.8 shows a new allocation (using $p = 0.25$) for ladder companies based on projected 1983 alarm rates. It should be recalled that the data base for 1983 includes a new region (Region 6), incorporating the area under industrial development in the southeastern part of the city. The most striking feature of the new allocation is that except for Region 6, the travel times throughout the city are relatively uniform. The reason is that the busy density is projected to be more uniform throughout the city in 1983 than it was in 1974. It should also be noted that while there is an imbalance in the existing allocations of ladder companies to Regions 2, 4, and 5, the projected changes in city conditions correct that imbalance without requiring a redistribution of ladder companies. The citywide average travel time increases because it is projected that, on the average,

TABLE 9.8. Projected 1983 allocation of ladder companies in Jersey City.

Region	1974 Allocation	1983 Allocation	Estimated Average Busy (1983)	Average Travel Time (min)	
				First-Arriving	Second-Arriving
1	3	1.7	0.18	1.93	2.62
2	3	3.2	0.30	1.99	2.70
3	1	1.4	0.10	2.10	2.86
4	2	2.1	0.19	1.99	2.70
5	2	1.9	0.12	2.18	2.95
6	–	0.7	0.03	2.45	3.33
Citywide	11	11.0	0.93	2.03	2.76

9.5 Using the Allocation Model to Reallocate Fire Companies

TABLE 9.9. Projected 1983 allocation of engine companies in Jersey City.

Region	1974 Allocation	1983 Allocation	Estimated Average Busy (1983)	Average Travel Time (min)	
				First-Arriving	Second-Arriving
1	5	2.9	0.30	1.63	2.17
2	5	5.3	0.49	1.69	2.24
3	1	2.2	0.16	1.80	2.39
4	4	3.5	0.32	1.70	2.25
5	3	3.0	0.20	1.86	2.46
6	–	1.1	0.05	2.09	2.77
Citywide	18	18.0	1.52	1.73	2.29

there will be more ladders busy and therefore unavailable to respond to new alarms. The major change in the allocation of companies is the removal of more than one ladder from Region 1, where improved conditions relative to the rest of the city are projected. The ladders removed from Region 1 should be moved closer to Regions 3 and 6, which are projected to require more fire protection in the future.

Table 9.9 shows a new allocation for engine companies. The remarks made for ladder companies are also true for these new allocations. The more drastic reduction of two engine companies in Region 1 reflects the fact that none of the new houses is considered to be consolidated under this allocation, although there was currently one consolidated house (with two engine companies) in the region. (With respect to travel time, the two engine companies currently in the consolidated house in Region 1 are effectively one company.)

9.5.4 Changing the Number of Ladder Companies

We can use the allocation model to evaluate the effect on travel times and workload per company, of changing the total number of ladder companies deployed in the city. We are interested in a prescription for the number of companies that should be assigned to each region and what the relative travel times in each region should be, given a total number of companies to be allocated citywide. Once a particular allocation to a region has been decided, the siting model (described in Chapter 10) can be used to evaluate alternative firehouse sites.

Table 9.10 compares the first-arriving ladder travel times resulting from allocations using 7, 9, and 11 ladders. It can be seen that the average travel times are relatively insensitive to changes in the number of companies deployed, although a reduction in companies from 11 to 9 involves

TABLE 9.10. Allocations and average first-arriving ladder travel times for different numbers of ladders (1983 alarm rates), Jersey City. All travel times are in minutes.

Region	11 Ladders		9 Ladders		7 Ladders	
	Number	Average Travel Time	Number	Average Travel Time	Number	Average Travel Time
1	1.7	1.93	1.4	2.05	1.1	2.23
2	3.2	1.99	2.7	2.12	2.1	2.30
3	1.4	2.10	1.1	2.24	0.9	2.43
4	2.1	1.99	1.7	2.12	1.3	2.30
5	1.9	2.18	1.5	2.32	1.2	2.51
6	0.7	2.45	0.6	2.61	0.4	2.83
Citywide	11.0	2.03	9.0	2.16	7.0	2.35

a 6 percent increase in average travel time, while a reduction from 9 to 7 causes a 15 percent increase. With 11 ladders, during the busiest time of the day the chance that a ladder company is working is 10 percent; with 9 ladders this increases to 13 percent; and with 7 ladders it increases to 17 percent, a relatively high figure.

We can evaluate a decision to reduce, for example, the number of ladder companies from 11 to 9 in the light of the factors mentioned above. The effect on average citywide first-arriving ladder travel time would be small, increasing by about 8 seconds from 2.03 minutes to 2.16 minutes. With 9 ladders, the greatest average travel time in a residential region is 2.32 minutes in Region 5. This figure compares favorably to other cities. The maximum regional workload in Region 1 would be 13 percent. This is high compared to the averages in most cities; however, it is not unusually large compared to the workloads found in the busy areas of many cities in the northeast. The final decision as to the level of protection a city should have, however, is usually determined by political and budgetary considerations.

9.5.5 Changing the Number of Engine Companies

The allocation model can be used to generate allocation policies for different numbers of engines. Table 9.11 compares the average first-arriving engine travel times resulting from allocations using 18, 16, 14, 12, and 10 engine companies citywide. The variations in these average travel times are even smaller than the variations in average citywide first-arriving ladder travel times when the number of ladders was varied. A drastic reduction of eight engine companies would result in an increase of less than 20 percent in average travel times. This insensitivity is a

TABLE 9.11. Allocations and average first-arriving ladder travel times for different numbers of engines (1983 alarm rates), Jersey City. All travel times are in minutes.

Region	18 Engines		16 Engines		14 Engines		12 Engines		10 Engines	
	Number	Average Travel Time	Number	Average Travel Time	Number	Average Travel Time	Number	Average Travel Time	Number	Average Travel Time
1	2.9	1.63	2.5	1.70	2.2	1.77	1.9	1.86	1.6	1.98
2	5.3	1.69	4.7	1.76	4.1	1.83	3.6	1.93	3.0	2.05
3	2.2	1.80	2.0	1.87	1.7	1.95	1.5	2.05	1.2	2.18
4	3.5	1.70	3.1	1.76	2.7	1.84	2.3	1.93	1.9	2.05
5	3.0	1.86	2.7	1.93	2.4	2.01	2.0	2.11	1.7	2.24
6	1.1	2.09	1.0	2.17	0.9	2.26	0.7	2.38	0.6	2.53
Citywide	18.0	1.73	16.0	1.79	14.0	1.87	12.0	1.97	10.0	2.09

result of the relatively high density of engine companies that existed in Jersey City. It is apparent that the removal of as many as four engine companies would have had little overall effect on travel time.

With 18 companies deployed, the average 1983 workload in Region 1 is projected to be about 10 percent. If only 10 engine companies were deployed, the companies in Region 1 would have a workload of about 19 percent (almost double). This level of work, while found in some areas of other cities, is relatively high. At a level of 14 companies, the Region 1 workload is 14 percent, which is reasonable for this region.

Workload, manning levels, dispatch policy, adequate coverage, and travel times must all be taken into consideration when deciding on the appropriate level of engine companies. Based on the criteria of workload and average travel time, however, it would appear that 14 engine company locations would provide adequate firefighting coverage in Jersey City.

9.5.6 Conclusions from the Allocation Model

The Parametric Allocation Model provided some quantitative information that can be used for deciding on (1) the number of engines and ladders required to provide adequate coverage in Jersey City and (2) how the companies should be distributed around the city. The primary results are presented in Table 9.12.

It should be kept in mind, when making the comparison between the 1974 and the 1983 allocations, that total workload is projected to increase by about 25 percent and that the occupied land area of the city is projected to increase by nearly 30 percent. Even under these additional burdens, however, the average travel times and workloads obtained under the suggested allocations compare quite favorably with those experienced in other cities.

The first stage in the two-stage analysis is complete. The next step is to consider the proposed allocations in detail by using a siting model (Chapter 10). The allocation stage has reduced the number of configurations that need be considered.

Availability of Computer Programs for the Parametric Allocation Model. Three versions of the Parametric Allocation Model have been developed: BASIC and FORTRAN versions for use in a time-sharing environment, and a PL/I version for use in a batch environment. The BASIC version is documented in Rider (1975), which provides details on the data requirements, output reports, and other considerations not discussed here. Copies of the programs and their documentation are available from the Rand Corporation.

TABLE 9.12. Comparison of existing 1974 and suggested 1983 allocations of fire companies in Jersey City. All travel times are in minutes.

Demand Region	11 Ladders (1974)			9 Ladders (1983)			18 Engines (1974)			14 Engines (1983)		
	Number	Workload[a]	Average First-Arriving Travel Time	Number	Workload[a]	Average First-Arriving Travel Time	Number	Workload[a]	Average First-Arriving Travel Time	Number	Workload[a]	Average First-Arriving Travel Time
1	3	0.07	1.63	1.4	0.13	2.05	5	0.07	1.48	2.2	0.14	1.77
2	3	0.05	1.93	2.7	0.11	2.12	5	0.05	1.64	4.1	0.12	1.83
3	1	0.06	1.89	1.1	0.09	2.24	1	0.10	1.87	1.7	0.09	1.95
4	2	0.10	2.00	1.7	0.11	2.12	4	0.09	1.60	2.7	0.12	1.84
5	2	0.06	2.12	1.5	0.08	2.32	3	0.06	1.86	2.4	0.08	2.01
6	–	–	–	0.6	0.05	2.61	–	–	–	0.9	0.06	2.26
Citywide	11	0.07	1.89	9.0	0.10	2.16	18	0.07	1.63	14.0	0.11	1.87

[a] Workload is the proportion of time that a unit can be expected to be busy.

APPENDIX A9
THE CALCULATION OF HAZARD FACTORS

In this Appendix we discuss how hazard factors can be calculated.

Multiple Hazards

Throughout Chapter 9 it is assumed that each region of the city has a hazard factor that is independent of how a fire department chooses to balance equal coverage (equal average travel times) and most efficient service (minimum average travel times). When calculating hazard factors, however, more detailed consideration must be given to this question.

If a given region i were to contain just one type of building, j, with a fire escalation rate represented by a hazard factor h_j, then the region itself would have a hazard factor $H_i = h_j$. But, if a region contains several types of buildings with different associated hazard factors, how is the hazard factor for the entire region to be calculated? The following example shows that the straightforward use of averages is inappropriate.

Assume that the department wants to give each region "equal coverage." Assume further that one region of the city is not completely built up, but does contain very "hazardous" buildings. The hazard factor for that region will reflect the high fire escalation rate of these buildings. If, however, the development of the region were completed by the construction of very safe occupancies, the average unweighted potential demand in the region would decrease even though all of the unsafe buildings remained. If an average hazard factor were used to determine deployment, this would have the unreasonable effect of indicating a need for less coverage than before the new structures were built.

Let us therefore reformulate the allocation model, explicitly considering the presence of different hazards in one region. The original formulation of the allocation model can be written:

minimize
$$\sum_i \bar{\lambda}_i (H_i \tau_i)^{1/p}$$

subject to
$$\sum_i n_i = m$$

where

τ_i = expected travel time in region i

H_i = hazard factor of region i

n_i = number of companies to be assigned to region i

m = total number of companies to be allocated

p = tradeoff parameter

$\bar{\lambda}_i$ = work content (number of hours of company work time) of one hour's alarms in region i (the alarm factor).

Appendix A9

This formulation can easily be generalized to the following:

minimize
$$\sum_i \sum_j \bar{\lambda}_{ij}(h_j\tau_i)^{1/p}$$

subject to
$$\sum_i n_i = m,$$

where

λ_{ij} = work content of one hour's alarms at type j incidents in region i

h_j = hazard factor for type j incidents.

It can be seen that this formulation splits incidents into various types and considers the resulting risk, associated with a given travel time, for each type of incident. The risks are then weighted, as before, by their work content. We calculate the regionwide hazard factor by the following series of rearrangements.

Let w_{ij} = the proportion of work time in region i spent at incidents of type j.

$$\sum_i \sum_j \bar{\lambda}_{ij}(h_j\tau_i)^{1/p} = \sum_i \sum_j \bar{\lambda}_i w_{ij} h_j^{1/p} \tau_i^{1/p}$$
$$= \sum_i \bar{\lambda}_i \tau_i^{1/p} \sum_j w_{ij} h_j^{1/p}$$
$$= \sum_i \bar{\lambda}_i (H_i(p)\tau_i)^{1/p},$$

where

$$H_i(p) = \left(\sum_j w_{ij} h_j^{1/p}\right)^p.$$

When all the h_j in region i are equal (called the common value h), this formula reduces to $H_i(p) = h$ for all values of the tradeoff parameter p. When $p = 1$, for minimizing average risk, the formula reduces to an average of the h_j weighted by w_{ij}. This is the only case for which an average of the hazards is justified. The average, however, is weighted by proportion of work content. When $p = 0$ (the equal coverage value), then $H_i(0) = \max_j(h_j)$. That is, travel times to the worst risks in each region are equalized. This condition is an interpretation of equal coverage to mean that all target hazards are equally protected, a strategy often found in smaller cities. An intermediate value, such as $p = \frac{1}{2}$, would reduce the formula to the following: $H_i(\frac{1}{2}) = (\Sigma w_{ij} h_j^2)^{1/2}$. In this case, more emphasis is placed on the larger hazards than would be the case if a simple average were taken. For purposes of illustration in the next section, we will use this last formula as the one appropriate to combining incident hazard factors to get a regional hazard factor.

Sample Calculations of Hazard Factors

In this section we attempt to estimate the values of hazard factors for a representative sample of battalions in New York City. Figure 9.9 shows the locations of these battalions. The calculations are based on a number of broad assumptions, but the results are sufficient to reach some significant conclusions.

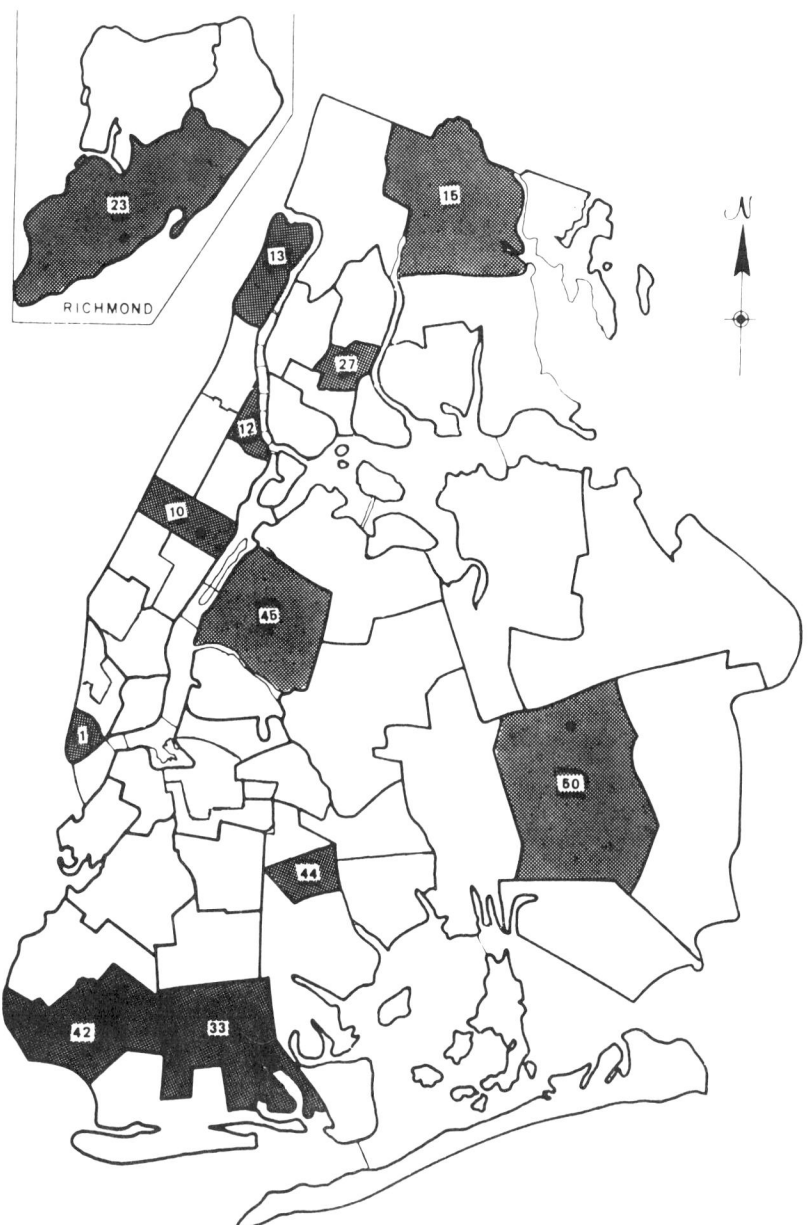

FIGURE 9.9. Map of sample battalions in New York City.

Appendix A9 369

A study conducted for New York City (Ignall et al., 1975) indicated that, for the range of travel distances encountered in the city, there was no discernable relationship between travel distance and fire severity in fireproof buildings. That study also indicated that for certain types of alarms, during certain times of day, the rate of escalation of fires for commercial structures was greater than that for multiple dwellings and private (including frame) residences. When a linear severity-travel distance model was used, no significant difference was found between fire escalation rates in private residences and multiple dwellings. The data used for that study were insufficient to determine precise escalation rates. For this example, however, we will use two estimates of the rate of escalation of fires in commercial occupanices relative to residential occupancies: a very large estimate of 2, and a smaller estimate of 1.414. These relative rates are almost certainly overestimates rather than underestimates.

For each of the sample battalions, we have calculated the proportion of fires that occurred in commercial structures. Data for these calculations were obtained by Held (1975). We calculated hazard factors for the sample battalions using the approximate formula

$$H_i = (f_i(1 - c_i)h_m^2 + f_i c_i h_c^2)^{1/2},$$

where

H_i = hazard factor for region i

f_i = fraction of fires that occurred in nonfireproof occupancies in region i

c_i = fraction of fires that occurred in commercial occupancies in region i

h_m = hazard factor for noncommercial occupanices

h_c = hazard factor for commercial occupancies.

This formula assumes, based on the severity study, that the hazard factor for fireproof occupancies is 0.[4] It also assumes that in any battalion, the fraction of fires occuring in nonfireproof buildings is the same for both commercial and noncommercial occupancies. The latter assumption is not true and would not be necessary if more detailed data were available, but its use will not alter the conclusions to be made from the calculations. The results of the calculations are listed in Table 9.13.

It can be seen that even with the high estimate of the commercial hazard factor, most of the regional hazard factors are close to 1. When the commercial hazard factor is reduced, all battalions but 1 and 10 have values very close to 1. Given the error in estimating the commercial hazard factor and the other assumptions used in the calculation, there is no reason to assume that the hazard factor for any of the battalions, except 1 and 10, is different from 1. The surprising result of this calculation is that he hazard factors for battalions 1 and 10 are calculated to be substantially *less* than 1. These are battalions in the downtown and midtown

---

[4] This is a simplification for expository purposes. Life hazard in fireproof buildings is not negligible (although it is quite low).

TABLE 9.13. Hazard factor calculations for battalions in New York City.

Battalion	Fraction of Fires in Nonfireproof Occupancies	Fraction of Fires in Commercial Occupancies	Hazard Factor (H)	
			$h_m = 1$ $h_c = 2$	$h_m = 1$ $h_c = 1.414$
1	0.453	0.399	1.00	0.80
10	0.655	0.042	0.86	0.83
12	0.882	0.033	0.98	0.95
13	0.910	0.080	1.06	0.99
15	0.742	0.123	1.01	0.91
23	0.980	0.112	1.14	1.04
27	0.971	0.035	1.04	1.00
33	0.955	0.183	1.22	1.06
42	0.988	0.164	1.21	1.07
44	0.927	0.056	1.04	0.99
45	0.758	0.255	1.16	0.98
50	0.894	0.159	1.15	1.02

areas of Manhattan that are usually assumed to have hazard factors substantially *greater* than 1.

The reason for this result is easy to see. Battalions 1 and 10 have relatively few fires in nonfireproof occupancies. The fraction of fires in nonfireproof occupancies in battalion 1 is only 0.435, and this small fraction offsets the larger proportion of commercial occupancy fires.

GLOSSARY OF SYMBOLS

A_i	=	Area of region i
$E(B_i)$	=	Average number of companies busy in region i
c	=	Travel coefficient
D	=	Response distance
F	=	Normalizing factor
f_i	=	Fraction of fires occurring in nonfireproof occupancies in region
H_i	=	Hazard factor for region i
h_j	=	Hazard factor for type j incidents
M	=	Total number of companies to be allocated
N	=	Normalizing factor
n_i	=	Number of companies assigned to region i
n_i^*	=	Optimal number of companies to assign to region i
p	=	Tradeoff parameter
s_i	=	Work time at type i incident
T	=	Travel time
w_i	=	Hazard weight for region i
Z	=	Value of objective function
α	=	Travel coefficient
β	=	Travel coefficient
η_i	=	Redefined hazard factor for region i $(= H_i^{1/\beta})$
λ_i	=	Average hourly alarm rate in region i
$\bar{\lambda}_i$	=	Alarm factor for region i
μ_i	=	Availability density of companies in region i
ν	=	Tradeoff parameter $(= p/(\beta + p))$
ξ	=	Lagrange multiplier
ρ_i	=	Busy density in region i
τ_i	=	Expected travel time in region i

Chapter 10
Locating Firehouses

Synopsis

This chapter continues the development of methods for deciding where to locate firehouses that was begun in Chapter 9. The methods in this chapter deal with ways of selecting specific sites at which to locate fire companies. Two descriptive models are discussed: the Firehouse Site Evaluation Model (the "siting model") and the Fire Station Location Package (FSLP). The models estimate the travel times and company workloads for any given arrangement of fire companies. By comparing the results from one arrangement to those from others, good fire company locations can be determined.

The chapter compares various characteristics of the two models in order to help a potential user choose the more appropriate model. Characteristics compared include their input data requirements, output reports, methods for estimating travel times, computer requirements, and the effort required to implement them.

The input data requirements of the two models differ considerably because they use very different approaches to estimating travel times. The FSLP estimates travel times using a street network. The approach used in the siting model is to estimate the travel distance between two points from grid coordinates assigned to the points, and to estimate the travel time using an experimentally determined relationship between travel distance and travel time. (Chapter 6 describes and compares these two approaches.)

Since the travel-time estimates produced by the FSLP and the siting model have never been directly compared, it is not possible to say which approach will produce the best estimates. However, certain aspects of the two approaches would make one or the other preferable in certain circumstances. For example, construction of the street network required by the FSLP is a time-consuming task. The siting model does not require such an elaborate data base. The assignment of grid coordinates is much *easier to accomplish. But, if a computer-readable street network of the community already exists, or if the street network is to be used for other purposes, the FSLP may be the better way to proceed.*

The FSLP approach is also preferred if the community contains a great many barriers to travel, or irregularly shaped areas. It may also be worthwhile to spend the extra time and effort in building the FSLP network if the FSLP is to be used for locating other public facilities, such as parks or ambulance garages. In addition, officials may feel more comfortable with the FSLP travel-time estimates since its calculations are based on imitating the path actually followed by fire companies. However, the siting model's travel-time estimates have been validated against actual travel times in several cities, and have been found to be accurate enough for firehouse site selection purposes.

The FSLP is more widely used. By late 1976, Public Technology, Inc., reported that 52 jurisdictions were known to have implemented the FSLP, while the siting model had been used by ten jurisdictions. The costs for using the two models have not been reported in comparable form. The total cost for a deployment study using the siting model has been reported to average $14,000, with a range from $10,000 to $35,000. PTI reports that an average of 30 person-months were expended by users of the FSLP, with a range from 3 to 528 person-months.

The chapter concludes with a detailed case study of how the siting model was used to analyze the firehouse location problem in Trenton, New Jersey.

10.1 INTRODUCTION

One of the most common and most important deployment problems facing a fire department is where it should place its firehouses. Even if a jurisdiction has only one or two firehouses, it would like to make sure that they are as well located as possible. In recent years, several approaches have been developed for helping fire departments decide where to place firehouses. Not surprisingly, most use essentially the same measures of effectiveness, have the same general data requirements, and are more or less based on the same principles. However, the specific models are actually quite different, and require different amounts of time and manpower to set up and use. This chapter discusses two of these models in detail.

Neither of these new models makes direct use of the *Grading Schedule for Municipal Fire Protection*. Instead, they use descriptive models (see Chapter 3) and require fire officials to look at the travel distances and times implied by different firehouse locations. The policy input to either model is an "arrangement" or a "configuration" of fire companies (i.e., a set of sites for fire companies). The model then estimates the values of a large number of performance measures that could be expected if that policy were actually implemented. By comparing the consequences of several different arrangements, a suitable arrangement of fire companies can be selected. One of the models can also be used in a prescriptive mode. In this case, the input to the model is a set of travel times required for various points in the city. The outputs are the number and locations of the fire companies needed to meet these requirements.

It should be pointed out that both of the firehouse siting models assume that it is possible to actually erect a firehouse on any of the sites under consideration. This means that before using any of these models, the analyst must spend some time discussing potential sites with the agency (or agencies) in the community that have information on where public land is available (or can be obtained), and which of these parcels of land could be used for a firehouse. If the two-stage approach described in Chapter 9 is used, it may not be necessary to compile a listing of all available parcels in the city. The output of the Parametric Allocation Model permits attention to be focused on finding sites in specific regions of the city.

10.2 TWO DESCRIPTIVE MODELS

Chapter 3 describes the types of models generally used in deployment studies. It defines descriptive models as ones that "predict the values of various performance measures for given deployment policies." Many recent studies to determine firehouse locations have used descriptive models to compare alternative arrangements.

One problem in using a descriptive model for this purpose is that there are often a large number of alternative configurations that have to be evaluated. This problem is especially severe in a large community. In some small communities it may not be difficult to determine the best configuration, even without the help of a mathematical model; simply studying maps on which the various alternative arrangements are displayed may be sufficient. However, in larger cities it is nearly impossible for a planner to look at a map and make accurate guesses regarding the workload of the units or areas where travel times will be too high. It may also be difficult to specify a small number of good alternative configurations to be evaluated with the help of a descriptive model simply by looking at a map (although this approach has been used successfully in a number of medium-sized cities).

The two-stage method discussed in Chapter 9 was developed to make easier the process of generating good alternatives. The Parametric Allo-

10.2 Two Descriptive Models

cation Model is used in the first stage to provide the planner with a general picture of the number of fire companies that should be located in different parts of the city. It is simple, easy to use, and requires very little data. But it cannot be used to determine specific locations for the firehouses. Once the fire department has chosen (at least tentatively) the number of companies to be assigned to each region of the city, it is not difficult to develop several alternative configurations of station sites that might lead to the desired levels of performance. These can then be compared by using a descriptive model. These models estimate the travel times and company workloads for any particular arrangement of fire companies. Although descriptive models do not suggest arrangements to be tried, experience indicates that examination of their output makes it easy to eliminate poor arrangements, and to zero in on good ones (Schneider, 1971).

There are two models of this type that have been widely applied to the problem of locating firehouses.[1] They are:

The Firehouse Site Evalutation Model (the "siting model"), developed by The New York City-Rand Institute under contracts with New York City and the U.S. Department of Housing and Urban Development (Walker, 1975, and Dormont et al., 1975).

The Fire Station Location Package (FSLP), developed by Public Technology, Inc. (PTI) under a contract with the U.S. Department of Housing and Urban Development (*Fire Station Location Package,* 1974).[2]

These two models have several features in common. For example, to use either model the city must be divided into small subareas, each no smaller than the area covered by a single alarm box, and sometimes an area up to four or five times this size. The subareas must be reasonably small, since the models assume that the demand for fire service in a subarea arises at only one point, and that travel times to any place in the subarea will be the same as to that point. Computational necessity dictates the need for using subareas—it would be infeasible to calculate the travel times to every location in a community. However, travel times do not vary much among locations that are close together. Thus, aggregating

---

[1] Several other models have been developed for this purpose as part of deployment studies in some cities. For example, the Station Configuration Information Model (SCIM) was developed by researchers studying the Denver Fire Department (Hendrick et al., 1974). These models are not well documented and are generally not able to be obtained for use in other cities. We have, therefore, limited our discussion to these two well-documented models.

[2] In October 1976, PTI released a new version of the FSLP. Documentation of the new version was not available at the time this book was written, so the description of the FSLP contained in this chapter is based upon *Fire Station Location Package,* 1974.

locations into small subareas makes the problem manageable while providing reasonably accurate travel-time estimates.

Both models permit the user to identify some subareas as being especially hazardous, so that the analysis can pay special attention to them. They differ primarily in the method used to estimate travel times and in the performance measures that are tabulated on the output reports.[3]

10.2.1 Estimating Travel Times

Travel time is the most important measure used in evaluating alternative arrangements of firehouses. Both the siting model and the FSLP calculate a number of different travel-time measures for a given arrangement of firehouses. But each model uses a different method for calculating the travel time between two points.

The FSLP estimates travel times using a street network (as described in Chapter 6, Section 6.3). Briefly, a street map of the region being studied is converted into a computer-readable network description in which street intersections are represented as nodes, and streets are the connecting arcs between the nodes. An estimate is made of the average speed at which a fire company would travel along each arc (using traffic surveys, experienced guesses, experimental trips by fire companies, etc.). The speed of travel and the length of the arc determine the average time for a fire company to traverse it. The travel time from any firehouse (a node in the network) to any subarea (another node) is then estimated by finding the set of arcs that form the shortest time path.

The approach used in the siting model is to assign grid coordinates to every potential station site and subarea. The travel distance between a firehouse and a subarea is then estimated from either the straight-line (Euclidean) distance or the right-angle distance between them. Let (x_1, y_1) be the coordinates of the firehouse, and (x_2, y_2) be the coordinates of the center of the subarea. One of the functions that can be used to estimate the distance between them is

$$D_1 = k\sqrt{(x_2 - x_1)^2 + (y_2 - y_1)^2}, \qquad (10.1)$$

---

[3] The Fire Station Location Package is available at no extra cost to PTI subscribers. Nonsubscribers can obtain the package for a fee from PTI or the National Technical Information Service (NTIS). PTI can also supply technical assistance to a jurisdiction, including telephone consultation, computer runs at PTI, or on-site visits. (Public Technology, Inc., 1140 Connecticut Avenue, N.W., Washington, D.C. 20036; National Technical Information Service, U.S. Department of Commerce, 5285 Port Royal Road, Springfield, Virginia 22151.)

Copies of the Firehouse Site Evaluation Model and its documentation are available from the Rand Corporation (1700 Main Street, Santa Monica, California 90406), or from NTIS.

Information on how to access the Firehouse Site Evaluation Model using a computer terminal also can be obtained from Rand.

10.2 Two Descriptive Models

where D_1 is the Euclidean (straight-line) distance between the two points, multiplied by a user-supplied constant, k. The constant depends on the street patterns and geography of the area being modeled. (Empirical data gathered in several cities has shown that the value of k varies only slightly from city to city, and that a value of $k = 1.15$ produces good estimates for most cities. However, a city can experimentally determine its own value of k.)

The right-angle distance between the firehouse and the subarea is given by

$$D_2 = |x_2 - x_1| + |y_2 - y_1|. \qquad (10.2)$$

If, in the region being studied, fire companies travel on streets that parallel the grid, D_2 will provide the best estimates of travel distances.

Given the travel distance, D (which may be either D_1 or D_2), the siting model estimates the travel *time*, T, by using Equation (6.4). That is,

$$T = \begin{cases} c\sqrt{D} & D \leq d \\ a + bD & D \geq d, \end{cases}$$

where a, b, c, and d are supplied to the siting model by the user. Experience in a wide range of cities has shown that the values of these parameters vary little from city to city. Therefore, at least until a travel-time experiment can be set up, run, and analyzed, a city may obtain useful travel-time estimates by using Equation (6.5), which is based upon experimental results in Trenton, Denver, Wilmington, and Yonkers:

$$T = \begin{cases} 2.10\sqrt{D} & D \leq 0.38 \text{ mile} \\ 0.65 + 1.70D & D \geq 0.38 \text{ mile}, \end{cases}$$

where D is the travel distance in miles and T is the travel time in minutes. If the user does not specify values for a, b, c, and d, the siting model will automatically use Equation (6.5) for estimating travel times.

Hickey (1977) compared some travel time estimates produced by the FSLP and the siting model for Alexandria, Virginia, and found that the estimates were extremely close to each other. However, certain aspects of the two approaches would make one or the other preferable in certain circumstances. For example, construction of the computer-readable street network required by the FSLP is a time-consuming task. (See *Fire Station Location Package* (1974) for a detailed description of the procedure and resources required.) The siting model does not require such an elaborate data base. The assignment of grid coordinates and subareas can be done manually by overlaying a transparent sheet of graph paper on a map showing the station sites and the centers of subareas (the grid need not have lines spaced any closer than a few hundred feet), and recording the x value and y value of the grid lines closest to each point. Alternatively, there are commercial service bureaus that will assign coordinates to points on a map accurate to within a few feet, for a cost of 10¢ to 20¢ per point. However it is done, the process of assigning grid coordinates should take only a few days to accomplish. Thus, if a computer-readable street network of the city has not already been developed, the siting model is the faster and less costly way to proceed.

The FSLP approach is to be preferred if the community contains a great many barriers to travel (e.g., hills, railroad tracks, rivers, airports, one-way streets), or irregularly shaped areas (e.g., peninsulas). In these cases, it would be difficult for the siting-model approach to produce accurate estimates of travel distances. It may also be worthwhile to spend the extra time and effort in building the FSLP network if the FSLP is to be used for locating other public facilities, such as parks, or ambulance garages. In addition, officials may feel more comfortable with the FSLP travel-time estimates since its calculations are based on imitating the path actually followed by fire companies. However, the siting model's travel-time estimates have been validated against actual travel times in several cities, and have been found to be quite accurate (more than adequately accurate for firehouse site selection purposes).[4]

Table 6.1 in Chapter 6 presents a comparison of the two approaches to travel-time estimation to assist in choosing between them.

10.2.2 Output Reports

For each input arrangement of fire companies, both the siting model and the FSLP calculate a set of descriptive performance measures. The measures are primarily based on the travel times of fire companies to subareas; but both include workload information that can be used to analyze the distribution of work among the fire companies.

The estimation of travel times in both models is based on the following two assumptions:

1. Units are always available in their firehouses to respond to an incoming alarm. (This is a reasonable assumption for most jurisdictions. The travel-time estimates produced by these models are useful for making deployment decisions as long as an average fire company is available at least 90 percent of the time.)
2. The closest units are always dispatched to an alarm. (There are very few jurisdictions in which this policy is not followed.)

Both programs perform separate calculations for ladder companies and for engine companies.

---

[4] One such validation is documented in Hendrick et al. (1974); another in an unpublished report by Walker (1973).

10.2 Two Descriptive Models

There are some important differences in the specific output measures calculated by the different programs. We discuss the output of the two programs in the following two subsections.

FSLP Output. The subareas in this model are called *fire demand zones* (FDZs). The point representing all the properties in a fire demand zone is called a *focal point*. For each demand zone, a required maximum travel time for the closest unit is specified, as well as the number of alarms that occurred within the zone during a selected time period.

Given a configuration of firehouses, the program estimates the travel times between firehouses and fire demand zones (actually, between firehouses and focal points) for that configuration and prints out three types of reports. One report shows the FDZs that the given configuration would leave "uncovered" (estimated travel time of the closest unit is greater than the specified maximum travel time). For each of the uncovered zones, the report also shows the required travel time of the (assigned) closest units to the zone (TIME) and the total alarm count for some historical period (INCI). Figure 10.1 is an example of this report. In this case, the trial configuration (which might be for engine companies or for ladder companies) resulted in seven uncovered FDZs (numbered 3, 4, 68, 69, 70, 71, and 77).

The second report consists of two parts. The first part shows the fire stations in the configuration being analyzed (a listing of the input configuration). The second part shows the resulting citywide frequency distribution of first-due travel times to fire demand zones (i.e., the number of zones with first-due travel times under one minute, between one and two minutes, etc.). This part also includes the citywide average first-due time to "covered" FDZs (estimated travel time of the closest unit is less than or equal to the specified maximum travel time), and the overall citywide average first-due travel time.[5] Figure 10.2 illustrates this report. It shows that a configuration with three firehouses is being analyzed. All demand zone first-due travel time requirements are four minutes or less. If this configuration were implemented, the FSLP estimates that 80 of the city's 87 fire demand zones would receive the required first-due travel time specified in the input data. Ten percent of these 80 travel times would be under one minute; 18.8 percent would be between three and four minutes; and, as we saw in Figure 10.1, the configuration would not be able to satisfy the travel time requirements of seven demand zones. The average first-due travel time for the covered zones (summing the 80 travel times and dividing by 80) is 1.98 minutes. The average citywide first-due travel time (summing all 87 travel times and dividing by 87) is 2.14 minutes.

---

[5] Note that the FSLP uses "response time" and "travel time" synonomously.

21 JUN 74   PTI FIRE STATION LOCATION   CURRENT COVERAGE ON NETWORK A

THESE ZONES WILL NOT BE COVERED IN THE NEXT SOLUTION

THEY CANNOT BE REACHED WITHIN THE ASSOCIATED RESPONSE TIME REQUIREMENTS

ZONE	TIME	INCI	ZONE	TIME	INCI	ZONE	TIME	INCI	ZONE	TIME	INCI	ZONE	TIME	INCI	ZONE	TIME	INCI
3	3.5	3.0	4	3.5	0.0	68	3.0	8.0	69	3.0	0.0	70	3.0	9.0	71	3.0	11.0
77	4.0	1.0															

FIGURE 10.1. FSLP: Analysis of uncovered fire demand zones.

10.2 Two Descriptive Models

```
21 JUN 74   PTI FIRE STATION LOCATION   CURRENT COVERAGE ON NETWORK A

HAVE REACHED A SOLUTION WITH   3 SITES

THE VALUE OF THE MAX RESPONSE TIME IS           4.00

THE SITES IN THIS SOLUTION ARE:
CURRENT STATION NO 1 AT A LEVEL   1
CURRENT STATION NO 2 AT A LEVEL   1
CURRENT STATION NO 3 AT A LEVEL   1

** NOTE- THERE MAY BE ALTERNATIVE SOLUTIONS **



21 JUN 74   PTI FIRE STATION LOCATION   CURRENT COVERAGE ON NETWORK A

THE DISTRIBUTION OF TRAVEL TIMES IS
         TIMES      # OF          % OF
                    FD ZONES      FD ZONES
            0         8             10.0
            1        27             33.8
            2        30             37.5
            3        13             16.3
            4         2              2.5
            5         0              0.0
            6         0              0.0
            7         0              0.0
            8         0              0.0
9 OR MORE             0              0.0
UNCOVERED             7              8.8

AVERAGE RESPONSE TIME FOR COVERED ZONES IS   1.98 MINUTES

OVERALL AVERAGE RESPONSE TIME IS   2.14 MINUTES

THE RESPONSE TIME VALUE IS   4.0
```

FIGURE 10.2. FSLP two part report showing (a) firehouse sites being analyzed and (b) citywide travel-time distribution for fire demand zones.

(From this information it can be determined that the average first-due travel time to the seven uncovered demand zones is 3.96 minutes.) Since the travel time to an FDZ is not weighted by the alarm rate in the zone in computing the average, the result is highly dependent on the manner in which the FDZs are defined.

The third type of report displays the fire demand zones in each fire company's first-due area, and shows the estimated travel times of the first-, second-, and third-due units to each zone, and the historical number of incidents that have occurred within each zone. The historical incidence for each zone is input by the user. Its appearance on this report provides an estimate of the potential first-due workload for the associated fire company. Figure 10.3 displays information on the 17 FDZs contituting the first-due area for the company assigned to Station 1. For example, the first-due travel time for FDZ 1 would be 2.5 minutes with this configuration. The second-due travel time would be 5.2 minutes (provided by the company in Station 2), and the third-due travel time would be 5.6 minutes (provided by the company in Station 3). The average first-due travel time in the area would be 2.3 minutes, and one of the FDZs would have a first-due travel time in excess of the maximum specified to the program for that FDZ.

Siting Model Output. The siting model uses the term *alarm box* to refer to a subarea. To help evaluate alternative arrangements of fire companies, each alarm box may be assigned to a demand region. (Demand regions are defined in Chapter 8.) The use of demand regions makes it possible to group alarm boxes having similar fire protection needs and to compare fire protection in regions of the city having similar characteristics, to see if imbalances exist. It also makes it easy to see whether the more hazardous regions have smaller travel times. (In the FSLP, the user may specify as input shorter travel-time requirements for the more hazardous locations, and determine whether or not they are met.) The model can be used interactively, with the user sitting at a computer terminal. The program provides a command language with which the user can specify new arrangements of fire companies and vary the types of output reports produced.

After receiving a specification of a proposed configuration of fire companies, the program calculates the resulting travel times to each of the alarm boxes in the city. It is possible to obtain all of these travel times as output, but it would be difficult to interpret so much information. Thus, the siting model provides aggregate information on the resulting travel times to various groupings of alarm boxes (including the citywide and company response area groupings provided by the FSLP). Similar information is printed out for each grouping. The groupings are:

1. *Citywide.* Citywide average and maximum travel times and travel distances are printed, that summarize the results for all alarm boxes in the city.
2. *By demand region.* Travel times and distances are printed separately for each of the previously defined demand regions constituting the city.
3. *By company response area.* The siting model divides the city into response areas based on the estimated distances that companies would have to travel to each alarm box. Summary statistics are printed for

21 JUN 74 PTI FIRE STATION LOCATION   CURRENT COVERAGE ON NETWORK A

ASSIGNMENT FOR CURRENT STATION NO 1 SITE

FDZ TO BE COVERED	TIME		SITE PROVIDING 2ND RESPONSE	TIME		SITE PROVIDING 3RD RESPONSE	TIME	ALARM #
1	2.5	*	CURRENT STATION NO 2	5.2	*	CURRENT STATION NO 3	5.6	2.0
2	2.9	*	CURRENT STATION NO 2	4.9	*	CURRENT STATION NO 3	5.5	4.0
* 3	3.9	*	CURRENT STATION NO 2	5.1	*	CURRENT STATION NO 3	6.7	3.0
8	3.4	*	CURRENT STATION NO 2	4.1	*	CURRENT STATION NO 3	4.7	2.0
9	2.1	*	CURRENT STATION NO 2	4.5	*	CURRENT STATION NO 3	5.1	6.0
10	2.7	*	CURRENT STATION NO 2	3.9	*	CURRENT STATION NO 3	4.5	4.0
13	1.5	*	CURRENT STATION NO 2	3.9		CURRENT STATION NO 3	4.2	r3.0
14	2.9	*	CURRENT STATION NO 2	3.3		CURRENT STATION NO 3	3.5	3.0
17	1.2	*	CURRENT STATION NO 3	4.2	*	CURRENT STATION NO 2	5.3	17.0
18	0.3	*	CURRENT STATION NO 3	4.1	*	CURRENT STATION NO 2	5.1	15.0
19	2.8		CURRENT STATION NO 3	3.7	*	CURRENT STATION NO 2	4.1	2.0
23	2.1		CURRENT STATION NO 3	3.5	*	CURRENT STATION NO 2	5.2	4.0
24	1.3		CURRENT STATION NO 3	2.9		CURRENT STATION NO 2	4.3	2.0
25	1.9		CURRENT STATION NO 3	3.4		CURRENT STATION NO 2	3.8	3.0
26	2.6		CURRENT STATION NO 3	2.8		CURRENT STATION NO 2	3.2	1.0
29	2.8		CURRENT STATION NO 3	3.7		CURRENT STATION NO 2	4.1	1.0
35	1.5	*	CURRENT STATION NO 3	4.1	*	CURRENT STATION NO 2	5.6	7.0

TOTAL ZONES	AVE TIME			AVE TIME			AVE TIME	TOTAL INCI
17	2.3			3.9			4.7	79.0

* SIGNIFIES A ZONE WITH INADEQUATE COVER

FIGURE 10.3. FSLP: Station site assignments.

each company's first-due response area, second-due response area, and so on. Once a new configuration of firehouses is chosen, this information is useful in making up new response assignments for each company.
4. *For the "affected region."* The data base for the siting model contains information on a previously defined arrangement of fire companies, that it calls the "current" configuration. In any use of the model, results are presented, side by side, for two configurations: the current configuration and the new one under consideration, called the "proposed" configuration. The *affected region* is the set of alarm boxes to which travel times in the proposed configuration are different from those in the current configuration. The affected region is automatically determined by the computer and will be different for each proposed configuration. Analysis of the effects of the new arrangement should focus on the affected boxes. A comparison of the current and proposed travel times to boxes in the affected region provides a better measure of the impact of the proposed arrangement than a comparison of the two citywide averages, since the citywide averages will generally include a large number of alarm boxes to which the travel time has not changed at all. (That is, the citywide impact may be small, but the impact in certain areas may be substantial.)
5. *For all boxes that are near significant hazards (target hazards).* Travel times are printed for each of these high-hazard boxes and are summarized for the whole group of boxes.

For each of the above groups of alarm boxes (except company response areas), the siting model provides the values of the following performance measures for both the current and proposed configurations:

1. Average travel time to an alarm box, giving equal weight to each box (AV. TR.T). These are comparable to the average travel times produced by the FSLP.
2. Average travel distance to an alarm box (AV. TR.D.).
3. Average travel time to a structural fire, taking into account that some alarm boxes have more structural fires than others (AV. TR.T. TO STRUCTURALS).
4. Average travel distance to a structural fire (AV. TR.D. TO STRUCTURALS).
5. The longest travel time among all boxes in the group (MAX TR.T.).

All of the above statistics are calculated separately for engine companies and ladder companies, and can be obtained for first-due, second-due, third-due, etc., responses, up to the response level requested by the user. Travel times are reported in minutes; travel distances, in miles.

A sample report showing citywide and demand-region results is given in Figure 10.4, which presents first-due engine results for a city that has

1ST DUE ENGINE RESPONSE

CITYWIDE	(398 BOXES)	CURRENT	PROPOSED	(4730 ALARMS,	1872 STRUCTS.)
AV. TR.T.		1.98	1.96		
AV. TR.D.		0.74	0.73		
AV. TR.T.	TO STRUCTURALS	1.45	1.46		
AV. TR.D.	TO STRUCTURALS	0.42	0.43		
MAX TR.T.		3.80	3.80		
REGION 1	(71 BOXES)	CURRENT	PROPOSED	(2215 ALARMS,	927 STRUCTS.)
AV. TR.T.		1.51	1.41		
AV. TR.D.		0.46	0.40		
AV. TR.T.	TO STRUCTURALS	1.35	1.26		
AV. TR.D.	TO STRUCTURALS	0.36	0.31		
MAX TR.T.		2.52	2.52		
REGION 2	(58 BOXES)	CURRENT	PROPOSED	(254 ALARMS,	86 STRUCTS.)
AV. TR.T.		2.09	2.09		
AV. TR.D.		0.80	0.80		
AV. TR.T.	TO STRUCTURALS	1.69	1.69		
AV. TR.D.	TO STRUCTURALS	0.57	0.57		
MAX TR.T.		3.59	3.59		
REGION 3	(173 BOXES)	CURRENT	PROPOSED	(1211 ALARMS,	492 STRUCTS.)
AV. TR.T.		2.29	2.14		
AV. TR.D.		0.93	0.83		
AV. TR.T.	TO STRUCTURALS	1.60	1.65		
AV. TR.D.	TO STRUCTURALS	0.51	0.54		
MAX TR.T.		3.80	3.80		
REGION 4	(96 BOXES)	CURRENT	PROPOSED	(1050 ALARMS,	367 STRUCTS.)
AV. TR.T.		1.70	1.98		
AV. TR.D.		0.57	0.74		
AV. TR.T.	TO STRUCTURALS	1.45	1.67		
AV. TR.D.	TO STRUCTURALS	0.43	0.56		
MAX TR.T.		2.47	3.43		

FIGURE 10.4. Siting model: Citywide and demand-region first-due engine statistics for the current and proposed configurations.

398 alarm boxes divided into four demand regions. The city currently deploys nine engine companies. Under the deployment policy proposed by the user, one of the engines is eliminated, and the remaining eight companies are rearranged. The siting model results show that the resulting configuration could be expected to reduce the citywide average first-due engine travel time by 0.02 minutes, while the average travel time to structural fires would increase by 0.01 minutes and the maximum travel time would remain unchanged. The proposed configuration would have a favorable impact on first-due engine travel times in Demand Region 1 (the region with the highest alarm rate and most structural fires in the city), while travel times in Demand Region 4 would be degraded.

Figure 10.5 shows the output produced for the region affected by the proposed change; in this case, the region covered by alarm boxes whose first-due engine travel time will be changed. (The affected region is divided into two parts: those boxes to which the first-due engine travel time would increase, and those whose first-due engine travel time would be reduced.) Similar reports are produced for the affected boxes within each demand region.[6] If the user desires, the program will produce a list of the affected boxes in each of the two categories (improved and degraded travel times). Figure 10.5 shows that if the proposed arrangement of engine companies is implemented, 64 boxes, which experienced 1091 alarms, including 414 structural fires, in the previous year, would receive degraded first-due engine travel times. The estimated average travel time to structural alarms at these boxes would increase by 0.60 minutes, or 36 seconds. It also shows that the first-due engine travel time would improve for 86 boxes that experienced 1093 alarms, including 441 structural fires, in the previous year. The estimated average travel time to structural alarms at these boxes would decrease by 0.51 minutes, or 31 seconds.

One way to use this information in analyzing deployment alternatives is the following. Suppose the arrangement of engine companies represented by the output in Figure 10.5 was implemented, and that the alarm rates at the 150 boxes affected by the change remained the same next year. Then 414 structural fires would receive an average first-due engine travel time increase of 0.60 minutes, for a total increase of 248.4 minutes (414 × 0.60 = 248.4); and 441 structural fires would receive an average first-due engine travel time decrease of 0.51 minutes, for a total decrease of 224.9 minutes (441 × 0.51 = 224.9). Thus, by eliminating one engine company and rearranging the others, this city will experience a net increase of 23.5 minutes of travel time to the 855 structural fires expected

---

[6] Depending on the changes being made to the current configuration, the affected boxes may be in several different parts of the city. The union of the subareas of the affected boxes defines the affected region.

1ST DUE ENGINE RESPONSE

CITYWIDE

64 DEGRADED BOXES		CURRENT	PROPOSED	(1091 ALARMS,	414 STRUCTS.)
AV. TR.T.		1.57	2.23		
AV. TR.D.		0.50	0.89		
AV. TR.T.	TO STRUCTURALS	1.32	1.92		
AV. TR.D.	TO STRUCTURALS	0.35	0.70		
MAX TR.T.		2.39	3.43		

86 IMPROVED BOXES		CURRENT	PROPOSED	(1093 ALARMS,	441 STRUCTS.)
AV. TR.T.		2.27	1.69		
AV. TR.D.		0.91	0.57		
AV. TR.T.	TO STRUCTURALS	1.88	1.37		
AV. TR.D.	TO STRUCTURALS	0.68	0.38		
MAX TR.T.		3.55	2.73		

150 AFFECTED BOXES		CURRENT	PROPOSED	(2184 ALARMS,	855 STRUCTS.)
AV. TR.T.		1.97	1.92		
AV. TR.D.		0.74	0.71		
AV. TR.T.	TO STRUCTURALS	1.61	1.63		
AV. TR.D.	TO STRUCTURALS	0.52	0.53		
MAX TR.T.		3.55	3.43		

FIGURE 10.5. Siting model: First-due engine citywide affected region statistics. Affected region statistics by demand region are also produced in the same format.

to occur per year at the affected boxes. An illustration of how to use such information is presented in Section 10.4.2.

Figure 10.6 shows the same set of output measures for the 15 alarm boxes in the city that were designated as target hazards. In this example, the proposed configuration would improve both the unweighted average first-due engine travel time to these hazards, and the average travel time to structural fires expected to occur at these 15 boxes. However, the maximum time for the first-due engine to reach any of these hazards is increased by almost 23 seconds. Figure 10.7 shows the effect of the proposed configuration on each of the 15 boxes identified as a target hazard. The first-due engine travel time to Box 1419, which had been the highest time to any of the 15 target hazards, would be reduced by one minute. But, the first-due engine travel time to Box 207 would be increased by almost one minute, making its time the highest of the 15.

Figure 10.8 is another type of report, which shows, for each demand region and citywide, the number of alarm boxes having a travel time that falls into each of a number of half-minute intervals under the proposed configuration. This information can be used to see how frequently very long travel times can be expected to occur with a particular configuration of companies. (The output from the FSLP includes a similar report showing the distribution of first-due travel times to fire demand zones citywide; see Figure 10.2b.) Figure 10.8 shows that, under the proposed configuration, over half of the boxes in the city would have first-due engine travel times between 1 and 2 minutes; and almost 80 percent would have travel times under 2.5 minutes. Six of the seven alarm boxes in the city that would have first-due travel times over 3.5 minutes are in Demand Region 3.

The last siting model report to be discussed presents information on company response areas. For each company response area (both current and proposed), the program prints the number of alarm boxes in the area, the average and maximum travel times, and the estimated alarm rates in the area. The alarm rates provide an estimate of the company's workload, indicating whether a proposed configuration will result in an undue strain on a particular company, or in large workload imbalances among the companies. Figure 10.9 presents this report for first-due engines. It shows that Engine 2 is eliminated in the proposed configuration and that Engine 9 is unaffected by the redeployment of companies. The workload of Engine 10 (which had been the highest in the city) is reduced, but Engine 8 picks up a considerable amount of work. At the user's option, lists of the alarm boxes constituting each company's response area can be produced.

The siting program can also be used to create a data file containing information needed to produce alarm assignment cards corresponding to the new arrangement of fire companies. The data file contains, for every

1ST DUE ENGINE RESPONSE

15 TARGET HAZARDS		CURRENT	PROPOSED (270 ALARMS, 102 STRUCTS.)
AV. TR.T.		1.69	1.56
AV. TR.D.		0.57	0.49
AV. TR.T.	TO STRUCTURALS	1.52	1.42
AV. TR.D.	TO STRUCTURALS	0.47	0.41
MAX TR.T.		2.71	3.09

FIGURE 10.6. Siting model: First-due engine statistics averaged over all 15 target hazards in the city.

	BOX	TRV. DIST.		TRV. TIME	
		CURR.	PROP.	CURR.	PROP.
*	207	0.84	1.40	2.14	3.09
*	506	0.12	0.83	0.93	2.13
	612	0.23	0.23	1.12	1.12
*	707	0.33	0.41	1.28	1.43
*	804	0.58	0.41	1.70	1.43
*	807	0.51	0.26	1.60	1.17
*	809	0.74	0.16	1.97	1.01
*	810	0.51	0.36	1.60	1.35
	901	0.84	0.84	2.14	2.14
	911	0.58	0.58	1.70	1.70
*	1011	0.81	0.62	2.09	1.78
	1210	0.41	0.41	1.43	1.43
*	1416	0.62	0.00	1.78	0.73
*	1419	1.17	0.58	2.71	1.70
	1704	0.23	0.23	1.12	1.12

FIGURE 10.7. Siting model: Detailed first-due engine statistics for each target hazard. Asterisks indicate target hazards with different first-due travel times in the current and proposed configurations.

FIGURE 10.8. Siting model: Histograms of first-due engine travel times, citywide and by demand region.

DISTRIBUTION OF TRAVEL TIMES TO BOXES- CITYWIDE

TR TIME	0.5	1.0	1.5	2.0	2.5	3.0	3.5	4.0
# BOXES		18	97	110	85	46	35	7

DISTRIBUTION OF TRAVEL TIMES TO BOXES- REGION 1

TR TIME	0.5	1.0	1.5	2.0	2.5	3.0
# BOXES		8	37	20	5	1

DISTRIBUTION OF TRAVEL TIMES TO BOXES- REGION 2

TR TIME	0.5	1.0	1.5	2.0	2.5	3.0	3.5	4.0
# BOXES		2	11	17	11	8	8	1

DISTRIBUTION OF TRAVEL TIMES TO BOXES- REGION 3

TR TIME	0.5	1.0	1.5	2.0	2.5	3.0	3.5	4.0
# BOXES		5	27	46	44	26	19	6

DISTRIBUTION OF TRAVEL TIMES TO BOXES- REGION 4

TR TIME	0.5	1.0	1.5	2.0	2.5	3.0	3.5
# BOXES		3	22	27	25	11	8

1ST DUE ENGINE RESPONSE

CO.	BOXES		AV. TR.T.		MAX TR.T.		ALARMS		STRUCTURALS	
	CURR.	PROP.	CURR.	PROP.	CURR.	PROP.	CURR.	PROP.	CURR.	PROP.
* 1	14	22	1.71	1.48	2.49	2.25	492	692	199	268
* 2	9	0	1.17	0.00	1.51	0.00	356	0	141	0
* 3	98	96	2.40	2.38	3.80	3.80	325	373	124	150
* 5	45	48	1.70	1.69	2.40	2.40	349	313	116	106
* 6	56	41	1.72	1.95	2.47	3.43	776	842	271	327
7	17	18	1.27	1.29	1.78	1.78	642	693	286	314
* 8	26	48	1.60	1.95	2.52	3.10	650	879	281	342
9	58	58	2.09	2.09	3.59	3.59	254	254	86	86
* 10	75	67	2.15	1.81	3.55	2.73	886	684	368	279

FIGURE 10.9. Siting model: First-due response area statistics for engine companies. Asterisks denote companies whose response areas are different in the current and proposed configurations.

alarm box, lists of engine companies and ladder companies located closest to the box, each list ordered by estimated travel distance. Another output option allows the user to create a data file for producing computer-generated maps of alarm density or of the distribution of travel times throughout the city. This option may also be used to display the locations of the boxes affected by the change in the arrangement of firehouses. Figure 10.10 is a computer-generated map of Jersey City, New Jersey, showing the geographic pattern of structural alarms that occurred in that city in 1973.

10.2.3 Evaluating Alternative Firehouse Arrangements

There are many ways to use the information provided as output by the descriptive models to evaluate alternative arrangements of fire companies. To make most effective use of the output from any of the programs, the department's planners would tabulate many different performance measures. They would then identify and summarize important results so that the relative rankings of the various arrangements of fire companies could be assessed. For example, a project team that used the siting model in Wilmington, Delaware (Walker et al., 1975) developed a matrix that provided a comparison of some of the key outputs from the model. Figure 10.11 presents a sample of such a matrix that compares first-due engine data for the then existing configuration of companies to six other configurations, each of which has one less engine company than the existing one.

The FSLP provides a form called the Location Run Abstract (Figure 10.12) on which users can record pertinent information for comparing the output from up to seven runs. The FSLP Project Operations Guide says: "Since any single . . . run can result in considerable quantities of output, particularly if several response time values are used, a simplifying system is needed to make the results comprehensible. The Location Run Abstract is designed to provide the project team with a 'quick look' at the premises and outcome of one or more computer runs."

Once the large amount of information in the output reports has been reduced and displayed in such matrices, some alternatives may be identifiable as clearly unacceptable. For example, two demand regions that have approximately the same fire hazards and demands might be found to have very different travel times. A new trial configuration would then be designed, and one of the models would be used to determine whether an adequate improvement has been made. In the Wilmington study, one criterion used to evaluate alternatives was that any change to the existing arrangement must result in no significant increase in the first-due travel times and no major increase in the imbalance of workloads among companies. This criterion led to the elimination of many alternatives. When

FIGURE 10.10. The geographic density of structural alarms in Jersey City, New Jersey, 1973.

Region	Existing	A	B	C	D	E	F
CITYWIDE							
Avg. travel time	1.98	2.00	2.07	1.99	2.01	2.00	1.96
Avg. travel time to structurals	1.44	1.44	1.43	1.43	1.42	1.44	1.50
Max. travel time	3.86	3.86	4.75	3.86	3.86	3.86	4.03
REGION 1							
Avg. travel time	1.49	1.75	1.58	1.72	1.72	1.75	1.59
Avg. travel time to structurals	1.36	1.39	1.37	1.38	1.38	1.39	1.44
Max. travel time	2.41	2.95	2.42	2.83	2.83	2.95	2.51
REGION 2							
Avg. travel time	2.08	2.03	2.08	2.04	2.04	2.03	2.06
Avg. travel time to structurals	1.63	1.65	1.68	1.66	1.66	1.65	1.79
Max. travel time	3.70	3.68	3.68	3.68	3.68	3.68	3.39
REGION 3							
Avg. travel time	2.31	2.30	2.51	2.30	2.30	2.30	2.22
Avg. travel time to structurals	1.57	1.55	1.56	1.55	1.55	1.55	1.59
Max. travel time	3.87	3.86	4.75	3.86	3.86	3.86	4.03
REGION 4							
Avg. travel time	1.72	1.63	1.63	1.63	1.67	1.63	1.71
Avg. travel time to structurals	1.42	1.35	1.35	1.35	1.32	1.35	1.46
Max. travel time	2.51	2.52	2.52	2.52	2.75	2.52	2.71
WORKLOADS							
Busiest engine (first-due alarms, FY 1973)	397	587	364	545	459	587	468
Least busy engine (first-due alarms, FY 1973)	116	129	116	104	104	104	116

FIGURE 10.11. A comparison of siting model results for seven configurations of engine companies. All travel times are first-due engine travel times, in minutes.

the number of alternatives had been reduced to a workable number, considerations such as second-due travel times, availability of land, land use, terrain, and traffic patterns came into more active consideration and led to the elimination of several more possibilities.

It is unlikely that the results for several configurations will produce a particular arrangement that is obviously the best to all the concerned parties. Tradeoffs must be made considering the relative values of first-due and second-due travel times, within regions, variations in travel times among regions, and the concerns and interests of community organizations, labor unions, and good-government groups. Therefore, a set of alternatives, together with their expected performance measures, would be presented to the decisionmaker for consideration. Ultimately, someone who understands the entire operational and political context of the department and the city must decide which of the arrangements studied appears best, all things considered, or whether still more arrangements should be analyzed.

10.2.4 Data Requirements

Siting Model. Most of the data required by the siting model are related to a set of subareas (alarm boxes) or to the current arrangement of fire companies. The data for each alarm box include:

Its location, given by its (x,y) coordinates on a grid map of the city.

Its identification number.

The number of alarms that occurred at that box in the past year (or that are projected to occur).

The number of structural alarms that occurred at that box (or that are projected to occur).

An indication of whether the box is considered a "target hazard" (more important than the others for achieving rapid response).

The demand region to which the box belongs.

The data on the current arrangement of fire companies include:

The location of each fire company, given by its (x,y) coordinates on the same grid as is used for locating alarm boxes.

An identifying name for each fire company.

An ordered list of the closest fire companies to each alarm box. (If this information is not easily available the program can generate it using the grid locations or the fire companies and alarm boxes.)

In addition, the function for estimating travel distances, and the relationship between travel distance and travel time, must be specified in terms of one of the functions described in Section 10.2.1.

Fire Station Location Package. The FSLP has similar data requirements related to the set of fire demand zones and firehouse sites (both current and proposed). It also has data requirements related to the street network of the city.[7]

---

[7] As indicated in Section 10.2.1, the street network consists of street segments called "arcs" that connect focal points, firehouse sites, and key street intersections, all of which are identified as "nodes" in the network.

PTI FIRE STATION LOCATION PACKAGE
LOCATION RUN ABSTRACT†

☐ Single Run   ☐ Multiple Run Comparison

Part 1: RUN NUMBER										
Part 2: NETWORK ASSUMPTIONS*										
☐ Network Name**										
☐ No. Focal Points										
☐ No. Station Sites										
Part 3: POLICY INPUTS**										
☐ Station Site Record*										
• No. Seeded Sites										
• No. Deleted Sites										
☐ Response Time*										
• Minimum										
• Maximum										
• Increment										
☐ Incident Tally Flag										

☐ Time Deviation File**

Part 4: SOLUTION RECORD*

☐ Uncovered Zones*
- Total No. Zones
- No. Uncovered Zones

☐ Sites in Solution*
- Total No. Sites
- No. Current Sites
- No. Potential Sites

☐ Response Time Analysis*
- Avg. for Covered Zones
- Avg. for all Zones

☐ Travel Time Dist.***

* Check block if additional comments are appended to this abstract.
** That is, the identifying code number or other designation.
*** Check block if LOCATION Display 3(B) is appended to this abstract.
† For a detailed explanation of the information that is to be placed on this form, see *Fire Station Location Package* (1974).

FIGURE 10.12. FSLP: Location Run Abstract

The data for each arc include:

Its origin and destination node identification number.

Its length.

The average speed at which a fire company would traverse it.

Its direction (indicating whether it is a one-way or two-way street).

The data for each firehouse site include:

Its node identification number.

Its firehouse site identification number (each site is assigned a number in sequence).

An alphanumeric name for the site.

The data for each fire demand zone include:

The node identification number for the focal point that represents all of the properties within the FDZ.

Its FDZ/focal point identification number (each FDZ is assigned a number in sequence).

The total number of alarms that occurred in the FDZ during a selected historical period (or a projection for a future period).

The relative travel-time requirement for the FDZ.

10.2.5 Resources Needed for Implementation

The FSLP and the siting model may both be run in batch mode on a medium-sized computer. The siting model is written in FORTRAN. On a PDP-10 computer it requires 27,000 words of core storage for a city with 750 alarm boxes and 30 fire companies (approximately equivalent to 108K bytes of core storage on an IBM System 360 or 370 computer).

The documented version of FSLP includes three programs, one of which is written in FORTRAN and the other two, in PL/1. The FORTRAN program (called PATH) calculates the travel time between pairs of points using a street network of the city. For a city with 1000 arcs in the network, the program requires 70K bytes of core storage. One of the PL/1 programs (called CONFORM) reads the table of travel times produced by PATH and reformats it for input into the other PL/1 program. It will generally require less than 40K bytes of core storage. The second PL/1 program (called LOCATION) produces the output described in Section 10.2.2. It requires 90K bytes of core storage for a city with 300 focal points and 25 firehouse sites.[8]

---

[8] The October 1976 version of the FSLP is composed of only two programs; PATH (written in FORTRAN) and LOCATION (written in COBOL). CONFORM has been made a part of LOCATION.

10.2 Two Descriptive Models 399

Agencies wishing to use either of these models in batch mode must have access to a computer on which the appropriate languages are available. Public Technology, Inc. offers to run the FSLP for those communities lacking the necessary computer resources.

The siting model is available for use through a national computer time-sharing service.[9] A department wishing to use the model in this way need only have access to a computer terminal that can be coupled to the computer via telephone.

The time and effort required to set up the siting model for use in a particular city depends on whether: (a) grid locations have been determined for alarm boxes and firehouse locations; (b) computerized files of reports on alarms have been maintained; and (c) the city has been divided into regions of similar firefighting demands. If these conditions are met, then a management analyst can set up the model in two or three man-weeks. Otherwise, an additional two or three man-months will probably be required to collect and process the data. The total cost for using the siting model in a study has been reported to average $14,000, with a range from $10,000 to $30,000 (Chaiken, 1977). For example, in a firehouse location study performed in Miami, Florida, in which over 75 runs of the siting model were examined before a final configuration was identified, the cost was $15,000. Less than one person-month was expended on the preparation of data, and ten person-months were expended on the analysis of output. The analysis included the evaluation of new firehouse locations, the addition of new apparatus, the moving of apparatus to respond to changing workloads, and possible company reductions and firehouse closings. (See Eichelberger and Farren (1977).)

The time and effort required to set up the FSLP for use in a city depends on whether or not a computer-readable street network for the city already exists. Public Technology, Inc. provides a table of estimated personnel requirements for implementing the FSLP. The figures (shown in Table 10.1) are estimates derived from their experience in a number of cities that did not already have street networks. The documentation of the FSLP states: "For most jurisdictions, the use of the PTI package requires 4 to 6 calendar months' work by staff people to develop the data base and other mathematical information needs for computer operation. Overall, project implementation can take from 3 to 6 additional calendar months, depending on the size of the jurisdiction. Personnel levels can range from 20 to 80 person-weeks of effort." (*Fire Station Location Package*, 1974). A more recent report shows that a median of 14 person-months were expended by users of the FSLP, with a range from 2 to 264 person-months (*The PTI Fire Station Location Package: Effectiveness Survey Analysis*, 1977). The causes for such a large range were not clearly identified, but the jurisdictions with low numbers of person-months ex-

---
[9] Compu-Serv Network, Inc., Columbus, Ohio.

TABLE 10.1. Estimated time and personnel requirements to implement the FSLP. Source: *Fire Station Location Package: Project Leader's Guide* (1974).

General Population Category	Minimum am Size	Minimum Calendar Weeks		
		Data Preparation	Data Analysis	Total Implementation Time
1,000,000 and above	5	20	16	36
500,000–1,000,000	4	16	14	30
250,000–500,000	3	12	10	22
100,000–250,000	2	10	8	18
50,000–100,000	2	6	8	14
25,000–50,000	1	4	6	10
10,000–25,000	1	4	6	10
5,000–10,000	1	2	4	6
5,000 and below	1	1	3	4

pended most likely had a serviceable computer-readable street network of the city prepared for other purposes.

10.2.6 History of Use

The Firehouse Site Evaluation Model was used in four cities with direct assistance from members of the staff of The New York City–Rand Institute: Jersey City (Rider et al., 1975); Trenton (Hausner and Walker, 1975; and Section 10.4 of this book); Wilmington (Walker et al., 1975; and Singleton, 1975); and Yonkers (Hausner, Walker, and Swersey, 1974; and Section 14.1 of this book). Both Jersey City and Yonkers installed the program on their own computer systems and have used the model for deployment studies performed without the help of the Institute's staff.

Subsequently, nine individuals or government agencies received copies of the program. Nearly all recipients have used it in deployment studies, and operational changes appear likely to occur eventually in every instance of use. Documented results have been published in two cases.

In Miami, Florida, analysts in the city's Planning Department and Fire Department used the siting model as part of their Master Planning work, with no outside technical assistance. They developed a ten-year plan for construction of firehouses (Eichelberger and Farren, 1977). A professor and a graduate student in the Industrial Engineering Department of Lehigh University used the siting model in a study designed to improve the effectiveness of the fire department in Allentown, Pennsylvania. They investigated a number of alternative firehouse configurations, and proposed several locations for new houses that would provide improved fire protection service (Groover and Fagan, 1977). A complete listing of all the users of the siting model as of May 1977 is given by Chaiken (1977).

The Fire Station Location Package has been used by Fire Departments in over 50 cities. In October 1976, PTI surveyed all the jurisdictions known to have implemented the FSLP as of that date. The results are reported in *The PTI Fire Station Location Package: Effectiveness Survey Analysis* (1977). They found that 36 jurisdictions had already completed a station location study, and that 31 of these had taken action as a result of the study (made a final location decision, acquired land, built a station, or closed a station). Many cities changed their future fire station plans in order to adopt plans, based on the results of the studies, that would have lower costs, better service or (in some cases) both. The use of the model in specific cities is not discussed in the report.

10.3 A PRESCRIPTIVE MODEL

The Fire Station Location Package also has a prescriptive mode of operation. In this mode the FSLP will choose from a large set of potential firehouse locations the smallest subset that will provide certain required travel times to a set of points in the community. The travel time requirements are specified in advance.

In order to determine this set of firehouse locations, the FSLP solves a mathematical problem known as a "covering problem." Numbering the potential firehouse sites $1, 2, \ldots, K$ and the set of focal points $1, 2, \ldots, M$, the covering problem is to:

minimize

$$\sum_{j=1}^{K} x_j$$

subject to

$$\sum_{j=1}^{K} a_{ij} x_j \geq 1, \quad i = 1, 2, \ldots, M,$$

where

$$a_{ij}(\text{input variable}) = \begin{cases} 1 & \text{if station } j \text{ would satisfy the first-due travel time requirement for demand point } i \\ 0 & \text{otherwise} \end{cases}$$

and

$$x_j(\text{output variable}) = \begin{cases} 1 & \text{if firehouse site } j \text{ is used} \\ 0 & \text{otherwise.} \end{cases}$$

It is possible to force some of the x_j to be 1 or 0 in the final solution (i.e., either they must be in the final solution ($x_j = 1$) or they cannot be allowed to appear in the final solution ($x_j = 0$)). For example, if a firehouse has been recently constructed, the city might want to require that it be part of any solution. So it would require that $x_j = 1$ for that firehouse.

In theory, solving the covering problem solves the firehouse location problem. In practice, however, there are several things that must be kept in mind when using the FSLP in this mode. First, and most important, there are no accepted standards to use in setting the travel-time requirements. Therefore, the requirements must be set subjectively. As David Gratz (1972) wrote in reviewing a forerunner of the FSLP: "In planning for the location of fire stations, the overriding consideration is to keep response time within accepted limits. Unfortunately, there is no specific definition of 'accepted limits'."

Second, instead of the number of fire companies being an input variable (since it is more or less fixed by the department's budget level), the number of companies (or company houses) is an output variable. So, for a given set of travel-time requirements, the number of firehouses needed may exceed any reasonable budget level. As a result, the problem generally must be solved several times with different travel-time requirements until the resulting solution conforms to the budget constraints. To facilitate this process, the FSLP contains a provision for solving the covering problem for a number of different travel-time requirements in a single run of the program.

Third, the FSLP does not distinguish between locations already having firehouses and potential new sites. The model will find a solution with the smallest number of firehouses. There may, however, be alternative solutions having the same number of houses, but with more existing firehouses included in the solution. Such solutions are to be preferred, since their capital cost requirements will be lower.

A project team at the Denver Urban Observatory, which was funded by the U.S. Department of Housing and Urban Development, modified the FSLP to eliminate the third difficulty, as part of their work on locating Denver's fire companies (Hendrick et al., 1974). They changed the objective function in the FSLP to be

$$\min \sum_{j=1}^{p} x_j + \sum_{j=p+1}^{K} (1 + \epsilon)x_j,$$

where firehouse sites numbered 1, 2, . . . , p are existing locations, and sites numbered $p + 1$, $p + 2$, . . . , K are new sites. If the value of ϵ is chosen small enough, solving the problem with the new objective function will produce a solution that minimizes the number of firehouses needed to satisfy the travel-time requirements while maximizing the number of existing houses in the minimum set. In their report, Hendrick et al. describe the Denver project's experience in using both the original FSLP and the modified version for locating firehouses in Denver.

10.4 USING THE SITING MODEL IN TRENTON, NEW JERSEY

We now turn to a specific example, the redeployment of fire companies in Trenton, New Jersey, to illustrate how one of the descriptive models can be used to evaluate alternative arrangements of fire companies.[10]

The immediate problem in Trenton was that all of its firehouses were old, and some were in serious need of renovation or reconstruction. This gave the city the opportunity to embark on a comprehensive examination of the deployment of all of its fire companies. In particular, the objective of the portion of the study described here was to find ways to deploy Trenton's nine engine companies and four truck companies to improve fire protection in the city.

Trenton was partitioned into six demand regions, based on homogeneity of population density, land use, housing stock, and alarm rates within each region. Figure 10.13 is a map of Trenton showing the boundaries of the six demand regions and the locations of all firefighting equipment deployed in the city at the start of the study.

Table 10.2 summarizes some of the demographic and alarm incidence characteristics of the six regions. Demand Region 4 is the most densely populated part of Trenton. This region also encompasses the central business district, as well as the state, county, and municipal office buildings, so that in the daytime, the population is swelled by shoppers and business people. As a result, the potential demand for fire protection is greater than in other regions. It also has a higher realized demand (alarm density); in particular, a higher density of structural fires. Demand Region 2 ranks second in terms of both population density and alarm density. Demand Regions 1, 3, 5, and 6 are all similar to each other; they have similar housing stock and relatively low population and alarm densities. Whatever criteria are used, a reasonable allocation of resources within the city would be one that produces similar travel times in each of these four regions.

Since little information was available at the time to indicate how quickly fire companies respond to fires and how travel times vary with

---

[10] A complete description of the Trenton study is presented in Hausner and Walker (1975).

TABLE 10.2 Summary of demand region characteristics.

Demand Region	Area (square miles)	Population			1970 Population Density (pop./square mile)	Alarm Incidence, 1973					
						Number of Alarms			Alarm Densities (Alarms per square mile)		
		1960	1970	Percent change		Total	Structural	False	Total	Structural	False
1	1.76	18,017	15,753	−12.8%	8,951	609	111	216	346	63	123
2	.92	18,147	17,408	− 4.1%	18,913	676	176	189	735	191	205
3	.48	6,700	6,015	−10.2%	12,521	139	29	15	290	60	31
4	.38	12,753	10,744	−15.7%	28,274	379	94	84	997	247	221
5	2.72	19,182	18,240	− 4.9%	6,706	1,123	323	268	413	119	99
6	2.20	39,370	36,278	− 7.8%	16,486	721	162	156	329	74	71
Total	8.46	114,169	104,438	− 8.5%	12,345[a]	3,650	895	928	431[a]	106[a]	110[a]

[a] Number is an average density, not a total.

10.4 Using the Siting Model in Trenton, New Jersey

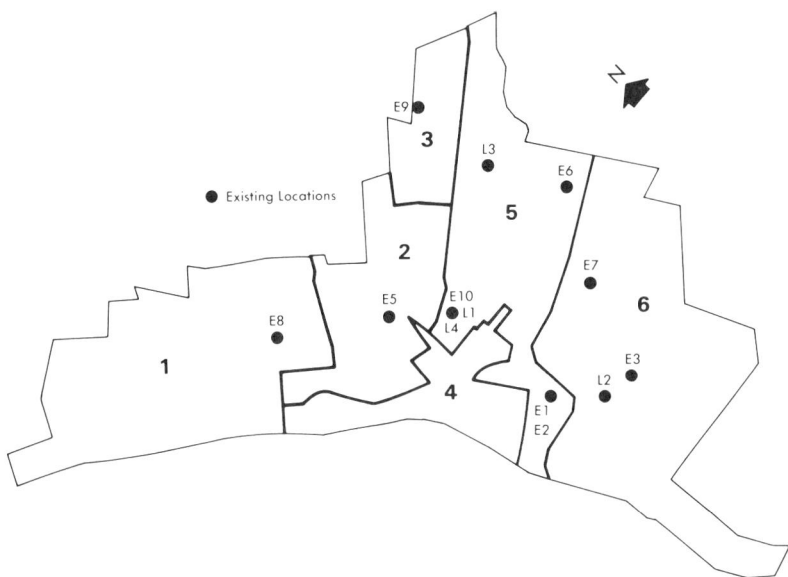

FIGURE 10.13. Trenton: Map of demand regions and fire company locations.

distance, an experiment was conducted to gather this information. (The experiment was similar to the one described in Chapter 6 for New York City.) Fire companies representing a cross section of all geographic and topographic areas in Trenton were equipped with stopwatches and coding forms, and asked to record data every time they responded to an incident. The data were keypunched and processed by computer to determine the relationship between travel time and travel distance. (The program used to obtain these estimates is given by Hausner, 1975.) The best estimates of travel time were given by the function:

$$T = \begin{cases} 1.914\sqrt{D} & D \leq 0.31 \text{ mile} \\ 0.533 + 1.719 \times D & D \geq 0.31 \text{ mile}, \end{cases} \quad (10.3)$$

where D is the travel distance in miles, and the travel time, T, is expressed in minutes. This relationship is shown graphically in Figure 10.14.

Trenton's Department of Planning and Development prepared a grid for a map of the city from which (x, y) coordinates were obtained for the city's 664 fire alarm boxes and 10 firehouses. The siting model estimated the distance D, between an alarm box with grid coordinates (x_1, y_1) and a firehouse with grid coordinates (x_2, y_2), as

$$D = 1.15 \sqrt{(x_2 - x_1)^2 + (y_2 - y_1)^2}. \quad (10.4)$$

Given an estimate of the travel distance, the resulting travel time was estimated by using Equation (10.3).

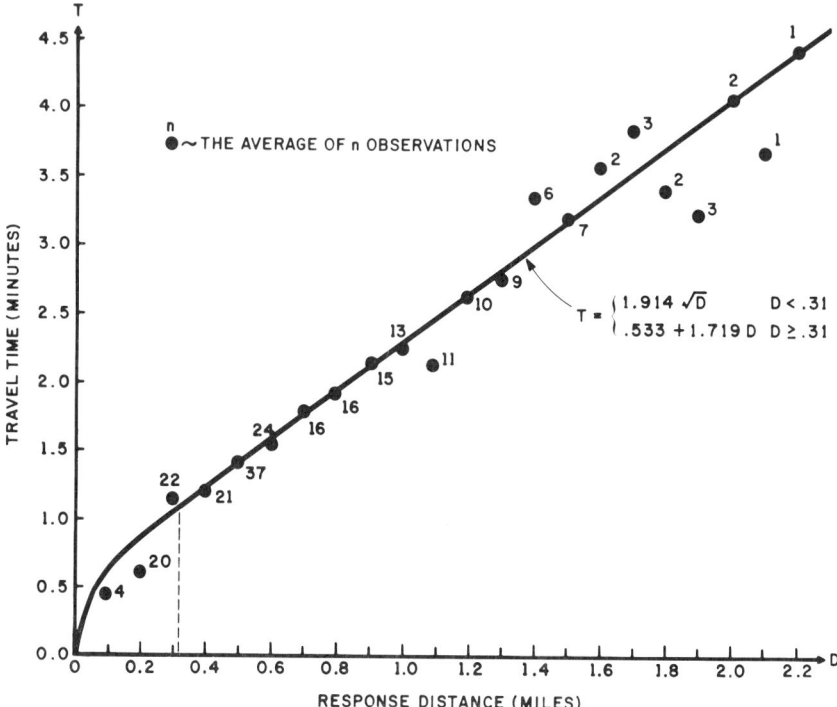

FIGURE 10.14. Trenton: Relationship between travel time and response distance.

10.4.1 The Existing Deployment of Fire Companies[11]

First-Due Engine Companies. Table 10.3 shows first- and second-due travel times obtained from the siting model for the configuration of engine and ladder companies in Trenton when the study began. The results show, for example, that at that time, the first-due engine travel times in the demand regions were not consistent with the relative population and alarm densities in the regions. Region 4, Trenton's downtown area, should have had enough engine companies assigned in and around it to produce the lowest average travel times in the city, since it had the greatest hazards, the highest population density, and the highest alarm density. However, Region 4 had the fifth highest average first-due engine travel time of the six demand regions. Therefore, an objective of the

---

[11] In the following material, "existing" refers to the situation in Trenton during the period of this study (i.e., 1974).

TABLE 10.3. Estimated existing first- and second-due travel times (in minutes).

Demand Region	First-Due Engine		Second-Due Engine		First-Due Ladder		Second-Due Ladder	
	Average Travel Time	Maximum Travel Time	Average Travel Time	Maximum Travel Time	Average Travel Time	Maximum Travel Time	Average Travel Time	Maximum Travel Time
1	2.00	5.01	3.82	7.50	4.02	6.52	4.02	6.52
2	1.41	3.35	2.28	4.24	1.75	3.25	1.80	3.25
3	1.15	1.85	2.79	4.03	1.74	2.34	2.93	4.05
4	1.62	3.38	1.68	3.91	1.65	3.02	1.77	3.02
5	1.19	1.80	1.82	2.69	1.35	2.66	2.11	3.97
6	1.53	4.17	1.91	3.63	1.68	3.60	3.28	5.79
Citywide	1.51	5.01	2.31	7.50	2.02	6.52	2.78	6.52

redeployment of the existing configuration of fire companies was to reduce the first-due engine travel time in Region 4 relative to the other demand regions.

Maximum first-due engine travel times varied considerably, ranging from 1.85 minutes in Region 3 to 5.01 minutes in Region 1. Region 6 had the second highest maximum first-due engine travel time—4.17 minutes—followed by Region 4, with 3.38 minutes. The travel-time frequency distributions obtained from the siting model show that of the 664 fire-alarm boxes located in Trenton, only 36 were more than three minutes from the closest engine. Eighteen of these 36 boxes were located in Region 1, eight in Region 6, five in Region 4, and five in Region 2. This information indicated that another objective of redeployment of fire companies should be to seek to reduce the number of such long travel times, particularly for responses in Region 4, the region with the highest level of potential and realized demand.

The citywide average second-due travel time was 2.31 minutes. By region, second-due average travel times for engines ranged from 1.68 minutes in Region 4 to 3.82 minutes in Region 1, and were more consistent with fire protection demands than the first-due engine travel times. Region 4, which was surrounded by five engine companies, had the lowest average second-due travel time, receiving protection that, in this case, reflects the firefighting hazards in the central business district, where more units must arrive at the scene of a fire quickly. The less populated, more residential areas, such as Regions 1 and 3, had higher second-due engine travel times, consistent with their lower hazards and alarm rates.

The maximum second-due engine travel time in Region 1 was 7.50 minutes. This is more than three minutes longer than the maximum second-due travel time in any other region of the city. Except for Region 1, maximum travel times were not unreasonably high, although a redeployment might be able to improve them somewhat. Region 4, which had the highest population and alarm densities, and Region 2, which ranked second in both densities, ranked third and fifth, respectively, in terms of maximum second-due travel time. Of the 53 fire-alarm boxes to which second-due engine travel times exceeded four minutes, 49 were located in Region 1, two in Region 2, and two in Region 3, emphasizing the magnitude of the second-due engine problem in Region 1.

First-Due Ladder Companies. An examination of the ladder travel times in Table 10.3 does not reveal as many problems as were found for engines. The only real difficulty was in Region 1, an area served by a ladder company that was moved from its original house when that house could no longer be used, without changing its area of responsibility. Therefore, the first-due ladder travel times to boxes in Region 1 when only one ladder is dispatched were very high, averaging 4.02 minutes, compared to well-balanced average travel times ranging from 1.35 minutes to 1.74 minutes in the other five regions.

Maximum first-due ladder travel times were also well-balanced. The exception, again, was Region 1, which had a maximum travel time of 6.52 minutes. There are 50 alarm boxes to which the first-due ladder travel time exceeded four minutes, and all 50 were located in Region 1.

In looking for alternative locations for the four ladder companies, an appropriate strategy would be to reduce the average and maximum first-due ladder travel times in Region 1, and to make the first-due ladder travel times in Regions 2 and 4 better than the other regions, because of the higher potential and realized demands in Regions 2 and 4.

10.4.2 The Redeployment of Fire Companies

In this section we show how the siting model was used to evaluate alternative redeployments of Trenton's existing fire companies. The objective was to find ways to improve fire protection levels and make them more consistent with the regional fire hazards and alarm rates. The siting model was used to examine several arrangements of fire companies, some of which were suggested by the Trenton Fire Department, some of which were suggested by analysts on the project team, and some of which were generated by the Parametric Allocation Model (Chapter 9). The results presented are for the configurations selected by the city as the best, based on a number of factors, including results from the siting model.

Ladders. In analyzing the deployment of the four ladder companies in Trenton, primary emphasis was placed on first-due ladder times for the reasons just stated. Results are presented for two alternative configurations, named Option 1 and Option 2, and a method for comparing them is described. In each configuration, Ladder 1 is moved to a new location west of its current location. Under Option 1 it is moved to Point A on the map in Figure 10.15. Under Option 2 it is moved to Point B.

Table 10.4 summarizes the effects on travel time in the various demand regions resulting from the two redeployments of ladder companies. Under Option 1, average citywide travel time drops from 2.02 minutes to 1.75 minutes, a decrease of 13 percent. Average travel times in the six demand regions range from 1.27 minutes in Region 2 to 3.00 minutes in Region 1. Region 4, the central business district, has an average travel time of 1.40 minutes. Thus, the average travel times in the more populous, high alarm rate regions are still substantially lower than the average travel time in Region 1.

Under Option 2, the average citywide travel time is further reduced. The average travel times in the six demand regions show less variability,

FIGURE 10.15. Proposed redeployment of ladder companies.

ranging from 1.35 minutes in Region 5 to 1.74 minutes in Region 3. In fact, the expected travel time for the first-due ladder is almost the same in each region; but the average and maximum travel times in Regions 2 and 4 are higher than under Option 1.

Both of these options offer better fire protection than the existing deployment of ladder companies, since most average and maximum travel times are reduced and none are increased. But the question of which of the two options is better is more difficult to answer. In attempting to answer it, we must look at the *affected region*[12] for each of the options, and then consider three aspects of fire protection:

1. travel time to structural fires (realized demand)
2. travel time to all points in the city (coverage)
3. travel time to hazards (potential demand).

Useful information for performing this analysis, which was obtained from the siting model, is presented in Table 10.5.

(1) Travel Times to Structural Fires. Option 1 reduces average travel time to the 198 alarm boxes in its affected region by an average of 0.90

---

[12] See Section 10.2.2.

10.4 Using the Siting Model in Trenton, New Jersey

TABLE 10.4. Average and maximum first-due ladder travel times (in minutes) for the three configurations of ladder companies.

Area	Existing		Option 1		Option 2	
	Average	Maximum	Average	Maximum	Average	Maximum
Citywide	2.02	6.52	1.75	5.41	1.60	3.60
Region 1	4.02	6.52	3.00	5.41	1.67	3.57
Region 2	1.75	3.25	1.27	2.18	1.66	2.25
Region 3	1.74	2.34	1.74	2.34	1.74	2.34
Region 4	1.65	3.02	1.40	2.36	1.54	2.94
Region 5	1.35	2.66	1.35	2.60	1.35	2.66
Region 6	1.68	3.60	1.68	3.60	1.68	3.60

minutes. Option 2 reduces average travel time to the 140 boxes in its affected region by 1.97 minutes. From a travel-time point of view, the importance of these improvements is reflected in the number of structural fires that can be expected to be reached with these improved travel times. We can estimate the total expected decrease in travel time to structural fires by taking the product of the change in travel time and the historical number of structural fires at these boxes. Under Option 1, where the affected region had 245 structural fires in 1973, the total reduction in travel time would be 0.90 minutes × 245 structural fires = 220.5 minutes. A similar calculation for Option 2, which had 155 structural fires in its affected region in 1973, yields a total reduction in travel time of 305.4 minutes. Thus, Option 2 is expected to have a better effect on travel times to structural fires than Option 1. (Note that the actual values of the travel time reductions are not very useful; it is the relative values that are of the most interest.)

(2) Travel Time to All Points in the City. To improve the general level of fire protection in the city, the more alarm boxes to which travel time improves, the better. One way to measure the change in this fire protection characteristic is to compute the product of the change in average travel time and the number of alarm boxes in the affected region. Under

TABLE 10.5. Summary of changes in the first-due ladder affected region for each option.

Affected Region Measure	Option 1	Option 2
Reduction in average travel time (minutes)	0.90	1.97
Number of alarm boxes	198	140
Number of alarms in 1973	1155	790
Number of structural fires in 1973	245	155

Option 1, coverage in the affected region improves by 0.90 minutes × 198 boxes = 178.2 minutes. Under Option 2, coverage improves by 1.97 minutes × 140 boxes = 275.80 minutes. Again, Option 2 is better than Option 1.

(3) Travel Time to Hazards. The results presented show that Option 2 is better in terms of both average travel time to structural fires, and coverage. However, under Option 1 the ladder company is located closer to the greater fire hazards in Demand Regions 2 and 4. The question of whether the difference in hazard levels is great enough to offset the improvements in coverage and average travel time has no clear answer. The determination of which of the two options to implement must include a subjective evaluation of the relative hazards (the potential loss of life and property) associated with the properties surrounding Ladder 1 in each location, and a consideration of the political constraints that enter such a policy decision, as well as the quantitative measures calculated above.

Engines. A three-phase redeployment of Trenton's nine engine companies was developed that would improve travel times throughout the city. The primary effect of Phase 1 is to reduce first- and second-due travel times in Regions 2 and 4. Phase 2 reduces average travel time in Region 1, but more importantly, it reduces the number of boxes to which the first-due travel time is greater than three minutes and the second-due travel time is greater than four minutes. Phase 3 reduces the number of long first-due and second-due travel times in Region 6.

Figure 10.16 shows each of the moves on a map of Trenton. Table 10.6 summarizes the effect of the moves on travel times, showing the results for the final configuration, as well as the results after each of the two intermediate steps. The final configuration results in a reduction in the average citywide first-due engine travel time from the current 1.51 minutes to 1.29 minutes, and provides more balanced fire protection over the city. The greatest improvement is in Region 4, where the average travel time goes from 1.62 minutes to 1.24 minutes, a reduction of 23 percent. Regions 1 and 2 benefit almost as much. Average first-due travel time falls from 2.00 minutes to 1.65 minutes in Region 1, and from 1.41 minutes to 1.10 minutes in Region 2. In Region 6, average first-due travel time drops to 1.29 minutes from the current 1.53 minutes. The moves do not affect the average first-due travel times in Regions 3 or 5, where the average travel times remain 1.15 minutes and 1.19 minutes, respectively.

The three-phase redeployment results in a reduction in citywide maximum first-engine travel time of almost 30 percent, from 5.01 minutes to 3.57 minutes. The maximum first-due engine travel times in Region 1, 2, and 4 are reduced by approximately 1.5 minutes in each region, and the

TABLE 10.6. Average and maximum engine travel times (in minutes) for four configurations of engine companies.

Area Covered	Existing Deployment		After Phase 1		After Phase 2		After Phase 3	
	Average Travel Time	Maximum Travel Time	Average Travel Time	Maximum Travel Time	Average Travel Time	Maximum Travel Time	Average Travel Time	Maximum Travel Time
FIRST-DUE ENGINES								
Citywide	1.51	5.01	1.41	4.32	1.36	4.17	1.29	3.57
Region 1	2.00	5.01	1.97	4.32	1.65	3.57	1.65	3.57
Region 2	1.41	3.35	1.09	1.91	1.10	1.91	1.10	1.91
Region 3	1.15	1.85	1.15	1.85	1.15	1.85	1.15	1.85
Region 4	1.62	3.38	1.22	1.76	1.24	1.76	1.24	1.76
Region 5	1.19	1.80	1.19	1.80	1.19	1.80	1.19	1.80
Region 6	1.53	4.17	1.53	4.17	1.53	4.17	1.29	3.06
SECOND-DUE ENGINES								
Citywide	2.31	7.50	2.01	5.41	2.02	5.41	2.06	5.41
Region 1	3.82	7.50	2.97	5.41	3.01	5.41	3.01	5.41
Region 2	2.28	4.24	1.41	2.35	1.42	2.35	1.42	2.35
Region 3	2.79	4.03	2.79	4.03	2.79	4.03	2.79	4.03
Region 4	1.68	3.91	1.53	2.27	1.55	2.27	1.63	2.36
Region 5	1.82	2.69	1.73	2.68	1.73	2.68	1.80	2.68
Region 6	1.91	3.63	1.91	3.63	1.91	3.63	1.99	4.17

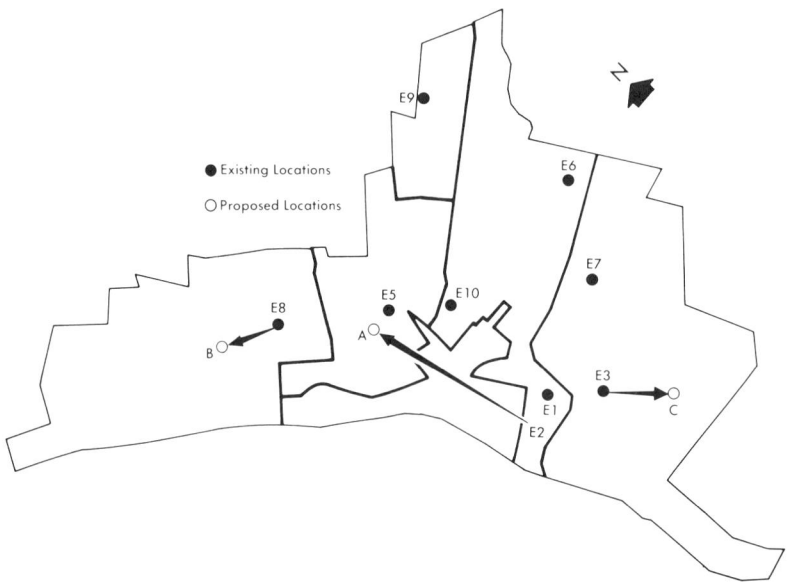

FIGURE 10.16. Proposed redeployment of engine companies.

maximum time in Region 6 is cut by over one minute, from 4.17 minutes to 3.06 minutes. More importantly, only eight of the 36 boxes that had first-due travel times of three minutes or more still have long travel times. Six of these boxes are located in Region 1 and two in Region 6.

Citywide travel time for second-due engines is also reduced. The average second-due travel time is improved from 2.31 minutes to 2.06 minutes. The greatest improvements occur in Regions 1 and 2. The average second-due travel time is reduced from 3.82 minutes to 3.01 minutes (21 percent) in Region 1 and from 2.28 minutes to 1.42 minutes (38 percent) in Region 2. Slight improvements also occur in Regions 4 and 5; there is no change in Region 3; and in Region 6, average second-due travel time is somewhat degraded, increasing from 1.91 minutes to 1.99 minutes (approximately 5 seconds, or 4 percent).

The citywide maximum second-due engine travel time is reduced by 28 percent, going from 7.50 minutes to 5.41 minutes. The greatest improvements occur in Regions 1, 2, and 4. In Region 6, the maximum travel time is increased by one-half minute, going from 3.63 minutes to 4.17 minutes. However, this higher maximum makes Region 6 comparable to two other regions of similar hazard, Regions 1 and 3, where the maximum second-engine travel times are 5.41 minutes and 4.03 minutes,

10.4 Using the Siting Model in Trenton, New Jersey 415

respectively. The redeployment leaves only 23 alarm boxes in Trenton to which the second-due engine travel time exceeds four minutes, compared to 53 alarm boxes prior to the redeployment. Of these, 18 are located in Region 1, two in Region 3, and three in Region 6. These are the three regions with the lowest population and alarm densities in Trenton.[13]

---

[13] A history of the implementation of the results of the Trenton study is given by Walker (1978).

Chapter 11
Initial Dispatch

Synopsis

Initial dispatch policies that worked well in the past may no longer be effective. Rising alarm rates, with an ever larger proportion of false alarms, have led to pressures for reducing the standard response. Should initial response be reduced? If so, should it be reduced to all locations and at all times of day?
  Improving initial dispatch policy requires:

1. *A suitable definition of a "serious" incident.*
2. *A scheme for classifying incidents according to the chance that they are serious, given the information that the dispatcher has when a decision is to be made.*

For initial dispatch, serious incidents are those to which speedy response is essential to prevent damage, injury, or death. Information that is useful in discriminating serious from nonserious incidents includes the time of day and whether more than one report of the incident has been received. The past history at the location (alarm box) in question can also be useful. In particular, the methods of Chapter 8 can give reliable predictions, from analysis of incidents in a region, of box-to-box differences in the chance that an alarm is serious.
  This chapter spells out the consequences of initially dispatching too few or too many units. Methods are given for quickly calculating the response times that would result from different kinds of dispatch policies, including traditional ones based on alarm assignment (running) cards. We find that, ideally, the initial dispatch to an incoming alarm should be based on the following four factors: the chance that the alarm is for a serious fire; the current alarm rate; the current availability of nearby companies; and the workload of companies. Some common dispatching policies ignore one or more of these factors; for example, reducing

response to "false alarm" boxes (which may also have many serious incidents) around the clock in an attempt to relieve a workload problem.

The first factor is the most important, and it forms the basis for a simple adaptive procedure that should be appropriate in many cities. This procedure attempts to get first and second ladders to serious fires quickly while controlling the total number of times a second ladder is dispatched. It can also be used similarly to improve engine company responses.

A computer procedure that is appropriate for regions with high alarm rates is developed. It determines both how many companies and which ones should be dispatched on the basis of the four factors just mentioned, incorporating the queuing considerations described in Chapter 7. Simulation tests of this procedure on an historical sequence of incidents show that it would improve second-engine and second-ladder response times to serious incidents significantly, while reducing some of the need for relocation.

11.1 INTRODUCTION

When an alarm is reported to a fire department, a decision must be made. How many of the department's fire companies, and which ones, should be sent to the alarm? Chapter 7 has presented simple models of these two aspects of the initial dispatch decision. In this chapter, we elaborate on them and tie them together.

The goal of an initial dispatch of fire companies is to get the necessary groups of men and equipment to an incident within an appropriate time. The resources needed and the appropriate response times differ from incident to incident. A small fire in a single-family dwelling, for example, might call for a quick response of two engines and a ladder. A serious fire in a large commercial structure might require a response of several engines and ladders. On the other hand, a rubbish fire would probably need only a single engine company within a reasonable length of time. How can the dispatch decision be tailored to the requirements of the incident?

In the past—when alarm rates were low and false alarms were relatively few—the decision was fairly simple. If the dispatcher had some information about the nature of the incident (based on a telephone call or other verbal report), he would dispatch what appeared to be required. If the alarm was received from a street box, the presumption was that it signaled a serious fire. A preplanned response, judged to be what was initially needed for serious fires in that area, was used.

Sending the full preplanned response to box alarms made obvious sense. If the fire turned out to be minor, the extra units simply returned to their houses. Since the alarm rate was low, there was little danger that they would be needed while they were out. If the fire was large, the required units were on the scene quickly. In addition, under the traditional dispatching policy, the closest companies were always sent—there was no reason to do otherwise.

Today we see rising alarm rates, tight municipal budgets, and, in some cities, individual fire companies that make thousands of responses annually. There is, therefore, more pressure to match the initial dispatch to what is needed at the fireground than there was years ago.

What are the stakes in this decision? On the one hand, there are increases in damage, injury, and death when too few units are sent. (We assume that, in these situations, the first units to reach the scene will call for reinforcements, so the losses result from delay in getting these units to the scene, not from their never being sent.) On the other hand, there are the direct and indirect costs of needless responses.

What can prevent an appropriate response from being achieved? There are two major factors. One is the dispatcher's uncertainty about the nature of the incident at the time he must make the decision. The other is how the dispatcher *uses* the available information (about the incident, company availability, etc.).

Consider first the dispatcher's uncertainty. If the dispatcher knew what resources were needed at the new incident, there would be no decision problem. The resources required could be dispatched (provided there was no disaster in progress that was already using most of the companies in the city) to the incident without any doubt as to whether the dispatch was appropriate.

Many cities use telegraph boxes for reporting incidents. When a signal is transmitted to the fire department, the dispatcher has no way of knowing what kind of incident is being reported. It may be a serious fire, a false alarm, or something in between. Even if an incident is reported by telephone, a dispatcher cannot rely on the informant to accurately communicate the seriousness of the incident. A large proportion of the fire might be out of sight; perhaps there are exposure dangers. On the other hand, the smoke might turn out to be a steam leak, or the report might be false.[1]

Therefore, the dispatcher is faced with making a decision based on incomplete information. The dispatch that is made, if it is a good dispatch, will make use of all the relevant information available. Anything that

---

[1] It is not possible to remove all uncertainty even when a firefighter or officer is on scene. The resources needed to control and extinguish are sometimes difficult to predict even after firefighting operations have begun. The occasional tragedies that take the lives of firefighters confirm the unpredictability of individual fires.

reduces uncertainty about the nature of the incident is relevant. This includes whatever information is provided by the report itself (what the callers say on a telephone alarm); the time of day (a telegraph box alarm just after school lets out is different from one at 4:00 A.M.); the weather; the location of the incident; and so forth. Also relevant (to the extent that the decision on the alarm in question affects the number of companies available to answer any alarms that might be received in the near future) is information about the current status of the city's companies. This leads us to the second major factor, how the information is used. The way in which all this information is incorporated into the decision process and used to determine a dispatch may be called a *policy*.

As in earlier chapters, we will discuss both engine and ladder companies. For brevity, we do not discuss the dispatch of rescue companies, other special-purpose units, and chief officers to the first report of an incident. We also will not consider the choice of follow-up dispatches in response to reports from firefighters and officers on the scene. Since we take the manning of fire companies as fixed, the situation at the scene determines the number of units needed. We also take the number and location of fire companies as fixed. Consequently, the response time of a needed unit will depend on whether it is dispatched initially. Response times and the number of units dispatched are therefore closely related. For purposes of explanation, we will emphasize one or the other factor as appropriate.

Section 11.2 discusses how to evaluate initial dispatch policies. The following three sections present a range of possible dispatching policies. One of the traditional policies discussed in Section 11.3 or the "adaptive response" policy of Section 11.4 is probably appropriate for a city with a low or moderate alarm rate. Such an alarm rate implies that if more units are sent than are needed, there is only a small chance that another alarm will occur before these extra companies become available. Consequently, considering only the current alarm is sufficient.

The adaptive response policy considers both the company workload and the chance that the alarm signals a serious fire. It tailors the size of the dispatch to the needs at the scene better than traditional policies do. It can be viewed as a way of assuring an adequate response to as many serious fires as possible, while limiting the total number of responses made.

If a city has a high alarm rate, it is probably worthwhile to consider a policy like the one described in Section 11.5. This initial dispatch algorithm considers the consequences at the current incident and at any others that may occur before companies are released from the current incident. All four factors listed in this section are taken into account. In contrast to the adaptive response policy, a computer is required for implementing this algorithm.

11.2 THE EVALUATION OF INITIAL DISPATCH POLICIES

To evaluate an initial dispatch policy or to compare different policies, we need to look in detail at possible "errors" and their consequences. There are two ways in which an initial dispatch can be "wrong" for a particular incident: (1) It can send fewer companies than are needed. The ensuing delay in getting the required companies to the scene can increase damage, injury or deaths. (2) It can send more companies than are needed. The resulting unnecessary responses cost something in themselves—chiefly strain on the firefighters. They also prevent the affected companies from responding to any alarm that is received before they are released from the current alarm.

11.2.1 Response Time and Losses Due to Inadequate Responses

The loss at an incident depends on the nature of the fire and how long it takes units to arrive (as well as other factors such as the time until discovery and the firefighting tactics used). It is not necessary to know the precise relationship between response time and fire loss to formulate an initial dispatch policy. A policy that reduces response times will, on the average, lead to diminished losses.

Since losses depend on both response time and the nature of the fire, we need to consider the seriousness of an incident. If, for instance, a particular policy results in delayed responses to 50 serious fires (e.g., because it does not send the second ladder initially), we can express that loss in terms of the additional response time to those fires (e.g., "the average additional response time for the second-arriving ladder company was three minutes").

A similar measure expresses loss in terms of the fraction of serious fires where there was a delay. For example, if there is a delay to 50 of 200 serious fires, we may say the initial response was adequate to 75 percent of the serious fires. It has been found that in some cases, *initial response adequacy* is more convenient to use than response time. When the alarm rate is low, we will see that these measures are nearly equivalent.

For both response time and response adequacy, different types of incidents should be separated. For example, short response times are important for structural fires but not for false alarms; and adequate responses are more important for structural fires than for rubbish fires.

How can we separate incidents into types so that response times and response adequacy are reasonable substitutes for dollar damage, injuries, and fatalities? The key is to classify incidents as *serious* or *nonserious*, according to the extent to which response times and adequacy affect life and property loss. The serious incidents are those structural fires (and other emergencies) at which slow or inadequate initial response will add to life and property loss. The nonserious incidents are false alarms, rubbish fires, fires in abandoned cars, and so forth, where no practical exposure hazard exists, so that the initial response matters little. Note that this notion of seriousness may not be the same as that used informally in a fire department. In fact, some fatal incidents are not serious according to this definition. For example, in the classic drinking and smoking fire, the victim is often dead and the fire smouldering in a chair when the incident is reported to the fire department. This kind of incident would not be considered serious from an initial dispatch point of view.

How can past incidents be classified as serious or not? This is something that has to be worked out in conjunction with experienced fire officers. A definition that proved workable in New York City: *any incident in a nonvacant structure that requires at least two ladders working is serious; all others are not serious.* (In New York, putting the second ladder to work usually indicates extensive search or overhaul, suggesting that an initial dispatch of two ladders instead of one would have some effect on the outcome.) The precise definition of seriousness is not crucial: the same incidents, more or less, are serious by any reasonable definition (see Ignall, Rider, and Urbach, 1977).

Calculating Response Time and Response Adequacy. For a precise calculation of response times and response adequacy, simulation is essential. The simulation model described in Chapter 13 was designed with initial dispatch questions in mind. However, there are simple approximate methods for calculating these performance measures. A good way is to:

1. Estimate travel times using one of the models from Chapter 6.
2. Estimate response adequacy.
3. Use response adequacy (and turnout times) to estimate response times from the travel times.

We will illustrate these calculations with a simple hypothetical example for ladder companies. Consider a city of 36 square miles in which alarms occur at an average rate of 2 per hour. Suppose that there are 10 ladder companies, and that an average alarm requires $\frac{1}{2}$ hour of ladder work. From this information we calculate that the average number of ladders busy is $2 \times .5 = 1$, leaving an average of 9 ladders available.

We can calculate the average first- and second-due travel times from the relationships given in Chapter 6. If the travel distance square-root law constants are $k_1 = 0.60$ and $k_2 = 1.00$ for first and second ladders, then the average travel distance from an incident to the first-arriving ladder is approximately:

$$E(D_1) = 0.60 \sqrt{36/9} = 1.20 \text{ miles},$$

and the average distance to the second-arriving ladder is approximately

$$E(D_2) = 1.00 \sqrt{36/9} = 2.00 \text{ miles}.$$

For illustration, we use the New York City travel time and distance relationship from Chapter 6. For distances greater than 0.88 mile, it is

$$T = 1.35 + 1.53 \times D.$$

Using this formula, we calculate the average first- and second-arriving travel times as $E(T_1) = 3.19$ minutes and $E(T_2) = 4.41$ minutes.

The estimation of response adequacy requires the classification of incidents by alarm type, and estimation of the rate at which each type occurs and of the fraction of each type that are serious. (Issues in the definition of alarm types are discussed in Section 11.2.3; the estimation problems are discussed in Chapter 8.)

Table 11.1 presents a classification by alarm types for the hypothetical city discussed above. (To actually assemble this classification would require perhaps a year's worth of data on past incidents.) Since these incidents occurred in the past, we know what response was needed.[2] We would like to evaluate the response adequacy for a given dispatch policy.

Suppose that the dispatch policy is to send two ladders to all telephone alarms that sound like structural fires, and one ladder to all other alarms. Under this policy, 344 of the 400 incidents that needed two ladders initially would have gotten two, and 56 would have gotten one ladder. Response adequacy would thus have been (344/400) × 100 = 86 percent for these incidents. (For other kinds of dispatch policies, the calculation of response adequacy may require more effort. One approach is described in Section 11.3.4.)

---

[2] The number of companies that eventually responded is often recorded. In some cities the initial dispatch is also recorded.

TABLE 11.1. Classification of alarms and incidents for a hypothetical city.

	Alarm Types		
Incident types	Telephone Report That Sounds Like a Structural Fire	All Other Alarms	All Alarms
Those that need two ladders initially	344	56	400
Those that need one ladder initially	2683	14,477	17,160
All incidents	3027	14,533	17,560

11.2 The Evaluation of Initial Dispatch Policies

Once the average travel times and the response adequacy have been calculated, we are able to calculate the resulting average response times. Assume that dispatching time is negligible, turnout time (u) is 1 minute, and setup time (S) is $\frac{1}{2}$ minute. The average first-arriving response time is then given by:

$$E(R_1) = u + E(T_1) + S$$
$$= 1.0 + 3.19 + 0.5 = 4.69 \text{ minutes.}$$

To get average second-arriving response times to incidents requiring two ladders, note that the response adequacy calculations indicate that about 86 percent of these incidents get a second ladder in the initial dispatch. For the other 14 percent, the second ladder will be delayed by approximately the time it takes the first ladder to reach the scene and call for help. Therefore, average second-arriving ladder response time to incidents that need two ladders is approximately

$$E(R_2) = 0.14(u + E(T_1)) + [u + E(T_2) + S]$$
$$= 0.14 \times 4.19 + 5.91$$
$$= 6.50 \text{ minutes.}$$

In general, if y_j is the probability that at least j units will be initially dispatched to a particular type of incident, then the average response times to that incident type are approximately

$$E(R_1) = u + E(T_1) + S$$
$$E(R_j) = [(1 - y_j) \times (u + E(T_1))] + [u + E(T_j) + S].$$

If the type of incident in question requires no more than j ladders, then y_j is the initial response adequacy for that type incident. Figure 11.1 shows these relationships for the second-arriving units.

11.2.2 Unnecessary Responses

The consequences of an unnecessary response depend on the situation. What can be termed the direct costs—the cost of an accident if one occurs, the gasoline and oil consumed, and the wear and tear on the apparatus—is small. The indirect costs—resulting from needless stress on firefighters or the chance that the company will be needed at another alarm—can be very large.

Consider the direct costs first. The cost of gasoline and oil for a two- or three-mile round trip would be less than a dollar. Wear and tear on the apparatus—tires, engine, etc.—would also be small. Typical accident

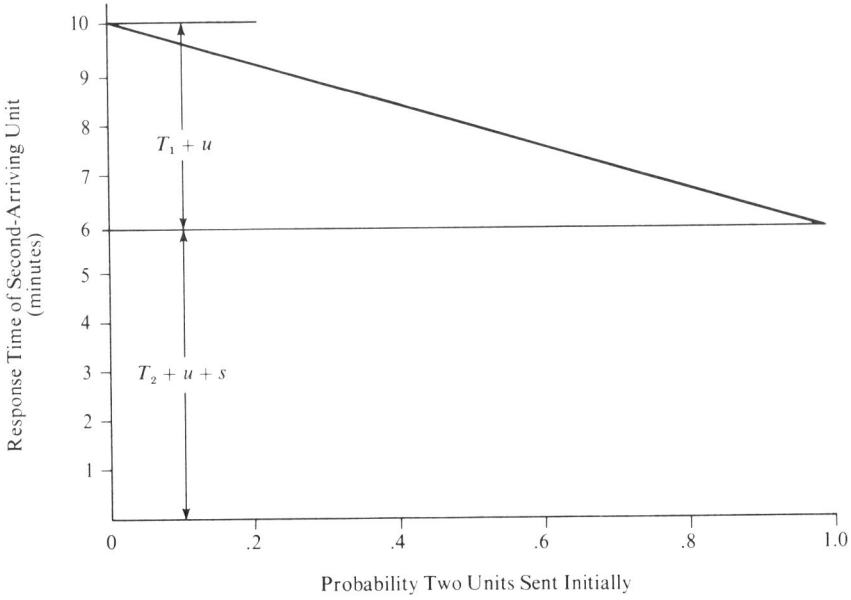

FIGURE 11.1. Relationship between dispatch policy and response time.

rates are very small, and would add less than a dollar to the cost of an unnecessary response.[3]

What about the indirect costs of firefighters responding to an incident where their services are not needed? The issue here is not a single such response, but the pattern of them. For the firefighter, there is a large difference between expecting to work on half the alarms to which he goes, and expecting to work on one in twenty. And there is a large difference between expecting to respond twenty times in a nine-hour tour, and expecting to respond twice.

When the number of responses per tour is high, turnout may be slower at the end of the tour, and firefighting may be less effective. Thus, response to several false alarms early in the tour can mean that a fire that occurs later will do more damage. In a similar way, when the chance that the response will not be necessary is large, turnout may be slower and morale may decline. In New York City in the late 1960s, this kind

---

[3] In New York City in 1973, there were 213 vehicle accidents involving units responding to and returning from 300,000 incidents. Most, but not all, involved engines or ladders. Figuring an average dispatch of four companies to each incident, the accident rate would be perhaps 200/1,200,000, or one for every 6000 responses. The loss at each accident would have to be $6000 to add a dollar to the cost of a response.

of morale problem was one of the factors behind union pressures for more fire companies. Thus, a large enough increase in needless responses in a year in an area could mean that a new fire company would be created. There is no way to determine exactly how large this measure would have to be, but 5000 responses is the right order of magnitude. At an annual cost of over $500,000 for a company, the indirect cost of each needless response in this case would be over $100.

In order to capture the cost of unnecessary responses in units that are compatible with losses at incidents, we define a factor (W) in units of time. This workload factor, which is associated with a company response, is a surrogate for the cost of that response (as discussed earlier). We will see that as W is increased, the initial dispatch algorithm will reduce the number of unnecessary responses and increase response times. Thus, the determination of this factor involves making a subjective judgment on the tradeoff between unnecessary responses and response time.

Another consequence of a needless response is the possibility that the unit in question will be needed at an alarm that occurs before it is released from the current one. If, in response to an incoming alarm, too many units are sent initially, the extra units will be unavailable to respond to other alarms that are received during the time it takes for the first units to arrive and determine that the extra units are not needed.[4] These later alarms may be subject to the costs of an inadequate or delayed response. In areas with high alarm rates, this is an important consideration.

Calculating Response Degradation. When alarm rates are low, the cost of needless responses is small. When alarm rates are moderately high, this cost may be large. There are some simple approximate calculations that can be used to determine if a potential response degradation problem exists. The basic measure to use is unit availability. This in turn can be used to estimate the degradation in response time due to unavailable companies.

Recall our hypothetical example. We will calculate the average first-arriving ladder response time for two situations. On the average, one ladder is busy and nine are available. Average availability is therefore given by $a = \frac{9}{10} = 0.9$. This means that approximately 10 percent of the alarms will not have the closest (first-due) ladder available to respond. What does this mean in terms of response time? With all 10 ladders available, we get for the average first-due ladder response distance:

$$E(D_1) = 0.60 \sqrt{36/10} = 1.14 \text{ miles},$$

---

[4] Alternatively, all but the first-arriving unit can be dispatched on a conditional basis. That is, if another alarm is received, one or more of those units can be diverted to the new incident before the nature of the first one is known.

and for average first-due ladder travel time:

$$E(T_1) = 1.35 + 1.54 \times D_1 = 3.09 \text{ minutes}.$$

The average travel time of the second-due ladder would be:

$$E(T_2) = 1.35 + 1.53 \times 1.00 \times \sqrt{36/10} = 4.25 \text{ minutes}.$$

Therefore, if the first-due ladder were unavailable to respond to a given alarm and the second-due ladder were the first to respond, the travel time would be 1.16 minutes longer. We would expect this to occur roughly 10 percent of the time.

If a fire department decided to dispatch two ladders to all alarms, instead of only to telephone alarms that "sound structural," as in the preceding example, the average time at an alarm might increase to 0.6 company hour. The average number of ladders busy would then be 1.2, and availability would decrease to 0.88. Increased response time would, in this case, be experienced by 12 percent of the alarms.

In formulating a dispatch policy, therefore, a fire department has to weigh the tradeoffs involved in reducing availability in order to obtain better response adequacy. This problem may be serious when alarm rates are high, and hence, company availability low. We note that the use of relocations (Chapter 12) will limit response degradation. Thus, when alarm rates are very high, response times may remain acceptable, but there will be a large number of relocations.

11.2.3 Information Available at the Time of the Dispatch

The preceding discussion of losses considers incidents only in terms of an after-the-fact assessment of the situation at the scene of the incident. However, to design a good initial dispatch policy, we need to know or estimate the requirements of an alarm that has just been received. Therefore, we need to be able to associate losses with incidents as they appear to the dispatcher, when he has to pick a set of companies to respond.

First, we have to systematically categorize what a dispatcher might know about an incoming alarm. We do this by defining various *alarm types* that reflect before-the-fact information. For example, we might define the following alarm types: street box alarm; telephone report—sounds like a structural fire; telephone report—sounds like a rubbish fire or similar minor incident. The alarm type, specifying the alarm as received, defines the information available to the dispatcher and relevant to the initial dispatch decision. We are interested in defining alarm types that provide as much information as possible about the requirements of the incident. In the three-way classification above, the "sounds structural" class comprises alarms that report flame or smoke; it will include some incidents that turn out to be steam-leaks and other nonfires. We

11.2 The Evaluation of Initial Dispatch Policies

will assume that the rate at which these alarms occur and their eventual response requirements can be estimated (Chapter 8 and Section 13.2)

In this chapter we emphasize the classification of street box alarms. It was found in New York City that street box alarms could be divided reliably into *risk* classes. The chance that an alarm from a high-risk box was a serious incident[5] was considerably higher than the chance that one from a low-risk box was serious. (This is discussed in detail in Section 8.6). Knowing whether a street box alarm is from a high- or a low-risk box is useful information for the dispatcher. In a similar way, the time of day provides information. A box alarm received at 3:00 P.M. on a school day is less likely to be serious (because it is more likely to be false) than one received at 3:00 A.M. And it has been found in New York City that an incident reported from more than one source—a telephone call and a pulled street box call or two (or more) telephone calls—is much more likely to be serious than one that gets a single report. (In areas of New York City where an adaptive response policy (Chapter 14) was in use, about half of all serious incidents in the late afternoon and evening that were first reported by box got a follow-up telephone report before the first companies arrived at the scene.) These observations suggest expansion of the three-way classification we began with to the one shown in Table 11.2.

The principal criterion to use in selecting a classification of alarms is minimization of the uncertainty with respect to the incident type. We will show how this criterion can be quantified. Consider the classification scheme shown in Table 11.1. Table 11.3 presents a matrix that shows the probability of each incident type given an alarm type.

If there were no information as to alarm type, when an alarm came in, the dispatcher would know only that the chance that it required two

---

[5] Defined as an alarm needing at least two engines and two ladders.

TABLE 11.2. A possible alarm classification.

Time of Day	Type of Report	Report Subtype
8 A.M. to 4 P.M.	Multiple report	None
	One report	Telephone, sounds structural
		Telephone, sounds minor
		Box, Risk Class 1
		Box, Risk Class 2
		: : :
		Box, Risk Class k
4 P.M. to 12 A.M.	Multiple report	None
	One report	Same as One report above
12 A.M. to 8 A.M.	Multiple report	None
	One report	Same as One report above

TABLE 11.3. A matrix of alarm and incident types.

	Alarm Types		
Incident Types	Telephone Report Sounds Structural	All Others	All Alarms
Needs two ladders	$\dfrac{344}{3,027}=0.1136$	$\dfrac{56}{14,533}=0.0039$	$\dfrac{400}{17,560}=0.0228$
Needs one ladder	$\dfrac{2,683}{3,027}=0.8864$	$\dfrac{14,477}{14,533}=0.9961$	$\dfrac{17,160}{17,560}=0.9772$
All incidents	$\dfrac{3,027}{17,560}=0.1724$	$\dfrac{14,533}{17,560}=0.8276$	

ladders is just under 2 percent. We can measure this uncertainty in information-theoretic terms. The uncertainty (in units of bits) is given by:

$$H = \sum_i P_i \log_2(P_i),$$

where P_i is the probability of the ith incident type. So

$$H = -0.0228 \log_2(0.0228) - 0.9772 \log_2(0.9772) = 0.1568 \text{ bits}.$$

If the dispatcher knows that a telephone report that sounds like a structural fire has an 11.4 percent chance of requiring two ladders, and that other alarms have only a 0.4 percent chance of requiring two ladders, then given that the telephone reports are 17 percent of all alarms, his uncertainty is given by

$$H_T = \sum_k g_k H_k$$

where g_k is the probability of the kth alarm type and H_k is the uncertainty once this alarm type is received.

$$H_T = 0.1724(-0.1136 \log_2(0.1136) - 0.8864 \log_2(0.8864))$$
$$+ 0.8276(-0.0039 \log_2(0.0039) - 0.991 \log_2(0.9961))$$
$$= 0.1184 \text{ bits}.$$

His uncertainty is therefore reduced by 0.0384 bits. Further classification of alarm types could further reduce the uncertainty. Perfect knowledge would give zero uncertainty. For example, if all two-ladder fires were reported by telephone and all one-ladder incidents by box, then

$$H_T = 0.0228(-1 \log_2 1 - 0 \log_2 0) + 0.9772(-0 \log_2 0 - 1 \log_2 1)$$
$$= 0 \text{ bits}.[6]$$

---

[6] $0 \log_2 0 = 0$, by L'Hopital's rule.

Many fire departments tape-record telephone reports of incidents. Analysis of the content of these calls and comparison with the subsequent situation at the scene (as judged from a fire report, for example) is then possible. This may lead to better predictions of seriousness. For example, the fire report may be expanded to include questions like:

What would have been the appropriate initial response to this incident?

What information (alarm type) was available at the time the incident was reported?

Data of this kind collected over perhaps a year would permit the construction of a matrix showing the probability of each incident type given an alarm type. The efficient construction of such a matrix for use in a dispatching policy would be assisted by the measures of uncertainty discussed previously.

11.2.4 Initial Dispatch Principles

Based on the preceding discussion and on the methods and models of Chapters 6 through 8, we can summarize several factors that are important in the initial dispatch decision. For simplicity, we consider only ladder companies. The following factors are relevant:

1. *The probability that the alarm represents a serious fire.* The greater the likelihood that the alarm represents a serious fire where at least two ladders are required, the more advisable it is to dispatch the two ladders closest to it.
2. *The availability of nearby ladder companies.* If two ladders are dispatched, the second ladder's response area must be covered by more distant companies. The fewer companies currently available, the larger the response area for the second ladder and, therefore, the more likely that another alarm occurs in its area. Since there are fewer remaining companies available, they will be further away and take longer to arrive. Therefore, the fewer companies available, the more advisable it is to dispatch only one ladder while saving the second one for a subsequent alarm.
3. *The alarm rate in the surrounding area.* The greater the alarm rate in the surrounding area, the more likely it is that another alarm will occur in the response area of the second ladder. As a result, the greater the alarm rate, the more advisable it is to either dispatch one ladder or dispatch the second ladder from a less busy area. For example, late at night when few alarms occur, two ladders should be dispatched since there is little chance of another alarm being received in the next few minutes. On the other hand, at eight o'clock on a summer evening,

the chance of another alarm occurring would be much higher and (perhaps) one ladder should be sent.
4. *Workload*. As we indicated in Section 11.2.2, the greater the company workload, the greater the possible need for reducing response.

It is important to identify factors that should *not* determine initial dispatch policy. We are aware of the following major pitfalls in formulating an initial dispatch policy:

Reducing response to solve a nonexistent workload problem. We have heard of blanket reductions in the number of units dispatched to some types of alarms, in cities where the busiest companies make four or five responses a day. It is not clear what real benefit comes from reducing this workload. In the meantime, response times to some serious fires are increased.

Reducing responses to "false alarm" boxes. This is often done on the basis of the annual number of false alarms. But, boxes that have many false alarms often have many serious fires. A proper identification of "problem" boxes would be based on the fraction of the alarms, reported from the box, that are serious.

Reducing response around the clock. There are few cities with workload problems in the late night hours. Reducing response in the hours when most people are sleeping runs a high risk to save very few responses.

These pitfalls seem to stem from confusing the objectives of the fire department in initial dispatch with what causes problems with traditional dispatch policies. For example, the growth in false alarms and rubbish fires, and the resulting workload problems, are often the initial reason for considering alternatives to traditional initial dispatch policies. However, it would be a mistake to take reducing responses to these incidents as the objective. It is better to view the "false alarm problem" as creating a constraint on the total number of responses, and to take providing the best responses to serious fires, within that constraint, as the objective.

11.3 TRADITIONAL APPROACHES AND THEIR IMPLICATIONS

In this section we discuss traditional approaches to dispatching fire companies. We distinguish between policies in which a predetermined number are always sent to an alarm of a given type (fixed policies), and those in which the number of companies in a dispatch may be reduced if some companies are not available (variable policies).

In most fire departments, alarm assignment cards (running cards) play a fundamental role in the initial dispatch and redeployment decisions. One such card is pictured in Figure 2.3 in Chapter 2. It lists the companies

11.3 Traditional Approaches and Their Implications

in order of their distance from the location (in this case, 15th and H Streets, NW). The companies on the first line constitute the full first-alarm assignment; those on the second line are the second-alarm assignment; and so forth. A typical initial dispatch policy might be (in part):

Type of Alarm	*Decision*
Telephone report—sounds like a rubbish or automobile fire	Send the first engine on the card
Telephone report—sounds like a structural fire	Send the engines and ladders on the first line of the card
Pulled street box alarm	Send the first two engines and first ladder on the card

This specification of a standard initial response for different kinds of alarms may vary in other ways as well: the number of companies to respond initially may vary from location to location, with more companies specified for locations with known high hazards (lumberyards, hospitals, etc.). Although few cities do so, the number can also change with the hour of the day, the season of the year, the weather, or the past history of alarms at the location.

An implicit assumption in the use of alarm assignment cards is that all the companies listed will be available for dispatch when the alarm is received. In the past, this was almost always true; but with recent increases in alarm rates, it is becoming more and more common that one or more of the companies to be dispatched are unavailable. This is particularly true in cities in which fire departments have emergency medical service responsibility. In some instances the dispatcher will replace an unavailable company by another company on the same (or the next) line of the running card; in others, he will not, and fewer companies will be sent to the incident. In some cities the dispatchers have some discretion in this matter. Sometimes additional information is used. For example, the dispatcher may be required to find a substitute for an unavailable company if there is an indication that the fire is serious (e.g., when two or more telephone calls report the same fire).[7]

The practice of sending a reduced response when some of the companies on the first line of the running card are unavailable may be more widespread than previously suspected. Because there is a natural reluctance to acknowledge that less than the standard response might some-

---

[7] Note that we are considering the question of replacing unavailable units only on the initial dispatch. We are not considering methods by which reports from units that reach the scene can be used to adjust the initial response.

times be dispatched, it may be necessary to observe dispatching operations or look at dispatching records to find out what the current dispatching procedures actually are.

11.3.1 Fixed Policies

Fixed policies are perhaps the most widely used type of dispatch policy. An example of such a policy is one that prescribes the dispatch of two engines and two ladders to every telephone report that sounds like a structural fire; one engine to every telephone report of a rubbish fire; and so forth. In many cities, blanket rules of this sort are applied around the clock. Fixed policies have the advantage of being simple and easy to implement. If the alarm rate of a community is sufficiently low, such a policy may be best.

When a fixed policy is to be used, the size of the standard dispatch must be determined. Should the standard response of years ago be maintained in the face of rising alarms? How is the size of the standard dispatch to be determined? The increase in alarms, especially in false alarms from street boxes, has led many cities to modify blanket-type fixed policies. One common modification is to vary the size of a dispatch with the time of day. During periods of peak demand, the size of a dispatch may, for example, be reduced from two engines and two ladders to one company of each type. Such a policy seeks to ease workload and have more companies available during the busy period. Another type of modification is to reduce responses only to "problem" boxes. Such a policy can provide better response to serious fires than a blanket reduction to all boxes.

What measures are appropriate for evaluating a particular fixed policy? We suggest the use of response times and response adequacy, calculated with the simulation model (Chapter 13), the siting model (Chapter 10), or the approximation procedure presented in Section 11.2.2.

Alarm types should be defined so that there is a cross-classification of different times of day with problem boxes, other boxes, and various telephone alarms as in Section 11.2.3.

If this is done, it will probably be seen, for example, that a blanket response reduction would severely reduce response adequacy to serious fires during the times it is in force. It is doubtful that the calculation will show that the benefits derived from increased availability will compensate for the need to wait for the additional companies required.

It will probably also be seen that it is unwise to reduce responses to problem boxes around the clock. Late at night, the reduction in company runs will be slight, and the chance of an inadequate response to a serious incident is likely to be large.

11.3.2 Variable Policies

The policies discussed above are fixed in that, at a given time or at a given box, the response policy to a given type of alarm is predetermined. In this section we discuss variable policies, in which the number of companies dispatched depends on certain other conditions. For example, a policy of this type might always send engines from the two closest houses to an incident if they are available. If one or more of these engines is unavailable, the (one) closest engine among those available at the time might be sent. The number of engines sent, therefore, would depend on the number available. We call this a *variable response policy*.

This policy is a natural one for a busy city to use. It does reduce workload and increase coverage. In comparison to the way a fixed policy might modify response by time of day, this policy modifies a dispatch depending on the actual conditions at the time of an alarm. The more companies that are busy fighting fires, the less chance there is that two companies of a given type will be dispatched to an alarm.

This policy, however, also has serious disadvantages. It is possible, for example, that almost all engines might be available except for one of the two closest to a given location. A reasonable policy would, in this case, send two engines to a new alarm at that location. But a variable "two-engine" policy would send only one. This could lead to a situation where a false alarm at a given location is sent two engines and two ladders, while a nearby serious structural fire reported over the phone a short time later would be sent one engine and one ladder. In this case the decision on how many companies are sent to an alarm is not controlled by the department, in the sense that it is determined by the sequence of recent alarms.

11.3.3 Determining the Policy a Department is Using

It may not be obvious what initial dispatch policy is in use by a fire department. (It may be a mixture of fixed and variable policies. For example, the "telephone—sounds structural" alarms may get a fixed response of three engines, while "street box" alarms may get whichever of the first three engines on the running card is available.) How can one find out? We indicate here some calculations that may be a helpful supplement to reading policy or procedure guidelines, discussing them with dispatchers and their supervisors, and observing communications office operations.

What should be done depends on what kind of records a department keeps. For New York City the calculation mentioned in this section provides evidence that a variable policy was in use during the late 1960s for street box alarms. At that time, individual companies in the city recorded their responses by incident type. (These included responses to higher alarms as well as initial dispatches.) Battalion chiefs' reports on all incidents were also tabulated. The company records did not distinguish street box alarms from those reported by telephone and other means. The chiefs' reports did.

Consider ladder companies. In the late 1960s, all alarm assignment cards listed two ladders on the first line of the card, and this was the nominal response to street box alarms. To try to separate street box alarms from the others, all false alarms were examined. The company records indicated a total of 87,665 ladder company responses to false alarms. Chiefs indicated 48,106 false alarms, all but 3329 of them reported by street box. The nonbox false alarms received a variety of responses, ranging from no ladders to two ladders. If all had received none, the average number of ladders per box false alarm would have been 1.96 = 87,665/(48,106 − 3,329). That is, not all of the box false alarms could have received the standard two ladders. (The 1.96 is consistent with 96 percent getting two ladders and 4 percent getting one). If, as is more likely, all the nonbox false alarms had been sent at least one ladder, then the average number of ladders per box false alarm would have been no more than 1.88 = (87,665 − 3,329)/(48,106 − 3,329).

Since the dispatchers did not know which box alarms would be false (in 1967 about half the box alarms were false, while about 15 percent of them were structural fires), this suggests that variable response was used to all street box alarms, at least in some parts of the city. Simply producing such figures, with their indication that fixed policies are not always used, is very useful in generating sensible discussion of variable response and its implications within the department.

11.3.4 Response Adequacy and Company Availability with Variable Response Policies

The preceding section describes one way in which the existence of variable response can be diagnosed. It is also useful to be able to predict the effects of using a variable response policy, since such a policy has some attractive features. We present here several relationships that were found to hold in situations of moderate to high availability in New York City.[8]

The relationships presume that average company availability can be specified (Chapters 7 and 8). For alarm types governed by a particular variable response policy, they predict the fraction for which one ladder will be dispatched initially, the fraction for which two will be dispatched initially, and so forth.

---

[8] The discovery and validation of Equation (11.1) is discussed in Section 7 of Chapter 13. Also see Ignall and Urbach (1975).

11.3 Traditional Approaches and Their Implications

We consider engines and ladders separately. Define a variable "k" policy as follows: a set of k units is associated with the incident; as many of those k units as are available are dispatched to the incident; if none are available, an available unit is found and dispatched.

Let p be the average unit availability in the area; that is, the average fraction of the time a unit is available. Define $x_k(n, p)$ as the probability that n units are dispatched initially to an incident at which the variable policy is used during a time period in which the average availability is p. Consider a variable "2" policy (it is a common one for ladders). Then

$$\left. \begin{array}{l} x_2(2, p) = p^2 \\ x_2(1, p) = 1 - p^2 \end{array} \right\} \text{ for } p \geq 0.4. \tag{11.1}$$

Equation (11.1) says that if variable "2" is in use for ladders and average ladder availability is 90 percent, then in 81 percent of the incidents, the initial response will be two ladders, and in 19 percent the initial response will be one ladder. Figure 11.2 shows how the fraction of incidents in which two ladders are initially dispatched depends on availability.

The relationship in Equation (11.1) would be true if (a) availability were the same for every unit in the region, and (b) the chance that any particular unit is available were independent of the status of all other units. Neither of these is true, yet the relationship appears to hold.

FIGURE 11.2. The performance of a variable 2 policy.

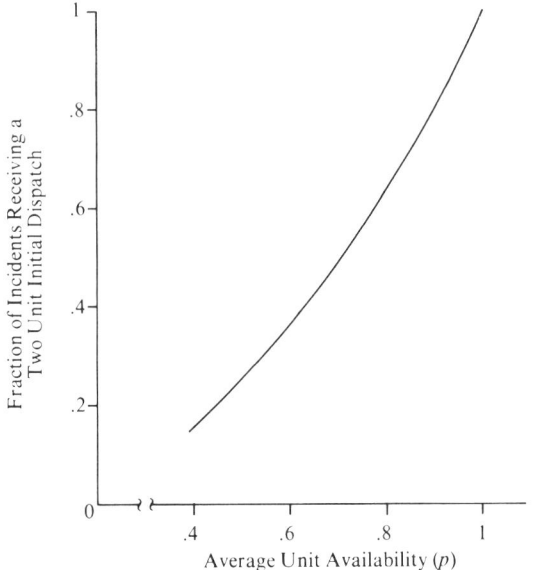

For the variable "3" policy, the result, valid for $p \geq 0.4$, is

$$x_3(3, p) = p^3 + 0.5p(1 - p)^2$$
$$x_3(1, p) = (1 - p)^3 + 3p(1 - p)^2 + 0.5p(1 - p) \quad (11.2)$$
$$x_3(2, p) = 1 - (x_3(3, p) + x_3(1, p)).$$

In this case, assumptions (a) and (b) would imply that $x_3(3, p) = p^3$. Ignall and Urbach found that this did not fit results from simulation experiments, however, and Equation (11.2) was chosen by trial and error. It was chosen to be a set of polynomial functions of p that fit well and satisfied the common-sense conditions $x_3(3, 0) = 0$; $x_3(3, 1) = 1$; $x_3(3, p)$ increasing in p; $x_3(1, 1) = 1$; and $x_3(1, p)$ decreasing in p. Figure 11.3 shows how the fraction of incidents that get three units and the fraction that get at least two units depend on availability.

11.4 A SIMPLE ADAPTIVE APPROACH

11.4.1 Background

Fixed policies are natural and attractive. However, increasing alarm rates have pressed some cities to reduce the predetermined response to some alarms. In contrast, a variable policy adapts to the current situation by adjusting the dispatch on the basis of company availability. As we have

FIGURE 11.3. The performance of a variable 3 policy.

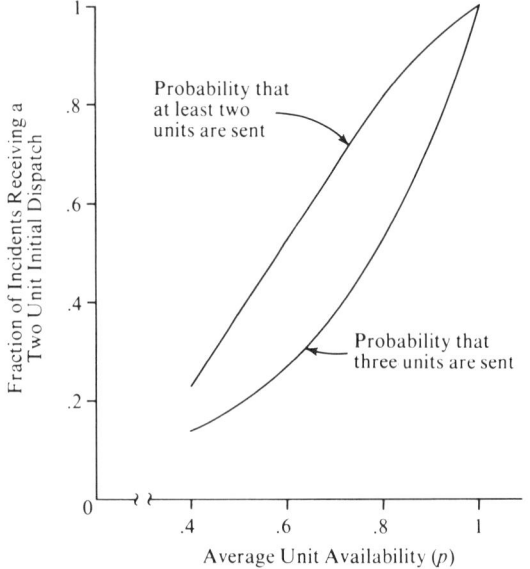

11.4 A Simple Adaptive Approach

just seen, variable dispatch policies are fallible in specific instances. In this section and in Section 11.5, we introduce some other ways of trying to tailor the dispatch to the needs of an incident. These other approaches can often be much better than either the fixed or the variable policies.

To develop these alternatives we use two of the models described in Chapter 7. The first is the "how many to dispatch" model of Section 7.4. The second is the "which companies to dispatch" model of Section 7.3. Insights from the "how many" model are used to develop an "adaptive response" policy. This policy can be implemented within existing alarm assignment card systems. It combines the advantages of modifying dispatches by time of day and location of alarm with the flexibility of variable response. It should be sufficient for all but the largest cities.

In Section 11.5 a more complicated policy is developed that requires a computer-aided dispatch system. This algorithm uses insights from the "which companies" model as well as the "how many" model. However, it is likely to be worthwhile only in cities with very high alarm rates.

11.4.2 What is an Adaptive Policy?

We begin by recalling the "how many" model developed by Swersey (1972), described in Section 7.4. The model takes the state of the system to be the number of ladders busy, distinguishing those dispatched as first-arriving from those dispatched as second-arriving.

For purposes of illustration, we will consider ladders—a fixed region that has n^* ladders in it,[9] and only two possibilities for each incident: sending one ladder or sending two ladders. The relevant feature of an alarm is the chance that it signals a serious fire. The objective is the minimization of the sum of long-run average losses at the incidents and the costs of company response. These losses occur only at serious incidents and are determined by first- and second-ladder response times at those incidents.

For this situation, the optimal dispatch policy is of the following form:

> *Swersey Cutoff Theorem:* For each state of the system (i, j), where i and j are the number of first- and second-arriving ladders busy respectively, there is a cutoff probability, $s^*(i, j)$, such that two ladders should be sent if an alarm occurs with a probability serious greater than $s^*(i, j)$; otherwise, one ladder should be sent.

The value of s^* depends on the total number of ladders busy, i and j, and s^* increases when i and j increase. The optimal cutoffs are larger when the alarm rate and the cost of a response are larger.

---

[9] The region should be large enough to include several ladders, but not so large that incidents in one part should not affect decisions in another. Swersey uses eight companies.

In this section we will expand the cutoff probability notion to engines and to the question of sending 1, 2, 3, or more units of each type. That is, we will consider adaptive response policies, which are policies of the following form: There will be cutoff probabilities $s_{1L}^*, s_{2L}^*, \ldots$ and $s_{1E}^*, s_{2E}^*, \ldots$. Suppose p is the probability that the alarm in question is serious. Then if

$$p < s_{1L}^*, \text{ send one ladder}$$
$$s_{1L}^* < p < s_{2L}^*, \text{ send two ladders}$$
$$s_{2L}^* < p < s_{3L}^*, \text{ send three ladders}$$
$$\vdots$$
$$p < s_{1E}^*, \text{ send one engine}$$
$$s_{1E}^* < p < s_{2E}^*, \text{ send two engines}$$
$$\vdots$$

In addition, however many companies are sent, send the closest ones.

An adaptive response policy, then, is a specification of a particular fixed policy for each alarm. If it is to work well, a prerequisite is a well thought out classification of alarms as in Section 11.2.3. Note that an adaptive response policy is static in that the local situation—how many companies are actually available nearby right now—is not considered. A dynamic policy is developed in Section 11.5.

We evaluate a particular adaptive response policy in terms of (1) The fraction of serious incidents to which one ladder is initially dispatched, the fraction to which two ladders are dispatched, and so forth; and (2) The number of responses made by companies in the region. Our first measure, then, is response adequacy. Response-time estimates can be obtained from it by using the procedures of Section 11.2.2.

As we have mentioned, we need to know the chance that the alarm, for which we must now make an initial dispatch decision, signals a serious incident. An adaptive response policy will be substantially better than fixed or variable policies if this probability can be estimated accurately and if it varies from alarm to alarm. That it does vary from alarm to alarm in some cities is evident from the following data from New York City. Considering only alarms reported from street alarm boxes, there are great local differences. Table 11.4 shows how boxes at locations near each other have widely varying histories of serious fires. In addition, the chance that a box alarm is serious will change by time of day and season. Table 11.5 shows how significant this effect is.

To see the possible effectiveness of an adaptive response policy, suppose the four boxes in Table 11.4 were the only ones in the city. A fixed policy of two ladders to all incidents would have generated 784 re-

11.4 A Simple Adaptive Approach

TABLE 11.4. Difference in the chance that a box alarm signals a structural fire. Data are from the Bronx, 1970. Boxes are a few blocks to one mile from one another.

Bronx Box Number	Predicted Probability Structural	Actual 1970 Data		
		Alarms	Structural Fires	Serious Fires
2277	0.004	96	0	0
2948	0.070	102	6	1
2786	0.135	100	15	3
2209	0.318	94	25	12
Totals		392	46	16

sponses[10] in 1970, and two ladders would have been sent to all 16 serious fires. A fixed policy of one ladder would have generated 408 responses,[11] and none of the serious fires would have received a two-ladder initial dispatch. To see the effect of a variable policy, suppose average ladder availability were 0.87. Then, from Equation (11.1), the chance that two ladders are dispatched to an alarm would be $0.75 (=(0.87)^2)$. This would apply to each of the four boxes, so we could expect about three-quarters of the incidents (and serious fires) at each box to get a two-ladder initial dispatch. That is, we could expect 690 responses, and two ladders would be initially dispatched to 12 of the 16 serious fires. An adaptive response policy with $s^* = 0.010$ would send two ladders to all but box 2277. It would generate 688 responses, and two ladders would be sent to all 16 of the serious fires. That is, the adaptive response policy would produce a workload comparable to the variable policy, while initially getting two ladders to more of the serious fires. The characteristics of fixed, variable, and adaptive response policies (the latter with various values of s^*) are summarized in Table 11.6.

---

[10] In this context, we are counting a "response" whenever a ladder is sent to an incident.
[11] 392 initial responses plus 16 second ladder responses to the serious fires results in 408 total responses.

TABLE 11.5. Percentage of all box alarms that are serious by season and time of day, South Bronx, 1970.

Winter			Spring and Fall			Summer		
0–8	8–16	16–24	0–8	8–16	16–24	0–8	8–16	16–24
6.6%			4.5%			4.8%		
	5.8%			3.5%			3.8%	
		3.5%			2.6%			3.1%

TABLE 11.6. A comparison of fixed, variable, and adaptive response policies.

Policy	Ladder Responses	Number of Serious Fires to Which Two Ladders Are Sent as the Initial Dispatch
Fixed 2	784	16
Fixed 1	408	0
Variable	690	12
Adaptive response		
$s^* = 0.002$	784	16
$s^* = 0.010$	688	16
$s^* = 0.100$	587	15
$s^* = 0.150$	490	12
$s^* = 0.350$	408	0

We now turn to the details of specifying an adaptive response policy and comparing it to fixed and variable policies.

11.4.3 Defining an Adaptive Response Policy

As an illustration, consider the policy to be used to dispatch ladder companies in response to alarms reported by street box in a particular region at a specified time of day. Assume that at least one ladder will always be dispatched, and that the problem is when to send a second ladder initially. An adaptive response policy will specify which alarm boxes will receive an initial dispatch of two ladders and which will receive only one ladder.

The procedure is as follows. We label the boxes in the region (1, 2, 3, ..., N) in increasing order of the probability that an alarm from the box signals a serious fire. Let p_i be the chance that an alarm from box i signals a serious fire, and λ_i be the hourly rate at which box alarms occur there. (Our labeling implies that $p_1 \leq p_2 \leq p_3 \leq \cdots \leq p_N$. The p_i and λ_i will be estimated values. Chapter 8 gives methods for getting them.) Let $\lambda = \lambda_1 + \cdots \lambda_N$ be the total rate at which box alarms occur in the region. A cutoff probability is then specified; this determines the boxes that will receive an initial dispatch of one ladder. If an alarm is received from box i and p_i is less than the cutoff value (s^*), one ladder is sent; if p_i is greater than or equal to s^*, two ladders are sent. The larger the value of s^*, the fewer the number of boxes to which two ladders are dispatched. By varying s^*, policies can be developed that dispatch an average number of ladders per box alarm anywhere in the range between 1.0 and 2.0. The ordered lists of alarm boxes make it easy to develop and evaluate such policies.

11.4 A Simple Adaptive Approach

For example, suppose that the probabilities of boxes $1, 2, \ldots, m - 1$ signaling a serious fire are all less than s^*, while $p_m \geq s^*$. The expected total number of ladder initial responses to these box alarms in an hour is given by

$$D(s^*) = \lambda + (\lambda_m + \cdots + \lambda_N). \tag{11.3}$$

The average initial dispatch to a box alarm is given by

$$d(s^*) = 1 + (\lambda_m + \cdots + \lambda_N)/\lambda. \tag{11.4}$$

The expected number of serious box incidents per hour to which two ladders are initially dispatched is given by

$$A(s^*) = \lambda_m p_m + \cdots + \lambda_N p_N. \tag{11.5}$$

The fraction of all the serious box incidents to which two ladders are sent initially is given by

$$a(s^*) = \frac{\lambda_m p_m + \cdots + \lambda_N p_N}{\lambda_1 p_1 + \cdots + \lambda_N p_N} \tag{11.6}$$

So, A and a are measures of response adequacy.

11.4.4 Example of a Simple Adaptive Policy

The following example is based on data from New York City. Table 11.7 gives the information on the boxes. The empirical Bayes methods of Section 8.6 were used with 1967–1969 data to estimate the value of p_i for every box in the region. The boxes with the smallest estimated values of p_i were put in class 1 until that class of boxes had at least 3000 alarms between 3 P.M. and midnight in 1970; the boxes with the next smallest

TABLE 11.7. 1970 alarms from boxes assigned to "super box" classes on the basis of 1967–1969 data for part of the Bronx (roughly Region 2 of Figure 8.17).

	3 P.M. to Midnight			
Class	Box Alarms in 1970	Serious Occupied Structurals in 1970	Proportion Serious	"Smoothed" Proportion Serious
1	3028	18	0.0059	0.0060
2	3017	33	0.0109	0.0090
3	3071	29	0.0094	0.0120
4	2905	43	0.0148	0.0150
5	3051	52	0.0170	0.0180
6	2954	61	0.0206	0.0210
7	3000	67	0.0233	0.0240

values were put in class 2 until that class had at least 3000 alarms; and so forth. These classes then define $N = 7$ "super" boxes, each with 3000 box alarms per year in the 3 P.M. to midnight period (or 0.913 alarms per hour). We use the "smoothed" proportion serious, rather than the actual, for computational convenience. Thus, for the super boxes we have $p_1 = 0.006$, $p_2 = 0.009$, $p_3 = 0.012, \ldots , p_7 = 0.024$ and $\lambda_1 = \lambda_2 = \cdots = \lambda_7 = 0.913$. To calculate a, it is helpful to have $\lambda_1 p_1 + \cdots + \lambda_N p_N$. This sum is 0.0959.

If $s^* = 0.005$ is chosen, then two ladders are dispatched to all alarms and $d(s^*) = d(0.005) = 2$, $a(0.005) = 1$. If $s^* = 0.008$, then one ladder responds to alarms from box 1, and all others get two. As a result, $d(0.008) = 1.857$ (i.e., $= 1 + 6/7$). From Equation (11.6), $a(0.008) = 1 - (0.913 \times 0.006)/0.959 = 0.950$. If $s^* = 0.010$, one ladder is dispatched to the alarms from boxes 1 and 2, and all others get two. Then $d(0.010) = 1.714$. From Equation (11.6), $a(0.008) = 0.857$. That is, sending a second ladder 71.4 percent of the time gets that second ladder to 85.7 percent of the serious fires. Using a procedure that did not take box classes into account would require sending a second ladder to 85.7 percent of the incidents, significantly more than the 71.4 percent required by the adaptive policy.

Figure 11.4 shows how the adaptive policy compares to variable response policies over a range of average dispatch sizes. Fixed responses are represented by points A and B. Suppose that the average ladder availability were 0.75. Then, by Equation (11.1), two ladders would be sent 57 percent of the time under a variable policy, so that its performance would be represented by point C. Note that moving to an adaptive response policy at point D will decrease total ladder responses while keeping the same response adequacy as the variable policy. Also note that by moving to an adaptive response policy at point E, response adequacy is improved while total ladder responses are unchanged.

11.4.5 Discussion and Extension

We have looked at how the choice of s^* induces a specific policy and the resulting value of $d(s^*)$, the average initial ladder dispatch to an incident, and $a(s^*)$, the average fraction of serious box incidents to which two ladders are initially dispatched. It is possible to choose either d or a, and let it determine s^*. For example, suppose we wish to have $d = 1.8$ ladders per alarm. Then we invert Equation (11.4); that is, we find m so that

$$\lambda_m + \lambda_{m+1} + \cdots + \lambda_N \simeq (1.8 - 1)\lambda. \qquad (11.7)$$

(It may not be possible to achieve exact equality.) That is easy to do—we calculate the right-hand side, and then add boxes, starting with the Nth until we get equality. With this value of m, we can compute A and a using Equations (11.5) and (11.6). (And, we can set $s^* = p_m$.) Simi-

11.4 A Simple Adaptive Approach

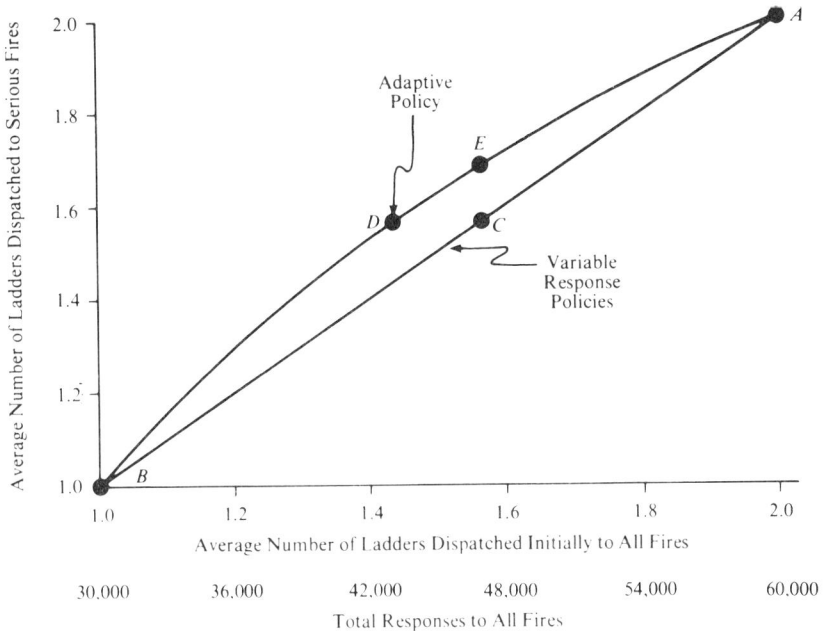

FIGURE 11.4. Comparison of fixed, variable, and adaptive response policies.

larly, suppose we want $a = 0.60$, that is, 60 percent of the serious box incidents are to receive a two-ladder initial dispatch. Then we invert Equation (11.6); that is, we find m so that

$$\lambda_m p_m + \cdots + \lambda_N p_N = 0.60(\lambda_1 p_1 + \cdots + \lambda_N p_N). \quad (11.8)$$

With this m, we compute D and d and s^*.

We now show how to determine total ladder responses—including those to higher alarms and those where two are needed but one is sent. Let π_j be the proportion of all box incidents at which j ladders work, and r_i be the proportion of box alarms at box i at which two ladders work. Then the expected total hourly number of responses is given by

$$\begin{aligned} M(s^*) = D(s^*) + (\pi_3 + 2\pi_4 + 3\pi_5 + \cdots)\lambda \\ + (\lambda_1 r_1 + \cdots + \lambda_{m-1} r_{m-1}). \end{aligned} \quad (11.9)$$

Note that the π terms do not depend on s^*. Also, $M(s^*)$ can be rewritten as

$$\begin{aligned} M(s^*) = \lambda(\pi_1 + 2\pi_2 + 3\pi_3 + \cdots) + [\lambda_m(1 - r_m) \\ + \cdots + \lambda_N(1 - r_N)], \end{aligned} \quad (11.10)$$

where the last term gives the needless second-ladder responses. (We are assuming that at least one ladder is necessary; i.e., $\pi_0 = 0$.)

Recall that this discussion has been for ladder company responses to box alarms in a given period and region. We can combine different time periods and develop a single ranked list of possible alarms (it might look like "box 1, evening; box 2, evening; box 1, midday; box 3, evening; . . . ; box N, late night") and use a single cutoff. Or, we can have separate cutoffs for different times of the day. A similar choice is possible for different regions.

Combination into a single list allows maximum benefit in the sense of highest response adequacy for a fixed number of company responses. However, we may not wish to create such a list. Serious fires late at night can be different from serious daytime fires. Workload is not the problem late at night that it may be during the day. And combining regions can lead to the kind of equity problems (discussed in Chapter 9) that arise when companies are allocated to regions.

In additon, other types of incidents can be combined with box alarms. If we want to retain the existing policy for the other alarms—for example, fixed two ladders to "telephone, sounds structural" and fixed one to "telephone, rubbish"—the previous formulas can be combined with the implications of this choice: Calculate the number of ladder responses to these alarms and add them to $D(s^*)$. It is more interesting to think of applying the adaptive response notions to these other alarms also. To do this, imagine that each of the other kinds of alarms can be characterized by its alarm rate and its value of p (the chance that an alarm signals a serious fire). Then treat each of them as if it were a single alarm box, combine them with the boxes, and follow the procedure outlined for box alarms.

As we have mentioned, the set of policies presented in Section 11.4.3 can be expanded to handle more than the dichotomy between dispatching one ladder or two. To do so, we expand the single cutoff probability s^* to several cutoffs, some for ladders and others for engines. To evaluate these more complicated policies, the formulas for D and d have to be extended. This can be done in a straightforward way. The response adequacy measures A and a require a redefinition that will depend on the needs of the city.

11.5 AN ALGORITHM FOR INITIAL DISPATCH

11.5.1 Background

The policy discussed in the preceding section should be adequate for all but the largest cities. However, when the alarm rate is very high, a more refined policy can be better than adaptive response. We have assumed up to this point that it is possible to preplan the size of a dispatch. The policy that we describe here attempts to consider the "current situation." It varies the cutoff probability s^* dynamically, depending on the availability of companies at the time of a new alarm. It also considers the

11.5 An Algorithm for Initial Dispatch

question of *which* companies to send. An algorithm implementing this policy is described in detail in Carter, Ignall, and Rider (1977). Their objective is to minimize losses at serious fires while ensuring that fire company workloads are not too high. They measure losses in terms of response time and handle the workload constraint by adding a workload factor (W) for each response made by a company. W is defined in units of response time and is chosen by the user. Increasing its value will decrease the total number of responses made. The parametric variation of W then produces a tradeoff curve of response time against company workload, similar to the tradeoff of realized and potential demands in the Parametric Allocation Model described in Chapter 9.

The algorithm is intended for situations where there is a significant chance of receiving another alarm (for a different incident) before the companies finish handling the current one. Therefore, the calculation of expected losses cannot consider only the current alarm. In fact, the real problem is to find workable ways of combining the current and future consequences of a particular dispatch decision.

That is, it is necessary to get expressions for the current loss C and future loss F of a possible dispatch decision, and then choose the decision that minimizes the sum $Z = C + F$. This is done by combining the approaches of Sections 7.4 and 7.3 in Chapter 7, which deal respectively with how many companies to dispatch, and which companies to dispatch. The ideas of the "how many" procedure of Swersey (1972) are extended to explicitly include the geography of the region and the companies in it. To this is added an additional future loss consideration, based on the "which" model of Carter, Chaiken, and Ignall (1972).

Because the development of the algorithm uses cases that go beyond the assumptions of the models and makes use of various approximations, the algorithm is necessarily an approximation to the best policy. With this in mind, the algorithm provides a number of parameters (in addition to W) that the user can vary. The initial dispatch algorithm therefore encompasses a set of policies (just as adaptive response is a set of policies).

For purposes of illustration, we describe the algorithm for ladder decisions only. We further suppose that either one or two ladders is to be sent.

11.5.2 General Loss Function

Before proceeding it is necessary to define "losses at serious fires" more precisely. For the purposes of a dispatching policy, the most direct definition of a serious fire is "a fire that requires two ladders (engines) quickly." This was discussed more fully in Section 11.2.1.

In general, the expected loss at a serious fire will be some (perhaps complicated) function of the time it takes all the needed fire companies to arrive at the scene. As we have previously indicated, this function is not yet known. Carter, Ignall, and Rider (1977) use a simple function that captures what appear to be major determinants of loss. Following Keeney (1973), they give more weight to the first-arriving unit than to the second. They also give more weight to serious fires than to other incidents. For simplicity, a linear function (Section 7.4; Swersey (1972); and Ignall, Rider and Urbach (1977)) was chosen. It uses the following concepts:

Quantities to be determined by choice of how many and which companies to dispatch:

R_1 = the estimated time it takes the first-arriving company to respond.

R_2 = the estimated time it takes the second-arriving company to respond.

$R(i)$ = the estimated time it takes company i to respond.

Information available at the time of dispatch:

$t_j(x)$ = the estimated travel time from the location of company j to location x.

$p(x, m)$ = the estimated probability that an alarm of type m, at location x, is serious.

Parameters chosen by the user:

β = the importance of second-arriving company response time relative to first-arriving response time.

r = the importance of response time to a nonserious incident relative to response time to a serious incident.

Response time includes the time it takes to dispatch a company after receipt of an alarm, the turnout time u, the travel time, and the setup time. Thus, if the second company is not immediately dispatched, the delay is included in the response time. For our purposes we neglect the dispatch time and the setup time.

The parameter β lies between 0 and 1; if $\beta = 1$, the response time for the second-arriving unit is weighted just as heavily as the first-arriving unit's response time; if $\beta = 0$, the second-arriving unit's response time is not considered at all. A typical value would be $\beta = 0.5$. It might be tempting to set the parameter $r = 0$; however, the procedure would take this literally and send a company from many miles away to a nonserious incident. This is prevented by assigning r some small value, typically 0.01 or 0.02.

The calculation of the loss is relatively straightforward. Consider an alarm of type m at location $\mathbf{x}$. If ladder i is the first-arriving ladder at the incident and ladder j is the second-arriving ladder, the expected loss is:

$$C = [p(\mathbf{x}, m) + [1 - p(\mathbf{x}, m)]r]R_1 + p(\mathbf{x}, m)\beta R_2,$$

11.5 An Algorithm for Initial Dispatch

where
$$R_1 = R(i) \text{ and } R_2 = R(j).$$

It is easier to work with C if we rewrite it as
$$C = q(\mathbf{x}, m)R_1 + p(\mathbf{x}, m)\beta R_2, \tag{11.11}$$

where
$$q(\mathbf{x}, m) = p(\mathbf{x}, m) + (1 - p(\mathbf{x}, m))r.$$

That is, C is a weighted sum of the first- and second-arriving ladder response times. Typical weights on the response times can be seen in Table 11.8.

To calculate the current loss at an alarm, the probability that the alarm is serious and the response times for the units selected (including the delay if only one unit is initially dispatched) would be used in this formula. Suppose that one ladder is sent initially and it is ladder i. Let ladder j be the closest of the other ladders. Then

$$R_1 = u + t_i(\mathbf{x})$$
$$R_2 = [u + t_i(\mathbf{x})] + u + t_j(\mathbf{x}).$$

(The delay represented by the first term in R_2 can be smaller if the first engine arrives before ladder company i. Thus, we may replace $(u + t_i)$ by $r_{\min}$ which is defined as u plus the smaller of t_i and the first-arriving engine time.)

Similarly, suppose two ladders are sent initially and they are ladders i and j, with i being closer than j. (The i and j here need have no relationship with the i and j in the previous paragraph.) Then

$$R_1 = u + t_i(\mathbf{x}).$$
$$R_2 = u + t_j(\mathbf{x}).$$

TABLE 11.8. Typical weights on first- and second-arriving ladder response times. $r = 0.02$, $\beta = 0.50$.

Alarm Type	p	Weight on First Unit Response Time q	Weight on Second Unit Response Time βp
Telephone, sounds structural	0.10	0.118	0.050
Box alarm	0.05	0.069	0.025
Telephone, sounds like a car fire	0.00	0.020	0.00

To consider future losses, we need the following definitions and concepts:

λ = the total alarm rate in the region.
$\bar{p}$ = the chance that an alarm in the region is serious.
$\bar{q} = \bar{p} + r(1 - \bar{p})$.
N = the number of ladders stationed in the region.
n = the number of those ladders that are now available (before any are sent to the incident).

Let $T_1(k)$ and $T_2(k)$ be expected travel times of the first- and second-arriving ladders, respectively, when k ladders are available, and let r_{min} be the response time of the first-arriving unit of any kind. For each value of k, these three times can be estimated using the models of Chapter 6 and the area of the region.

It is not practical to calculate F exactly. Therefore, Carter, Ignall, and Rider compromise between ignoring the future and treating it exhaustively. As was first suggested by Swersey (1972), a reasonable approximation is to look at the interval from now until the first unit arrives on the scene, and at the next alarm, if any, received in that interval. The future loss is taken to be the loss at that alarm times the chance that it occurs.

The significance of this interval is that once the first unit arrives at the scene, the number of companies actually needed will be determined by the officer. Extra units will be sent back or additional units will be called for as needed. Thus, the major effect of the initial dispatch decision (as opposed to the actual situation at the scene) on company availability, and thus on future losses, is felt in that interval.

The loss at the next alarm will depend on the expected seriousness of that alarm, and the expected initial dispatch and resulting response times to it. If there are k ladders available then and the average dispatch is d ladders,[12] then the expected cost of the next alarm, should it occur, is

$$L(k) = \bar{q}\{T_1(k) + u\} + \bar{p}\beta\{T_2(k) + u + (2 - d)r_{min}\}. \quad (11.12)$$

This formula is an extension of the formula for current costs.

The probability that an alarm comes in during time r_{min} when the alarm stream is Poisson, is $1 - \exp(\lambda r_{min})$. This may be approximated by λr_{min}, the expected number of new alarms in the interval.

The expected future loss on the basis of the number of ladders sent to the current alarm thus becomes:

$$\text{Send One:} \quad F_1 = L(n - 1)\lambda r_{min}; \quad (11.13)$$

$$\text{Send Two:} \quad F_2 = L(n - 2)\lambda r_{min}. \quad (11.14)$$

---

[12] d is calculated on the basis of Equation (11.1).

11.5 An Algorithm for Initial Dispatch

Combining Equations (11.11), (11.12), (11.13), and (11.14) so that

$$Z_1 = C_1 + F_1 \text{ and } Z_2 = C_2 + F_2 \qquad (11.15)$$

gives the loss in terms of response times to fires. We now add the workload factor. It is $2W$ if two ladders are sent and $W + p(\mathbf{x}, m)W$ if one is sent (since the second ladder will eventually be sent if the alarm is serious). Thus, it is sufficient to add the difference, $W(1 - p(\mathbf{x}, m))$, to Z_2, to obtain

$$Z_2 = C_2 + F_2 + (1 - p(\mathbf{x}, m))W. \qquad (11.16)$$

Note that C_1 and C_2 depend on the companies chosen for the dispatch. There is no restriction to the closest and second-closest units. However, the "future" losses F_1 and F_2 represent the regional response time degradation, assuming that this degradation depends only on the number of companies dispatched, and not on which ones are dispatched. The formulation can be extended to take into account specific differences between response time degradations if different companies are dispatched.

Recall the two-company model of Carter, Chaiken, and Ignall (1972) discussed in Section 7.3. In this model, one company is sent to each alarm, and the question is how to divide the region into "response areas." An optimal dispatch rule is of the following form. Company 1 rather than Company 2 should be dispatched to an alarm of type m at location $\mathbf{x}$ if

$$c_1(\mathbf{x}, m) - c_2(\mathbf{x}, m) \leq (C_1 - C_2)\rho/(\rho + 1), \qquad (11.17)$$

where $c_j(\mathbf{x}, m)$ is the expected damage if Company j responds to an alarm of type m at $\mathbf{x}$, C_j is the expected loss at an average alarm in the region if it is served by Company j, and $\rho = \lambda/u$, where λ is the alarm rate in the region and $1/\mu$ is the service time. Under the assumptions of this chapter,

$$c_j(\mathbf{x}, m) = p(\mathbf{x}, m)t_j(\mathbf{x}).$$

It will be helpful to define T_j as the expected loss in the region if Company j is *not* sent (so that the other company serves all incidents). This gives $T_1 = C_2$ and $T_2 = C_1$. Rewriting Equation (11.17), we get: dispatch Company 1 if

$$p(\mathbf{x}, m)t_1(\mathbf{x}) + \frac{\rho}{\rho + 1} T_1 \leq p(\mathbf{x}, m)t_2(\mathbf{x}) + \frac{\rho}{\rho + 1} T_2. \qquad (11.18)$$

This has the following interpretation. If Company 1 is sent to the incoming alarm and does not return before the next alarm, then the next alarm will be served by Company 2 and the loss will be T_1. If the alarms are Poisson and service is exponential, then $\rho/(\rho + 1)$ is the probability that the next alarm occurs before Company 1 returns. Therefore,

$\rho/(\rho + 1)T_1$ on the left-hand side of Equation (11.18) is the expected loss at the next alarm if Company 1 is sent in response to the incoming alarm. (The loss at the next alarm if it occurs *after* Company 1 returns is not considered, because both companies will be available and the system starts over from scratch.)

Thus, the left-hand side of Equation (11.18) can be seen as the sum of a current loss ($p(\mathbf{x}, m)t_2(\mathbf{x})$) and a future loss ($T_1\rho/(\rho + 1)$) if Company 1 is sent to the incoming alarm. The right-hand side is similarly a current loss plus a future loss if Company 2 is sent. We interpret Equation (11.18) as saying: choose the company that minimizes the sum of current and future losses. It is this interpretation that is preserved in developing the algorithm that will handle a region with many companies and the possibility that more than one company will be sent to each incident.

Define $\theta_j = T_j\rho/(\rho + 1)$. The details of the calculation of θ_j are given in Carter, Ignall, and Rider (1977). What is important for our purposes is that the size of the region plays a significant role. In particular, the larger the region used in this computation, the smaller the role of any particular company and so the smaller the values of the θ_j's. Thus, choosing the size of the region determines how much weight future losses receive. A region size factor (G) is included in the calculation of θ_j, and it turns out that θ_j is nearly proportional to G. In particular, if G is set equal to zero, all of the θ_j's are zero.

The appropriate θ is added to the values of Z_1 and Z_2 obtained from Equations (11.15) and (11.16). Specifically, in evaluating the consequences of sending only Company j, θ_j is added to Z_1. If Companies j and k are sent initially, and k would arrive second, θ_k is added to Z_2.

In choosing dispatches, it may be desirable to forego strict optimality in terms of minimum average response times over a period of time by discounting future costs. The reason for this is what we call the *principle of accountability*. This principle states that a public official will be held more accountable for what has happened than for what might happen. If it turns out that a fire with a fatality was not sent the closest fire company, it will do the responsible official little good to argue that the closest company was being held in reserve for a potentially more serious fire.

Therefore, the algorithm incorporates a number of parameters (W, G, β, r) and choices that can be adjusted so that individual dispatches will be defensible while average performance is improved. Section 11.5.3 shows the effect of adjusting these parameters on dispatch decisions. The algorithm performs the following steps separately for engines and for ladders:

1. A unit that definitely will be sent to the alarm is selected. Because of the principle of accountability, parameters will be set so that this is almost certainly the closest unit for occupied structural fires.

11.5 An Algorithm for Initial Dispatch

2. A candidate second unit is selected. This unit may not be the second closest available unit.
3. A decision is made whether or not to send the candidate (second) company.

In mathematical terms we have the series of steps described below. (Note that times shown with a small t are retrieved from a data file, and those shown with a capital T are calculated estimates.)

Step 1
Calculate

$$Z_1'(k) = q(\mathbf{x}, m)t_k(\mathbf{x}) + \theta_k,$$

and choose the company k^* that minimizes Z_1'.

Step 2
After an engine and a ladder are selected in Step 1, the first response time can be found by adding u to the shorter travel time; call this $r_{\min}$.

Step 3
Calculate the send-one cost

$$Z_1'(k^*) = q(\mathbf{x}, m)t_k^*(\mathbf{x}) + \theta_k^* + p(\mathbf{x}, m)\beta\{t_i(\mathbf{x}) + r_{\min}\},$$

where company i is the closest ladder other than k^*.

Step 4
Given that company k^* is being sent, attempt to select the best company j to send as the second company if two companies are sent. Calculate for all $j \neq k^*$:

$$\begin{aligned}Z_2'(k^*, j) &= q(\mathbf{x}, m)\min\{t_k^*(\mathbf{x}), t_j(\mathbf{x})\} \\ &+ \beta p(\mathbf{x}, m)\max\{t_k^*(\mathbf{x}), t_j(\mathbf{x})\} \\ &+ \theta_j + \{F_2(j) - F_1(j)\} \\ &+ \{1 - p(\mathbf{x}, m)\}W.\end{aligned} \quad (11.19)$$

The minimum and maximum terms are in Z_2' because, if j is closer to $\mathbf{x}$ than k^*, j will be arriving first if both units are sent. Future costs F_2 and F_1 are obtained from Equations (11.13) and (11.14) by considering an N-company region centered about company j. Thus, the appropriate value of n depends on j, which is the reason for our notation $F_2(j)$ and $F_1(j)$. Including θ_j allows a company-specific choice of the appropriate second ladder if one is sent. The W term adds the workload factor.

Select the company j^* that minimizes $Z_2'(k^*, j)$. Note that W plays no role in this choice.

Step 5

In this step we calculate $Z(k^*, j^*)$ the actual send-two cost with candidate j^*. This is the same as $Z'(k^*, j^*)$ in Equation (11.19) except that θ_j^* is replaced by θ_k^* if company k^* is closer than company j^*. If $Z(k^*, j^*) \leq Z(k^*)$, dispatch both k^* and j^*. If not, send only k^*.

The four parameters play the following roles:

(a) *How Many Companies are Sent*

Send two if and only if

$$r_{\min}\beta p(\mathbf{x}, m) > (F_2 - F_1) + \{1 - p(\mathbf{x}, m)\}W.$$

For a given incident (and its corresponding p and $r_{\min}$), $F_2 - F_1$ is usually very small so that the ratio β/W usually determines how many companies are sent. The larger this ratio, the larger the average number of ladders dispatched.

(b) *Which Companies are Sent*
  (i) If two companies are sent, the candidate second-arriving companies are ranked on the value of

  $$\beta p(\mathbf{x}, m)t_k(\mathbf{x}) + \theta_k.$$

  Since θ is almost proportional to G, the larger the ratio G/β, the more often the algorithm will choose, on the basis of future losses, a second ladder that is not the closest available.
  (ii) If one company is sent, the candidate companies are ranked on the values of

  $$\{p(\mathbf{x}, m) + r(1 - p(\mathbf{x}, m))\}t_k(\mathbf{x}) + \theta_k.$$

  Roughly, then, the larger the ratio G/r, the more the algorithm will choose, on the basis of future losses, a first ladder that is not the closest one available.

The algorithm will choose the more distant of a pair of companies only when their response times are at most a few seconds different. For additional details, see Section 5 of Carter, Ignall, and Rider (1977).

11.5.3 Results of Simulation Tests in New York City

Table 11.9 gives summary response-time and workload statistics that allow us to compare the performance of the traditional initial dispatch policy in New York City to the dispatch algorithm, as various parameters of the algorithm are varied. These statistics come from simulation of department operations in response to actual alarms in the Bronx for the four-week period (672 hours) beginning July 5, 1972.

11.5 An Algorithm for Initial Dispatch

The simulation model used is the one described in Chapter 13. The traditional policy was a variable two-engine and two-ladder response to street box alarms and telephone or verbal alarms that sounded structural. (All telephone and verbal alarms that were structural, as well as those that were sent more than one engine and one ladder, were classified as "sounding structural.") Other telephone and verbal alarms were sent one engine and/or one ladder, as needed. The initial dispatch algorithm handled these other alarms in the same way as the traditional policy. For street box and telephone/verbal "sounds structural" alarms, the procedure given in Section 11.5.2 was used. The parameter values chosen were $\beta = 0.4$, $r = 0.01$, and a region containing eight ladder companies. The values of $p(\mathbf{x}, m)$ for box alarms were determined from 1967–1970 data using the empirical Bayes procedures described in Section 8.6. For telephone/verbal alarms, boroughwide estimates of p were assumed to apply to all locations. In both cases, the values of p were adjusted to the time of day (Section 8.6). For all policies simulated, the relocation policy of Chapter 12 was used. Travel times were determined from the square root-linear time-distance relationship of Chapter 6.

Table 11.9 shows that the algorithm improves second-arriving engine and second-arriving ladder response times to occupied structure fires that need them, while keeping workload about the same as under the traditional policy. These improvements result from the algorithm's attempt to consider the chance that the alarm is a fire in an occupied structure. Thus, although in the $G = \frac{1}{2}$ case, for example, fewer responses are made with the algorithm, and so fewer incidents receive a two-engine and two-ladder initial response, more *occupied structure fires* receive two and two initially. In this case, two engines were initially dispatched to 457 of the 702 occupied structure fires under the traditional policy; this rose 30 percent to 596 fires with the algorithm.

The slight degradation (about one to two seconds) in first-engine and first-ladder times to occupied structure fires with the algorithm results from the closest company being in-house slightly more often under the traditional policy. For ladders, one reason that the closest company was in its house more often is the more frequent relocations under the traditional policy. This policy resulted in five times as many ladder relocations as the algorithm did, and the total time spent relocated was at least four times as large.

The different values of the θ_j's induced by the differences in G led to very little variation in average response times. The smallest values of first-engine and ladder response times occur when $G = 0$, which makes all of the θ's zero. The smallest values of second-engine and ladder response times occur when $G = \frac{1}{2}$.

The different values of G have minor effects on average workload, as

TABLE 11.9. Response-time and workload statistics simulated for the Bronx during four weeks in July 1972.

		Traditional Policy	Policies With Approximately the Same Total Workload As the Traditional Policy				Policies That Vary the Total Workload (All With $G = 1$)		
			Always Send Closest Company		→	Sometimes Send a Farther Company	Make More Responses		Save Responses
			$G = 0$	$G = 1/2$	$G = 1$	$G = 2$	$W = 132$	$W = 265$	$W = 397$
Average response times to fires in occupied structures:	RESPONSE TIME								
	First-arriving engine	3.95 min	3.96	3.96	3.97	3.98	3.97	3.97	3.96
	Second-arriving engine (when needed)	5.57 min	4.87	4.75	4.81	4.87	4.55	4.85	5.57
	First-arriving ladder	4.01 min	4.02	4.03	4.04	4.04	4.03	4.04	4.03
	Second-arriving ladder (when needed)	5.49 min	5.04	5.02	503	5.07	4.59	5.01	5.47
Number of fires in occupied structures that were dispatched:	RESPONSE ADEQUACY								
	Two engines initially	457	589	596	598	599	653	588	513
	Two ladders initially	474	598	598	601	602	654	588	514

WORKLOAD									
Average number of responses by Bronx companies to all incidents in the 28 day period	Engines	330	318	321	323	326	357	314	283
	Ladders	385	369	373	375	377	413	361	325
The number of responses made by the company that made the most	Engines	712 (E82)[a]	653 (E82)	623 (E85)	634 (E85)	638 (E85)	733 (E85)	637 (E85)	553 (E85)
	Ladders	714 (L31)	673 (L31)	655 (L58)	681 (L58)	697 (L58)	813 (L58)	674 (L58)	595 (L58)
The total operating hours of the company that had the most	Engines	202.5 hrs (E82)	195.4 (E82)	187.7 (E82)	183.8 (E82)	179.8 (E73)	183.2 (E82)	185.1 (E82)	179.9 (E82)
	Ladders	189.5 hrs. (L31)	188.0 (L31)	180.1 (L31)	177.1 (L42)	177.2 (L42)	180.3 (L42)	177.9 (L42)	174.5 (L42)
RELOCATIONS									
Total number of relocations made	Engines	372	294	283	284	288	293	287	283
	Ladders	226	43	39	38	41	22	43	66
Total hours spent relocated	Engines	335 hrs	374	368	361	373	359	363	350
	Ladders	280 hrs	67	63	60	66	42	68	97

[a] Engine Company 82; other companies labeled similarly.

measured by the average number of responses made by Bronx engines and ladders. Among themselves and relative to the traditional policy, they do have a significant effect on the arrangement of that workload. Comparing the four values of G to the traditional policy, we see that:

1. Even when $G = 0$, the busiest engine and ladder companies make fewer responses and spend fewer hours traveling and at incidents.
2. As G is increased, the number of responses and operating hours of the busiest engine and ladder companies first decrease and then increase. Responses of the busiest engine and ladder companies are smallest at $G = \frac{1}{2}$; operating hours of the busiest engine are smallest at $G = \frac{1}{2}$; operating hours of the busiest ladder are smallest at $G = 1$. Note that when $G = 1$, the algorithm gave many responses to Engine 85, making it run more than Engine 82; but 82 still spends more time operating.

We have already mentioned that the algorithm substantially reduced ladder company relocations. For engines it reduced the number of relocations, but not the time spent by the relocatees filling in for other companies. Relocation implies a trip to another firehouse and back; and while there, possible responses to incidents in a less familiar area. Thus, all else being equal, less relocating is an advantage. In this regard the algorithm offers a significant advantage.

GLOSSARY OF SYMBOLS

$A(s^*)$ = Expected number of serious box incidents getting two ladders initially if the cutoff probability is s^*
$a(s^*)$ = Fraction of all box serious incidents getting two ladders
c_i = Square-root law constant for the ith company
C = Current "cost" of a dispatch decision
C_i = Current "cost" of sending i ladders
$C_1(i)$ = Send-one "cost" if ladder i is sent to an incident
D_i = Average travel distance for ith company
$D(s^*)$ = Expected total hourly number of initial ladder responses when cutoff probability is s^*
$d(s^*)$ = Average dispatch to a box alarm when cutoff probability is s^*
F = Future "cost" of a dispatch decision
F_i = Future "cost" of a dispatch decision if i units are dispatched initially
g_k = Probability of kth alarm type
G = Multiplier for "which" future cost
H = Measure of uncertainty
$M(s^*)$ = Expected total hourly number of ladder responses when cutoff probability is s^*
n^* = Number of ladders located in a region
N = Number of boxes in a region
n = Number of ladders currently available in a region
p = Average unit availability in an area
p_j = Probability that an alarm at box j signals a serious fire
$p(\mathbf{x}, m)$ = Estimated probability that an alarm of type m at location $\mathbf{x}$ is serious
P_i = Probability of the ith incident type
$q(\mathbf{x}, m)$ = Coefficient for the travel time of the first-arriving company at an incident with probability serious $p(\mathbf{x}, m)$
r = The importance of response time to a nonserious incident relative to response time to a serious incident
r_i = Proportion of box alarms at box i that work two ladders
$r_{\min}$ = Travel time plus turnout time of closest unit, whether engine or ladder, to an incident
R_i = Average response time of ith-arriving company
$R(i)$ = Response time of company i
S = Setup time
s^* = Cutoff probability
T_i = Average travel time of ith-arriving company

$t_j(\mathbf{x})$ = Travel time from the location of company j to location $\mathbf{x}$
u = Turnout time
W = Workload "cost"
x_j = Probability that an initial dispatch will send j ladders to an incident
y_j = Probability that an initial dispatch will send at least j ladders to an incident
Z = Total "cost" of a dispatch decision
$Z_1(i)$ = Total "cost" of sending only ladder i to an incident in an initial dispatch
$Z_2(i, j)$ = Total "cost" of sending ladders i and j to an incident in an initial dispatch
$Z(j)$ = Total "cost" of sending company j to an incident
β = The importance of second-company response time relative to first-company response time
α_j = Expected degradation of travel time to serious fires if company j is working at an average incident
λ_i = Alarm rate in ith region
μ = Service (return) rate for an average incident
π_j = Proportion of all box incidents that work j ladders

Chapter 12
Relocation

Synopsis

When most or all of the fire companies in a region are fighting fires, protection against future fires in the same region is considerably reduced. It is standard practice in most urban fire departments to protect the exposed region by temporarily relocating fire companies from outside the region into some of the vacant houses. Most departments currently make relocations that are planned in advance and recorded on alarm assignment cards. At low alarm rates, such preplanned relocations can work well, since they are usually based on the assumption that only one fire of any significance is in progress at any time. At high alarm rates this assumption is not true; and preplanned relocations can become impossible, or (in some circumstances) actually harmful though possible, just at the time when effective relocations are most needed.

This chapter describes a relocation procedure that is designed to overcome the difficulties of the preplanned system. It can be used in two ways. It was originally designed to be implemented in a real-time computerized command and control system, where it would exploit the ability of the computer to (1) keep abreast of the current status of all fires in progress and all units on duty; and (2) generate and compare many alternative relocation plans very quickly. The method has been designed to be very fast and to use a modest amount of computer memory. It has been implemented in this way in New York City. The second way to use the relocation method is to generate preplanned relocations. Because of its flexibility, more scenarios can be considered in creating preplanned relocations than might otherwise be possible. The resulting preplanned relocations should be better than those currently being used on alarm assignment cards.

12.1 INTRODUCTION

A very large fire is raging. Many fire companies, both engine and ladder, are hard at work controlling and extinguishing the blaze. They will be occupied by these tasks for many hours; meanwhile, their firehouses will be empty and the region in which they ordinarily respond to alarms will be left unprotected.

When this happens in a large city, the fire department usually temporarily relocates (moves) some fire companies from their firehouses in parts of the city that are still adequately protected, to some of the empty houses. In smaller cities it may be necessary to achieve the same effect by borrowing companies temporarily from neighboring communities via a mutual assistance agreement. The purpose of such temporary relocations is clear—to spread out the still available firefighting resources in order to reduce and balance the risks and consequences that would result if other fires occur. The dilemma of relocation is equally clear: How much can be borrowed? When is the borrowing (or lending) jusified? Precisely which companies should be relocated? Which of the empty houses should be filled?

When alarm rates are low, those fires requiring relocations of firefighting units are rare. They occur one at a time, and when they occur, typically no other fires are in progress. Thus, under low alarm rate conditions it is possible to plan in advance for relocations with a reasonable expectation that the plan will be able to be carried out. Experienced fire officers imagine a hypothetical incident, say a three-alarm fire at a particular alarm box. Using their judgment, and assuming that all other fire companies not called to the third alarm will be available, they formulate a specific relocating plan. The plan consists of a list of temporary transfers of engine companies and ladder companies. When these plans are made by experienced and talented officers, and when the alarm rate is low, these plans work well. When the alarm rate is high, the plans—however well conceived originally—often break down. The reason for the breakdown is simply that at high alarm rates, several incidents (even first alarms) may be in progress simultaneously, and the officers who created a relocation plan for one particular incident could not have anticipated this. Making a good and implementable relocation in this situation requires knowledge of the status of all of the fire companies at the department's disposal, and the nature of incidents in progress *at the time action must be taken*. There are so many possible variations of the situation that can be encountered that there is no way to do this in advance.

In this chapter we present a mathematical method for solving relocation problems using a computer. The method can be used in two ways. The first is to assist planners in the preparation of preplanned relocations

12.1 Introduction   461

for alarm assignment cards, in cities where alarm rates are low enough for such advance plans to be generally implementable. The method we develop incorporates most of the considerations that experienced officers make in developing relocation plans, and can be a great help whenever major revisions of relocation plans are desired—for example, if a new firehouse is being built, or if some companies are being moved into new locations.

The second way to use the relocation method is as part of an on-line real-time computer-assisted command and control system that keeps accurate status information on fire companies and incidents moment by moment. In this type of application, the computer system is programmed to recognize a relocation problem as soon as it appears. The computer then quickly makes calculations that compare alternative relocations. The results suggest to a human decisionmaker the one or several relocations that look best.

The relocation problem is closely related to the dispatching problems already discussed in Chapter 11. In our discussion we view the relocation algorithm (that is, the organized mathematical procedure by which the relocation is specified) and the dispatch method as the two main components of a computerized Management Information and Control System (MICS). The two procedures must operate in parallel.

It should be noted that, while the (temporary) relocation problem has some apparent relation to the fire resource allocation problems and firehouse siting problems discussed in Chapters 9 and 10, in this discussion we assume that the fire department has already allocated its resources and located its firehouses more or less as it deems appropriate. We thus take these allocations and locations as our starting point, and develop an approach that tries as far as possible to preserve the key characteristics of the fire company distribution implicitly defined by the department as being "good."

12.1.1 Some Relocation Examples

At this point some specific examples will clarify our concerns. First, we must ask whether relocation is still needed, or if it is needed as much today with modern apparatus and communications as it was 50 or more years ago. Relocation originated in the days of horse-drawn wagons, steam-powered pumpers, and telegraph (only) signal systems. It was crucial then because the speed with which the fire department could react to new incidents in an area already depleted of protection was severely limited by vehicular speed, the distance the apparatus could move, and the inability to keep close communication with companies on the move and on the firegrounds.

A fire and the resulting relocations that occurred in Harlem on the Fourth of July, 1886 concretely illustrate the concerns. The details of this fascinating incident are vividly given in Galvin (1971). For our purposes, the significant facts are that on that Fourth of July afternoon, a multiple-alarm fire broke out in a fireworks stand at Third Avenue and 125th Street in Harlem, then a prosperous "suburb." In the initial response, the second-due engine company and the third-due ladder company had to travel over a mile and a quarter—horse-drawn, of course. The fire quickly spread to four other buildings. As the third alarm was transmitted, the Assistant Chief for the area was summoned from his home in Greenwich Village, far south of the fire. He rode by chief's wagon to the nearest station of the elevated train that ran up Third Avenue, boarded it, and rode to 116th Street, the closest station to the fire. It was the fastest way he could get to the scene, yet it took him forty minutes! By this time the fire had engulfed eight buildings and the chief had ordered a special signal (known as the "three-sixes") to get more units on the scene. The resulting action stripped Manhattan of all firefighting units north of 14th Street, which was about five miles south of the fire. In addition, relocations were made on special orders of the Assistant Chief on the scene—none had been preplanned. When the Chief of Department arrived on the scene he countermanded the three-sixes signal, and the fire was eventually extinguished by the firefighting forces on the scene. The consequences of depleting the area north of 14th Street of its protection were so serious that a departmental trial was held for the chief who ordered the three-sixes signal.

Eighty-three years later, on the Fourth of July, 1969, the fundamental deployment problem still existed and was experienced in a series of major fires, this time in the Bronx. These incidents were so strenuous a test of the capabilities of the city's fire department that the history of that day was used as one of the tests of the relocation algorithm we describe here. The day is described in detail in subsequent sections. Two hundred and eighty-eight alarms were received, almost twice as many as on a typical day. Over 100 alarms were received during a single four-hour period. There were seven very serious fires, each of which could have justified a relocation decision on its own; and several of these fires were in progress simultaneously. The planned relocations given on the alarm assignment cards were of little help. In many cases, the companies listed to move were themselves at working fires. In other cases, relocating a company would have created an unprotected area as large as the one to be filled. Moreover, with the alarms coming in at a rate of nearly one every two minutes (many of them for structural or other serious fires), the dispatchers did not have the luxury of coolly reflecting on the relocation problems. They were completely occupied by dispatching, and by trying to keep up with the status of units and incidents in the field. All

12.1 Introduction

of this, despite the advantages of radio communications and fast modern apparatus.

Events do not have to progress so dramatically for relocations to be needed or for a manual relocation system to be strained. In 1972, a relatively simple small fire filled much of the Hotel Commodore on 42nd Street with smoke. So many companies were involved in the massive rescue operations that a very significant part of Manhattan would have been left unprotected for many hours, had relocations not been made. Relocations may have to be made fairly often in a city with high alarm rates. For example, at 1975 alarm rates, fires requiring relocations occur about ten times a day in New York City, and it can (and does) happen that more than one of these fires is in progress at the same time.

The remainder of this chapter is devoted to an analysis of the relocation problem and to the design and testing of an algorithm creating relocation suggestions. The algorithm is of greatest benefit when used as part of an on-line computerized command and control system in a city with a high alarm rate. It can also be used in cities with low alarm rates, to aid fire officers or dispatchers in creating or modifying preplanned relocations for alarm assignment.

12.1.2 Difficulties in Defining the Objectives

Before proceeding to the largely mathematical discussion of how the relocation problem was formulated and solved by Kolesar and Walker (1972), we discuss the reason behind the particular approach that was taken. The goal was a procedure for relocating fire companies that would overcome the problems of preplanned relocations, that could be implemented within the computer-time and space constraints of a real-time system,[1] and that would produce "good" relocations. It was by no means clear at the outset what "good" meant. It was decided jointly, by the analysts working on the relocation algorithm and fire department management, that the definition would have to be operational. That is, the analysts, the fire department, and the public would all have to agree that the procedure was making the right kind of relocations.

It is not difficult to formulate relocation objectives. The problem is that they may lead to policies that are unacceptable to the fire department. We have already had (in Chapter 9) an extensive discussion of the dilemmas encountered when formulating criteria for deployment. For example, one objective may be to provide equal first-due travel times to all of the city. If so, the available units should be spread out rather

---

[1] Relocation is only one of several functions that an MICS must handle, and dispatching takes precedence.

uniformly. This might be loosely termed an "equity oriented" criterion—it gives similar protection to all, regardless of different needs. If, however, the goal is to minimize the citywide average travel time of first-arriving engines and ladders to alarms, the companies should be concentrated in the areas where the fire incidence is greatest. This is the "efficiency" criterion. (See Chapter 9 for a more extensive discussion of these alternatives.)

Most fire departments' resource allocation policies achieve a compromise between these two extremes. A mathematical statement of the objectives of these policies, however, is hard to determine. In constructing a solution to the relocation problem, therefore, it was decided to model the problem as a sequential decision process, with different objectives being used at each step of the process.

The objectives from the citizen's point of view must also be taken into account. Consider the reaction of a community to the relocation of its "own" fire company to another part of the city. These citizens are likely to feel they *need* their fire company, and that they are paying for it. Lending it out is likely to be justifiable to them only if done infrequently and in situations of dramatic need to the borrowing region. A formal algorithm, whatever its broad criteria, will also have to make sense when examined from this point of view.

The quantification of the objectives is discussed in the following section, which also presents a mathematical formulation of the relocation problem and a heuristic method of solution. In Section 12.3, a sample relocation problem is used to demonstrate the way the algorithm works.

12.2 MATHEMATICAL FORMULATION OF THE PROBLEM

12.2.1 Summary of the Algorithm

We begin by defining a relocation as a set of individual company moves made at one time. Our formulation of the relocation problem separates the problem into subproblems that are solved sequentially. The subproblems answer each of the following questions:

1. When should a relocation be made?
2. How many companies should be relocated?
3. Which available companies should be relocated?
4. To which house should each relocating company go?

All of these questions have to be answered by any relocation method. They are interrelated and, if optimization were the goal, should be dealt with simultaneously. We have found it much easier to treat the problems sequentially, and our testing indicates that there is no important practical disadvantage to doing so.

12.2 Mathematical Formulation of the Problem

Since engines and ladders both provide crucial services, we perform computations and analysis separately for engines and ladders. A brief description of how the algorithm answers each of the questions is presented below.

1. *When should relocations be made?* A call for relocations is made whenever the fire protection being provided in an area of the city falls below some minimum level. The minimum standards are based on maintaining the *relative* densities of fire companies throughout the city rather than on specifying maximum travel-time or travel-distance standards for every area of the city. The standards can be varied in any particular application, but relocations may be made, for example, whenever some location in the city has both its first-due and second-due companies (ladders or engines) unavailable, and they are expected to be unavailable for some extended period of time. Such a location is said to be *uncovered*.
2. *How many companies should be relocated?* Enough empty houses should be filled to assure that no location remains uncovered, while moving as few companies as possible.
3. *Which companies should be relocated?* The companies to be relocated are chosen to satisfy four general principles:

    A company should not be moved if moving it will cause new locations to become uncovered.

    A company should not be moved if it is "too busy." A busy company is more likely to have an alarm occur in its area while it is relocated than is a less busy company. If its house is empty, a substitute company will have to respond from further away.

    A company should not be moved if it is protecting "too large" a region. If such a company is moved and an alarm occurs in its area while it is away, the resulting travel time for the substitute company will be excessive.

    A company should not be moved "too far." A company that is relocated a long distance will spend a long time traveling, and will therefore be out of its area longer than if a closer company were moved. The long relocation time increases the chance that an alarm will occur in the company's area while it is away, or that one will occur in the area to which it is traveling while it is traveling, resulting in long travel times to the alarm.

We use a single number to measure the "penalty" or "cost" of a particular relocation plan. This cost is the average travel time of first-arriving units, to alarms expected to occur in the area affected by the moves, during the time the moves are in effect. It takes into account whether a company is "too busy" by including the alarm rate in its first-due area. It takes into account whether it is protecting "too large" a region by including the size of the company's first-due area. It takes into account whether it is moving "too far" by including the travel time between its present location and the location of the vacant house it would be filling.

The relocation procedure, then, is to select those available companies to move that will produce the lowest "cost" without uncovering any of their home areas.

4. *To which house should each relocating company go?* Step 2 chooses the set of houses to be filled. Step 3 chooses the set of companies to be moved. It also specifies how the companies should be assigned to the empty houses to obtain the smallest "cost." However, it can be improved by applying a further objective: minimizing the time that the relocating companies will spend traveling.

There are several reasons why fire departments would want to do this. First, shorter relocation times are less of a burden on the relocating companies and increase their availability. Second, moving companies shorter distances tends to keep them in areas in which they are familiar with the street patterns as well as the firefighting problems.

12.2.2 Defining the Objectives

One way of balancing considerations of equity and efficiency is to set a minimum coverage standard for every area of a city. One such standard is to guarantee that there is at least one firefighting company within x minutes (or y miles) of every structure or point in the city (Toregas et al., 1971). Since all alarms are generally referenced to the nearest alarm box, and since alarm boxes are usually distributed widely and relatively uniformly across the city, we found it convenient to apply the standard to alarm boxes (street intersections would work equally well). It would not be difficult to provide a minimum coverage standard if x (or y) were specified and were constant over the city. In practice, however, the minimum coverage standard should probably be different in different areas depending on the hazards associated with the areas, and it would be difficult in practice for the fire department to specify the value of x (or y) for each area.

An attractive alternative is to let the way firefighting units are already allocated to areas implicitly define the minimum coverage standards for those areas. Usually fire companies are not uniformly distributed over a city, but are concentrated in some areas and spread out in others. This distribution is the result of complex forces—some political, some operational, others historical. In working with its existing distribution of resources, a fire department has implicitly decided how it wishes to balance equity against efficiency, at least in the short run. In the long run, of

12.2 Mathematical Formulation of the Problem

course, the fire department may modify the distribution by building new firehouses. By assuming that the department is satisfied with the distribution of fire companies, we can define a minimum coverage standard for the relocation problem that will maintain approximately the same relative geographic distribution of fire companies as currently exists. This, in turn, will maintain approximately the same variation in travel times (or distances) that currently exists among the areas.

Therefore, the minimum coverage standard requires that, for every alarm box in the city, at least one of the k closest engine houses and at least one of the p closest ladder houses contain an available company. k and p are parameters that have to be set by fire department policy. Various values could be tested and compared; New York City has generally used $k = 3$ and $p = 2$. Relocations are recommended whenever minimum coverage is not being provided. The houses to be filled and the companies that relocate are selected so as to guarantee minimum coverage, as well as to meet the objectives we are about to discuss.

While the standard of coverage defined by $k = 3$ and $p = 2$ applies in most regions of New York City, it need not be applied inflexibly to all regions of a city. It can be varied in order to provide appropriate coverage to areas that are particularly isolated or have other special characteristics. For example, some areas might require that the closest ladder company be available, while in others only one of the three closest ladders need be available. The algorithm is flexible enough to accommodate such variations. However, in order to keep the following discussion simple and concrete, we proceed as if a uniform criterion were applied in all parts of the city. No loss of generality is involved, for the framework allows the user to define and implement a minimum coverage standard requiring that m_j out of the closest n_j units of a specified type be available to alarm box j.

It is possible to simplify the application of the minimum coverage standard by noticing that, in general, several—perhaps many—alarm boxes will have the same k closest engines or the same p closest ladders. We call the aggregate of all alarm boxes having the same k closest engines an *engine response neighborhood* (written "engine RN" for brevity). A *ladder response neighborhood* ("ladder RN") is defined as the set of alarm boxes having the same p closest ladders. The set of engines and ladder response neighborhoods each form nonoverlapping partitions of the city. They are defined separately, since the coverage standard is to be applied separately to engines and ladders in order to keep a balance

---

[2] Readers familiar with optimization and computers will recognize that variants are conceptually easy to implement, but they could make the algorithm difficult to implement if applied with abandon. Good results may usually be obtained even if the standard is kept as simple as possible.

of each unit type in each region. The definition of minimum coverage can now be restated as: *there must be no engine response neighborhood with all of its k engines unavailable, and no ladder response neighborhood with all of its p ladders unavailable.*

Figure 12.1 illustrates how response neighborhoods are constructed. For simplicity, the figure assumes that $p = 2$ and that Euclidean distance determines travel times. The first-due area of Ladder A is the square area enclosed by dotted lines, which has Ladder A at its center. The response neighborhood defined by Ladder A and Ladder B is the shaded area between the two companies. Notice that the RN includes a portion of each company's first-due area, and that the companies are located on the boundary of the RN.

The use of response neighborhoods considerably reduces the calculations required to check on coverage. For example, in the Bronx there are over 2000 alarm boxes; but with $p = 2$, fewer than 50 ladder RNs. Figure 12.2 shows the ladder RNs in the Bronx. Note that in regions where the ladder companies are close together, the RNs are small; and where the companies are far apart, they are larger.

We have delayed giving, until now, a precise definition of unit "availability" for purposes of minimum coverage. It makes no sense to relocate a unit into the house of a company responding to (but not yet working at) an alarm, returning from an alarm, or due back soon from a working fire. Therefore, we consider a company to be unavailable only if it is

FIGURE 12.1. An example of a response neighborhood.

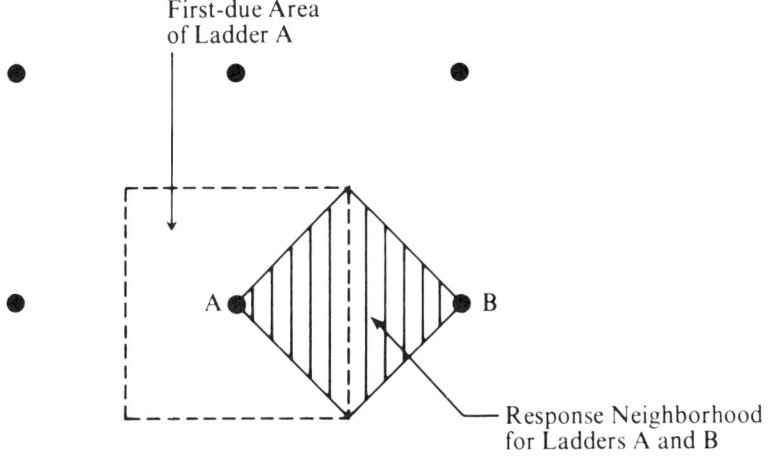

12.2 Mathematical Formulation of the Problem

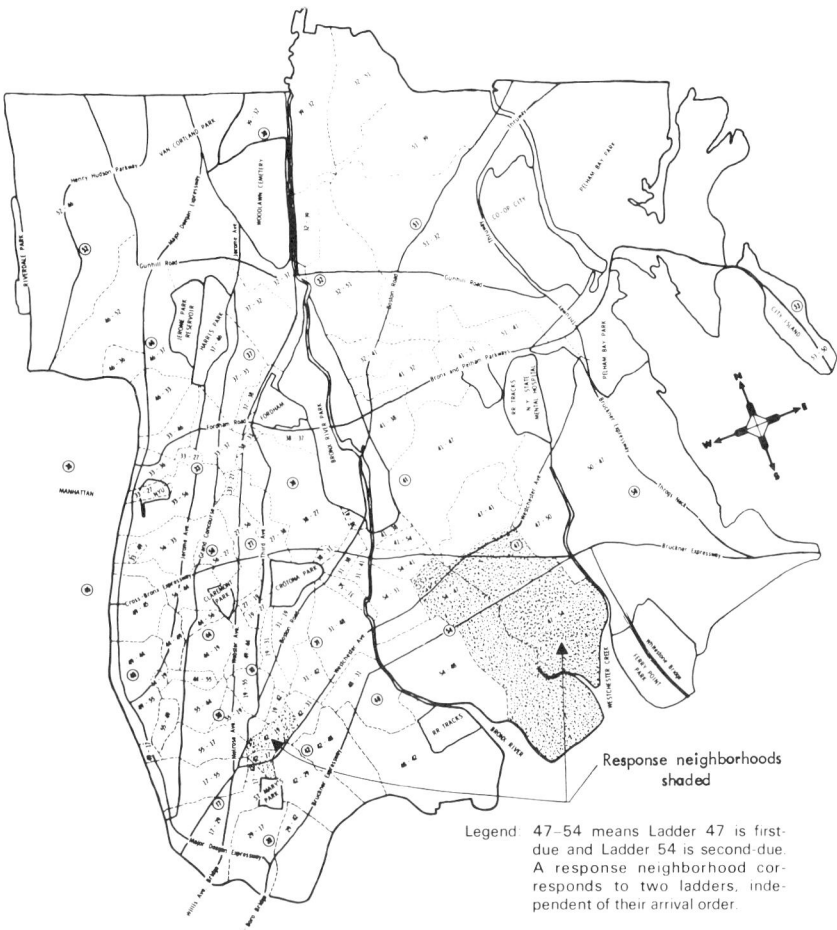

FIGURE 12.2. Ladder response neighborhoods in the Bronx.

working at a fire expected to last for a "considerable" length of time, a concept to be precisely defined later in this section.

The primary objective of the relocation algorithm is to maintain minimum coverage as just defined. It makes sense to do this by moving as few companies as possible, since moving companies increases communication problems, places them in regions with which they may not be familiar, and takes them away from their home bases, food, and dry clothes. Therefore, keeping the number of moves to a minimum becomes one of our secondary objectives.

Once the houses to be filled have been selected on the basis of the minimum coverage criterion, there may be many available companies that could be moved into those houses. Of course, no company should be moved if, by moving it, the minimum coverage criterion is violated. We therefore only consider moves that do not violate the standard. In addition, we wish to apply the following secondary criteria:

1. Do not move a company "too long" a distance.
2. Do not move a company that is "too busy."
3. Do not move a company that is protecting "too big" an area.

The way to trade off among these criteria is not immediately clear. A function that measures travel time was found to take all these secondary factors into account.

12.2.3 Developing a Cost Function

Since the minimum coverage standard primarily satisfies the fire department's equity objective (alarm rates are not considered, and the standard prevents protection in any region from being severely degraded), an efficiency measure is used to choose the companies that should be moved. In this step, we find the relocation that yields the minimum total expected travel time to alarms that occur in the regions affected by the moves (that is, the regions that gain and lose companies during the incident). The following simplified scenario provides the background for the development of the objective function for this step.

Referring to Figure 12.3, suppose Ladder 31 has just responded to a serious fire. Its house is now empty and we wish to evaluate possible relocations into it. The houses of Ladder Companies 37 and 38 are currently covered, and either one may be moved into Ladder 31's house. We want to evaluate which move is superior and if indeed any move should be made.

First, consider the data required to make the evaluation. Let R_{31} denote the region in which Ladder 31 would be closest company to all alarm boxes if it were available in its house. We must take into account which of Ladder 31's neighbors are currently available when we decide what constitutes R_{31}. Let A_{31} and λ_{31} denote respectively the physical area and the alarm rate of this region. (Note that this region changes as the pattern of available and busy companies changes.) Let R_{37} denote the region in which Ladder 37 is *currently* the closest available company, and let A_{37} and λ_{37} be, respectively, the area and alarm rate in R_{37}. Once again, in deciding what constitutes a region—namely, R_{37}—we must take into account which of Ladder 37's neighbors are available.[3] Similar

---

[3] In this example, involving ladders and a one of two minimum coverage standard, they would have to be available or Ladder 37 could not be moved. However, with a different standard (e.g., one out of three), a particular company would still be eligible to move if some of its immediate neighbors were unavailable.

12.2 Mathematical Formulation of the Problem

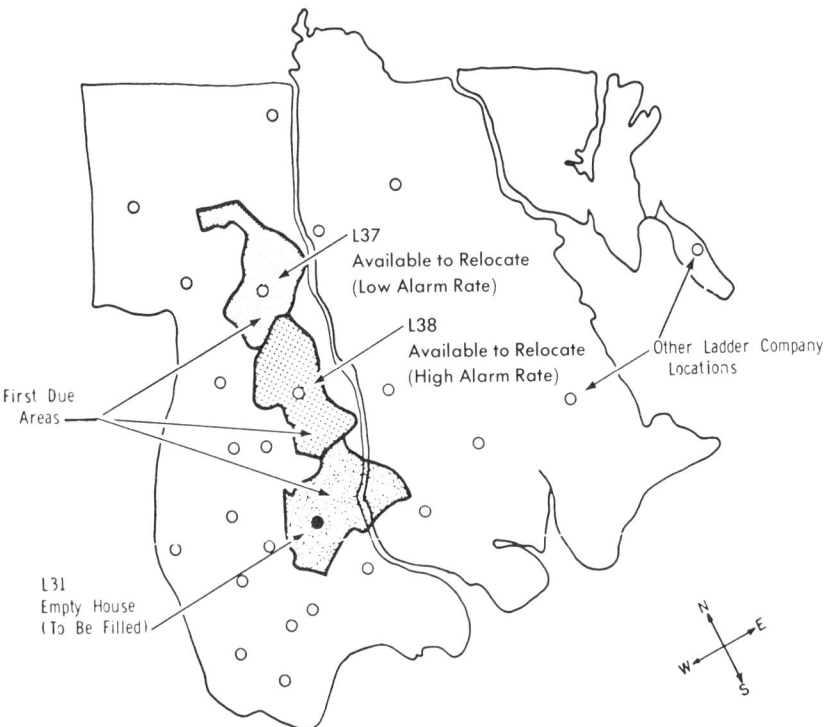

FIGURE 12.3. A simple relocation problem: Which of the two available companies should fill the empty house?

definitions apply for R_{38}, A_{38}, and λ_{38}. We assume that the alarm arrivals are a Poisson process and that all of the above parameters have been estimated. In addition, r_{ij}, the time required to relocate a company from location i to location j, is assumed to be known.

The expected travel time of the first-arriving company to an alarm in the regions served by these companies depends on which companies are available to respond to the alarm. If the closest company is not in quarters, the second closest company must play the role of the closest company, and consequently the travel time will be longer. Exact calculations of expected travel times for the first-arriving fire company in any region can be made if the alarm rates and travel times associated with individual alarm boxes are known. Alarm rates can be estimated from historical data, and actual response distances or travel times to each box can be measured directly (Chapters 6 and 8). The computation would be

$$E(T) = \sum_{k=1}^{n} a_k T_k \qquad (12.1)$$

where a_k is the proportion of alarms in the region that occur at alarm box k, T_k is the expected travel time of the first-arriving company to alarm box k, and $k = 1, \ldots, n$ indexes all the alarm boxes in the region.

Of course, the data and computation requirements for doing this in real time are formidable, so we will approximate travel times using the analysis of Chapter 6. The approximation used here is based on two models: (1) travel distances are proportional to the square-root of the size of the area served by a company (the square-root model of Section 6.4); and (2) average travel times increase linearly with distance (Section 6.3).

The travel-distance model estimates the regional average travel distance, for the first-arriving unit as $c_1\sqrt{A/N}$ when the region has area A and N units available. To estimate the average second-arriving travel distance, c_1 is replaced by c_2. (Estimation of these constants is discussed in Section 6.4.) The approximation has been tested, and works well for fairly large regions. We use it here for small one-company regions, even though it may not be very accurate.[4]

Travel times in regions served by a single company, such as R_{31}, R_{37}, and R_{38}, are approximated as follows: $c_1\sqrt{A_i}$ estimates the expected response distance of the closest responding unit in region R_i when Company i is available. If it is unavailable, but its neighbors are available (as is more or less the case if minimum coverage is being guaranteed), then $c_2\sqrt{A_i}$ is the expected response distance of the closest responding unit. If alarms in region i are arriving according to a Poisson process with an alarm rate λ_i, then $\lambda_i t$ alarms, on the average, would occur in the region during a period of length t hours. Denoting the average response speed in R_i by v_i, and ignoring some of the complicated dynamic behavior that could occur in region R_i during the fire, we have $c_1\sqrt{A_i}\,\lambda_i t/v_i$ or $c_2\sqrt{A_i}\,\lambda_i t/v_i$ as the expected total first-arriving travel time to alarms occurring in R_i during an interval of length t—the duration of the fire that is causing the relocation problem.

What complications are we avoiding? We are assuming that any other alarms that occur during the interval are not serious enough to require the service of one of the other companies for a long period of time. If any alarm were serious, another relocation problem might occur, other companies might have to respond from further away, etc. Our deliberately myopic view of the problem ignores such second-order effects by taking a snapshot of a dynamic system.

We now return to the simple scenario of Figure 12.3 (where Ladder companies 37 and 38 are candidates to relocate into Ladder 31's house), and evaluate the cost of relocating Ladder 37 in terms of expected total travel time. Let t denote the duration of the fire at which Ladder 31 is

---

[4] Recall that the estimates need only be good enough to suggest good relocations.

12.2 Mathematical Formulation of the Problem

working, and let $T > t$ be an arbitrary time interval long enough for any company that might be relocated to return to its own quarters before T has elapsed. That is, T has to be long enough to encompass all the effects of any relocations in the system. Then, letting $\alpha_i = \lambda_i \sqrt{A_i}/v_i$, the expected total first-arriving ladder travel time to alarms occurring over the interval $[0, T]$ in regions R_{31}, R_{37}, and R_{38}, is given by the formula

$$(c_2 - c_1)\{\alpha_{37}(t + r_{37,31}) + \alpha_{31}r_{37,31}\} + c_1 T\{\alpha_{31} + \alpha_{37} + \alpha_{38}\}. \quad (12.3)$$

This calculation is based on the assumption that Ladder 37 spends a time $r_{37,31}$ traveling to Ladder 31's house, stays at that house until Ladder 31 returns from the fire at time t, and then returns home. Thus, R_{31} is covered by a second-closest company during the interval $[0, r_{37,31}]$ and by a closest company during the interval $[r_{37,31}, T]$; R_{37} is covered by a second-closest company during the interval $[0, t + r_{37,31}]$; and R_{38} is covered by a closest company during the interval $[0, T]$. We are using an important property of the Poisson process, namely, that when two or more independent processes are observed simultaneously, the "joint process" (the results of both taken together) is also a Poisson process and has as its rate the sum of the rates of the individual processes.

If Ladder 38 were relocated into Ladder 31's house, the expected total first-arriving ladder travel time over the interval $[0, T]$ would be

$$(c_2 - c_1)\{\alpha_{38}(t + r_{38,31}) + \alpha_{31}r_{38,31}\} + c_1 T\{\alpha_{31} + \alpha_{37} + \alpha_{38}\}; \quad (12.4)$$

while, if no relocation were made, we would have

$$(c_2 - c_1)\alpha_{31}t + c_1 T\{\alpha_{31} + \alpha_{37} + \alpha_{38}\}. \quad (12.5)$$

The last term of each travel time expression is the same, so the alternatives can be compared by comparing only the first terms, which can now be written in a general form. Letting c_{ij} denote the "cost" or "penalty" in expected total travel time of relocating available company i into empty house j, we have

$$c_{ij} = (c_2 - c_1)\{\alpha_i(t + r_{ij}) + \alpha_j r_{ij}\}, \quad (12.6)$$

and the cost of making no relocation is $(c_2 - c_1)\alpha_j t$. Using similar reasoning, it is possible to calculate the cost of more complicated actions, such as moving available company k to the house of available company i while the latter relocates into empty house j. The cost of this "successive moveup" is

$$(c_2 - c_1)\{r_{ij}\alpha_j + r_{ki}\alpha_i + (t + r_{ij} + r_{ki})\alpha_k\}. \quad (12.7)$$

Before we use these functions to evaluate some actual relocation plans, notice that each of the three secondary criteria—relocation travel distance (r_{ij}), the "busyness" of a company (λ_i), and the size of the region protected by a company (A_i)—are all explicitly included in the cost functions. In addition, another element appears that perhaps had not been anticipated: the duration of the fire causing the relocation problem. According to the cost function, it is possible that a different relocation would be suggested for a short incident than for a long incident. In fact, using this function, it is possible to determine what the predicted length of the incident must be before it becomes advantageous to relocate.

Figure 12.4 illustrates the typical relocation costs for a situation in which Ladder Company 31 is working at a fire and Ladder Companies 37 and 38 are available to relocate. The average total first-arriving ladder travel time for fires that occur during the duration of the incident leading

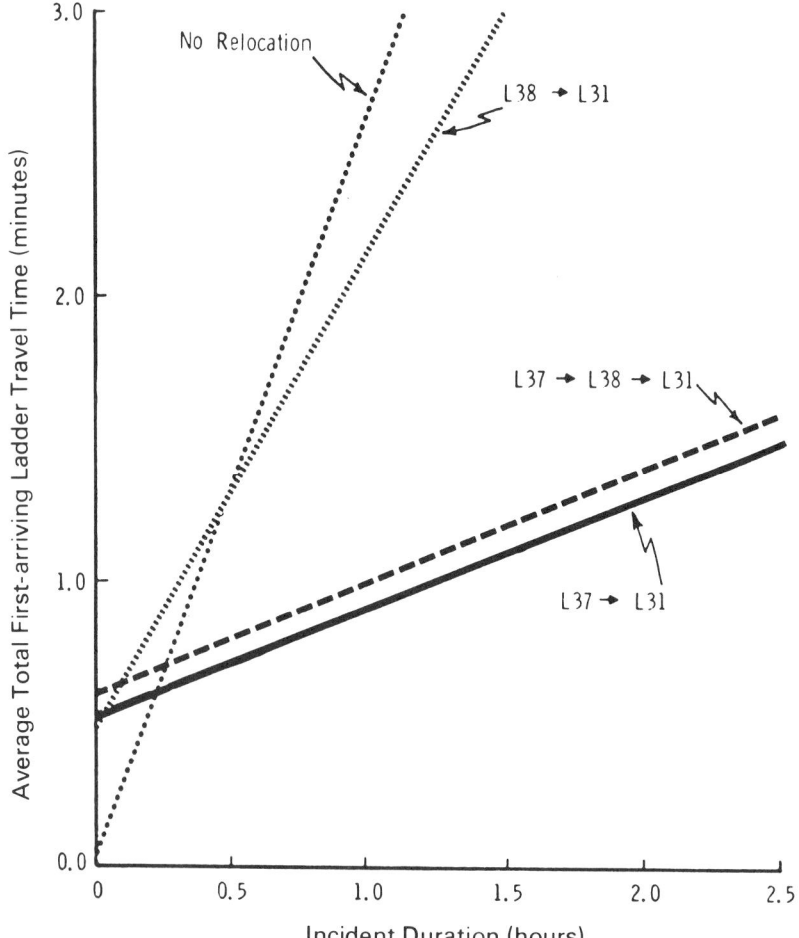

FIGURE 12.4. A comparison of relocations into the house of Ladder 31.

12.2 Mathematical Formulation of the Problem

to the relocation is shown for four alternatives:

1. No relocation (Ladder 31's house remains uncovered).
2. Move Ladder 38, which is closer to Ladder 31, but is a busy company.
3. Move Ladder 37, which is farther away from Ladder 31, but is less busy.
4. Relocate Ladder 37 into Ladder 38's house, and relocate Ladder 38 into Ladder 31—called a "successive moveup."

For any given value of t, the best relocation is the one for which the function is the smallest. Examination of the graph indicates that it certainly does not pay to make a relocation for an incident whose predicted duration is less than 15 minutes. If the fire lasts longer than that, the best plan is to move Ladder 37 into Ladder 31's house. If the incident lasts more than a half-hour, there is a clear advantage to this relocation. Note that if Ladder 37 could not be moved, it would not be worthwhile to make any relocation for a fire lasting a half-hour or less. Figure 12.4 also shows that the successive moveup of L37 to L38 to L31 is slightly worse than simply relocating Ladder 37 to Ladder 31's house.

Of course, these observations depend on the characteristics of the particular New York City problem we have been examining. Nevertheless, examination of cost functions for many situations suggests some generalizations. First, successive moveups have about the same travel-time cost as simple relocations. They are sometimes a little better, more often a little worse. But, they also move twice as many companies, thereby increasing the inconvenience to the men—as well as increasing communication and control problems. For these reasons, and after consultation with fire department senior officers, successive moveups were eliminated from further consideration in New York City. Second, in most situations in the city there seemed to be a clear travel-time advantage to relocating only if the relocation were to last more than one hour. (In the example, the advantage showed at about a half-hour, but this was due to the fact that Ladder 31 was at that time the busiest ladder company in the city.) In general, an incident that will last an hour or more is identifiable by a chief when he first arrives at the fire. So, rather than requiring the exact duration of all incidents (the value of t in the cost function), it was suggested that relocations be made only for fires expected to last more than one hour.[5]

The actual duration of such "serious" fires does not change the *relative* travel-time cost rankings very much. In other words, if moving Ladder

---

[5] Roughly speaking, this conforms to the New York City Fire Department practice of calling for relocations on "all hands" fires (all first-alarm companies working) and higher alarm fires.

37 to the Ladder 31 house looks better than moving Ladder 38 there for a one-hour fire, it also looks better for a two-hour fire. This is important since, if it were not true, the identities of the relocating companies would depend on accurate predictions of fire duration (which are generally not possible). Therefore, in the following method, travel-time cost calculations are based on the average duration of a serious fire—about one hour.[6]

12.2.4 Mathematical Formulation

The solution to the relocation problem involves a series of decisions: whether a relocation is called for; if so, which empty houses are to be filled, and by which available companies. Moreover, these decisions must be made for both engines and ladders. The mathematical formulation of the relocation problem presented below breaks the problem into four decision stages, which are solved sequentially:

1. Determination of the need for a relocation by establishing if uncovered response neighborhoods exist.
2. Determination of the empty houses to be filled in order to cover all response neighborhoods with a minimum number of moves.
3. Determination of the available companies to be relocated to minimize total travel time to incidents expected to occur during the duration of the relocation.
4. Determination of relocation assignments to minimize total travel distance of the relocating companies.

Stages 2, 3, and 4 are formulated as integer linear programming problems that either can be solved exactly using standard algorithms, or approximately using heuristic procedures.

Stage 1. Determination of the Need for a Relocation. A call for relocations should be made whenever an uncovered response neighborhood exists anywhere in the city. In a computerized command and control system, uncovered RNs can be detected by a monitoring program that is called upon periodically or whenever the computer system learns that a large fire is in progress. If the program finds that no RNs are uncovered, the next stage of the relocation algorithm is not called. If there is at least one uncovered RN, the second stage of the algorithm is entered with the list of uncovered RNs as input data.

---

[6] If a department or a chief can make better predictions of incident duration, those predictions could, of course, be used to make accurate cost estimates, and hence, possibly better relocations.

12.2 Mathematical Formulation of the Problem

In general, the rest of the relocation algorithm will be executed twice, once for engines (if there are uncovered engine RNs) and once for ladders (if there are uncovered ladder RNs). The discussion that follows applies equally well to either case.

Stage 2. Determination of the Empty Houses to be Filled. The second stage of the algorithm determines which of the uncovered houses should be filled so that the number of companies relocated is minimized. Formally, this problem belongs to a class of integer linear programming problems known as "covering problems." For more background on covering problems, see Garfinkle and Nemhauser (1972).

Suppose there are K uncovered RNs, and L vacant houses whose busy companies cover or serve these RNs. For our decision variables let $x_j = 1$ if house j is to be filled, and $x_j = 0$ otherwise. Then the problem can be stated as:

minimize
$$\sum_{j=1}^{L} x_j$$

subject to
$$\sum_{j=1}^{L} a_{ij} x_j \geq 1 \qquad i = 1, 2, \ldots, K$$

$$x_j = 0, 1 \qquad j = 1, 2, \ldots, L,$$

where

$$a_{ij} = \begin{cases} 1 & \text{if the } j\text{th house's busy company covers} \\ & \text{or serves the } i\text{th RN,} \\ 0 & \text{otherwise.} \end{cases}$$

The matrix of the a_{ij} is known as the *incidence matrix* for the covering problem. Each row of the matrix corresponds to an uncovered RN. There will be p elements equal to 1 in each row when we consider ladders, and k elements equal to 1 in each row when we consider engines. The columns correspond to the houses of the unavailable companies. There will be a 1 in each row-column position that marks the correspondence between an unavailable company and an RN it is supposed to cover when it is available. The output of stage 2 is a set of M ($M \leq L$) vacant houses to be filled, which is the input to stage 3.

Stage 3. Determination of the Available Companies to Relocate. The next decision to be made is, which available companies should relocate? The problem is formulated as if we were not only selecting the companies to relocate, but also, at the same time, assigning them to the empty houses. However, the specific assignments will not actually be used (they will be generated in stage 4); only the set of companies to be relocated will be determined. The problem is quite similar in structure to special linear programming problems called "assignment" and "transportation" problems, but with additional constraints needed to assure that the coverage criteria are not violated.

Let $j = 1, 2, \ldots, M$ refer to the empty houses to be filled, $j = M + 1, \ldots, M + N$ refer to the available companies, and $k = 1, 2, \ldots, L$ refer to the RNs associated with the available companies.

The objective function to be minimized is the total expected travel time during the relocation incident. As shown in the discussion of relocation costs given in Section 12.2.3, we have a cost to relocate available company i into empty house j given by

$$c_{ij} = (c_2 - c_1)\{\alpha_1(t + r_{ij}) + \alpha_j r_{ij}\}.$$

Consider the total cost of the M simultaneous moves needed to fill the M empty houses selected by stage 2. If we fill empty house j with available company i_j ($j = 1, 2, \ldots, M$), the total cost of this set of moves is

$$\sum_{j=1}^{M} c_{i_j,j} = (c_2 - c_1) \sum_{j=1}^{M} \{\alpha_{i_j}(t + r_{i_j,j}) + \alpha_j r_{i_j,j}\}.$$

The decisions are framed in terms of which available company is assigned to which empty house. The decision variables will be x_{ij}, where $x_{ij} = 1$ if available company i is assigned to relocate into empty house j, and $x_{ij} = 0$ otherwise. A "dummy" empty house ($j = 0$) is used so that if available company i is to remain in its own house, $x_{i0} = 1$. The integer linear program to be solved is:

Find $\{x_{ij}\}$ to

minimize
$$\sum_{j=1}^{M} \sum_{i=M+1}^{M+N} c_{ij} x_{ij}$$

subject to
$$\sum_{i=M+1}^{M+N} x_{ij} = 1 \qquad j = 1, 2, \ldots, M$$

$$\sum_{j=0}^{M} x_{ij} = 1 \qquad i = M+1, M+2, \ldots, M+N$$

$$\sum_{i=M+1}^{M+N} a_{ik} x_{i0} + \sum_{i=M+1}^{M+N} \sum_{j=1}^{M} a_{jk} x_{ij} \geq 1 \qquad k = 1, 2, \ldots, L$$

$$x_{ij} = 0, 1 \quad \text{for all } i, j.$$

The objective function and the first two sets of constraints have the structure of an assignment or transportation problem. The first set of

12.2 Mathematical Formulation of the Problem

constraints requires that all M of the empty houses be filled. The second set of constraints guarantees that all available companies are assigned somewhere. As in stage 2, the coefficients a_{ij} form an incidence matrix between firehouses and response neighborhoods. $a_{ik} = 1$ if available company i serves response neighborhood k, and is zero otherwise. The last set of constraints requires that none of the RNs that are being covered by available companies be uncovered.

Stage 4. Specific Relocation Assignments. The output of stage 3 is a specific set of assignments or "moves" of available companies to the empty houses being filled. However, the assignments sometimes make the relocating companies travel further than might another possible assignment of the same set of companies to the same empty houses. In some rare instances the assignment can even make relocating companies travel on paths that cross. This is because travel distance is only one of the components of c_{ij}. While the relocating travel distance matters, it is actually the distance times the alarm rate times the square-root of the area that is being considered, and so the algorithm can sacrifice relocation travel distance for gains in expected travel times to alarms.

Yet, for several reasons, fire departments are concerned with the distance that relocating companies must move. One reason is that shorter relocation distances mean less of a burden on relocating companies, and larger availability times. Another is that keeping the relocation distance down tends to keep companies in areas where they are familiar with street patterns as well as with particular firefighting problems. To solve this problem we view stage 3 as a device for selecting the companies to relocate, and ignore the specific moves it suggests. We then determine the specific assignments that minimize total travel distance. Of course, this would not make sense if the travel-time cost were much higher. But in most cases the resulting "reassignment" increases the relocation cost very little, and can significantly reduce the total distance traveled (Section 12.5).

We now let the index $j = 1, 2, \ldots, M$ refer to the M empty houses selected by stage 2 and the index $i = 1, 2, \ldots, M$ refer to the M available companies selected by stage 3. Again, r_{ij} denotes the time required for a unit to relocate from "full" house i to "empty" house j, and the decision variable $x_{ij} = 1$ if available company i is assigned to empty house j and is zero otherwise.

Mathematically, stage 4 involves solving a traditional assignment problem:

Find $\{x_{ij}\}$ to

minimize

$$\sum_{j=1}^{M} \sum_{i=1}^{M} r_{ij} x_{ij}$$

subject to

$$\sum_{j=1}^{M} x_{ij} = 1 \qquad i = 1, 2, \ldots, M$$

$$\sum_{i=1}^{M} x_{ij} = 1 \qquad j = 1, 2, \ldots, M$$

$$x_{ij} = 0, 1.$$

12.3 SOLVING THE PROBLEM: A HEURISTIC ALGORITHM

In this section a method is described for solving the optimization problems previously formulated. All these problems are integer linear programs in zero-one variables. Stage 2 has the special structure of a set-covering problem, stage 3 is a transportation problem with additional constraints, and stage 4 is an assignment problem. All these problems can be solved exactly using one of several special integer programming algorithms. Unfortunately, except for the assignment problem, the exact algorithms require more computation time and computer memory than can be afforded in a real-time system. (By an exact algorithm we mean one that is guaranteed to find an optimal solution in a finite number of iterations.) The state of the art in integer programming is changing rapidly, but at present it would be too costly in terms of computer time to guarantee exact solution of these integer programming problems.[7] Relocation is only one of many on-line functions to be carried out by an MICS, so one must be frugal with computer time and storage.

Heuristic algorithms were designed to obtain solutions to the problems. By their very nature these algorithms, although designed to find optimal solutions, are not guaranteed to do so. In testing the algorithms, the results obtained using exact algorithms were compared to those obtained using the heuristics, in order to check how far from optimal the heuristic solutions were likely to be. Fortunately, in our tests the optimal solution was always obtained using the heuristic methods.

12.3.1 Stage 2. Determination of the Empty Houses to Be Filled

The basic heuristic rule for selection of a house to fill is to select first the house associated with the largest number of uncovered RNs. After application of this rule, the covering problem is reduced by the elimination of the house just selected to be filled and all RNs that will be covered as

---

[7] Often most of the computing effort of exact algorithms is spent guaranteeing the optimality of a solution obtained early in the calculations.

12.3 Solving the Problem: A Heuristic Algorithm

a consequence of filling it. In the same way, another house is selected to be covered. This procedure continues until all RNs are covered. The rule may be applied several times using alternate starting points. The method can be summarized as follows:

1. Set $j = 1$.
2. Fill the empty house associated with the jth largest number of uncovered RNs. If there is a tie, fill the house of the company with the highest alarm rate in its first-due area.
3. Fill the house that now belongs to the largest number of uncovered RNs. If there is a tie, fill the house of the company with the highest alarm rate in its first-due area. Keep going until no RNs are uncovered. Count the number of houses that are filled.
4. Repeat steps 2 and 3 for $j = 2, 3, \ldots, P$.[8]
5. If there are no ties, the set of empty houses to be filled will be the one that requires the fewest number of houses to be filled. If several sets are tied with the same number of houses to be filled, solve stage 3 separately for each set and select the set that produces the minimum stage 3 cost.

12.3.2 Stage 3. Determination of the Available Companies to Relocate

The heuristic rule by which we determine the available company to move into a given house is to try to fill each empty house with the available company having the lowest relocation cost associated with the move. The relocation costs are the c_{ij} described above. To help select the relocatees (companies to be relocated) a ranked list of candidate relocatees can be created for each house to be filled. The companies on the list are the available ones, ordered by their c_{ij} values.

Each move must be checked against the coverage criterion to assure that no RNs become uncovered. A company on any relocatee list may be relocated without violating minimum coverage. But, if the selections are made independently for each vacant house to be filled, the resulting set of moves might have the same company moving into more than one house, or might leave one or more RNs uncovered by moving neighboring companies.

A feasible relocation is generated by successive applications of the heuristic test and the feasibility test. The procedure begins with one house to be filled, and progresses in sequence through the others, one by

---

[8] The value of P is arbitrary—the larger it is, the greater the certainty of obtaining an optimal solution, but the more time that is used. In New York City, P = max (6, number of empty houses) was used, thus determining a maximum of six covering sets.

one. If the lowest-cost move for each house produces a feasible relocation, that relocation is optimal and no further computations are necessary. Otherwise, since the algorithm is fast, several feasible relocations are produced by changing the order in which houses being filled are considered, and by changing the heuristic for the first house being considered to "choose the available company with the kth lowest relocation cost." The least-cost relocation generated after all trials is used as the stage 3 solution. The method may be summarized as:

A. Obtain an initial solution and see if it is optimal.
   1. Find the minimum value of c_{ij} over all the relocatee lists. Imagine that the move it represents is made.
   2. Search the lists of the remaining houses to be filled for the smallest c_{ij} that represents a feasible move. Add this move to the relocation being generated.
   3. Repeat step 2 until a relocatee has been selected for each house to be filled.
   4. If each of the companies in this relocation is associated with the lowest c_{ij} element in the relocatee list of the house it is filling, this relocation is optimal: Exit. Otherwise, go to part B.

B. Generate a series of feasible relocations.
   1. Assign the numbers 1, 2, . . . , M to the M vacant houses to be filled. Set the house indicator i to 1.
   2. Imagine that the lowest-cost move into house i is made.
   3. Sequence in order through the remaining houses to be filled ($j = 1, 2, \ldots, M; j \neq i$). For each house j, find the feasible move associated with the smallest cost element on house j's relocatee list (it must be feasible with respect to the other moves already included in the relocation now being generated). This set of moves produces a feasible relocation.
   4. Repeat step 3, first filling house i with the company associated with the second-lowest cost element on house i's relocatee list.[9] This produces a second feasible relocation starting with house i.
   5. Steps 1–4 produce two feasible relocations. They are generated by first finding the best and second-best relocatees for house 1. Repeat steps 2–4 for each of the other houses ($i = 2, 3, \ldots, M$).

Part A of this method generates one relocation and Part B generates $2M$ relocations. Thus, a total of $2M + 1$ candidate relocations are generated

---

[9] One need not stop after the second-lowest cost. In general, step 3 may be repeated for each of the first Q lowest-cost relocatees on house i's relocatee list. Tests in New York City indicated that going below the second does not lead to a better solution.

from which the one with the lowest cost is selected. The relocation so selected provides the set of M available companies that relocate.

12.3.3 Stage 4. Specific Relocation Assignments

Having selected relocatees as above, an assignment problem is solved to minimize total relocation distance. For small problems—say, up to $M = 5$—solutions can quickly be obtained by complete enumeration of all $M!$ permutations (5! = 120). For larger problems a more efficient algorithm may be used.[10] (We have employed the method of Balinski and Gomory (1964), which appears to be very efficient.) In real-time applications it would be unusual to have to make even five relocations at one time. Usually a fire progresses gradually through a number of stages (first alarm, second alarm, third alarm, etc.). At each stage, the number of relocations needed would be small (two or three at most).

12.4 AN EXAMPLE

In this section we present a hypothetical situation to illustrate how the algorithm works. Suppose that two serious fires, one a two-alarm and the other a three-alarm fire, are announced almost simultaneously in the Bronx. To keep the discussion simple, but without any loss of generality, we analyze the relocation problem for ladders only and consider only Bronx ladder companies (none from other boroughs) as possible relocatees. In reality, we would also solve the engine relocation problem and we might consider relocatees from the neighboring boroughs of Manhattan and Queens.

Figure 12.5 shows the locations of the two fires, the locations of the houses of the seven ladder companies working at the fires, and the region left uncovered as a result. All but three of the other ladder companies are assumed to be available to relocate. These three companies are identified as "reserved" because fire department policy dictates that, due to geographical isolation, they are not candidates for relocation. Within the computer the ranked lists of available companies would reflect this policy.

Stage 1 of the algorithm finds that there are nine uncovered ladder RNs. Since there are seven empty houses, a 9×7 covering problem must be solved in stage 2. There are two solutions; each requires that four of the seven empty houses be filled to provide a minimum covering. Filling (either set of) these four houses leaves no RNs uncovered and moves a minimum number of companies. The two sets differ by only one

---

[10] 6! = 720, and 10! = 3,628,800.

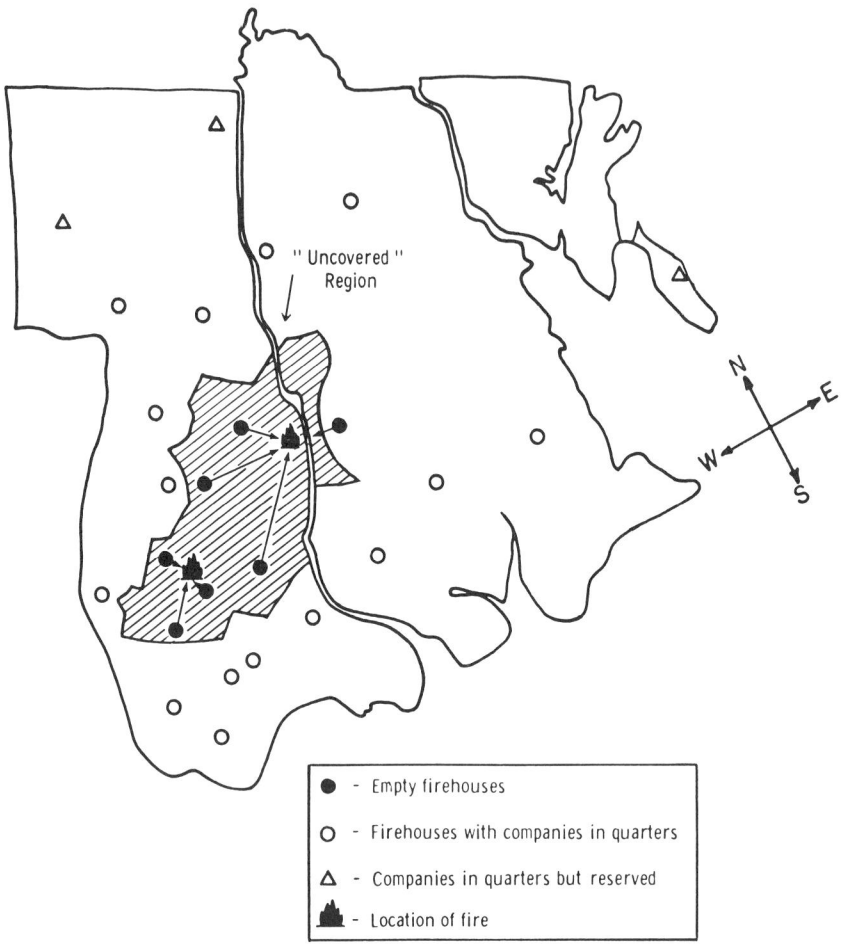

FIGURE 12.5. A sample relocation problem.

house. Stage 3, which selects the companies to relocate, was solved using both solutions to stage 2 as input. The same set of relocatees was found by stage 3 regardless of the stage 2 solution used. This result is not atypical of other examples that have been run, and indicates a desirable robustness of the model. The least-cost assignment resulting from stage 3 is indicated by dotted arrows in Figure 12.6. The least travel-distance solution produced by stage 4 is, of course, a permutation on the least-cost solution and is shown in Figure 12.6 by solid arrows. The solution produced by stage 4 results in a reduction of 22 percent in travel distance with only a 9 percent increase in the cost function.

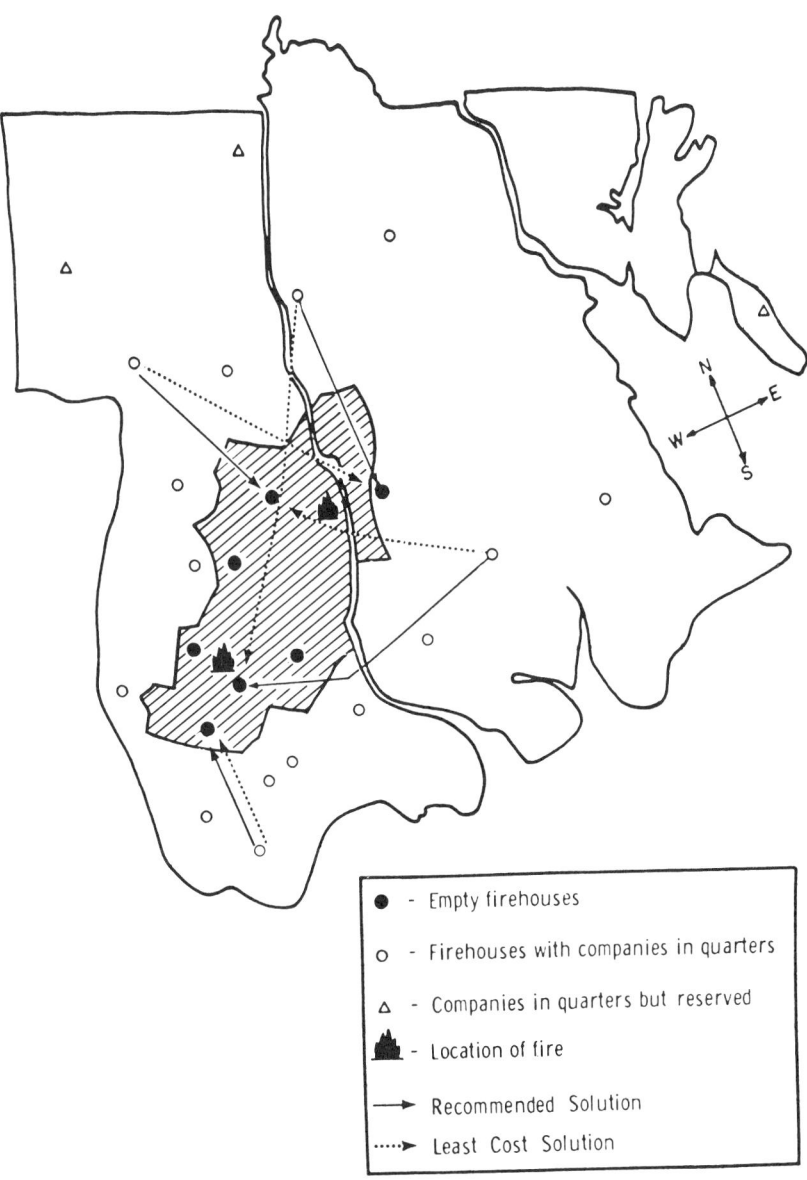

FIGURE 12.6. Solutions to the sample relocation problem.

This problem was also solved using the exact integer programming computer code of Geoffrion (1967). The result obtained was identical to the minimum cost solution found by the heuristic algorithm. However, the heuristic required only one-quarter of the CPU time and only one-half the amount of computer core storage.

12.5 TESTING THE ALGORITHM

The algorithm has been tested extensively: first, with problems that were designed to present difficult or interesting situations; second, in a simulation model in which over 3600 alarms were generated at random according to historical patterns; and third, to provide a strenuous realistic test, in specifying relocations for one of the worst evenings ever experienced in the Bronx. In the last of these, the sequence of incidents was reconstructed and a simulation was run to determine what would have occurred if the relocation algorithm had been operating. Finally, the algorithm was run in parallel with the existing manual system in one of the fire department's communications offices.

We describe here the test of the algorithm on an actual stream of alarms, received in the Bronx on July 4, 1969. This was one of the most trying periods in recent departmental history. Our objective was to determine exactly what happened that day and evening; to reconstruct moment-by-moment, in detail, the events of that night. The required data included the precise times at which alarms were received, dispatches were made, higher alarms were signaled, relocations were ordered, and units were returned to service. Typically, the Fourth of July is a very busy day for the fire department in the Bronx; a large number of false alarms are received and many fires are fought that have been purposely set. This particular Fourth was one of the worst ever experienced in the Bronx up until that time. There were 288 alarms turned in, almost twice as many as during a normal day. To make matters worse, these alarms did not occur uniformly during the day; over 40 percent occurred in the four-hour period from 8:00 P.M. to midnight.

The alarms that were received during the period from 8:00 P.M. July 4 to 3:00 A.M. July 5 are summarized in Table 12.1. In this seven-hour period, an average of 24 alarms per hour were received. There were 33 structural fires, including two 3-alarm fires. In addition to the multiple alarm fires, there were five other very serious fires that occurred during this period. A summary of these seven serious fires is given in Table 12.2. Five of the fires broke out within an hour of each other (11:38 P.M. to 12:38 A.M.). The number of fire companies needed to put out the serious fires was almost equal to the total number of companies stationed in the Bronx.

Not only did the fires occur closely in time, but they were grouped

12.5 Testing the Algorithm

TABLE 12.1. Alarms received in the Bronx from 8 P.M. on July 4, 1969 to 3 A.M. on July 5, 1969.

Time	Number of Alarms			
	Total	Structural	Serious	False
8–9 P.M.	35	4		8
9–10	31	2		14
10–11	38	6	1	16
11–12	30	6	3	11
12–1 A.M.	7	4	2	1
1–2	14	8	1	1
2–3	12	3		5
Total	167	33	7	56

geographically in the South Bronx (Figure 12.7). Thus, it is clear that the relocation of a significant number of units into the South Bronx was required in order to maintain adequate coverage.

The manual alarm assignment card relocation system was unable to effectively handle the situation. It could not take into account the existence of other fires in progress that involved the companies specified to be relocated by the card. In addition, the relocations for two alarms, when taken together, would have uncovered the neighborhoods that were protected by these units. These problems and others were experienced at several points. The simulation of the period showed that, had it been operating then, the computerized relocation algorithm, which would have based its suggestions on the status of the entire system at any given time, would have significantly out-performed the manual system. The simulation was carried out using the computer simulation model of the Bronx discussed in Chapter 13. Instead of an input stream of randomly generated alarms, the actual alarms of July 4, 1969 were used.

TABLE 12.2. Serious fires in the Bronx, July 4–5, 1969.

Time	Box No.	Number of Working Units	
		Engines	Ladders
10:45 P.M.	2791	3	2
11:38	4789	8	3
11:56	2732	10	5
11:59	3131	2	2
12:27 A.M.	2240	2	2
12:35	2550	7	4
1:12	2916	3	2
2.5 hours		35	20

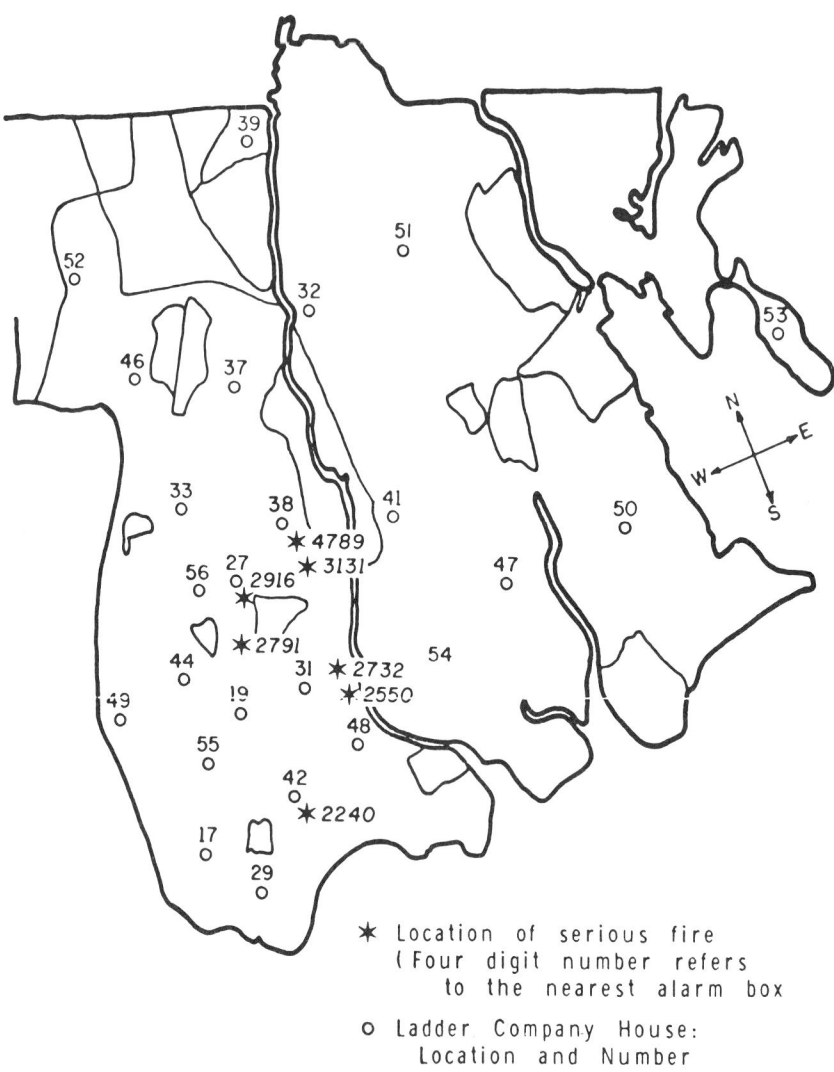

FIGURE 12.7. Location of serious fires in the Bronx, July 4-5, 1969.

The period simulated lasted from 9:52 P.M. on July 4, 1969 to 4:00 A.M. on July 5. During this period, which begins well before any serious alarms were received and lasts until well after they were ended, a total of 107 alarms were received. The simulated results were compared to the actual performance of the system during that period as reconstructed from fire department logs and other official records. Some of the more interesting comparisons between the simulated and actual performances

12.5 Testing the Algorithm 489

are described below. The reader should bear in mind that the dispatchers who actually worked that night were using a system that was not designed to handle the volume or complexity of alarms received.

Number of Relocations Made. The algorithm would have made a total of 35 relocations; in reality, only 25 relocations were made. Five relocations listed on the alarm assignment cards could not be made because the units specified to be relocated were not available. Of the 25 relocations made, 10 were specified on the alarm assignment cards. The other 15 were made by the dispatchers because they felt that coverage in the South Bronx was bad and additional companies were needed to provide protection. The alarm assignment cards afforded them no help in determining how many extra units were needed, when the relocations should be made, or which companies should be moved.

Timing of Relocations. The algorithm generated its relocations gradually and continually over time, while relocations made by the dispatchers were generally made in spurts. Thus, although by 1:08 A.M. each method had made a total of 23 relocations, the algorithm had called for relocations to be made at 16 separate times, while the dispatchers had made their relocations at only 5 different times. The dispatchers made 7 relocations at 11:45 P.M. and 10 relocations (only one of which was specified on the alarm assignment cards) at 12:49 A.M.

Coverage. Under the definition of minimum coverage used as the primary objective in the relocation algorithm, every alarm box should always have at least one of its closest three engines, and at least one of its closest two ladders, available. "Available" in this case includes responding to an alarm, returning from an alarm, due back from a working fire soon, or actually in quarters. Much stronger measures of the coverage provided to an area are the percentage of alarm boxes in the area for which at least one of the closest three engines companies is *available in quarters*, and the percentage of alarm boxes with at least one of the two closest ladders *available in quarters*. We will use these as our measures in comparing the coverage actually provided.

During the first two hours of the scenario, the algorithm and the actual system performed comparably. The simulation made 10 relocations, compared to 9 in the real system, and the coverage provided at 11:52 P.M. is given in Table 12.3.

After midnight, the actual coverage began to deteriorate. Because of the large number of alarms in progress, the alarm assignment cards became less and less useful. It became increasingly difficult for the dispatchers—who were under intense time pressure—to manage both their dispatching and relocation functions, so relocations began to suffer.

TABLE 12.3 Coverage at 11:52 P.M., July 4, 1969.

	11:52 P.M.	
	Engine Coverage	Ladder Coverage
Simulation (using algorithm)	98%	100%
Actual	97.5%	88%

The algorithm, however, was able to keep up with the situation and to maintain a high level of coverage. Table 12.4 below shows the coverage levels (where coverage is defined as above) at 12:54 A.M. and 1:36 A.M., July 5, 1969.

The algorithm never leaves a response neighborhood without minimum coverage. However, on that night, a total of 16 RNs were actually left uncovered for periods ranging from 30 minutes to 1.6 hours. Figure 12.8 shows the actual status of the ladder houses in the Bronx at 12:54 A.M. on July 5, 1969. The shaded areas represent the uncovered response neighborhoods. There were four uncovered RNs at that time. These can be labeled (44,49), (32,41), (32,37), and (33,37). The RN labeled (44,49) was left uncovered after both ladder companies were dispatched to the third alarm fire at box 2732 (neither company appeared on the alarm assignment card), and since no relocations were made, this RN was left uncovered for a total of 1 hour and 38 minutes.

Figure 12.9 shows the status of the ladder houses in the Bronx at 12:54 A.M. in the simulation. There are no uncovered response neighborhoods. It should be noted that the simulation put two more ladder companies in the Bronx at this time than were actually there. These are Manhattan ladders that the simulation relocated into the Bronx. Eventually, the dispatchers in the Bronx moved the same number of Manhattan ladders into their boroughs, but considerably later.

Response Times. Response times to actual alarms and area coverage are closely related, but not equivalent, measures of effectiveness. Coverage is a geographical measure, while response times are associated with actual responses to incidents. While there are no data on the actual

TABLE 12.4 Coverage at 12:54 A.M. and 1:36 A.M., July 5, 1969.

	12:54 A.M.		1:36 A.M.	
	Engines	Ladders	Engines	Ladders
Simulation (using algorithm)	88%	100%	94%	90%
Actual	78%	88%	82%	79%

12.5 Testing the Algorithm

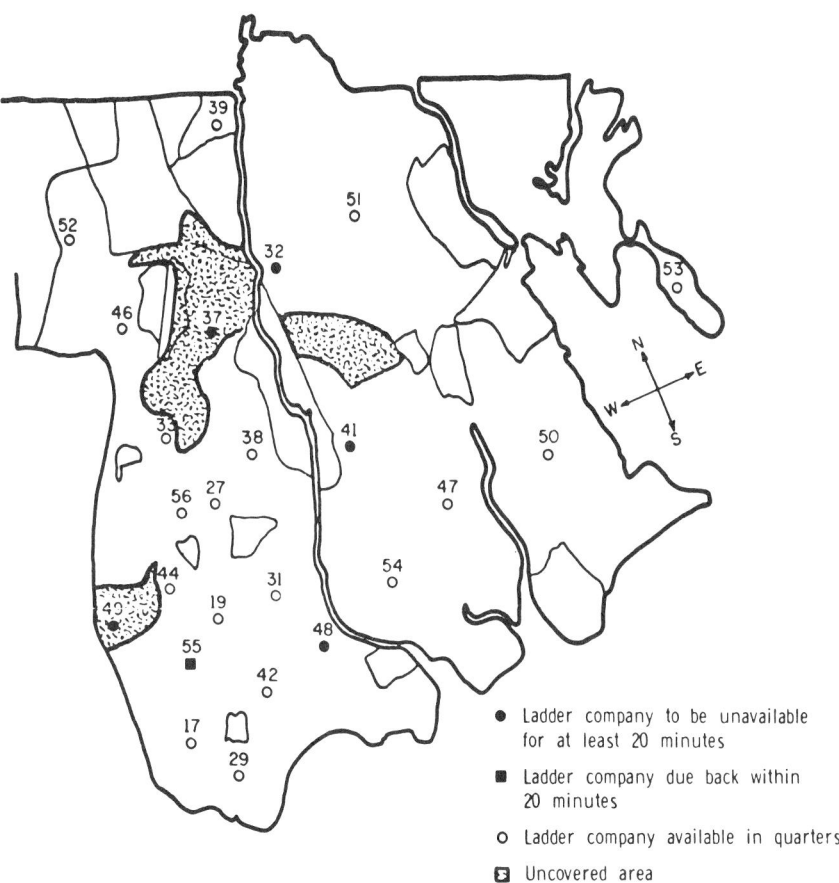

FIGURE 12.8. Actual Bronx ladder company status, July 5, 1969, 12:54 A.M.

response times to the incidents of July 4, 1969 (response times are not routinely recorded by the department), we can look at the units that were actually dispatched to the incidents and see how close they were to the alarm boxes to which they were sent. We compare these to the closeness of the units dispatched in the simulation. Our measure of closeness is the position on the alarm assignment card of the house from which the unit responded, since the houses are generally listed on the card in order of closeness to the box.

In making these comparisons it was found that the algorithm almost never required dispatch of units further from the alarm box than those actually dispatched; often it was possible to dispatch closer units. In one case, the effect was dramatic. For one of the three-alarm fires, the manual system dispatched the fifth-closest ladder, while the simulation, using the

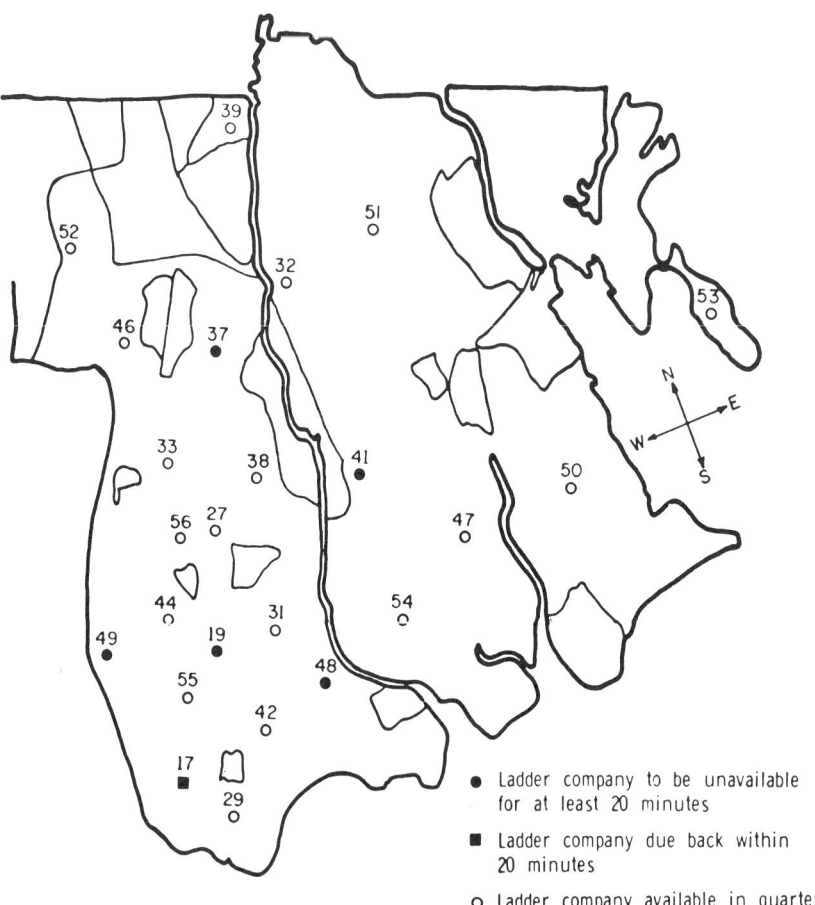

FIGURE 12.9. Simulated Bronx ladder company status, July 5, 1969, 12:54 A.M.

algorithm, was able to dispatch the closest ladder and hence reduce the response time to the fire by an estimated two minutes.

The improvement in response times was primarily due to the fact that the algorithm produced more and earlier relocations, resulting in better availability in the busy area than with the alarm assignment card method. The algorithm also positioned relocated units in houses where the probability that they would be needed was high.

12.6 ON-LINE IMPLEMENTATION OF THE ALGORITHM IN NEW YORK CITY

The relocation algorithm was implemented as part of a real-time computer-based Management Information and Control System (MICS) by the Fire Department of New York in the middle of 1977. In addition to

12.6 On-line Implementation of the Algorithm in New York City 493

recommending relocations, the MICS recommends dispatches, maintains the status of fire companies and alarms in progress, and updates statistical records. The system was implemented in the Brooklyn communications office, and is to be expanded citywide by 1981.

In order to give an idea of how the algorithm can be used and of its flexibility, we describe some of the ways in which the dispatcher is able to interact with it. Changes in alarm and company status are entered into the computer at a terminal. The system determines whether there are any uncovered response neighborhoods, and makes an indication to the dispatcher if there are any. The computer will then generate a relocation recommendation if requested to do so by the dispatcher.

At this point, the dispatcher has several options available. He can implement the suggested relocation by pushing the appropriate button at his terminal, or he can ignore the suggestion and make no relocations. The system will simply remind him again later if any response neighborhoods remain uncovered after the next status changes. No relocations are made automatically. The computer only suggests relocations to the dispatcher.

The dispatcher has several other options available:

He can modify the suggested relocation in whole or in part, based on considerations that he may be aware of but that are not included in the model. For example, he may know that a company which the computer suggested as a relocatee has itself just returned from a very arduous fire. If he modifies part of the suggestion, he can then ask the computer to re-solve the problem, taking this change into account.

The dispatcher may temporarily exclude one or more of the recommended relocatees and ask the computer to re-solve the problem without them.

To help him make modifications in the recommended set of relocations, the dispatcher can ask that the computer provide him with a ranked list of desirable and available candidates for relocation into any given house.

The dispatcher can delay making the relocation. He might do this if he thinks or has information that an incident will soon escalate. There are several reasons for wanting to delay a relocation decision, including the fact that some companies which are selected to be relocatees might soon be needed at the incident, and the fact that fewer relocations will generally be needed if relocations are held up until all higher alarms are in for an incident.

The algorithm does not make any "unrelocation" suggestions. Under the current New York City Fire Department system, a company remains in its relocated quarters until the company that belongs there returns from fighting its fire. Thus, no dispatching decision need be made to unrelocate a company. However, if a neighboring company were to return to quarters first, the relocated company might be able to be unrelocated without uncovering an RN. In fact, his presence in another area might be more important for coverage.

12.7 USING THE ALGORITHM TO GENERATE PREPLANNED RELOCATIONS

The discussion of the formulation and testing of the algorithm has been given in the context of its use in a real-time computerized command and control system. We mentioned earlier that the same algorithm can be used to create or modify the preplanned relocations included on alarm assignment cards. How can this be done? A computer program documented in Shanesy (1975), which implements the algorithm, can be used to do this directly.[11] The user would have to create the data base for the computer program, including company identities, first-due areas, alarm boxes and their alarm assignments, travel distances, and alarm rates. The user would then specify a relocation problem, or a series of relocation problems, for which solutions are required to be put on alarm assignment cards. The computer would be requested to solve the problems and give its relocation suggestions. This computing process could be carried out on-line in an interactive mode, or off-line in batch mode. It might be better to do it on-line since the analyst and managers could then interact more easily with the program. They could ask for the same type of modifications as do dispatchers who use the program on-line. A series of escalating situations at the same alarm box could be presented to the computer and a series of solutions obtained. They could be recorded on the alarm assignment cards as is, or modified, according to judgment. In this way the analyst and managers could proceed, alarm box by alarm box, to create a set of relocation plans for each likely scenario at each box. Alternative plans, for different times of day or different projected company availabilities, could be readily obtained by redoing the analysis with the appropriate modifications made to the data.

---

[11] A FORTRAN version of the relocation algorithm is documented in Shanesy (1975). Data requirements and other considerations not discussed here are presented in detail.

Chapter 13
The Fire Operations Simulation Model

Synopsis

This chapter describes the design of a simulation model of fire department operations and its use in evaluating deployment policies. The model is a computer program that imitates events in the real operations of a fire department. These events include what happens as alarms are received, as companies are dispatched, and as they are subsequently returned to service. They do not include fireground operations.

Such a model can represent the features of the system—for example, the geography of the city—with more detail and accuracy than the models presented in previous chapters. It can also produce more detailed output information, such as response times to particular incidents. It is, however, more expensive to get the information needed to make the model work, and to actually run it.

The added expense can be worthwhile in three situations: (1) to evaluate deployment policies that are too complicated for other models to handle; (2) to verify the predictions of simpler models, so that the latter can be used with confidence; and (3) to satisfy the preference of city officials for a more "lifelike" test of proposed policy changes. Each of these uses is illustrated in detail elsewhere in the book. The first use—evaluation of complex policies—is illustrated in the evaluation of initial dispatch policies (Section 12.5), and in the evaluation of alternative policies for alleviating workload problems in the New York City Fire Department (Section 14.4). The second use—verification of simpler models—is illustrated for the "square-root law" in Section 6.4.3. The third use—for "lifelike" testing of policies—is illustrated in the Denver case study in Section 14.2.4.

This chapter describes a particular model, the Fire Operations Simulation Model. The overall design of the computer program is outlined, and its input needs and output capabilities are illustrated. One important feature of the model is that it can either use a sequence of incidents that have actually occurred in the past, or it can generate a sequence of incidents with a given probabilistic distribution in time and geography.

Effective use of the simulation model depends on recognizing that it is an experimental tool. The major emphasis in the chapter is on the design and analysis of experiments that evaluate and compare deployment policies. Examples are given of how the questions to be answered should influence the features of the system that are represented, the input data used, and the output information provided. Statistical techniques that are needed to analyze output results are discussed and illustrated.

13.1 OVERVIEW

A simulation model is a powerful tool for analyzing almost any kind of system or operation that can be described numerically. It consists of a computer program that imitates, step by step, the essential aspects of what actually happens in the real operation. The simulation model described in this chapter follows a large number of incidents from the time the fire begins, through the time it is reported to the department by telephone or alarm box, on through the dispatch of companies, their arrival at the scene, their work at the incident, and their release, to (finally) their return to quarters and their availability for another dispatch. The simulation acts like an "all-knowing" dispatcher who keeps track of all the companies and incidents, but does not pay attention to firefighting tactics or activities at the fire scene.

The simulation differs in several important respects from the models described in previous chapters. First, the features of the fire response system are represented with far more detail and accuracy. For example, detailed representation of the geography (as in Chapter 10) can be combined with accurate representation of the initial dispatch policy (as in Chapter 11). Very detailed output is possible—for example, response time to individual incidents (as well as in aggregate), or individual company workloads. These advantages come at a price. The model is a complicated computer program. Using it requires help from programmers who understand the special language used (SIMSCRIPT I.5). It also requires a moderately large computer (at least 228K bytes of core storage and two auxiliary storage devices, tape or disk), is expensive to operate (around $100 for each run), and requires a substantial amount of detailed data as input.

Consequently, the simulation is not the model to use for preliminary evaluations and comparisons—it requires too much time, effort, and money. The models described in the preceding seven chapters, and others like them, will suffice during the initial stages of analysis.

13.1 Overview

It has been found worthwhile to use simulation in three general situations: (1) to evaluate deployment policies that are too complicated for simpler models; (2) to validate simpler models; and (3) to give fire chiefs and other officials evidence that proposed policy improvements already evaluated using simpler models are workable and effective.

Complicated deployment policies or situations may call for simulation if the desired performance measures are more detailed than the simpler models can provide. Even when aggregate output would be sufficient, it may be that none of the simpler models are appropriate because:

1. Many simple models assume that all of the fire companies are always available when a demand for service occurs. Therefore, they are not adequate to evaluate policies at high alarm rates, when companies are frequently busy.
2. Some kinds of proposed deployment changes cannot be analyzed to any degree with available simple models. The policies may be more complex than those for which analytic solutions are available, or the interaction of several policy variables that can be analyzed separately may produce joint effects that are difficult to predict.

Analytic models are much cheaper to use than simulation. In addition, they often "tell you something." For example, the square-root law shows that it is hard to reduce response times by adding companies. But analytic models are often derived under very restrictive assumptions—assumptions that almost surely do not hold in any particular city. However, it is still possible that the analytic model may predict well in any particular city. One way to tell is to compare the analytic model's prediction to simulation results. For example, to test the validity of the square-root law, simulations should be run for varying numbers of companies on duty, and the average response distances of first-arriving engines, for example, should be compared to those predicted by the square-root law. That is, the simulation may be used to see if it is safe to use the square-root law. If so, we say the model has been "validated by simulation."

Simulation has been used to validate many of the models described earlier in this book. Among them are the square-root law (Chapter 6), the relationships between response adequacy and company availability (Section 11.3.4), and the queuing model of the number of busy companies (Section 7.2.2). For a description of these validations see Ignall, Kolesar, and Walker (1978). To indicate what is involved, we include the validation of one of the models in Section 13.7.

Simulation may also be useful in providing governmental decisionmakers with the necessary confidence that a proposed new policy will actually work in the way predicted. For example, in Denver the simulation model was used after other methods of analysis had suggested that a reduction from 44 to 39 fire companies, together with construction of six new fire stations, could provide almost the same level of fire protection as the then-current configuration (Hendrick et al., 1975). However, these conclusions were based on the assumption that every fire company would almost always be available for dispatch at its station. At this point, the simulation model was run to see whether the real performance of the new configuration would be as good as anticipated, taking into account the unavailability of companies.

Denver's Deputy Finance Director has said that "one of our main concerns was what effect the changed configuration of fire companies would have on response times if the number of fire alarms continued to increase. The Rand simulation told us that, even at double our present peak alarm rate, there would be no significant deterioration in service. This was important in presenting our recommendations to the mayor and the City Council."[1]

There is a potential benefit in starting to build or adapt a simulation, even if the program is not completed or run. Building the model forces the analyst to observe the system in a focused way, which often leads to worthwhile discoveries. For example, in order to simulate the operations of the New York City Fire Department, a representation of the then-current dispatching policy was needed. A field study was undertaken, which included observing communications office operations and riding with fire companies. Those on the project felt that this led to the discovery of the existence of "variable response" (Chapter 11) sooner than it would have been found otherwise. This discovery and its documentation were at least as important to the evaluation of the existing initial dispatch policy and the development of better policies as were any of the simulation runs.

In short, if complex policies or conditions of high workload are to be analyzed, a simulation model is the most effective tool to use. But, if one is only interested in policy alternatives for which a model exists or can be easily derived, if the alarm rate is so small that the assumption that companies are available is reasonable, and if the additional detail provided by the simulation is not necessary, then one need not use simulation at all. In fact, it is likely that many departments need never use an existing simulation model or build their own.

The simulation model discussed here is The New York City–Rand Institute's Fire Operations Simulation Model. It was used for seven years on a variety of New York City problems.[2] The Fire Operations Simulation Model is organized in a flexible manner, and its application in Denver by Hendrick et al. (1975) shows that analysts who were not involved in its original development can adapt it to other situations in other cities. More

---

[1] C. Tomasides, private communication, 1975.
[2] For examples, see Carter and Ignall (1970); Carter, Ignall, and Walker (1975); Sections 11.4, 14.4; and the Research History of the Rand Fire Project in this book.

importantly, the issues in the design and use of any simulation model can be illustrated with this one.

The model will be described in detail in the next section. A complete program listing of the simulation is available.[3] Succeeding sections discuss the model's input needs (Section 13.3), the output that it gives (Section 13.4), and how to design and analyze simulation experiments (Sections 13.5 and 13.6). We give a great deal of attention to this last topic. Simulation is an experimental tool, and its successful use depends on tailoring the input, output, and features of the program itself to the questions that are to be answered. It also requires working with statistical output, so that statistical techniques are needed.

13.2 PROGRAM DESIGN

The Fire Operations Simulation Model is a computer representation of a fire department's units and the incidents to which they respond. Key happenings in the system are represented by events. These events include the reporting of a fire, the dispatch of fire units, the arrival of a fire unit at the scene of the incident, and many others. By means of a simulation clock, the computer keeps track of the time at which events would happen in the real world. After each event is finished, the computer checks to see when the next event would occur in the real world, and updates the clock to this time before processing the new event. In this way, time is compressed so that activities that take several days in the real world can be simulated in a few seconds on the computer.

In the simulation, firehouses, firefighting companies, and fires are each described by a set of *attributes*. For example, an attribute of a firehouse is its location, which is specified as input to a particular simulation run; such attributes may be changed to evaluate several policies. Thus, one could run the simulation once, with all the firehouses located as they currently are in a city; then, by changing the coordinates and response areas of one or more firehouses, one could simulate a possible new configuration of firehouses. Afterward, the output of the two simulation runs could be compared.

This section describes the major features of the Fire Operations Simulation Model. They are: the incident generator; the simulation program; and post-simulation analysis programs. The heart of the Fire Operations Simulation Model is the *simulation program*. It imitates the response of

---

[3] A complete listing of the programs comprising the Fire Operations Simulation Model, and a user's manual for the programs are contained in Carter (1974), which presents in detail the data requirements and output reports, and provides descriptions of each subprogram. Copies of the program and its documentation are available from The Rand Corporation, 1700 Main Street, Santa Monica, California 90406.

the fire department to a sequence of incidents for a particular deployment policy. This program is a set of subroutines and events that describe the major activities in the dispatch and control of firefighting companies. The simulation program reads a file containing descriptions of the incidents to be simulated. It produces output that often needs statistical analysis before policy decisions can be reached.

Consider first the input file, which is called the "exogenous events" tape. It can be prepared in two ways. A separate program—the *incident generator*—is available to generate incidents according to a set of probability distributions that describe the characteristics of incidents. Or, a tape describing an actual sequence of incidents can be prepared.

There are advantages to the flexibility inherent in using a separate input file instead of generating the incidents inside the simulation program. First, it allows different deployment policies to deal with exactly the same set of incidents. This substantially reduces the number of incidents that must be simulated to detect a significant difference in response times (or other performance measures) between the two policies. The same statistical reliability can be achieved with one-quarter the number of incidents, when the same set of incidents is used instead of two different sets with the same probabilistic properties (Section 13.6). The second advantage to using a separate input file is that it allows an actual sequence of incidents to be simulated. To do so, the incidents that actually occurred would be described by the exogenous events tape.

To ease the statistical analysis of the output of the simulation program, there are several *postsimulation analysis programs*. These programs help the user to efficiently compare the response times and other performance measures obtained under one deployment policy, to those obtained under another policy. For each alarm, the simulation program writes an output file of response times and other "raw" output information, that will be processed at some later time by one or more of the postsimulation analysis programs.

Response times are determined as much by how close particular incident locations are to fire stations, as by dispatch policy. So the differences between response times under different policies, on an incident-by-incident basis, are the appropriate raw material for statistical analysis. The writing of an output file for each policy makes this analysis easier.[4]

This approach also makes a given simulation run more likely to be useful for purposes other than the one for which it was first planned. For example, a run may be part of a study of citywide response times. If, in

---

[4] The average difference can be obtained without incident by incident comparison. However, to see whether this difference is statistically significant, an estimate of its variance is needed. It is the estimation of this *variance of the average difference* that requires the postsimulation analysis.

13.2 Program Design

the future, there is interest in the response times in a particular region of the city, the output file of response times can be sorted to give the desired organization of response times. If the output of the run had simply been the average (and other features of the distribution) of response times citywide, another run would be necessary.

We now describe the three parts of the model—the incident generator, the simulation program, and the postsimulation analysis routines—in more detail. For complete information, see Carter (1974), which contains flowcharts, a complete program listing, sample data decks, and sample output reports.

13.2.1 The Incident Generator

The incident generator converts a probabilistic description of the incidents that may occur into a particular sequence of incidents, and writes a description of these incidents onto a tape. This tape is then used as the input file for one or more simulation runs. The characteristics of each incident include the following:

1. *Location.*
2. *Information class,* as indicated by what kind of information is available to the dispatcher when the alarm is turned in.
3. *Incident type,* as indicated by the nature of the situation at the scene, including the number and kinds of companies needed to handle the incident, and the length of time each company is required.

In addition, the following information can be included in the incident characteristics:

4. The delay between the start of a fire and the receipt of the alarm by the department.
5. Whether the ultimate size of the incident depends on when the companies arrive. If it does, the conditions that determine the final size, the eventual number of companies needed, the time each is required, and the resulting damage and injury must be supplied.[5]

The first three characteristics are essential for running the simulation and learning from its output. First of all, the location and the "work content" of incidents are needed to make the simulation adequately represent the patterns of company availability and workload. Second, the dispatcher's information about the incident is needed to properly represent dispatching policy (and the response times that are determined

---

[5] The program listed in Carter (1974) assumes that incident size does not depend on when the fire companies arrive. It can be modified to allow such escalation.

by it). Third, for output purposes, similar alarms should be grouped together.

We will speak of a simulation incident type (SI type) as being defined by these three characteristics:

1. The output class of the incident.
2. Its requirement for companies.
3. Its information class.

This seems to imply the need for an enormous number of SI types, but such is not the case. The necessary number is determined by the purpose of the simulation runs. This is discussed further in Sections 13.3 and 13.5.1.

The probabilistic description of alarms that is required is the rate at which incidents of each SI type occur at each location. (The program assumes that incidents occur according to independent Poisson processes.) Chapter 8 describes how to estimate these rates for each type of alarm.

This framework allows the level of detail to be adjusted to suit the part of the policy that is of concern. For example, to test decision rules for which companies to dispatch, simulating every street corner in a relatively small area is appropriate. To compare relocation policies, aggregating neighboring alarm boxes into groups (of 5, 10, or more) but treating a large area is appropriate. The *rates* at which incidents occur can be adjusted for the purposes of the experiment. For example, if improvements in prevention are anticipated, alarm rates can be lowered. Or, if detectors are to be installed at some locations, the delay from the start of the fire until the alarm is turned in can be decreased.

Companies can respond to incidents outside the region being simulated (mutual aid responses). To make this easier, a special event called DOWN is included in the program. Less information is required for these incidents than for incidents occurring inside the region being simulated (Section 13.5).

13.2.2 The Simulation Program

The major events in the simulation program are the eight events pictured in Figure 13.1. This simplified flow chart shows many of the events that could be triggered by an incident.

Each event is a subprogram that schedules one or more other events. For example, the delay in the communications office is specified in the ALARM event (which simulates the report of the incident to the fire department). Consequently, if simulation is to be used to compare the

13.2 Program Design

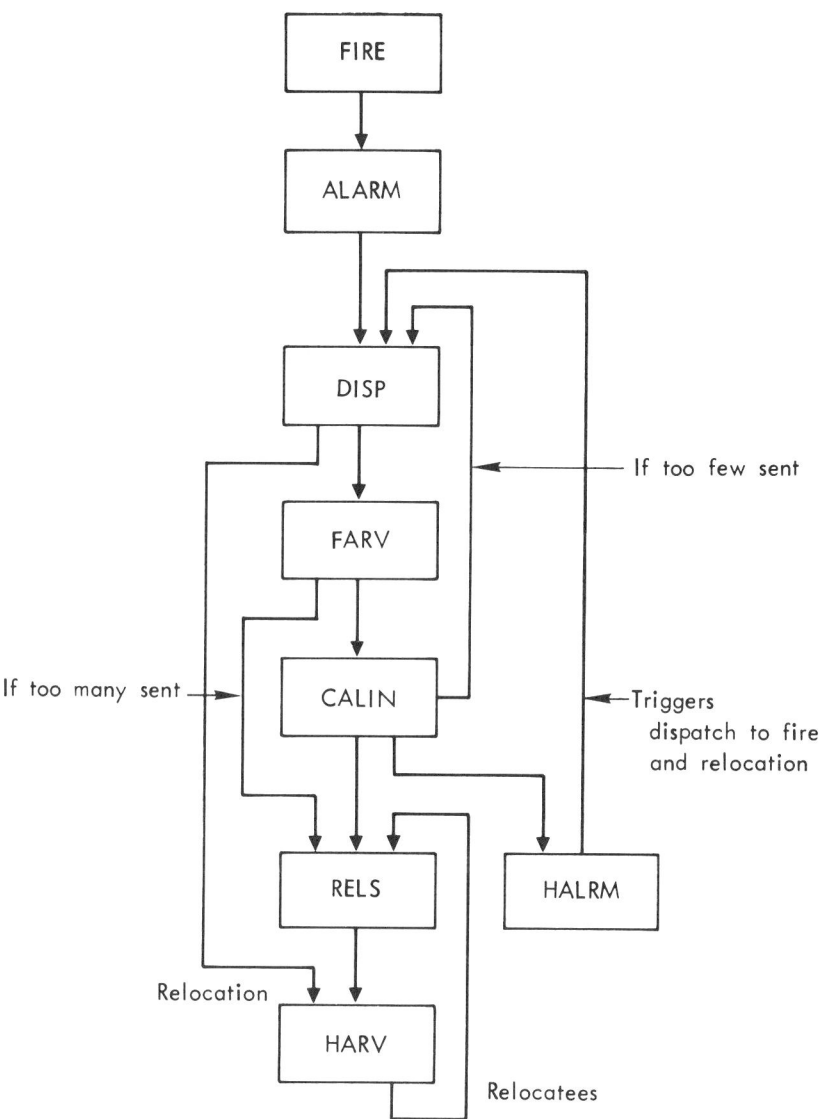

FIGURE 1. Flow of events in the Fire Operations Simulation Model.

current situation to one in which communications operations would be changed, the ALARM event must be modified to reflect that change.

This example shows the relationship between events and deployment questions. To spell out these relationships for all deployment issues and all the features of the model would require too much space here. Instead we indicate the important aspects of each of the events, and the subrou-

TABLE 13.1 Major events in the Fire Operations Simulation Model.

Events	Definition and Discussion
FIRE	The start of the incident. The delay until the incident is reported appears on the input tape. The tape can be modified if, for example, the introduction of detectors reduces the delay.
ALARM	The receipt of the alarm at the dispatching office. Schedules the dispatch of fire companies. Therefore, it can reflect the possible dependence of the delay, from alarm receipt until dispatch on the number of incidents then active (Section 14.5). Or, it can reflect the possible changes in this delay that would occur if communications office operations were changed (for example, by the installation of a computer-aided dispatch system).
DISP	The notification of companies to respond to an alarm or to relocate.
FARV	The arrival of fire companies at the scene. A fire escalation model or a dollar-damage calculation would use this company arrival information together with the FIRE event time.
CALIN	The first report to the communications office from a company at the scene of the incident. If too many units were sent, those not needed will be turned back. If too few were sent, others will be sent (see HALRM).
HALRM	The request from the scene for a second-alarm, third-alarm, and so forth. Will induce dispatch of companies to the scene and relocations of companies into empty houses.
RELS	The release of companies from the scene. They are usually available during the trips back to their houses. (If it is necessary to recognize standby status—a company on the scene but available for dispatch to another incident—a new type of event would be needed.) The release of companies is dependent on the work times specified. A unit's work time can begin when it arrives or when the last of the needed companies arrives, as specified by the user.
HARV	The arrival of a company at a firehouse. It can be a company returning from an incident or a relocatee returning home. Or, it can be a relocatee getting to the house it will cover. The company may be available for dispatch at this time, or it may be given some time to recover.

tines and functions that serve them. The eight major events are described in Table 13.1.

There are other events of importance to the user. They are described in Table 13.2.[6]

These events are supported by the subroutines and functions described in Tables 13.3 and 13.4.

---

[6] We have omitted some housekeeping and initialization events.

TABLE 13.2. Other important events in the Fire Operation Simulation Model

Event	Definition and Discussion
AVAIL	The return to service of a company that is granted a recovery period after return from an incident.
DOWN	The dispatch of companies to an incident outside the area of primary concern. The units to be sent are specified by the exogenous events tape (rather than by the ALARM event).
ACC	The occurrence of an accident during a company's trip.
INSER	The return to service of a company, following DOWN or ACC.
SMPCV	Used to determine the coverage being provided. Called periodically for output purposes (Section 13.4.3).

13.2.3 Postsimulation Analysis Programs

The purpose of these programs is to perform efficient statistical analysis of either the output of a particular simulation run, or (more importantly) the differences between two or more simulation runs. Carter (1974) describes one such program, called COMPARE, that can be used to obtain information about the difference between two runs. This program is written in FORTRAN IV. It provides a histogram of the response time

TABLE 13.3. Major Subroutines in the Fire Operations Simulation Model.

Subroutine	What It Does, and Why
DATAT	Used for aggregating alarms for output purposes. Determines which output class the response times and response adequacy for this alarm belong in.
DCDE	Chooses the companies to dispatch to an incident in response to a call from the ALARM, CALIN, HALRM, or ACC.
SEND	Determines the length of every trip by a company.
LCTCO	Calculates the location of a company that is currently traveling. Can be used to consider dispatching companies that are returning from incidents, or relocating.
STOPCO	Changes the destination of a company that is currently traveling. Used to turn back excess companies if the first-arriving unit finds no need for them, to redirect companies (that are relocating or returning) to a new incident, and in case of accident.
TESTA	Determines whether an accident will occur on this trip.
DECDR	Makes the relocation decisions.
DORLT	Does the relocations (if any) that DECDR picks.
UNRLCT	Returns relocatees to home stations. (If any are working at alarms, assures that they will return home rather than to the houses they responded from.)

TABLE 13.4. Major function subprograms in the Fire Operations Simulation Model.

Function	Purpose
DIST	Determines a travel distance given the (x, y) coordinates of the starting point and the destination.
TRVLT	Determines the travel time of a trip on the basis of the distance to be covered. If a matrix of travel times between points is available, it can replace this function and DIST.
DSPT	Determines the time required to make the dispatch decision and notify the companies.
AVLT	Determines the time a unit will be out of service following an accident.

differences between the two policies. An example of its output and the appropriate statistical methods are described in Section 13.6.4. The cost of a typical use of the COMPARE program is less than $20.00. Other programs to perform the comparisons needed by a user can be written in a straightforward manner, using COMPARE as a model.

13.3 INPUT NEEDS

In order to run the simulation program, it is necessary to:

Represent the geography of the area being simulated. This involves specifying the locations of fire companies and the possible locations of alarms.

Specify the travel time for each possible origin and destination.

Specify a sequence of incidents. For each incident include the number of units required, their work times, and the information given to the dispatcher upon receipt of the initial alarm.

Specify the deployment policy. This will include the number and location of companies, the initial dispatch policy, and the relocation policy.

Each of these inputs should be chosen in accordance with what the user wishes to learn from the simulation run or runs. That is, the input specifications chosen are part of the experimental design; they will be discussed further in Section 13.5. Here we will emphasize the computer and data collection aspects of these choices, rather than their content.

13.3.1 The Representation of Geography and Travel Time

There are two choices here. One is the representation of fire stations and possible incident locations on a grid coordinate system. Roughly speaking, this means providing the latitude and longitude of each location. The

13.3 Input Needs

other approach is a network representation, in which the distances or travel times (sometimes both) between pairs of locations are constructed by finding the shortest path through the network. The pros and cons of each approach are discussed in Chapter 6, and we will not repeat that discussion here. The listing in Carter (1974) assumes that a grid coordinate system is used.

One special feature of the simulation imposes an additional requirement if used. This is the ability to change the destination of a company that is traveling. Thus, a responding company can be turned back before it reaches the scene if the first-arriving units find that it will not be needed. More important, a company that is returning from an incident (or a relocation, or making a relocation) can be redirected to another incident. If this feature is used, it is necessary to be able to locate, at least approximately, a company that is traveling.

13.3.2 Information about Incidents

As indicated in Section 13.2, an actual historical alarm sequence may be used in the simulation program. Alternatively, the incident generator can be given incident rates and allowed to generate the alarm sequence. The definition of simulation incident alarm types requires a combination of information about work content, seriousness, and what the dispatcher knows. These definitions are not likely to correspond to any particular department's current classification scheme. So the user must devise a way of mapping the scheme currently in use into one suitable for simulation, even if a historical alarm sequence is to be used.

We will give an example, because this process can be complicated. (In Denver, Hendrick et al. (1975) found it conceptually more difficult than any of the features of the simulation program.) This example is intended to suggest ways of constructing simulation incident types. It may also be helpful to read Hendrick et al. (1975), and Carter and Ignall (1970), before constructing SI types.

It is easiest to begin with the classification of incidents used by fire departments to record incidents after they occur. (We will refer to this as the department's "after-the-fact" classification.) In the Denver study, the 43 classifications in Table 13.5 were the starting point for the construction of SI types. First, these types were compressed into 19 aggregates by combining similar incidents. For example, all the false alarms were combined. To develop the SI types, these incident aggregates were cross-classified with their work content, what the dispatcher knows about them when the alarm is turned in, and their seriousness.

We next consider the work content. In Denver over 99.9 percent of all incidents required one of the eight combinations of engines and ladders listed in Table 13.6.

TABLE 13.5. Denver Fire Department's "after-the-fact" incident classification.

Code	Incident Type	Code	Incident Type
	FIRES (NONBUILDING)		SERVICE CALLS
12	Trees, brush, grass fire	71	Lock-out
13	Vehicle fire	72	Water evacuation
14	Refuse fire	73	Smoke or odor removal
15	Outside structures	74	Animal rescue
16	Explosion, no afterfire	75	Assist police
17	Outside spill or leak		BUILDING FIRES
	FALSE ALARMS	81	Residential, single-family duplex (including private garages)
21	Malicious or mischievous		
22	Bomb scare, no bomb	82	Multifamily residential (apartment, condominium, etc.)
23	System malfunction		
24	Unintentional	83	Institutions (schools, hospitals, nursing homes, etc.)
	RESCUE CALLS		
31	Resuscitation	84	Stores, offices, restaurants, etc.
32	First aid	85	Manufacturing facility
33	Lock-in	86	Warehouse, storage facility, etc.
		87	Motels and hotels
	OVERPRESSURE RUPTURES (No Combustion)		NOT OTHERWISE CLASSIFIED
41	Steam rupture		
42	Air or gas rupture	10	Nonbuilding fire, not otherwise classified
	HAZARDOUS CONDITIONS		
51	Spill or leak	20	False alarm, not otherwise classified
52	Explosive removed	30	Rescue call, not otherwise classified
53	Excessive heat	40	Overpressure rupture, not otherwise classified
54	Power lines down		
55	Arcing or shorted electrical equipment	50	Hazardous condition, not otherwise classified
	GOOD INTENT CALLS	60	Good intent call, not otherwise classified
61	Smoke scare where no action is needed	70	Service call, not otherwise classified
		80	Building fire, not otherwise classified
62	Wrong location		
63	Control burn		

Statistical analysis of the 18,000 incidents that occurred in Denver in 1972 was used to associate work content with incident aggregates. For example, the numbers in the right-hand column of Table 13.6 give the chance that a "multifamily residential fire" required each combination of companies. Similar estimates were developed for the other 18 incident aggregates.

The eight work-type classifications now need to be cross-classified with the amount of time the companies work, what the dispatcher knows, and seriousness, before SI types can be obtained.

13.3 Input Needs

TABLE 13.6. Definition of work types used in Denver.

Work Type	Companies Needed	Chance that a Multifamily Residential Fire Needed the Indicated Number of Companies
1	None (false alarm)	0.000
2	1 Engine	0.083
3	1 Ladder	0.000
4	1 Engine, 1 ladder	0.041
5	2 Engines, 1 ladder	0.315
6	3 Engines, 2 ladders	0.466
7	3 Engines, 2 ladders	0.000
8	4 Engines, 2 ladders	0.041

Before illustrating the cross-classification, we note that the chance that an incident at a particular location is of a given work type can be found by estimating the probability distribution of the after-the-fact incident types. Consider the following hypothetical example. Suppose 60 percent of the incidents at a given location are "multifamily residential" and 40 percent are false (which are work type 1). Then, the chance that an incident at that location would be work type 1 is 0.40; the chance that it is work type 2 is 0.050 (= 0.60 × 0.083); and so forth. (In Denver, each possible incident was classified as being one of three "box types"; the box types were defined by the specification of the probability distribution of work types.)

It is easier to continue the development of SI types by switching to an example from a study for New York City (Carter and Ignall, 1970). The specification will be incomplete, because only engines are considered. The seven work types used in that study are given in Table 13.7, along with the average work times for the companies.[7] (These average work times were obtained from analysis of a sample of several hundred incidents.)

If work times are to be generated from work-time distributions, the following method can be used. For each work type, find an appropriate distribution for the work time of the first-arriving engine. When an alarm of that type occurs:

1. Generate the work time for the first-arriving engine from its probability distribution.

---

[7] Only five work types are actually required, because types 1, 2, and 3 all require only one engine working. The reason for their separation is described in this section.

TABLE 13.7. Definition of work types used in New York City.

Work Type	Engines Required	Average Work Times (minutes)
1	1	5
2	1	18
3	1	18
4	2	75, 45
5	3	150, 105, 60
6	7	240, 180, 120, 90, 90, 60, 60
7	11	360, 300, 270, 240, 180, 150, 120, 120, 90, 90

2. The work time for the second-arriving engine (if required at the incident) is obtained by multiplying the generated work time of the first-arriving engine by the ratio of the average work time of the second-arriving engine to the average first-arriving time. Repeat with third-arriving engine, first-arriving ladder, etc., playing the role of the second-arriving engine.

For example, suppose a work type 4 incident occurs. Assume that a specific sample drawn from the probability distribution for the first engine at a type 4 fire produces a work time of 60 minutes. The mean work time for first-arriving engines for this type of incident has been estimated to be 75 minutes, and the mean for the second-arriving engine, 45 minutes. The ratio is 45/75 or 0.6, so that the work time assigned to the second-arriving engine would be 36 minutes (60 × 0.6).

The cross-classification with what the dispatcher knows at the time he makes an initial dispatch decision is, conceptually, perhaps the most difficult part of developing SI types. It is usually easier for box-reported incidents. If the dispatch policy is the same for all boxes, then all box-alarms get the standard dispatch initially, regardless of their actual work type.[8] Telephone-reported alarms require more care. For example, there are telephone false alarms that are mischievous or malicious. If the dispatcher knew what the companies he sends would find out in a few minutes, he would not send them. Similarly, if he knew that the "I smell smoke" call would turn out to be a temporarily malfunctioning incinerator that needed no action (rather than a real fire), he would not send any companies.

This "before-the-fact" classification of incidents can best be defined in terms of the dispatch policy. For example, we might label these inci-

---

[8] If a policy depends on the "risk class" of the box (Chapters 8 and 11), then this is not so.

dents as: "seems like a one-engine incident", "seems like a three-engine-and-two-ladder incident", and so forth. Analysis of the number of companies actually sent to incidents and their after-the-fact classification makes it possible to estimate the chance that a "seems like a three-engine-and-two-ladder incident" actually needs 3 and 2 (or 1 and 1, or 11 and 4, etc.). The cross-classification with work types (which are after-the-fact) yields the seven SI types for telephone-reported incidents that are given in Table 13.8. The distinction between types 2 and 3, then, is that type 2 "seems like" a one-engine incident, while type 3 "seems like" a three-engine incident. For example, a typical type 2 incident would be a refuse fire; a typical type 3 would be a small structural fire. We have separated type 1 (false alarm) from type 2 because locations may differ in the chance that an alarm is false. If we did not separate the two types, the average work time would depend on the mix of the two types of incidents.

For box-reported incidents, only six types would be needed (1, and 3–7), but to parallel the telephone alarms, we define seven. This gives 14 SI types.

To complete the definition of SI types, the seriousness of incidents must be considered. In the New York City study, Carter and Ignall did not explicitly define serious incidents. For illustration, it would be reasonable to assume that SI types 4–7 (box alarms) and 11–14 (telephone alarms) would be serious, and the others would not.

13.4 OUTPUT INFORMATION

The ability to provide as output almost any information on system performance is what makes simulation most useful. In this section we describe the kinds of output that are available with no modification in

TABLE 13.8. Definition of simulation incident types used in New York City.

SI Type		Engines Required (After-the-Fact)	Engines That Seem to Be Required (Before-the-Fact)
Box Reported	Telephone Reported		
1	8	1	1
2	9	1	1
3	10	1	3
4[a]	11[a]	2	3
5[a]	12[a]	3	3
6[a]	13[a]	7	3
7[a]	14[a]	11	3

[a] Serious incident.

TABLE 13.9. Definition of dispatch policies.

Alarm Reported By	Area or Simulation Incident Type	Dispatch Policy
Box	Busy area	Variable, 2 engines and 1 ladder
	Low area	Variable,[a] 3 engines and 2 ladders
Telephone	SI types 8 and 9	1 engine and 1 ladder
	SI types 10–14	Fixed,[b] 3 engines and 2 ladders

[a] A variable 3 and 2 policy sends whichever is available of the first 3 engines and 2 ladders on the alarm assignment card. Special calls are made if necessary, to get at least 1 and 1.

[b] A fixed 3 and 2 policy sends exactly 3 engines and 2 ladders (if that many are available among the approximately 10 and 5 listed on the card). See Chapter 11 for a further explanation of these dispatching policies.

Carter (1974), as well as some modifications that the user may wish to make.

It is easier to display sample output and explain it than to talk about the output in general. The run described here simulated the response to 1209 incidents over a 360-hour period. There were 14 simulation incident types (the same as those given in Table 13.8). The region being simulated was divided into two areas—"busy" and "low." The dispatch policy that was used is given in Table 13.9.

13.4.1 Response Times

We begin with response times.[9] Table 13.10 shows the organization of response-time output and presents some of the results. There are 14 simple output classes, corresponding to the seven input types (no distinction is made between box-reported and telephone incidents) and in the two different areas. Incidents in these 14 classes are combined in different ways to produce ten other output groups. We call the resulting 24 groups "aggregate types." For example, aggregate 16, "BUSY AREA ALL ALARMS," gives the response times for each incident in aggregates 8 through 14.

Consider the entries for each aggregate type. There were 57 incidents of aggregate type 1—false alarms in the low area. The average time from report of the incident until the first engine arrived was 6.87 minutes, and the standard deviation of those times was 1.80 minutes. On 56 of those incidents, the first ladder arrived before the CALIN event. The average first-arriving ladder response time was 6.88 minutes with standard deviation 1.88. The average time to get a unit to the scene (sometimes an

---

[9] In this simulation run, response time is the sum of travel time and a one-minute turnout time.

13.4 Output Information

engine arrived first, sometimes a ladder did) was 6.62 minutes, and the average time to get the "required" units to the scene (both, on those occasions when both arrived; or just the engine in the case where only it came) was 7.13 minutes.

Now turn to aggregate type 4—"STRUCT, ETC." incidents in the low area. There were seven of them. In addition to the first-arriving engine and first-arriving ladder times, there are second-arriving engine and second-arriving ladder times, because these incidents require two engines and two ladders. The "OVERALL MAX" entry is the average time to get the last of these four units to the scene. (From the numbers, it is clear that the second ladder was always the last to arrive.)

To see how the grouped aggregates function, look at number 15, all incidents in the low area. There were 433 of them. The average time for the first-arriving engine to reach these incidents was 7.01 minutes. The average time for the second-arriving engine to reach the 13 incidents *that needed at least two engines* was 8.31 minutes. The average third-arriving engine time was 9.82 minutes to the six incidents that needed at least three engines, and so forth. The average "OVERALL MIN" of 6.65 minutes represents the average time to get the first unit (of any type) to the scene. The "OVERALL MAX" represents the time to get all the units that were needed to the scene. As such, it mixes incidents needing many companies with those that need few, and so is not very meaningful. This example of response-time output illustrates the ability to display separately the response times for different types of incidents in different areas. Another useful possibility, not shown here, would be to display separately the responses during different periods of the day.

A word about statistical analysis: the usual formula for the standard deviation of average response time may not apply here. For example, the standard deviation of first-arriving engine times of the 433 low area incidents was 1.97 minutes. This would seem to imply that the standard deviation of the average would be 0.095 minutes ($=1.97/\sqrt{433}$). But this assumes that response times to successive incidents are independent of each other. Dividing 433 incidents by 360 hours gives an average of a little more than one per hour, indicating that some of these incidents may be occurring before others are over. Consequently, assuming independence is not wise, and modifications are in order. (These modifications are discussed in Section 13.5.) When the response times are not independent, the true standard deviation is larger than that produced by the naive calculation that uses the square-root of the sample size.[10] That is, in this case, the 0.095 would, if anything, be an underestimate of the true standard deviation of average first-arriving engine response time.

---

[10] This assumes positive covariances, which are to be expected from sequences of response times (Section 13.6.1).

TABLE 13.10. Response Time Vectors from Sample Simulation.

SAMPLE DECK
RESPONSE TIME VECTORS

	\multicolumn{3}{c}{AGGREGATE TYPE}									
	1 LOW AREA, FALSE ALARMS			2 LOW AREA, RUBBISH, ETC			3 LOW AREA, SIMPLE STRUCT			4 LOW AREA, STRUCT, ETC		
MEAS TYPE	NO OF MEASUR MENTS	AVG RESPONSE TIME	STD DEV RESPONSE TIME	NO OF MEASUR MENTS	AVG RESPONSE TIME	STD DEV RESPONSE TIME	NO OF MEASUR MENTS	AVG RESPONSE TIME	STD DEV RESPONSE TIME	NO OF MEASUR MENTS	AVG RESPONSE TIME	STD DEV RESPONSE TIME
1E	57	6.87	1.80	184	7.24	2.22	179	6.87	1.77	7	6.45	0.91
2E	0	0.	0.	0	0.	0.	0	0.	0.	7	8.21	0.91
3E	0	0.	0.	0	0.	0.	0	0.	0.	0	0.	0.
4E	0	0.	0.	0	0.	0.	0	0.	0.	0	0.	0.
5E	0	0.	0.	0	0.	0.	0	0.	0.	0	0.	0.
6E	0	0.	0.	0	0.	0.	0	0.	0.	0	0.	0.
7E	0	0.	0.	0	0.	0.	0	0.	0.	0	0.	0.
8E	0	0.	0.	0	0.	0.	0	0.	0.	0	0.	0.
1L	56	6.88	1.88	184	7.04	2.07	179	6.72	1.59	7	6.33	0.91
2L	0	0.	0.	0	0.	0.	0	0.	0.	7	8.81	1.75
3L	0	0.	0.	0	0.	0.	0	0.	0.	0	0.	0.
4L	0	0.	0.	0	0.	0.	0	0.	0.	0	0.	0.
OVERALL MIN	57	6.62	1.77	184	6.81	2.02	179	6.52	1.57	7	6.33	0.91
OVERALL MAX	57	7.13	1.86	184	7.47	2.23	179	7.07	1.75	7	8.81	1.75

	AGGREGATE TYPE														
	5 LOW AREA. 1 FULL ALARM			6 LOW AREA. 2 FULL ALARMS			7 LOW AREA. 3 FULL ALARMS			8 BUSY AREA. FALSE ALARMS		
MEAS TYPE	NO OF MEASUR MENTS	AVG RESPONSE TIME	STD DEV RESPONSE TIME	NO OF MEASUR MENTS	AVG RESPONSE TIME	STD DEV RESPONSE TIME	NO OF MEASUR MENTS	AVG RESPONSE TIME	STD DEV RESPONSE TIME	NO OF MEASUR MENTS	AVG RESPONSE TIME	STD DEV RESPONSE TIME
1E	5	6.63	1.44	0	0.	0.	1	6.00	0.	219	6.47	1.42
2E	5	8.20	2.07	0	0.	0.	1	9.56	0.	0	0.	0.
3E	5	9.67	1.82	0	0.	0.	1	10.59	0.	0	0.	0.
4E	0	0.	0.	0	0.	0.	1	30.99	0.	0	0.	0.
5E	0	0.	0.	0	0.	0.	1	32.66	0.	0	0.	0.
6E	0	0.	0.	0	0.	0.	1	33.25	0.	0	0.	0.
7E	0	0.	0.	0	0.	0.	1	38.82	0.	0	0.	0.
8E	0	0.	0.	0	0.	0.	1	43.25	0.	0	0.	0.
1L	5	6.53	1.31	0	0.	0.	1	6.00	0.	220	6.82	1.65
2L	5	9.02	2.09	0	0.	0.	1	9.56	0.	0	0.	0.
3L	0	0.	0.	0	0.	0.	1	29.05	0.	0	0.	0.
4L	0	0.	0.	0	0.	0.	1	40.99	0.	0	0.	0.
OVERALL MIN	5	6.53	1.31	0	0.	0.	1	6.00	0.	224	6.27	1.18
OVERALL MAX	5	9.67	1.82	0	0.	0.	1	43.25	0.	224	6.99	1.78

continued

TABLE 13.10. Response Time Vectors from Sample Simulation, *continued*

	AGGREGATE TYPE											
	9 BUSY AREA. RUBBISH, ETC			10 BUSY AREA. SIMPLE STRUCT			11 BUSY AREA. STRUCT, ETC			12 BUSY AREA. 1 FULL ALARM		
MEAS TYPE	NO OF MEASUR MENTS	AVG RESPONSE TIME	STD DEV RESPONSE TIME	NO OF MEASUR MENTS	AVG RESPONSE TIME	STD DEV RESPONSE TIME	NO OF MEASUR MENTS	AVG RESPONSE TIME	STD DEV RESPONSE TIME	NO OF MEASUR MENTS	AVG RESPONSE TIME	STD DEV RESPONSE TIME
1E	299	6.63	1.58	219	6.25	1.31	20	6.37	1.45	11	6.26	1.23
2E	0	0.	0.	0	0.	0.	20	10.02	5.60	11	8.76	2.86
3E	0	0.	0.	0	0.	0.	0	0.	0.	11	10.50	3.67
4E	0	0.	0.	0	0.	0.	0	0.	0.	0	0.	0.
5E	0	0.	0.	0	0.	0.	0	0.	0.	0	0.	0.
6E	0	0.	0.	0	0.	0.	0	0.	0.	0	0.	0.
7E	0	0.	0.	0	0.	0.	0	0.	0.	0	0.	0.
8E	0	0.	0.	0	0.	0.	0	0.	0.	0	0.	0.
1L	299	6.87	1.75	219	6.67	1.62	20	6.48	1.70	11	6.43	1.46
2L	0	0.	0.	0	0.	0.	20	11.92	6.39	11	10.15	4.16
3L	0	0.	0.	0	0.	0.	0	0.	0.	0	0.	0.
4L	0	0.	0.	0	0.	0.	0	0.	0.	0	0.	0.
OVERALL MIN	299	6.40	1.38	219	6.14	1.26	20	6.36	1.46	11	6.19	1.25
OVERALL MAX	299	7.10	1.85	219	6.78	1.62	20	12.11	6.67	11	10.66	3.87

AGGREGATE TYPE

MEAS TYPE	13 BUSY AREA, 2 FULL ALARMS			14 BUSY AREA 3 FULL ALARMS			15 LOW AREA, ALL ALARMS			16 BUSY AREA ALL ALARMS		
	NO OF MEASUR MENTS	AVG RESPONSE TIME	STD DEV RESPONSE TIME	NO OF MEASUR MENTS	AVG RESPONSE TIME	STD DEV RESPONSE TIME	NO OF MEASUR MENTS	AVG RESPONSE TIME	STD DEV RESPONSE TIME	NO OF MEASUR MENTS	AVG RESPONSE TIME	STD DEV RESPONSE TIME
1E	2	5.98	0.06	1	7.66	0.	433	7.01	1.97	771	6.46	1.46
2E	2	6.99	0.77	1	8.34	0.	13	8.31	1.49	34	9.38	4.68
3E	2	7.79	0.09	1	10.83	0.	6	9.82	1.69	14	10.13	3.39
4E	2	23.70	0.43	1	23.30	0.	1	30.99	0.	3	23.57	0.40
5E	2	25.43	0.68	1	26.32	0.	1	32.66	0.	3	25.72	0.70
6E	2	28.14	0.47	1	29.88	0.	1	33.25	0.	3	29.72	0.91
7E	0	0.	0.	1	30.22	0.	1	38.82	0.	1	30.22	0.
8E	0	0.	0.	1	35.94	0.	1	43.25	0.	1	35.94	0.
1L	2	5.98	0.06	1	7.66	0.	432	6.87	1.84	772	6.78	1.69
2L	2	6.99	0.77	1	10.83	0.	13	8.95	1.84	34	11.03	5.60
3L	2	22.27	2.47	1	23.30	0.	1	29.05	0.	3	22.62	2.07
4L	0	0.	0.	1	30.22	0.	1	40.99	0.	1	30.22	0.
OVERALL MIN	2	5.98	0.06	1	7.66	0.	433	6.65	1.79	776	6.29	1.29
OVERALL MAX	2	28.14	0.47	1	35.94	0.	433	7.39	2.65	776	7.25	2.72

continued

TABLE 13.10. Response Time Vectors from Sample Solution. *continued*

	17 ALL FALSE ALARMS			AGGREGATE TYPE 18 ALL RUBBISH, ETC			19 ALL SIMPLE STRUCT			20 ALL TYPE 4		
MEAS TYPE	NO OF MEASUR MENTS	AVG RESPONSE TIME	STD DEV RESPONSE TIME	NO OF MEASUR MENTS	AVG RESPONSE TIME	STD DEV RESPONSE TIME	NO OF MEASUR MENTS	AVG RESPONSE TIME	STD DEV RESPONSE TIME	NO OF MEASUR MENTS	AVG RESPONSE TIME	STD DEV RESPONSE TIME
1E	276	6.56	1.51	483	6.86	1.87	398	6.53	1.57	27	6.39	1.34
2E	0	0.	0.	0	0.	0.	0	0.	0.	27	9.55	4.91
3E	0	0.	0.	0	0.	0.	0	0.	0.	0	0.	0.
4E	0	0.	0.	0	0.	0.	0	0.	0.	0	0.	0.
5E	0	0.	0.	0	0.	0.	0	0.	0.	0	0.	0.
6E	0	0.	0.	0	0.	0.	0	0.	0.	0	0.	0.
7E	0	0.	0.	0	0.	0.	0	0.	0.	0	0.	0.
8E	0	0.	0.	0	0.	0.	0	0.	0.	0	0.	0.
1L	276	6.83	1.70	483	6.94	1.88	398	6.69	1.61	27	6.44	1.54
2L	0	0.	0.	0	0.	0.	0	0.	0.	27	11.11	5.74
3L	0	0.	0.	0	0.	0.	0	0.	0.	0	0.	0.
4L	0	0.	0.	0	0.	0.	0	0.	0.	0	0.	0.
OVERALL MIN	281	6.34	1.32	483	6.55	1.66	398	6.31	1.42	27	6.35	1.34
OVERALL MAX	281	7.02	1.80	483	7.24	2.01	398	6.91	1.69	27	11.25	5.98

AGGREGATE TYPE

MEAS TYPE	21 ALL 1 FULL ALARM			22 ALL 2 FULL ALARMS			23 ALL 3 FULL ALARMS			24 ALL ALARMS		
	NO OF MEASUR MENTS	AVG RESPONSE TIME	STD DEV RESPONSE TIME	NO OF MEASUR MENTS	AVG RESPONSE TIME	STD DEV RESPONSE TIME	NO OF MEASUR MENTS	AVG RESPONSE TIME	STD DEV RESPONSE TIME	NO OF MEASUR MENTS	AVG RESPONSE TIME	STD DEV RESPONSE TIME
1E	16	6.38	1.31	2	5.98	0.06	2	6.83	0.83	1204	6.66	1.63
2E	16	8.58	2.65	2	6.99	0.77	2	8.95	0.61	47	9.09	4.09
3E	16	10.24	3.23	2	7.79	0.09	2	10.71	0.12	20	10.04	2.99
4E	0	0.	0.	2	23.70	0.43	2	27.15	3.84	4	25.42	3.23
5E	0	0.	0.	2	25.43	0.68	2	29.49	3.17	4	27.46	3.07
6E	0	0.	0.	2	28.14	0.47	2	31.56	1.69	4	29.85	2.11
7E	0	0.	0.	0	0.	0.	2	34.52	4.30	2	34.52	4.30
8E	0	0.	0.	0	0.	0.	2	39.60	3.66	2	39.60	3.66
1L	16	6.46	1.41	2	5.98	0.06	2	6.83	0.83	1204	6.81	1.74
2L	16	9.80	3.68	2	6.99	0.77	2	10.20	0.63	47	10.15	4.95
3L	0	0.	0.	2	22.27	2.47	2	26.18	2.87	4	24.23	3.31
4L	0	0.	0.	0	0.	0.	2	35.61	5.39	2	35.61	5.39
OVERALL MIN	16	6.30	1.28	2	5.98	0.06	2	6.83	0.83	1209	6.42	1.50
OVERALL MAX	16	10.35	3.40	2	28.14	0.47	2	39.60	3.66	1209	7.30	2.70

Table 13.10 gives averages and standard deviations of response times. More information about the distribution of response times is contained in the histograms of response time illustrated in Table 13.11. (Table 13.11 is an excerpt from the full histogram.) Table 13.11 indicates that for aggregate type 1, one incident had a first-arriving engine response time between 2 and 3 minutes, six incidents had first-arriving engine response times between 4 and 5 minutes, and so forth. If you are interested in how many incidents (of all types in both areas) had first-arriving engine times of more than 10 minutes, adding the entries in the first 14 rows in the columns to the right of (but not including) column 10 gives 54 of them, or 4 percent of the 1209 incidents.

13.4.2 Response Adequacy

The output report shown in Table 13.12 gives initial dispatch adequacy information. Here the seven incident types and two areas are cross-classified with two ways in which incidents are reported. For example, in the "STRUCT, ETC." incidents in the low area—aggregate type 4—three engines and two ladders were sent to each incident initially. The incidents of the same type in the busy area—aggregate 10—had varying responses. There were 219 alarms: 46 reported by box and 173 reported by phone. Of the box alarms, one engine was initially dispatched to 19 of them and two engines were sent to the other 27. Of the telephone alarms, two engines were initially dispatched to one of them and the other 172 got three. (Since these incidents need two engines, 20 of the 219 received an inadequate engine response.)

13.4.3 Coverage

Table 13.13 gives "coverage" information. Response times measure performance at incidents that actually occur. Coverage (to be defined below) measures how well the department could respond to an incident, if one occurred. That is, response times measure "realized" performance; coverage measures "potential" performance.

Coverage is measured by periodically interrupting the simulation, and seeing which houses have companies available and which do not. There were 476 such "samples" taken in this run, one every 45 minutes. Each time the simulation is interrupted, every potential incident location is examined to see whether or not there is an available engine in the house closest to it. The results of these samplings are reported in the first column of Table 13.13.[11] The first column indicates that (for example) on

---

[11] These coverage samples are also used in "virtual estimation," a variance reduction technique described in Section 13.6.

13.4 Output Information

one interruption (of the 476), less than 10 percent of the incident locations had an engine available in the closest house (so over 90 percent did not); on six interruptions, between 10 and 20 percent of the locations had an engine available in the closest house, and so forth. The 476 entries averaged 76.97 percent closest engine coverage, with a standard deviation of 21.58 percent. That is, over the whole simulation run, on the average just under 77 percent of the incident locations had an engine available in the closest house. Further, for the complete sequence of 476 samples, the standard deviation was just under 22 percent.

Coverage measured in this way provides information about equity among different areas of the city. For example, it might be possible to reduce overall average response times by temporarily moving companies into the busy area. But the 77 percent average first-due engine coverage would probably decrease. Coverage also indicates relocation effectiveness. An improved relocation policy should increase coverage levels. Note that there are many occasions on which few incident locations have their first-due engine available; this implies poor distribution of companies, regardless of the average (which in this case was 77 percent).

The other columns contain similar information. The second column gives the percentage of potential incident locations for which an engine is available in the closest or second-closest house. On the average over the simulation, almost 90 percent of the incident locations had an engine company available in the closest or second-closest house; on one occasion, however, less than 10 percent did; on four occasions, between 20 and 30 percent did; and so forth. The third column shows that, if a location is thought of as "covered" when there is an engine in the closest, second-closest, or third-closest house then just over 95 percent were covered, on the average. The next two columns report similar figures for ladder coverage.

The next six columns report a different sort of coverage measure, namely, the availability of companies without regard to the coverage of specific locations. For example, the "ALL ENG" column indicates that on one occasion, fewer than 10 percent of the engines were available; on two, between 10 and 20 percent were available; and so forth. Overall, on the average, over 76 percent were available. The other columns have similar figures for ladders, and for the two areas separately.

13.4.4 Workload

Table 13.14 gives workload information. The far left-hand column gives the company identification numbers used inside the simulation; the far right-hand column gives the name by which the company is known by the fire department (or any other identifier the user specifies). Company 1, which is really Engine 15, made 234 responses in the 15-day period

TABLE 13.11. Response Time Histograms from Sample Simulation Run.

SAMPLE DECK
HISTOGRAMS OF RESPONSE TIME. DELTA 1
TIME INCREMENT

AGGREGATE TYPE	MEAS TYPE	1	2	3	4	5	6	7	8	9	10	11	12	13	14	15	16	17	18	19	20
1	1E	0	0	1	0	6	11	117	12	5	0	2	2	1	0	0	0	0	0	0	0
2	1E	0	0	1	0	13	42	59	22	16	9	7	6	3	2	3	1	0	0	0	0
3	1E	0	0	1	0	17	42	55	30	13	9	6	2	1	3	0	0	0	0	0	0
4	1E	0	0	0	0	1	0	5	1	0	0	0	0	0	0	0	0	0	0	0	0
5	1E	0	0	0	0	1	1	1	1	1	0	0	0	0	0	0	0	0	0	0	0
6	1E	0	0	0	0	0	0	0	0	0	0	0	0	0	0	0	0	0	0	0	0
7	1E	0	0	0	0	0	1	0	0	0	0	0	0	0	0	0	0	0	0	0	0
8	1E	0	0	0	0	32	49	90	17	21	7	0	0	2	0	0	0	0	0	0	0
9	1E	0	0	0	0	40	67	114	28	28	13	2	0	2	1	0	0	1	0	0	0
10	1E	0	0	0	0	50	46	79	18	20	3	3	4	0	0	0	0	0	0	0	0
11	1E	0	0	0	0	3	8	4	2	0	0	0	0	0	0	0	0	0	0	0	0
12	1E	0	0	0	0	3	0	5	2	1	3	0	0	0	0	0	0	0	0	0	0
13	1E	0	0	0	0	0	1	1	0	0	0	0	0	0	0	0	0	0	0	0	0
14	1E	0	0	0	0	0	0	0	1	0	0	0	0	0	0	0	0	0	0	0	0
1	2E	0	0	0	0	0	0	0	0	0	0	0	0	0	0	0	0	0	0	0	0
2	2E	0	0	0	0	0	0	0	0	0	0	0	0	0	0	0	0	0	0	0	0
3	2E	0	0	0	0	0	0	0	3	0	2	0	0	0	0	0	0	0	0	0	0
4	2E	0	0	0	0	0	0	2	1	2	0	0	0	0	0	0	0	0	0	0	0
5	2E	0	0	0	0	0	0	0	1	1	0	0	1	0	0	0	0	0	0	0	0

	2E-6	2E-7	2E-8	2E-9	2E-10	2E-11	2E-12	2E-13	2E-14	3E-1	3E-2	3E-3	3E-4	3E-5	3E-6	3E-7	3E-8	3E-9	3E-10	3E-11	3E-12	3E-13	3E-14	4E-1	4E-2	4E-3	4E-4
	0	0	0	0	2	0	0	0	0	0	0	0	0	0	0	0	0	0	0	0	0	0	0	0	0	0	0
	0	0	0	0	0	0	0	0	0	0	0	0	0	0	0	0	0	1	0	0	0	0	0	0	0	0	0
	0	0	0	0	0	0	1	0	0	0	0	0	0	0	0	0	0	0	1	0	0	0	0	0	0	0	0
	0	0	0	0	0	0	0	0	0	0	0	0	0	0	0	0	0	0	0	0	0	0	0	0	0	0	0
	0	0	0	0	0	0	0	0	0	0	0	0	0	0	0	0	0	0	0	0	0	0	0	0	0	0	0
	0	0	0	0	0	0	0	0	0	0	0	0	0	0	0	0	0	0	0	0	0	0	0	0	0	0	0
	0	0	0	0	0	0	0	0	0	0	0	0	1	0	0	0	0	0	0	0	0	0	0	0	0	0	0
	0	0	0	0	0	0	0	0	0	0	0	0	0	0	0	0	0	0	0	0	0	0	0	0	0	0	0
	0	0	0	0	0	0	0	0	0	0	0	0	0	0	0	0	0	0	0	0	0	0	0	0	0	0	0
	0	0	0	0	0	0	0	0	0	0	0	0	1	0	1	0	0	0	0	1	0	1	0	0	0	0	0
	0	1	0	0	0	4	2	0	0	0	0	0	0	0	0	0	0	0	3	0	0	0	0	0	0	0	0
	0	0	0	0	0	6	2	0	1	0	0	0	0	2	0	0	0	0	0	3	0	0	0	0	0	0	0
	0	0	0	0	0	7	4	1	0	0	0	0	0	1	0	0	0	0	0	2	2	0	0	0	0	0	0
	0	0	0	0	0	1	2	1	0	0	0	0	0	0	0	0	0	0	0	0	0	0	0	0	0	0	0
	0	0	0	0	0	0	0	0	0	0	0	0	0	0	0	0	0	0	0	0	0	0	0	0	0	0	0
	0	0	0	0	0	0	0	0	0	0	0	0	0	0	0	0	0	0	0	0	0	0	0	0	0	0	0
	0	0	0	0	0	0	0	0	0	0	0	0	0	0	0	0	0	0	0	0	0	0	0	0	0	0	0
	0	0	0	0	0	0	0	0	0	0	0	0	0	0	0	0	0	0	0	0	0	0	0	0	0	0	0
	0	0	0	0	0	0	0	0	0	0	0	0	0	0	0	0	0	0	0	0	0	0	0	0	0	0	0
	0	0	0	0	0	0	0	0	0	0	0	0	0	0	0	0	0	0	0	0	0	0	0	0	0	0	0

TABLE 13.12. Initial response adequacy information from sample simulation run.

SAMPLE DECK
NUMBER INITIALLY DISPATCHED TO ALARMS

AGGREGATE TYPE	ENGINES						LADDERS					
	DISP 1		DISP 2		DISP 3		DISP 1		DISP 2		DISP 3	
	BOX	PHONE	BOX	PHONE	BOX	PHONE	BOX	PHONE	BOX	PHONE	BOX	PHONE
1	8	0	10	0	27	12	12	0	33	12	0	0
2	11	131	9	1	33	0	16	131	37	0	0	0
3	7	0	9	0	24	138	15	0	25	139	0	0
4	0	0	0	0	1	6	0	0	1	6	0	0
5	0	0	0	0	1	4	0	0	1	4	0	0
6	0	0	0	0	0	0	0	0	0	0	0	0
7	0	0	0	0	0	1	0	0	0	1	0	0
8	68	0	110	1	0	45	170	0	0	46	0	0
9	34	198	67	0	0	0	101	198	0	0	0	0
10	19	0	27	1	0	172	46	0	0	173	0	0
11	2	0	3	0	0	15	5	0	0	15	0	0
12	1	0	1	0	0	9	2	0	0	9	0	0
13	0	0	0	0	0	2	0	0	0	2	0	0
14	0	0	0	0	0	1	0	0	0	1	0	0

that was simulated. It "worked" at 147 of the incidents to which it responded. It spent 47 hours and 20 minutes traveling. For 23 hours and 10 minutes of that travel time, it was available to respond to an incident (presumably because it was returning from somewhere); for 1 day (24 hours) and 10 minutes of that travel time, it was unavailable. It spent 2 days, 19 hours, and 33 minutes working at incidents.[12] It spent no time at incidents outside the region (i.e., at DOWN events). It spent two hours in repairs. The total time spent in travel, at work outside the region, and under repair was 4 days, 20 hours, 53 minutes.[13]

The companies can be grouped as desired for computation of average workload statistics. In this case, engines are separated from ladders; and for each type of unit, those stationed in the busy area are separated from those stationed in the low area and outside the region being simulated. (We allow these units from outside the region for the same reason as we permit DOWN events. They allow interaction with the outside region without detailed representation of it (Section 13.5).)

During the fifteen days of simulated time, the six engine companies in the busy area (numbered 1 through 6 in the simulation) made an average of 237 responses (almost 16 per day) and worked at an average of 131 incidents (almost 10 per day). By comparison, the seven engine companies in the low area and outside the region being simulated (numbered 7 through 13) averaged only 11 responses per day, and just over 5 workers per day. The engine companies in the busy area averaged just over 24 hours in available travel, which was 6.8 percent of the 15 days, and just over $2\frac{1}{2}$ days working at incidents, which was 17.0 percent of the simulated time. The companies in the low area spent 4.7 percent of their time in available travel, and 9.2 percent of their time working at incidents.

13.4.5 Relocation

Table 13.15 gives relocation information. It indicates that there were two relocations made from Engine House 9, for a total of 9.52 hours spent out-of-house. There was one relocation made into House 5, and the company that relocated there was assigned to House 5 for 7.34 hours. (Some of that time was spent traveling to and from House 5.)

Note that this report is indexed by houses, not companies. This is because the company that relocates from a house because of a particular fire need not be stationed there—it could have relocated *into* that house because of a previous fire.

The association between houses and companies stationed in them is

---

[12] The way SIMSCRIPT I.5 reports time, 2.19.33 means 2 days, 19 hours, 33 minutes.
[13] All of these figures are for the company itself, whether acting from its own house or from another house (as a relocatee).

TABLE 13.13. Coverage information produced by periodic interruption of the sample simulation run.

COVERAGE VECTOR 476 SAMPLES AT INTERVALS OF 0 HOURS AND 45 MINUTES

TYPE	FIRST ENG	FIRST 2 ENG	FIRST 3 ENG	FIRST LDR	FIRST 2 LDR	ALL ENG
AVERAGE	0.769790	0.898550	0.950525	0.746933	0.894538	0.767938
STD DEV	0.215823	0.160338	0.116352	0.202107	0.147768	0.194201

HISTOGRAMS

LOWER BOUND						
0.	1	1	1	0	0	1
0.10	6	0	0	4	0	2
0.20	13	4	0	10	0	6
0.30	17	5	4	15	8	20
0.40	19	10	4	20	7	18
0.50	48	14	3	62	14	33
0.60	53	22	7	68	21	98
0.70	77	44	25	77	40	72
0.80	106	62	39	89	90	62
0.90	5	175	254	29	202	81
1.00	131	139	139	94	94	83

TYPE	ALL LDR	LOW AREA ENG	HIGH AREA E	LOW AREA LDR	HIGH AREA L
AVERAGE	0.790298	0.720238	0.808824	0.693803	0.845438
STD DEV	0.165061	0.270282	0.208561	0.284617	0.163014

HISTOGRAMS

LOWER BOUND					
0.	0	6	2	18	0
0.10	0	30	3	0	0
0.20	1	0	13	61	4
0.30	11	42	0	0	0
0.40	16	0	30	0	12
0.50	31	61	49	83	41
0.60	59	72	0	0	0
0.70	79	0	71	162	96
0.80	102	118	131	0	132
0.90	85	0	0	0	0
1.00	92	147	177	152	191

TABLE 13.14. Workload information from sample simulation run (Company statistics).

SAMPLE DECK
SIMULATION ENDS AT TIME 15.00.00

COMPANY	RUNS	WORKERS	TRVL AV	TRVL UNAV	WORK	DOWN	REPAIR	TOTAL	TYPE	HOME	LCN	NAME
1	234	147	0.23.10	1.00.10	2.19.33	0.00.00	0.01.60	4.20.53	ENG	2.50	1.75	E15
2	89	65	0.08.59	0.09.15	1.07.22	0.00.00	0.00.00	2.01.37	ENG	2.50	1.75	E26
3	248	143	1.00.59	1.01.53	2.21.40	0.00.00	0.00.60	5.01.32	ENG	2.	3.75	E10
4	376	177	1.15.27	1.18.08	3.08.09	0.00.00	0.00.60	6.18.44	ENG	3.90	3.20	E101
5	197	114	0.21.32	0.22.26	2.05.21	0.00.00	0.01.60	4.02.20	ENG	3.90	3.20	E17
6	283	144	1.05.26	1.06.29	2.17.36	0.00.00	0.01.60	5.07.31	ENG	4.90	1.80	E16
AVG	237.83	131.67	1.00.36	1.01.43	2.13.17	0.00.00	0.01.10	4.16.46				
AVG UTILIZATION			0.06832	0.07145	0.17023	0.	0.00324	0.31325				
7	209	135	0.21.59	0.23.41	2.11.20	0.00.00	0.00.60	4.10.01	ENG	6.85	3.75	E34
8	151	68	0.18.04	0.18.21	1.08.30	0.00.00	0.00.60	2.21.55	ENG	6.	6.75	E202
9	220	107	1.00.40	1.02.20	2.01.41	0.00.00	0.00.60	4.05.41	ENG	4.50	6.	E2
10	223	102	1.01.17	1.01.56	2.02.08	0.07.10	0.00.00	4.12.31	ENG	2.75	5.50	E1
11	116	64	0.13.09	0.12.58	1.02.33	0.03.25	0.00.00	2.08.05	ENG	2.25	7.	E4

12	51	7	0.07.06	0.07.03	0.02.17	0.18.10	0.00.00	1.10.36	ENG	2.25	8.25	OE1
13	54	14	0.07.31	0.07.42	0.10.54	0.19.35	0.00.60	1.22.43	ENG	0.10	5.50	OE2
AVG	146.29	71.	0.16.49	0.17.26	1.09.03	0.06.54	0.00.34	3.02.47				
AVG UTILIZATION			0.04673	0.04842	0.09182	0.01918	0.00159	0.20775				
14	212	172	0.20.21	0.21.03	2.19.02	0.00.00	0.00.60	4.13.27	LDR	2.50	1.75	L1
15	228	185	0.21.59	0.22.47	2.23.54	0.00.00	0.01.60	4.22.41	LDR	2.	3.75	L2
16	295	223	1.05.34	1.07.43	3.13.24	0.00.00	0.00.00	6.02.40	LDR	3.90	3.20	L56
17	238	183	0.23.27	1.00.40	3.02.22	0.00.00	0.01.60	5.04.29	LDR	4.90	1.80	L17
AVG	243.25	190.75	0.23.51	1.01.03	3.02.40	0.00.00	0.01.15	5.04.49				
AVG UTILIZATION			0.06623	0.06960	0.20743	0.	0.00347	0.34673				
18	188	151	0.19.58	0.20.30	2.16.48	0.00.00	0.00.60	4.10.15	LDR	6.85	3.75	L106
19	126	59	0.14.25	0.14.26	1.01.53	0.00.00	0.00.00	2.06.44	LDR	6.	6.75	L219
20	119	77	0.12.33	0.12.59	1.05.33	0.00.00	0.00.00	2.07.06	LDR	5.	7.	L305
21	181	124	0.19.36	0.19.54	2.07.02	0.07.10	0.00.00	4.05.41	LDR	2.75	5.50	LXX
22	94	64	0.09.25	0.09.28	1.03.25	0.03.25	0.00.00	2.01.43	LDR	2.25	7.	LYYZ
23	17	4	0.01.55	0.01.53	0.01.01	0.15.15	0.00.00	0.20.04	LDR	2.25	8.25	OL1
24	29	15	0.04.09	0.04.29	0.10.04	0.19.35	0.00.60	1.15.18	LDR	0.10	5.50	OL2
AVG	107.71	70.57	0.11.43	0.11.57	1.06.32	0.06.29	0.00.17	2.12.59				
AVG UTILIZATION			0.03255	0.03319	0.08483	0.01802	0.00079	0.16939				

part of the input to the simulation program. In this instance, companies 1, 2, and 14 occupy House 1; 3 and 15 occupy House 2; and so forth.

13.4.6 Designing Additional Output

The output we have described may already seem too voluminous, but it may not be enough for some user's purposes. We discuss here some possible outputs that could be added.

Utility Calculation. The response times, as presented in Tables 13.10 and 13.11, permit comparison of the average and the distribution of first-arriving engine times for different types of incidents. They also permit comparison of second-arriving engine times, first-arriving ladder times, etc. This is very useful; chiefs want to see this kind of information. On the other hand, how does one compare one policy to another? What if one policy does better on average first-arriving engine time to structurals at which two engines work, but worse on average second-arriving engine time to two-alarm fires? Or, what if one policy does better on *average* first-arriving engine time but produces more long travel times? A single figure of merit for an entire simulation would be very helpful here.

As discussed in Chapter 3, Keeney (1973) has begun the task of getting a single figure. His utility function for response times to structural fires gives one number as the "value" of the response time vector for each incident. The underlying theory implies that averaging these values at different incidents is sufficient, in the sense that the policy that maximizes the average is best. For example, if long response times are inordinately bad, the utility function will assign a high weight to them, and it is therefore unlikely that the best policy will have many of them. The utility function approach involves making a number of assumptions that may be unpalatable to some potential users. When this is the case, a direct attempt at comparison, as described in the previous paragraph, is necessary.

Escalation Calculation. Suppose it is possible to work out a relationship that indicates what kind of response will allow fires of a given type to grow. Then, an escalation report should be designed. It would count the number of incidents that could have escalated, the number that did, and what features of the response led to escalation.

Damage Calculation. Similarly, if the user can find a relationship between response times and damage, a report is in order. If the damage falls into a few discrete classes—for example, none, light, medium, heavy—then a count on the number of incidents in each damage class

TABLE 13.15. Relocation information from sample simulation run (reported by house).

SAMPLE DECK
RELOCATION REPORT BY HOUSE

HOUSE	ENG				LDR			
	OUT OF		IN TO		OUT OF		IN TO	
	NO.	DURATION IN HOURS	NO.	DURATION IN HOURS	NO.	DURATION IN HOURS	NO.	DURATION IN HOURS
1	0	0.	0	0.	0	0.	0	0.
2	0	0.	2	9.52	0	0.	2	8.58
3	0	0.	1	2.16	0	0.	1	1.91
4	0	0.	0	0.	0	0.	0	0.
5	0	0.	1	7.34	1	1.91	0	0.
6	0	0.	0	0.	0	0.	0	0.
7	0	0.	0	0.	0	0.	0	0.
8	1	2.16	0	0.	0	0.	0	0.
9	2	9.52	0	0.	2	8.58	0	0.
10	1	7.34	0	0.	0	0.	0	0.
11	0	0.	0	0.	0	0.	0	0.
12	0	0.	0	0.	0	0.	0	0.

is logical. If the damage is in dollars or square feet, then it is also sensible to report the total damage.

13.5 EXPERIMENTAL DESIGN

In this section, we return to issues raised in Chapter 3. To decide what features to put in the simulation model, what policies to try, what alarm sequence to use, and similar questions, it is necessary to start with the purpose of the study and go through the steps in a systems analysis study.

The theme of this section has been well put by Hamming (1962): "The purpose of computing is insight, not numbers."

13.5.1 Features of the Simulation Model

The flexibility of simulation means that there are many choices to make in deciding how to represent the system. There are no hard-and-fast rules for what to do; some obvious points follow. A model that will be used to see how well a particular deployment policy will work in practice needs more detail than one that is exploring the effect of a purely hypothetical policy. The policy should be specified in detail for common and important incidents; for unusual or uninteresting incidents, approximate treatment is sufficient, particularly if no one is contemplating changing the way they are handled. To be more specific, we discuss some of the considerations that determine the features of the Fire Operations Simulation Model.

Most of the uses that were identified for the simulation model had as their main requirement a reasonable representation of the pattern of company availability. Differences in this pattern are, in some sense, the primary differences between dispatch policies (or relocation policies). This view, and the need for less detail about uncommon and unimportant alarms, leads to discarding some types of incidents. For example, suppose 3 percent of a department's actual incidents are reported by people walking into a firehouse, but the reports are otherwise pretty much like telephone-reported alarms. It is probably not important to distinguish them from telephone alarms. As a first approximation they may be ignored entirely, while the rate of telephone alarms is increased to make the total alarm rate appropriate. The need to represent availability well is the reason for the DOWN event and for the inclusion of companies outside the region of interest. They allow consideration of a relatively small region without sacrificing accurate representation of company availability.

Let us consider in more depth the question of choosing a region to simulate, and then handling its interaction with the rest of the city and/or

13.5 Experimental Design 533

neighboring cities.[14] To include an entire city and its environs may imply a large number of companies (counting both engines and ladders); and simultaneously representing the activities of all of them implies a burdensome, slow-running simulation. While the regions that pose major problems are usually relatively small, no group of fire companies singled out for study is independent of the others. Since interactions are greatest near the border of any area we wish to study, the problem is one of *edge effects*.

The approach taken in the simulation model to minimize these edge effects is as follows: First, the region to be studied and the companies inside it are distinguished. When an incident occurs inside this area, it is followed in detail. The units to be sent are determined (from the initial dispatch policy) and all response times are measured. Incidents outside the area are also treated, but are followed in much less detail. The identities of the companies that respond from outside the area of interest are fixed, regardless of the dispatch policy inside the distinguished area, and their response times are not measured. The DOWN event is used to handle these outside incidents. Various workload measures are incorporated to keep track of companies, both inside and outside the area. However, the workloads of the inside companies are of the most concern.

Another question related to edge effects is, what action should be taken when an incident occurs and all the simulated units are busy? In the real world such a condition is unlikely, since additional fire resources would be brought into the area from neighboring regions or by recalling off-duty firemen. The assumption built into the simulation model is that units not being simulated will respond to such an incident. Consequently, the simulation model does not keep a queue of incidents or a record of response times to incidents that occur when all units are busy.

The model documented in Carter (1974) does not allow fires to escalate. (A few runs have been made with a rudimentary escalation model.) In most of the simulation runs in New York City, no escalation model was used, and none is included in the sample program that produced the output described in Section 13.4. There were two reasons for this choice: (1) it is difficult to obtain accurate parameters for an escalation model; and (2) escalation adds complexity to the model in return for a degree of realism that is not normally necessary to distinguish between alternative deployment policies.

To see why (2) is true, consider the following. Let $\mathbf{x} = (x_1, x_2, \ldots)$ and $F_1(\mathbf{x})$ be the (simulated) proportion of incidents that have response

---

[14] In New York City, the initial notion of simulating only part of the city troubled most fire officers. After some results (using a very rough approximation to one of the five boroughs) showed that insights to citywide policies could be obtained from simulating a small part of the city, the question never came up again (see Section 14.2 and Carter and Ignall (1970)).

times that are $\leq x$ when Policy 1 is used. (That is, the first-arriving engine time is $\leq x_1$, and the second-arriving engine time is $\leq x_2$, and so forth.) Let $F_2(\mathbf{x})$ be the proportion when Policy 2 is used. If it turns out that $F_1(\mathbf{x}) \geq F_2(\mathbf{x})$ for all $\mathbf{x}$, then under Policy 1, fires will be less likely to escalate. If we added an escalation model to the simulation, we would find that Policy 2 would require a larger additional commitment of fire resources. The result would be that response times under Policy 2 would increase more than under Policy 1, and therefore the new distributions of response time would still obey $F_1(\mathbf{x}) \geq F_2(\mathbf{x})$. Thus, Policy 1 would remain the superior policy.

Clearly, the simulation includes many approximations to how the system really works. Given these approximations, is the model safe to use? Is it an adequate representation of the true situation when some alarms are discarded and only a small region of the city is used? What about the lack of an escalation feature? These and related questions are about the model's *validity*, which it is now appropriate to discuss.

13.5.2 Validity

For policy analysis purposes, determining the validity of a model means determining the answer to the question: Are the features of the simulation adequate to justify the policy implications that may be drawn from the results? To quote Van Horn (1971): "The users of simulators are seldom concerned with the 'truth' of a model . . . . Instead the simulator produces some specific insight which needs validation . . . . The objective is to validate a specific set of insights, not necessarily the mechanism that generated the insights . . . ." Taking this view should be helpful in making all of the simulation design choices. It also suggests that features that are appropriate for one purpose can be unnecessary for another, and inadequate for a third.

This view of validity applies to all of the models in this book. The potential user of any of the models should maintain a healthy skepticism about their validity. Before applying any model to a particular problem he should observe in person the different aspects of the system, and should discuss each part of the model with people who know the operation well.

Next the model should be checked to see whether it behaves the way it is expected to behave. In any simulation run, for example, a "trace" of the first few (10, 20, or more) incidents should be printed. This should show when they occurred, which units responded, and which units were available before each dispatch. The availability of companies should also be tracked. If possible, the model's behavior should be compared to the real world. For example, a real alarm sequence should be run and compared to what actually happened—which companies worked at which incidents, response times, and so on.

13.5.3 Sources of Policies to be Tested

If the best policy is not included in the simulation runs, neither the beauty of the model nor any amount of statistical ingenuity will identify it. Therefore, effort is needed to get good policies to be tested in the simulation. Where does one get such policies? There are two important sources: (1) fire officers and (2) analysts.

The existence of a project team will surely evoke proposals from officers. Analysts working with models of the kind discussed in Chapters 6–12 will yield others. Iterative use of the simulation model may also help. The combination of the officers' ideas and the models has special value. While using the models often leads to new deployment policy ideas, it does not uncover many of the complications and policy constraints. Experienced chiefs are much better at identifying and resolving these problems than are the analysts.

13.5.4 Choice of Alarm Sequence

Should an historical sequence of incidents or one generated probabilistically be used? If the latter, should it imitate one period of the day repeatedly, or cycle through the whole day? (That is, should the alarm sequence be steady-state or time-varying?) A related question is whether, in comparing two policies, to use the same incident sequence in both runs or to use two different ones. In this section we will consider the first two questions, leaving the last one for Sections 13.5.5 and 13.6.

The simulation model can handle any choice about the incident sequence that the user cares to make. The simulation program uses an exogenous events tape to describe the incidents to be simulated, so it is totally unaware of the time-varying or steady-state nature of the input alarm sequence. The procedure for gathering statistics on the response times to incidents is flexible enough so that they can be easily examined by the time of day in which the alarms occurred. Thus, the simulation program is well suited to a simulation of either steady-state or transient behavior.

Many of the problems that require deployment analysis—problems of coverage due to many units being busy at incidents, and workload problems stemming from repeated runs to false alarms and small incidents—occur only during the hours of peak demand. Many of the dispatch and relocation algorithms that should be considered are aimed at these problems of the peak demand period. During periods of light demand they perform exactly the same as the current practices of the fire department. In order to understand the properties of these algorithms, it is more efficient to simulate only the peak periods in which one is interested than to simulate incidents for the entire day.

For convincing the chief, the unions, the budget bureau, the mayor (and the analyst) that a particular policy will work, using an historical alarm sequence can be vital. It may also be desirable to approximate the effect of an increase in alarm rate, to reflect what might be expected in the future. For example, suppose the idea is to see what happens when the rate is 20 percent higher than the historical period being used as input, and the plan is to simulate a particular one-week test period. The following procedure may be used: Take the incidents in the week before (or after) the test week and "overlay" 20 percent of them on the ones from the test week. This may be done by sampling a (new) random number for each alarm received the week before (or after). If the random number is less than 0.20, add that alarm to the alarm sequence of the test week. (That is, move it up or back exactly 168 hours.) If the random number is greater than 0.20, do not add it.

13.5.5 Initial Conditions

The most convenient way to start the simulation is with all companies available in their houses. If the starting point is in a very slow period, for example 6 A.M., these initial conditions are reasonable because it is very likely that no incidents are in progress. If the starting point is a busy time with these initial conditions, the first few incidents will be simulated in a better situation that could be expected in reality—and we would expect the corresponding response times to be lower. In this case, it is recommended practice to discard the first hour or so (and all of the incidents in that *run-in-period*). (Section 10.4 of Fishman (1973).) In other words, the first few incidents should be used to "prime" the system, and only then should the recording of response times, coverage, company workloads, and so forth, begin.

13.5.6 Variance Reduction—Statistical Efficiency

Making inferences about future performance from the output of a simulation run involves statistical inference. Consequently, good experimental design may permit the user to achieve a given statistical reliability (standard error of estimate, confidence interval width, test power) with a shorter simulation run. Section 13.6 has several suggestions for doing so. The most important of these are the use of the same incidents whenever two or more policies are being compared, and the use of "virtual" estimation.

13.6 STATISTICAL ANALYSIS

The best reference on the statistical analysis of simulation is Fishman (1973), especially Chapters 10 and 11. We summarize some of the most important points here.

If the question is simply which policy performs best on a particular historical alarm sequence, there is no statistical problem. A more likely problem, however, is inferring which policy can be expected to perform best in the future. In this situation, a particular simulation run may be viewed as producing a sequence $\mathbf{X}_1, \mathbf{X}_2, \ldots, \mathbf{X}_n$ of response time vectors to the first, second, ..., and nth incidents. We make the assumption (to be discussed in Section 13.6.1) that all the $\mathbf{X}_j$ are samples from the same distribution, and for brevity we let $\mathbf{X}$ be a (vector) random variable with this distribution. Then, to estimate future performance (assuming future alarms will have the same probabilistic properties as those in the simulation run), we want to know $E(\mathbf{X})$, Var $(\mathbf{X})$, and other features of the distribution of $\mathbf{X}$. If we want to infer which of two policies will be better in the future, and the second one gives response time vectors $\mathbf{Y}_1, \mathbf{Y}_2, \ldots, \mathbf{Y}_m$, we are interested in $E(\mathbf{X}) - E(\mathbf{Y})$ and other features of the response time *differences*. (Similar remarks apply to other performance measures, both here and for the remainder of this chapter.)

What special problems, if any, does simulation pose in the statistical analysis of these questions? First of all, there is the fact that the $\mathbf{X}_j$ are vectors rather than one-dimensional random variables. A more serious problem would exist even if we were interested only in (say) first-arriving engine response time for which $X_1, X_2, \ldots, X_n$ would be ordinary random variables. This problem is that $X_1, X_2, \ldots, X_n$ will generally *not* be a sequence of independent random variables. (Because, for example, higher-than-average response times now usually mean many busy companies, a circumstance that is likely to cause higher-than-average response times in the near future.) Consequently, the usual formulas for confidence intervals and tests of hypothesis about $E(\mathbf{X})$ do not apply. To be specific, let

$$\bar{X} = \sum_{i=1}^{n} X_i/n$$

be the average first-arriving engine response time, and let

$$S^2 = \sum_{i=1}^{n} (X_i - \bar{X})^2/(n-1)$$

be the sample variance of first-arriving engine response times. Then (under certain assumptions—see Section 13.6.1) $\bar{X}$ is a good estimator of $E(X)$ and S^2 is a good estimator of Var(X), but S^2/n will be a poor estimator of Var($\bar{X}$). In particular, it can be very low, with the result that the usual (normal) confidence interval—namely $\bar{X} \pm t_{\alpha/2, n-1} \sqrt{S^2/n}$ as an interval for $E(X)$—can be much too narrow.

13.6.1 Assumptions

We begin by considering first-arriving engine response times only. (Our reasoning applies to second-arriving engine times, or to first-arriving ladder times or the like, so long as each is considered by itself.) Let the first-arriving engine response times be represented by $X_1, \ldots, X_n$. We will return to the simultaneous consideration of the entire response time vector $(\mathbf{X}_1, \ldots, \mathbf{X}_n)$ later.

Suppose that incidents are generated probabilistically with no time-of-day variation in the alarm rate. Suppose also that the first hour or more of incidents are discarded, so that the effect of the initial conditions can be ignored. Let X_1 be the first response time after observations begin, X_2 be the second, and so on. Then, if we observe n response times,

$X_1, X_2, \ldots, X_n$ all have the same distribution;

$X_1, X_2, \ldots, X_n$ will not, in general, be independent of each other.[15]

Let F be the (common) distribution functions of the individual X_j's. That is, $F(x) \equiv P(X_j \leq x)$, for all x and all j. Then $X_1, \ldots, X_n$ can be used to estimate $E(X)$, $\text{Var}(X)$, $\text{Cov}(X_j, X_{j+k})$ and other features of the distribution of $(X_1, \ldots, X_n)$. For example:

$\bar{X}$ is a good estimator of $E(X)$.

X^2 is a good estimator of $\text{Var}(X)$.

Because of dependence, the problem is to estimate $\text{Var}(\bar{X})$, which is given by

$$\text{Var}(\bar{X}) = \frac{\text{Var}(X)}{n} + 2 \sum_{j<k} \text{Cov}(X_j, X_k)/n^2.$$

We discuss how to estimate $\text{Var}(\bar{X})$ in the following section.

What is likely to be true is that the covariances in the expression for $\text{Var}(\bar{X})$ are positive. Thus S^2/n, which is the usual estimator of $\text{Var}(\bar{X})$ in the independent case, will be an underestimate in this situation.

13.6.2 How to Estimate $\text{Var}(\bar{X})$

Estimate the Covariance. Under our assumptions, $\text{Cov}(X_1 X_2) = \text{Cov}(X_2 X_3) = \cdots = \text{Cov}(X_{n-1} X_n)$; and $\text{Cov}(X_1 X_3) = \text{Cov}(X_2 X_4) = \cdots$

---

[15] Technically, $(X_1, \ldots, X_n)$ will be a *covariance stationary process*.

13.6 Statistical Analysis

; etc. So

$$\hat{R}(1) = \frac{(X_1 - \bar{X})(X_2 - \bar{X}) + \cdots + (X_{n-1} - \bar{X})(X_n - \bar{X})}{n}$$

is a good estimator of $\text{Cov}(X_1 X_2)$. Similarly,

$$\hat{R}(2) = \frac{(X_1 - \bar{X})(X_3 - \bar{X}) + \cdots + (X_{n-2} - \bar{X})(X_n - \bar{X})}{n}$$

is a good estimator of $\text{Cov}(X_1 X_3)$. See Fishman (1973) for more on this. He discusses spectral analysis, which is equivalent to the estimation of covariances.

Avoid the Problem: Find Some Independent Variables. The idea is to divide the run into K segments, each with M incidents. M should be large enough that the segments are, more or less, independent of each other. For practical purposes, since few incidents last over an hour, M equal to twice the hourly incident rate should be sufficient.

Formally, pick K and M so that $KM = n$.

Define

$$V_1 = (X_1 + \cdots + X_M)/M,$$
$$V_2 = (X_{M+1} + \cdots + X_{2M})/M,$$
$$\vdots$$
$$V_K = (X_{(K-1)M+1} + \cdots + X_{KM})/M.$$

Then $\bar{X} = \bar{V}$, so $\text{Var}(\bar{X}) = \text{Var}(\bar{V})$; and $\text{Var}(\bar{V})$ may be estimated by S_V^2/K, where

$$S_V^2 \equiv \frac{(V_1 - \bar{V})^2 + \cdots + (V_K - \bar{V})^2}{K - 1}.$$

Pick M *large* enough so that V_1 is (more or less) independent of V_2, V_2 is independent of V_3, etc.; and *small* enough so that K is not too small. To see if M is large enough, compute the sample covariance lag 1 (i.e., $\hat{R}(1)$, using V's); if the covariance is near zero, then the V's are at least close to independent of each other.

13.6.3 Comparison of Different Situations

To make the explanation in this section easier, we continue with the notions in the second part of Section 13.6.2. Assume each run is divided into K segments that are independent of each other. Let V_j and W_j be the average response times in segment j for Policy 1 and Policy 2, respectively.

If Different (and Independent) Incidents Are Used for the Two Policies. We want to estimate $E(V - W)$. A good estimator is $\bar{V} - \bar{W}$. Because of independence,

$$\text{Var}(\bar{V} - \bar{W}) = \text{Var}(\bar{V}) + \text{Var}(\bar{W}),$$

so that

$$\text{Var}(\bar{V} - \bar{W}) \simeq \frac{S_V^2}{K} + \frac{S_W^2}{K}.$$

If the Same Incidents Are Used for Both of the Policies. Again, $V - W$ is a good estimator of the expected difference in response time. $\text{Var}(\bar{V} - \bar{W}) = \text{Var}(\bar{V}) + \text{Var}(\bar{W}) - 2\,\text{Cov}(\bar{V}\bar{W})$. This covariance is likely to be positive, so this procedure should be better than using independent incident sequences. To estimate $\text{Var}(\bar{V} - \bar{W})$ it helps to define $\Delta_j = V_j - W_j$. Then

$$\bar{\Delta} = \frac{(\Delta_1 + \cdots + \Delta_K)}{K} = \bar{V} - \bar{W}.$$

Then, if M is large enough so that the Δ's are independent of each other,

$$\text{Var}\,\bar{\Delta} = \text{Var}(\Delta)/K \simeq S_\Delta^2/K,$$

where

$$S_\Delta^2 \equiv \frac{\Sigma(\Delta_j - \bar{\Delta})^2}{K - 1}.$$

Note that writing output files (Section 13.2) makes it easy to compute $(\Delta_1, \Delta_2, \ldots, \Delta_K)$.

This second procedure, having both policies face the same incident sequence, can reduce $\text{Var}(\bar{V} - \bar{W})$ to about a quarter of its value for independent sequences, if K and M are fixed. Alternatively, K can be reduced by a factor of four (that is, the run can be shortened by 75 percent, while the statistical confidence in the results remains the same), leading to a significant saving in the cost of running the simulation program. To illustrate, and also to show an example of the use of the COMPARE program (Section 13.2.3), we consider response-time statistics for the third-arriving engine under the "base case" and "proposed" policies discussed in the first set of simulations in Section 14.4 (also, pages 27–31 of Carter and Ignall (1970)). We first look at the response times for third-arriving engines under each of the policies considered individually. Histograms, which summarize these response times for the 49 incidents that needed three or more engines, are given in Figures 13.2 and 13.3. Letting $V_1, \ldots, V_{49}$ and $W_1, \ldots, W_{49}$, be the times under

13.6 Statistical Analysis

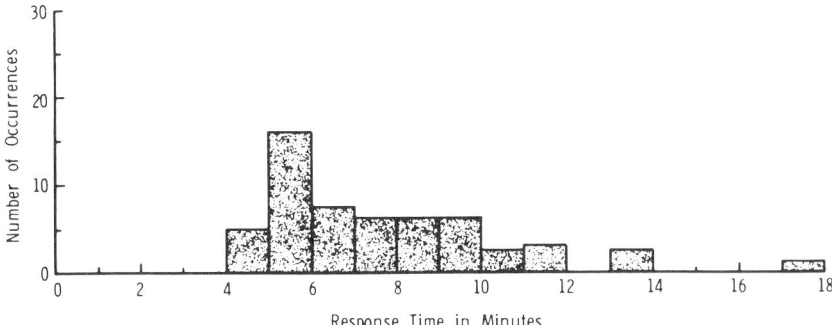

FIGURE 13.2. Base case: Histogram of third-arriving engine response times (the average is 7.26 minutes).

the base case and proposed policies, respectively, we calculate

$$\bar{V} = (V_1 + \cdots + V_{49})/49 = 7.26,$$

$$\bar{W} = 6.57,$$

$$S_V^2 = \{(V_1 - \bar{V})^2 + \cdots + (V_{49} - \bar{V})^2\}/(49 - 1) = 7.3,$$

$$S_W^2 = 4.3.$$

It is reasonable to suppose that the V_i are independent[16] of each other (so we have $M = 1$ and $K = 49$). Therefore, $S_V^2/49$ provides a good estimate of Var($\bar{V}$). If $\bar{V}$ and $\bar{W}$ were independent of each other (that is, if the two policies faced independent sets of incidents), an estimate of the standard deviation of ($\bar{V} - \bar{W}$) would be $\sqrt{(7.3 + 4.3)/49} = 0.49$. Now $(7.26 - 6.57)/0.49 = 1.4$, so that, assuming that $\bar{V}$ and $\bar{W}$ are normally distributed, the difference between $\bar{V}$ and $\bar{W}$ would appear to be significant at the 10 percent level but not at the 5 percent level. However, the two policies were run against the same sequence of incidents. In Figure 13.4 we show the histogram of the differences in response time. For the individual differences $\Delta_i = V_i - W_i$ we get $\bar{\Delta} = 0.69$ and $S_\Delta^2 = 3.1$. The large fraction of zeros—usually meaning the same engine was dispatched under both policies—implies that the Δ_i are not normally distributed. However, $\bar{\Delta}$ should be approximately normal and the standard deviation of $\bar{\Delta}$ is approximately $\sqrt{S_\Delta^2/49} = \sqrt{3.1/49} = 0.25$. Since $(7.26 - 6.57)/0.25 = 2.8$, we see that, in fact, the difference is significant at the 1 percent level. Note that to get the standard deviation of ($\bar{V} - $

---

[16] The average time between fires that require three or more engines is 4.8 hours, and the average duration of such events is 3 hours (see Section 14.4). Considering the geographical dispersion of these alarms and that most engines at work at such fires stay much less than three hours, there is good reason to suppose that our samples of these response times are independent. The "runs" test was used to confirm independence.

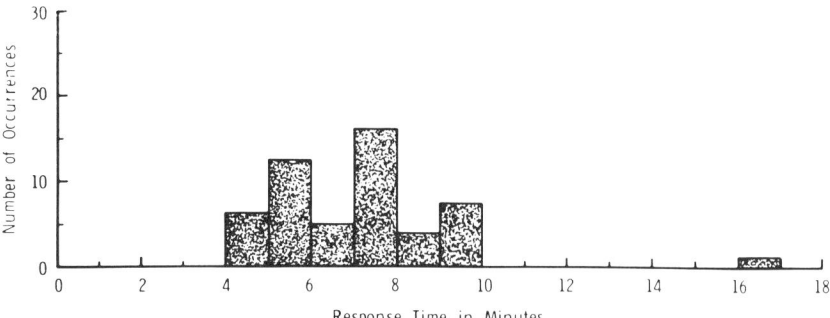

FIGURE 13.3. Proposed policy: Histogram of third-arriving engine response times (the average is 6.57 minutes).

$\bar{W}$) to be 0.25 in the independent case would require about 190 incidents that need a third engine ($\sqrt{(7.3 + 4.3)}/190$ =0.25). This is almost four times the 49 needed when both policies faced the same incidents.

13.6.4 Virtual Estimation

There were only 49 response times in the preceding example. The simulation run that produced them consisted of several thousand incidents,

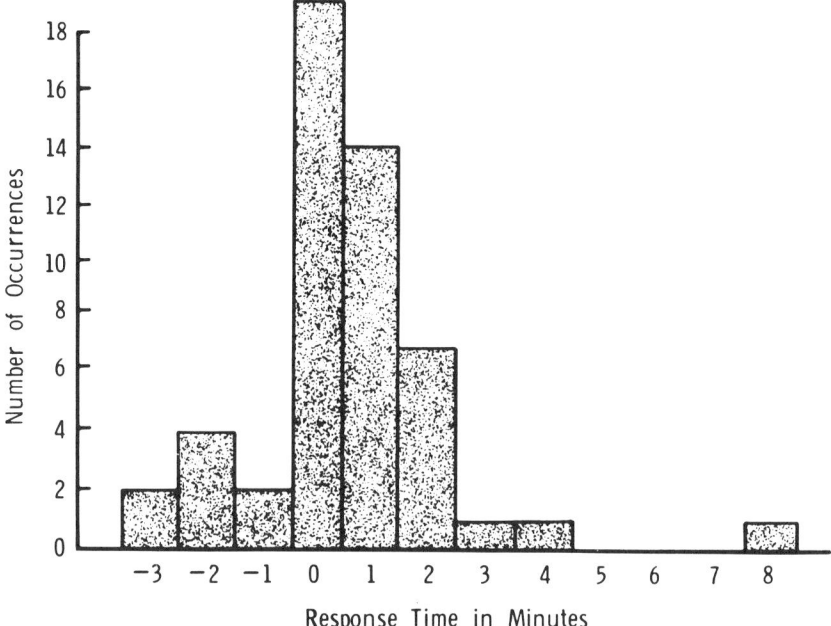

FIGURE 13.4. Histogram of differences in third-arriving engine response times (base case − proposed policy).

13.6 Statistical Analysis

but very few of them needed a third engine. So despite a long (and costly) simulation, it is possible to get relatively little information about the kinds of incidents of greatest concern.

For those unusual situations where a precise estimate of third-arriving engine response time (or some other measure determined by a relatively small number of incidents) is needed, there is an alternative to simply increasing the run length. We call this approach "virtual estimation." We describe it briefly here, and refer the reader to Carter and Ignall (1975) and Section 11.2 of Fishman (1973) for details.

Virtual estimates depend on the state of the system at any given time, but not on what happens at the actual incidents. Suppose, for example, that we interrupt the simulation at some point in time and ask, what is the expected third-arriving engine response time at incidents reported within the next five minutes? The answer clearly depends on:

1. The probabilities of incidents of various types at each of the boxes in our area.
2. Which companies are available.
3. How many and which companies the dispatching policy would send to each incident that occurred.

Note that we do not cause any of these incidents to occur; we only ask what would happen if each of them did. Hence, the term "virtual."

Carter and Ignall (1975) have applied this technique to the estimation of expected second-arriving ladder response times in the Bronx. They recorded which ladders were available when the simulation was interrupted. The simulation had 24 firehouses with ladder companies assigned. They were numbered 1, 2, . . . , 24, and a coverage vector **a** was defined with a_i being number of available ladders in house i. From the point of view of any particular box, the whole coverage vector is not of concern. The state of the eight closest ladder companies is sufficient to determine the second-arriving ladder response time in almost all cases. Since several boxes shared the same group of eight ladder companies, there were only 91 ladder groups of interest in the Bronx.

For each group there are $2^8 = 256$ possible states. Let $H_m(j) \equiv$ the number of times that group m is in state j in the N coverage vectors sampled. Then, for each box k that belongs to ladder group m (denoted by $k \in G_m$), they calculated r_{kj}, defined as the second-arriving ladder response time to box k if the group were in state j, for the given dispatch policy. Let $\pi(k)$ be the probability that a serious incident occurs at box k given that one occurs somewhere. Then a virtual estimate of the expected second-arriving ladder is given by:

$$\bar{R} = \sum_m \sum_{k \in G_m} \sum_j \frac{H_m(j)}{N} r_{kj} \pi(k).$$

How Much is Variance Reduced? A 17-day period with 5436 total alarms and 185 serious alarms was simulated. Both serious fires and other alarms occurred, according to independent stationary Poisson processes. The average second-arriving ladder response time to the serious alarms was 4.76 minutes with a standard deviation of 1.86 minutes. Since the second-arriving ladder response times were uncorrelated, the appropriate estimate of the standard deviation of the mean response time is $1.86/\sqrt{185} = 0.136$. The coverage matrix was sampled every 15 minutes during the simulation. These samples were then grouped into 16 sets of 100 matrices each, and $\bar{R}$ was calculated for each set. Since the time span of any set is more than one day, the virtual response times of each set are effectively independent. The mean second-arriving response time was 4.50 minutes and the standard deviation, 0.12 minutes. Thus, the standard deviation of the mean was 0.030. In order to determine the mean from the simulation to the same degree of precision would require a sample of T serious fires, where $1.86/\sqrt{T} = 0.030$ or $T = 3844$, which is over 20 times the 185 serious fires which were processed.

The simulation required 373 seconds of CPU time in a 220K byte region on an IBM 360/65. Producing the virtual response times required an additional 367 seconds in a 160K region. Since the computer charges depended on region size as well as CPU time consumed, the extra cost of the virtual response time calculation was 75 percent of the cost of the simulation run. Thus, the savings in using the virtual response calculation rather than direct simulation were $(3844/185)/(1 + 0.75)$, or a factor of 12, in computing cost.

13.6.5 Miscellany

Treatment of response times as vectors requires looking at covariances between elements of the vector for each incident (e.g., between first-arriving and second-arriving response times). Such an analysis can be done, but it is often unnecessary. Instead, we have focused on ways to reduce each response time vector to a single number; for example, using response adequacy or utility theory.

The nonindependence problem affects almost everything one might want to measure—response adequacy, company workloads, relocations, and coverage (as measured by the vector **a** in Section 13.6.4). Dividing the run into segments that are two or more hours long, treating average values of adequacy (or whatever measure is chosen) over these segments as the basic observations, and then assuming independence, is the simplest way to proceed (Section 13.6.3). (For response adequacy, segments should be defined in terms of incident counts. For workloads, segments should be defined in terms of elapsed time.)

13.7 The Use of Simulation to Validate an Analytic Model 545

TABLE 13.16. Example: dividing an alarm sequence for statistical analysis. Alarm rate is 0.2 per hour from 0000 to 0800, 0.4 per hour from 0800 to 1600, 0.5 per hour from 1600 to 2400.

Day	Time			First-arriving Engine Response Time (minutes)			
	0000–0800	0800–1600	1600–2400				
1	0215			2.81			
	0633			3.41			
		0919			2.65		
		1147			3.03		
		1313			3.29		
			1725				2.96
			2008				3.13
			2016				2.12
			2106				3.85
			2249				3.13
2	0413			2.17			
		0851			3.09		
		1010			2.65		
		1238			3.29		
		1411			3.60		
			1848				3.06
			1922				2.56
			2150				2.77

For the 0000–0800 period there are three incidents in two days, and $y_1 = 2.81$, $y_2 = 3.41$, $y_3 = 2.17$. For the 0800-1600 period there are seven incidents: $w_1 = 2.65$, $w_2 = 3.03$, $w_3 = 3.29$, $w_4 = 3.09$, $w_5 = 2.65$, $w_6 = 3.29$, $w_7 = 3.60$. The remaining eight incidents are in 1600–2400. Call them z's. Then the y's are treated as the X's are in Section 13.6.1; so are the w's and the z's.

Using an alarm sequence with a rate that varies throughout the day would invalidate the assumptions of Sections 13.6.1. In particular, X_1, $X_2, \ldots, X_n$ would not all have the same distribution. One solution is to divide the run into time segments within which the alarm rate is roughly constant. Then, roughly speaking, the incidents inside can be treated as if they satisfied the assumptions of Sections 13.6.1. The different time periods or segments can then be analyzed separately (Table 13.16).

13.7 THE USE OF SIMULATION TO VALIDATE AN ANALYTIC MODEL

In New York City in the mid-60s, the traditional policy for alarms turned in by box was to send whichever of the companies listed on the first line of the alarm assignment card were available, "special calling" companies further down on the card (if necessary) to assure a response of at least one engine and one ladder. As discussed in Chapter 11, as a result of this policy (a "variable" dispatching policy) the number of engines or the number of ladders actually sent to a box alarm is a random variable that depends on the number of available fire companies in the area surrounding the box at the moment the box is activated. (For example, as many as three engines or as few as one engine might in fact be dispatched.)

Ignall and Urbach (1975) were concerned with predicting how the actual number of units dispatched depended on the alarm rate and the number of units stationed in the region; that is, how the number dispatched depended on the average unit availability. By analyzing some fire simulation runs that had been made for other purposes, they derived a simple relationship between the number of units sent to incidents in a region for which a "variable" dispatching policy is used, and the average unit availability in a region. Ignall, Kolesar, and Walker (1975) report the use of simulation to derive that relationship, and, more to the point of our discussion, to confirm its validity.

Let "a" be the average unit availability in a given region; i.e., "a" is the average fraction of the time a unit is available. Define $P(n, a)$ as the probability that n ladder units are dispatched to an incident at which the variable policy is used during a time period in which the average availability is a; there are two ladder companies listed on the first line of the alarm assignment card.

A good fit to the simulation data was found by using:

$$P(2, a) = a^2$$
$$P(1, a) = 1 - a^2.$$

This relationship would be true if

1. The average availability were the same for every unit in the region.
2. The event that any particular unit is available were independent of the status of all other units.

Neither of these is true, yet the relationship appears to hold to a good approximation. In fact, the validity of the relationship was discovered in the course of attempting to see how poor a^2 was as an estimate of $P(2, a)$.

The relationship was developed from a set of simulation runs that had originally been made to test the effects, at different alarm rates, of both adding new companies to an area and modifying the dispatching policy. The simulation models the Bronx and, for data collection purposes, it was partitioned into two regions: the South Bronx, a very high-activity region (which we shall call Region 2), and the rest of the Bronx (Region 1). Nine simulation runs were analyzed, in which four different alarm rates and five different allocations of fire companies were used.

For each simulation run, the fraction of time each ladder company was available was calculated. The average of these availabilities over all the ladder companies in the region was then obtained (and called "a"). For

13.7 The Use of Simulation to Validate an Analytic Model

TABLE 13.17. Derivation of New York 2 relationship.

	Region 1			Region 2	
	Observed and Predicted (From Availability) Percent of NY2 Alarms Receiving the Indicated Number of Ladders (Observed/Predicted)			Observed and Predicted (From Availability) Percent of NY2 Alarms Receiving the Indicated Number of Ladders (Observed/Predicted)	
Observed Availability	One Ladder	Two Ladders	Observed Availability	One Ladder	Two Ladders
0.952	13.2/9.3	86.8/90.7	0.898	19.3/19.4	80.7/80.6
0.951	21.8/9.6	78.2/90.4	0.882	24.7/22.7	75.3/77.9
0.877	24.3/23.1	75.7/76.9	0.769	35.1/40.9	64.9/59.1
0.875	25.0/23.3	75.0/76.7	0.752	41.9/43.4	58.1/56.6
0.871	26.5/24.1	73.5/75.9	0.739	45.8/45.4	54.3/54.6
0.869	27.5/24.4	72.5/75.6	0.718	52.5/48.5	47.5/51.6
0.776	47.3/39.7	52.7/60.3	0.555	72.3/69.2	27.7/30.8
0.666	58.7/55.7	41.3/44.3	0.466	72.7/78.3	27.3/21.7
0.623	66.2/61.2	33.8/38.8	0.379	85.1/85.6	14.9/14.4

all incidents in the region for which the variable policy was used, they found $P(2, a)$, the proportion that received two ladders as their initial dispatch (these data had been part of the normal output from all simulation runs.) The results in Table 13.17 show that $P(2, a)$ was very close to a^2. In particular, in the first simulation run, based on an observed availability in Region 2 of 0.898, it would be predicted by this relationship

TABLE 13.18. Verification of the New York 2 relationship.

	Region 1			Region 2	
	Observed and Predicted (From Availability) Percent of NY2 Alarms Receiving the Indicated Number of Ladders (Observed/Predicted)			Observed and Predicted (From Availability) Percent of NY2 Alarms Receiving the Indicated Number of Ladders (Observed/Predicted)	
Observed Availability	One Ladder	Two Ladders	Observed Availability	One Ladder	Two Ladders
0.945	16.2/10.8	83.8/89.2	0.849	27.8/27.9	72.2/72.1
0.882	29.8/22.2	70.2/77.8	0.705	49.8/50.3	50.2/49.7
0.948	16.2/10.2	83.8/89.8	0.847	28.1/28.3	71.9/71.7
0.888	30.7/21.1	69.3/78.9	0.699	50.7/51.1	49.3/48.9
0.738	57.5/45.6	42.5/54.4	0.494	75.5/75.6	24.5/24.4
0.745	55.0/44.5	45.0/55.5	0.485	75.8/76.4	24.2/23.6
0.689	61.9/52.6	38.1/47.4	0.469	86.1/78.1	13.9/21.9

that two ladders would be sent 80.6 percent of the time; in fact, two were sent to 80.7 percent of the box alarms.

The relationship was then validated by analyzing the results on a different set of simulations that had also been run previously, but had not been examined during the derivation of the relationship. The original objective of these runs had been to study the effects of matching the number of fire engines on duty more closely to the time-varying alarm rate. Results of four simulations were analyzed and compared to the results predicted by the relationship (Table 13.18). On the basis of this comparison, the relationship did provide a useful approximation to the more accurate simulated dispatching behavior. Thus, this relationship can be used instead of the simulation to analyze the effects of various deployment options on the number of units initially dispatched.

Chapter 14
Deployment Case Studies

Synopsis

The five case studies in this chapter illustrate applications of the models and methods discussed in previous chapters. The first three studies cover different approaches to choosing locations for firehouses. In the Yonkers study, a team consisting of researchers and city personnel were able to achieve significant results without major expenditure of time or money. The case illustrates the data analysis methods described in Chapters 6 and 8, and documents the early development of the siting model described in Chapter 10. The project team developed a new response policy and recommended new locations for two fire companies. Equally important, the study documented the methods and tools used in analyzing alternative deployment options. Thus, when Yonkers was faced with a severe fiscal crisis more than a year after the completion of the study, city personnel were able to employ the siting model in helping them determine which companies to disband.

The Denver case illustrates a somewhat different approach to firehouse siting. This study concentrated on analyzing the city's fire hazards and grouping them into fire demand zones. The computer model was then used to estimate travel times to demand zones for different fire station configurations. The process of choosing a final "solution" involved close continuous interaction between the Chief, his staff, and the analysts. The result was the recommended reduction of five companies and a redistribution to maintain fire protection service levels.

The Tacoma case describes how, with only a few weeks' work, the Parametric Allocation Model (described in Chapter 9) was used to analyze the deployment of the city's fire companies. This "ministudy" illustrates how meaningful insights can be developed quickly, using approximate methods and rough data. Here again, the prescriptions of the model were evaluated in the light of the experience and perceptions of the Chief and his staff.

The fourth case in this chapter—workload problems in the New York City Fire Department—involved a team of analysts using new methods to test proposed solutions, working under the pressures of labor negotiations. At the time of the study, the simulation model (described in Chapter 13) was incomplete, providing a very rough representation of the geography of the Bronx. The analysts felt, however, that the model captured the essential elements of the system, and they were confident that its results were meaningful. These findings (later confirmed by the completed simulation model) were instrumental in shaping the final agreement.

The last case is about fire engine dispatching delays. It shows how one researcher discovered a serious bottleneck in a dispatching operation, and illustrates how a mathematical model is developed in a systems analysis study. This case illustrates both the step-by-step procedure and recursive nature of a systems analysis study.

One purpose of presenting these case studies is to indicate the practical problems that arise in conducting deployment analyses. The actual use of a model is seldom as neat and accurate as their theoretical descriptions might suggest. As the work progresses, new insights are developed and models are redefined. In some case, an improvement is discovered after the work is finished, when the analyst turns to a new study or contemplates the results of a completed one. In some instances, the analysts in the case examples used models in ways that have not been recommended in the preceding chapters. These variations are instructive in showing how methodology must be adapted, in order to be effective in the real world.

A second reason for presenting these case studies is to describe how the work was organized, the level of effort involved, the working environment, and the impacts of the studies on the fire departments. This should further illustrate the implementation issues discussed in Chapter 5 and help the reader to evaluate the work and methods described in preceding chapters.

14.1 THE DEPLOYMENT OF FIREFIGHTING RESOURCES IN YONKERS, NEW YORK[1]

Needing to choose sites for two new firehouses, Yonkers officials recognized that the time was right for a broader study of its fire defenses. A team of analysts from The New York City–Rand Institute worked with a local project team that included an assistant chief, a captain, a lieutenant, and a civilian analyst. The project team received its policy direc-

---

[1] This section is based upon the report by Hausner, Walker, and Swersey (1974).

tion from the Chief of the Yonkers Fire Department and the Director of the Bureau of the Budget. The entire study cost about $40,000 to perform, including computer time and the time of the Institute personnel, but not including the time spent by the Yonkers personnel.

The primary deployment model employed in the study was the Firehouse Site Evaluation Model (Chapter 10), which was used to evaluate a range of alternative arrangements of fire companies. The team recommended new locations for the two firehouses and devised an improved dispatching policy. More than a year later, in response to a severe fiscal crisis, the city used the siting model (which had been installed on its own computer system) to help determine how to eliminate three fire companies while minimizing the impact on the city's fire protection.

14.1.1 Background

As part of its 1973-1974 Capital Improvement Program, the City of Yonkers, recognizing that the time was right for a study of its general fire defenses, asked The New York City-Rand Institute to examine the allocation of its firefighting resources and to recommend improvements. A highway to be constructed was to run through the location of one of the city's firehouses, while another firehouse had been declared unsafe and was condemned by the city. A study was then undertaken with the joint sponsorship of Yonkers and the U.S. Department of Housing and Urban Development (HUD), as part of a contract with The New York City-Rand Institute for analyzing deployment problems in a number of cities.

In early 1973, a team of Institute analysts began the study with the cooperation and assistance of an assistant chief and a captain in the Yonkers Fire Department. The project was completed over a period of about eight months. The total effort was moderate: during the eight months, one Institute researcher spent most of his time on the project; another worked two months, while three others spent periods of several weeks to a month.

Although the analysts had never before looked at the question of specific fire station locations, they were able to build upon the New York City experience. For example, extensive work had already been done analyzing fire demand (described in Chapter 8), and the methods for relating travel time to travel distance (Chapter 6) had already been used in New York. Also, the initial dispatch analyses (Chapter 11) were to prove useful. Some new efforts were needed; in particular, the siting model (Chapter 10) was still under development.

The project team recommended new locations for the two firehouses that were being replaced, and devised an improved dispatching policy.

In addition, the siting model allowed the analysts to evaluate the consequences of a range of alternative firehouse configurations. The most potentially attractive of these were presented to city officials for their consideration. These options (and the siting model itself, which was installed on the city's computer) provided the city with the ability to evaluate the deployment of fire companies in the light of changing circumstances. For example, more than a year later, city personnel used the siting model to help evaluate a range of possible fire company deployment changes in reaction to a serious fiscal crisis.

14.1.2. Fire Protection in Yonkers

Yonkers, New York is a city of about 200,000 people, covering about 18 square miles just north of New York City. Figure 14.1 is a map of the city that shows the locations of its engine and ladder companies. At the time of the study there were 21 fire companies (13 engine companies, 7 ladder companies, and 1 rescue company) located in 13 fire stations. Each company was manned by three men and one officer. There were 405 uniformed personnel and the fire department's operating budget was about $7.5 million per year. (Its operating budget for fiscal year 1978 was about $8.4 million.)

FIGURE 14.1. Demand regions and fire company locations, Yonkers, New York, 1973.

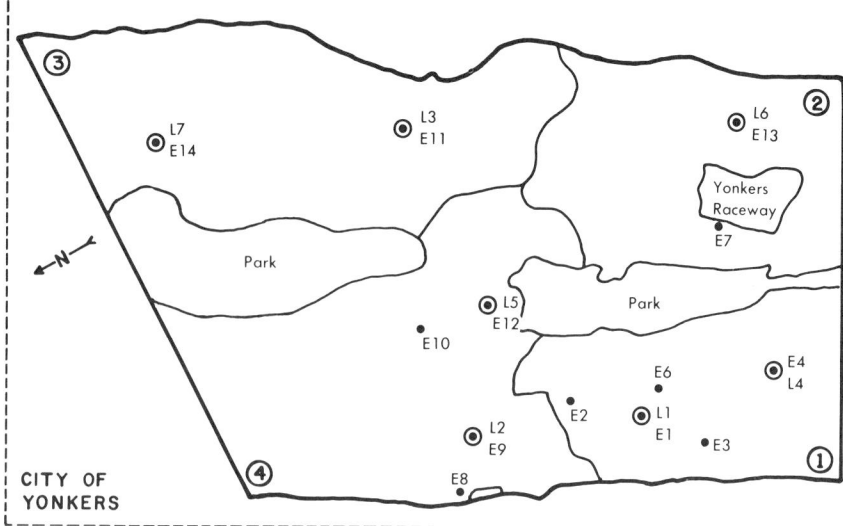

14.1.3 Analyzing the Data

The first step in the analysis was to examine the demand for fire protection services. The city was divided into demand regions having similar demographic characteristics, and the alarm data were analyzed using methods described in Chapter 8. An experiment was run to determine the relationship between travel time and travel distance. The alarm data and travel-time results were then used as input to the siting model (described in Chapter 10), and the consequences of alternative firehouse locations were examined.

Demand Region Characteristics. Project staff and fire department officers partitioned Yonkers into four demand regions (Figure 14.1) that seemed fairly homogeneous with respect to the fire demands within each region. To simplify computations, the boundaries of the demand regions were constructed to coincide with first-due engine response boundaries.

Figures 14.2 and 14.3 show the geographic distribution of the total alarms and structural fires in 1971. The analysts divided the city into squares, each about 0.06 square miles in area and containing from three

FIGURE 14.2. Distribution of fire alarms in Yonkers, 1971.

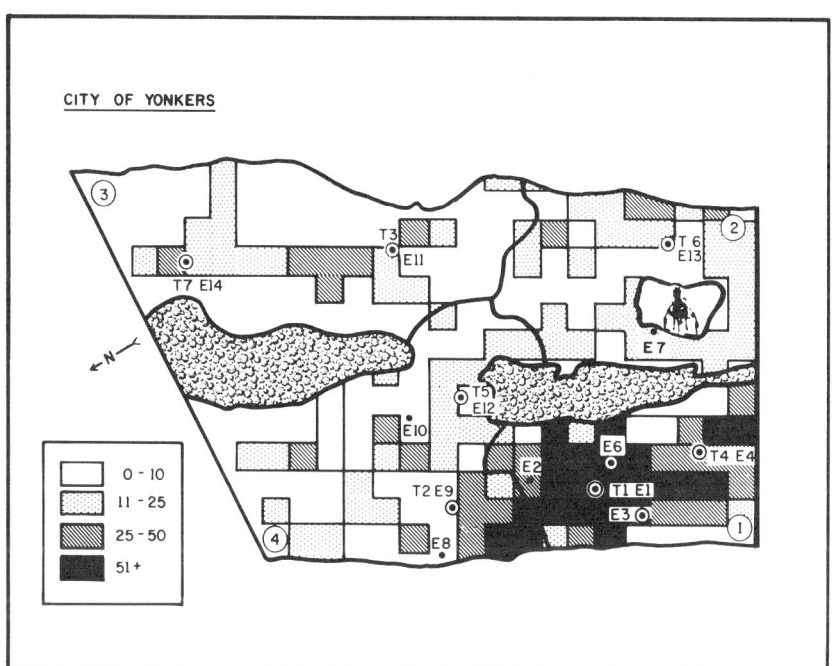

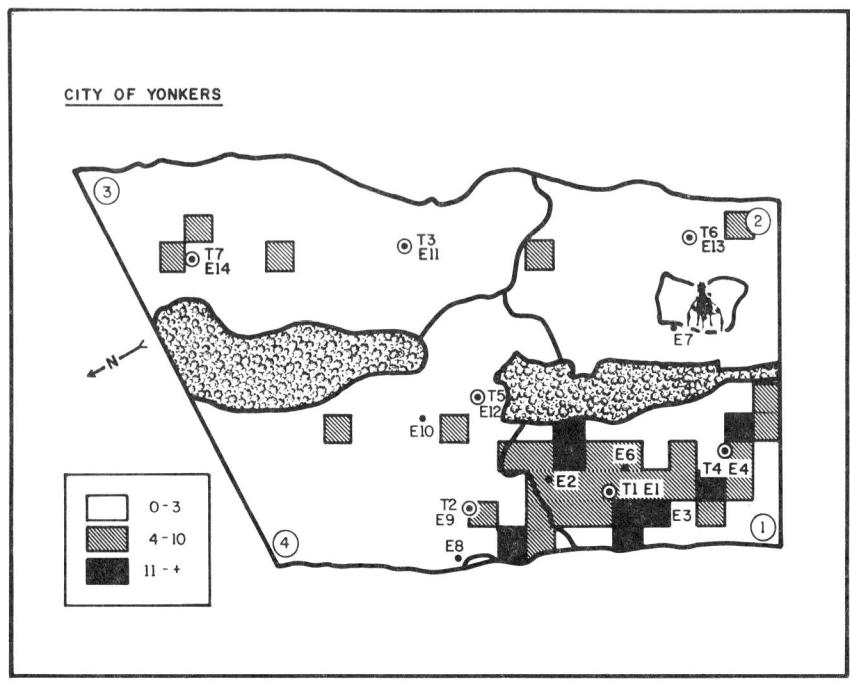

FIGURE 14.3. Distribution of structural fires in Yonkers, 1971.

to five alarm boxes, and determined the number of alarms (total and structural) that occurred in each square. More than one-half of the total alarms and structural fires occurred in Region 1 (the southwest section of Yonkers), and a similar pattern (not shown) held for false alarms.

Table 14.1 summarizes some geographic, demographic, and alarm data for the four demand regions. Region 1 includes the oldest and most densely populated part of Yonkers. Most of the structures are old and of frame construction. This region also contains the principal business district of the city, so in the daytime the population is swelled by the shoppers and others whose business is downtown. Regions 2, 3, and 4 have lower population densities and are more residential than Region 1, although all contain some commercial establishments. The existing deployment of fire companies already reflected the disparity in fire protection demand among the regions. More units were allocated to Region 1 than any of the others—eight of the department's 21 units (including the rescue company, which was located in the same house as Engine 1 and Ladder 1)—even though Region 1 contained only 16 percent of the total area served by the department.

The overall population of Yonkers increased by 7 percent in the ten

14.1 Deployment of Firefighting Resources in Yonkers, New York

TABLE 14.1. Demographic and alarm data for Yonkers demand regions.

Characteristic	Region				
	1	2	3	4	Citywide
Area (square miles)	2.90	3.80	5.36	5.96	18.02
Total alarms (1971)	2,875	728	746	1,225	5,574
Structural fires (1971)	243	49	62	89	443
Number of engines	5	2	2	4	13
Number of ladders	2	1	2	2	7
Number of engines per square mile	1.72	0.53	0.37	0.67	0.72
Number of ladders per square mile	0.69	0.26	0.37	0.34	0.39
Population: 1960	69,240	39,996	36,848	44,522	190,604
1970	64,457	42,628	43,801	53,051	203,937
Percent change	−6%	+6%	+18%	+19%	+7%
1970 Population density (population/square mile)	23,876	11,217	8,171	8,901	11,317
Housing units	23,422	15,263	14,274	17,499	70,458
Housing units per square mile	8,076	4,017	2,663	2,935	3,910

years between 1960 and 1970. There has been a clear pattern of northward migration. More and more people are leaving south Yonkers for the semisuburban environment of north Yonkers. In the north, the population in Regions 3 and 4 increased 18 percent and 19 percent, respectively, between 1960 and 1970; in the same decade in south Yonkers, the population decreased by 6 percent in Region 1 and rose by 6 percent in Region 2.

The city has a large white middle-class population in the areas serving as bedroom communities to New York (its median family income is over $12,000, and in 1969 only 6 percent of its families had incomes that fell below the poverty level). However, it also has increasing populations of the elderly and the poor and minority groups, especially in Region 1. (Although in 1970 blacks accounted for only 6 percent of the population, their numbers grew by over 70 percent between 1960 and 1970.)

Other Alarm Data. The analysts examined changes in alarm rates between 1961 and 1972 (Figure 14.4). Total alarms increased from 2651 in 1961 to 5785 in 1972, due primarily to a sharp jump in false alarms (from 280 in 1961 to 1699 in 1972). Structural fires remained fairly stable during this period. Nonstructural fires showed considerable variation from year to year. The sharp drop in such alarms in 1967, which led to a decrease in total alarms, was the result of a decrease in the number of brush fires. During the period 1961–1972, nonfire emergency alarms con-

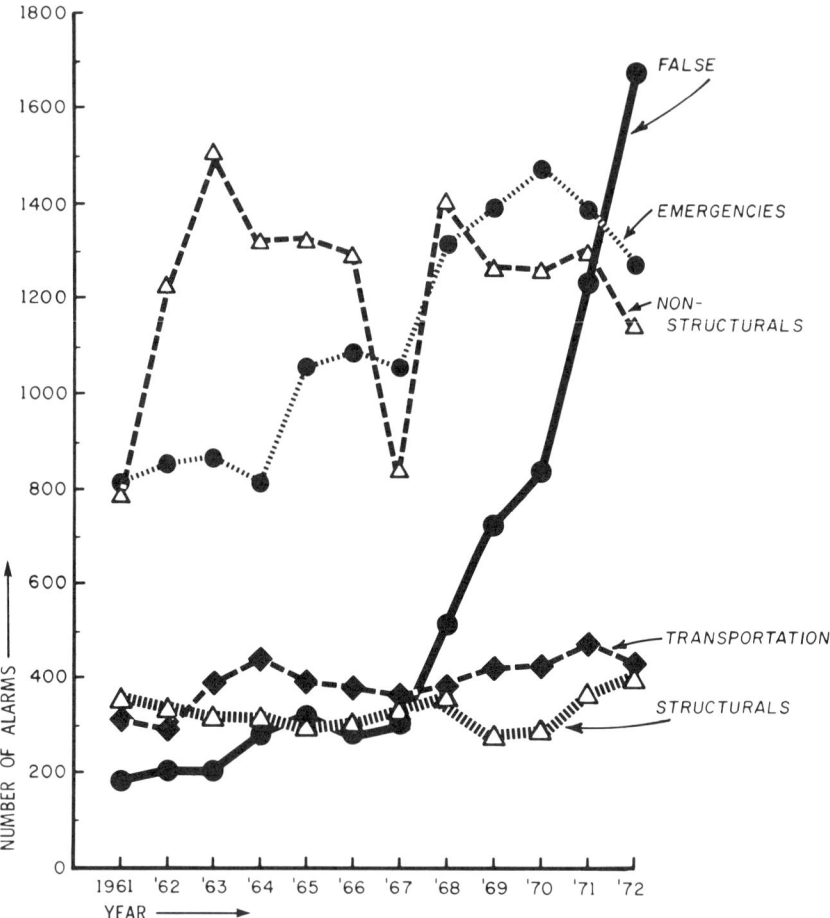

FIGURE 14.4. Alarm rates by type, Yonkers, 1961–1972.

sistently represented between 25 and 30 percent of total alarms. Despite the substantial increase in alarms over the past decade, the alarm rate in Yonkers in 1972 was still fairly low. A total of 5785 alarms per year is an average of only 0.66 alarms per hour. By 1976 the alarm rate had increased to 7321 alarms, 2347 (32 percent) of which were false.

The analysts examined the time-of-day pattern of alarms in 1971 (Figure 14.5). Although there was considerable variation over a day, the peak rate of 1.1 alarms per hour between 8 P.M. and 10 P.M. was still quite low. At any time the average number of engines or ladders busy was less

14.1 Deployment of Firefighting Resources in Yonkers, New York

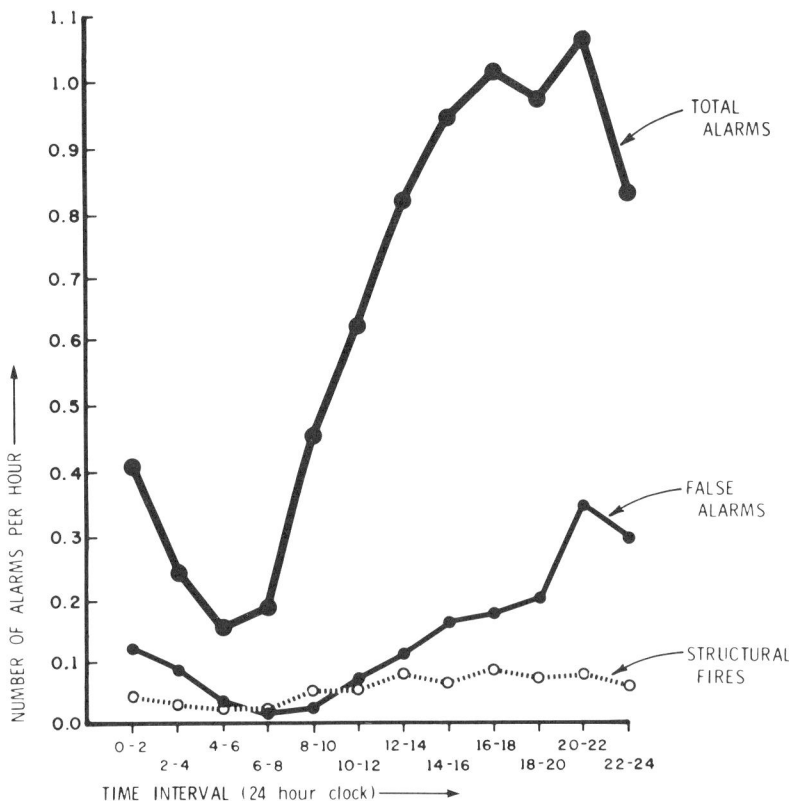

FIGURE 14.5. Average alarm rate in each two-hour time interval, Yonkers, 1971.

than one.[2] Therefore, the assumption used in the siting model that all units are available was, in this case, quite appropriate. The time-of-day data were used later to formulate a new initial response policy for the Yonkers Fire Department.

The analysts projected annual alarm rates to 1984 based upon the rate of growth in the period 1966 to 1972 (Figure 14.6). Although the total number of alarms is expected to almost double between 1972 and 1984, this will not unduely strain the city's existing resources since, for ex-

---

[2] Recall from Chapter 7 that the average number of units busy is equal to the alarm rate times the average unit hours (engine or ladder) worked at an alarm. Although the analysts did not gather work time data, it is safe to say that the relevant average work times for both engines and ladders were considerably less than one hour.

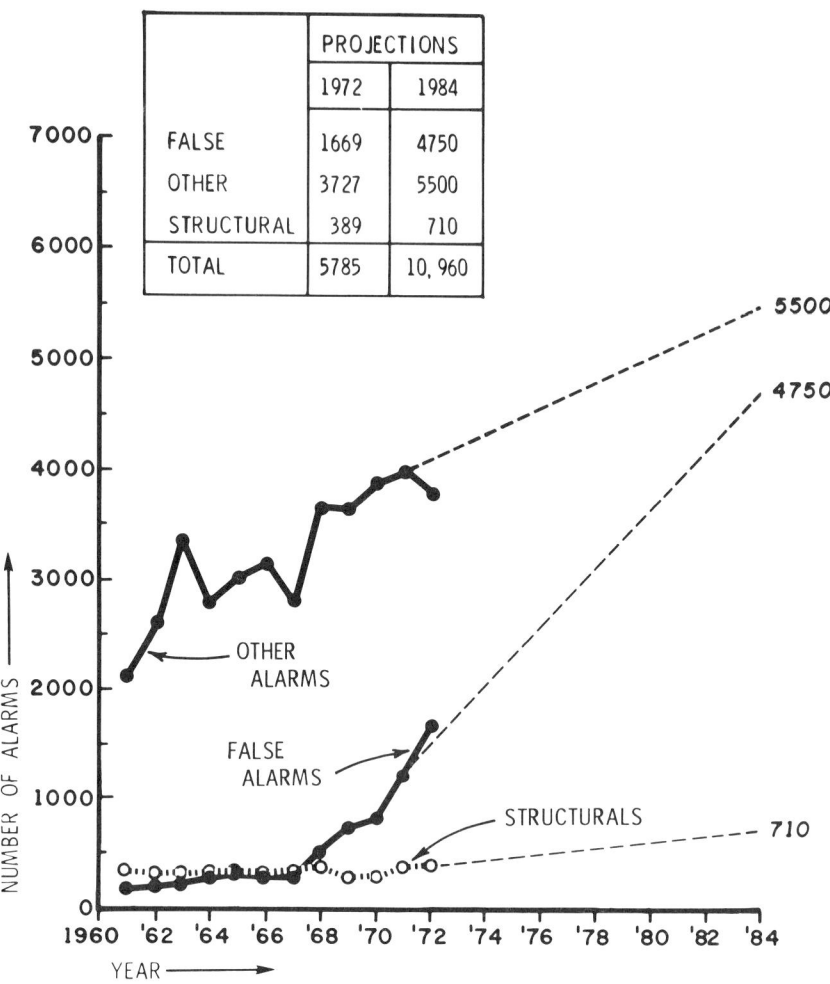

FIGURE 14.6. Alarm rate projections for Yonkers, 1984.

ample, the total number of structural alarms is expected to increase from 389 in 1972 to 710 (fewer than two per day) in 1984.

Turnout and Travel Time Data. An experiment to estimate average turnout time in Yonkers was designed and conducted by fire department personnel. It revealed that turnout time was relatively constant—about 60 seconds—at all firehouses but one. At the remaining station, which houses Engine 7, turnout took about 20 seconds longer because of slow-moving automatic doors.

In another experiment, nine fire companies measured travel times with

14.1 Deployment of Firefighting Resources in Yonkers, New York

stopwatches in order to find the relationship between travel time and travel distance. The response areas of the companies selected for participation in this experiment (Ladders 2, 4, 5, 6, and 7; Engines 8, 9, and 10; and the Rescue Company) represented a cross-section of all geographic and topographic areas of Yonkers. The best estimates of travel time were obtained from the linear function:

$$\text{travel time} = 0.66 + 1.77 \times \text{distance}.$$

This fit is shown in Figure 14.7 and is consistent with the results from other cities discussed in Chapter 6.

The response data were also analyzed to determine what effect the time of day had on response speed and hence, on travel time. It was found that a time-of-day effect did exist, but that it was less significant than expected. There were no apparent practical differences in travel speed between daylight hours and nighttime hours, or even between rush

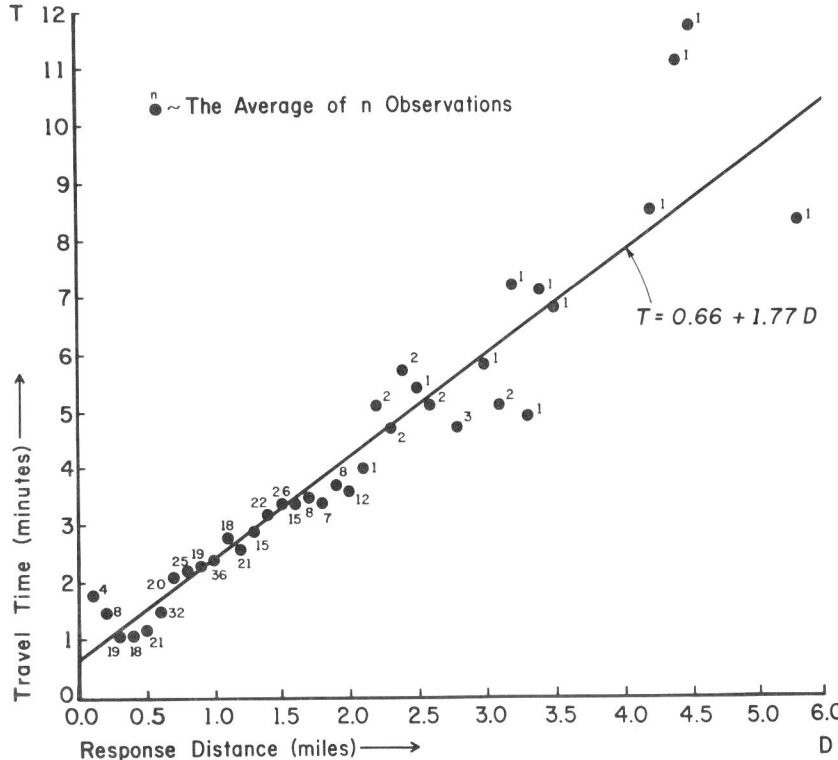

FIGURE 14.7. Relationship between travel time and response distance, Yonkers, 1973.

hours and nonrush hours. The average speeds in different two-hour periods are given in Chapter 6, Table 6.4.

14.1.4 Evaluating the Deployment of Fire Companies

Existing Protection Levels. The first step in the analysis was to determine the existing level of service in each of the city's four demand regions. At a cost of under $100, a commercial service bureau produced a set of punched cards giving the (x,y) coordinates of the firehouse locations and the approximately 900 alarm boxes. Using the siting model (described in Chapter 10) and the results of the travel-time experiment, average and maximum first-due response times to alarm boxes (unweighted by alarms or structural fires) were estimated for each demand region and for the city as a whole.[3] The results are shown in Table 14.2. (It would have been useful to estimate second-due response times as well. This capability was not yet in the siting model, but was subsequently added.)

Average first-due engine response times were about the same in all regions, except Region 1 where it was significantly lower. This reflects the fire department's perception of the relatively greater hazards in Region 1, which contains the central business district, compared to the more residential sections of the city. Average first-due ladder response time was lowest in Region 1, about the same in Regions 3 and 4, and highest in Region 2 (there is only one ladder company there).

---

[3] Response time in this study was defined to mean travel time plus a one-minute turnout time.

TABLE 14.2. Estimated existing first-due engine and ladder response times (in minutes) in demand regions of Yonkers, 1973.

Demand Region	First-Due Engine		First-Due Ladder	
	Average Response Time	Maximum Response Time	Average Response Time	Maximum Response Time
1	2.7	4.2	3.0	4.9
2	3.4	4.9	3.8	4.9
3	3.4	4.9	3.4	4.9
4	3.2	5.3	3.5	6.1
Citywide	3.0	5.3	3.4	6.1

14.1 Deployment of Firefighting Resources in Yonkers, New York

The maximum first-due engine and ladder response times were highest in Region 4. A glance at the map in Figure 14.1 shows why. The four engine companies and two ladder companies in Region 4 were all located in the southern half of the region. Response times to incidents in the northern section must, therefore, be fairly long. It was clear that changing the firehouse configuration in this region could do much to improve coverage.

A New Location for Engine 10. In a city as small as Yonkers, good alternative arrangements of fire companies can usually be developed for the siting model without the aid of the Parametric Allocation Model (Chapter 9). Given existing response-time levels, the analyst can quickly determine whether improvements will result from adding units or rearranging existing ones. The effect of disbanding one or more units also can easily be determined. The first step in the Yonkers analysis was to seek a new location for Engine 10. Moving it to the vicinity of point A in Figure 14.8 would improve both the average and maximum response times in Region 4. The particular site chosen was city-owned property that was large enough to accommodate the department's proposed new training center.

The effect of the move would be to increase response time in Engine 10's old first-due region and to decrease response time in its new first-due region. The entire region affected by the move consisted of 104 alarm

FIGURE 14.8. Existing and proposed firehouse locations, Yonkers, 1973.

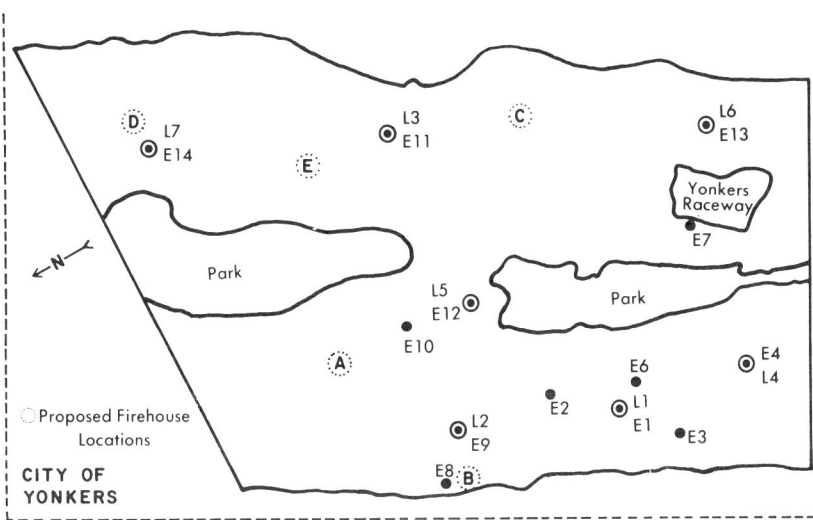

boxes that reported a total of 435 alarms in 1971. By implementing this option at the cost of constructing a new firehouse, the average response time in the affected region would drop from 3.4 minutes to 3.2 minutes. The maximum response time would be reduced by almost a full minute, from 5.3 minutes to 4.4 minutes. Note that the 0.2 minute improvement in average response time is, by itself, not a sufficient measure of the resulting change in fire protection. As discussed in Chapter 10, the change in response time multiplied by the number of alarm boxes in the affected region (in this case, $0.2 \times 104 = 20.8$) is a measure of the improvement in coverage, while the change in response time multiplied by the number of alarms in the affected region (in this case, $0.2 \times 435 = 87.0$) is a measure of the change in response time to alarms. A better measure, discussed in Chapter 10 but not used in the Yonkers study, is the change in response time to structural fires in the affected region (the change in average response time multiplied by the number of structural alarms in the affected region).

A New Location for Engine 8. Next, the analysts sought a new location for Engine 8. Engine Company 8 had first-due responsibility in a long, narrow, north-south corridor on the west side of Yonkers. The boundaries of the area are determined by certain physical and geographic characteristics peculiar to this section. Except for the fact that its quarters were scheduled for demolition, Engine 8 was almost perfectly placed. Therefore, rebuilding on the same site was considered, along with several alternative sites. The one selected (location B on the map in Figure 14.8) possessed ample additional space for construction of a repair shop. This site also provided easy and quick access to Warburton Avenue, a major north-south thoroughfare. Moreover, Engine 8 could continue to respond from its current quarters while its new house was being built, which would not be possible if the new firehouse were to be built on the old site.

Other Siting Options. The preceding two changes were the only recommendations submitted to Yonkers officials. A number of other options were presented to the city as the most attractive of the many possibilities considered. Table 14.3 summarizes the resulting response-time changes for the two recommendations and the other options. In the remainder of this section, we discuss the major characteristics of these alternatives.

It seemed clear to the analysts (and the allocation model described in Chapter 9 confirmed this) that Region 1 was the only area from which units might logically be transferred. Removing a company from another region would cause too great an increase in response time. If a company were to be disbanded or removed from Region 1, Engine 1 seemed the

TABLE 14.3. Summary of response-time changes in the affected regions for several siting options in Yonkers.

Option	Effect on Response Time	No. of Alarms	No. of Boxes	Average Response Time		Maximum Response Time	
				Old	New	Old	New
1. Move Engine 10 to location A[a]	Improved	435	104	3.4	3.2	5.3	4.4
2. Move Engine 8 to location B	No change	—	—	—	—	—	—
3. Disband Engine 1	Worsened	503	46	2.4	2.9	2.8	3.4
4a. Add an engine company at location C	Improved	226	56	4.2	2.8	4.9	3.6
4b. Move Engine 1 to location C	Improved (same as 4a)	226	56	4.2	2.8	4.9	3.6
	Worsened (same as 3)	503	46	2.4	2.9	2.8	3.4
5a. Add a ladder company at location A.	Improved	359	90	4.3	3.1	6.1	4.3
5b. Move Ladder 5 to location A	Improved	917	146	3.7	3.4	6.1	5.2
5c. Convert Engine 1 to a ladder company and locate at location A	Improved (same as 5a)	359	90	4.3	3.1	6.1	4.3
	Worsened (same as 3)	503	46	2.4	2.9	2.8	3.4
6. Assuming Option 4, move Engine 14 to location D and Engine 11 to location E	Improved	749	226	3.3	3.1	4.9	4.1
Move Ladder 7 to location D	Improved	424	130	3.4	3.3	4.9	4.7

[a] Letters refer to locations on the map in Figure 14.8.

logical choice. Removing any other unit would cause a greater degradation in response time.

From Table 14.3 we see that the region affected by removing Engine 1 contained 46 alarm boxes, which transmitted a total of 503 alarms in 1971. This region was Engine 1's old first-due area, which would have to be absorbed by the surrounding companies (Engine 2, Engine 3, and Engine 6). Assuming Engine 1 were disbanded, the average response time in the affected region would increase from 2.4 minutes to 2.9 minutes. The maximum response time would increase from 2.8 minutes to 3.4 minutes.

The removal of Engine 1 would result in savings of about $450,000 per year, but at the expense of an increase in response time in the affected region. The question (which has no clear answer) is whether the savings would be worth the increase in response time. The trade off involved can be sharpened somewhat in the following manner. Of the 509 alarms in the affected region, 43 were structural fires. A reasonable estimate of the number of serious structural fires would be about ten. Is the average 30 seconds in response time to these ten (or so) fires worth $450,000? The decision depends on the judgment of the decisionmaker.

The analysts investigated a number of other options. Once the new firehouse for Engine 10 at location A was built, significant improvements in ladder response times would result from moving Ladder 5 to the new house (Option 5b). Alternatively, a new ladder company could be created, with the need for additional manpower and equipment, and be located at A (Option 5c). Or, Engine 1 could be converted to a ladder company (the men would have to be retrained) and moved to location A (Option 5c).

Locating an engine company at C on the map in Figure 14.8 would significantly improve response times in that area. A new company could be created (Option 4a), or Engine 1 could be moved to C (Option 4b). Consider the tradeoffs involved in Option 4b (Table 14.3). Moving Engine 1 would result in a net improvement in response time to alarms (an improvement of 1.4 minutes per alarm $\times$ 226 alarms = 316.4 minutes in its new first-due region, and a degradation of $0.5 \times 503 = 251.5$ minutes in its old first-due region), as well as a net improvement in coverage (an improvement of 1.4 minutes per box $\times$ 56 boxes = 78.4 minutes in its new first-due region, and a degradation of $0.5 \times 46 = 23.0$ minutes in its old first-due region). But these gains may be offset by the fact that the hazards are relatively greater in Region 1. Should Engine 1 be moved to location C? Again the choice must be based on the subjective judgment of the decisionmaker. The analysis can only present the tradeoffs.

Putting Engine 1 at C or creating a new company there suggested another option to the project team, moving Engine 11 to E and Engine 14 to D (Option 6).

14.1.5 A Proposed Dispatching Policy

The dispatching changes instituted in Yonkers are a good illustration of the methods discussed in Chapter 11. The dispatching policy in use at the time of the study was designed primarily to combat the dramatic increase in false alarms in the city during the preceding few years. Between the hours of noon and midnight, when false alarms were most frequent, box alarms received an initial response of one engine and one ladder. At other times the initial response was three engines and one ladder. Table 14.4 shows the breakdown of box alarms by type of incident. We see that the percentage of box alarms that were false was about 50 percent from midnight to noon, and 60 percent from noon to midnight. However, during the same periods, the percentages of box alarms that signaled structural fires were 13 percent and about 9 percent. Sending one engine or one ladder initially would result in a delay, for the second and third engine and the second ladder, to these structural fires when they were needed. (The delay would be about 3 minutes, the citywide average first-engine response time. This assumes that the first-arriving unit is always an engine, and ignores the differences in response times from region to region.)

The then-current policy sacrificed this response time to save more unnecessary runs to false alarms and other incidents. But the analysts reasoned that these savings were not worth the loss in fire protection that results from the reduced response. Despite the increase in false alarms in the preceding few years, there were still fewer than an average of five false alarms per day. Also, there was no workload problem for the reduced response policy to relieve. The busiest fire company in Yonkers (Engine 2) made 1120 runs in 1972, i.e., an average of three responses per day. Finally, because of the low alarm rate, there was no reason to reduce a response in expectation that the units held back would soon be needed at another alarm.

TABLE 14.4. Distribution of box alarms by incident type, Yonkers, 1971.

Alarm Type	Midnight to Noon		Noon to Midnight	
	Number	Percent	Number	Percent
Structural	59	13.0	118	8.7
False alarm	222	49.0	824	60.3
Emergency	41	9.0	100	7.3
Other	131	29.0	324	23.7
Total	453	100.0	1366	100.0

Therefore, the reduced response merely reduced fire protection and permitted fire companies to spend more time in their firehouses. A new dispatching policy for box alarms was proposed; in Table 14.5, it is shown in comparison to the then-current policy.

An immediate result of the proposed policy would be a substantial increase in the number of runs made by fire companies. All box alarms received between midnight and noon would result in one additional ladder response, while all box alarms received between noon and midnight would require one additional engine and one additional ladder. (This is approximately correct but not strictly true. A small percentage of box-reported incidents require a second engine and a second ladder. These responses would be made under both the old and new policy.)

Table 14.6 compares the number of runs made by each fire company in 1972 with the expected number of runs under the new policy. As expected, the greatest increase in responses would be experienced by ladder companies. Even so, the busiest company under the new policy—Ladder 1, with 1506 responses—would still average only four runs per day. Engine companies would average 743 responses under the new policy, as compared to 637 responses under the current policy. Ladder company responses would increase from an average of 572 to 832.

14.1.6 Implementation

Recommendations were presented to the city manager, the budget director, and fire department officials at a briefing in December 1973. The proposed dispatching policy was implemented in the summer of 1974 and the two new firehouses were included in Yonkers' capital budget for 1974–1979. However, the situation changed dramatically in October 1975, when the city was faced with a severe financial crisis. The city was unable to renew short-term notes that were to come due in October and November, and was therefore on the verge of default. The State of New York instituted emergency financial procedures, in part requiring the city to develop a new financial plan with a reduced budget. An estimated budget deficit of $19 million for the following 18 months had to be eliminated, which amounted to reducing spending by approximately $1 million per month. The financial plan, developed by the city manager in

TABLE 14.5. Initial dispatch to box alarms, Yonkers, 1973.

Time Period	Current Policy	Proposed Policy
Midnight to noon	3 engines	3 engines
	1 ladder	2 ladders
Noon to midnight	1 engine	2 engines
	1 ladder	2 ladders

TABLE 14.6. Comparison of 1972 company workloads to expected workloads under the new response policy in Yonkers.

Demand Region	Engines				Ladders			
	Unit	1972 Runs	Expected Runs Under New Policy	Expected Additional Runs	Unit	1972 Runs	Expected Runs Under New Policy	Expected Additional Runs
Region 1	E1	1059	1243	184	L1	866	1506	640
	E2	1120	1311	191	L4	550	960	410
	E3	819	964	145				
	E4	733	863	130				
	E6	682	797	115				
Region 2	E7	383	447	64	L6	423	617	194
	E13	498	582	84				
Region 3	E11	498	571	73	L3	313	362	49
	E14	385	442	57	L7	203	235	32
Region 4	E8	481	556	75	L5	656	822	166
	E9	609	703	94	L2	992	1240	248
	E10	519	600	81				
	E12	501	575	74				

consultation with the budget director and the heads of each agency, called on the fire department to eliminate its rescue company and two additional companies. A three-man team from the budget bureau and fire department, without outside assistance, used the siting model to evaluate alternative proposals for eliminating fire companies. As a result of their analysis, in January 1976, three companies were eliminated (Engine 1, Ladder 3, and the rescue company) and a freeze was placed on plans to construct the two new firehouses.[4]

14.2 LOCATING FIREHOUSES IN DENVER, COLORADO[5]

A provision of the Denver firefighters' 1972–1973 contract provided for the performance of a management study of the Denver Fire Department. The city's Budget and Management Office asked the Denver Urban Observatory to aid them in developing a multidisciplinary research team to conduct the study. The project was directed by Denver's Deputy Finance Director and the Director of the Denver Urban Observatory. The two principal investigators were faculty members at the University of Colorado. A high-level Policy Review Committee was formed to provide policy direction. In January 1973, HUD agreed to support the study. The project budget was approximately $140,000, of which about $30,000 was an in-kind contribution of the City and County of Denver.

The project team recommended locations for engine and ladder companies that would leave the level of service in Denver almost unchanged, while reducing the number of companies from 44 to 39. An 11-stage timetable was developed that would achieve the recommended changes by January 1979, with firefighter reductions being accomplished by attrition. It was estimated that the reductions would eventually save the city $1.25 million annually.

As of the end of 1977, four of the nine stages that were to have been carried out had been completed, resulting in a reduction of three fire companies and a reduction in the authorized strength of the department by 25 men (a savings of over $500,000 per year).

14.2.1 Background

Soon after Chief Myrle Wise assumed his responsibilities as Denver's Fire Chief in late 1970, he indicated to the city's Director of Management Research the pressing need for management tools to aid him in administering Denver's Fire Department.

---

[4] A more complete description of the history of the implementation of these changes is contained in Walker (1978).
[5] This section is based upon the report by Hendrick et al. (1975).

14.2 Locating Firehouses in Denver, Colorado

In June 1971, the City and County of Denver passed a charter amendment that required the city to bargain collectively with the recognized union representatives of the Denver Fire Department. During the first negotiations, which took place in the summer of 1971, the city negotiators realized that they knew very little about the operations of the department. There were questions about whether the current level of expenditure in fire protections services was excessive, too low, or about right. The bargaining in 1972 (for 1973) failed to reach an agreement and went to arbitration. A management study was recommended in the arbitration decision. As a result, one of the provisions of the 1972-1973 contract provided for the performance of a management study of the Denver Fire Department. The Budget and Management Office asked the Denver Urban Observatory to aid them in developing a multidisciplinary research team to attack the problem.

Such a team was formed in late 1972. It consisted of: operations research specialists, computer specialists, and statisticians from the College of Business and Administration, University of Colorado; management and budget analysts in the Budget and Management Office of the City and County of Denver; and members of the Denver Fire Department. The team was directed and administered by the Deputy Finance Director of the City and County of Denver and the Director of the Denver Urban Observatory. Also, a Policy Review Committee was formed to guide the activities of the research team. It consisted of the Finance Director of the City and County of Denver, the Denver Fire Chief, the Dean of the Graduate School of Public Affairs of the University of Colorado, an Administrative Assistant to Denver's Mayor, and the Director of Denver's Career Service Authority.

The preceding chain of events led to a research proposal to HUD that was funded in January 1973. The project budget was approximately $140,000; of this total, about $30,000 were in-kind contributions of the City and County of Denver. The main objectives of the project were to assess the current level of fire protection and to develop alternative fire station configurations that might provide approximately the same level of fire suppression service at a lower cost. The proposal explicitly called for the involvement of the fire department and other city personnel in the study, and recognized the importance of creating an ongoing capability for analysis.

The research resulted in a long-term plan, calling for a five-company (85-firefighter) reduction. It specified in detail the number of engine and ladder companies necessary for Denver to maintain approximately the level of service prevailing in 1974; where these companies should be located; which stations should be built, consolidated, or closed; and a budgetary timetable for these changes.

The approach to analyzing fire station locations used in this study is considerably different from the one used in the Yonkers study (Section

14.1). The method used in Denver is similar to the Public Technology, Incorporated (PTI) approach described in Chapter 10. The major steps involved grouping properties into fire demand zones, assigning a hazard rating to each demand zone, setting maximum travel times for each hazard rating, and solving an optimization problem to find the minimum number of fire companies required to satisfy the travel-time requirements. This approach does not consider actual fire incidence explicitly (except insofar as high-fire incidence in a demand zone may tend to increase its hazard rating).

The study also used a model similar to the Firehouse Site Evaluation Model (described in Chapter 10) to compare travel times under various alternative configurations of fire companies, and the Fire Operations Simulation Model (Chapter 13) to examine the availability of fire companies and to determine travel times at different alarm rates for both the current and proposed configurations.

The City and County of Denver, with a population of approximately 515,000 people, occupies a rather square and flat 115 square miles in the middle of a metropolitan area with a population of 1,300,000 people. The Denver Fire Department's 1974 operating budget was approximately $14 million. (Its 1978 operating budget was approximately $19 million.) The department is organized into seven districts. On January 1, 1974, there were 27 firehouses, 46 fire companies[6] (27 engines, 17 ladders, and 2 rescue companies), and 929 firefighters. Each company was staffed by four firefighters. The location of the seven districts (numbered 2 to 8) and the 27 firehouses are shown in the map in Figure 14.9.

For the previous few years, alarms had been increasing at a rate of approximately 13.5 percent per year. The total number of alarms in 1972 was almost 18,000, with a false alarm rate of approximately 25 percent. Since 1973, the alarm rate has remained rather stable at approximately 22,000 alarms per year.

14.2.2 Converting Travel Distance to Travel Time

A travel-time experiment was conducted in Denver, similar to experiments described in Section 6.3. However, an important difference is that no data were collected by firefighters. Instead, travel times were estimated by dispatchers, and travel distances were estimated by determining the (x,y) coordinates of each incident and firehouse, using an address-matching program developed by the U.S. Bureau of the Census. Since the deployment models estimate travel times from (x,y) coordinates also, this approach seemed well-suited for purposes of analysis, even if (per-

---

[6] A special-purpose airport company is excluded.

14.2 Locating Firehouses in Denver, Colorado

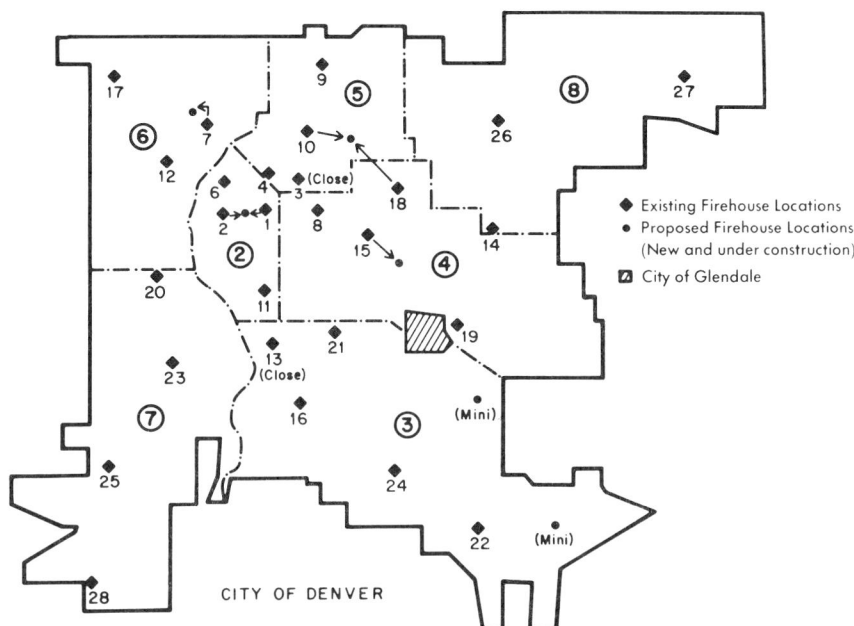

FIGURE 14.9. Firehouse locations, Denver, 1974.

haps) less well-matched to reality than direct measurements of travel distances, as in Section 6.3.

An electric timer installed in Fire Alarm Headquarters was used to measure the time from the end of the dispatch to the arrival of the first vehicle at the scene. It was assumed that this provided a reasonable approximation to the actual travel time. Data on nearly 1600 responses were obtained and analyzed.

The analysis showed that the data were fit well by two linear equations, one for the downtown area (i.e., where response distances are typically short):

$$T = 0.304 + 2.01 D,$$

and one for the remainder of the city:

$$T = 0.438 + 1.70 D.$$

Here D is the travel distance in miles and T is the travel time in minutes. A square-root/linear equation of the form described in Section 6.3 also provided a good fit:

$$T = \begin{cases} 1.95 \sqrt{D} & D \leq 0.40 \text{ miles} \\ 0.62 + 1.53 D & D \geq 0.40 \text{ miles}. \end{cases}$$

The project team also investigated differences in travel times between rush-hour periods and other times of the day. As in other cities, there were no statistically significant differences between these periods in Denver.

14.2.3 Analysis Using Static Models

The basic approach in the first part of the study was to establish a maximum allowable engine and ladder travel time for every point in the city. Then a computer program would determine the smallest number of engine companies needed to achieve the desired travel-time levels, assuming every company is always available.[7] Since many different configurations of firehouse locations could satisfy the requirements, the program chose configurations that included as many existing stations as possible. These configurations were then evaluated using another computer program, which calculates second-due and higher order travel times, as well as first-due. A key step in the analysis was establishing maximum allowable travel times, which will be described in this section.

Identification of Focal Points. The first step in developing the fire demand zones was to identify and classify hazards. The approach was to have each fire company assign a hazard rating to each structure in its inspection district that was considered to be some sort of hazard. This procedure produced a total of 800 hazards. These individual buildings were then grouped into classes requiring similar travel times because of their approximately equal hazard ratings. Initially, three travel-time classes were established: red (most hazardous, such as a run-down hotel or a chemical plant), yellow (such as a public building with sprinklers and automatic fire detection devices), and green (some types of retail establishments).[8] Figure 14.10 shows the location and class of each of the 800 hazards. The classification was performed by the assistant fire chiefs and reviewed by a group of senior assistant chiefs and fire protection personnel.

Next, the 800 hazard points were grouped into 246 focal points. A focal point, as in the PTI approach, was defined as a point that is taken to represent all hazards in the fire demand zone surrounding it. These demand zones were determined by the district chiefs in the following way: Each hazard was marked with a dot of the appropriate color (red, yellow, or green) on a map. The chiefs were given plastic diamonds of

---

[7] The analysis was also conducted for ladder companies, but only the analysis for engines will be described here.

[8] One other class, "super red," was subsequently defined, and is described later in this section.

14.2 Locating Firehouses in Denver, Colorado

FIGURE 14.10. Fire hazard grid for Denver.

three different sizes that were scaled to the map and represented travel times of approximately 20 seconds (for red), 30 seconds (for yellow) and 45 seconds (for green). They were instructed to place one of the diamonds over each focal point. The size of the diamond chosen for a focal point would correspond to the chiefs' subjective evaluation of the time difference that would be unimportant for that group of hazards. After all of the areas were covered by a diamond of some color, the empty spaces (containing structures that need some fire protection) were assigned a blue code. Figure 14.11 shows the resulting focal point map for Denver.

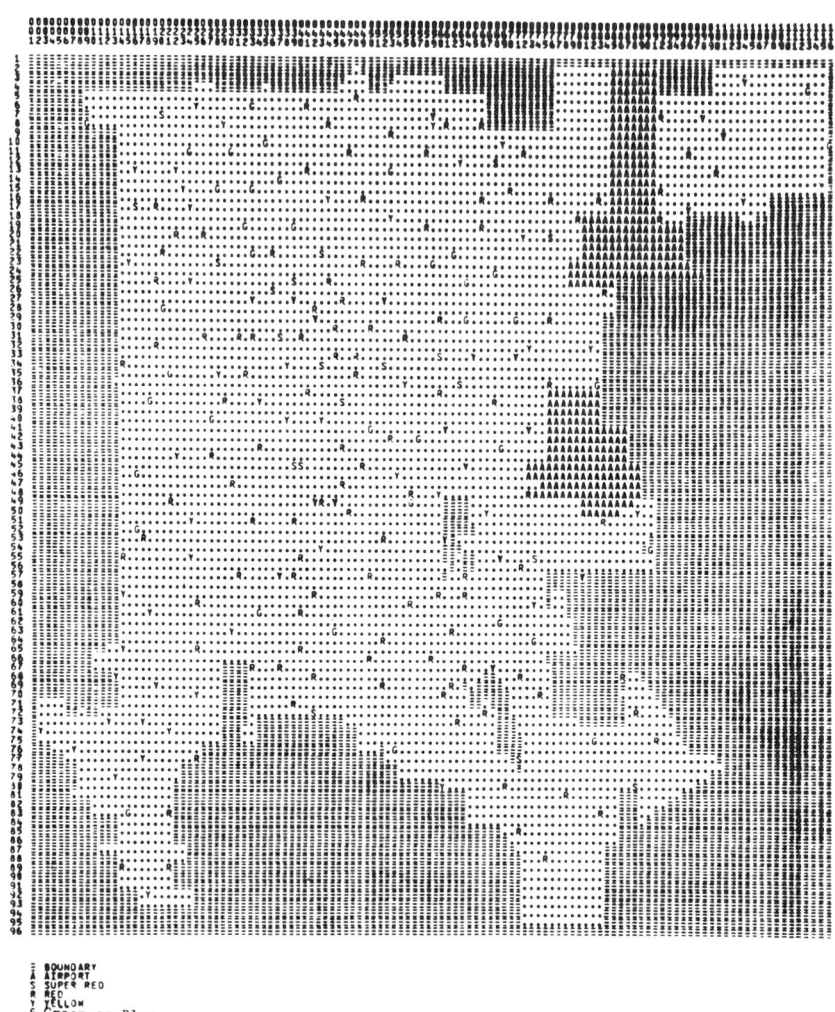

FIGURE 14.11. Focal point grid for Denver.

Travel-Time Requirements for Each Focal Point Class. The next set of data requirements was the maximum first-due engine (and, separately, first-due ladder) travel time for each of the focal points, or for each class of focal points. Instead of stating specific time requirements for each class, attention was focused upon determining approximate travel-time *differentials* for each focal-point class.

All assistant fire chiefs were given a diagram similar to Figure 14.12 and were asked to indicate where they would build one firehouse to serve these three hazards. Nineteen of the 21 chiefs chose a location in the

14.2 Locating Firehouses in Denver, Colorado

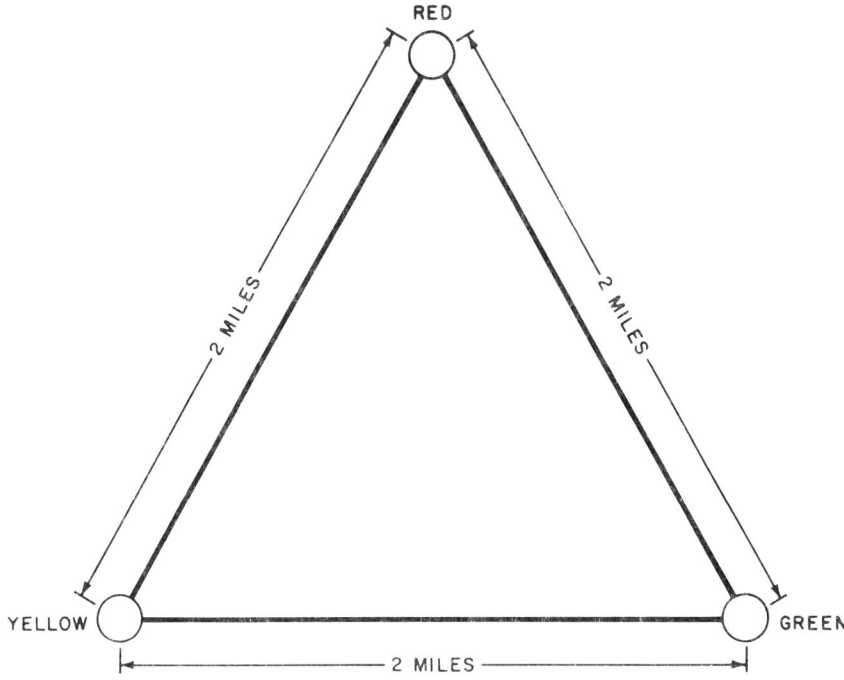

FIGURE 14.12. Triangle experiment for determining travel-time differentials.

upper-left part of the triangle; closest to the red, second closest to the yellow, and farthest from the green focal point. The centroid of this cluster of responses implied a 90-second difference between red and yellow, and a 30-second difference between yellow and green. Although there are many pitfalls to this procedure, it did yield a consensus among experienced officers that was readily accepted by the fire department personnel. An interesting aspect of this approach is that the necessary data were obtained by rephrasing the original question about travel-time differentials in familiar terminology. Instead of speaking in terms of travel-time differentials (which is not a common area of thought for fire chiefs), the question was rephrased in terms of firehouse location, which is a typical matter of concern. The fire chiefs concurred with these results and, in addition, set the travel-time differentials between green and blue equal to zero.

Determining a maximum travel time for a focal point of a particular color was more difficult. The general approach was to start with a requirement of two minutes for red focal points and then "sweep" a range of time requirements, keeping the difference between color codes constant.

Alternative Locations for Firehouses. Each district chief was asked to provide an unspecified number of places that he would consider for locating firehouses if there were no existing firehouses in the city. Access and other favorable characteristics, such as topography and lack of barriers, were to be considered. This yielded a list of 100 possible candidate sites, including the existing 27 stations. Since several areas of the city were not covered with enough alternative locations, additional sites were added at locations suggested by fire department members of the project team. At this point, there were 112 candidate sites throughout the city. (At later points in the study, this number was increased to a total of 120 candidate sites.)

Using the Models. When the computer programs (which were similar to PTI's FSLP) were first used to determine where the engine companies should be located, the results were not acceptable to the Fire Chief. The great number of red focal points and a maximum travel time of two minutes to each produced the need for too many stations. By increasing the maximum time, a solution was found using close to the existing number of stations, but it had unacceptably long travel times to some red focal points. The project team solved the problem by identifying the most hazardous of the red focal points. Based on the judgment of the 21 district chiefs, the Chief and his staff specified 20 "super red" focal points. The final list of 246 focal points consisted of 20 super reds, 117 reds, 69 yellows, and 40 blues and greens. A time difference of one minute between super red and red focal points was used at the suggestion of the Fire Chief.

Nine different runs were made with this data base. The maximum first-due engine travel time to super red focal points was varied from 1.8 minutes to 2.6 minutes, in increments of 0.1 minutes. The results of these solutions are indicated in Table 14.7. There were 27 engine companies in the city of Denver at the time, so the results implied that these resources could be deployed to provide maximum travel times of approximately 2.2 minutes for super reds.

The five configurations that resulted from varying the super red travel-time requirement between 2.1 and 2.5 minutes were discussed with the Fire Chief and several of his officers. They found the results to be unacceptable in two ways. First, the model tended to draw stations to the extreme corners of the city's boundaries in response to super red focal points located near the boundaries. This was not surprising, nor necessarily a bad policy, but it was unacceptable to the Fire Chief. Secondly, the solutions resulted in an insufficient level of fire protection in the downtown area. This happened because the exclusive use of first-due engine travel times provided no special consideration to the require-

TABLE 14.7. Number of engine companies needed in Denver to meet varying standards of maximum first-due engine travel time.

Maximum First-due Engine Travel Time to Super Reds (minutes)	Total Number of Locations	Number of New Locations
1.8	36	21
1.9	36	20
2.0	32	17
2.1	28	14
2.2	27	12
2.3	25	14
2.4	23	14
2.5	23	10
2.6	22	9

ment for more than one vehicle at fires in the congested downtown area. (This same problem also arose in Tacoma, discussed in Section 14.3.)

The Chief was then asked to compose a configuration of engines that he thought would provide approximately the current level of fire protection with (if possible) a smaller number of companies. The project team then used the Chief's suggested configuration in the downtown area as a given constraint in subsequent runs of the model.

A computer program named the Station Configuration Information Model, or SCIM (which was similar to the Firehouse Site Evaluation Model), was run with the configuration of stations suggested by the Chief. This configuration left 30 focal points uncovered within the Chief's target first-due engine travel time of 2 minutes for super red, 3 minutes for red, 4.5 minutes for yellow, and 5.0 minutes for blue or green. Each focal point whose time requirement was not satisfied was examined by the Chief and his staff. They found that the resulting travel times to each of these focal points was acceptable; i.e., all "violated" constraints could be safely violated. In making these determinations, they considered specific streets and their traffic conditions and directions, which was impossible to do using the distance-time conversion equations to predict travel time.

An additional constraint suggested by the fire department and the city was that stations constructed within the preceding eight years should be in the final solution. A new solution was obtained that required the same number of pumper companies as the previous solution. Furthermore, the new configuration was identical to the Chief's solution, except that one station recommended by the Chief was not actually needed to meet any of the constraints.

Results and Recommendations. The combination of the use of mathematical modeling and informed judgment resulted in a set of recommendations for the location of engine companies in the City and County of Denver. The SCIM results showed that this set of recommendations, which uses 25 engine companies rather than the 27 companies existing at the beginning of the project, provides approximately the existing level of fire suppression service. Table 14.8 shows the average first-due engine travel times to focal points of different hazard classes for the two configurations. These two sets of travel times are essentially the same except for the super red class, where the new configuration is slightly better. The analysis would have been even more meaningful if travel-time figures were obtained for the set of focal points to which travel time would change. (This is analogous to the "affected region" discussed in Chapter 10 and in the Yonkers case.) The citywide figures may mask some important effects, since travel times to the majority of focal points remain unchanged. It also would have been useful to examine the incidence of structural fires at the various focal points. Average travel times to focal points of a given hazard class, weighted by the number of structural fires, is a meaningful measure that was not used in this study.

Although the research did not use an "absolute" standard for first-due engine travel time for any class of focal points, Table 14.9 compares the two configurations using the Chief's suggested "target" response time of 2 minutes for super red focal points and appropriate differentials for the other classes.

14.2.4 Dynamic Analysis

The Fire Operations Simulation Model described in Chapter 13 was used by the Denver project team to check whether the configurations of station locations considered potentially desirable at the completion of the static

TABLE 14.8. Average travel times of first-due engines (minutes) in Denver.

Type of Focal Point	Existing Configuration (27 Engines) (1972)	Proposed Configuration (25 Engines)
Super red	1.8	1.7
Red	2.3	2.3
Yellow	2.2	2.2
Blue, green	2.5	2.5
Citywide	2.3	2.2

14.2 Locating Firehouses in Denver, Colorado

TABLE 14.9. Percentage of focal points for which first-due engine travel times are less than or equal to target maximum travel times in Denver.

Type of Focal Point	Number of Focal Points	Target Travel Time (Minutes)	Percent of Focal Points Meeting Target	
			Existing Configuration (27 Engines)	Proposed Configuration (25 Engines)
Super red	20	2.0	65	75
Red	117	3.0	80	81
Yellow	69	4.5	96	97
Blue, green	40	5.0	98	98
Citywide	246		86	88

analysis would prove suitable under realistic operating conditions.[9] The simulation model takes into account a number of characteristics of fire department operations that were not considered during the static analysis. For example, companies may sometimes be unavailable when alarms occur in their response area; they may be relocated on higher alarms; second-due travel times are interesting only at incidents that need a second company; the direction of the street grid differs between downtown Denver and the rest of the city; and the travel time for the first-arriving company (engine or ladder) may be interesting for certain incidents. As the overall alarm rate changes, performance measures estimated by the simulation model also change, which is not the case for static models.[10] Since the annual number of alarms was increasing in Denver, the project team wanted to know how satisfactory the proposed configurations would be at alarm rates that were much higher than those experienced in 1974.

The results of static models, like the Firehouse Site Evaluation Model or the Station Configuration Information Model, had not yet been compared with simulation results at the time of this study. Therefore, the dynamic analysis in Denver can be considered an historically important step in the validation of the static models. Fortunately, the outcome was that the simulation results did confirm those obtained from simpler models. None of the impressions of those involved, regarding the relative desirability of different proposed configurations, were changed by the simulation results; rather, they were strengthened.

However, using the simulation model was difficult, lengthy, and ex-

---

[9] Seven different configurations were considered in the dynamic analysis.
[10] The results of the static models change only if there is a change in the *relative* numbers of alarms in different parts of the city.

pensive. Over half of the entire cost of the Denver project can probably be attributed to the process of learning to use the model, adapting the computer program to match the requirements of local computer systems and fire department operational characteristics, collecting data for the simulation, running the program, and analyzing the output. The unique contribution of the Denver team was their method for defining incident types, which has already been described in Section 13.3.2.

The lesson for other fire deployment analysts is that a simulation model is not needed for studying configurations of firehouses if the average company is available more than 90 percent of the time (an average fire company in Denver was available to respond to a alarm from its quarters over 95 percent of the time.) The primary use of the simulation model described in Chapter 13 would be for analysis of dispatching and relocation strategies that have not previously been tested by simulation. However, it is worth bearing in mind that the political value of a simulation in supporting a new policy may be critical (see Section 13.1).

14.2.5 Implementation

The project produced recommendations for the location of engines and ladders in Denver that would leave the level of service almost the same, with the reduction of five companies—from 44 companies to 39 companies (a reduction of 85 firefighters). These proposed reductions were accompanied by an 11-stage timetable for the construction of firehouses, closing of existing houses, and equipment changes that would achieve the recommended changes, with no layoffs of firefighters,[11] by January 1979.

By the end of 1977, nine of the eleven stages of the plan were to have been carried out, resulting in the closing of six stations and the building of three new ones, with a net reduction of three companies. In fact, four of the nine stages were carried out, resulting in the elimination of three fire companies and a reduction in the authorized strength of the department by 25 firefighters (a savings of over $500,000 per year). A severe budget squeeze in Denver in 1975 facilitated the elimination of two of the companies. Political opposition to the recommendations, particularly from members of the City Council, is likely to prevent the implementation of any additional parts of the recommendations. Nonetheless, the plan

---

[11] One guideline specified by the city for the implementation of changes was that there would be no layoffs due to a reduction in the number of fire companies. Hence, attrition became the determining factor for the rate of company reduction.

developed through analysis in 1974 is a "living document" and serves as one basis for each year's deliberation on the fire department budget.[12]

14.3 USING THE PARAMETRIC ALLOCATION MODEL IN TACOMA, WASHINGTON

In 1974, at the request of Tacoma's City Manager and Fire Chief, staff members of The New York City-Rand Institute examined the allocation of engine companies in the city. Because of limited funding, it was decided to use the Parametric Allocation Model (Chapter 9), but not the Firehouse Site Evaluation Model. The study required less than two person-weeks' effort, including seven person-days of effort by Institute staff, and incurred computation costs of under $30.

The Parametric Allocation Model is a useful tool for analyzing allocation questions quickly, without the need for large amounts of data. In this application, it reinforced the chief's opinion that one engine company could be eliminated with little impact on travel time. Two months after the study, the engine company was taken out of service. The chief later stated that this change would have been difficult to implement without the information provided by the model.

14.3.1 Background

This study was conducted in 1974, when William Donaldson was the City Manager of Tacoma. Known for his innovative approach to improving municipal services, Mr. Donaldson was in the process of sponsoring a variety of technological projects related to transit routing, court scheduling, sewage treatment, refuse collection, police services, and municipal planning, as well as to the fire department. Earlier, as City Manager of Scottsdale, Arizona, he had successfully introduced such innovations as Godzilla, a vehicle that increased productivity in refuse collection (Baer et al., 1976).

Mr. Donaldson, with the concurrence of the Fire Chief, James Reiser, had repeatedly offered Tacoma as a test site for any methods or models that the fire project staff at The New York City-Rand Institute might wish to try in cities other than New York. However, his offer did not include a commitment of either personnel time or resources of the fire department, since he felt that the department's administrators should

---

[12] A more complete description of the history of the implementation of these changes is contained in Walker (1978).

decide whether such a commitment was warranted, taking into account the other innovative projects already under way.

At the time, the Institute had HUD funding to develop a training course on the deployment of emergency services, and to test its deployment models in several cities. Thus, it was possible for the Institute to accept Tacoma's invitation, and to carry out a training course and the initial stages of a fire deployment study under HUD funding. The understanding, however, was that HUD funding was not adequate to support a complete deployment analysis, and a later decision would determine whether the city could commit its own resources, or find alternative sources of funding for a complete study.

Under this arrangement, and in direct negotiations with Chief Reiser, two members of the Institute staff organized and presented a training course, based on drafts of lecture materials that were subsequently published (Chaiken, Ignall, and Walker, 1975). After the training course was completed, the Chief expressed great interest in proceeding with a deployment study to see if the allocation of his engine companies could be improved. He appointed a deputy chief as project director.

Thereafter, one analyst carried out a few days work over a period of several weeks. He met several times with members of the fire department and arranged for the collection of appropriate data. He and another analyst then carried out the analysis described below, taking only about two days to complete the work. Not including the training course, the entire study consumed about 7 man-days of time by Institute staff and consultants, and 5 man-days of time by fire department personnel. This case study is, therefore, an example of what can be accomplished in a relatively quick and uncomplicated deployment study.

Located on an inlet of Puget Sound, Tacoma is a city of 48 square miles and 150,000 people. It has major industrial and port facilities. Its fire department had a budget of $5.6 million in 1974, with 15 engine companies, 4 ladder companies, 2 rescue companies, and a fireboat. It responded to about 4400 fire alarms a year and an equal number of other emergencies (mostly medical).

14.3.2 Preparation of the Data

The model used in the analysis was the Parametric Allocation Model (Chapter 9). One important step in using this model is to divide the city into demand regions. This was accomplished at a meeting attended by more than ten high-ranking chiefs and representatives of the Institute. A large map of the city with a plastic overlay was prepared for this meeting. Demand regions were tentatively drawn on the map by Chief Reiser and then modified in response to suggestions from the audience, whose members, collectively, were intimately familiar with all parts of the city.

14.3 Using the Parametric Allocation Model in Tacoma, Washington

The basic criteria used in designing the demand regions were those mentioned in Chapter 8. First, each region had to contain more than one engine company. (The number of ladder companies was too small to permit a meaningful division of the city into regions containing several.) Second, the regions had to distinguish among industrial, commercial, and residential parts of the city. This criterion could not always be applied to everyone's satisfaction, since primarily residential areas always contain commercial subareas that the local chiefs consider substantially different in their requirements for firefighting. Third, the boundaries of the demand regions had to follow natural barriers to travel whenever possible. Two major barriers of this type in Tacoma are Interstate Highway 5 and the Puyallup River. The result of this process was the definition of five demand regions as shown in Figure 14.13.

The next data needed were the areas (in square miles) of each demand region. These were obtained by laying a transparent grid over the city map and counting the number of grid boxes in each region. The number of square miles in each grid box was known from the scale of the map.

To determine the number of engine companies currently located in each region, it is not appropriate to count each company according to the region in which its station is located, since companies located near region boundaries serve more than one region. An appropriate approach would divide each engine company according to the fraction of its first-due area that is included in each region. However, maps of the first-due areas of engine companies were not available in Tacoma. Each company did have an assigned "hydrant district," within which it was responsible for inspections and other administrative matters. Since maps of hydrant districts were available, the analysis was expedited by dividing engine companies according to their hydrant districts. (This was recognized as an approximation that should be repaired in a more careful analysis.) For example, Region 5 contained the entire hydrant district of Engine Companies 14 and 16, 85 percent of the hydrant district of Engine Company 9, and 90 percent of the hydrant district of Company 13. Thus, Region 5 had approximately $2 + 0.85 + 0.90 = 3.75$ engine companies located in it.

The existing field incident reporting system of the Tacoma Fire Department also identified the locations according to hydrant districts. Again, although a correct analysis would involve determining the demand region in which each incident had occurred, alarm rates were estimated by an approximation: incidents were assumed to be evenly distributed over each hydrant district. Thus, for example, the number of incidents in Region 5 was estimated as the sum of all the incidents in the hydrant districts for Engines 14 and 16, plus 85 percent of the incidents in the hydrant district of Engine 9 and 90 percent of those in the hydrant district of Engine 13. Of course, it could happen, for instance, that only

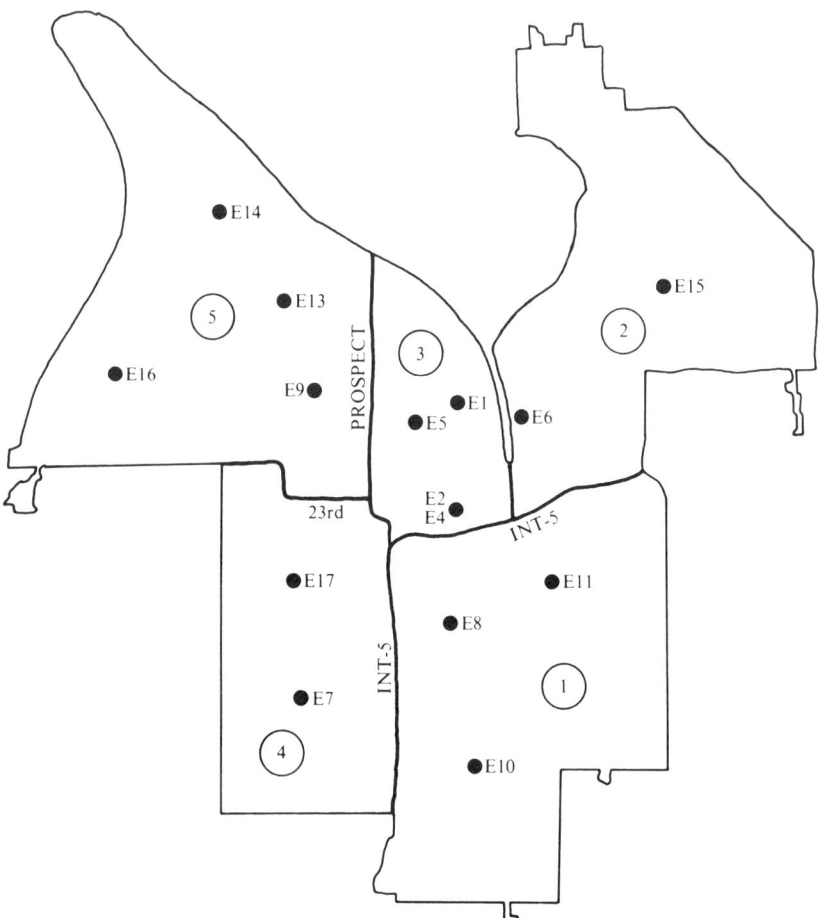

FIGURE 14.13. Demand regions and engine company locations, Tacoma, Washington, August 1974.

60 percent of the incidents in the hydrant district for Engine 9 were actually in Region 5—which is why the method is an approximation.

The data for each hydrant district were obtained by making a special tabulation for the most recent 12-month period (June 1973 through May 1974). These figures were not projected into the future, either by extrapolation of past trends, or by considering planned redevelopment in various parts of the city. (Again, this study was intended to be a quick, rough analysis.)

The method used to estimate the average number of engine company hours per alarm (another item of data needed as input for the Parametric

14.3 Using the Parametric Allocation Model in Tacoma, Washington 585

Allocation Model) was even rougher. The total number of responses and work hours for each engine company had been previously tabulated for the year 1973. (Note that this period of time is different from the one used in the alarm-rate estimates.) The responses were assumed to be divided among demand regions according to the companies' hydrant districts, an admittedly poor approximation, since companies can work long hours at incidents located far from their stations (as at a third-alarm fire). This permitted an estimate of the number of work-hours per response in each region, which was then multiplied by an average of 1.43 engines working per incident (a citywide figure). As shown in Table 14.10, the results appeared sensible, since large work-hour figures occurred in the same demand regions that had a large percentage of fires.

The department had previously collected data showing travel times for first-arriving companies, so the parameters for converting travel distance to travel time were easily determined, as follows:

$$T = 3.44\ D^{0.675},$$

where, as usual, T is the travel time in minutes, and D is the travel distance in miles.

Hazard factors for each demand region were determined subjectively by the analysts, based on experience in other cities. Regions 1 and 5 (residential) were assigned a hazard factor of 1.0, Regions 3 and 4 (commercial) a factor of 1.1, and Region 2 (industrial) a factor of 1.2.

14.3.3 Results from the Parametric Allocation Model

The Parametric Allocation Model was first used to estimate the then-current (base case) travel time for first and second-arriving engine companies. Note that Engines 2 and 4 occupied the same firehouse. It was necessary, therefore, to estimate the number of firehouses serving each demand region, rather than the number of engine companies. If N is the

TABLE 14.10. Comparison between estimated engine company hours per alarm and the relative frequency of fires. Data for Tacoma, 1973.

Demand Region	Average Engine Company Hours	Percent of Alarms That Are Fires
1	0.785	20.5
2	1.050	32.5
3	0.851	21.1
4	1.001	25.4
5	0.891	22.8

number of stations in a region, the discussion in Section 7.2.4 shows that the correct estimate of $\bar{N}$ is $N - \{(N-1)/N\}\bar{B}$, which is slightly larger than $N - \bar{B}$. Here $\bar{N}$ is the average number of firehouses with an available company, and $\bar{B}$ is the average number of busy companies. However, the allocation model estimates $\bar{N} = N - \bar{B}$, so the resulting estimates for average first-arriving engine travel times should be slightly high. To obtain estimated second-arriving engine travel times, $\bar{N}$ was set equal to the number of engine companies, rather than the number of stations. This yields a slight underestimate. The results are shown in Table 14.11.

The match between the model and reality was fairly good, except in Region 2. To interpret the disparity, the knowledge of local fire officials is vital. In this case, it turns out that Tacoma had mutual-aid agreements with nearby communities, whose companies were first-due in parts of Region 2. The model estimated what the first-arriving engine travel times would be if Tacoma companies were the only ones to respond, whereas the data indicated the travel times to those incidents where a Tacoma company actually arrived before companies from elsewhere. Thus, an unintended benefit from using the model was an indication of the value of the mutual aid agreements.

The Parametric Allocation Model was subsequently operated in the prescriptive mode (with the tradeoff parameter $p = 0.25$), varying the number of companies. The recommended allocation for 14 engine companies is compared to the base case in Table 14.12.

The results indicated that a lower average first-arriving engine travel time could be achieved with one less engine company. However, it is not immediately obvious which companies should be moved. Since the recommended allocation is based on the model's assumption that each engine occupies a firehouse without any other engines in it, the company to eliminate is evidently Engine 4 (or Engine 2; it doesn't matter).[13] By trying out different designs on the map, it was found that by eliminating Engine 4 and moving Engine 5 to a location where it serves Regions 1, 3, and 4, the desired allocation can be achieved. (The desired reduction in the number of engines in Region 5 occurs automatically with the removal of Engine 5, since the first-due area of Engine 9 expands into Region 3.)

Using the descriptive capabilities of the allocation model, the consequences of various specific combinations of eliminations and moves were considered. Each case involved drawing a map of the proposed configuration to estimate the number of companies in each demand region, as in the base case. Both first- and second-arriving engine travel times were

---

[13] The small increase in average travel time accompanying a large reduction in the number of companies in Region 3 (Table 14.12) can be attributed to the change to single-engine houses.

14.3 Using the Parametric Allocation Model in Tacoma, Washington

TABLE 14.11. Travel time (in minutes) for the base case (15 engine companies) in Tacoma.

Demand Region	Average First-Arriving Engine Travel Time (From Data)	Average First-Arriving Engine Travel Time (From Parametric Allocation Model)	Average Second-Arriving Engine Travel Time (From Parametric Allocation Model)
1	3.73	3.64	4.99
2	3.30	4.40	6.19
3	2.78	3.01	3.81
4	3.49	3.83	5.42
5	3.48	3.49	4.89
Citywide	3.36	3.53	4.83

reviewed, although Table 14.12 shows only the first-arriving engine travel times. For example, the allocation model showed that if Engine 5 were eliminated, first-arriving engine travel times would increase by 12 percent in Region 3 and 2 percent in Region 5, while second-arriving engine travel times would increase by 10 percent in Region 3 and 2 percent in Region 5. Nonetheless, average travel times in both regions would still be at or below the then-current citywide averages. This finding, to which the analysts paid no particular attention at the time, was most important to city officials, as we shall see.

14.3.4 Implementation

The department's reception of the analysis was influenced by the fact that a tentative decision to eliminate Engine 5 had already been made. This fact had not been brought to the attention of the analysts, either to preserve their objectivity or because a reversal of the decision was genuinely possible if the analysis indicated it was unwise.

TABLE 14.12. Recommended allocation of 14 engine companies in Tacoma.

		Base Case		Recommended	
Demand Region	Hazard Factors	Number of Engines	Estimated First-Arriving Engine Travel Time (Minutes)	Number of Engines	Estimated First-Arriving Engine Travel Time (Minutes)
1	1.0	3.40	3.64	3.52	3.52
2	1.2	2.40	4.40	2.74	3.61
3	1.1	3.45	3.01	2.16	3.05
4	1.1	2.00	3.83	2.18	3.48
5	1.0	3.75	3.49	3.41	3.61
Citywide		15.00	3.53	14.00	3.42

The chiefs already realized that travel times were low in Region 3 (downtown). (Remember, the department had data showing the average first-due travel time in each hydrant district.) However, they did not know what would happen to travel times if Engine 5 were removed, and the model's results proved illuminating and gratifying on that score. Thus, the preexisting decision was reinforced.

The analysts felt that the model had indicated a clear penalty in travel time for having two engines in a single firehouse, but the chiefs were not convinced. They correctly pointed out that the model did not take into account the fact that Engines 2 and 4 were located near hazards that were most likely to require a second engine in the event of a fire. In other words, the allocation model gives estimated second-arriving engine travel times for all incidents (or all structural fires, depending on how it is used) in a region; but one really wants to know the second-arriving engine travel times to *incidents that need a second engine*. Even the Firehouse Site Evaluation Model (Chapter 10) does not provide this information, unless the data are prepared with this particular purpose in mind.

Engine 5 was taken out of service two months after the study was completed. The Institute analysts played no role in this decision, nor were they mentioned publicly in connection with it. On the contrary, the department's annual report stated that the change was based on "the recommendation of the Insurance Services Office." Two years later, Chief Reiser, then retired, and his successor, Chief Tony Mitchell, made a joint statement that quite clearly explained the role of analysis in the political process. "Use of the deployment model in Tacoma was most helpful," they said. "A prior decision had already been made to eliminate a fire company. Political and neighborhood opposition to this change would have been difficult to deal with if we had not had the information provided by the deployment model . . . ."

At the conclusion of the preliminary study, the Fire Chief and the City Manager both expressed interest in pursuing a more careful analysis— one that would use the Firehouse Site Evaluation Model. Interesting questions remained to be settled: What would be the actual effect of removing Engine 4 from the firehouse with Engine 2 in it? Where was the best location for a new firehouse for Engine 4? But various attempts to obtain funding for such a study were unsuccessful, and no further deployment analysis was conducted in Tacoma.

14.4 WORKLOAD PROBLEMS IN THE NEW YORK CITY FIRE DEPARTMENT

One of the New York City Fire Department's major concerns at the time The New York City–Rand Institute was formed was the increasingly heavy workload of its fire companies. A few companies were responding

14.4 Workload Problems in the New York City Fire Department

to so many alarms that occasional physical exhaustion of the firefighters was fast becoming a distinct possibility. These companies were sometimes experiencing entire tours that offered no opportunity for a meal. The firefighters' unions were bringing pressure on the city to add more companies to relieve workload; the department was interested in reducing the number of units dispatched to an initial alarm.

These competing proposals were the focus of the contract negotiations between the unions and the city in 1969. Analysts at The New York City–Rand Institute tested a range of alternative workload-reduction policies using an early version of the Fire Operations Simulation Model (see Chapter 13). The results showed the clear benefits of a policy that both reduced the initial dispatch and added companies. These results had a major impact on the final labor agreement. A new dispatching policy was put into effect in a high alarm-rate area of the city, and five full-time and six peak-hour companies were added in high alarm-rate areas.

14.4.1 Background

Workload was a major issue in the 1969 contract negotiations between the firefighters' unions and the city of New York. The unions argued that a large number of units were overworked "as a regular condition of employment." They demanded that the city relieve this condition, preferably by pairing one new unit with each "overworked" unit to split the workload. The city had already added companies—one in 1967 and nine in 1968—each at a cost of about $600,000 per year. But apparently this "solution" was doing little to relieve workload. For example, in 1966, Engine Company 82 in the South Bronx responded to over 6000 alarms and was the busiest engine company in the city. The company added in 1967 was placed in the firehouse of Engine 82 to relieve its workload. But in 1968, its first full year of operation, Engine 82 was still the busiest engine company in the city (responding over 9000 times) and the new company became the second busiest.

The increase in fire company workload was the result of a rapid increase in alarms—from about 100,000 in 1960 to 180,000 in 1967, and to 223,000 in 1968. Furthermore, the increased total workload was not evenly distributed; for example, an engine company less than one mile from Engine 82 made 3900 responses in 1968.

Given this situation, the pressure from the unions was to add more companies. The fire department recognized that much of the workload resulted from the traditional dispatching policy of attempting to send three engine companies and two ladder companies to box alarms. Therefore, they sought a reduction in the number of units dispatched initially. If companies were to be added, they preferred that these companies work only during the peak afternoon and evening hours when they would provide the most workload relief.

At that time (early summer of 1969), the Institute's fire project had been working with the New York City Fire Department for about 18 months. Ten researchers were at work—analyzing fire demands, beginning to develop relocation and dispatch models, and building a computer simulation of firefighting operations. At that point, the work was beginning to gain management acceptance and support—a dispatching office study (described in Section 14.5) had been completed, and the fire project staff had prepared the groundwork for a computer-aided Management Information and Control System. The workload problems and the labor negotiations were to be the first test of whether the analysis could provide timely and useful input to deployment decisionmaking.

At the height of the negotiations, the fire project staff was actively working at developing the simulation (Chapter 13) and other analytical models. Although the simulation was not complete, it was obvious it would have to be used and relied upon. The version used to test policies that were proposed in the negotiations did not represent the actual geography of the city. Rather, company and alarm box locations were specified in a fictional square region with highly regular "geography." (This fictional region is described later in the text.) By the end of 1969, the representation of the geography of the Bronx was completed and incorporated into the model, and the range of policies tested. The results of these tests confirmed the earlier results obtained from the incomplete model. They were also used to determine the locations for a number of companies added in 1970.

In presenting this case study, we first discuss the results obtained using the early version of the simulation model. These results—obtained for the fictional region—suggested the usefulness of a new dispatching policy called *adaptive response*, when the alarm rate is high. They also indicated that adding new companies was most effective at peak hours of the day. We then describe the later simulations that used the geography of the Bronx. These runs were made to see if the earlier results were valid for the city, and to measure the likely effectiveness of adaptive response.

14.4.2 The Early Simulation Model

A number of options for relieving workload were presented by both fire department management and union representatives. The most obvious solution, perhaps—and the one preferred by the unions—was to add full-time companies. Department management argued that the workload problems were, in large part, the result of a traditional dispatching policy that sought to dispatch three engine companies and two ladder companies to each incoming box alarm. (The traditional policy, which is described and

14.4 Workload Problems in the New York City Fire Department 591

discussed in Chapter 11, specified that the three closest engines and two closest ladders would be sent *if they were available,* with a minimum dispatch of the closest available engine company and ladder company.) Therefore, they sought to reduce the initial response to box alarms (about half of all alarms were received directly from street boxes). A third set of options resulted from combining these two extremes, i.e., adding companies and reducing response. The earliest runs with the simulation model varied the number of companies on duty, the number dispatched initially to different kinds of alarms, and the alarm rate.

Before we discuss the results of these runs, let us describe the simulation model as it then existed. When these policies were being considered, the geographic representation of the Bronx was not complete, so a fictional region shown in Figure 14.14 was used. It was six miles long and six miles wide, and divided into 36 one-mile squares. In the base

FIGURE 14.14. Fictional geographic region used in early simulation runs in New York City. The base case is represented here.

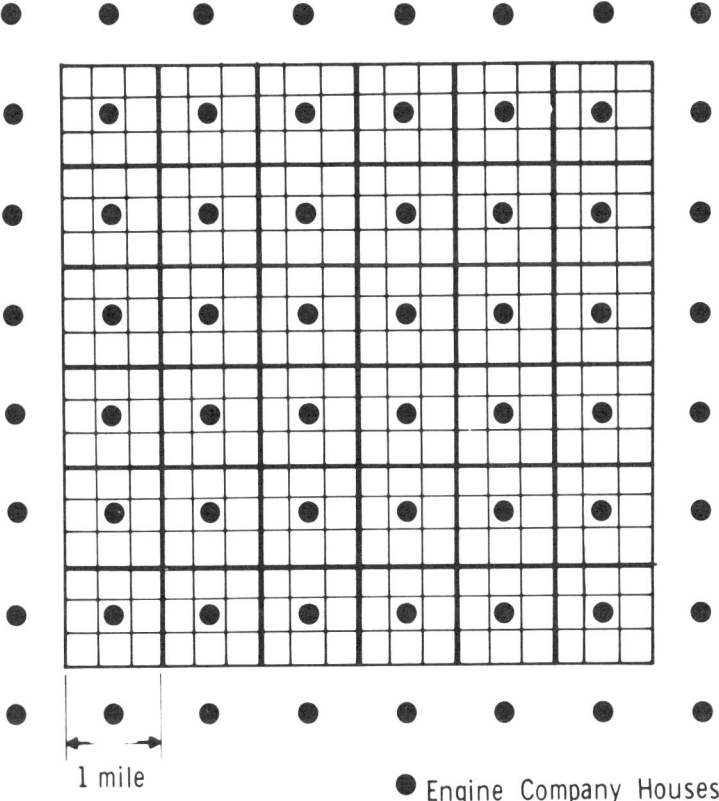

case (the situation to which the various runs were compared), an engine company was located at the center of each of these squares. (We concentrate here on the engine simulations; similar runs were made for ladders.) In addition, 28 engine companies were located around the outer perimeter of the area. Each of the 36 squares was subdivided into nine smaller squares. The centers of each of these 324 smaller squares were the potential incident locations: the hypothetical alarm boxes.

The engines were assumed to travel at 20 mph, and right-angle distance was used. It was assumed that one minute was required to get a message through the dispatching office and start a unit on its way.

The area was divided into regions of high, medium and low demand as indicated in Figure 14.15. The ratio of total alarm rates per box in the three regions was assumed to be 20:5:1. The proportions of the various incident types are given in the last four columns of Table 14.13[14]; they were modeled on two of the battalion districts in the Bronx. The total alarm rate was 16.7 incidents per hour, roughly comparable then to a summer evening in the Bronx. The simplified picture was devised to approximate the configuration of fire companies and alarms in the Bronx.

FIGURE 14.15. The same fictional region as in Figure 14.14, divided into areas of high, medium, and low demand.

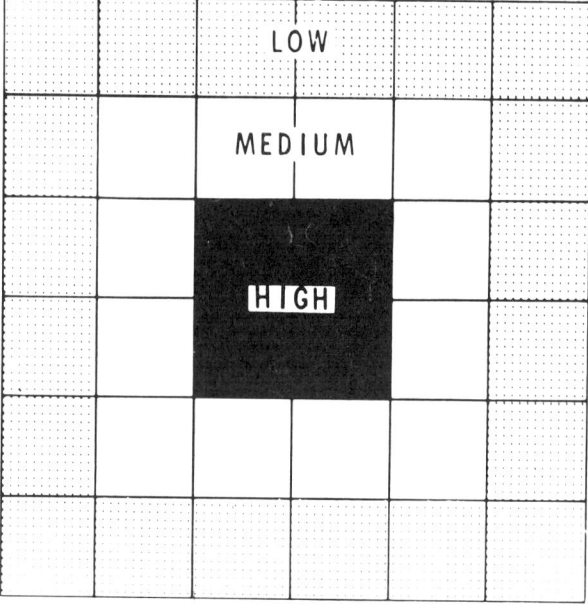

---

[14] The information in the rest of Table 14.13 is discussed later in this section.

TABLE 14.13. Characteristics of simulations used to test alternative deployment policies designed to reduce company workload.

	Number of Engines Nominally Dispatched					Typical Work Times (Minutes)	Percentage of All Alarms in:			
	Existing		Proposed		Required		Heavy and Medium Region		Low Region	
Incident Type	Box	Phone	Box	Phone			Box	Phone	Box	Phone
False alarm	3	1	2	1	1	5	27.70	2.30	14.60	3.00
Rubbish fire, etc.	3	1	2	1	1	18	27.40	15.70	14.00	29.30
Minor structural	3	3	2	3	1	18	13.10	10.80	7.40	28.40
Structural fire	3	3	2	3	2	75, 45	1.02	0.68	0.51	1.36
Structural fire	3	3	2	3	3	150, 105, 60	0.60	0.40	0.30	0.80
Structural fire	3	3	2	3	7	240, 180, 120, 90, 90, 60, 60	0.12	0.08	0.06	0.16
Structural fire	3	3	2	3	11	360, 300, 270, 240, 240, 180, 150, 120, 120, 90, 90	0.06	0.04	0.03	0.08
Total							70.00	30.00	37.00	63.00

The North Bronx is a low-alarm rate area; the South Bronx contains a high-alarm rate center surrounded by a medium alarm rate region.

Three basic strategies were tested: (1) adding companies; (2) reducing response; and (3) adding companies and reducing response. The first policy improved fire company response time, of course, but the workload relief given to busy companies was far less than might be imagined. The additional units served to increase overall availability, and under the traditional three-engine two-ladder dispatching policy more units were initially dispatched. Thus, the total workload increased and the number of responses saved were fewer than expected. This was why the company that had been added to relieve Engine 82 became a busy unit itself, and offered little relief to Engine 82. The second policy saved a substantial number of responses, but at alarm rates comparable to average evenings in the Bronx, the second- and third-arriving engine companies (and the second-arriving ladder company) took, on the average, longer to arrive.

The third strategy—adding companies and reducing response—seemed to be one that potentially could both reduce workloads and improve response times. The proposed policy would:

1. Establish new units to work mainly during the hours of peak demand.
2. Send two engines (and one ladder) to incidents reported from street alarm boxes during those hours.[15]
3. Treat each new unit and the busy one with which it would be paired as a two-section company, meaning that both would never go to the same incident. (If both were engines closest to an incident, and two or more engines were desired, only one of them would go.)

Let us examine the rationale underlying this policy, and the questions about it that were answered by simulating it. It has been customary in paid fire departments (at least, in the United States) to have around-the-clock companies, and to staff them uniformly throughout the day. However, there appeared to be good reasons to match the companies on duty to demand. For example, it seemed that three units working only the peak eight hours of the day do more to relieve the workload of existing units than one around-the-clock unit. However, it is precisely during the peak hours that new units are drawn more to filling out responses (that otherwise would have been less than three engines and two ladders) than to relieving the original units. Consequently, the issue was not so clear. Similarly, it seemed clear that, as a result of adding new units and modifying the nominal response to street box alarms, the total number

---

[15] This is a variable response policy (Chapter 11). If the two closest engines were not available, only one would be sent.

14.4 Workload Problems in the New York City Fire Department

of responses per unit would go down; and the concept of the two-section company seemed to ensure that more relief would go to the busy unit. How much relief there would be and how (in detail) it would be distributed among the units, however, was not clear.

Because there would be more units, and because each original unit would be available more of the time, the first two engines (and the first ladder) should, on the average, arrive sooner. What would happen to the response time of the third-arriving engine (and the second-arriving ladder) was quite unclear. They would not be dispatched to a street box alarm until a unit was on the scene. On the other hand, under the existing dispatch policy, street box and telephone alarms often did not get a third engine or second ladder on initial dispatch anyway; and under the proposed policy, telephone alarms would have more chance of getting them initially.

Compared to the existing fire company deployment, the deployment policy to be tested had four additional engine companies, one at each of the four houses in the high-demand region (Figure 14.15). Within each of the resulting two-section companies, each of the two units will make an equal number of responses, although this is not necessary. How the two deployment policies differ in the number of engines nominally sent is shown in Table 14.13. Under both policies, relocation of units occurs on second and higher alarms.

The incident generator of the simulation model (Section 13.2.1) prepared a sequence of incidents, covering a 240-hour period equivalent to a month of evenings. The incidents were generated assuming that the various incident types at the various boxes are realized as independent Poisson processes. In these particular runs there were 4141 incidents in the resulting sequence. Both policies dealt with the same sequence of incidents.

The simulations gave the following workload results: response by the engines inside the area totaled 7940 under the base case and 7213 under the proposed one, with the four new engines making 1454 responses and the original 36 making 5754 responses. To examine the way the reductions were distributed under the proposed policy, the original 36 engines were classified into the following four groups:

1. The original companies in the high-incidence area.
2. The eight companies in the medium-incidence area which were closest to the high-incidence area.
3. The other four companies in the medium-incidence area.
4. The 20 companies in the low-incidence area.

The average number of responses under each of the policies is displayed by group in Figure 14.16, where one box in each group is highlighted.

Average response times are given in Table 14.14. The response times

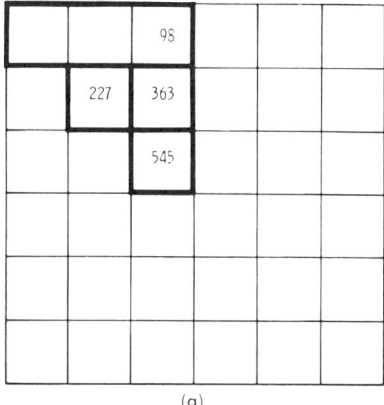

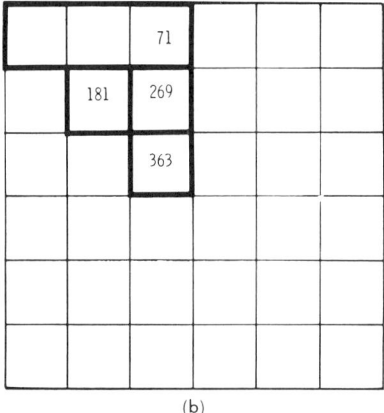

FIGURE 14.16. Average number of responses per engine company by group: (a) Original policy—send three closest engines to box alarms if they are available, but send at least one engine; (b) Proposed policy—add four engine companies in the high-demand region; send two engine companies if they are available, but send at least one engine.

shown for second- and third-arriving engines are only for those incidents that needed them, since the times are irrelevant in other cases. The improvements observed in first- and second-arriving engine response times under the proposed policy were expected. The improvement observed in third-arriving engine response time is more interesting, since there was no obvious prediction. Further, the improvement was found to be statistically significant.

On the basis of these two simulation runs, the new policy would be expected to: (1) Reduce the total number of responses made, with the

14.4 Workload Problems in the New York City Fire Department

TABLE 14.14. Average simulated response times (in minutes) for engines under the traditional and proposed dispatch policies.

Policy	First-Arriving Engine	Second-Arriving Engine	Third-Arriving Engine
Traditional	3.21	5.27	7.26
Proposed	2.71	4.48	6.57

bulk of the reduction going to units that originally responded most; and (2) Improve the distribution of the response-time vector, component by component, and thus reduce both loss of life and fire damage. Since all incidents received the number of units needed, usually more quickly than before, none of the eliminated responses were needed. The new policy could thus be expected both to enhance the actual service provided, and to reduce needless responses.

14.4.3 Policy Changes

The simulation results discussed in the last section and the results of other runs that treated related policies had a direct impact on the final labor agreement. Briefings were presented, both to fire department management and to officials of the unions representing firefighters and fire officers. The overall implications—that both reducing nominal response and adding companies at the peak hours would improve fire protection and reduce workload—seemed clear, despite the deficiencies of the model. The policy that was adopted and put into practice was similar to the one described in the preceding section. A new response policy—termed *adaptive response*, or "AR" (Chapter 11)—was instituted in a high-alarm incidence region of the Bronx. Under this plan, most street alarm boxes (except about 20 percent that were judged most likely to signal a structural fire, which retained the traditional response) were designated to receive *exactly* two-and-one, as opposed to the possibility of one-and-one under the "variable" two-and-two dispatching policy that had been simulated. In addition, the affected areas received around-the-clock units as well as peak-hour units.

In all, five full-time units and six peak-hour units were added. The peak-hour units, called *tactical control units,* were manned by volunteers and operated from 3 P.M. to 1 A.M. The program necessarily was voluntary, since provisions of the State Constitution prevented the implementation of work schedules providing for more coverage during particular times of the day. The addition of the full-time units was a concession to union demands, and a necessary bargaining lever for obtaining their agreement to the tactical control unit program.

As selection of the alarm boxes for AR and the specific locations for the new units proceeded (performed primarily by Department personnel), the representation of geography of the Bronx in the simulation was completed. The new policies were then simulated to verify the original conclusions. Recall that the simulations of the fictional region suggested that AR would be a useful policy at high alarm rates; but they had not explicitly evaluated AR (which applied in one region, at selected boxes). We therefore turn to the simulation tests of AR made using the Bronx geography.

14.4.4 Using the Bronx Simulation to Test Policies

The simulation model described in Chapter 13 is more realistic than the simpler version just described, since it includes a representation of the actual geography of the Bronx. Using this model, more precise estimates of the effects of alternative policies were obtained. However, these results are consistent with the insights and conclusions drawn from the earlier model.

As with the earlier model, comparisons were made of the effects of adding units, changing the response policy, and both adding units and changing the response policy. An important difference in the new runs was that the proposed response policy was AR. In the previous simulations the new response tested was a "variable" two and one policy, in which fewer than two engines, on the average, would be dispatched initially to box alarms. Under AR at a sufficiently high alarm rate, the average number of engines sent (i.e., two) could be greater than the average number sent under the traditional three-engine two-ladder policy.

AR was simulated for several different numbers of fire companies and for four different alarm rates—5, 13.5, 21, and 30 alarms per hour. These alarm rates roughly correspond to the average alarm rates for early morning, midday, evening, and a peak evening. All runs at the same alarm rate used the same sequence of incidents (numbering about 2000). The results are given in Tables 14.15 and 14.16. For example, we see that at 21 alarms per hour (an average Bronx evening), adding three ladder companies improved first- and second-arriving ladder response times significantly. However, the addition results in only a 10 percent reduction in workload (an estimated 1.51 responses per ladder per hour, compared to the base of 1.678). Adding three ladders and using AR reduces the workload to about 26 percent of the base, but with a smaller improvement in second-arriving ladder response time.

We now discuss the effects of the new policies in the South Bronx. The response time results for the 12 South Bronx ladders are displayed in Figure 14.17. The first-arriving ladder response times were slightly better under AR at all alarm rates. This is a result of the increased

TABLE 14.15. South Bronx simulation results for engines, from adaptive response (AR) tests.

Bronx Alarm Rate (Alarms/Hour)	Policy	Average Response Time (Minutes)			Workload (Number of Responses Per Hour Per Engine)
		First-Arriving Engine	Second-Arriving Engine (When Needed)	Third-Arriving Engine (When Needed)	
5	18 engines, no AR[a]	2.30	3.26	4.32	0.533
	19 engines, no AR	2.30	3.26	4.28	0.474
13.5	18 engines, no AR[a]	2.56	3.55	4.81	1.174
	18 engines, AR	2.55	3.43	5.35	1.079
	21 engines, no AR	2.41	3.42	4.72	1.068
	21 engines, AR	2.39	3.33	5.16	0.943
21	18 engines, no AR[a]	2.92	4.47	6.13	1.649
	18 engines, AR	2.89	4.07	6.13	1.649
	21 engines, no AR	2.64[b]	3.65[b]	5.60[b]	1.534[b]
	21 engines, AR	2.62	3.78	5.80	1.468
30	18 engines, no AR[a]	3.57	6.12	8.07	2.052
	18 engines, AR	3.57	5.33	8.05	2.224
	21 engines, no AR	3.13	5.05	6.76	1.940
	21 engines, AR	3.10	4.62	6.75	2.041
Range of number of incidents		1820–2208	50–78	25–31	
Range of raw standard deviation of indicated response times		0.81–1.93	1.72–2.39	2.56–2.74	

[a] This is the existing situation and represents the base case.
[b] Estimated; simulation was not run for this case.

TABLE 14.16. South Bronx simulation results for ladders, from adaptive response (AR) tests.

Bronx Alarm Rate (Alarms/Hour)	Policy	Average Response Times (Minutes)		Workload (Number of Responses per Hour per Ladder)
		First-Arriving Ladder	Second-Arriving Ladder (When Needed)	
5	12 ladders, no AR[a]	2.58	4.02	0.547
	14 ladders, no AR	2.53	3.81	0.480
13.5	12 ladders, no AR[a]	2.93	4.42	1.196
	12 ladders, AR	2.90	5.07	0.969
	15 ladders, no AR	2.67	3.90	1.046
	15 ladders, AR	2.66	4.61	0.794
21	12 ladders, no AR[a]	3.47	5.67	1.678
	12 ladders, AR	3.44	6.12	1.473
	15 ladders, no AR	3.02[b]	4.94[b]	1.51[b]
	15 ladders, AR	2.99	5.44	1.238
30	12 ladders, no AR[a]	4.45	8.11	2.072
	12 ladders, AR	4.37	7.94	1.927
	15 ladders, no AR	3.61	6.82	1.942
	15 ladders, AR	3.55	6.72	1.710
Range of number of incidents		1820–2211	50–78	
Range of raw standard deviations of indicated response times		0.97–2.07	1.94–3.41	

[a] This is the existing situation and represents the base case.
[b] Estimated; simulation was not run for this case.

14.4 Workload Problems in the New York City Fire Department

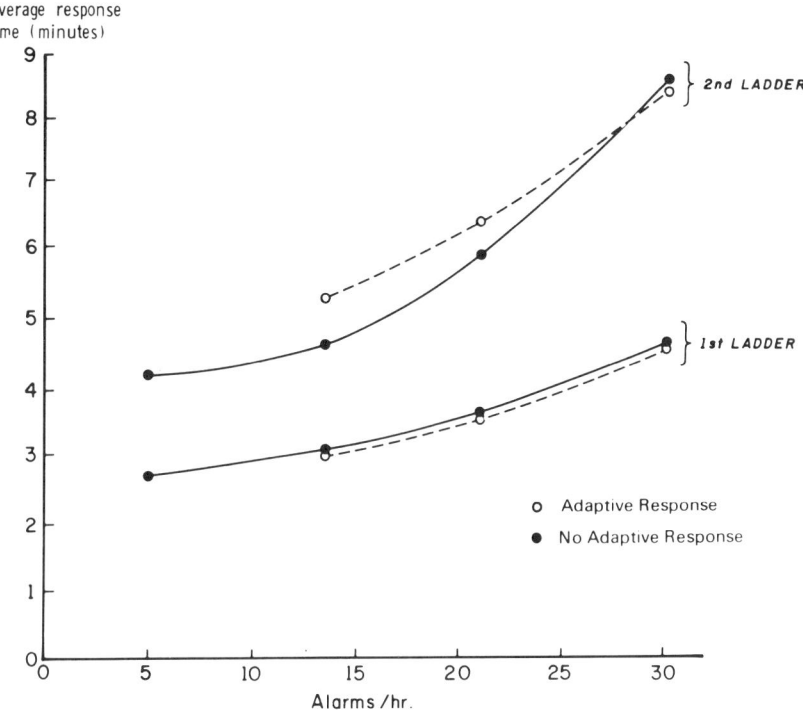

FIGURE 14.17. Simulated average response times for 12 ladders in the South Bronx.

availability of ladder companies under AR at all alarm rates. More importantly, at the highest alarm rate the average second-arriving ladder response time was also better. Since the workload of the ladders was also reduced under AR (Table 14.16), this policy apparently dominates the traditional one for ladders. (We say "apparently" because neither response time reduction was statistically significant.)

For engines, the response-time results were similar (Table 14.15). For 18 engines in Region 1, average first-arriving engine response time decreased under AR at all alarm rates. For the two highest alarm rates, average second- and third-arriving engine response times also decreased under AR. However, average workload increased in these cases.

The decreases in second- and third-arriving engine response times can be explained (as in the example for second-arriving ladders, which follows) by looking at the response to each class of alarm under both the traditional and the AR policies:

1. *Telephone Alarms.* Both policies initially send two ladders, but

under AR the second ladder is closer, on the average, because of increased availability.
2. *Box Alarms.* There are two classes of box alarms to consider:
   (a) Alarms that received one ladder under the traditional policy and still receive one under AR. The one ladder dispatched under adaptive response is closer, on the average. Therefore, if a second ladder is needed, it will get there faster, on the average, under adaptive response.
   (b) Alarms that received two ladders initially under the traditional policy, but only one under AR. This is the only class of alarms for which the traditional policy is better than adaptive response. But, as the alarm rate increases, this class includes a smaller and smaller proportion of the box alarms since, as availability decreases, the two closest ladders are *both* available less and less often.

Thus, as the alarm rate increases, those classes of alarms to which the second-arriving ladder response time is better under AR begin to predominate.

For ladders, AR reduces the workload of units at all alarm rates. However, as the alarm rate increases, the relative reduction decreases. This is because, with increasing alarm rate, the average number of ladders initially sent to alarms under the traditional policy approaches the number sent under AR.

For engines, Table 14.15 shows that at high alarm rates, the average number of responses per hour *increases* under AR, which implies that without AR, engine availability would be so low that, on the average, fewer than two engines would be dispatched.

Adding Companies. From Tables 14.15 and 14.16 it can be seen that under either the traditional policy or AR, adding new units has a greater effect on response times at high alarm rates than at low ones. Under the traditional policy, for example, the reduction in the average first-arriving ladder response time was about one second per additional ladder at five alarms per hour; five seconds per additional ladder at 30 alarms per hour.

The workload reductions for busy units, when companies were added under the traditional response policy, turned out to be considerably less than might be expected if the same work were distributed among more companies. Figure 14.18 shows the simulated workloads that resulted from using the traditional policy with 12 and 15 ladders, respectively, at different alarm rates, in the South Bronx. Below these curves is a curve that represents the anticipated average workload for the 15 ladder companies if the work performed by the 12 ladders were split among 15 companies. Notice, for example, that at 30 alarms per hour, each of the

14.4 Workload Problems in the New York City Fire Department

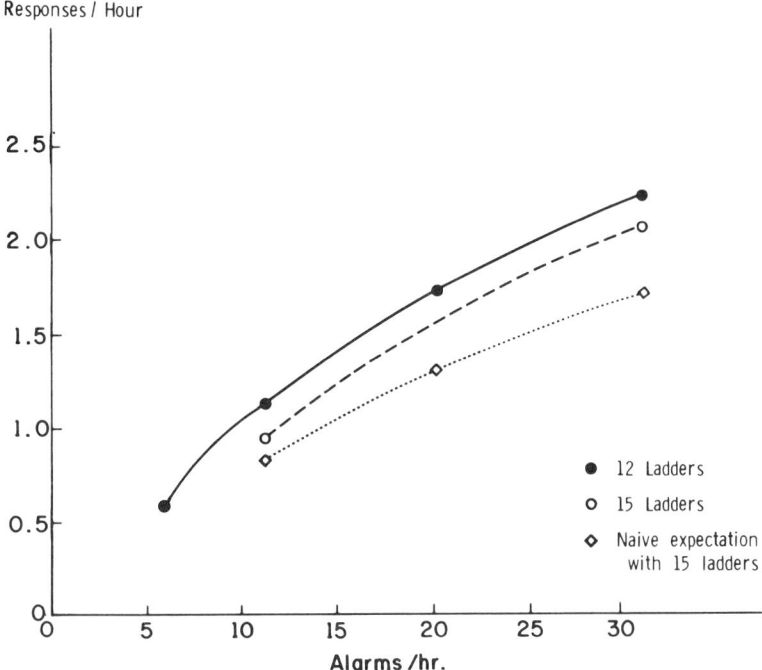

FIGURE 14.18. Simulated workload for South Bronx ladders under the traditional dispatching policy (no adaptive response).

12 ladders made an average of 2.072 responses. When three ladders are added, if the same work were to be redistributed, one would expect ($\frac{12}{15}$) × 2.072, or 1.658, responses per ladder per hour—a 20 percent reduction. However, the simulation with 15 ladders resulted in 1.942 responses per ladder per hour—only a 6 percent reduction. These results indicated that the main effect of the new ladders on the original ones was to make them available to answer alarms that had previously received only one ladder from the South Bronx, or had received a ladder from outside the region. (This effect can be predicted using the model described in Section 11.3.4.)

Combining the Two Policies. In mid-1969, at the time these simulation runs were made, there were 12 ladders and 18 engines in the South Bronx. Figures 14.19 and 14.20 show the effect on average response time of adding three ladders and three engines, and implementing adaptive response in the region. At low alarm rates, there were small improvements in the response times of the first-arriving ladder and the first- and second-arriving engines, coupled with a small worsening of the second-

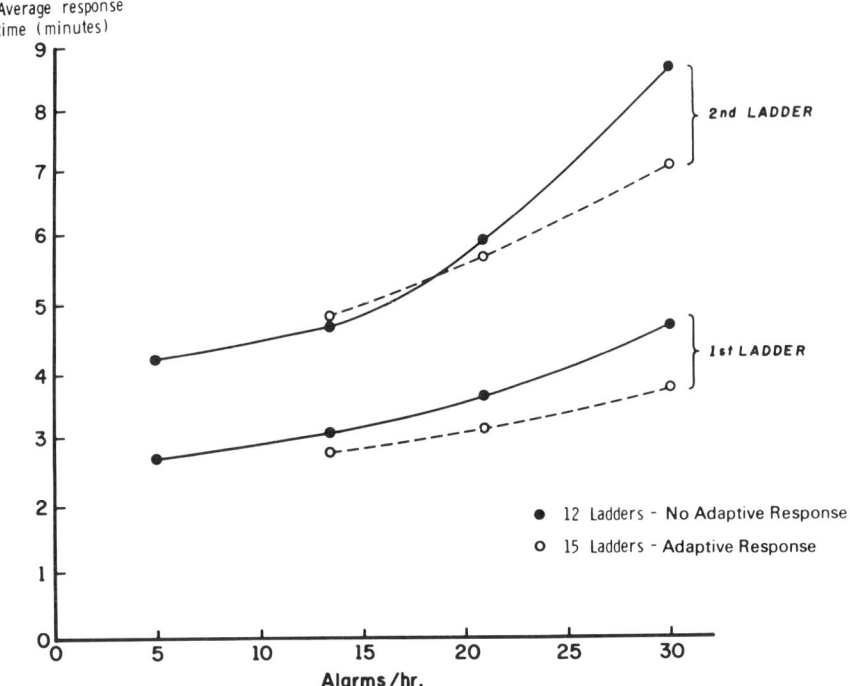

FIGURE 14.19. Simulated average ladder response times for the South Bronx. The two policies being compared are defined by the legend.

arriving ladder response time and a large worsening of third-arriving engine response time. At higher alarm rates, there were considerable improvements in the first-arriving ladder response time and the first- and second-arriving engine response times (especially in the latter). More importantly, above about 18 alarms per hour, the second-arriving ladder and third-arriving engine response times are also improved.

These results indicate that, from the point of view of response time, the new policy would be better than the traditional one during busy times of day, and not as good when the alarm rates were low.

Additional support for the policy of adding part-time companies and implementing AR only during the hours of high alarm rates came from a workload analysis. First it was assumed that a day consists of three eight-hour periods at each of the three highest alarm rates (with these high alarm rates meant to correspond to what could be expected in the near future). Next the result of adding one 24-hour unit was compared to adding three units that would work only eight hours each evening. The

14.4 Workload Problems in the New York City Fire Department

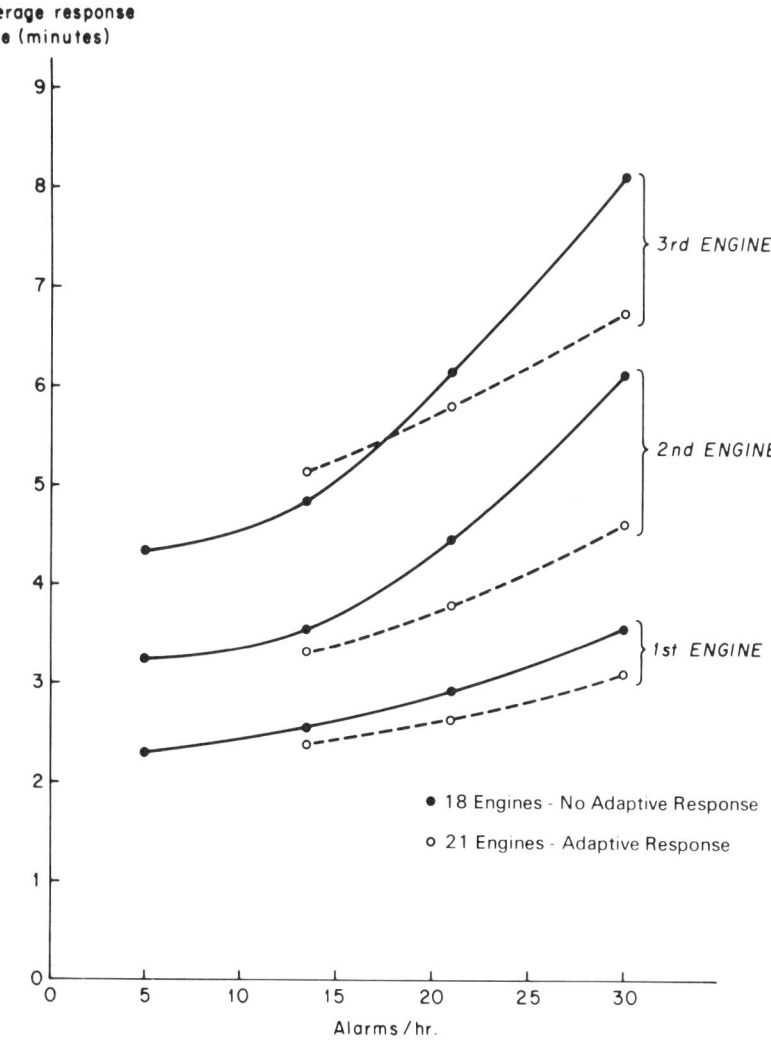

FIGURE 14.20. Simulated average engine response times for the South Bronx. The two policies being compared are defined by the legend.

base case average daily workload (with no additions) for South Bronx companies was 35 responses per ladder and 40 per engine. The workload reduction achieved by adding three ladder companies in the South Bronx in the evening was calculated to be about 1.74 responses per ladder per day (8 × (1.927 − 1.710)). Under AR, the addition of one ladder around the clock would reduce the average workload of a South Bronx ladder company by about 1.67 responses per day.[16] For South Bronx engines, the reduction from 40 average daily responses would be about 1.35 for one full-time engine were added, and about 1.46 if three evening-only engines were added.

Overall, by adding new companies and using AR during evening hours, there would be both a reduction in company workload and an improvement in average response time relative to the traditional policy. Using methods described in Chapter 13, the response-time improvements were found to be statistically significant.

14.4.5 Implementation

The tactical control units operated successfully for about two and a half years. Then, under union pressure arising out of contract negotiations, men stopped volunteering for service and the program was discontinued. Although a successful program ended, there were positive long-term effects. The loss of these units increased the pressure on the fire department to search for other means of improving deployment, eventually leading to a major reallocation of resources in November 1972. (See Ignall et al., 1975.) These changes—the disbanding of six companies and the permanent relocation of seven others—were based on an analysis using the square-root model described in Chapter 6. The initial AR program operated on a pilot basis in the South Bronx for about hree years, and was then expanded and extended to other areas of the city.

The simulation had an impact beyond its use in the negotiations. Department management began to accept—and would later rely on—analytical tools in making policy decisions. Important measures of performance were beginning to emerge. For the first time, estimates of fire company response times were developed and used. The notion of initial response adequacy became a new concern. The fact that department management questioned the assumption of constant travel speed in the simulation led to the travel-time experiments described in Chapter 6.

The simulation had a significant effect not only on the department, but on the fire project team as well. The insights derived from the early simulation runs suggested the structure of some analytical models later developed for initial dispatch and relocation. In short, in many ways the simulation analyses described in this case set the stage for the deployment work that was to follow.

---

[16] $1.67 = 8 \text{ hours} \times \sum_{i=1}^{3}$ (responses/hour/ladder in period i with 12 ladders − responses/hour/ladder in period i with 15 ladders)/$(15 - 12) = 8 \times (\frac{1}{3})$ {$(0.969 - 0.794) + (1.473 - 1.238) + (1.927 - 1.710)$}.

14.5 REDUCING DISPATCHING DELAYS IN A NEW YORK CITY COMMUNICATIONS OFFICE[17]

When this study began, in the summer of 1968, both the management and the dispatchers of the New York Fire Department recognized that there was a problem in the Brooklyn Communications Office: delays were beginning to occur in handling incoming alarms at certain times of the day.

The department's proposed solution was to improve the equipment in the office for the short run, and to introduce computer-aided dispatch for the long run. The dispatchers wanted more manpower.

An analyst at The New York City-Rand Institute was assigned to study the operations of the communications office. He observed the system over a period of several weeks, collected data, and developed a model of the dispatching operation. His analysis showed that the Brooklyn Communications Office was rapidly approaching an overloaded condition. Simple suggestions for improving the dispatching operation were tested, both in the model and at the office, and were found to reduce dispatching delays dramatically.

14.5.1 Background

This case deals with dispatching time. This is the critical interval between the receipt of an alarm in the communications office and the notification of units that they are to respond. It illustrates many of the steps in the systems analysis process discussed in Chapter 3. In particular, it stresses problem identification, and the development and use of a model in composing alternatives.

In the summer of 1968 when this study began, both the management and the dispatchers of the New York City Fire Department recognized a problem in the communications offices (C.O.s). Management's view was that the problem could be solved by updating equipment in the short run—for example, by replacing telegraph transmission with voice transmission, and through computerization in the longer run. At the same time, the dispatchers were demanding increases in manpower.

The New York City-Rand Institute became involved in 1968 when it was realized that the C.O.s were vulnerable to disruption or overload; that is, if one of the five borough offices were unable to function, the others might be unable to take on the additional load. With this in mind, one Institute analyst began studying the operations of the Brooklyn C.O.

---

[17] A more complete description of this case study is contained in Swersey (1973).

He observed the system over a period of several weeks, collecting data for both day and evening periods, and developing a model of the dispatching operations. In time he found that the Brooklyn office was, indeed, rapidly approaching the point of overload.

14.5.2 A Model of the Dispatching Operation

At the time of the study, six men worked in the Brooklyn C.O. When someone in Brooklyn pulled the handle of an alarm box it "rang" on a panel, and a dispatcher would count the number of rings to identify the number of the alarm box. When telephone reports of fires were received in the C.O., the reported street address of the incident was looked up in a street index file to determine the number of the nearest alarm box.

In either case, once the alarm box was identified, another man would retrieve the alarm assignment card for that box and pass it on to the dispatcher. The dispatcher would then check the status of the units listed on the card by looking at a status board, where each fire company was represented by a plastic chip. If he decided that the alarm represented a new incident and there were units available in quarters to respond, the box number would be transmitted by telegraph to the units in the firehouses. Other units in the field might be contacted by radio.

The dispatching procedure shown in Figure 14.21 is not entirely sequential, since some of its elements often occur simultaneously; yet the essence of the system is captured by the model shown in Figure 14.22. The model assumes that the process can be divided into three stages: (1) receipt of the alarm, (2) decisionmaking, and (3) transmission of the orders. An alarm is received at the first stage. If the dispatchers are busy, it waits, joining a queue. After the alarm assignment card is retrieved, it goes to the decisionmaker at Stage 2. He looks at the status board and decides whether it is a new alarm, and if so, which units to send. Here again, if the decisionmaker is busy, the alarm waits. Finally, it goes to a third stage, transmission of orders, which is the actual notification of units to respond.

A visitor to a C.O. might not initially perceive the flow of alarms as shown in the model. Busy dispatching offices are typically noisy places where a great deal of simultaneous activity creates an atmosphere of apparent confusion. A key part of this analysis was the insight (based on days of observation) that the system could be represented as shown. The model is not, however, exact in every detail. It assumes that an alarm progresses through the three stages in sequence. In reality, there were times when two or more stages occurred at once, particularly during slow periods. For example, when all units were in quarters and an alarm was received, the telegraph signal was sometimes sent immediately. How-

14.5 Reducing Dispatching Delays in a Communications Office

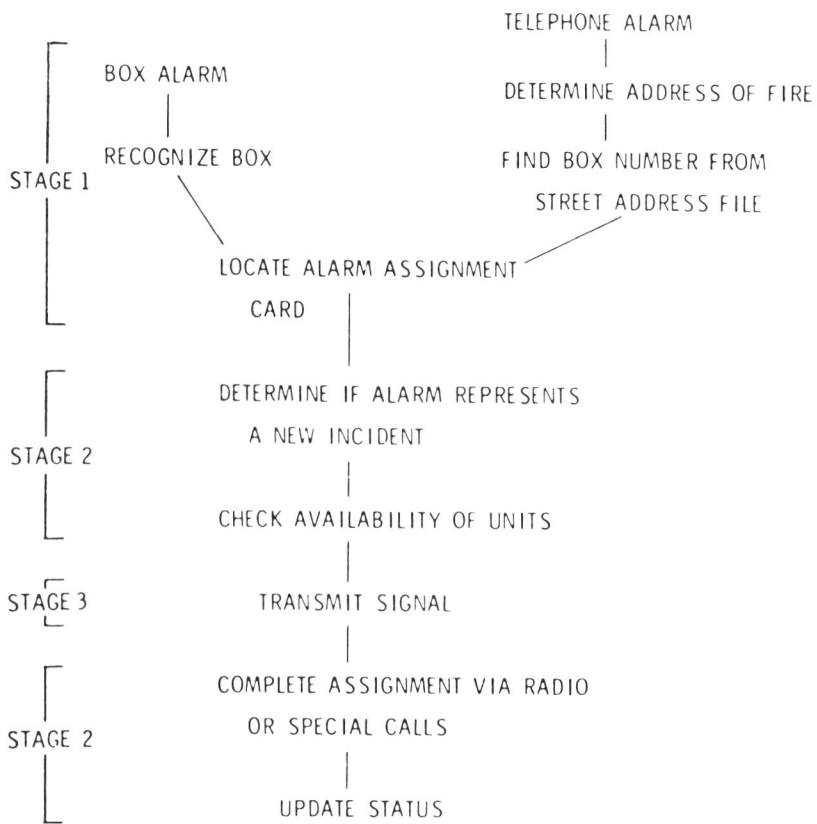

FIGURE 14.21. Dispatching procedure used in the Brooklyn C.O.

ever, as the alarm rate increased, the system operated more and more in the way that the model indicates.

Given this model, the variable of interest is dispatching time, the time from receipt of the alarm to its transmission to the companies. The dispatching time is the sum of the waiting time and service time for all stages. It takes a certain amount of time to identify the alarm box, to answer the telephone, to figure out who to send, and so on. Each of these times is distributed probabilistically; that is, there is a certain probability that any one of them will be longer than 10 seconds, longer than 20 seconds, and so on. The total dispatching time will also have a distribution that depends on how quickly alarms come in, whether they are telephone or box alarms, the number of men who are answering phones or identifying alarm boxes, and the distributions of service times at each stage.

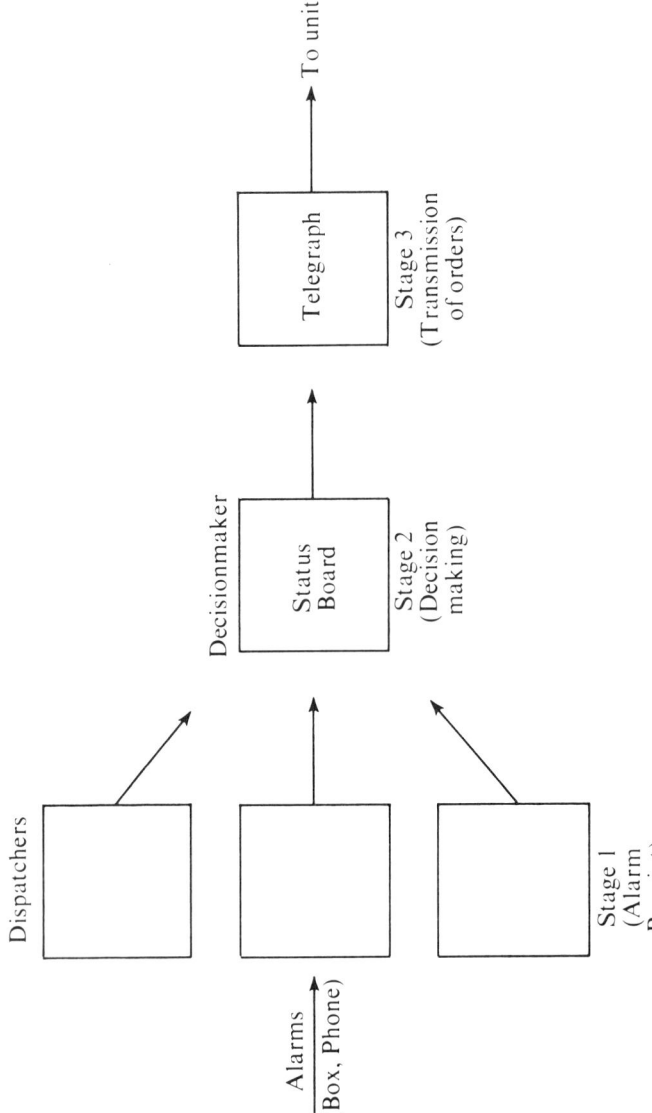

FIGURE 14.22. A multistage queuing model of the dispatching process outlined in Figure 14.21.

14.5 Reducing Dispatching Delays in a Communications Office

As input to the model, information was required on alarm rates and on how long it takes to perform Stages 1 and 2. Data collection took about three months. Collecting data for Stage 1 of the model was straightforward; but for Stage 2, the task was more difficult and was done in several phases, as is discussed later in this section.

Exponential distributions were used in the model, since they were found to fit the data quite well in most cases. The particular form of the distributions is not crucial to the results and insights obtained from the study, since the latter derive from the fact that Stage 2 service time increases as a function of the number of incidents in progress.

Arrivals of Alarms. It was assumed that alarms occur according to a Poisson process with a rate that is constant over intervals of about one hour. Figure 14.23 shows the observed distribution having a mean of 1.66 arrivals per five-minute interval, which was the average observed during that period. The Poisson distribution fits the observed data extremely well, as is shown, not only by the figure, but also by a chi-square test (Swersey, 1973).

The Distribution of Service Time at Stage 1. It was found that, for each task, exponential random variables, offset by what appears to be the minimum time to perform the task, fit the observed data well. Table 14.17 presents summary statistics on the observed data for each of the four

FIGURE 14.23. Distribution of alarm arrivals in Brooklyn, C.O. October 21, 1968, 5 to 8 P.M. Dotted line represents actual; unbroken line represents Poisson distribution.

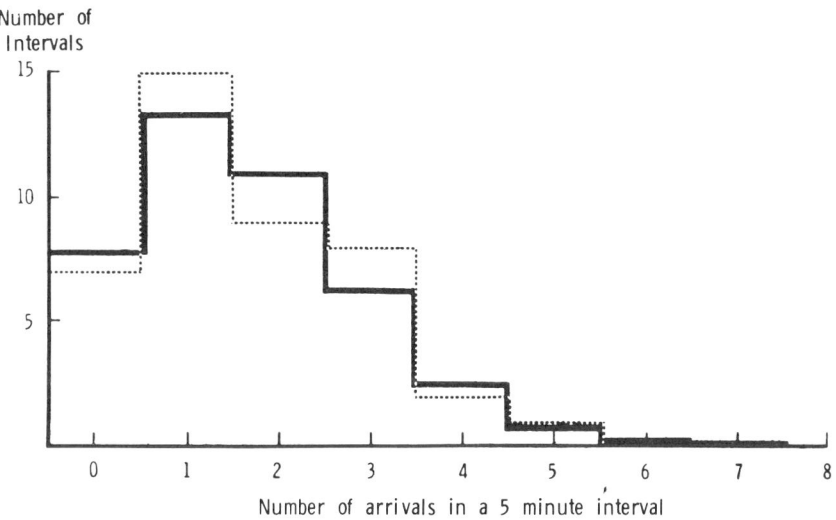

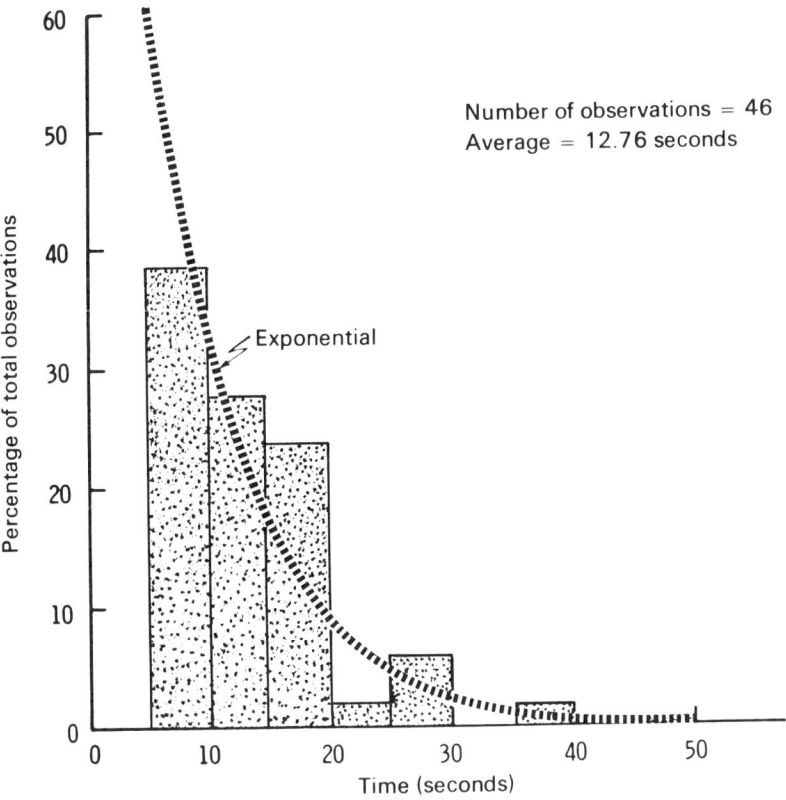

FIGURE 14.24. Histogram of the required time to identify an incoming alarm box.

tasks in Stage 1. Figures 14.24–14.27 show graphically how well an exponential distribution fits the observed data for each of the tasks. In each case a chi-square test of the goodness of fit led to acceptance of the hypothesis that the data were a sample from the exponential distribution shown in the figure.

The Distribution of Service Times at Stage 2. The critical part of the model is the second stage. While observing the system in operation, it appeared that the time between the dispatcher looking at the alarm assignment card and the transmission of the signal by telegraph was usually quite short. This was because the alarm rate during the observation periods was comparatively low. It was apparent, however, that the service time at the second stage did not end with the transmission of the alarm. The dispatcher had to spend some additional time before he was ready to process another alarm. This time was used to contact units on

14.5 Reducing Dispatching Delays in a Communications Office

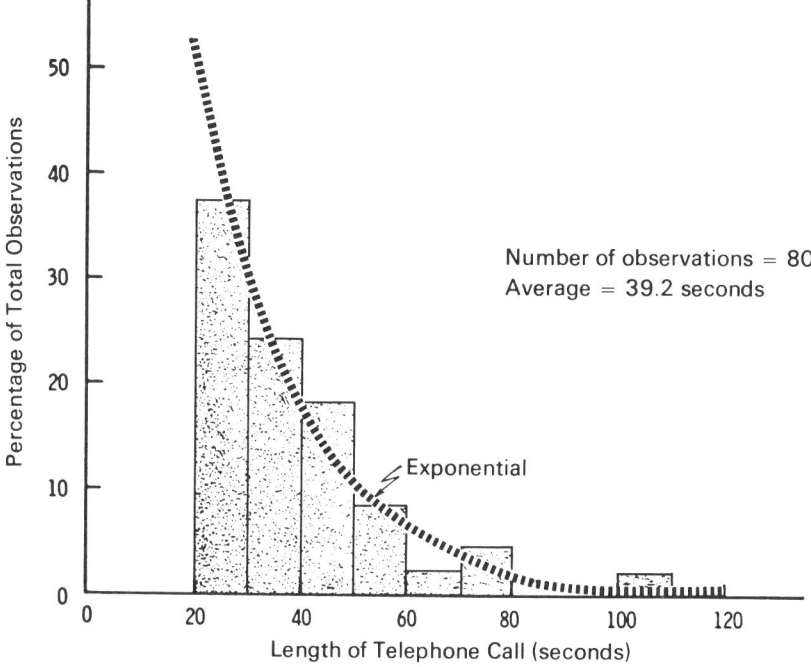

FIGURE 14.25. Histogram of the length of telephone calls.

the radio and to update the status of the units sent to the alarm. Therefore, the service time at the second stage was divided into two parts: T_1, the time until initial dispatch of units, and T_2, the time from initial dispatch until completion of the assignment and updating of the status board.

It also became apparent that the time to dispatch units (T_1) increased with the number of incidents in progress. (Actually, it increased with the number of companies busy, but it is simpler to look at the number of incidents in progress than to count the number of busy companies.) The

TABLE 14.17. Service times for Stage 1 tasks at the Brooklyn Communications Office.

Task	Minimum Time (seconds)	Average Time (seconds)	Number of Observations
Identify incoming alarm box	5	12.76	46
Receive telephone report of fire	20	39.2	80
Find closest alarm box using street address file	9	24.6	43
Locate alarm assignment card	5	9.45	62

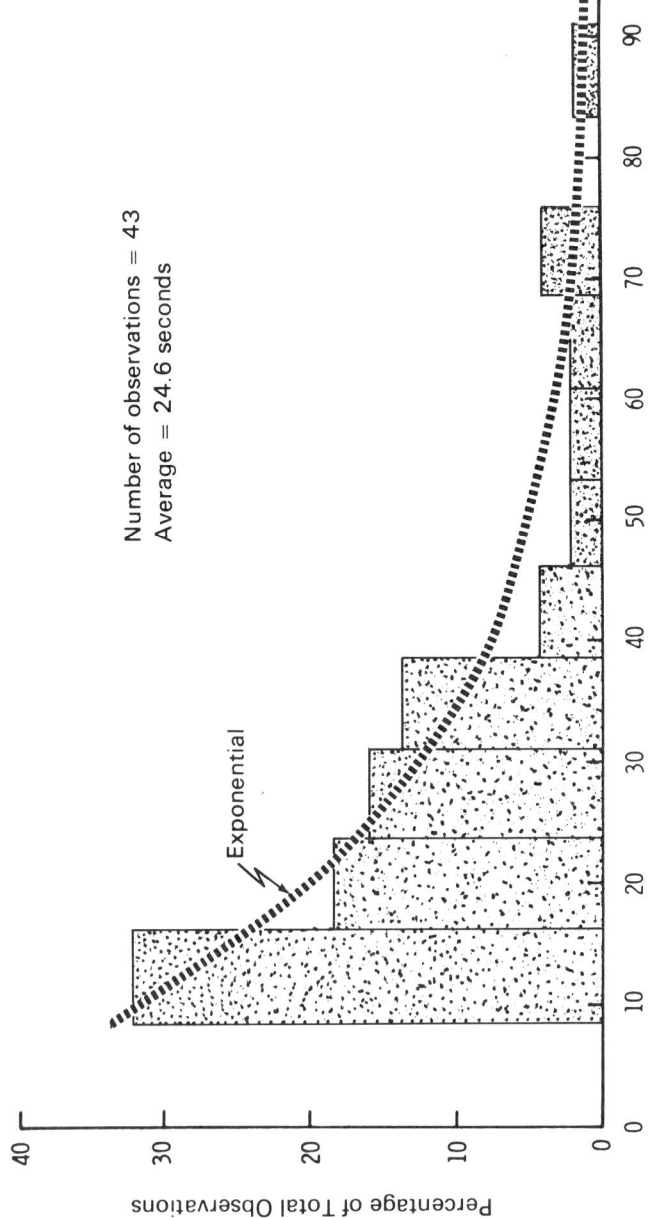

FIGURE 14.26. Histogram of the time to find the closest alarm box using street address file.

14.5 Reducing Dispatching Delays in a Communications Office

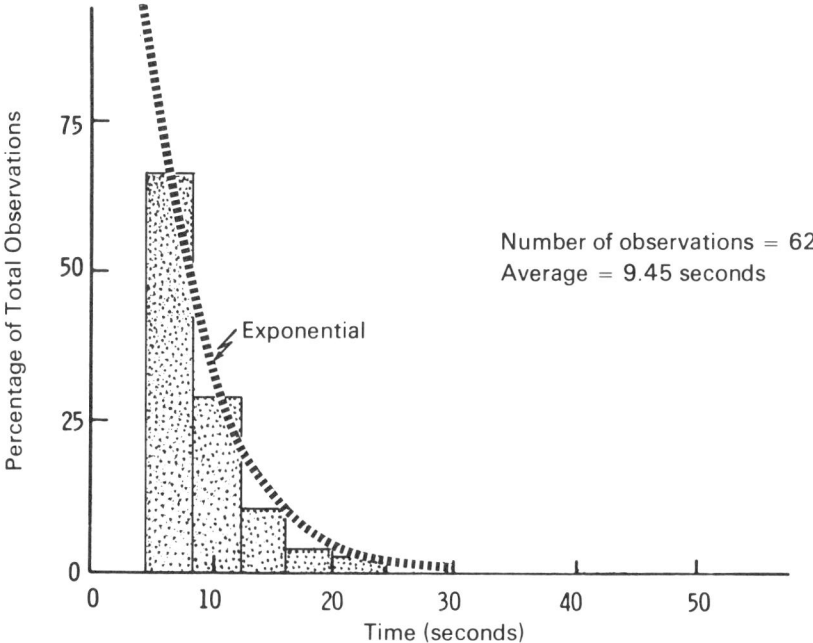

FIGURE 14.27. Histogram of the time to locate the alarm assignment card.

dispatcher had to check the availability of the units in quarters. With more incidents in progress, this takes longer. Also, the dispatcher had to determine whether or not an alarm was a new one. If nothing was happening in the field, he would know that each alarm is a new alarm. But if there were five or ten incidents in progress, each new incident had to be checked against old ones. Figure 14.28 shows how T_1 increased with the number of incidents in progress. In this case, we fit a straight line to the data. Given a certain number of in-progress incidents, the time to make the decision is assumed to be exponentially distributed (Figure 14.29).

The second part of the Stage 2 service time, T_2, also increased with the number of incidents in progress. It did so first because of the greater probability of having to call units on the radio. The more busy units there were, the higher was the probability that it would be necessary to call one. At the same time, radio communication slowed down because more units were competing to use the same radio channel. In addition, companies returning to their quarters from incidents would telephone the C.O. to report their new status. The dispatcher at the status board would not want to interrupt what he was doing, but he needed this new status information to make decisions. To facilitate data collection, T_2 was de-

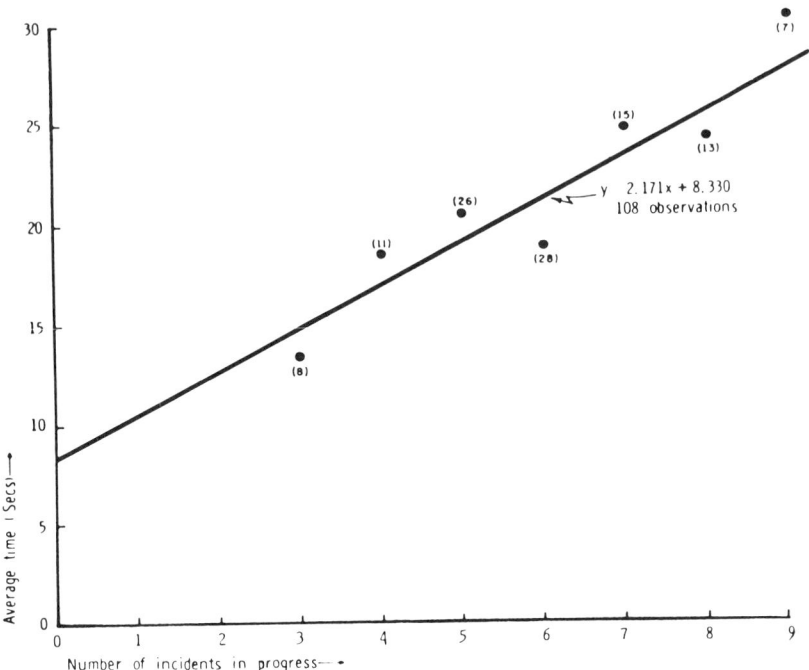

FIGURE 14.28. Relationship at Stage 2 between time until initial dispatch and number of incidents in progress.

termined by measuring the total Stage 2 time (Figure 14.30) and subtracting T_1 from it (Figure 14.28). Again it was assumed that, for a given some number of incidents in progress, T_2 is exponentially distributed.

To simulate the decisionmaking time at Stage 2, it was necessary to keep track of the number of incidents in progress. To do so, the duration of incidents had to be estimated. Figure 14.31 shows the distribution of the duration of incidents, not including alarms for which three engines or two or more ladders were needed. (Such fires were rare, occurring about 1 percent of the time; their durations were obtained from other data.)

14.5.3 Simulation Experiments and Recommended Improvements

A computer model that simulated the operation of the first two stages of the queuing system in Figure 14.22 was written in SIMSCRIPT I.5. It uses the task-time and incident-duration distributions developed in the previous section.

The simulation was checked by seeing how well the simulated dispatching times matched some actual dispatching times. To do so, actual dis-

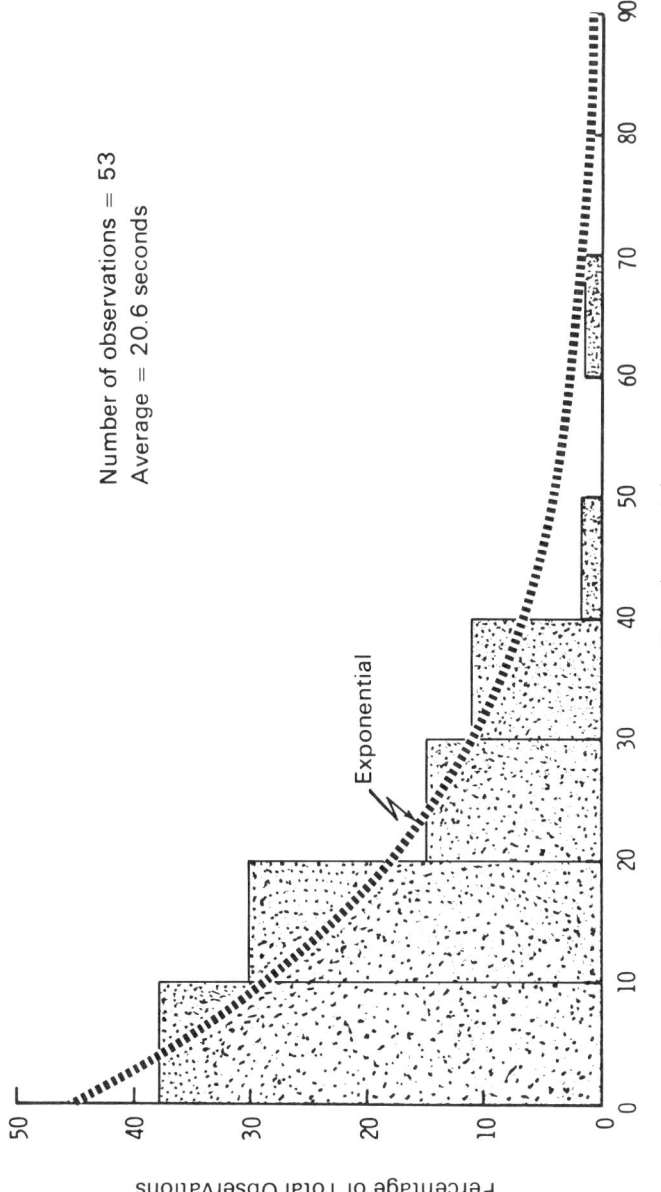

FIGURE 14.29. Histogram of the time at Stage 2 until initial dispatch with five or six incidents in progress.

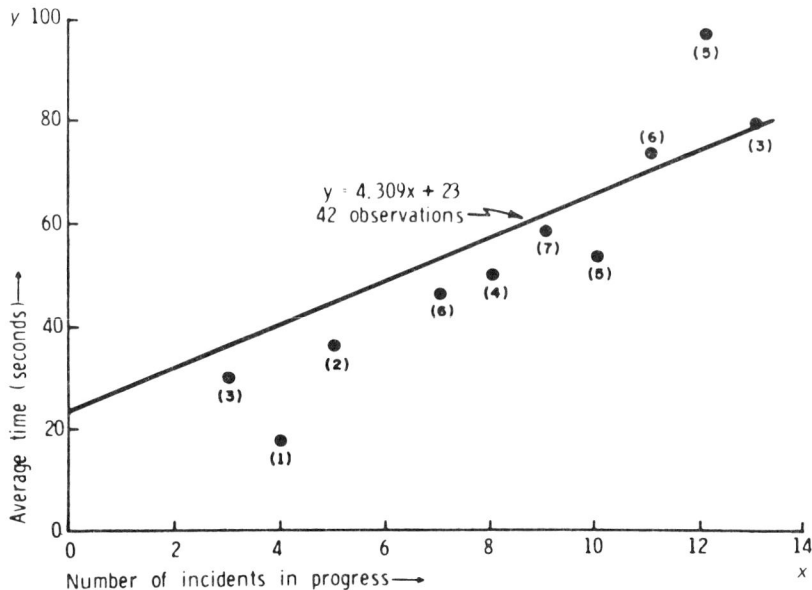

FIGURE 14.30. Relationship between the total time at stage 2 and the number of incidents in progress.

patching time (the time from the first ring of the box or telephone until the first tap of the telegraph) was measured at the Brooklyn C.O. over a three-hour period on October 22, 1968. For the test period, the alarm rate was 22.4 alarms per hour, with 26.8 percent telephone alarms. The simulation was run at the same rate with the same percentage of telephone alarms, and 5000 alarms[18] were simulated. In Figure 14.32 the simulation results are compared to the actual test data. The simulation predicted an average dispatching time of 90.6 seconds with an estimated standard deviation of the mean of 2.06. The actual average dispatching time was 87.1 seconds, with an estimated standard deviation of 8.9. The fit between the actual distribution and the simulation curve thus appears to be quite good. An exception is the interval 20–30 seconds. The simulation underestimated the probability that dispatching time falls in this interval because it assumed that each alarm is processed sequentially through Stages 1 and 2. When few incidents were in progress, the two stages often took place simultaneously. However, this "error" was not a serious one, since the tail of the dispatching time distribution is the main concern.

---

[18] The number of dispatchers on duty during the test period was about equivalent to having two dispatchers at Stage 1. We say "equivalent" since during actual operations, one dispatcher may perform tasks relating to both stages.

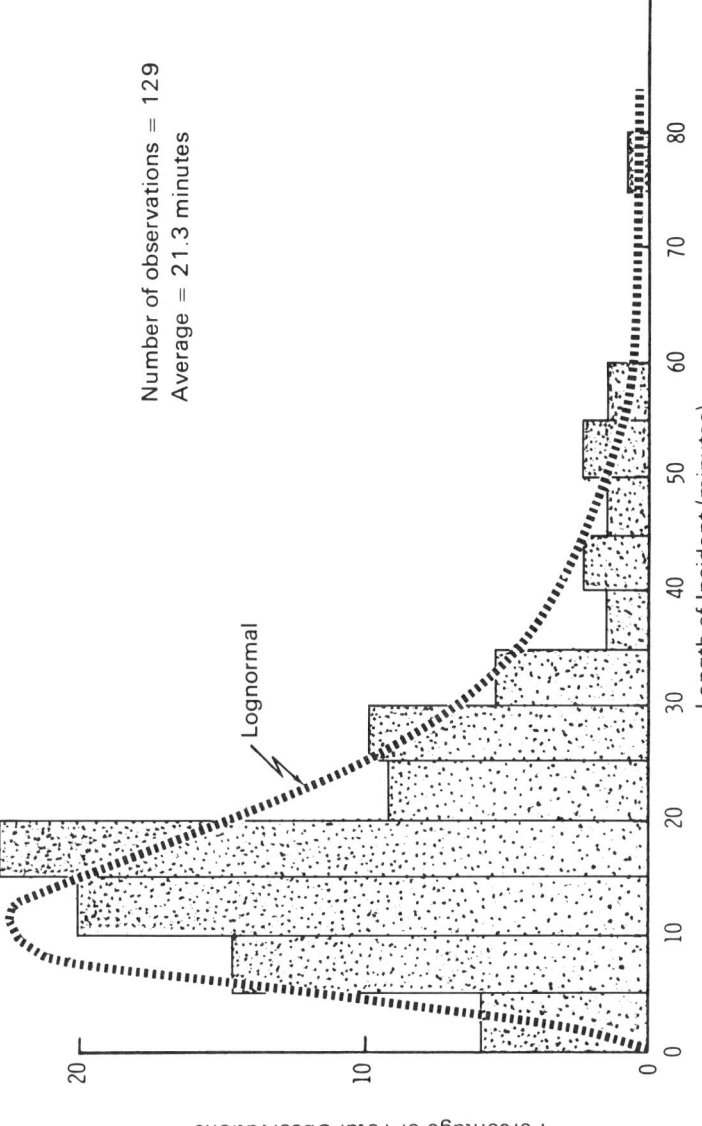

FIGURE 14.31. Histogram of the duration of incidents that required less than three engines and two ladders. Incident duration was measured from initial dispatch until the incident was removed from status board.

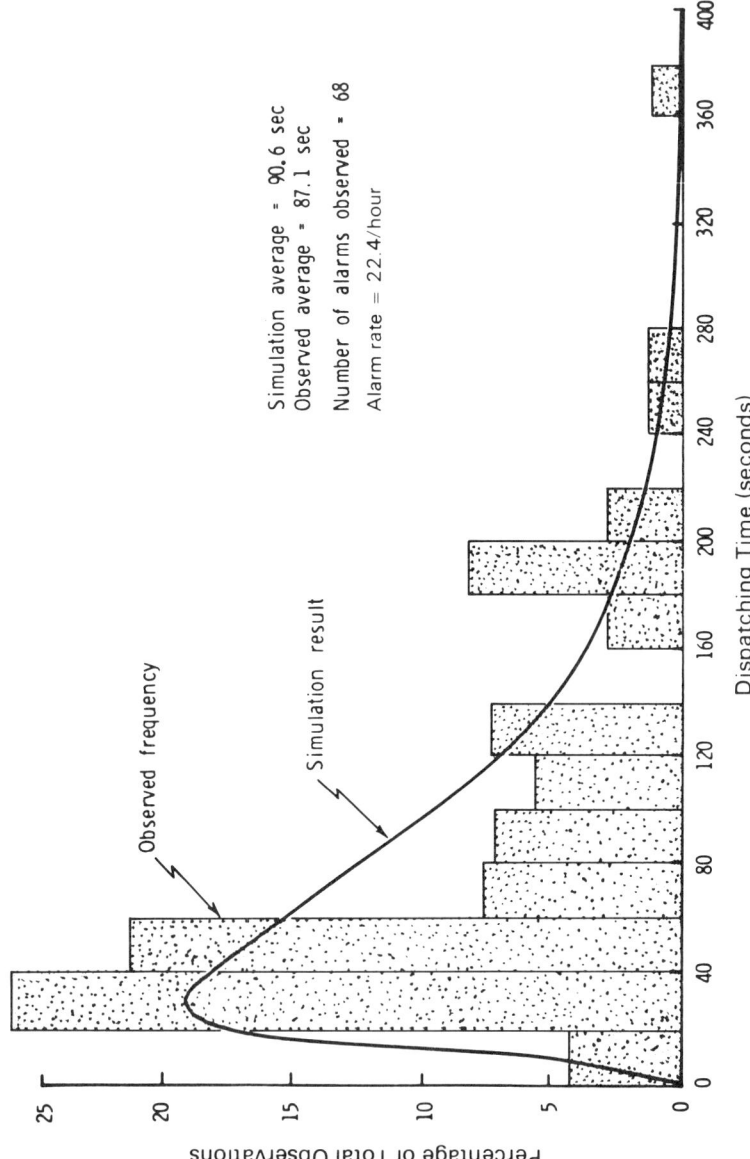

FIGURE 14.32. Comparison of the simulation predictions to actual.

14.5 Reducing Dispatching Delays in a Communications Office

Further simulation runs were made for different alarm rates with two dispatchers at Stage 1 and 25 percent telephone alarms. Table 14.18 shows the results of these runs and gives, for each alarm rate, the average dispatching time and the number of alarms simulated. The relationship between alarm rate and the simulation predictions of average dispatching time is shown graphically in Figure 14.33. The y-intercept for this curve was determined by calculating the sum of the expected service time at Stage 1 and the expected service time until initial dispatch (T_1), both given zero incidents in progress. This value is 40.9 seconds, and the curve passes through this point. The curve rises fairly slowly as the alarm rate increases up to a value of 25 alarms per hour, at which point the average dispatching time is 1.7 minutes. Here the dispatching-time curve starts to become steeper. Average dispatching time reaches about 3 minutes at 30 alarms per hour, and about 9 minutes at 35 alarms per hour.

These results do not imply that if someone called to report his house on fire during a period when the arrival was 35 alarms per hour, it would

FIGURE 14.33. Relationship between average dispatching time and arrival rate of alarms.

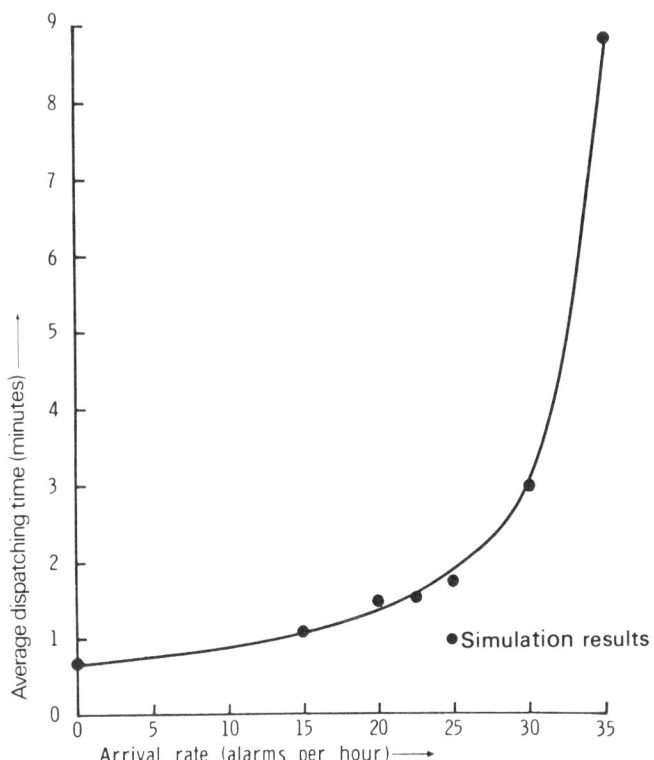

TABLE 14.18. Brooklyn Communications Office Simulation Results: Average dispatching times at various alarm rates.

Alarm Rate	Number of Alarms Simulated	Average Dispatching Time (Seconds)	Estimated Standard Deviation of Average Dispatching Time
15	5,000	65.2	1.03
20	5,000	87.4	2.70
22.4	5,000	90.6	2.20
25	20,000	104.5	2.25
30	5,000	177.7	13.15
35	5,000	528.2	75.80

take 9 minutes to transmit the alarm. On the contrary, telephone alarms for house fires would and did receive immediate priority. However, house fires reported by street box (and not followed by telephone calls) obviously did not.

Table 14.19 gives simulation results for the tail of the distribution of dispatching time for varying alarm rates, all with 25-percent telephone alarms and two dispatchers at Stage 1. At 20 alarms per hour, about 20 percent of the alarms took longer than 2 minutes to get a response. At 25 alarms per hour, the figure is 29 percent; at 30 alarms per hour, it increased to 49 percent; and at 35 alarms per hour, more than 75 percent of the alarms had dispatching times greater than 2 minutes.

Only 2.5 percent of the alarms required more than 5 minutes dispatch-

TABLE 14.19. Brooklyn Communications Office Simulation Results: Percentage of alarms with dispatching time greater than T minutes for various alarm rates.

	Alarm Rate (alarms per hour)			
T	20	25	30	35
2	20.7	28.9	49.1	76.1
3	9.0	14.0	32.7	65.8
4	4.5	7.4	22.8	57.9
5	2.5	4.1	16.3	51.0
8	0	1.0	6.8	34.7

14.5 Reducing Dispatching Delays in a Communications Office

ing time at a rate of 20 alarms per hour. At 30 alarms per hour, about 15 percent fell into this category, and at 35 alarms per hour, about 50 percent.

Finally, none of the alarms required more than 8 minutes for a response at a dispatching rate of 20 alarms per hour, while at 30 alarms per hour, about 7 percent experienced delays of that length; and at 35 alarms per hour, the system became so busy that about 35 percent did.

That the problem arises at Stage 2 is illustrated in Figure 14.34, which breaks down the components of average dispatching time. At 30 alarms per hour, there was an average delay of about 1 second at Stage 1, with two dispatchers receiving incoming alarms. This average results from a probability of delay of only 0.04, and an average delay of 17 seconds for those alarms that were delayed. The average service time at Stage 1 was 35 seconds. The major component of dispatching time was contributed by the delays at the status board, which averaged almost 2 minutes; the second longest time was the total service time at Stage 2, which averaged 74 seconds. Thus, at 30 alarms per hour, less than 20 percent of the total

FIGURE 14.34. Average duration of component times at key points in the dispatching system.

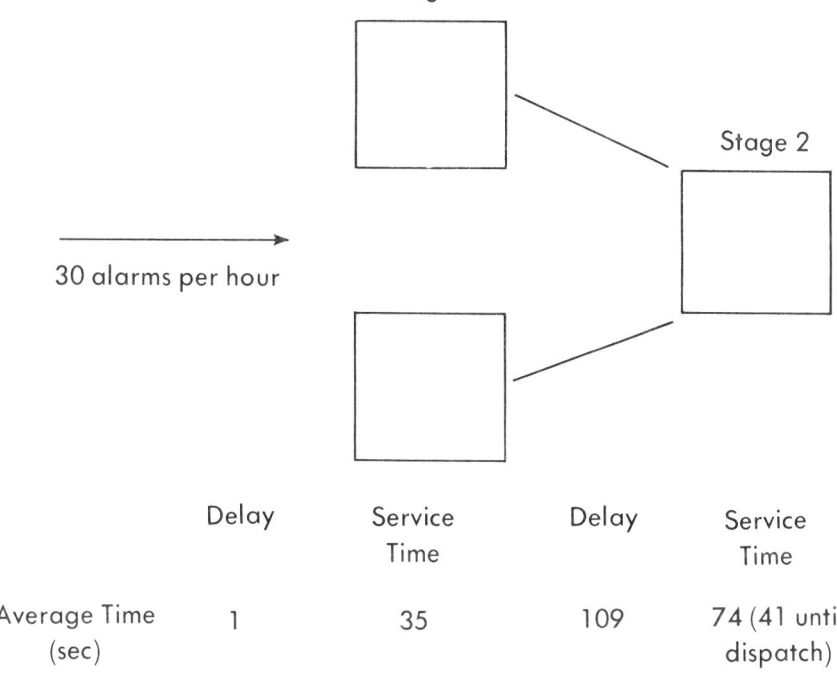

time that an alarm spent in the system was spent in Stage 1; more than 80 percent was spent waiting for service and being served at Stage 2.

14.5.4 Observations

The simulation results of the preceding sections should not be viewed as an exact description of the behavior of the Brooklyn C.O., or of C.O.s in general. Data for the model were gathered at the Brooklyn C.O., and consisted of observations of several different groups of dispatchers with no attempt to differentiate between the performance of the different groups. However, after allowing for these uncertainties, the following observations are inescapable.

The system capacity was being approached. At the time of this study, an alarm rate of 20 per hour in Brooklyn was considered a busy night, while a rate of 25 per hour was considered extremely busy. This means that the alarm rate was approaching the neck of the curve (Figure 14.33) as well as the capacity of the system (i.e., the point at which delays become intolerable). The curve is so steep because the Stage 2 service time increased with the number of incidents in progress.

Thus, although as many as 180 telegraph signals per hour could be transmitted, the capacity of the system was reached long before the rate reached this level, because of the Stage 2 bottleneck.

Adding dispatchers at Stage 1 would have had little effect on dispatching time. Once the probability of a delay at Stage 1 is reduced almost to zero (as in Figure 14.34), there would be no advantage in adding men. The model did, however, assume that all alarms that were received, were transmitted. In reality, there were additional alarms that were received but that did not go beyond Stage 1. Examples are the same box ringing one or more times in a short period of time, and a single fire generating several telephone calls reporting it. The difference is not great, however, and the conclusion remains the same: that the problem was not at Stage 1 but at Stage 2, the status board position.

A visitor to a C.O. is easily misled. Attention is drawn to those areas where box alarms are received. There is a great deal of noise associated with ringing boxes and telephones, and there is much activity related to identifying alarm boxes, answering telephones, and determining the locations of incidents reported by telephone. However, the problem is not in receiving the alarms, but in sending them out.

Major delays occurred at Stage 2. The bottleneck in the system was at the status-board position. Decisions were essentially made one at a time, by one man, and the decision time increased with the number of incidents in progress.

One of the major reasons for this was that the status board did not reflect the true status of units. As the number of incidents in progress increased, the probability increased that one or more units on the first line of the alarm assignment card were not available in quarters. In most cases, these units were listed on the status board as being at an incident and, therefore, technically unavailable. However, unless a unit was actually working at an incident, there was a good chance that it was available to respond to a new incident. Because of this, the decisionmaker could contact the units on the radio, determine their status, and direct them to the new incident if they were available. If this procedure was not followed, either an incomplete response would result, or the decisionmaker would search down the alarm assignment card for units that were farther away from the incident.

The System Adapted to Heavy Workloads. The simulation predicted that at alarm rates beyond 30 per hour, the average dispatching time would increase rapidly. There is evidence that at such alarm rates the system began to be severely strained, and that it reacted to the strain in two important ways. During several heavy alarm periods at the Brooklyn C.O., it was observed that some incoming street-box alarms were not counted by a dispatcher, and were therefore lost. This results partly from deficiencies in manpower and equipment, but it is also a means of reducing the strain on the system. By losing some alarms, the system adapts to an arrival rate that it is better able to handle.

An inspection of alarm records at the Brooklyn office showed that at times, a reduced response was sent to some street-box alarms during high-alarm periods. Although this procedure was inconsistent with the department policy, sending only one engine, or one engine and one ladder, reduced the service time at the status board and therefore the dispatching time as well.

14.5.5 Alternatives for Improving the System

Reductions in dispatching time, especially during peak periods, could have been achieved by either (1) reducing the service time at Stage 2, or (2) increasing the number of Stage 2 dispatchers.[19]

---

[19] A peak period is somewhat arbitrarily defined as four or more hours where the alarm rate averages at least 25 per hour. There were ten such periods in July, 1972.

Reducing the Service Time at the Status Board. The service time at the status board position could have been decreased in the following ways:

1. *Provision of more current status information.* A substantial part of the decisionmaker's time was spent in determining the availability of units that were not in quarters, but were on the air. An electronic status reporting system would have enabled units to transmit this status information rapidly without using the radio channel. An automatic system also could have been used by units in quarters to replace the then-current voice method.
2. *Faster status updating.* Status information was received from units both in the field and in quarters. Within the C.O. this information was relayed to the status board (either verbally or by messenger) or, particularly in the case of radio reports, it was lost. It would have been an improvement if the dispatcher receiving new status information could transfer it directly onto the status board; for example, by activating switches connected to lights on the status board.
3. *Improved radio usage.* As the alarm rate and the number of busy units increased, the single radio channel in each borough began to overload. The capacity of the radio system could have been increased somewhat by coding radio messages; for example, by replacing the message "available on the air" by the code 10-8. Beyond that, further improvement requires an additional radio channel.
4. *Improvements in physical layout.* The communications offices generally were not arranged to facilitate an orderly flow of information. Because they were designed at a time when the alarm rate was extremely low, and because verbal communication is not difficult during such periods, there was little reason to consider the configuration of men and equipment. However, with increasing alarm rates, this becomes essential.

Adding a Stage 2 Dispatcher. In conjunction with the possible improvements cited above, dispatching time in busy periods could have been significantly reduced by adding another decisionmaking dispatcher at Stage 2 of the queuing system. This could have been accomplished by dividing the borough into two parts, with a separate decisionmaking dispatcher responsible for the alarms and units in each half (Figure 14.35). At the point in the process after the alarm assignment card has been located, it could be presented to the dispatcher responsible for the area in which the box lies. (The cards could be marked to facilitate this.)

Ideally, one would divide the borough so that the alarm rate in each half is about he same. However, because of the steepness of the average dispatching time curve, it would not be necessary to do so to achieve

14.5 Reducing Dispatching Delays in a Communications Office

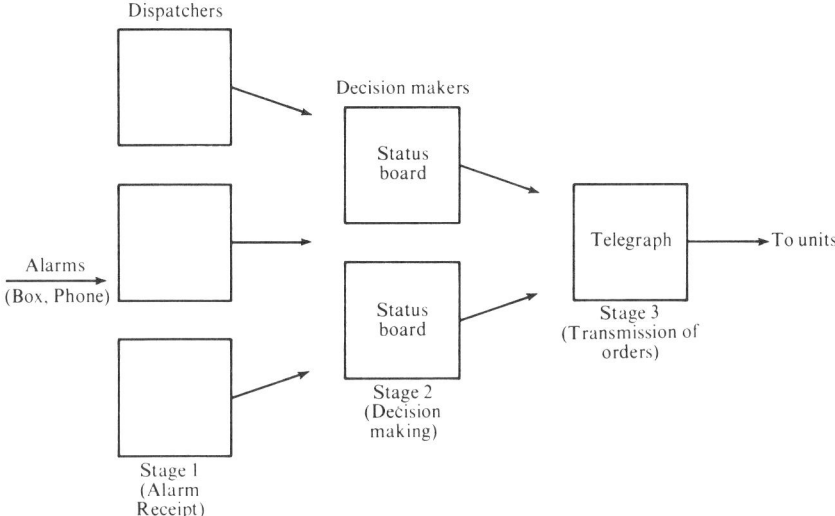

FIGURE 14.35. A new dispatching configuration with two decisionmaking dispatchers in Stage 2.

significant reductions in dispatching time. For example, for a rate of 35 alarms per hour, if the borough were divided so that 70 percent of the alarms fell in one half, the rate through the dispatcher handling that half would be only 21 alarms per hour, with a rate of 14 alarms per hour through the other dispatcher.

In dividing the borough, a difficulty might arise when an alarm draws on units from both halves. However, tests of the procedure (described in the following section) show that this overlap problem is not serious.

14.5.6 Testing the New Procedures

A series of tests were performed at the Brooklyn C.O. during February and May of 1969. The borough was divided into two parts, with approximately a 60 percent–40 percent split in the alarm rate. A more even division, which was avoided, would have caused the dividing line to fall in a high-demand area.

Initially, the concept of two decisionmaking dispatchers was tested using two separate status boards. After three evenings of experimentation, a single status board was used—divided, but with all units listed in the center section. The advantages of this arrangement were that it eased communication between the two decisionmakers and allowed one decisionmaker to operate alone during slow periods. Because the two decisionmakers were side by side, and because each had access to all the companies, each could easily locate and dispatch units from outside his area, thereby lessening the boundary problem. During this same time, 27 alarms were transmitted in one half-hour period, and 43 in one hour-long period, with no appreciable delays. Except for special evenings (e.g., on July 4th), when a reduced response policy was in effect, these were the highest dispatching rates ever experienced until that time.

14.5.7 Implementation

In July of 1969, Brooklyn was split into two parts for dispatching purposes, and the divided status board was introduced. The insights derived from this study also had an effect on the department's plans for a computerized dispatching system. Plans were developed for a new system, rather than for computerization of the old one. The new plans recognized the need for faster Stage 2 service time and included digital status reporting from the field. In addition, procedures were developed to allow for several decisionmakers and the simultaneous processing of alarms.

As a result of the work, there was a greater recognition by department management of the importance of C.O. operations. Although the dispatchers' union asked in the past, and has continued to ask, for more personnel, the new procedures now enable more effective use to be made of additional manpower.

In addition to providing answers to a particular problem, the analysis well illustrates the feedback "loop" in the systems analysis procedure. The study began with the formulation of the problem. But what was seen as the original problem—the vulnerability of the system to overloading—was actually part of a larger problem. It became clear that the system inherently had a limited capacity and that major improvements could be made. The process was continuous: developing a model, collecting data, improving the model, collecting more data, and so on. The model served as a framework for observation, giving the analyst a structured way of looking at the system. To build a realistic model, one must understand the operation of the system; trying to construct the model aids in developing such understanding. In all of the work that has been described in this book, observing the system has played an important role; but never more so than in this study.

Research History of the Rand Fire Project

INITIAL DEPLOYMENT RESEARCH FOR THE NEW YORK FIRE DEPARTMENT

Our work began in January 1968, in a political context that has been well described by Greenberger, Crenson, and Crissey (1976, Chapter 8). The first tasks for Edward Blum, the first project leader, were to establish the scope of work and to assemble a project team. Most of us[1] were hired from outside Rand and had no previous experience with fire-related research. In fact, there was virtually no opportunity for the project team to have previously worked on fire deployment analysis, since this field was practically nonexistent at the time. The only major exceptions were studies being conducted in Great Britain at the Fire Research Station and the Home Office.

Our initial research topics naturally focused on the problems of our client, the New York City Fire Department. As described by Blum (1972), we recognized the need to develop a strong analytical basis for our work—which would require several years' effort—and at the same time, we were under pressure to provide immediate solutions to pressing problems. The scope of research was therefore designed to cover a mix of short-term and long-term studies.

One reason for urgency was that the Fire Department was facing a rapid increase in alarm rates. The number of fire alarms per year had

---

[1] By early 1969, the project staff included Archibald, Blum, Carter, Chaiken, Dodd, Ignall, Held, Keeney, Rolph, Shanesy, Stevenson, and Swersey. See Preface for the full list of project members.

tripled over the preceding decade and, as if to underscore the point, during 1968 the alarm rate skyrocketed (Section 14.4 and Figure 8.19). As described in Chapter 8, the 1968 phenomenon turned out to be a one-year aberration that was subsequently handled in our demand analysis by including an "indicator variable" that equaled one for dates after 1967, and equaled zero for dates in 1967 and earlier years. But at the time, prudent adminstrators had to consider the possibility that the numbers of fire alarms might continue to increase as they had in 1968, as well as how to meet the deployment problems that had already become serious by 1968.

With the increasing alarm rate as a driving force, the major initial deployment-related research issues were quite clear:

How could future alarm rates be predicted so that realistic planning could take place? What were the underlying causes of the increase in alarm rates?

How could the communications offices (dispatch centers) adapt to the increasing workload? Not only were delays occurring in handling incoming alarms, but the simultaneous unavailability of nearby companies was creating a need for relocations that had not been preplanned. In the context of the late 1960s, the possibility of purposive physical disruption of the communications office was also a matter of concern. The consensus generally was that new equipment, including some form of computer assistance for the dispatchers, would be needed.

How could firefighting resources be reallocated, especially to improve service and balance workload? A few companies were responding to so many alarms that occasional physical exhaustion of the firefighters was a distinct future possibility. These companies were sometimes experiencing entire tours that offered no opportunity for a meal. Evidently, either additional companies would be needed, the existing companies would have to become more efficient through changes in deployment or technology, or part of the workload would have to be transferred from the busiest companies to less busy ones.

While there was some change in emphasis over the ensuing years, these remained the primary topics of deployment research for the New York Fire Department: analysis of incidence and the underlying causes of changes in incidence; management information and control systems; and allocation of firefighting resources.

Some of the topics proposed for research in 1968 and 1969 still remain important questions for future research. For example, we had intended to include in the simulation model (described in Chapter 13) a subroutine that would imitate the escalation of fires according to the arrival time of companies. Moreover, we anticipated that what happened at a simulated fire would vary according to the sizes, as well as the arrival times, of the responding companies; thus, the model could have been used to examine the consequences of policies such as a reduction in the number of firefighters on an engine company from five to four. These hopes were not realized, partly due to the general lack of understanding of critical details, which hampered the conceptual and modeling effort; and partly due to our later assessment that added complexities in the model would not necessarily enhance its value for policy analysis (Section 13.5.1).

Other issues grew less important when it became clear that the Fire Department itself had little control over the relevant policy levers. What can be done to decrease the number of false alarms? Why do some neighborhoods have many more fires than other physically similar neighborhoods where the population has different socioeconomic characteristics? These are important questions, but they proved less susceptible to quantitative analysis than did deployment questions, and by itself, the Fire Department could not do much about them in the short run. Thus, our attention to them waned with the passage of time.

HUD-FUNDED DEPLOYMENT RESEARCH

After the work for the Fire Department had been under way for a year, the U.S. Department of Housing and Urban Development funded a parallel effort on the deployment of emergency services. This contract capitalized on ongoing work and permitted the project staff to generalize their findings to police and medical services, as well as fire services, and to prepare publications applicable to all cities, not just New York. Thus, results which had been developed in rough form for the New York City Fire Department were extended to include more general mathematical assumptions and proofs, and to eliminate terminology and data specific to New York.

This initial contract, completed in 1970, was intended to permit other cities to apply the insights and models developed by the Fire Project. The basic content of the work, however, focused on the same fire service problems that we and the Fire Department had identified as important in New York. We had only then begun to recognize that most cities had little use for models that would help alleviate workload for busy companies, or adjust dispatching and relocation practices in accordance with current unavailabilities. In fact, in most fire departments, alarms rarely do occur when companies are already busy.

Later HUD contracts specifically provided for field testing of our models in selected smaller cities. During this work, which was initially directed by Edward Blum, next by Jan Chaiken, and later by Warren Walker, we began to appreciate the value of static models—those based on assuming, as a reasonable approximation, that all companies are always available. In most cities this assumption is so close to reality that using more elaborate dynamic models is generally unnecessary, except to reassure decisionmakers about the validity of static models. Thus, at the start of the field tests, our interest focused on queuing models (Chapter 7), dynamic relocation (Chapter 12), and the simulation model (Chapter 13). Gradually, these were deemphasized. Responding to the deployment problems posed by smaller cities, we turned to development of the siting model (Chapter 10). This model is one of the "youngest" presented in this book. New York had not wanted such a model, so it did not even exist at the start of our field test; and it was applied in New York City only after the HUD-funded field tests were over. But it proved to be the "work horse" for our deployment studies in other cities.

INTERFACES

If we have been successful, the reader may feel that the topic organization presented in this book's chapters is based on obvious logical distinctions. Historically, however, these topics developed together as parts of an evolution of the research; only later did the distinctions become clear and important. In our work, many pieces of research were being conducted simultaneously, with the results from one feeding back into another. For example, the twin difficulties of organizing analysis teams and implementing the results of analysis were nearly continual concerns of our project leaders, even though in most instances the responsibility for these activities rested outside the Fire Project. Most of us did not view them as *general* topics we were studying, but rather as a series of *specific* questions: Who would be the best leader for *this* city's analysis team? To whom should he report? What steps could we take to persuade the department that *this* finding is important and should lead to changes in operations?

However, Rae Archibald was observing all these developments from the perspective of the general framework described in Chapters 4 and 5. His research on organizational structure and implementation practices drew on his personal experiences, first as a member of the Fire Project; then as our second project leader ; and later as Deputy Fire Commissioner in New York. The material presented in this book also reflects the experiences of later project leaders—Arthur Swersey, Kenneth Rider, and Warren Walker—and of the project teams in Denver, Jersey City, Tacoma, Trenton, Wilmington, and Yonkers.

Similarly, there was a strong interface between our work on incidence analysis and our modeling efforts. The incidence analysis not only provided methods for obtaining the data needed in models, but also illuminated the kinds of models that might be fruitful. For example, the observation that alarm rates could vary substantially over short distances— only a few blocks, in some cases—led us to explore the model of response boundaries presented in Section 7.3. In fact, our initial idea was that the response areas of companies with heavy workload could be decreased somewhat in size for the sole purpose of relieving the companies' potential problems of overwork in the future. We anticipated that average response times would suffer (i.e., become higher) under such a policy. Thus, the model provided us with an unexpected bonus when we discovered that the opposite could be true in some circumstances.

Another discovery during incidence analysis—that one could reliably predict the probability of a serious alarm at a particular location (Section 8.5)—motivated the development of initial dispatch strategies based on a cutoff probability (Section 7.4 and Chapter 11). Moreover, the basic idea of how to define a "serious" incident emerged from the incidence analysis itself and not from the modeling work. So it was not at all fortuitous that the data needed by the initial dispatch algorithm could be obtained from the incidence analysis—both pieces of work progressed in tandem.

As a final example of interface, we should mention the important role the simulation model played in relation to other models. Several chapters (especially Chapter 6, and Sections 12.5, 13.7, and 14.2) describe how the simulation model was used to validate the results from other models or to stimulate the development of good approximations. These examples, however, merely illustrate the pervasive influence of the simulation model on nearly all of our work. An important ingredient in the repeated use of the simulation model is the fact that its designers, Grace Carter and Edward Ignall, were among the few Fire Project members who were present at the beginning of the work and continued their participation until the end.

It is somewhat ironic that the simulation model proved so useful that it made itself unnecessary for most future applications. The simpler models that it stimulated and validated can now be used with confidence in most applications. The history of this model will be further described in the next section.

SIMULATION MODEL

Work on the simulation model described in Chapter 13 began in the earliest days of the Fire Project. We knew that only a sustained effort, over many years, would permit careful design, testing, and application of a simulation model, so we had no expectations for early results. Considerable time was spent on selection of the SIMSCRIPT I.5 language for the model (SIMSCRIPT II had not yet been fully tested), design of the modular subroutine structure that separates the decision rules from the logic of the "housekeeping" portions of the program, and techniques for statistical analysis of the output. Some of these techniques, such as virtual estimation (Section 13.6.4), were so advanced that they had not yet been documented in the simulation literature.

A key question that arose when the simulation program was first being written was, what geographical area should be simulated? The data base is flexible enough so that any arrangement of fire companies and any pattern of alarms can be simulated. Initially, the geography consisted of an imaginary square city, which has been shown in Figures 14.14 and 14.15. When real geography was being discussed, the Fire Project staff argued that modeling one borough would be adequate to capture everything of interest for deployment analysis, especially considering the added cost of a larger data base. But the initial reaction of the New York Fire Department was that the whole city would have to be simulated or the results would not be meaningful. After the analysis based on a square city proved useful in the 1969 union negotiations, as described in Section 14.4, the possibility of simulating the whole city never arose again. The Bronx was chosen as the borough to simulate, primarily because it is geographically separated from the other boroughs and displays the full range of alarm patterns found in other areas of the city.

Incidence analysis had, until that time, focused on the borough of Brooklyn, where there was concern about the capability of the communications office to meet rising demands (Section 14.5). But the previously developed computer programs that aggregated and mapped counts of incidents were equally applicable to the Bronx, and they provided a basis for defining 358 alarm box groups. Reduction of data storage requirements in the simulation model was the main reason for considering groups of alarm boxes, rather than every alarm box separately. However, it was also true that predicting the alarm rates at individual boxes would have been much more difficult.

The simulation program was not fully completed and documented until 1974. Even then it was not a fixed, unvarying program. Many subroutines were altered for specific purposes, and the version described by Carter (1974) is only one of the many that have been used.

The Denver project team adopted this model even before final documentation was available (Hendrick and Plane, 1974). They alerted us to several difficulties that can occur when transferring the program to another computer system, and they contributed several valuable ideas concerning the preparation of data for the program and the interpretation of its output.

The many applications of this model have been described in the previous section and throughout this book.

ANALYSIS OF DEMANDS FOR SERVICES

The historical progression of our incidence analysis was from exploratory data processing through sophisticated statistical techniques, and then back to simple tabulations of data. The main lesson of this work was that incidence analysis can be a lengthy and uncertain undertaking. More particularly, we observed the following:

Initially it is necessary to get a rough "feel" for the patterns that are important for deployment analysis. Just because a pattern is present and can be studied is not sufficient justification for spending time on it. By the time Chapter 8 was written, we were able to provide advice intended to prevent future analysts from repeating the unfruitful explorations we undertook.

Typically, available incident records contain many errors of documentation or keypunching that can be misleading if they are not cleaned up or reinterpreted. The codes used by fire departments to record information can change in meaning when administrative boundaries or alarm boxes are moved or data forms are updated, leading to perils for the analyst who tries to use files that are several years old. Attention to details is important if the results are to be trustworthy.

The level of accuracy to be provided from analysis of demands should depend on the degree to which policy decisions will be influenced by the data. Sometimes a rough guess at certain alarm rates or service times will suffice, because the analyst can show that wide variations in the input data for this model—within reason—lead to the same policy recommendation. This process, a guess followed by sensitivity analysis, can sometimes be much less costly and more meaningful than careful estimation procedures.

We felt that the requirements of a real-time Management Information and Control System (MICS) in New York City justified quite accurate estimates of alarm rates and service times. This belief motivated the work described in Sections 8.5 and 8.6, which was the culmination of several years' research by Grace Carter and John Rolph. Yet these techniques proved too complex for full inclusion in New York's MICS, and have not yet been applied in any other city.

In our later work with smaller cities which experience fewer alarms, we focused more on basic issues or sources of change—e.g., anticipated changes in land use, demographic characteristics of the population, or even jurisdictional boundaries. Future demands cannot be predicted well from past data when there are dominant changes, even with the most sophisticated techniques. Therefore our most recent work, involving applications of the siting model, has rested on simple aggregations of alarm counts from past data, without any attempt at projection except for "reasonable guesses." This method is quite similar to the early exploratory data analysis we performed in New York, and it brings us full circle to the beginning.

ALLOCATION AND SITING OF FIRE COMPANIES

With our initial focus on workload problems in New York, it appeared that queuing models could determine the number of companies needed in different areas of a city. However, this conceptualization did not include the important considerations of efficiency and equity described in Chapter 9. This mismatch between allocation objectives and models proposed for allocation remained for several years, until the models described in Chapter 6 were developed—the square-root law for travel distances and the conversion of travel distance to travel time. The basic idea underlying the square-root law was proposed early by Edward Blum. It developed into a useful and trustworthy model once Peter Kolesar derived the precise form of the equations and validated them.

The resulting simple and accurate equation for estimating the average travel time in a region encompasses both the geographical characteristics of the region and the unavailability of the companies stationed there. Once we developed the square-root law into an important tool of deployment analysis (in 1972), it became possible to formulate a *simple* model that had the desirable properties for allocation purposes: the larger a region is, the more companies it should have; and the busier the companies are, the more of them should be assigned to the region.

Thus the square-root law for travel distances and the conversion from travel distance to travel time were essential ingredients needed for Kenneth Rider to propose the Parametric Allocation Model. However, he also brought to this topic a variety of conceptual advancements. He operationalized the notion of "hazard." He also devised a mathematical formulation of the tradeoff between allocating for "equal coverage" and allocating for "efficiency." The final step in proving the utility of this model was his empirical discovery that a single value of the tradeoff parameter captured the main features of the current allocation policy of the New York Fire Department and therefore reflected, in unknown but satisfactory fashion, a myriad of factors traditionally considered by fire department planners.

The Parametric Allocation Model was subsequently used in most of our HUD-funded field tests. Still later it was applied—without direct assistance from the Rand Fire Project—by analysts working on emergency medical services in South Florida (Meredith and Shershin, 1975), and on fire allocation studies in Maryland and in Allentown, Pennsylvania.

The Firehouse Site Evaluation Model was developed around the same time, to handle the details of station location that are ignored by the Parametric Allocation Model. At the time this work began, in late 1973, the Fire Station Location Package had already been designed by Public Technology, Inc. (PTI), but it had not yet been documented and was not available for our use. Both of these models were funded by the same office at HUD, and their common features are the result of a series of interactions between the Rand team and the PTI team. However, they do differ in certain important characteristics that have been described in Chapter 10.

MANAGEMENT INFORMATION AND CONTROL SYSTEM

The work by Arthur Swersey on operations at the communications offices (reported in Section 14.5) and the design of initial dispatch and relocation algorithms (Chapters 11 and 12) were all motivated by the requirements of the proposed MICS for the New York Fire Department. The basic objectives were to design a flexible system that avoided incorporating inappropriate or outmoded dispatching procedures in the computer software, and to meet realistic constraints on the cost and rapidity of response of the computer system. Thus, for example, we could not recommend an "optimal" algorithm that might use the full resources of the computer system for two minutes in order to recommend a relocation. The emphasis was on fast, approximately correct, algorithms.

The first functional specification for the MICS was produced in a two-month crash effort in 1969 by Rae Archibald, Arthur Swersey, and other members of the Rand Fire Project, working with IBM and Fire Department personnel. The communications office study was substantially completed by that time. At the heart of the MICS plan was an allowance for initial dispatch and relocation algorithms that did not yet exist and were not even well-formulated conceptually.

For the initial dispatch algorithm, work began separately on the questions of how many companies to dispatch and which companies to dispatch. The basic problem was to find an appropriate tradeoff between the response to the current alarm and the adequacy of coverage provided for future alarms by the remaining companies.

Keeney (1972) developed a utility function approach for weighting the "utility" of first- and second-due responses. Swersey (1972), building on this approach and using the square-root law for average travel distance, developed a Markov decision model (described in Section 7.4) for deciding whether or not to dispatch the second closest available company to an alarm along with the closest available company. He formulated an exact solution to the Markov model in terms of a linear programming problem, and showed that a simpler and more computationally feasible approximation could be used to achieve nearly the same decisions.

Swersey showed that the "how many" decision could be made on the basis of the probability that a given alarm was serious. His work led to the development of adaptive response (described in Section 11.4.2), and also formed the basis of the initial dispatch algorithm.

The idea that sometimes it might pay not to dispatch the closest companies was stimulated by the two-company response area model of Carter, Chaiken, and Ignall (1971). This work was extended to the case in which several companies are dispatched and alarms may be of different types by Ignall, in a 1971 paper that was not published but is briefly summarized in Section 7.3.

An algorithm combining the two decisions (which and how many companies to dispatch) was developed by Ignall and Rider. In addition to the problem of extending Swersey's algorithm to apply to two candidate companies that are not necessarily the closest ones available, and incorporating the selection of the companies to send so that neither the "how many" nor the "which" decisions were suboptimized, Ignall and Rider had to confront the Department's natural reluctance to withhold the closest available company from an alarm. Simulations run by Grace Carter showed that the original algorithm would almost always send the closest available unit of a given type to an alarm (although the second unit, if two were sent, was not always the second closest). Therefore, the algorithm was modified to *always* send the closest unit of each type to a box alarm and to a reported structural fire. Simulation tests showed that the final algorithm (described in Section 11.5) would substantially reduce the average response time of second-arriving units to a serious structural fire, would help balance company workloads, and would reduce the number of relocations that were necessary (Carter, Ignall, and Rider, 1977).

Our first ideas concerning the relocation algorithm were very different from its final form as described in Chapter 12. The basic concept was that whenever m companies were unavailable, a certain arrangement of empty and occupied firehouses would be "optimal." Substantial effort was devoted by Arthur Swersey to formulating the optimization problem and then, when it was found to be expensive to solve on the computer, to producing faster, special-purpose algorithms that obtained nearly optimal solutions.

The results from these models indicated that firehouses could be ranked in order of the desirability of having a company located in them, independent of the number of unavailable companies. The ranked lists were then used in a relocation algorithm that was tested in the simulation model. The tests showed that the algorithm had many undesirable features. First, it would either suggest too many relocations or too few, depending on general unavailability levels and the values chosen for certain parameters in the model. Second, the same companies were always the ones selected for relocations (because they had a low ranking), quite independent of the location of the fire. Thus, in the simulation, these companies spent much of their time traveling to other firehouses, often at long distances.

Based on these problems and a study of the methods actually used by the staff of the Department's alarm assignment bureau, Jan Chaiken suggested the concept of a "response neighborhood" and the notions of "covered" and "uncovered" neighborhoods. The objective of a relocation algorithm was then reoriented to deemphasize optimal locations and to focus on guaranteeing a specified minimum level of coverage to all areas of the city.

This concept, however, was not adequate for producing a workable relocation algorithm, a task that occupied Peter Kolesar and Warren Walker for several months. The four-stage algorithm presented in Chapter 12 was the result of a series of trials and iterations. The first important step was to blend the ranked lists into the formulation of the algorithm. Simply maintaining minimum levels of coverage led to too few relocations; in particular, firehouses that had a high ranking could be left uncovered. Kolesar and Walker therefore developed the cost function described in Section 12.2.3 and included relocations based on cost in stage 3 of the ultimate algorithm.

Simulation tests of this improved formulation revealed the problem that was later solved in stage 4—some companies were traveling "too far" to relocate into other firehouses, in some cases passing right by empty houses which were to be filled by other companies. There was some concern, however, that adding stage 4 would defeat the cost minimization incorporated in stage 3. Further simulation tests were required to determine that this was not a serious problem. Finally, the entire algorithm was checked for reasonableness by comparing its recommendations for relocations with those made by fire department personnel for single multiple-alarm fires (Chaiken, Ignall, and Walker, 1975), and for complicated combinations of small and large fires (Section 12.5). The final algorithm was incorporated into the MICS, which was placed in operation in the Brooklyn communications office in the spring of 1977.

KUDOS

The work of the Fire Project has won recognition from our professional colleagues. Peter Kolesar and Warren Walker were awarded the 1974 Lanchester prize of the Operations Research Society of America for their relocation paper. The paper by Ignall et al. (1975), which summarizes the deployment research of the project, won second prize in a competition on the Practice of Management Science in 1974, sponsored by The Institute of Management Sciences College on the Practice of Management Science. The same paper won the 1976 NATO System Science Price Competition. We also take satisfaction from the fact that our work has already proved practical and useful to several fire departments, and we hope that this book will help other fire departments improve their deployment practices in the future.

Glossary*

adaptive response (AR)   A dispatching policy for *box alarms* (see) in which the number of companies initially sent to answer an alarm is predetermined according to time of day, to geographic area, and to *alarm type* (see). Compare *fixed response* and *variable response*.
administrative battalion   A *battalion* (see).
administrative district   A *district* (see).
aerial ladder   An extendable ladder anchored to a turnable base on a ladder truck, which is used to gain access to upper floors and roofs, and also to deliver water through a detachable pipe. Typically, hydraulically operated and used in common sizes ranging from 65 to 100 feet or more. Also called "aerial." Compare *elevating platform* and see *ladder*.
affected region   In the Firehouse Site Evaluation Model, the set of alarm boxes to which travel times in a proposed configuration of fire companies are different from those in the current configuration.
alarm   1. Any notification of the fire department that a situation that requires a response exists, or may exist. Following the response to the first alarm, the officer in charge of fireground operations at the scene may issue additional alarms: a "second alarm" making the incident a "two-alarm fire," a "third alarm" making it a "three-alarm fire," and so on. See *multiple alarm*. 2. Broadly, the fire or other incident causing the alarm.
alarm assignment card   A card, kept for a particular alarm box or location, that

---

* The purpose of this Glossary is to assist readers in reviewing the meanings of words encountered in the text. Therefore, the entries have been selected from the text itself, with only a small number of additions representing more general fire vocabulary, and the definitions give the meanings that appear in the book. While these are usually common meanings, the reader should recognize that others may exist. The superscripts that appear in some entries are cross references to numbered definitions in other entries.

shows the specific companies, chief officers, and special units assigned to respond to each successive alarm (usually the first through the fifth) associated with that box or location. Also called "running card." See *alarm*.

alarm box 1. A device using a telegraph, telephone, or radio to automatically transmit its identifying code number, and sometimes to transmit voice, to a fire department communications office when activated by pulling a handle, using a telephone handset, or pushing buttons. 2. In the Firehouse Site Evaluation Model, a *subarea* (see). Also called "box."

alarm factor In the Parametric Allocation Model, a measure of the *realized demand* (see) in a region. In practice, the alarm factor is usually calculated as the total work time of all companies at an average incident in the region. Compare *hazard factor*.

alarm rate The average number of alarms per hour received by a fire department dispatching office. Only one alarm for each incident is used to compute the average, regardless of how many notifications of the incident are received or of multiple alarms that may be issued by officers at the fireground.

alarm type A class of incidents defined on the basis of information available at the time of the *initial dispatch* (see). For example, an alarm type may be a telephone report of what appears to be a structural fire, or it might be a street box alarm from a location with a history of serious fires reported by box. Compare *incident type*.

algorithm A finite set of ordered steps, rules, or procedures used to achieve a computational result, typically employing repetition of at least some of the steps.

allocation 1a. The distribution of fire companies citywide. b. The number of fire companies assigned to a particular region of a city. 2. The process by which such a distribution or such an assignment is made. Compare *deployment*.

analytic model A *model* (see) that is derived mathematically from theoretical statements of relationships that hold in the real world; broadly, a model in which the results are achieved by mathematical analysis.

apparatus A motor vehicle on a truck chassis, such as an engine or ladder, especially as distinguished from the *equipment* (see) that it carries.

AR *Adaptive response* (see).

arc A street segment beween any two intersections in a computer representation of a street network. Compare *node*.

availablity The fraction of time that a company is available to respond to an alarm. Compare *unavailability*.

battalion 1. A group of fire companies and the geographic area to which they are administratively assigned. Also called "administrative battalion." 2. The groupof companies so assigned.

box An *alarm box* (see).

box alarm An alarm signaled by *alarm box* (see), especially one unaccompanied by a verbal report describing the nature of the incident.

bubble diagram A graphic representation of a queuing system in which each state of the system is a labeled circle ("bubble"), arrival and service rates are labeled on arrows connecting the states, and the relationships among these elements represent a collection of equations that can be solved for the probability of a specific state occurring.

building fire   A *structural fire*² (see).

change agent   An individual who acts to bring about or to manage change in an organization.

C.O.   *Communications office* (see).

communications office.   A center where alarms are received, responses are determined, the availability status of all units is maintained, and dispatching orders are transmitted to companies selected to respond to alarms. Also called "dispatching office." See *dispatch*.

company   1. A basic firefighting unit consisting of one or more pieces of *apparatus* (see) and a complement of firefighters led by an officer, often a lieutenant or captain. The number of men on duty on a given tour varies from city to city, but often an engine company has three to five men, and a ladder company has four to six. 2. This unit with the total roster of men assigned to it (rather than just those on duty at a given moment). Rosters also vary from city to city, but often an engine company may have 15 to 25 men and a ladder company of 25 to 30. Also called "fire company" or "unit."

constraint   The highest or lowest permissible value of a *parameter* (see). More generally, any restriction on the possible values a parameter or set of parameters can take on.

coverage   1. The protection that a fire department provides to a region of a city by having companies available to respond to an alarm in that region, especially as distinguished from the protection provided by actual firefighting operations. 2a. A measure of this protection, estimated by the unweighted average travel time to all locations in the region, assuming that all companies assigned to the region are available to respond. b. The probability that a location or group of locations is *covered* (see).

covered   1. Having a fire company sufficiently nearby. 2. In the Fire Station Location Package, a focal point is covered if it has a fire station within x minutes' travel time, where x is a number specified for that focal point. 3. In the relocation algorithm, a neighborhood is covered if it has both the first-due and second-due companies available. 4. In the Fire Operations Simulation Model, an alarm box is covered if the first-due engine (ladder) is available, or alternatively, if its first- or second-due engine (ladder) is available, and so on.

cutoff   1. A number that separates values into two groups according to whether they are larger or smaller than the number. 2. One of a collection of numbers that separate values into groups according to their size.

demand   Latent demand, potential demand, or *realized demand* (all of which see).

demand region   Any of the areas into which a city may be divided such that within each one neither realized demand nor potential demand vary substantially, even if there are variations from area to area. Also called "region."

demand zone   A *fire demand zone* (see).

deployment   1a. The strategic assignment and placement of firefighting resources, especially firehouses, companies, and manpower. b. This assignment along with the tactical control of dispatch, response, and relocation. 2. A specific configuration of firehouses, companies, or other resources. 3. Broadly, *allocation* (see).

deployment analysis The application of *systems analysis* (see) to deployment problems.

descriptive model A *model* (see) that predicts the values of one or more performance measures for a given deployment policy. Compare *optimization model* and *prescriptive model*.

detection The discovery of a fire by a person or a mechanical device, especially this discovery regarded as a stage in the evolution of a fire from ignition to extinguishment.

dispatch 1. To determine the appropriate response to an alarm and to notify the fire companies that are to respond to it; broadly, to send firefighting units to the scene of a reported fire. 2a. The process by which this is accomplished, or an instance of it. b. A particular *response*[1] (see).

dispatcher A fire department employee stationed in the communications office, whose responsibilities include receiving alarms, determining their type and location, dispatching firefighting units, maintaining information on unit availability, and keeping records of activities.

dispatching office See *communications office*.

dispatching time The elapsed time from the receipt of an alarm, to the notification of specific fire companies that they are to respond. See *response time*.

district An area of a city to which a group of fire companies are assigned for administrative purposes. Also called "administrative district."

dynamic 1. Changing with time. 2. Involving, depending upon, or characteristic of changes with time. Compare *static*.

elevating platform A hydraulically operated platform used for both firefighting and rescue, mounted on a folding or telescoping boom, equipped with a heavy stream nozzle (turret) for delivering water to upper floors and roofs, typically anchored to a turntable base on a truck, and available in common sizes from 50 to 90 feet or more. Compare *aerial ladder*.

empirical model A *model* (see) based on the assumption that the output or performance measure of a system is related to input variables in a particularly simple fashion. Empirical data is used to estimate the parameters of such a model.

engine 1. The basic piece of firefighting *apparatus* (see) used to draw water from a hydrant, directly from a reservoir such as a lake, or from its own water tank, and pump it through a hose line for delivery to a fire. A common engine configuration, the "triple combination," consists essentially of a large fire pump, a hose body carrying a supply of hose, and a small booster pump and tank with a capacity of approximately 500 gallons. Also called "fire engine," "pumper." 2. An *engine company* (see). Compare *ladder*.

engine company A fire *company* (see) whose primary apparatus is the engine and whose primary function is to extinguish fires. Also called "engine," or "pumper company." Compare *ladder company*.

equipment Firefighting instruments such as hoses, water tanks, pumps, ladders, fire extinguishers, portable tools, and protective clothing, especially as distinguished from *apparatus* (see).

Glossary 645

exponential smoothing A procedure for updating alarm rate predictions as a function of how much past and present predictions have erred.
extinguishment 1. The point in time at which there is no longer any abnormal heat or smoke being generated in material that previously was burning. 2. The process or operation by which this is achieved.
false alarm An alarm that is determined not to have required a response. In some cities, the alarm is not considered a false alarm unless the person(s) turning it in knew a response was not required. The purpose of this qualification is to distinguish between malicious false alarms and honest mistakes.
fire A rapid, persistent chemical reaction that releases heat and light; especially, the heat-induced exothermic combination of a fuel with oxygen. An "unfriendly" fire is any instance of uncontrolled burning, including explosion, of combustible solids, liquids, or gases.
fire company See *company*.
fire demand zone In the Fire Station Location Package, a *subarea* (see). Also called "demand zone."
fire engine An *engine*[1] (see).
fire flow The amount of water delivered or available for delivery to a fire, usually expressed in gallons per minute or gallons per minute for a specific period of time.
fireground An area in which a fire is being fought, operations are under the direction of the ranking officer present, and both operating and standby apparatus are present.
firehouse A structure providing space for firefighting resources and home-base operations, including administration, communications, housing of on-duty personnel, garaging of vehicles, equipment storage, maintenance, training, and supply. Also called "fire station."
fire management area A *demand region* (see). Used chiefly in master planning literature.
fire prevention That part of *fire protection* activities that are undertaken in advance of the outbreak of a fire to avoid its occurrence and to reduce loss should one occur.
fire protection The effort, or specific measures regarded collectively, to reduce loss of life, injury, and property damage by fire, including both prevention and suppression activities by public and private means.
fire station See *firehouse*.
fire suppression That part of *fire protection* activities that are undertaken after a fire has begun, in order to extinguish it.
first-alarm assignment The specification of which companies, officers, and special units are to respond to the first alarm received from a specific box or location. This specification is the first line on an *alarm assignment card* (see).
first-alarm response The actual response to a first alarm, potentially differing from the response specified in the first-alarm assignment as a function of dispatching policy, unit availability, or information in the alarm.
first-arriving Arriving first in response to an alarm, whether or not first-due. Compare *first-due*.
first-due Assigned to arrive first in an area in response to an alarm. The first-

due company is expected to be the one first-arriving, the second-due company second-arriving, and so on. Arrivals may, however, be influenced by circumstances (availability, traffic) so that, for example, the first-arriving ladder might be the one that was third-due.

first-due area The *response area* (see) in which a company is first-due, usually defined by the set of alarm boxes to which the company is closest (in time, if not distance). Also called "first-due response area."

fixed response Any dispatching policy for box alarms (see) in which the number of companies initially sent to answer an alarm is predetermined without regard to *alarm type* (see) or the number of companies that may be available when the alarm is received. Compare *variable response* and *adaptive response*.

flashover The phenomenon or stage of a fire in which flames suddenly appear on and sweep over the upper walls and ceiling of a room.

focal point In the Fire Station Location Package, the point representing all of the hazards in a fire demand zone. See *subarea*.

gpm gallons per minute.

hazard 1. Anything that can cause or contribute to injury, damage, or loss by burning. 2. The extent to which injury, damage, or loss will occur if there is a fire that is not promptly extinguished.

hazard factor In the Parametric Allocation Model, a measure of the *potential demand* (see) in a region. The hazard factor reflects the rate of fire escalation in the region. It is multiplied by the average travel time in the region when calculating the objective function for this model. Compare *alarm factor*.

higher alarm See *multiple alarm*[1].

hose A flexible tube attached at one end to a water pump or to a supply of water under pressure, at the other end to a nozzle, and used to deliver a stream or spray of water. Firefighting hose is commonly available in 50-foot lengths capable of being coupled, with inside diameters ranging from 3/4 inch to 6 inches, and when made for heavy regular use consists of an inner rubber lining protected by one or more outer fabric jackets. Also called "line" or "hose line."

ignition 1. The stage in the evolution of a fire at which it becomes self-sustaining, with or without the appearance of flames. 2. The physical and chemical processes directly causing this stage.

implementation The entire process, including economic, logistic, and political activity, by which change in policy or operations is brought into practice.

incident An occurrence or event resulting in an alarm, especially a fire or other emergency.

incident type A class of incidents defined on the basis of the situation at the scene. For example, an incident type may be a rubbish fire, or it may be a structural fire that requires two engines and two ladders. Compare *alarm type*.

initial dispatch 1. The *dispatch* (see) made upon receipt of the first alarm from a particular box or location. 2. A policy specifying how this dispatch is to be made.

initial response adequacy The appropriateness of the response specified in an

Glossary

initial dispatch, measured by comparing the number of each type of unit initially dispatched to an alarm to the number of each type of unit judged as a sufficient initial dispatch to the alarm.

interarrival time The time interval between two successive arrivals in a queuing system.

ladder 1. A *ladder company* (see). 2. A *ladder truck* (see). 3. Any of various fixed or extendible devices used for climbing or descending, and characterized by parallel, equally spaced rungs securely fastened at right angles to each of two long structural members. Compare *engine*.

ladder company A fire *company* (see) whose primary apparatus is the ladder truck and whose primary functions are rescue and ventilation. Also called "ladder" or "truck company." Compare *engine company*.

ladder pipe A heavy stream nozzle attached to an aerial ladder, usually supplied by a 3-inch hose and capable of being mechanically directed from the ground.

ladder truck A piece of firefighting *apparatus* (see) equipped with substantial lengths of ladders for external access to upper floors and with a variety of special tools for forcible entry, rescue, ventilation, overhaul, and salvage. Also called "ladder" or "truck." Compare *engine*.

latent demand 1. A requirement for fire protection created by the existence of a hazard. 2. *Potential demand*^{2} (see). Also called "demand." Compare *potential demand*, *realized demand*.

line See *hose*.

linear Related in a fashion that can be graphed as a straight line (for two variables), a plane, or a similar flat surface.

manning 1. The number of men assigned to a firefighting unit, such as an engine company or a ladder company. 2. The process of making such assignments.

Markov decision theory A method for finding an optimal policy for queuing and other probabilistic systems in which the conditional probability distribution for the states of the system, given the present state of the system, is assumed to be independent of the past history of the system.

matrix A mathematical device used to manipulate mathematical elements related in certain specific ways, usually represented as a rectangular array formed by rows and columns of the elements.

minipumper A relatively small, maneuverable *engine* (see), typically carrying a 250-gallon water tank, manned by two firefighters, and used in situations not requiring the full capabilities of the larger standard engines.

model A conceptual or physical representation of reality that may be used to study the behavior of a real system without altering it.

move-up See *relocation*.

multiple alarm 1. A second or higher order alarm signaled by an officer on the fireground to request additional assistance. 2. A multiple alarm fire. See *alarm*.

NFPA National Fire Protection Association

NFPCA National Fire Prevention and Control Administration

node A street intersection in a computer representation of a street network. Compare *arc*.

objective function A performance measure to be maximized or minimized by an optimization procedure.

optimization A procedure for finding the values of decision variables that make a certain performance measure as high or as low as possible.

optimization model A *model* (see) used to select a policy that will produce the highest or lowest possible value of a particular performance measure.

overhaul The final stage of extinguishment in which hidden fires, in walls for example, are sought and extinguished, steps are taken to prevent recurrence, and information about the ignition sequence is gathered.

parameter A number characterizing some aspect of a mathematical model or its input, that is held constant for a particular calculation but may be varied from calculation to calculation.

Poisson process A sequence of discrete events characterized by a parameter λ such that in a sufficiently short time interval, say of length T, the probability of exactly one event occurring is approximately λT, the probability of two or more events occurring is negligible, and the occurrence of an event in one interval has no effect on the occurrence of events in other nonoverlapping intervals. Events in a Poisson process are often said to occur "at random."

policy A concept that guides action, including decisionmaking, designed to achieve specific objectives under given constraints, and often embodied in a set of rules or procedures.

potential demand 1. An event that may occur in the future, that would require a response from the fire department. 2. The extent to which the resources of the fire department would be engaged should such an event occur. Also called "demand." Compare *realized demand*, and *latent demand*.

prescriptive model A *model* (see) that recommends a particular deployment policy or group of policies. Usually the prescribed policies optimize some performance measure, or come closest to producing given measures. Compare *descriptive model*, and *optimization model*.

proxy measure A measure that characterizes a system in a way that makes it a practical substitute for another measure that has not been or cannot in practice be evaluated. For example, response time is a proxy measure for property damage in measuring the performance of a fire department. Also called "proxy."

pumper An *engine*[1] (see).

queue A waiting line, as of customers at a checkout counter or alarms to be handled by a dispatcher.

queuing theory A collection of mathematical techniques that are used to analyze the behavior of queues.

realized demand 1. An event requiring a response by the fire department; an *alarm;* an *incident*. 2. The extent to which such events occur, or the extent to which they require fire department resources, often measured by alarm rate or workload. Also called "demand." Compare *potential demand,* and *latent demand*.

recovery A situation in which a fire company is unavailable for dispatch because its firefighters must rest after their work at a previous incident, or because its equipment must be replaced, replenished, dried, or repaired.

Glossary 649

redeployment 1. The process of changing the *deployment* (see) of firefighting resources. 2. *Relocation* (see).

region An area or portion of a city, especially a *demand region* (see).

regression A statistical technique that fits a smooth curve to empirical data so as to minimize some measure of the error. Used to estimate an unknown relationship between variables for purposes of analysis or prediction.

relocation 1. The moving of fire companies into temporarily vacant firehouses to provide coverage for the duration of the incident occupying the companies normally assigned to those houses. Also called "move-up" or "redeployment." 2. Broadly, the changing of firehouse sites or the deployment of companies; redeployment.

rescue company A fire company trained, equipped, and provided with a special vehicle to perform rescues and render emergency medical services at both fire and nonfire incidents. Also called "rescue squad."

response 1. The entire complement of firefighting resources, including personnel, apparatus, and equipment, sent to answer an alarm. Also called "dispatch." 2. The actual movement of these units to the scene of the alarm. 3. The activities, regarded collectively, of the fire department upon receipt of an alarm.

response area An area of a city assigned to a company for response in case of an alarm from that area. In general, each company will have several response areas. A company will be first-due in one response area, second-due in another, and so on.

response distance See *travel distance*.

response neighborhood (RN) A collection of alarm boxes that have the same unordered pair of ladders (or engines) as first-due and second-due. An RN can also be defined by unordered sets of three ladders (or engines).

response time The elapsed time from the receipt of an alarm to the completion of setup operations at the scene of a fire, including *dispatching time*, *turnout time*, *travel time*, and *setup time* (all of which see).

risk 1. The likelihood (chance) of a fire, especially the likelihood at, or associated with, a particular hazard. 2. *Hazard* (see). 3. In fire insurance, the property insured.

RN *Response neighborhood* (see).

run 1. A single instance of a fire company responding to and returning from an alarm. 2. A single execution of a computer program.

running card An *alarm assignment card* (see).

salvage The activity of minimizing damage to structures and their contents by heat, smoke, flames, water, and weather, commencing as soon as possible during firefighting and continuing after extinguishment.

second-arriving Arriving second in response to an alarm, regardless of the assigned order of arrivals. Compare *second-due* and see *first-due*.

second-due Assigned to arrive second in an area in response to an alarm. Compare *second-arriving* and see *first-due*.

seriousness A property or characteristic used to classify alarms for the purposes of analysis, and defined in terms, for example, of the size or growth rate of the fire, or the resources that may be required in the response.

service rate The inverse of the average *service time* (see). For example, the service rate is two per hour when the average service time is a half hour (30 minutes).

service time The amount of time a server spends providing a single customer with service in a queuing system.

setup time The elapsed time between the arrival of a fire company at the scene of a fire and the commencement of firefighting, during which interval apparatus is positioned and equipment is made ready for use. See *response time*.

severity The extent of the injury, damage, or loss resulting from a fire; the degree of destructive consequences.

simulation 1. The process of representing the behavior of a real system with a *simulation model* (see). 2. A computer run of a simulation model. 3. A simulation model.

simulation model A *model* (see) embodied in a computer program that permits all the critical resources, processes, and events that characterize a system to be internally represented so that, under various policy assumptions, a variety of detailed performance measures may be calculated at any instant.

squad company A unit that provides additional manpower to companies at a working incident, or for separate responses during peak periods, and that is assigned either to a vehicle used principally for transportation or to an engine or ladder.

square-root law 1. The relationship expressed by the equation $E(D) = k\sqrt{A/N}$, where $E(D)$ is the estimated average travel distance of companies to alarms in a region of area A when N companies are available for response in the region, and k is a constant that depends on street geometry and the distribution of companies in the region. 2. A similar relationship in which N is replaced by $E(N)$, the average number of available companies in the region.

state The condition of a queuing system as specified by the number of servers occupied in specific ways at a specific time.

state diagram A graphic representation of the *states* (see) of a system and the relationships among them. See also *bubble diagram*, which is a type of state diagram.

state space The collection of all the *states* (see) of a system.

static Not changing with time; constant. Compare *dynamic*.

status 1. The condition of availability or unavailability for dispatch characterizing a company, or each company in a group of companies, at a particular moment. 2. The current information about this condition, maintained by dispatchers, and sometimes divided into categories of availability by the type of activity in which each company is engaged.

steady-state solution The probabilistic behavior of a queuing system after a long time has passed, while underlying conditions (such as arrival and service rates) remain unchanged. The steady-state solution is independent of the state of the system at the initial moment. Compare *transient solution*.

strategic Involving or requiring long-range planning. Said of deployment issues such as firehouse siting, manning, and the allocation of companies by region. Compare *tactical*.

street alarm box An *alarm box* (see) available for public use in the street, as

Glossary 651

contrasted to one inside a building or otherwise not readily accessible to the public.

structural fire 1. A fire inside, on, under, or touching a structure (an assembly of materials forming a constructed whole for a specific purpose, including buildings, bridges, tunnels, tents, platforms, grandstands, etc.). 2. A fire occurring inside, or involving, a building (a structure with walls and a roof, and having a defined height), whether or not structural members are involved. In this sense only, also called "building fire."

subarea In the Fire Station Location Package and the Firehouse Site Evaluation Model, an area of the city sufficiently small that it may be assumed for computational purposes that all the demand for fire service in the area arises from a single point, and that travel times to any place in the area will be the same as to that point.

suboptimization An approximation to the optimal solution to a problem, usually derived by simplifying the original problem.

systems analysis A methodical, iterative technique for choosing among alternative actions in a complex system, characterized by a series of steps that include careful identification of the problem and of the objectives of analysis, choosing policy evaluation criteria, selecting alternative policies, analyzing the policies using a model of the system, comparing the alternative policies, implementing the chosen alternative, and monitoring its performance.

tactical Involving or requiring planning for activities, including decision making, during the course of a day. Said of deployment issues in dispatching and relocation. Compare *strategic*.

telegraph box An *alarm box* (see) that transmits alarms by telegraph.

third-arriving Arriving third in response to an alarm, regardless of the assigned order of arrivals. Compare *third-due* and see *first-due*.

third-due Assigned to arrive third in an area in response to an alarm. Compare *third-arriving* and see *first-due*.

tour A period of time during which the same group of firefighters is on duty; for example, 9 A.M. to 6 P.M. or 9 A.M. to 9 P.M.

tradeoff parameter In the Parametric Allocation Model, a number chosen by the user to specify the objective to be optimized.

transient solution The probabilistic behavior of a queuing system as a function of the time since the initial moment. The transient solution depends on the state of the system at the initial moment, but dependence weakens as time passes, eventually approaching the *steady-state solution* (see).

travel distance The distance a fire company must travel from its firehouse (or wherever it is when told to respond) to the scene of a fire (or the location from which the original alarm was signaled). Also called "response distance."

travel time The elapsed time between a fire company's departure from its firehouse (or wherever it is when notified to respond) and its arrival at the scene of a fire (or the location from which the original alarm was signaled). See *response time*.

trend 1. The change over time in some quantity; annual alarms, for example.

2. A line in a graph representing such a change. 3. A statistical estimate of such a change.

truck   A *ladder truck* (see).

truck company   A *ladder company* (see)

turnout time   The elapsed time between the notification of a company that it is to respond and its actual departure from quarters. See *response time*.

unavailability   The fraction of time that a company is busy and, hence, unavailable to respond to an alarm. Compare *availability*.

unit   A *company* (see) or any other firefighting entity (such as a chief, his aide, and their vehicle).

USFA   United States Fire Administration

variable response   Any dispatching policy for *box alarms* (see) in which the number of companies initially sent to answer an alarm depends on the number of companies available. Compare *fixed response,* and *adaptive response*.

ventilation   The systematic removal of heat, smoke, and fire gases from a structure, performed to improve visibility and reduce the risk of injury, damage, or explosion. Ventilation is normally performed just before putting water on a fire.

weight   Any of a set of numbers by which the quantities in a mathematical expression are multiplied to indicate how important each of those quantities is in the expression.

workload   1. The number of company-hours or person-hours consumed per unit time in responding to and working at incidents. 2. Broadly, the extent to which the fire department or its personnel are actually engaged in responding to incidents and extinguishing fires.

work time   1. The total amount of time spent unavailable by a company that responds to and works at the scene of an incident. 2. The total time spent unavailable by all companies at an incident. 3. In the Fire Operations Simulation Model, the time spent working at the scene only, excluding travel time and recovery time.

Bibliography

A Basic Guide for Fire Prevention and Control Master Planning. Stock No. 003-000-00528-3. Washington, D.C.: Government Printing Office, 1978.

America Burning. The Report of the National Commission on Fire Prevention and Control. Stock No. 052-000-00004-1. Washington, D.C.: Government Printing Office, 1973.

Archibald, R. and Hoffman, R. *Introducing Technological Change in a Bureaucratic Structure.* Paper P-4025. Santa Monica: The Rand Corporation, February 1969.

Baer, W. et al. *Analysis of Federally Funded Demonstration Projects: Supporting Case Studies.* Report R-1927-DOC. Santa Monica: The Rand Corporation, April 1976.

Balinski, M. "Integer Programming: Methods, Uses, Computation." *Management Science,* Vol. 12, No. 3, pp. 253-313, 1965.

Balinski, M. and Gomory, R. "A Primal Method for the Assignment and Transportation Problems." *Management Science*, Vol. 10, No. 3, pp.578-593, 1964.

Barnard, C. *The Function of the Executive.* Cambridge, Massachusetts: Harvard University Press, 1949.

Bennis, W. "Theory and Method in Applying Behavioral Science to Planned Organizational Change." *The Journal of Applied Behavioral Science,* Vol. 1, No. 4, pp. 337-359, 1965.

Berl, W. G., Fristrom, R. M., and Halpin, B. M. "Research on Fire Related Problems." *APL Technical Digest*, Vol. 14, No. 2, pp. 2-28, 1975.

Berlin, G. and Liebman, J. "Mathematical Analysis of Emergency Ambulance Location." *Socio-Economic Planning Sciences*, Vol. 8, pp. 323-328, 1974.

Blum, E. *Deployment Research of the New York City Fire Project.* Report R-968. Santa Monica: The Rand Corporation, May 1972; also in Drake, Keeney, and Morse, (eds.). *Analysis of Public Systems,* Chapter 7, Cambridge, Massachusetts: MIT Press, 1972.

Brown, R. *Smoothing, Forecasting and Prediction.* Englewood Cliffs, New Jersey: Prentice Hall, 1962.
Burke, P. "The Output of a Queuing System." *Operations Research,* Vol. 4, pp. 669–704, 1958.
Burns, T. and Stalker, G. *The Management of Innovation.* London: Tavistock, 1961.
Carter, G. *Simulation of Fire Department Operations: Program Description.* Report R-1188/2-HUD/NYC. Santa Monica: The Rand Corporation, December 1974.
Carter, G., Chaiken, J., and Ignall, E. *Response Areas for Two Emergency Units.* Report R-532-NYC/HUD. Santa Monica: The Rand Corporation, 1971; also in *Operations Research,* Vol. 20, No. 3, pp. 571–594, 1972.
———, *Simulation Model of Fire Department Operations: Executive Summary.* Report R-1188/1-HUD. Santa Monica: The Rand Corporation, December 1974.
Carter, G. and Ignall, E. *A Simulation Model of Fire Department Operations: Design and Preliminary Results.* Report R-632-NYC. Santa Monica: The Rand Corporation, December 1970; also in *IEEE Transactions on Systems Science and Cybernetics,* Vol. SSC-6, No. 4, pp. 282–293, October 1970.
———, "Virtual Measures: A Variance Reduction Technique for Simulation." *Management Science,* Vol. 21, No. 6 pp. 607–616, 1975.
Carter, G., Ignall, E., and Rider, K. *An Algorithm for the Initial Dispatch of Fire Companies.* Report R-1997. Santa Monica: The Rand Corporation, 1977.
Carter, G., Ignall, E., and Walker, W. *A Simulation Model of the New York City Fire Department: Its Use in Deployment Analysis.* Paper P-5110-1. Santa Monica: The Rand Corporation, July 1975.
Carter, G. and Rolph, J. *New York City Fire Alarm Prediction Models: I. Box Reported Serious Fires.* Report R-1214-NYC. Santa Monica: The Rand Corporation, May 1973.
———, *New York City Fire Alarm Prediction Models: II. Alarm Rates.* Report R-1215-NYC. Santa Monica: The Rand Corporation, January 1975.
Casey, J. (ed.). *The Fire Chief's Handbook,* 3rd edition. New York: Dun–Donnelly, 1967.
Chaiken, J. *The Number of Emergency Units Busy at Alarms Which Require Multiple Servers.* Report R-531-NYC/HUD. Santa Monica: The Rand Corporation, 1971.
———, "Boundary Effects in Square Root Laws for Travel Distances." Unpublished, 1973.
———, *Hypercube Queuing Model: Executive Summary.* Report R-1688/1-HUD. Santa Monica: The Rand Corporation, 1975.
———, "Transfer of Emergency Service Deployment Models to Operating Agencies." *Management Science,* Vol. 24, No. 7, pp. 719–731, 1978.
Chaiken, J. and Ignall, E. *An Extension of Erlang's Formulas Which Distinguishes Individual Servers.* Report R-567-NYC/HUD. Santa Monica: The Rand Corporation, 1971; also in *J. Applied Probability,* Vol. 9, No. 1, pp. 192–197, 1972.
Chaiken, J., Ignall, E., and Walker, W. *A Training Course in Deployment of*

Emergency Services: Instructor's Manual. Report R-1784/1-HUD. Santa Monica: The Rand Corporation, September 1975.

Chesler, L. and Goeller, B. *The Star Methodology for Short-Haul Transportation: Transportation System Impact Assessment.* Report R-1359-DOT. Santa Monica: The Rand Corporation, December 1973.

Chesnais, J. "La Mortalité par Accidents en France depuis 1826." *Population,* Vol. 29, No. 6, pp. 1097–1135, 1974.

Christian, W. and Dubivsky, P. "Household Fire Detection and Warning: The Key to Improved Life Safety." *Fire Journal,* Vol. 67, pp. 55–61, January 1973.

Churchman, C. *The Systems Approach.* New York: Dell Publishing Company, 1968.

Corman, H., Ignall, E., Rider, K., and Stevenson, S. "Fire Casualties and Their Relation to Fire Company Response Distance and Demographic Factors." *Fire Technology,* Vol. 12, No. 3, 193–203, August 1976.

Cox, D. *Analysis of Binary Data.* London: Methuen and Company, 1970.

Cox, D. and Lewis, P. *The Statistical Analysis of Series of Events.* London: Methuen and Company, 1966.

Cramer, H. *Mathematical Methods of Statistics.* Princeton, New Jersey: Princeton University Press, 1946.

Criteria for Master Planning and Resource Allocation. Report PTI-78/503. Washington, D.C.: Public Technology, Inc., 1978.

Derry, L. "A Study of U. S. Fire Experience, 1976." *Fire Journal,* Vol. 71, No. 6, pp. 50–53, November 1977.

Dormont, P., Hausner, J., and Walker, W. *Firehouse Site Evaluation Model: Description and User's Manual.* Report R-1618/2-HUD. Santa Monica: The Rand Corporation, June 1975.

Downs, A. *Inside Bureaucracy.* Boston: Little Brown and Company, 1967.

Dreyfus, S. "An Appraisal of Some Shortest Path Algorithms." *Operations Research,* Vol. 17, No. 3, pp. 395–412, 1969.

Dreyfus, S. and Law, A. *The Art and Theory of Dynamic Programming.* New York: Academic Press, 1977.

Drucker, P. *Management: Tasks, Responsibilities, Practices.* New York: Harper and Row, 1973.

Eichelberger, P. and Farren, T. "Miami Uses Station Locator Model to Prepare 10-Year Master Plan." *Fire Engineering,* Vol. 130, No. 6, pp. 30–33, June 1977.

Evaluating the Organization of Service Delivery: Fire. Research Triangle Institute, International City Management Association, and National Fire Protection Association, 1977.

Finnerty, J. "How Often Will the Firemen Get Their Sleep?" *Management Science,* Vol. 23, No. 11, pp. 1169–1173, 1977.

Fire Station Location Package: Chief Executive's Report, Fire Chief's Report, Project Leader's Guide, Project Operations Guide. Washington, D.C.: Public Technology, Inc., 1974.

Fire in the United States: Washington, D.C.: National Fire Data Center, U.S. Fire Administration, U.S. Department of Commerce, December 1978.

Fishman, G. *Concepts and Methods in Discrete Event Digital Simulation.* New York: John Wiley and Sons, 1973.

Fyffe, D. and Rardin, R. *Fire Protection Service Management.* Atlanta: Georgia Institute of Technology, October 1974.

Galvin, J. "Judgment Decision in Harlem." *W.N.Y.F.,* 2nd issue, pp. 20–23, 1971.

Garfinkel, R. and Nemhauser, G. *Integer Programming.* New York: John Wiley and Sons, 1972.

Geoffrion, A. *Implicit Enumeration Using an Imbedded Linear Program.* Report RM-5406-PR. Santa Monica: The Rand Corporation, September 1967.

Goeller, B., Abrahamse, A., Bigelow, J., Bolten, J., de Ferranti, D., De Haven, J., Kirkwood, T., and Petruschell, R. *Protecting an Estuary from Floods— A Policy Analysis of the Oosterschelde, Summary Report.* Report R-2121/1-NETH. Santa Monica: The Rand Corporation, December 1977.

Grading of Municipal Fire Protection Facilities—Its Relation to Fire Insurance and to the Municipality's Fire Protection Policy. Washington, D.C.: National League of Cities, 1967.

Grading Schedule for Municipal Fire Protection. New York: Insurance Services Office, 1974.

Gratz, D. *Fire Department Management: Scope and Method.* Beverly Hills: Glencoe Press, 1972.

Greenberger, M., Crenson, M. and Crissey, B. *Models in the Policy Process.* New York: Russell Sage Foundation, 1976.

Groover, M. and Fagan, J. *An Analysis of Fire Service Delivery for Master Planning in Allentown, Pennsylvania.* Allentown, Pennsylvania: Allentown Urban Observatory, January 1977.

Gross, B. *The Managing of Organizations.* New York: The Free Press, 1964.

Hage, J. and Aiken, M. *Social Change in Complex Organizations.* New York: Random House, 1970.

Hall, J., Karter, M., Koss, M., Schainblatt, A., and McNerney, T., *Fire-Code Inspections and Fire Prevention: What Methods Lead to Success?* Washington, D.C.: The Urban Institute, December 1978.

Hamming, R. *Numerical Methods for Scientists and Engineers.* New York: McGraw-Hill, 1962.

Hausner, J. *Determining the Travel Characteristics of Emergency Service Vehicles.* Report R-1687-HUD. Santa Monica: The Rand Corporation, April 1975.

Hausner, J. and Walker, W. *An Analysis of the Deployment of Fire-Fighting Resources in Trenton, New Jersey.* Report R-1566/1-TRNTN. Santa Monica: The Rand Corporation, February 1975.

Hausner, J., Walker, W., and Swersey, A. *An Analysis of the Deployment of Fire-Fighting Resources in Yonkers, New York.* Report R-1566/2-HUD/CY. Santa Monica: The Rand Corporation, October 1974.

Held, J. "Fire Data Handbook." Unpublished report. Santa Monica: The Rand Corporation, August 1975.

Hendrick, T. et al. *Denver Fire Services Research Project Report; Feasibility Test of Applying Emergency Service Deployment and Facility Location Methods to Assist in Municipal Budget Decisions in the Fire Service.* Denver,

Colorado: Denver Urban Observatory, 1974; modified version, *An Analysis of the Deployment of Fire-Fighting Resources in Denver, Colorado*. Report R-1566/3-HUD. Santa Monica: The Rand Corporation, May 1975.

Hickey, H. *A Comparative Analysis of Resource Allocation Plans For Urban Fire Safety*. Report APL/JHU FPP B 77-1. Laurel, Maryland: The Johns Hopkins University Applied Physics Laboratory, August 1977.

Hogg, J. "The Siting of Fire Stations." *Operations Research Quarterly*, Vol. 19, pp. 275-287, 1968.

———, *Station Siting in Peterborough and Market Deeping*. Fire research report 7/70. London: Home Office, November 1970.

———, *Losses in Relation to the Fire Brigade's Attendance Time*. Fire research report 5/73. London: Home Office, 1973.

———, *Methods of Planning Fire Cover Using Cost Effectiveness Criteria*. Fire research report 7/75. London: Home Office, 1975.

Hogg, J. and Morrow, D. *The Siting of Fire Stations in Northampton and Northamptonshire*. Fire research report 4/73. London: Home Office, 1973.

Home Office. *Report of the Majesty's Chief Inspector of Fire Services for the Year 1973*. London: Her Majesty's Stationery Office, Cmnd. 5674, October 1974.

Homer, P., Lawton, J., and Toregas, C. "Challenging the ISO Fire Rating System." *Public Management*, Vol. 59, No. 7, pp. 2-6, July 1977.

Horton, R. *Municipal Labor Relations in New York City: Lessons of the Lindsay-Wagner Years*. New York: Praeger Publishers, 1973.

Ignall, E., Kolesar, P., Swersey, A., Walker, W., Blum, E., Carter, G., and Bishop, H. "Improving the Deployment of New York City Fire Companies." *Interfaces*, Vol. 5, No. 2, pp. 48-61, February 1975.

Ignall, E., Kolesar, P. and Walker, W. *Using Simulation to Develop and Validate Analytical Emergency Service Deployment Models*. Paper P-5463. Santa Monica: The Rand Corporation, 1975; revised version in *Operations Research*, Vol. 26, No. 2, pp. 237-253, 1978.

Ignall, E., Rider, K., and Urbach, R. *Fire Severity and Response Distance: Initial Findings*. Report R-2013-NYC. Santa Monica: The Rand Corporation, 1978.

Ignall, E. and Urbach, R. *The Relationship Between Firefighting Unit Availability and the Number of Units Dispatched*. Paper P-5420. Santa Monica: The Rand Corporation, May 1975.

Insurance Services Office. *Grading Schedule for Municipal Fire Protection*. New York: Insurance Services Office, 1974.

ISO Today. New York: Insurance Services Office, February 1972.

Jarvis, J. *Optimization in Stochastic Service Systems with Distinguishable Servers*. Report TR-19-75. Cambridge: Massachusetts Institute of Technology, 1975.

Keeney, R. "A Utility Function for the Response Times of Engines and Ladders to Fires." *J. Urban Analysis*, Vol. 1, No. 2, pp. 209-222, 1973.

Kendall, M. and Stuart, A. *The Advanced Theory of Statistics*. New York: Hafner Publishing Company, 1961.

Khintchine, A. *Mathematical Methods in the Theory of Queuing*. London: Charles Griffin, 1960.

Kimball, W. *Fire Attack/Command Decisions and Company Operations.* Boston: National Fire Protection Association, 1966.

Kleinrock, L. *Queuing Systems, Volume I: Theory.* New York: John Wiley and Sons, 1975.

Kolesar, P. *A Model for Predicting Average Fire Company Travel Times.* Report R-1624-NYC. Santa Monica: The Rand Corporation, June 1974; also in *Operations Research,* Vol. 23, No.4, pp. 603–613, 1975.

Kolesar, P. and Blum, E. "Square Root Laws for Fire Engine Response Distances." *Management Science,* Vol. 19, No. 12, pp. 1368–1378, 1973; revised and updated version, *Square-Root Laws for Fire Company Travel Distances.* Report R-895-NYC. Santa Monica: The Rand Corporation, June 1975.

Kolesar, P. and Walker, W. *An Algorithm for the Dynamic Relocation of Fire Companies.* Report R-1023-NYC. Santa Monica: The Rand Corporation, September 1972; also in *Operations Research,* Vol. 22, No. 2, pp. 249–274, 1974.

———, *Measuring the Travel Characteristics of New York City's Fire Companies.* Report R-1449-NYC. Santa Monica: The Rand Corporation, April 1974. See also Kolesar, Walker, and Hausner (1975).

Kolesar, P., Walker, W., and Hausner, J. "Determining the Relation Between Fire Engine Travel Times and Travel Distances in New York City." *Operations Research,* Vol. 23, No. 4, pp. 614–627, 1975. This is an abridged version of Kolesar and Walker (1974).

Kotler, P. *Marketing for Nonprofit Organizations.* Englewood Cliffs, New Jersey; Prentice-Hall, 1975.

La Protection Civile. Paris: Ministère de l'Interieur, Service National de la Protection Civile, 1975.

Larson, R. "Improving the Effectiveness of New York City's 911." In Drake, Keeney, and Morse (eds.), *Analysis of Public Systems.* Cambridge, Massachusetts: MIT Press, 1972.

———, *A Hypercube Queuing Model for Facility Location and Redistricting in Urban Emergency Services.* Report R-1238-HUD. Santa Monica: The Rand Corporation, 1973; also in *Computers and Operations Research,* Vol. 1, No. 5, pp. 67–95, 1974.

———, *Urban Emergency Service Systems: An Iterative Procedure for Approximating Performance Characteristics.* Report R-1493-HUD. Santa Monica: The Rand Corporation, 1974; revised version in *Operations Research,* Vol. 23, No. 5, pp. 845–868, 1975.

———, *Hypercube Queuing Model: User's Manual.* Report R-1688/2-HUD. Santa Monica: The Rand Corporation, 1975.

Larson, R. and Stevenson, K. *On Insensitivities in Urban Redistricting and Facility Location.* Report R-533-HUD. Santa Monica: The Rand Corporation, March 1971; also in *Operations Research,* Vol. 20, No. 3, pp. 595–612, 1972.

Leamer, E. "Locational Equilibria." *Journal of Regional Science,* Vol. 8, No. 2, pp. 229–242, 1968.

Leavitt, H. *Managerial Psychology,* 2nd edition. Chicago: The University of Chicago Press, 1964.

Lerup, L., Cronrath, D, and Liu, J. *Learning from Fire: A Fire Protection Primer for Architects*. Berkeley: College of Environmental Design, University of California, 1977.

Lindgren, B. and McElrath, G. *Introduction to Probability and Statistics*. New York: The Macmillan Company, 1967.

March, J. and Simon, H. *Organizations*. New York: John Wiley and Sons, 1958.

"Master Planning Community Fire Protection." Prepared by Mission Research Corporation, Santa Barbara, for the Institute of Local Self Government. Berkeley, California, July 1976.

McGuire, J. and Ruscoe, B. *The Value of a Fire Detector in the House*. Fire Study No. 9. Ottawa: Division of Building Research, National Research Council of Canada, December 1962.

Meredith, J. and Shershin, A. *EMS and Fire Activities in the South Florida Region*. Working Paper 75-4. Miami, Florida: School of Business and Organizational Sciences, Florida International University, November 1975.

Morris, C. and Rolph, J. *Introduction to Data Analysis and Statistical Inference*. Paper P-5819. Santa Monica: The Rand Corporation, June 1977.

Morse, P. *Queues, Inventories, and Maintenance*. New York: John Wiley and Sons, 1967.

Municipal Fire Insurance: An Alternative to Private Fire Indemnity at Public Expense in Fire Prevention and Suppression. Berkeley: Institute for Local Self-Government, September 1977.

Munson, M. and Ohls, J. *Indirect Costs of Residential Fires*. Report 78-05. Princeton: Mathematica Policy Research, Inc., February 1978.

National Fire Incident Reporting System Handbook. Washington, D.C.: National Fire Prevention and Control Administration, U.S. Department of Commerce, February 1976.

Nelson, H. *The Application of Systems Analysis to Building Firesafety Design*. Chicago: Sixth Annual Fire Protection Seminar, Illinois Institute of Technology, March 1973.

Nerlove, M. and Press, S. J. *Univariate and Multivariate Log Linear and Logistic Models*. Report R-1306. Santa Monica: The Rand Corporation, December 1973.

The New York City–Rand Institute, "Research in 1970–1971." *Operations Research*, Vol. 20, No. 3, pp. 474–515, 1972.

NFPA (National Fire Protection Association). See *Uniform Coding* and *Uniform Fire Incident Reporting System*.

NFPCA. See *National Fire Incident Reporting System Handbook*.

O'Hagan, J. "Improving the Deployment of Fire-Fighting Resources." *Fire Journal*, Vol. 67, No. 4, pp. 42–46, July 1973.

O'Hagan, J. and Blum, E. *Technology Aids Fire Service*. Paper P-4872. Santa Monica: The Rand Corporation, June 1972; also in *Nation's Cities*, June 1972.

Perrow, C. *Complex Organizations*. Glenview, Illinois: Scott Foresman and Company, 1972.

Pigeon, C. "Police, Fire, and Refuse Collection and Disposal Departments: Manpower, Compensation, and Expenditures," *The Municipal Year Book, 1979*. Washington, D.C.: International City Management Association, 1979.

The PTI Fire Station Location Package: Effectiveness Survey Analysis. Washington, D.C.: Public Technology, Inc., 1977.
Public Technology, Inc. See *Fire Station Location Package* and *The PTI Fire Station Location Package.*
Quade, E. *Analysis for Public Decisions.* New York: American Elsevier, 1975.
Quade, E. and Boucher, W. *Systems Analysis and Policy Planning: Applications in Defense.* New York: American Elsevier, 1968.
Radnor, M. and Neal, R. "The Progress of Management-Science Activities in Large U. S. Industrial Corporations." *Operations Research,* Vol. 21, No. 2, pp. 427–540, 1973.
Rardin, R. and Mitzner, M. "Determinants of International Differences in Reported Fire Loss: Preliminary Investigation." Washington, D.C.: Final Technical Report. Atlanta: Georgia Institute of Technology, June 1977.
Rider, K. *A Parametric Model for the Allocation of Fire Companies: Executive Summary.* Report R-1646/1-HUD; and *User's Manual.* Report R-1646/2-HUD. Santa Monica: The Rand Corporation, August 1975.
———, "A Parametric Model for the Allocation of Fire Companies in New York City." *Management Science,* Vol. 23, No. 2, pp. 146–158, October 1976.
———, "An Analysis of Fire Hazards in New York City." The New York City-Rand Institute, unpublished.
———, "The Economics of The Distribution of Municipal Fire Protection Services." *Review of Economics and Statistics,* Vol. LXI, No. 2, pp. 249–258, 1979.
Rider, K. et al., *An Analysis of The Deployment of Fire-Fighting Resources in Jersey City, New Jersey.* Report R-1566/4-HUD. Santa Monica: The Rand Corporation, August 1975.
Rider, K. and Walker, W. "Prediction of Fire Alarms for 1975–1988." The New York City-Rand Institute, unpublished.
Rogers, E. *Modernization among Peasants: The Impact of Communication.* New York: Holt, Rinehart, and Winston, 1969.
Rogers, E. and Agarwala-Rogers, R. *Communication in Organizations.* New York: The Free Press, 1976.
Salzberg, F. *Fire Department Operations Analysis.* Chicago: IIT Research Institute, June 1970.
Salzberg, F., Vodvarka, F., and Maatman, G. "Minimum Water Requirements for Suppression of Room Fires." *Fire Technology,* Vol. 6, No. 1, pp. 22–28, 1970.
Santone, L. and Berlin, G. *A Computer Model for the Evaluation of Fire Station Location.* Report 10 093. Washington, D.C.: National Bureau of Standards, August 1969.
Schaenman, P., Hall, J., Schainblatt, A., Swartz, J., and Karter, M. *Procedures for Improving the Measurement of Local Fire Protection Effectiveness.* Boston: National Fire Protection Association, 1977.
Schaenman, P. and Swartz, J. *Measuring Fire Protection Productivity in Local Government.* Boston: National Fire Protection Association, 1974.
Schneider, J. "Solving Urban Location Problems: Human Intuition vs. the Computer." *Journal of the American Institute of Planners,* Vol. 37, No. 2, 1971.

Bibliography

Shanesy, C. *An On-Line Program for Relocating Fire-Fighting Resources.* Report R-1506-NYC. Santa Monica: The Rand Corporation, June 1975.

Simon, H., Shephard, R., and Sharp, F. *Fire Losses and Fire Risks.* Berkeley: Bureau of Public Administration, University of California, 1943.

Singleton, D. "Firefighting Productivity in Wilmington: A Case History." *Public Productivity Review,* Vol. 1, No. 1, pp. 19–29, 1975.

Spero, S. and Capozzola, J. *The Urban Community and Its Unionized Bureaucracies.* New York: Dunellen, 1973.

Swersey, A. *A Markovian Decision Model for Deciding How Many Units to Dispatch.* In "Models for Reducing Fire Engine Response Times." Ph.D. Thesis. New York: Columbia University, 1972.

———, *Reducing Fire Engine Dispatching Delays.* Report R-1458-NYC. Santa Monica: The Rand Corporation, December 1973; also in Quade (1975).

Swersey, A., Ignall, E., Corman, H., Armstrong, P., and Weindling, J. *Fire Protection and Local Government: An Evaluation of Policy-Related Research.* Report R-1813-NSF. Santa Monica: The Rand Corporation, September 1975.

Toregas, C., Swain, R., ReVelle, C., and Bergman, L. "The Location of Emergency Service Facilities." *Operations Research,* Vol. 19, No. 6, pp. 1363–1373, 1971.

Tukey, J. "Discussion Emphasizing the Connection Between Analysis of Variance and Spectrum Analysis." *Technometrics,* Vol. 3, No. 2, pp. 191–219, 1961.

UFIRS. See *Uniform Fire Incident Reporting System.*

Uniform Coding for Fire Protection. Publication No. 901-1976. Boston: National Fire Protection Association, 1975.

Uniform Fire Incident Reporting System (UFIRS)—Management Guide. Boston: National Fire Protection Association, 1977.

Urban Guide for Fire Prevention and Control Master Planning. Stock No. 003-003-01749-3. Washington, D.C.: U.S. Government Printing Office, 1977.

Van Horn, R. "Validation of Simulation Results." *Management Science,* Vol. 17, No. 5, pp. 247–258, 1971.

Walker, W. "Analysis of an Experiment to Determine the Effect of Moving New York's Engine Company 74 to a New Location." Unpublished report. Santa Monica: The Rand Corporation, December 1973.

———, *Firehouse Site Evaluation Model: Executive Summary.* Report R-1618/1-HUD. Santa Monica: The Rand Corporation, June 1975.

———, "Applying Systems Analysis to the Fire Service." *Fire Engineering,* Vol. 128, No. 8, pp. 38–64, August 1975c.

———, *The Deployment of Emergency Services: A Guide to Selected Methods and Models.* Report R-1867-HUD. Santa Monica: The Rand Corporation, September 1975b.

———, *Changing Fire Company Locations: Five Implementation Case Studies.* Stock No. 023-000-00456-9. Washington, D.C.: Government Printing Office, 1978.

Walker, W., Singleton, D., and Smith, B. *An Analysis of the Deployment of Firefighting Resources in Wilmington, Delaware.* Report R-1566/5-HUD. Santa Monica: The Rand Corporation, July 1975. See also, Singleton.

Walsh, C. and Marks, L. *Firefighting Strategy and Leadership,* 2nd edition. New York: McGraw-Hill, 1977.
Watts, J., *A Theoretical Rationalization of a Goal-Oriented Systems Approach to Building Fire Safety.* College Park, Maryland: Department of Fire Protection Engineering, University of Maryland, February 1978.
Wildavsky, A. "Principles for a Graduate School of Public Policy." *J. Urban Analysis,* Vol. 4, No. 1, pp. 3–28, 1977.
Winston, W. "Optimal Assignment of Customers in a Two-Server Congestion System." *Management Science,* Vol. 24, pp. 702–705, February 1978.
Wrightson, C. *Stochastic Models for Emergency Service Systems.* Report ORC 76-18. Berkeley: Operations Research Center, University of California, 1976.
Yin, R. "On the Equitable Outcome of Municipal Services: Street Cleanliness." Paper presented at the Operations Research Society of America annual meeting, Boston, April 1974.
Yin, R. Heald, K., Vogel, M., Fleischauer, P., and Vladek, B. *A Review of Case Studies of Technological Innovations in State and Local Services.* Report R-1870-NSF. Santa Monica: The Rand Corporation, 1976.
Zaltman, G., Duncan, R., and Holbek, J. *Innovations in Organizations.* New York: John Wiley and Sons, 1973.

Index

A

Adaptive response (AR), see Response
Alarm assignment card, 54, 57, 388, 430, 431, 434, 459, 487, 489, 491, 494, 608, 609, 612, 613, 641–642
Alarm factor, 341–342, 345–349, 371, 642
Alarm rates, 630, 642
   Data collection, see Incident reporting systems
   Data displays, 265–281, 553–558
   Estimating, 272–276, 279, 281–319
   Geographic variation, 256, 266–271, 350–356, 553–555
   Long range predictions, 283–284, 355–356, 557–558
   Temporal variation, 256–259, 272–278, 284–286, 557
   Trends, 282–283
Alarm types, 265–266, 420–423, 426–429, 431, 507–511, 642 (see also Incident types)
Allocating fire companies, 73, 323–371, 630, 636–637, 642
   Cost-benefit approaches, 326–327
   Response distance standards, 327–329
   Use of models, 329–339, 349–365, 581, 588
Analytical team, 100–124
   Established in Fire Department of New York, 113–124
   Position in organization, 108–110
   Staffing, 100–101, 102–108, 111–113, 119–124

Archibald, Rae, 125, 629, 632, 637, 665
Availability, 15–16, 43, 85, 642

B

Blum, Edward, 3, 629, 631, 665
Brooklyn (NY) Communications Office, 74, 75, 493, 608–628, 639
Bubble diagram, 215, 642
Building codes, 66

C

Carter, Grace, 255, 631, 633, 635, 665
Chaiken, Jan, 202, 629, 631, 665
Change agent, 125–127, 642
Change process, see Management of change
Codes, building and fire, 3, 66
Communications Office (C.O.), 30, 53–58, 492–494, 630, 643
   Brooklyn, see Brooklyn (NY) Communications Office
   Model of dispatching operations in New York City, 608–616
   Simulation of dispatching operations in New York City, 616–625
Computer-aided dispatching, 58–60 (see also Management information and control systems)
Cost
   Of fire, 4, 22–25
   Of fire protection, 2, 12–15, 86–87
   Of unnecessary responses, 423–425
   Of using models, 228, 339, 399–400, 496, 568–569, 581–582

Coverage, 31, 85, 520–521, 526–527, 643
Criteria, 40–42, 79–87

D

Data collection, 168–170, 261–265, 339, 397–398, 506–511, 635 (see also Incident reporting systems)
Deaths, fire-related
  International, 5, 32–37
  United States, 4, 5, 32–37
Demand regions, 256, 270–271, 297–299, 329, 336, 350–365, 382, 384–395, 403–415, 552–555, 560–564, 567, 583–588, 643
Demand zone, see Fire demand zone
Demands for fire services, 255–319, 634–635
  Latent demand, 7–9, 11, 267, 647
  Potential demand, 7, 267, 336–338, 341–344, 348, 410, 648 (see also Latent demand)
  Realized demand, 7, 10–11, 267, 336–338, 341–344, 348, 410, 648 (see also Alarm rates)
Denmark, 16, 36
Denver, Colorado, 59
  Deployment case study, 568–581
  Travel time estimation, 166, 174–177, 570–572
  Use of Fire Operations Simulation Model, 507–509, 578–580, 634
Denver Urban Observatory, 402, 568–569
Deployment analysis, 7, 68–99 (see also Systems analysis)
  Definition, 68–72, 644
  Steps in a deployment analysis study, 70–72
Detectors, smoke and fire, 22, 66–67
Dispatching, 52–60
  Computer-aided, 58–60 (see also Management information and control systems)
  Office, see Communications office
  Policy, see Response policy and Initial dispatch
  Time, 82, 83, 607, 609, 616–627, 644

E

Effectiveness, 40–45, 65–66, 80–81
Efficiency, 40–41, 77–79, 330–334, 340, 464, 466, 470
Empirical Bayes estimation (of alarm rates), 311–319
Engine company, 48–49, 644
Equity, 40–41, 77–79, 270, 330–334, 340–341, 464, 466, 470

Exponential distribution, 210–213, 295–296, 611–617
Exponential smoothing, 305–306, 645

F

Falck–Zonen, 16, 36
Fire demand zone (FDZ), 379–382, 398, 645
Fire department
  Organization, 63–64
  Activities, 52–62, 64–67
  Resources, 11–15, 48–52
  Costs, 12–15
Fire management area (FMA), 271, 645
Fire prevention, 8, 28–30, 36, 64–67, 645
Fire Station Location Package (FSLP), 372–373, 375, 636
  Data requirements, 395, 398
  History of use, 401
  Output reports, 379–382, 383
  Prescriptive use, 401–403
  Resources needed for implementation, 398–408
  Travel time estimation, 165–167, 168–169, 376–378
Firehouse location, 73, 372–425 (see also Firehouse Site Evaluation Model and Fire Station Location Package)
  In Denver, Colorado, 568–581
  In Trenton, New Jersey, 403–415
  In Yonkers, New York, 550–568
Firehouse Site Evaluation Model, 372–373, 375, 636
  Data requirements, 395
  History of use, 400–401
  Output reports, 382–392
  Resources needed for implementation, 39C
  Travel time estimation, 165–167, 168–169, 376–378
  Use in Trenton, New Jersey, 403–415
  Use in Yonkers, New York, 550–568
Focal point, 379, 646
Forecasting, see Alarm rates, estimating, and Alarm rates, Long range predictions
France, 3–4, 17, 32, 33, 34, 36

G

Germany, 5, 16, 17, 26, 36, 37
Great Britain, 17, 32, 33, 34, 36, 45, 196–197, 629

H

Hazard factor, 341–349, 355, 366–371, 646
Hazards, 7–9, 11, 29, 267, 270–271, 340–345, 384, 388–390, 395, 408, 412, 572–574, 646

Index

Hogg, Jane, 196, 326
HUD (U.S. Dept. of Housing and Urban Development), xiii, xix, xx, 375, 551, 568, 582, 631, 632, 636

I

Ignall, Edward, 629, 633, 666
Implementation, 97, 151–153, 646 (see also Innovation)
Incident reporting systems, 62–63, 262–265 (see also Data collection)
  NFIRS, 63, 262–265
  UFIRS, 262–263
Incident types, 420–423, 426–429, 507–511, 646 (see also Alarm types)
Initial dispatch, 54–56, 74, 416–458, 506, 637–638, 646–647
  Adaptive policies, 443–444, 597–606, 641
  Algorithm for, 444–456, 637–638
  Fixed policies, 432, 433, 646
  Measures for evaluating policies, 420–430
  Variable policies, 433–436, 652
Innovation, 37–39, 126, 144–151
Inspections, 16, 65–67
Insurance, fire, 23, 24, 25–27
Insurance Services Office (ISO), 26, 80, 327
  Grading Schedule for Municipal Fire Protection, 25, 26, 327, 373
Institute for Local Self-Government, 27
International Association of Fire Fighters (IAFF), 130, 134, 135
International City Management Association (ICMA), 136

J

Japan, 19, 24, 33
Jersey City, New Jersey, 177, 179, 271, 272, 400
  Alarm rates, 268–269, 276–279, 350, 354–356
  Deployment case study, 349–365
  Use of Parametric Allocation Model, 339, 349, 356–365

K

Kolesar, Peter, 157, 639, 666

L

Labor-management relations, 119, 140–142
Ladder company, 49, 647
Lindsay, John V., xx, 113

M

Management
  Of change, 125–153
  And labor relations, see Labor-management relations
  Of deployment analysis project, 100–114
Management information and control systems (MICS), 58–60, 461, 463, 492–493, 590, 635, 637–639
Manning of fire companies, 14–15, 26, 31, 51–52, 61–62, 73, 647
Manpower scheduling, 31, 64
Markov decision theory, 202, 203, 245, 637, 647
  Use in deciding how many fire companies to dispatch, 243–246
Master planning for community fire protection, 69, 271
Measures of performance, 39–46, 65–66, 71, 80–87, 329, 334, 384, 392–395, 420–430, 463–476, 489–492, 511–532
Metropolitan Toronto Ambulance Service, 31
Models, 89–96, 647 (See also Fire Station Location Package; Firehouse Site Evaluation Model; Initial dispatch algorithm; Parametric Allocation Model; Relocation algorithm; Station Configuration Information Model)
  Descriptive analytic, 93–94, 180–185, 642–643
  Empirical, 91–93, 164–177, 644
  For determining response boundaries, 234–243
  For estimating alarm rates, 272–319
  For travel time and travel distance, 157–201
  Prescriptive, 95, 340–349, 401–403, 648
  Principles of modeling, 286–291
  Probabilistic, 202–254, 308–318 (see also Queuing theory)
  Queuing, 218–248
  Simulation, 94–95, 495–548, 616–624, 650 (see also Simulation Model of Fire Operations)
  Types of, 90–96
  Use in a systems analysis study, 88–96
  Validation, 185–199, 292, 314–318, 534–535, 545–548
Move-up, see Relocation

N

National Fire Academy, 122
National Fire Data System (NFDS), 255
National Fire Incident Reporting System (NFIRS), 63, 262–265

National Fire Prevention and Control Administration, 38 (See also U.S. Fire Administration)
National Fire Protection Association (NFPA), 4, 5, 38, 39, 63, 134, 136, 150, 263
Netherlands, 97
Network, street, 162–169
New York City
  Alarm rates, 278, 280, 281, 282, 283–286, 288, 289, 290, 291–308, 438–439, 629–630
  Dispatching policy, 433–434, 452–456, 545–548, 590–591, 593, 594, 597–606
  Fire Department (F.D.N.Y.), xiii, xix, xx, 74, 84, 87, 113, 160, 283, 475, 492, 493, 495, 588, 629–631, 634–637
  Hazard factors, 367–370
  Reducing fire company workload (deployment case study), 588–606
  Reducing dispatching delays (deployment case study), 607–628
  Travel time estimation, 172–174, 177, 178, 179
New York City–Rand Institute, xii, xiii, 339, 375, 400, 498, 550–551, 581, 588, 589, 607 (See also Rand Corporation)

O

Objectives, 43, 77–79
Organizations
  As interest groups, 132–137
  Characteristics of, 130–132
  Fire departments as, 119, 123, 130–132
  Introducing change in, 137–153

P

Parametric Allocation Model (PAM), 324–325, 330–365, 374–375, 549, 582–588, 636
  Alarm factors, 341–342, 345–349, 371, 642
  Data and resources needed, 339
  Hazard factors, 341–349, 355, 366–371, 646
  History of use, 339–340
  How it works, 334–339
  Mathematical formulation and solution, 340–349
  Tradeoff parameter, 334–338, 340–341, 345–347, 358–360, 586, 651
  Treatment of conflicting objectives, 330–339
  Use in Jersey City, New Jersey, 349–365
  Use in New York City, 336–338
  Use in Tacoma, Washington, 581–588
Performance measurement, see Measures of Performance
Poisson distribution, 212, 220, 611
Poisson process, 203, 209–213, 236, 243, 257, 260, 287, 291–296, 297, 299, 473, 502
  Definition, 209–213, 648

Used for modeling alarm rates, 291–296
Validity for alarm occurrences, 291–296, 611
Prevention, see Fire prevention
Private fire protection, 16, 17, 24, 25, 36
Probabilistic models, 91, 202–254 (see also Queuing models)
  Deciding how many fire companies to dispatch, 243–246
  Of dispatching operation, 608–616
  Predicting alarm rates, 291–308
  Predicting the number of fire companies that will be dispatched, 435–436
  Predicting the probability that an alarm signals a serious fire, 308–318, 633
Probability distribution, 205–206, 222, 379, 381, 388, 538, 609–624
Problem definition in systems analysis, 72–77, 114–118
  Strategic problems, 73
  Tactical problems, 74
Productivity improvement in fire departments, 15–17, 30–32
PTI, see Public Technology, Inc.
Public Technology, Inc. (PTI), 373, 375, 376, 399, 570, 572, 576, 636–637

Q

Queuing models
  Deciding which fire companies to dispatch, 234–243, 252–254
  Estimating travel distances, 224–234
  Number of alarms in progress, 218–222
  Number of fire companies busy, 218–234, 247–251
Queuing theory, basic elements, 204–217, 246

R

Rand Corporation, 114, 393, 663 (see also New York City–Rand Institute)
Rand Fire Project, research history, 629–639
Relocation, 58, 74, 296, 426, 459–494, 638–639, 649
  Algorithm for solving problem, 464–466, 480–483, 638–639
  Defining objectives, 463–464, 466–470
  In Fire Operations Simulation Model, 525, 530, 531
  Mathematical formulation of problem, 464–480
  Testing the algorithm, 486–492, 639
  Use of the algorithm in New York City, 492–494
  Use of the algorithm to generate preplanned relations, 494
Response, 649
  Adaptive (AR), 31, 436–444, 597–606, 641
  Adequacy, 86, 420–423, 432, 434–436, 441, 520, 524, 647

Index

Area, 51–52, 235, 241, 243, 382, 384, 388, 391, 649
Policy, 31, 54–58, 74, 426–458, 565–566 (see also Initial dispatch)
Time, 82–83, 153, 260–261, 649
Response Neighborhood (RN), 467–469, 476–483, 490, 493, 494, 649
Richman, Barry, 666
Rider, Kenneth, 632, 666

S

Scottsdale, Arizona, 16, 31
Serious fires, 3, 32–35, 265–266, 420–421, 650
Setup time, 82, 83, 650
Simulation, 94–95, 650
  Of dispatching office, 607–628
  Of fire operations, see Simulation Model of Fire Operations
Simulation Model of Fire Operations, 495–548
  Data requirements, 506–511
  Description of program, 499–532
  Development, 633–634
  Estimation of travel distances, 163
  Output reports, 511–532
  Use in Denver, Colorado, 507–509, 578–580, 634
  Used to analyze workload problems in NYC, 588–628
  Used to test new dispatch policies, 452–456, 545–548
  Used to test relocation algorithm, 486–492
  Used to validate square-root law, 94, 187–196
  Validity, 534–535
Sprinklers, 8, 30, 67
Square-root law, 177–199, 224–234, 332–333, 636, 650
  Derivation, 180–185
  Use in Parametric Allocation Model, 341
  Validation, 185–199
State diagram, 215, 650
Station Configuration Information Model (SCIM), 577–578
Statistical inference, 280–291
  For predicting alarm rates, 291–319
  Use in analyzing simulation output, 537–545
Steady state, 214
Street network, see Network
Swersey, Arthur, 47, 549, 629, 632, 637, 666
Systems analysis, 5–7, 68–72, 628, 651

T

Tacoma, Washington, 34
  Alarm rates, 287, 583–584
  Deployment case study, 581–588
  Travel time estimation, 585
  Use of Parametric Allocation Model, 339, 581, 582, 585–587
Tradeoff parameter, see Parametric Allocation Model
Travel Distance, 157–164, 651
  Average in region, see Square-root law
  In Fire Operations Simulation Model, 163
  In Firehouse Site Evaluation Model, 376–377
  Point-to-point, 157–158, 161–164
  Right-angle, 162–163
  Straight-line (Euclidean), 162–163
  Street network, 163–164
Travel time, 82, 83, 157–162, 164–177, 651
  As a performance measure, 84–87
  Average in region, 159–160, 199–201
  Estimating relationship for Denver, Colorado, 174, 176, 570–572
  Estimating relationship for New York City, 172–174
  Estimating relationship for Tacoma, Washington, 585
  Estimating relationship for Trenton, N.J., 174–176, 405–406
  Estimating relationship for Wilmington, Delaware, 92
  Estimating relationship for Yonkers, N.Y., 174, 176, 559
  Estimating relationship from several cities, 166
  Experiment, 167–177
  In Fire Station Location Package, 376–378
  In Firehouse Site Evaluation Model, 376–378
  In Parametric Allocation Model, 341
  Point-to-point, 92–93, 158–159, 164–177
Trenton, New Jersey, 34
  Alarm rates, 272, 273, 403–404
  Deployment case study, 403–415
  Travel time estimation, 166, 174–177, 179, 405–406
  Use of Firehouse Site Evaluation Model, 400, 406–415
Turnout time, 82, 83, 652

U

Unavailability, 85, 652
Uniform Fire Incident Reporting System (UFIRS), 262–263
United Kingdom, 5, 326–327
United States Fire Administration, 4, 6, 38, 43, 62, 65, 69, 134, 135, 263, 339, 375, 400, 550–551, 581, 589, 607
United States fire data, 4, 5, 23, 32–35
University of Colorado, 568, 569
U.S. Bureau of the Census, 164, 570
U.S. Department of Defense, 70
U.S. Department of Housing and Urban Development, see HUD
U.S. General Services Administration (GSA), 69–70
Utility, 83–84, 530

W

Walker, Warren, 68, 631; 632, 638, 639, 666
Washington, D.C., 31, 51, 52, 53, 54, 56, 57, 63–64, 196
Wilmington, Delaware, 34, 141, 339, 392
  Alarm rates, 272, 274, 275, 283, 392–393
  Travel time estimation, 92, 93, 166, 174–177, 179
  Use of Firehouse Site Evaluation Model, 400
Workload, 10, 11, 12, 71, 79, 630, 631, 632–633, 652
  Analysis of policies to reduce, 588–628
  As a measure of performance, 45, 86
  In output of Fire Operations Simulation Model, 521, 525, 528–529
  In output of Firehouse Site Evaluation Model, 388, 391
Work time, 258, 342, 509–511, 652

Y

Yonkers, New York, 339
  Alarm rate, 75–76, 553–558
  Deployment case study, 550–568
  Dispatching policy, 565–567
  Travel time estimation, 166, 174–177, 179, 558–560
  Use of Firehouse Site Evaluation Model, 400, 551, 560–564

Selected Rand Books

Armor, David J., Polich, J. Michael, and Stambul, Harriet B. *Alcoholism and Treatment.* New York: John Wiley and Sons, Inc., 1978.

Bellman, Richard. *Dynamic Programming.* Princeton, New Jersey: Princeton University Press, 1957.

Bellman, Richard, ed. *Mathematical Optimization Techniques.* Berkeley and Los Angeles: University of California Press, 1963 (out of print).

Brewer, Garry D., and Kakalik, James S. *Handicapped Children: Strategies for Improving Services.* New York: McGraw-Hill Book Company, Inc., 1979.

Cohen, Bernard, and Chaiken, Jan M. *Police Background Characteristics and Performance.* Lexington, Massachusetts: D. C. Heath and Company, 1973 (out of print).

Dalkey, Norman C. *Studies in the Quality of Life: Delphi and Decision-Making.* Lexington, Massachusetts: D. C. Heath and Company, 1972.

Dantzig, G. B. *Linear Programming and Extensions.* Princeton, New Jersey: Princeton University Press, 1963.

Fisher, Gene H. *Cost Considerations in Systems Analysis.* New York: American Elsevier Publishing Company, Inc., 1971.

Ford, L. R., Jr. and Fulkerson, D. R. *Flows in Networks.* Princeton, New Jersey: Princeton University Press, 1962.

Goldhamer, Herbert. *The Adviser.* New York: Elsevier-North Holland, Inc., 1978 (a Rand Graduate Institute book).

Greenwood, Peter W., Chaiken, Jan M., and Petersilia, Joan. *The Criminal Investigation Process.* Lexington, Massachusetts: D. C. Heath and Company, 1977 (hardbound and paperback).

Kakalik, James S., and Wildhorn, Sorrel. *The Private Police: Security and Danger.* New York: Crane, Russak & Company, Inc., 1977.

McKean, Roland N. *Efficiency in Government through Systems Analysis: With Emphasis on Water Resource Development.* New York: John Wiley and Sons, Inc., 1958.

Newhouse, Joseph P., and Alexander, Arthur J. *An Economic Analysis of Public Library Services.* Lexington, Massachusetts: D. C. Heath and Company, 1972

Novick, David (ed.). *Current Practice in Program Budgeting (PPBS): Analysis and Case Studies Covering Government and Business.* New York: Crane, Russak, and Company, Inc., 1973.

Pascal, Anthony H. (ed.). *Thinking About Cities: New Perspectives on Urban Problems.* Belmont, Calif.: Dickenson Publishing Company, Inc., 1970 (out of print).

Quade, Edward S. *Analysis for Public Decisions.* New York: American Elsevier Publishing Company, Inc., 1975.

Wildhorn, Sorrel, Lavin, Marvin, and Pascal, Anthony. *Indicators of Justice: Measuring the Performance of Prosecution, Defense and Court Agencies Involved in Felony Proceedings.* Lexington, Massachusetts: D. C. Heath and Company, 1977 (hardbound and paperback).

Wirt, John G., Lieberman, Arnold J., and Levien, Roger E. *R&D Management: Methods Used by Federal Agencies.* Lexington, Massachusetts: D. C. Heath and Company, 1975.

Yin, Robert K. and Yates, Douglas *Street-Level Governments: Assessing Decentralization and Urban Services.* Lexington, Massachusetts: D. C. Heath and Company, 1975.

Yin, Robert K., Heald, Karen A., and Vogel, Mary E. *Tinkering with the System: Technological Innovations in State and Local Services.* Lexington, Massachusetts: D. C. Heath and Company, 1977.

Biographies

Rae W. Archibald Currently Director of Fiscal Operations of The Rand Corporation, he served as a staff member and then second Project Leader of The New York City-Rand Institute's Fire Project. Subsequently, he was Deputy Fire Commissioner of the New York City Fire Department with responsibility for executive management planning, budgeting, and communications. He also created an innovative policy analysis program for the Fire Department. He has a Ph.D. in City and Regional Planning from the University of California at Berkeley.

Edward H. Blum Founder of The New York City-Rand Institute's Fire Project, he served as Project Leader for nearly three years and codirected the Institute's early HUD-sponsored work on the deployment of municipal emergency services. He subsequently became Vice-President of The New York City-Rand Institute and then, on leave from Rand, spent two years at the International Institute for Applied Systems Analysis in Austria. There he studied the applicability of the emergency service deployment methods in cities throughout the world. Currently a manager of research and analysis in the U.S. Department of Energy, he holds a Ph.D. in Chemical Engineering from Princeton University.

Grace M. Carter Currently a Senior Policy Analyst at The Rand Corporation, she is codeveloper of The New York City-Rand Institute's Fire Operations Simulation Model and has extensive experience in the statistical analysis of simulation results. She also has been instrumental in developing statistical methods for predicting the demand for fire services. She has a Ph.D. in Policy Analysis from the Rand Graduate Institute for Policy Studies.

Jan M. Chaiken (Editor and Author) Currently a Senior Mathematician at The Rand Corporation where he is involved in criminal justice research, he has worked extensively on the development of analytical deployment methods for urban emergency services and was codirector of The New York City-Rand Institute's HUD-funded deployment studies for several years. As part of the HUD project he was involved in applications of fire deployment models and the development of training materials. He has a Ph.D. in mathematics from the Massachusetts Institute of Technology.

Edward J. Ignall (Editor and Author)   Currently Chairman of the Department of Industrial Engineering and Operations Research at Columbia University, and a professor in the department, he is codeveloper of The New York City-Rand Institute's Fire Operations Simulation Model and author of numerous papers on emergency service deployment. He has a Ph.D. in Operations Research from Cornell University.

Peter J. Kolesar   A professor in the Graduate School of Business at Columbia University, he has worked on the development, application, and validation of several models for emergency service deployment analysis. He was a consultant to the New York State Special Deputy Controller's Office where he developed long-term models of the New York City budget. He has a Ph.D. in Operations Research from Columbia University.

Barry Richman (Editorial Consultant)   Formerly Editorial Director of The New York City-Rand Institute, he is now associated with the Professional and Reference Book Division of the McGraw-Hill Book Company.

Kenneth L. Rider   Currently a member of the Management Advisory Services staff of Deloitte Haskins & Sells, he was Director of Special Projects in the Office of the New York State Special Deputy Comptroller and served as Project Leader of The New York City-Rand Institute's Fire Project. He has done extensive work in the fields of municipal finance and the distribution of municipal services, including the development of methods for the allocation and dispatch of fire companies. As part of the HUD project, he directed a study of the deployment of fire companies in Jersey City, New Jersey, He has a M.S. in operations research from Columbia University and a Ph.D. in Chemical Physics from Yale University.

John Rolph   Currently a Senior Statistician at The Rand Corporation, he has developed statistical methods for predicting fire alarm rates and estimating the probability that a particular alarm signals a serious fire. His other interests include the application of statistical methods to problems in health and criminal justice. He has a Ph.D. in Statistics from the University of California at Berkeley.

Arthur J. Swersey   Currently an Associate Professor at the Yale School of Organization and Management, where he teaches quantitative methods as well as production and operations management, he served as Project Leader of The New York City-Rand Institute's Fire Project for two years. He has done extensive work on fire deployment methods, and has been a court-appointed expert in a fire protection equity case. He has a D. Eng. Sci. in Operations Research from Columbia University, where his dissertation dealt with the dispatching of fire companies.

Warren E. Walker (Editor and Author) Currently a Senior Policy Analyst at The Rand Corporation where he is involved in criminal justice and water resources research, he played a major role in the development of methods for emergency service deployment analysis at The New York City-Rand Institute. He was Director of Fire Protection and Emergency Service Studies at the Institute, Project Leader of the Fire Project, and directed the Institute's work for HUD on the deployment of municipal emergency services. As part of the HUD project, he supervised deployment analyses of the Yonkers, New York, Wilmington, Delaware, and Trenton, New Jersey fire departments. He has a Ph.D. in Operations Research from Cornell University.